computer science

AN OVERVIEW

12th Edition

J. Glenn Brookshear

Dennis Brylow

with contributions from

David T. Smith

Indiana University of Pennsylvania

Pearson

Original edition, entitled *Computer Science: An Overview*, 12th Edition, by Brookshear, Glenn; Brylow, Dennis, published by Pearson Education, Limited. Copyright © 2015 by Pearson Education, Inc.

Indian edition

ISBN: 978-93-325-8761-8

First Impression, 2018

Published by Pearson India Education Services Pvt. Ltd, CIN: U72200TN2005PTC057128.
Formerly known as TutorVista Global Pvt. Ltd, licensees of Pearson Education in South Asia

Head Office: 15th Floor, Tower-B, World Trade Tower, Plot No. 1, Block-C, Sector 16, Noida 201301, Uttar Pradesh, India.
Registered Office: 4th Floor, Software Block, Elnet Software City, TS -140, Block 2 & 9 Rajiv Gandhi Salai, Taramani, Chennai, Tamil Nadu 600113.

Fax: 080-30461003,Phone: 080-30461060,
Website : in.pearson.com
Email: companysecetary.india@pearson.com

Printed in India by Rahul Print O Pack

Preface

This book presents an introductory survey of computer science. It explores the breadth of the subject while including enough depth to convey an honest appreciation for the topics involved.

Audience

We wrote this text for students of computer science as well as students from other disciplines. As for computer science students, most begin their studies with the illusion that computer science is programming, Web browsing, and Internet file sharing because that is essentially all they have seen. Yet computer science is much more than this. Beginning computer science students need exposure to the breadth of the subject in which they are planning to major. Providing this exposure is the theme of this book. It gives students an overview of computer science—a foundation from which they can appreciate the relevance and interrelationships of future courses in the field. This survey approach is, in fact, the model used for introductory courses in the natural sciences.

This broad background is also what students from other disciplines need if they are to relate to the technical society in which they live. A computer science course for this audience should provide a practical, realistic understanding of the entire field rather than merely an introduction to using the Internet or training in the use of some popular software packages. There is, of course, a proper place for that training, but this text is about educating.

While writing previous editions of this text, maintaining accessibility for nontechnical students was a major goal. The result was that the book has been used successfully in courses for students over a wide range of disciplines and educational levels, ranging from high school to graduate courses. This 12th edition is designed to continue that tradition.

New in the 12th Edition

The underlying theme during the development of this 12th edition has been incorporating an introduction to the Python programming language into key chapters. In the earliest chapters, these supplementary sections are labeled optional.

By Chapter 5, we replace the previous editions' Pascal-like notation with Python and Python-flavored pseudocode.

This represents a significant change for a book that has historically striven to sidestep allegiance to any specific language. We make this change for several reasons. First, the text already contains quite a bit of code in various languages, including detailed pseudocode in several chapters. To the extent that readers are already absorbing a fair amount of syntax, it seems appropriate to retarget that syntax toward a language they may actually see in a subsequent course. More importantly, a growing number of instructors who use this text have made the determination that even in a breadth-first introduction to computing, it is difficult for students to master many of the topics in the absence of programming tools for exploration and experimentation.

But why Python? Choosing a language is always a contentious matter, with any choice bound to upset at least as many as it pleases. Python is an excellent middle ground, with:

- a clean, easily learned syntax,
- simple I/O primitives,
- data types and control structures that correspond closely to the pseudocode primitives used in earlier editions, and
- support for multiple programming paradigms.

It is a mature language with a vibrant development community and copious online resources for further study. Python remains one of the top 10 most commonly used languages in industry by some measures, and has seen a sharp increase in its usage for introductory computer science courses. It is particularly popular for introductory courses for non-majors, and has wide acceptance in other STEM fields such as physics and biology as the language of choice for computational science applications.

Nevertheless, the focus of the text remains on broad computer science concepts; the Python supplements are intended to give readers a deeper taste of programming than previous editions, but not to serve as a full-fledged introduction to programming. The Python topics covered are driven by the existing structure of the text. Thus, Chapter 1 touches on Python syntax for representing data—integers, floats, ASCII and Unicode strings, etc. Chapter 2 touches on Python operations that closely mirror the machine primitives discussed throughout the rest of the chapter. Conditionals, loops, and functions are introduced in Chapter 5, at the time that those constructs are needed to devise a sufficiently complete pseudocode for describing algorithms. In short, Python constructs are used to reinforce computer science concepts rather than to hijack the conversation.

In addition to the Python content, virtually every chapter has seen revisions, updates, and corrections from the previous editions.

Organization

This text follows a bottom-up arrangement of subjects that progresses from the concrete to the abstract—an order that results in a sound pedagogical presentation in which each topic leads to the next. It begins with the fundamentals of information encoding, data storage, and computer architecture (Chapters 1 and 2); progresses to the study of operating systems (Chapter 3) and computer networks

(Chapter 4); investigates the topics of algorithms, programming languages, and software development (Chapters 5 through 7); explores techniques for enhancing the accessibility of information (Chapters 8 and 9); considers some major applications of computer technology via graphics (Chapter 10) and artificial intelligence (Chapter 11); and closes with an introduction to the abstract theory of computation (Chapter 12).

Although the text follows this natural progression, the individual chapters and sections are surprisingly independent and can usually be read as isolated units or rearranged to form alternative sequences of study. Indeed, the book is often used as a text for courses that cover the material in a variety of orders. One of these alternatives begins with material from Chapters 5 and 6 (Algorithms and Programming Languages) and returns to the earlier chapters as desired. I also know of one course that starts with the material on computability from Chapter 12. In still other cases, the text has been used in "senior capstone" courses where it serves as merely a backbone from which to branch into projects in different areas. Courses for less technically-oriented audiences may want to concentrate on Chapters 4 (Networking and the Internet), 9 (Database Systems), 10 (Computer Graphics), and 11 (Artificial Intelligence).

On the opening page of each chapter, we have used asterisks to mark some sections as optional. These are sections that cover topics of more specific interest or perhaps explore traditional topics in more depth. Our intention is merely to provide suggestions for alternative paths through the text. There are, of course, other shortcuts. In particular, if you are looking for a quick read, we suggest the following sequence:

Section	Topic
1.1–1.4	Basics of data encoding and storage
2.1–2.3	Machine architecture and machine language
3.1–3.3	Operating systems
4.1–4.3	Networking and the Internet
5.1–5.4	Algorithms and algorithm design
6.1–6.4	Programming languages
7.1–7.2	Software engineering
8.1–8.3	Data abstractions
9.1–9.2	Database systems
10.1–10.2	Computer graphics
11.1–11.3	Artificial intelligence
12.1–12.2	Theory of computation

There are several themes woven throughout the text. One is that computer science is dynamic. The text repeatedly presents topics in a historical perspective, discusses the current state of affairs, and indicates directions of research. Another theme is the role of abstraction and the way in which abstract tools are used to control complexity. This theme is introduced in Chapter 0 and then echoed in the context of operating system architecture, networking, algorithm development, programming language design, software engineering, data organization, and computer graphics.

To Instructors

There is more material in this text than students can normally cover in a single semester so do not hesitate to skip topics that do not fit your course objectives or to rearrange the order as you see fit. You will find that, although the text follows a plot, the topics are covered in a largely independent manner that allows you to pick and choose as you desire. The book is designed to be used as a course resource—not as a course definition. We suggest encouraging students to read the material not explicitly included in your course. We underrate students if we assume that we have to explain everything in class. We should be helping them learn to learn on their own.

We feel obliged to say a few words about the bottom-up, concrete-to-abstract organization of the text. As academics, we too often assume that students will appreciate our perspective of a subject—often one that we have developed over many years of working in a field. As teachers, we think we do better by presenting material from the student's perspective. This is why the text starts with data representation/storage, machine architecture, operating systems, and networking. These are topics to which students readily relate—they have most likely heard terms such as JPEG and MP3; they have probably recorded data on CDs and DVDs; they have purchased computer components; they have interacted with an operating system; and they have used the Internet. By starting the course with these topics, students discover answers to many of the "why" questions they have been carrying for years and learn to view the course as practical rather than theoretical. From this beginning it is natural to move on to the more abstract issues of algorithms, algorithmic structures, programming languages, software development methodologies, computability, and complexity that those of us in the field view as the main topics in the science. As already stated, the topics are presented in a manner that does not force you to follow this bottom-up sequence, but we encourage you to give it a try.

We are all aware that students learn a lot more than we teach them directly, and the lessons they learn implicitly are often better absorbed than those that are studied explicitly. This is significant when it comes to "teaching" problem solving. Students do not become problem solvers by studying problem-solving methodologies. They become problem solvers by solving problems—and not just carefully posed "textbook problems." So this text contains numerous problems, a few of which are intentionally vague—meaning that there is not necessarily a single correct approach or a single correct answer. We encourage you to use these and to expand on them.

Other topics in the "implicit learning" category are those of professionalism, ethics, and social responsibility. We do not believe that this material should be presented as an isolated subject that is merely tacked on to the course. Instead, it should be an integral part of the coverage that surfaces when it is relevant. This is the approach followed in this text. You will find that Sections 3.5, 4.5, 7.9, 9.7, and 11.7 present such topics as security, privacy, liability, and social awareness in the context of operating systems, networking, software engineering, database systems, and artificial intelligence. You will also find that each chapter includes a collection of questions called *Social Issues* that challenge students to think about the relationship between the material in the text and the society in which they live.

Thank you for considering our text for your course. Whether you do or do not decide that it is right for your situation, I hope that you find it to be a contribution to the computer science education literature.

Pedagogical Features

This text is the product of many years of teaching. As a result, it is rich in pedagogical aids. Paramount is the abundance of problems to enhance the student's participation—over 1,000 in this 12th edition. These are classified as Questions & Exercises, Chapter Review Problems, and Social Issues. The Questions & Exercises appear at the end of each section (except for the introductory chapter). They review the material just discussed, extend the previous discussion, or hint at related topics to be covered later. These questions are answered in Appendix F.

The Chapter Review Problems appear at the end of each chapter (except for the introductory chapter). They are designed to serve as "homework" problems in that they cover the material from the entire chapter and are not answered in the text.

Also at the end of each chapter are the questions in the Social Issues category. They are designed for thought and discussion. Many of them can be used to launch research assignments culminating in short written or oral reports.

Each chapter also ends with a list called Additional Reading that contains references to other material relating to the subject of the chapter. The websites identified in this preface, in the text, and in the sidebars of the text are also good places to look for related material.

Support Material

Instructors may access additional teaching support material from Pearson's website. Some of these are password protected and instructors using the book can obtain a password by registering on the Pearson website.

The material available includes :

- Instructor's Guide with answers to the Chapter Review Problems
- PowerPoint lecture slides

You can access this material at **www.pearsoned.co.in/GlennBrookshear**

To Students

Glenn Brookshear is a bit of a nonconformist (some of his friends would say *more* than a bit) so when he set out to write this text he didn't always follow the advice he received. In particular, many argued that certain material was too advanced for beginning students. But, we believe that if a topic is relevant, then it is relevant even if the academic community considers it to be an "advanced topic." You deserve a text that presents a complete picture of computer science—not a watered-down version containing artificially simplified presentations of only those topics that have been deemed appropriate for introductory students. Thus, we have not avoided topics. Instead, we've sought better explanations. We've tried to provide enough depth to give you an honest picture of what computer science is all about. As in the case of spices in a recipe, you may choose to skip some of the topics in the following pages, but they are there for you to taste if you wish—and we encourage you to do so.

We should also point out that in any course dealing with technology, the details you learn today may not be the details you will need to know tomorrow. The field is dynamic—that's part of the excitement. This book will give you a current picture of the subject as well as a historical perspective. With this background you will be prepared to grow along with technology. We encourage you to start the growing process now by exploring beyond this text. Learn to learn.

Thank you for the trust you have placed in us by choosing to read our book. As authors we have an obligation to produce a manuscript that is worth your time. We hope you find that we have lived up to this obligation.

Acknowledgments

First and foremost, I thank Glenn Brookshear, who has shepherded this book, "his baby," through eleven previous editions, spanning more than a quarter century of rapid growth and tumultuous change in the field of computer science. While this is the first edition in which he has allowed a co-author to oversee all of the revisions, the pages of this 12th edition remain overwhelmingly in Glenn's voice and, I hope, guided by his vision. Any new blemishes are mine; the elegant underlying framework is all his.

I join Glenn in thanking those of you who have supported this book by reading and using it in previous editions. We are honored.

David T. Smith (Indiana University of Pennsylvania) played a significant role in co-authoring revisions to the 11th edition with me, many of which are still visible in this 12th edition. David's close reading of this edition and careful attention to the supplemental materials have been essential. Andrew Kuemmel (Madison West), George Corliss (Marquette), and Chris Mayfield (James Madison) all provided valuable feedback, insight, and/or encouragement on drafts for this edition, while James E. Ames (Virginia Commonwealth), Stephanie E. August (Loyola), Yoonsuck Choe (Texas A&M), Melanie Feinberg (UT-Austin), Eric D. Hanley (Drake), Sudharsan R. Iyengar (Winona State), Ravi Mukkamala (Old Dominion), and Edward Pryor (Wake Forest) all offered valuable reviews of the Python-specific revisions.

Others who have contributed in this or previous editions include J. M. Adams, C. M. Allen, D. C. S. Allison, E. Angel, R. Ashmore, B. Auernheimer, P. Bankston, M. Barnard, P. Bender, K. Bowyer, P. W. Brashear, C. M. Brown, H. M Brown, B. Calloni, J. Carpinelli, M. Clancy, R. T. Close, D. H. Cooley, L. D. Cornell, M. J. Crowley, F. Deek, M. Dickerson, M. J. Duncan, S. Ezekiel, C. Fox, S. Fox, N. E. Gibbs, J. D. Harris, D. Hascom, L. Heath, P. B. Henderson, L. Hunt, M. Hutchenreuther, L. A. Jehn, K. K. Kolberg, K. Korb, G. Krenz, J. Kurose, J. Liu, T. J. Long, C. May, J. J. McConnell, W. McCown, S. J. Merrill, K. Messersmith, J. C. Moyer, M. Murphy, J. P. Myers, Jr., D. S. Noonan, G. Nutt, W. W. Oblitey, S. Olariu, G. Riccardi, G. Rice, N. Rickert, C. Riedesel, J. B. Rogers, G. Saito, W. Savitch, R. Schlafly, J. C. Schlimmer, S. Sells, Z. Shen, G. Sheppard, J. C. Simms, M. C. Slattery, J. Slimick, J. A. Slomka, J. Solderitsch, R. Steigerwald, L. Steinberg, C. A. Struble, C. L. Struble, W. J. Taffe, J. Talburt, P. Tonellato, P. Tromovitch, P. H. Winston, E. D. Winter, E. Wright, M. Ziegler, and one anonymous. To these individuals we give our sincere thanks.

As already mentioned, you will find Java and C++ manuals at the text's Companion Website that teach the basics of these languages in a format compatible with the text. These were written by Diane Christie. Thank you, Diane. Another thank you goes to Roger Eastman who was the creative force behind the chapter-by-chapter activities that you will also find at the companion website.

I also thank the good people at Pearson who have supported this project. Tracy Johnson, Camille Trentacoste, and Carole Snyder in particular have been a pleasure to work with, and brought their wisdom and many improvements to the table throughout the process.

Finally, my thanks to my wife, Petra—"the Rock"—to whom this edition is dedicated. Her patience and fortitude all too frequently exceeded my own, and this book is better for her steadying influence.

D.W.B.

Contents

**Asterisks indicate suggestions for optional sections.*

CHAPTER

0

Introduction

In this preliminary chapter we consider the scope of computer science, develop a historical perspective, and establish a foundation from which to launch our study.

Computer science is the discipline that seeks to build a scientific foundation for such topics as computer design, computer programming, information processing, algorithmic solutions of problems, and the algorithmic process itself. It provides the underpinnings for today's computer applications as well as the foundations for tomorrow's computing infrastructure.

This book provides a comprehensive introduction to this science. We will investigate a wide range of topics including most of those that constitute a typical university computer science curriculum. We want to appreciate the full scope and dynamics of the field. Thus, in addition to the topics themselves, we will be interested in their historical development, the current state of research, and prospects for the future. Our goal is to establish a functional understanding of computer science—one that will support those who wish to pursue more specialized studies in the science as well as one that will enable those in other fields to flourish in an increasingly technical society.

0.1 The Role of Algorithms

We begin with the most fundamental concept of computer science—that of an **algorithm.** Informally, an algorithm is a set of steps that defines how a task is performed. (We will be more precise later in Chapter 5.) For example, there are algorithms for cooking (called recipes), for finding your way through a strange city (more commonly called directions), for operating washing machines (usually displayed on the inside of the washer's lid or perhaps on the wall of a laundromat), for playing music (expressed in the form of sheet music), and for performing magic tricks (Figure 0.1).

Before a machine such as a computer can perform a task, an algorithm for performing that task must be discovered and represented in a form that is compatible with the machine. A representation of an algorithm is called a **program.** For the convenience of humans, computer programs are usually printed on paper or displayed on computer screens. For the convenience of machines, programs are encoded in a manner compatible with the technology of the machine. The process of developing a program, encoding it in machine-compatible form, and inserting it into a machine is called **programming.** Programs, and the algorithms they represent, are collectively referred to as **software,** in contrast to the machinery itself, which is known as **hardware.**

The study of algorithms began as a subject in mathematics. Indeed, the search for algorithms was a significant activity of mathematicians long before the development of today's computers. The goal was to find a single set of directions that described how all problems of a particular type could be solved. One of the best known examples of this early research is the long division algorithm for finding the quotient of two multiple-digit numbers. Another example is the Euclidean algorithm, discovered by the ancient Greek mathematician Euclid, for finding the greatest common divisor of two positive integers (Figure 0.2).

Once an algorithm for performing a task has been found, the performance of that task no longer requires an understanding of the principles on which the algorithm is based. Instead, the performance of the task is reduced to the process of merely following directions. (We can follow the long division algorithm to find a quotient or the Euclidean algorithm to find a greatest common divisor without

Figure 0.1 An algorithm for a magic trick

Effect: The performer places some cards from a normal deck of playing cards face down on a table and mixes them thoroughly while spreading them out on the table. Then, as the audience requests either red or black cards, the performer turns over cards of the requested color.

Secret and Patter:

Step 1. From a normal deck of cards, select ten red cards and ten black cards. Deal these cards face up in two piles on the table according to color.

Step 2. Announce that you have selected some red cards and some black cards.

Step 3. Pick up the red cards. Under the pretense of aligning them into a small deck, hold them face down in your left hand and, with the thumb and first finger of your right hand, pull back on each end of the deck so that each card is given a slightly *backward* curve. Then place the deck of red cards face down on the table as you say, "Here are the red cards in this stack."

Step 4. Pick up the black cards. In a manner similar to that in step 3, give these cards a slight *forward* curve. Then return these cards to the table in a face-down deck as you say, "And here are the black cards in this stack."

Step 5. Immediately after returning the black cards to the table, use both hands to mix the red and black cards (still face down) as you spread them out on the tabletop. Explain that you are thoroughly mixing the cards.

Step 6. As long as there are face-down cards on the table, repeatedly execute the following steps:

6.1. Ask the audience to request either a red or a black card.

6.2. If the color requested is red and there is a face-down card with a concave appearance, turn over such a card while saying, "Here is a red card."

6.3. If the color requested is black and there is a face-down card with a convex appearance, turn over such a card while saying, "Here is a black card."

6.4. Otherwise, state that there are no more cards of the requested color and turn over the remaining cards to prove your claim.

Figure 0.2 The Euclidean algorithm for finding the greatest common divisor of two positive integers

Description: This algorithm assumes that its input consists of two positive integers and proceeds to compute the greatest common divisor of these two values.

Procedure:

Step 1. Assign M and N the value of the larger and smaller of the two input values, respectively.

Step 2. Divide M by N, and call the remainder R.

Step 3. If R is not 0, then assign M the value of N, assign N the value of R, and return to step 2; otherwise, the greatest common divisor is the value currently assigned to N.

understanding why the algorithm works.) In a sense, the intelligence required to solve the problem at hand is encoded in the algorithm.

Capturing and conveying intelligence (or at least intelligent behavior) by means of algorithms allows us to build machines that perform useful tasks. Consequently, the level of intelligence displayed by machines is limited by the intelligence that can be conveyed through algorithms. We can construct a machine to perform a task only if an algorithm exists for performing that task. In turn, if no algorithm exists for solving a problem, then the solution of that problem lies beyond the capabilities of machines.

Identifying the limitations of algorithmic capabilities solidified as a subject in mathematics in the 1930s with the publication of Kurt Gödel's incompleteness theorem. This theorem essentially states that in any mathematical theory encompassing our traditional arithmetic system, there are statements whose truth or falseness cannot be established by algorithmic means. In short, any complete study of our arithmetic system lies beyond the capabilities of algorithmic activities. This realization shook the foundations of mathematics, and the study of algorithmic capabilities that ensued was the beginning of the field known today as computer science. Indeed, it is the study of algorithms that forms the core of computer science.

0.2 The History of Computing

Today's computers have an extensive genealogy. One of the earlier computing devices was the abacus. History tells us that it probably had its roots in ancient China and was used in the early Greek and Roman civilizations. The machine is quite simple, consisting of beads strung on rods that are in turn mounted in a rectangular frame (Figure 0.3). As the beads are moved back and forth on the rods, their positions represent stored values. It is in the positions of the beads that this "computer" represents and stores data. For control of an algorithm's execution, the machine relies on the human operator. Thus the abacus alone is merely a data storage system; it must be combined with a human to create a complete computational machine.

In the time period after the Middle Ages and before the Modern Era, the quest for more sophisticated computing machines was seeded. A few inventors began to experiment with the technology of gears. Among these were Blaise Pascal (1623–1662) of France, Gottfried Wilhelm Leibniz (1646–1716) of Germany, and Charles Babbage (1792–1871) of England. These machines represented data through gear positioning, with data being entered mechanically by establishing initial gear positions. Output from Pascal's and Leibniz's machines was achieved by observing the final gear positions. Babbage, on the other hand, envisioned machines that would print results of computations on paper so that the possibility of transcription errors would be eliminated.

As for the ability to follow an algorithm, we can see a progression of flexibility in these machines. Pascal's machine was built to perform only addition. Consequently, the appropriate sequence of steps was embedded into the structure of the machine itself. In a similar manner, Leibniz's machine had its algorithms firmly embedded in its architecture, although the operator could select from a variety of arithmetic operations it offered. Babbage's Difference Engine

Figure 0.3 Chinese wooden abacus (Pink Badger/Fotolia)

(of which only a demonstration model was constructed) could be modified to perform a variety of calculations, but his Analytical Engine (never funded for construction) was designed to read instructions in the form of holes in paper cards. Thus Babbage's Analytical Engine was programmable. In fact, Augusta Ada Byron (Ada Lovelace), who published a paper in which she demonstrated how Babbage's Analytical Engine could be programmed to perform various computations, is often identified today as the world's first programmer.

The idea of communicating an algorithm via holes in paper was not originated by Babbage. He got the idea from Joseph Jacquard (1752–1834), who, in 1801, had developed a weaving loom in which the steps to be performed during the weaving process were determined by patterns of holes in large thick cards made of wood (or cardboard). In this manner, the algorithm followed by the loom could be changed easily to produce different woven designs. Another beneficiary of Jacquard's idea was Herman Hollerith (1860–1929), who applied the concept of representing information as holes in paper cards to speed up the tabulation process in the 1890 U.S. census. (It was this work by Hollerith that led to the creation of IBM.) Such cards ultimately came to be known as punched cards and survived as a popular means of communicating with computers well into the 1970s.

Nineteenth-century technology was unable to produce the complex gear-driven machines of Pascal, Leibniz, and Babbage cost-effectively. But with the advances in electronics in the early 1900s, this barrier was overcome. Examples of this progress include the electromechanical machine of George Stibitz, completed in 1940 at Bell Laboratories, and the Mark I, completed in 1944 at Harvard University by Howard Aiken and a group of IBM engineers. These machines made heavy use of electronically controlled mechanical relays. In this sense they were obsolete almost as soon as they were built, because other researchers were applying the technology of vacuum tubes to construct totally

Figure 0.4 Three women operating the ENIAC's (Electronic Numerical Integrator And Computer) main control panel while the machine was at the Moore School. The machine was later moved to the U.S. Army's Ballistics Research Laboratory. (Courtesy U.S. Army.)

electronic computers. The first of these vacuum tube machines was apparently the Atanasoff-Berry machine, constructed during the period from 1937 to 1941 at Iowa State College (now Iowa State University) by John Atanasoff and his assistant, Clifford Berry. Another was a machine called Colossus, built under the direction of Tommy Flowers in England to decode German messages during the latter part of World War II. (Actually, as many as ten of these machines were apparently built, but military secrecy and issues of national security kept their existence from becoming part of the "computer family tree.") Other, more flexible machines, such as the ENIAC (electronic numerical integrator and calculator) developed by John Mauchly and J. Presper Eckert at the Moore School of Electrical Engineering, University of Pennsylvania, soon followed (Figure 0.4).

From that point on, the history of computing machines has been closely linked to advancing technology, including the invention of transistors (for which physicists William Shockley, John Bardeen, and Walter Brattain were awarded a Nobel Prize) and the subsequent development of complete circuits constructed as single units, called integrated circuits (for which Jack Kilby also won a Nobel Prize in physics). With these developments, the room-sized machines of the 1940s were reduced over the decades to the size of single cabinets. At the same time, the processing power of computing machines began to double every two years (a trend that has continued to this day). As work on integrated circuitry progressed, many of the components within a computer became readily available on the open market as integrated circuits encased in toy-sized blocks of plastic called chips.

A major step toward popularizing computing was the development of desktop computers. The origins of these machines can be traced to the computer hobbyists who built homemade computers from combinations of chips. It was within this "underground" of hobby activity that Steve Jobs and Stephen Wozniak

Babbage's Difference Engine

The machines designed by Charles Babbage were truly the forerunners of modern computer design. If technology had been able to produce his machines in an economically feasible manner and if the data processing demands of commerce and government had been on the scale of today's requirements, Babbage's ideas could have led to a computer revolution in the 1800s. As it was, only a demonstration model of his Difference Engine was constructed in his lifetime. This machine determined numerical values by computing "successive differences." We can gain an insight to this technique by considering the problem of computing the squares of the integers. We begin with the knowledge that the square of 0 is 0, the square of 1 is 1, the square of 2 is 4, and the square of 3 is 9. With this, we can determine the square of 4 in the following manner (see the following diagram). We first compute the differences of the squares we already know: $1^2 - 0^2 = 1$, $2^2 - 1^2 = 3$, and $3^2 - 2^2 = 5$. Then we compute the differences of these results: $3 - 1 = 2$, and $5 - 3 = 2$. Note that these differences are both 2. Assuming that this consistency continues (mathematics can show that it does), we conclude that the difference between the value $(4^2 - 3^2)$ and the value $(3^2 - 2^2)$ must also be 2. Hence $(4^2 - 3^2)$ must be 2 greater than $(3^2 - 2^2)$, so $4^2 - 3^2 = 7$ and thus $4^2 = 3^2 + 7 = 16$. Now that we know the square of 4, we could continue our procedure to compute the square of 5 based on the values of 1^2, 2^2, 3^2, and 4^2. (Although a more in–depth discussion of successive differences is beyond the scope of our current study, students of calculus may wish to observe that the preceding example is based on the fact that the derivative of $y = x^2$ is a straight line with a slope of 2.)

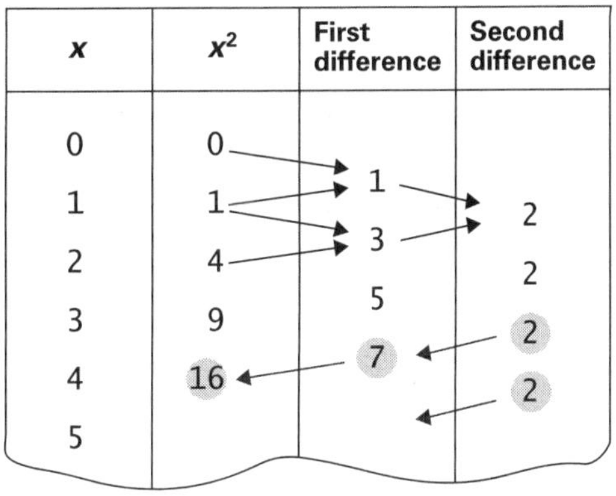

built a commercially viable home computer and, in 1976, established Apple Computer, Inc. (now Apple Inc.) to manufacture and market their products. Other companies that marketed similar products were Commodore, Heathkit, and Radio Shack. Although these products were popular among computer hobbyists, they were not widely accepted by the business community, which continued to look to the well-established IBM and its large mainframe computers for the majority of its computing needs.

In 1981, IBM introduced its first desktop computer, called the personal computer, or PC, whose underlying software was developed by a newly formed company known as Microsoft. The PC was an instant success and legitimized

Augusta Ada Byron

Augusta Ada Byron, Countess of Lovelace, has been the subject of much commentary in the computing community. She lived a somewhat tragic life of less than 37 years (1815–1852) that was complicated by poor health and the fact that she was a nonconformist in a society that limited the professional role of women. Although she was interested in a wide range of science, she concentrated her studies in mathematics. Her interest in "compute science" began when she became fascinated by the machines of Charles Babbage at a demonstration of a prototype of his Difference Engine in 1833. Her contribution to computer science stems from her translation from French into English of a paper discussing Babbage's designs for the Analytical Engine. To this translation, Babbage encouraged her to attach an addendum describing applications of the engine and containing examples of how the engine could be programmed to perform various tasks. Babbage's enthusiasm for Ada Byron's work was apparently motivated by his hope that its publication would lead to financial backing for the construction of his Analytical Engine. (As the daughter of Lord Byron, Ada Byron held celebrity status with potentially significant financial connections.) This backing never materialized, but Ada Byron's addendum has survived and is considered to contain the first examples of computer programs. The degree to which Babbage influenced Ada Byron's work is debated by historians. Some argue that Babbage made major contributions, whereas others contend that he was more of an obstacle than an aid. Nonetheless, Augusta Ada Byron is recognized today as the world's first programmer, a status that was certified by the U.S. Department of Defense when it named a prominent programming language (Ada) in her honor.

the desktop computer as an established commodity in the minds of the business community. Today, the term PC is widely used to refer to all those machines (from various manufacturers) whose design has evolved from IBM's initial desktop computer, most of which continue to be marketed with software from Microsoft. At times, however, the term PC is used interchangeably with the generic terms *desktop* or *laptop*.

As the twentieth century drew to a close, the ability to connect individual computers in a world-wide system called the **Internet** was revolutionizing communication. In this context, Tim Berners-Lee (a British scientist) proposed a system by which documents stored on computers throughout the Internet could be linked together producing a maze of linked information called the **World Wide Web** (often shortened to "Web"). To make the information on the Web accessible, software systems, called **search engines,** were developed to "sift through" the Web, "categorize" their findings, and then use the results to assist users researching particular topics. Major players in this field are Google, Yahoo, and Microsoft. These companies continue to expand their Web-related activities, often in directions that challenge our traditional way of thinking.

At the same time that desktop and laptop computers were being accepted and used in homes, the miniaturization of computing machines continued. Today, tiny computers are embedded within a wide variety of electronic appliances and devices. Automobiles may now contain dozens of small computers running Global Positioning Systems (GPS), monitoring the function of the engine, and providing

Google

Founded in 1998, Google Inc. has become one of the world's most recognized technology companies. Its core service, the Google search engine, is used by millions of people to find documents on the World Wide Web. In addition, Google provides electronic mail service (called Gmail), an Internet-based video-sharing service (called YouTube), and a host of other Internet services (including Google Maps, Google Calendar, Google Earth, Google Books, and Google Translate).

However, in addition to being a prime example of the entrepreneurial spirit, Google also provides examples of how expanding technology is challenging society. For example, Google's search engine has led to questions regarding the extent to which an international company should comply with the wishes of individual governments; YouTube has raised questions regarding the extent to which a company should be liable for information that others distribute through its services as well as the degree to which the company can claim ownership of that information; Google Books has generated concerns regarding the scope and limitations of intellectual property rights; and Google Maps has been accused of violating privacy rights.

voice command services for controlling the car's audio and phone communication systems.

Perhaps the most revolutionary application of computer miniaturization is found in the expanding capabilities of **smartphones,** hand-held general-purpose computers on which telephony is only one of many applications. More powerful than the supercomputers of prior decades, these pocket-sized devices are equipped with a rich array of sensors and interfaces including cameras, microphones, compasses, touch screens, accelerometers (to detect the phone's orientation and motion), and a number of wireless technologies to communicate with other smartphones and computers. Many argue that the smartphone is having a greater effect on global society than the PC revolution.

0.3 An Outline of Our Study

This text follows a bottom-up approach to the study of computer science, beginning with such hands-on topics as computer hardware and leading to the more abstract topics such as algorithm complexity and computability. The result is that our study follows a pattern of building larger and larger abstract tools as our understanding of the subject expands.

We begin by considering topics dealing with the design and construction of machines for executing algorithms. In Chapter 1 (Data Storage), we look at how information is encoded and stored within modern computers, and in Chapter 2 (Data Manipulation), we investigate the basic internal operation of a simple computer. Although part of this study involves technology, the general theme is technology independent. That is, such topics as digital circuit design, data encoding and compression systems, and computer architecture are relevant over a wide range of technology and promise to remain relevant regardless of the direction of future technology.

In Chapter 3 (Operating Systems), we study the software that controls the overall operation of a computer. This software is called an operating system. It is a computer's operating system that controls the interface between the machine and its outside world, protecting the machine and the data stored within from unauthorized access, allowing a computer user to request the execution of various programs, and coordinating the internal activities required to fulfill the user's requests.

In Chapter 4 (Networking and the Internet), we study how computers are connected to each other to form computer networks and how networks are connected to form internets. This study leads to topics such as network protocols, the Internet's structure and internal operation, the World Wide Web, and numerous issues of security.

Chapter 5 (Algorithms) introduces the study of algorithms from a more formal perspective. We investigate how algorithms are discovered, identify several fundamental algorithmic structures, develop elementary techniques for representing algorithms, and introduce the subjects of algorithm efficiency and correctness.

In Chapter 6 (Programming Languages), we consider the subject of algorithm representation and the program development process. Here we find that the search for better programming techniques has led to a variety of programming methodologies or paradigms, each with its own set of programming languages. We investigate these paradigms and languages as well as consider issues of grammar and language translation.

Chapter 7 (Software Engineering) introduces the branch of computer science known as software engineering, which deals with the problems encountered when developing large software systems. The underlying theme is that the design of large software systems is a complex task that embraces problems beyond those of traditional engineering. Thus, the subject of software engineering has become an important field of research within computer science, drawing from such diverse fields as engineering, project management, personnel management, programming language design, and even architecture.

In the next two chapters we look at ways data can be organized within a computer system. In Chapter 8 (Data Abstractions), we introduce techniques traditionally used for organizing data in a computer's main memory and then trace the evolution of data abstraction from the concept of primitives to today's object-oriented techniques. In Chapter 9 (Database Systems), we consider methods traditionally used for organizing data in a computer's mass storage and investigate how extremely large and complex database systems are implemented.

In Chapter 10 (Computer Graphics), we explore the subject of graphics and animation, a field that deals with creating and photographing virtual worlds. Based on advancements in the more traditional areas of computer science such as machine architecture, algorithm design, data structures, and software engineering, the discipline of graphics and animation has seen significant progress and has now blossomed into an exciting, dynamic subject. Moreover, the field exemplifies how various components of computer science combine with other disciplines such as physics, art, and photography to produce striking results.

In Chapter 11 (Artificial Intelligence), we learn that to develop more useful machines computer science has turned to the study of human intelligence for insight. The hope is that by understanding how our own minds reason and perceive, researchers will be able to design algorithms that mimic these processes and thus transfer comparable capabilities to machines. The result is the area of computer science known as artificial intelligence, which leans heavily on research in such areas as psychology, biology, and linguistics.

We close our study with Chapter 12 (Theory of Computation) by investigating the theoretical foundations of computer science—a subject that allows us to understand the limitations of algorithms (and thus machines). Here we identify some problems that cannot be solved algorithmically (and therefore lie beyond the capabilities of machines) as well as learn that the solutions to many other problems require such enormous time or space that they are also unsolvable from a practical perspective. Thus, it is through this study that we are able to grasp the scope and limitations of algorithmic systems.

In each chapter, our goal is to explore the subject deeply enough to enable true understanding. We want to develop a working knowledge of computer science—a knowledge that will allow you to understand the technical society in which you live and to provide a foundation from which you can learn on your own as science and technology advance.

0.4 The Overarching Themes of Computer Science

In addition to the main topics of each chapter as listed above, we also hope to broaden your understanding of computer science by incorporating several overarching themes.

The miniaturization of computers and their expanding capabilities have brought computer technology to the forefront of today's society, and computer technology is so prevalent that familiarity with it is fundamental to being a member of the modern world. Computing technology has altered the ability of governments to exert control; had enormous impact on global economics; led to startling advances in scientific research; revolutionized the role of data collection, storage, and applications; provided new means for people to communicate and interact; and has repeatedly challenged society's status quo. The result is a proliferation of subjects surrounding computer science, each of which is now a significant field of study in its own right. Moreover, as with mechanical engineering and physics, it is often difficult to draw a line between these fields and computer science itself. Thus, to gain a proper perspective, our study will not only cover topics central to the core of computer science but also will explore a variety of disciplines dealing with both applications and consequences of the science. Indeed, an introduction to computer science is an interdisciplinary undertaking.

As we set out to explore the breadth of the field of computing, it is helpful to keep in mind the main themes that unite computer science. While the codification of the "Seven Big Ideas of Computer Science"[1] postdates the first ten editions of this book, they closely parallel the themes of the chapters to come. The "Seven Big Ideas" are, briefly: Algorithms, Abstraction, Creativity, Data, Programming, Internet, and Impact. In the chapters that follow, we include a variety of topics, in each case introducing central ideas of the topic, current areas of research, and some of the techniques being applied to advance knowledge in that realm. Watch for the "Big Ideas" as we return to them again and again.

---

[1] `www.csprinciples.org`

Algorithms

Limited data storage capabilities and intricate, time-consuming programming procedures restricted the complexity of the algorithms used in the earliest computing machines. However, as these limitations began to disappear, machines were applied to increasingly larger and more complex tasks. As attempts to express the composition of these tasks in algorithmic form began to tax the abilities of the human mind, more and more research efforts were directed toward the study of algorithms and the programming process.

It was in this context that the theoretical work of mathematicians began to pay dividends. As a consequence of Gödel's incompleteness theorem, mathematicians had already been investigating those questions regarding algorithmic processes that advancing technology was now raising. With that, the stage was set for the emergence of a new discipline known as *computer science.*

Today, computer science has established itself as the science of algorithms. The scope of this science is broad, drawing from such diverse subjects as mathematics, engineering, psychology, biology, business administration, and linguistics. Indeed, researchers in different branches of computer science may have very distinct definitions of the science. For example, a researcher in the field of computer architecture may focus on the task of miniaturizing circuitry and thus view computer science as the advancement and application of technology. But, a researcher in the field of database systems may see computer science as seeking ways to make information systems more useful. And, a researcher in the field of artificial intelligence may regard computer science as the study of intelligence and intelligent behavior.

Nevertheless, all of these researchers are involved in aspects of the science of algorithms. Given the central role that algorithms play in computer science (see Figure 0.5), it is instructive to identify some questions that will provide focus for our study of this big idea.

- Which problems can be solved by algorithmic processes?
- How can the discovery of algorithms be made easier?

Figure 0.5 The central role of algorithms in computer science

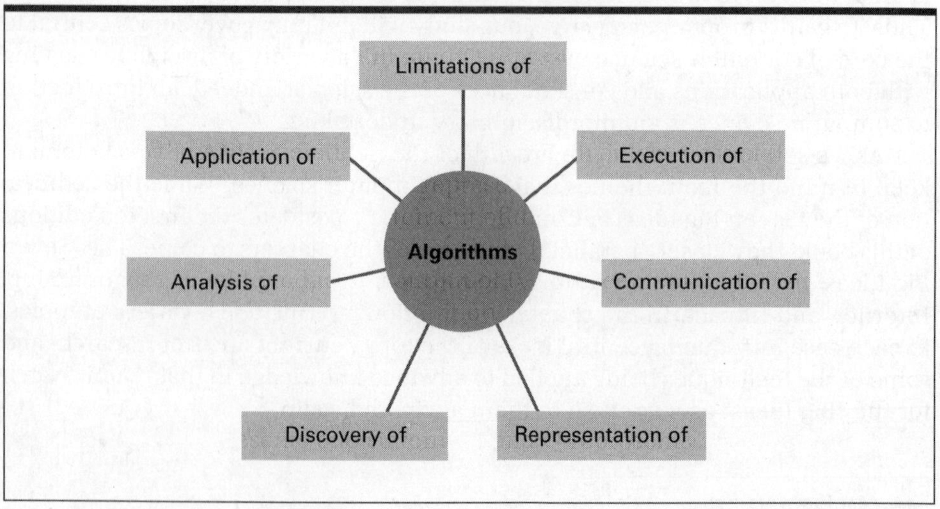

- How can the techniques of representing and communicating algorithms be improved?
- How can the characteristics of different algorithms be analyzed and compared?
- How can algorithms be used to manipulate information?
- How can algorithms be applied to produce intelligent behavior?
- How does the application of algorithms affect society?

Abstraction

The term **abstraction,** as we are using it here, refers to the distinction between the external properties of an entity and the details of the entity's internal composition. It is abstraction that allows us to ignore the internal details of a complex device such as a computer, automobile, or microwave oven and use it as a single, comprehensible unit. Moreover, it is by means of abstraction that such complex systems are designed and manufactured in the first place. Computers, automobiles, and microwave ovens are constructed from components, each of which represents a level of abstraction at which the use of the component is isolated from the details of the component's internal composition.

It is by applying abstraction that we are able to construct, analyze, and manage large, complex computer systems that would be overwhelming if viewed in their entirety at a detailed level. At each level of abstraction, we view the system in terms of components, called **abstract tools,** whose internal composition we ignore. This allows us to concentrate on how each component interacts with other components at the same level and how the collection as a whole forms a higher-level component. Thus we are able to comprehend the part of the system that is relevant to the task at hand rather than being lost in a sea of details.

We emphasize that abstraction is not limited to science and technology. It is an important simplification technique with which our society has created a lifestyle that would otherwise be impossible. Few of us understand how the various conveniences of daily life are actually implemented. We eat food and wear clothes that we cannot produce by ourselves. We use electrical devices and communication systems without understanding the underlying technology. We use the services of others without knowing the details of their professions. With each new advancement, a small part of society chooses to specialize in its implementation, while the rest of us learn to use the results as abstract tools. In this manner, society's warehouse of abstract tools expands, and society's ability to progress increases.

Abstraction is a recurring pillar of our study. We will learn that computing equipment is constructed in levels of abstract tools. We will also see that the development of large software systems is accomplished in a modular fashion in which each module is used as an abstract tool in larger modules. Moreover, abstraction plays an important role in the task of advancing computer science itself, allowing researchers to focus attention on particular areas within a complex field. In fact, the organization of this text reflects this characteristic of the science. Each chapter, which focuses on a particular area within the science, is often surprisingly independent of the others, yet together the chapters form a comprehensive overview of a vast field of study.

Creativity

While computers may merely be complex machines mechanically executing rote algorithmic instructions, we shall see that the field of computer science is an inherently creative one. Discovering and applying new algorithms is a human activity that depends on our innate desire to apply our tools to solve problems in the world around us. Computer science not only extends forms of expression spanning the visual, language and musical arts, but also enables new modes of digital expression that pervade the modern world.

Creating large software systems is much less like following a cookbook recipe than it is like conceiving of a grand new sculpture. Envisioning its form and function requires careful planning. Fabricating its components requires time, attention to detail, and practiced skill. The final product embodies the design aesthetics and sensibilities of its creators.

Data

Computers are capable of representing any information that can be discretized and digitized. Algorithms can process or transform such digitally represented information in a dizzying variety of ways. The result of this is not merely the shuffling of digital data from one part of the computer to another; computer algorithms enable us to search for patterns, to create simulations, and to correlate connections in ways that generate new knowledge and insight. Massive storage capacities, high-speed computer networks, and powerful computational tools are driving discoveries in many other disciplines of science, engineering and the humanities. Whether predicting the effects of a new drug by simulating complex protein folding, statistically analyzing the evolution of language across centuries of digitized books, or rendering 3D images of internal organs from a noninvasive medical scan, data is driving modern discovery across the breadth of human endeavors.

Some of the questions about data that we will explore in our study include:

- How do computers store data about common digital artifacts, such as numbers, text, images, sounds, and video?
- How do computers approximate data about analog artifacts in the real world?
- How do computers detect and prevent errors in data?
- What are the ramifications of an ever-growing and interconnected digital universe of data at our disposal?

Programming

Translating human intentions into executable computer algorithms is now broadly referred to as *programming*, although the proliferation of languages and tools available now bear little resemblance to the programmable computers of the 1950s and early 1960s. While computer science consists of much more than computer programming, the ability to solve problems by devising executable algorithms (programs) remains a foundational skill for all computer scientists.

Computer hardware is capable of executing only relatively simple algorithmic steps, but the abstractions provided by computer programming languages allow humans to reason about and encode solutions for far more complex problems. Several key questions will frame our discussion of this theme.

- How are programs built?
- What kinds of errors can occur in programs?
- How are errors in programs found and repaired?
- What are the effects of errors in modern programs?
- How are programs documented and evaluated?

Internet

The Internet connects computers and electronic devices around the world and has had a profound impact in the way that our technological society stores, retrieves, and shares information. Commerce, news, entertainment, and communication now depend increasingly on this interconnected web of smaller computer networks. Our discussion will not only describe the mechanisms of the Internet as an artifact, but will also touch on the many aspects of human society that are now intertwined with the global network.

The reach of the Internet also has profound implications for our privacy and the security of our personal information. Cyberspace harbors many dangers. Consequently, cryptography and cybersecurity are of growing importance in our connected world.

Impact

Computer science not only has profound impacts on the technologies we use to communicate, work, and play, it also has enormous social repercussions. Progress in computer science is blurring many distinctions on which our society has based decisions in the past and is challenging many of society's long-held principles. In law, it generates questions regarding the degree to which intellectual property can be owned and the rights and liabilities that accompany that ownership. In ethics, it generates numerous options that challenge the traditional principles on which social behavior is based. In government, it generates debates regarding the extent to which computer technology and its applications should be regulated. In philosophy, it generates contention between the presence of intelligent behavior and the presence of intelligence itself. And, throughout society, it generates disputes concerning whether new applications represent new freedoms or new controls.

Such topics are important for those contemplating careers in computing or computer-related fields. Revelations within science have sometimes found controversial applications, causing serious discontent for the researchers involved. Moreover, an otherwise successful career can quickly be derailed by an ethical misstep.

The ability to deal with the dilemmas posed by advancing computer technology is also important for those outside its immediate realm. Indeed, technology is infiltrating society so rapidly that few, if any, are independent of its effects.

This text provides the technical background needed to approach the dilemmas generated by computer science in a rational manner. However, technical knowledge of the science alone does not provide solutions to all the questions involved. With this in mind, this text includes several sections that are devoted to social, ethical, and legal impacts of computer science. These include security concerns, issues of software ownership and liability, the social impact of database technology, and the consequences of advances in artificial intelligence.

Moreover, there is often no definitive correct answer to a problem, and many valid solutions are compromises between opposing (and perhaps equally valid) views. Finding solutions in these cases often requires the ability to listen, to recognize other points of view, to carry on a rational debate, and to alter one's own opinion as new insights are gained. Thus, each chapter of this text ends with a collection of questions under the heading "Social Issues" that investigate the relationship between computer science and society. These are not necessarily questions to be answered. Instead, they are questions to be considered. In many cases, an answer that may appear obvious at first will cease to satisfy you as you explore alternatives. In short, the purpose of these questions is not to lead you to a "correct" answer, but rather to increase your awareness, including your awareness of the various stakeholders in an issue, your awareness of alternatives, and your awareness of both the short- and long-term consequences of those alternatives.

Philosophers have introduced many approaches to ethics in their search for fundamental theories that lead to principles for guiding decisions and behavior. Character-based ethics (sometimes called virtue ethics) were promoted by Plato and Aristotle, who argued that "good behavior" is not the result of applying identifiable rules, but instead is a natural consequence of "good character." Whereas other ethical bases, such as consequence-based ethics, duty-based ethics, and contract-based ethics, propose that a person resolve an ethical dilemma by asking, "What are the consequences?", "What are my duties?", or "What contracts do I have?," character-based ethics proposes that dilemmas be resolved by asking, "Who do I want to be?" Thus, good behavior is obtained by building good character, which is typically the result of sound upbringing and the development of virtuous habits.

It is character-based ethics that underlies the approach normally taken when "teaching" ethics to professionals in various fields. Rather than presenting specific ethical theories, the approach is to introduce case studies that expose a variety of ethical questions in the professionals' area of expertise. Then, by discussing the pros and cons in these cases, the professionals become more aware, insightful, and sensitive to the perils lurking in their professional lives and thus grow in character. This is the spirit in which the questions regarding social issues at the end of each chapter are presented.

Social Issues

The following questions are intended as a guide to the ethical/social/legal issues associated with the field of computing. The goal is not merely to answer these questions. You should also consider why you answered as you did and whether your justifications are consistent from one question to the next.

1. The premise that our society is *different* from what it would have been without the computer revolution is generally accepted. Is our society *better* than it would have been without the revolution? Is our society worse? Would your answer differ if your position within society were different?
2. Is it acceptable to participate in today's technical society without making an effort to understand the basics of that technology? For instance, do members of a democracy, whose votes often determine how technology will be supported and used, have an obligation to try to understand that technology?

Does your answer depend on which technology is being considered? For example, is your answer the same when considering nuclear technology as when considering computer technology?

3. By using cash in financial transactions, individuals have traditionally had the option to manage their financial affairs without service charges. However, as more of our economy is becoming automated, financial institutions are implementing service charges for access to these automated systems. Is there a point at which these charges unfairly restrict an individual's access to the economy? For example, suppose an employer pays employees only by check, and all financial institutions were to place a service charge on check cashing and depositing. Would the employees be unfairly treated? What if an employer insists on paying only via direct deposit?
4. In the context of interactive television, to what extent should a company be allowed to retrieve information from children (perhaps via an interactive game format)? For example, should a company be allowed to obtain a child's report on his or her parents' buying patterns? What about information about the child?
5. To what extent should a government regulate computer technology and its applications? Consider, for example, the issues mentioned in questions 3 and 4. What justifies governmental regulation?
6. To what extent will our decisions regarding technology in general, and computer technology in particular, affect future generations?
7. As technology advances, our educational system is constantly challenged to reconsider the level of abstraction at which topics are presented. Many questions take the form of whether a skill is still necessary or whether students should be allowed to rely on an abstract tool. Students of trigonometry are no longer taught how to find the values of trigonometric functions using tables. Instead, they use calculators as abstract tools to find these values. Some argue that long division should also give way to abstraction. What other subjects are involved with similar controversies? Do modern word processors eliminate the need to develop spelling skills? Will the use of video technology someday remove the need to read?
8. The concept of public libraries is largely based on the premise that all citizens in a democracy must have access to information. As more information is stored and disseminated via computer technology, does access to this technology become a right of every individual? If so, should public libraries be the channel by which this access is provided?
9. What ethical concerns arise in a society that relies on the use of abstract tools? Are there cases in which it is unethical to use a product or service without understanding how it works? Without knowing how it is produced? Or, without understanding the byproducts of its use?
10. As our society becomes more automated, it becomes easier for governments to monitor their citizens' activities. Is that good or bad?
11. Which technologies that were imagined by George Orwell (Eric Blair) in his novel *1984* have become reality? Are they being used in the manner in which Orwell predicted?
12. If you had a time machine, in which period of history would you like to live? Are there current technologies that you would like to take with you? Could your choice of technologies be taken with you without taking others? To what

extent can one technology be separated from another? Is it consistent to protest against global warming yet accept modern medical treatment?

13. Suppose your job requires that you reside in another culture. Should you continue to practice the ethics of your native culture or adopt the ethics of your host culture? Does your answer depend on whether the issue involves dress code or human rights? Which ethical standards should prevail if you continue to reside in your native culture but conduct business with a foreign culture on the Internet?
14. Has society become too dependent on computer applications for commerce, communications, or social interactions? For example, what would be the consequences of a long-term interruption in Internet and/or cellular telephone service?
15. Most smartphones are able to identify the phone's location by means of GPS. This allows applications to provide location-specific information (such as the local news, local weather, or the presence of businesses in the immediate area) based on the phone's current location. However, such GPS capabilities may also allow other applications to broadcast the phone's location to other parties. Is this good? How could knowledge of the phone's location (thus your location) be abused?

Additional Reading

Goldstine, J. J. *The Computer from Pascal to von Neumann*. Princeton, NJ: Princeton University Press, 1972.

Kizza, J. M. *Ethical and Social Issues in the Information Age*, 3rd ed. London: Springer-Verlag, 2007.

Mollenhoff, C. R. *Atanasoff: Forgotten Father of the Computer*. Ames, IA: Iowa State University Press, 1988.

Neumann, P. G. *Computer Related Risks*. Boston, MA: Addison-Wesley, 1995.

Ni, L. *Smart Phone and Next Generation Mobile Computing*. San Francisco, CA: Morgan Kaufmann, 2006.

Quinn, M. J. *Ethics for the Information Age*, 5th ed. Boston, MA: AddisonWesley, 2012.

Randell, B. *The Origins of Digital Computers*, 3rd ed. New York: SpringerVerlag, 1982.

Spinello, R. A., and H. T. Tavani. *Readings in CyberEthics*, 2nd ed. Sudbury, MA: Jones and Bartlett, 2004.

Swade, D. *The Difference Engine*. New York: Viking, 2000.

Tavani, H. T. *Ethics and Technology: Ethical Issues in an Age of Information and Communication Technology*, 4th ed. New York: Wiley, 2012.

Woolley, B. *The Bride of Science: Romance, Reason, and Byron's Daughter*. New York: McGraw-Hill, 1999.

CHAPTER

1

Data Storage

In this chapter, we consider topics associated with data representation and the storage of data within a computer. The types of data we will consider include text, numeric values, images, audio, and video. Much of the information in this chapter is also relevant to fields other than traditional computing, such as digital photography, audio/video recording and reproduction, and long-distance communication.

**Asterisks indicate suggestions for optional sections.*

We begin our study of computer science by considering how information is encoded and stored inside computers. Our first step is to discuss the basics of a computer's data storage devices and then to consider how information is encoded for storage in these systems. We will explore the ramifications of today's data storage systems and how such techniques as data compression and error handling are used to overcome their shortfalls.

1.1 Bits and Their Storage

Inside today's computers information is encoded as patterns of 0s and 1s. These digits are called **bits** (short for *binary digits*). Although you may be inclined to associate bits with numeric values, they are really only symbols whose meaning depends on the application at hand. Sometimes patterns of bits are used to represent numeric values; sometimes they represent characters in an alphabet and punctuation marks; sometimes they represent images; and sometimes they represent sounds.

Boolean Operations

To understand how individual bits are stored and manipulated inside a computer, it is convenient to imagine that the bit 0 represents the value *false* and the bit 1 represents the value *true*. Operations that manipulate true/false values are called **Boolean operations,** in honor of the mathematician George Boole (1815–1864), who was a pioneer in the field of mathematics called logic. Three of the basic Boolean operations are AND, OR, and XOR (exclusive or) as summarized in Figure 1.1. (We capitalize these Boolean operation names to distinguish them from their English word counterparts.) These operations are similar to the arithmetic operations TIMES and PLUS because they combine a pair of values (the operation's input) to produce a third value (the output). In contrast to arithmetic operations, however, Boolean operations combine true/false values rather than numeric values.

The Boolean operation AND is designed to reflect the truth or falseness of a statement formed by combining two smaller, or simpler, statements with the conjunction *and*. Such statements have the generic form

P AND *Q*

where *P* represents one statement, and *Q* represents another—for example,

Kermit is a frog AND Miss Piggy is an actress.

The inputs to the AND operation represent the truth or falseness of the compound statement's components; the output represents the truth or falseness of the compound statement itself. Since a statement of the form *P* AND *Q* is true only when both of its components are true, we conclude that 1 AND 1 should be 1, whereas all other cases should produce an output of 0, in agreement with Figure 1.1.

In a similar manner, the OR operation is based on compound statements of the form

P OR *Q*

where, again, *P* represents one statement and *Q* represents another. Such statements are true when at least one of their components is true, which agrees with the OR operation depicted in Figure 1.1.

Figure 1.1 The possible input and output values of Boolean operations AND, OR, and XOR (exclusive or)

The AND operation

0	0	1	1
AND 0	AND 1	AND 0	AND 1
0	0	0	1

The OR operation

0	0	1	1
OR 0	OR 1	OR 0	OR 1
0	1	1	1

The XOR operation

0	0	1	1
XOR 0	XOR 1	XOR 0	XOR 1
0	1	1	0

There is not a single conjunction in the English language that captures the meaning of the XOR operation. XOR produces an output of 1 (true) when one of its inputs is 1 (true) and the other is 0 (false). For example, a statement of the form *P* XOR *Q* means "either *P* or *Q* but not both." (In short, the XOR operation produces an output of 1 when its inputs are different.)

The operation NOT is another Boolean operation. It differs from AND, OR, and XOR because it has only one input. Its output is the opposite of that input; if the input of the operation NOT is true, then the output is false, and vice versa. Thus, if the input of the NOT operation is the truth or falseness of the statement

Fozzie is a bear.

then the output would represent the truth or falseness of the statement

Fozzie is not a bear.

Gates and Flip-Flops

A device that produces the output of a Boolean operation when given the operation's input values is called a **gate.** Gates can be constructed from a variety of technologies such as gears, relays, and optic devices. Inside today's computers, gates are usually implemented as small electronic circuits in which the digits 0 and 1 are represented as voltage levels. We need not concern ourselves with such details, however. For our purposes, it suffices to represent gates in their symbolic form, as shown in Figure 1.2. Note that the AND, OR, XOR, and NOT gates are represented by distinctively shaped symbols, with the input values entering on one side, and the output exiting on the other.

Gates provide the building blocks from which computers are constructed. One important step in this direction is depicted in the circuit in Figure 1.3. This is a particular example from a collection of circuits known as a **flip-flop.** A flip-flop

Figure 1.2 A pictorial representation of AND, OR, XOR, and NOT gates as well as their input and output values

AND

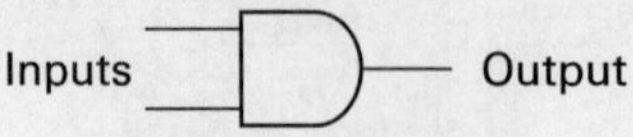

Inputs	Output
0 0	0
0 1	0
1 0	0
1 1	1

OR

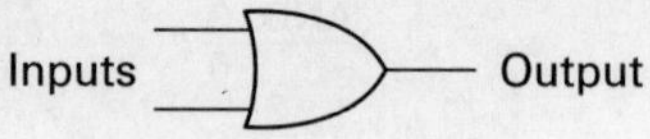

Inputs	Output
0 0	0
0 1	1
1 0	1
1 1	1

XOR

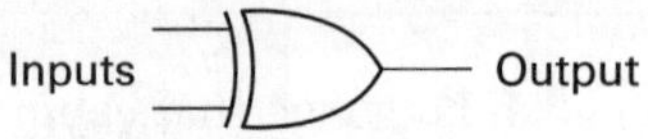

Inputs	Output
0 0	0
0 1	1
1 0	1
1 1	0

NOT

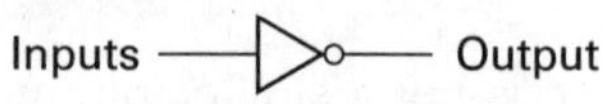

Inputs	Output
0	1
1	0

is a fundamental unit of computer memory. It is a circuit that produces an output value of 0 or 1, which remains constant until a pulse (a temporary change to a 1 that returns to 0) from another circuit causes it to shift to the other value. In other words, the output can be set to "remember" a zero or a one under control of external stimuli. As long as both inputs in the circuit in Figure 1.3 remain 0, the output (whether 0 or 1) will not change. However, temporarily placing a 1 on the upper input will force the output to be 1, whereas temporarily placing a 1 on the lower input will force the output to be 0.

Let us consider this claim in more detail. Without knowing the current output of the circuit in Figure 1.3, suppose that the upper input is changed to 1 while the lower input remains 0 (Figure 1.4a). This will cause the output of the OR gate to be 1, regardless of the other input to this gate. In turn, both inputs to the AND gate will now be 1, since the other input to this gate is already 1 (the output produced by the NOT gate whenever the lower input of the flip-flop is at 0). The output of the AND gate will then become 1, which means that the second input to the OR gate will now be 1 (Figure 1.4b). This guarantees that the output of the OR gate will remain 1, even when the upper input to the flip-flop is changed back to 0 (Figure 1.4c). In summary, the flip-flop's output has become 1, and this output value will remain after the upper input returns to 0.

Figure 1.3 A simple flip-flop circuit

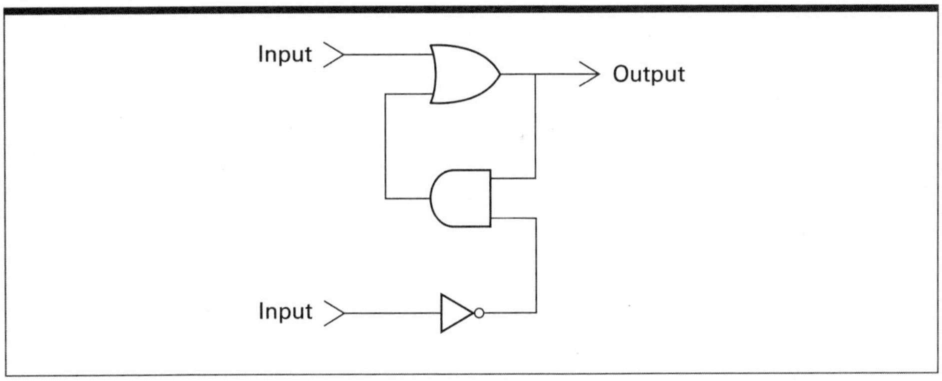

In a similar manner, temporarily placing the value 1 on the lower input will force the flip-flop's output to be 0, and this output will persist after the input value returns to 0.

Our purpose in introducing the flip-flop circuit in Figures 1.3 and 1.4 is threefold. First, it demonstrates how devices can be constructed from gates, a process known as digital circuit design, which is an important topic in computer

Figure 1.4 Setting the output of a flip-flop to 1

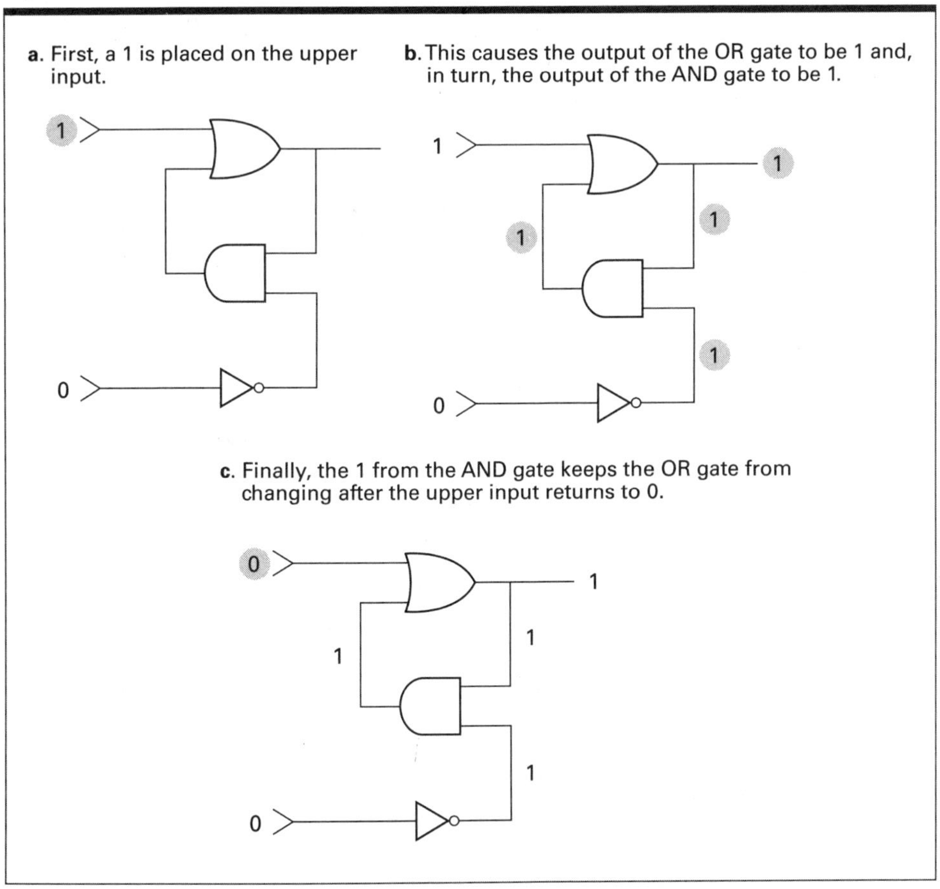

engineering. Indeed, the flip-flop is only one of many circuits that are basic tools in computer engineering.

Second, the concept of a flip-flop provides an example of abstraction and the use of abstract tools. Actually, there are other ways to build a flip-flop. One alternative is shown in Figure 1.5. If you experiment with this circuit, you will find that, although it has a different internal structure, its external properties are the same as those of Figure 1.3. A computer engineer does not need to know which circuit is actually used within a flip-flop. Instead, only an understanding of the flip-flop's external properties is needed to use it as an abstract tool. A flip-flop, along with other well-defined circuits, forms a set of building blocks from which an engineer can construct more complex circuitry. In turn, the design of computer circuitry takes on a hierarchical structure, each level of which uses the lower level components as abstract tools.

The third purpose for introducing the flip-flop is that it is one means of storing a bit within a modern computer. More precisely, a flip-flop can be set to have the output value of either 0 or 1. Other circuits can adjust this value by sending pulses to the flip-flop's inputs, and still other circuits can respond to the stored value by using the flip-flop's output as their inputs. Thus, many flip-flops, constructed as very small electrical circuits, can be used inside a computer as a means of recording information that is encoded as patterns of 0s and 1s. Indeed, technology known as **very large-scale integration (VLSI),** which allows millions of electrical components to be constructed on a wafer (called a **chip**), is used to create miniature devices containing millions of flip-flops along with their controlling circuitry. Consequently, these chips are used as abstract tools in the construction of computer systems. In fact, in some cases VLSI is used to create an entire computer system on a single chip.

Hexadecimal Notation

When considering the internal activities of a computer, we must deal with patterns of bits, which we will refer to as a string of bits, some of which can be quite long. A long string of bits is often called a **stream.** Unfortunately, streams are difficult for the human mind to comprehend. Merely transcribing the pattern 101101010011 is tedious and error prone. To simplify the representation of such bit patterns, therefore, we usually use a shorthand notation called **hexadecimal notation,** which takes advantage of the fact that bit patterns within a machine

Figure 1.5 Another way of constructing a flip-flop

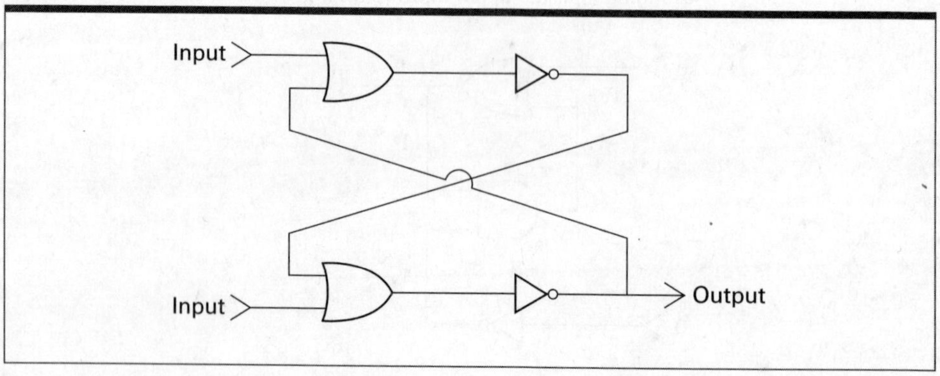

Figure 1.6 The hexadecimal encoding system

Bit pattern	Hexadecimal representation
0000	0
0001	1
0010	2
0011	3
0100	4
0101	5
0110	6
0111	7
1000	8
1001	9
1010	A
1011	B
1100	C
1101	D
1110	E
1111	F

tend to have lengths in multiples of four. In particular, hexadecimal notation uses a single symbol to represent a pattern of four bits. For example, a string of twelve bits can be represented by three hexadecimal symbols.

Figure 1.6 presents the hexadecimal encoding system. The left column displays all possible bit patterns of length four; the right column shows the symbol used in hexadecimal notation to represent the bit pattern to its left. Using this system, the bit pattern 10110101 is represented as B5. This is obtained by dividing the bit pattern into substrings of length four and then representing each substring by its hexadecimal equivalent—1011 is represented by B, and 0101 is represented by 5. In this manner, the 16-bit pattern 1010010011001000 can be reduced to the more palatable form A4C8.

We will use hexadecimal notation extensively in the next chapter. There you will come to appreciate its efficiency.

Questions & Exercises

1. What input bit patterns will cause the following circuit to produce an output of 1?

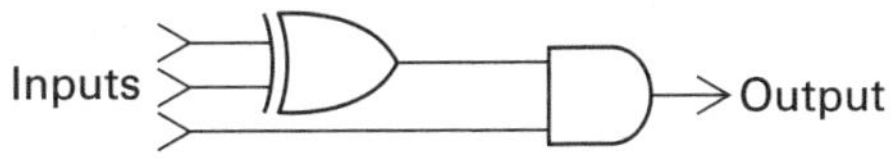

2. In the text, we claimed that placing a 1 on the lower input of the flip-flop in Figure 1.3 (while holding the upper input at 0) will force the flip-flop's output to be 0. Describe the sequence of events that occurs within the flip-flop in this case.

3. Assuming that both inputs to the flip-flop in Figure 1.5 begin as 0, describe the sequence of events that occurs when the upper input is temporarily set to 1.

4. a. If the output of an AND gate is passed through a NOT gate, the combination computes the Boolean operation called NAND, which has an output of 0 only when both its inputs are 1. The symbol for a NAND gate is the same as an AND gate except that it has a circle at its output. The following is a circuit containing a NAND gate. What Boolean operation does the circuit compute?

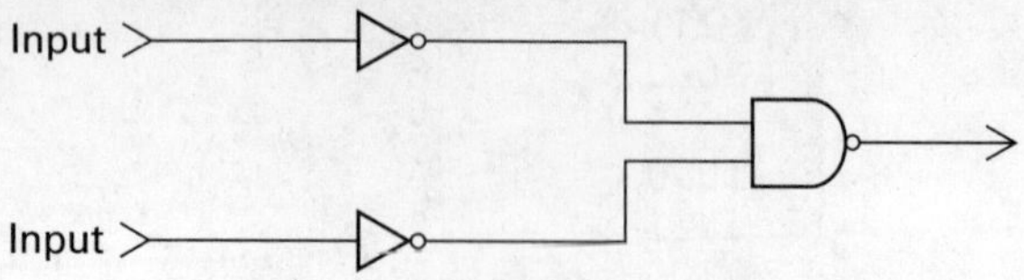

b. If the output of an OR gate is passed through a NOT gate, the combination computes the Boolean operation called NOR that has an output of 1 only when both its inputs are 0. The symbol for a NOR gate is the same as an OR gate except that it has a circle at its output. The following is a circuit containing an AND gate and two NOR gates. What Boolean operation does the circuit compute?

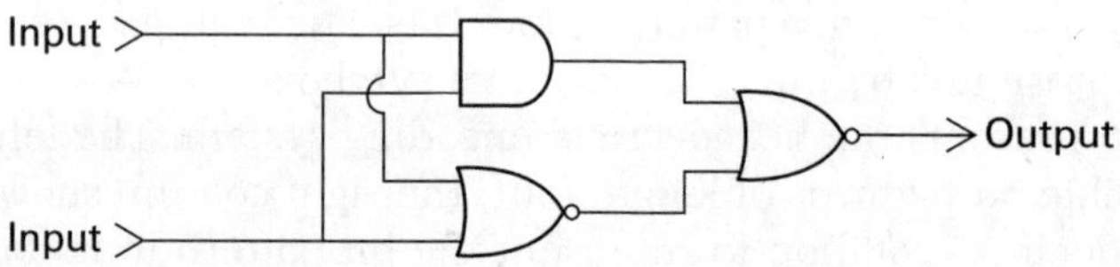

5. Use hexadecimal notation to represent the following bit patterns:

a. 0110101011110010
b. 111010000101010100010111
c. 01001000

6. What bit patterns are represented by the following hexadecimal patterns?

a. 5FD97
b. 610A
c. ABCD
d. 0100

1.2 Main Memory

For the purpose of storing data, a computer contains a large collection of circuits (such as flip-flops), each capable of storing a single bit. This bit reservoir is known as the machine's **main memory.**

Memory Organization

A computer's main memory is organized in manageable units called **cells,** with a typical cell size being eight bits. (A string of eight bits is called a **byte.** Thus, a typical memory cell has a capacity of one byte.) Small computers embedded in such household devices as microwave ovens may have main memories consisting

Figure 1.7 The organization of a byte-size memory cell

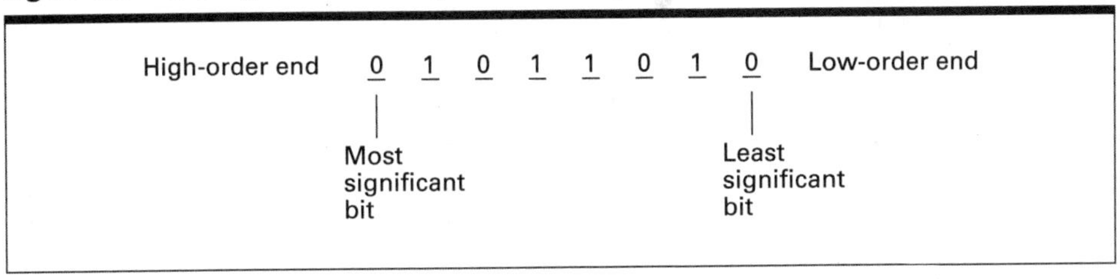

of only a few hundred cells, whereas large computers may have billions of cells in their main memories.

Although there is no left or right within a computer, we normally envision the bits within a memory cell as being arranged in a row. The left end of this row is called the **high-order end,** and the right end is called the **low-order end.** The leftmost bit is called either the high-order bit or the **most significant bit** in reference to the fact that if the contents of the cell were interpreted as representing a numeric value, this bit would be the most significant digit in the number. Similarly, the rightmost bit is referred to as the low-order bit or the **least significant bit.** Thus we may represent the contents of a byte-size memory cell as shown in Figure 1.7.

To identify individual cells in a computer's main memory, each cell is assigned a unique "name," called its **address.** The system is analogous to the technique of identifying houses in a city by addresses. In the case of memory cells, however, the addresses used are entirely numeric. To be more precise, we envision all the cells being placed in a single row and numbered in this order starting with the value zero. Such an addressing system not only gives us a way of uniquely identifying each cell but also associates an order to the cells (Figure 1.8), giving us phrases such as "the next cell" or "the previous cell."

An important consequence of assigning an order to both the cells in main memory and the bits within each cell is that the entire collection of bits within a computer's main memory is essentially ordered in one long row. Pieces of this long row can therefore be used to store bit patterns that may be longer than the

Figure 1.8 Memory cells arranged by address

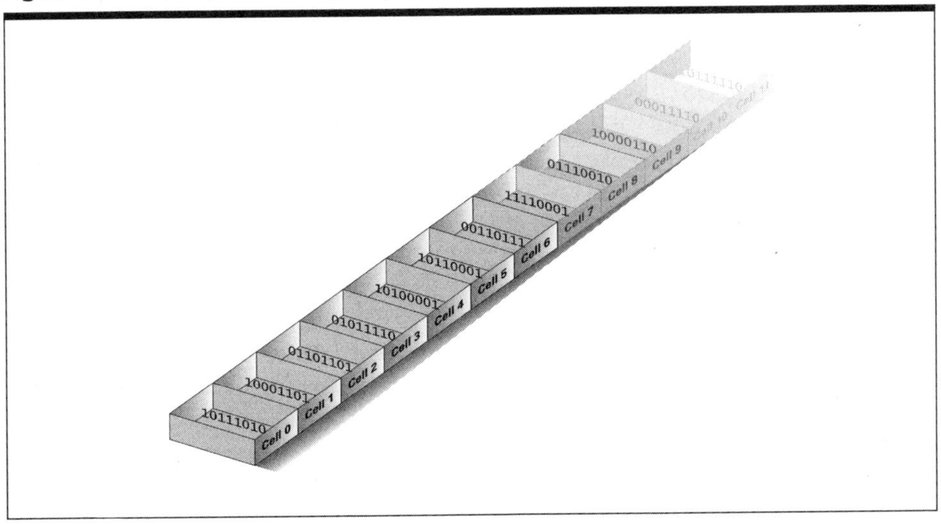

length of a single cell. In particular, we can still store a string of 16 bits merely by using two consecutive memory cells.

To complete the main memory of a computer, the circuitry that actually holds the bits is combined with the circuitry required to allow other circuits to store and retrieve data from the memory cells. In this way, other circuits can get data from the memory by electronically asking for the contents of a certain address (called a read operation), or they can record information in the memory by requesting that a certain bit pattern be placed in the cell at a particular address (called a write operation).

Because a computer's main memory is organized as individual, addressable cells, the cells can be accessed independently as required. To reflect the ability to access cells in any order, a computer's main memory is often called **random access memory (RAM).** This random access feature of main memory is in stark contrast to the mass storage systems that we will discuss in the next section, in which long strings of bits are manipulated as amalgamated blocks.

Although we have introduced flip-flops as a means of storing bits, the RAM in most modern computers is constructed using analogous, but more complex technologies that provide greater miniaturization and faster response time. Many of these technologies store bits as tiny electric charges that dissipate quickly. Thus these devices require additional circuitry, known as a refresh circuit, that repeatedly replenishes the charges many times a second. In recognition of this volatility, computer memory constructed from such technology is often called **dynamic memory,** leading to the term **DRAM** (pronounced "DEE–ram") meaning Dynamic RAM. Or, at times the term **SDRAM** (pronounced "ES-DEE-ram"), meaning Synchronous DRAM, is used in reference to DRAM that applies additional techniques to decrease the time needed to retrieve the contents from its memory cells.

Measuring Memory Capacity

As we will learn in the next chapter, it is convenient to design main memory systems in which the total number of cells is a power of two. In turn, the size of the memories in early computers were often measured in 1024 (which is 2^{10}) cell units. Since 1024 is close to the value 1000, the computing community adopted the prefix *kilo* in reference to this unit. That is, the term *kilobyte* (abbreviated KB) was used to refer to 1024 bytes. Thus, a machine with 4096 memory cells was said to have a 4KB memory ($4096 = 4 \times 1024$). As memories became larger, this terminology grew to include MB (megabyte), GB (gigabyte), and TB (terabyte). Unfortunately, this application of prefixes *kilo-*, *mega-*, and so on, represents a misuse of terminology because these are already used in other fields in reference to units that are powers of a thousand. For example, when measuring distance, *kilometer* refers to 1000 meters, and when measuring radio frequencies, *megahertz* refers to 1,000,000 hertz. In the late 1990s, international standards organizations developed specialized terminology for powers of two: *kibi-*, *mebi-*, *gibi-*, and *tebi-*bytes denote powers of 1024, rather than powers of a thousand. However, while this distinction is the law of the land in many parts of the world, both the general public and many computer scientists have been reluctant to abandon the more familiar, yet ambiguous "megabyte." Thus, a word of caution is in order when using this terminology. As a general rule, terms such as *kilo-*, *mega-*, etc. refer to powers of two when used in the context of computer measurements, but they refer to powers of a thousand when used in other contexts.

Questions & Exercises

1. If the memory cell whose address is 5 contains the value 8, what is the difference between writing the value 5 into cell number 6 and moving the contents of cell number 5 into cell number 6?
2. Suppose you want to interchange the values stored in memory cells 2 and 3. What is wrong with the following sequence of steps:

   Step 1. Move the contents of cell number 2 to cell number 3.

   Step 2. Move the contents of cell number 3 to cell number 2.

   Design a sequence of steps that correctly interchanges the contents of these cells. If needed, you may use additional cells.
3. How many bits would be in the memory of a computer with 4KB memory?

1.3 Mass Storage

Due to the volatility and limited size of a computer's main memory, most computers have additional memory devices called **mass storage** (or secondary storage) systems, including magnetic disks, CDs, DVDs, magnetic tapes, flash drives, and solid-state disks (all of which we will discuss shortly). The advantages of mass storage systems over main memory include less volatility, large storage capacities, low cost, and in many cases, the ability to remove the storage medium from the machine for archival purposes.

A major disadvantage of magnetic and optical mass storage systems is that they typically require mechanical motion and therefore require significantly more time to store and retrieve data than a machine's main memory, where all activities are performed electronically. Moreover, storage systems with moving parts are more prone to mechanical failures than solid state systems.

Magnetic Systems

For years, magnetic technology has dominated the mass storage arena. The most common example in use today is the **magnetic disk** or **hard disk drive (HDD),** in which a thin spinning disk with magnetic coating is used to hold data (Figure 1.9). Read/write heads are placed above and/or below the disk so that as the disk spins, each head traverses a circle, called a **track.** By repositioning the read/write heads, different concentric tracks can be accessed. In many cases, a disk storage system consists of several disks mounted on a common spindle, one on top of the other, with enough space for the read/write heads to slip between the platters. In such cases, the read/write heads move in unison. Each time the read/write heads are repositioned, a new set of tracks—which is called a **cylinder**—becomes accessible.

Since a track can contain more information than we would normally want to manipulate at any one time, each track is divided into small arcs called **sectors** on which information is recorded as a continuous string of bits. All sectors on a disk contain the same number of bits (typical capacities are in the range of 512 bytes to a few KB), and in the simplest disk storage systems each track contains the same

Figure 1.9 A disk storage system

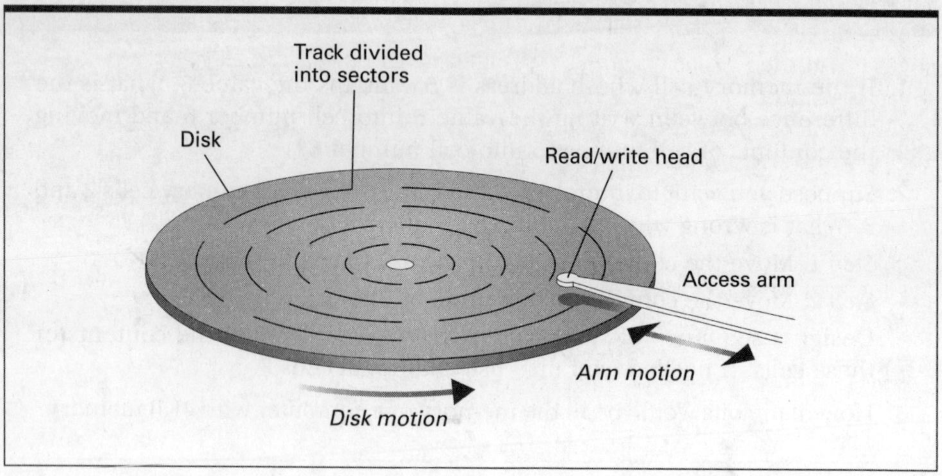

number of sectors. Thus, the bits within a sector on a track near the outer edge of the disk are less compactly stored than those on the tracks near the center, since the outer tracks are longer than the inner ones. In contrast, in high-capacity disk storage systems, the tracks near the outer edge are capable of containing significantly more sectors than those near the center, and this capability is often used by applying a technique called **zoned-bit recording.** Using zoned-bit recording, several adjacent tracks are collectively known as zones, with a typical disk containing approximately 10 zones. All tracks within a zone have the same number of sectors, but each zone has more sectors per track than the zone inside of it. In this manner, efficient use of the entire disk surface is achieved. Regardless of the details, a disk storage system consists of many individual sectors, each of which can be accessed as an independent string of bits.

The capacity of a disk storage system depends on the number of platters used and the density in which the tracks and sectors are placed. Lower-capacity systems may consist of a single platter. High-capacity disk systems, capable of holding many gigabytes, or even terabytes, consist of perhaps three to six platters mounted on a common spindle. Furthermore, data may be stored on both the upper and lower surfaces of each platter.

Several measurements are used to evaluate a disk system's performance: (1) **seek time** (the time required to move the read/write heads from one track to another); (2) **rotation delay** or **latency time** (half the time required for the disk to make a complete rotation, which is the average amount of time required for the desired data to rotate around to the read/write head once the head has been positioned over the desired track); (3) **access time** (the sum of seek time and rotation delay); and (4) **transfer rate** (the rate at which data can be transferred to or from the disk). (Note that in the case of zone-bit recording, the amount of data passing a read/write head in a single disk rotation is greater for tracks in an outer zone than for an inner zone, and therefore the data transfer rate varies depending on the portion of the disk being used.)

A factor limiting the access time and transfer rate is the speed at which a disk system rotates. To facilitate fast rotation speeds, the read/write heads in these systems do not touch the disk but instead "float" just off the surface. The spacing is so close that even a single particle of dust could become jammed between the head and disk surface, destroying both (a phenomenon known as a head crash). Thus, disk systems are typically housed in cases that are sealed at the factory. With this construction, disk systems are able to rotate at speeds of several hundred times per second, achieving transfer rates that are measured in MB per second.

Since disk systems require physical motion for their operation, these systems suffer when compared to speeds within electronic circuitry. Delay times within an electronic circuit are measured in units of nanoseconds (billionths of a second) or less, whereas seek times, latency times, and access times of disk systems are measured in milliseconds (thousandths of a second). Thus the time required to retrieve information from a disk system can seem like an eternity to an electronic circuit awaiting a result.

Magnetic storage technologies that are now less widely used include **magnetic tape,** in which information is recorded on the magnetic coating of a thin plastic tape wound on reels, and **floppy disk drives,** in which single platters with a magnetic coating are encased in a portable cartridge designed to be readily removed from the drive. Magnetic tape drives have extremely long seek times, just as their cousins, audio cassettes, suffer from long rewind and fast-forward times. Low cost and high data capacities still make magnetic tape suitable for applications where data is primarily read or written linearly, such as archival data backups. The removable nature of floppy disk platters came at the cost of much lower data densities and access speeds than hard disk platters, but their portability was extremely valuable in earlier decades, prior to the arrival of flash drives with larger capacity and higher durability.

Optical Systems

Another class of mass storage systems applies optical technology. An example is the **compact disk (CD).** These disks are 12 centimeters (approximately 5 inches) in diameter and consist of reflective material covered with a clear protective coating. Information is recorded on them by creating variations in their reflective surfaces. This information can then be retrieved by means of a laser that detects irregularities on the reflective surface of the CD as it spins.

CD technology was originally applied to audio recordings using a recording format known as **CD-DA (compact disk-digital audio),** and the CDs used today for computer data storage use essentially the same format. In particular, information on these CDs is stored on a single track that spirals around the CD like a groove in an old-fashioned phonograph record, however, unlike old-fashioned phonograph records, the track on a CD spirals from the inside out (Figure 1.10). This track is divided into units called sectors, each with its own identifying markings and a capacity of 2KB of data, which equates to 1/75 of a second of music in the case of audio recordings.

Note that the distance around the spiraled track is greater toward the outer edge of the disk than at the inner portion. To maximize the capacity of a CD, information is stored at a uniform linear density over the entire spiraled track, which means that more information is stored in a loop around the outer portion of the spiral than in a loop around the inner portion. In turn, more sectors will be read in a single revolution of the disk when the laser is scanning the outer portion of the spiraled track than when the laser is scanning the inner portion of the track. Thus, to obtain a uniform rate of data transfer, CD-DA players are designed

Figure 1.10 CD storage format

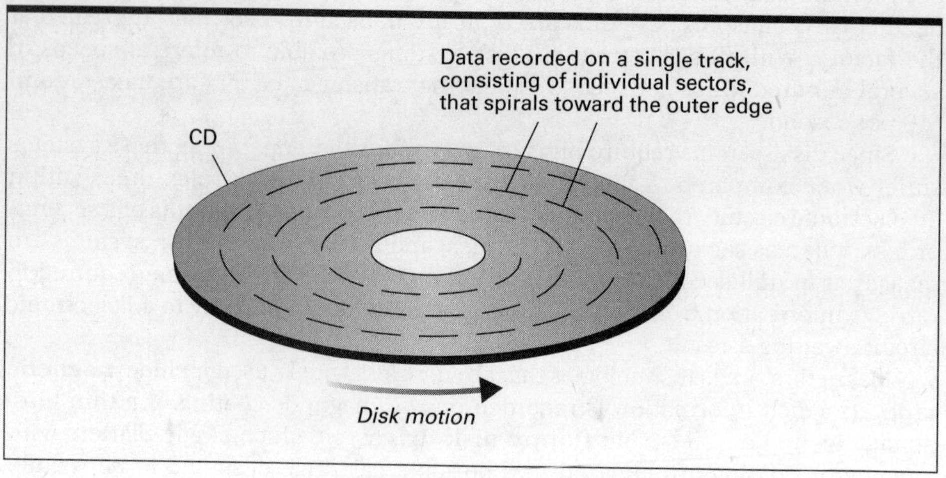

to vary the rotation speed depending on the location of the laser. However, most CD systems used for computer data storage spin at a faster, constant speed and thus must accommodate variations in data transfer rates.

As a consequence of such design decisions, CD storage systems perform best when dealing with long, continuous strings of data, as when reproducing music. In contrast, when an application requires access to items of data in a random manner, the approach used in magnetic disk storage (individual, concentric tracks divided into individually accessible sectors) outperforms the spiral approach used in CDs.

Traditional CDs have capacities in the range of 600 to 700MB. However, **DVDs (Digital Versatile Disks),** which are constructed from multiple, semi-transparent layers that serve as distinct surfaces when viewed by a precisely focused laser, provide storage capacities of several GB. Such disks are capable of storing lengthy multimedia presentations, including entire motion pictures. Finally, Blu-ray technology, which uses a laser in the blue-violet spectrum of light (instead of red), is able to focus its laser beam with very fine precision. As a result, **BDs (Blu-ray Disks)** provides over five times the capacity of a DVD. This seemingly vast amount of storage is needed to meet the demands of high definition video.

Flash Drives

A common property of mass storage systems based on magnetic or optic technology is that physical motion, such as spinning disks, moving read/write heads, and aiming laser beams, is required to store and retrieve data. This means that data storage and retrieval is slow compared to the speed of electronic circuitry. **Flash memory** technology has the potential of alleviating this drawback. In a flash memory system, bits are stored by sending electronic signals directly to the storage medium where they cause electrons to be trapped in tiny chambers of silicon dioxide, thus altering the characteristics of small electronic circuits. Since these chambers are able to hold their captive electrons for many years without external power, this technology is excellent for portable, nonvolatile data storage.

Although data stored in flash memory systems can be accessed in small byte-size units as in RAM applications, current technology dictates that stored data be erased in large blocks. Moreover, repeated erasing slowly damages the silicon dioxide chambers, meaning that current flash memory technology is not suitable for general main memory applications where its contents might be altered many times a second. However, in those applications in which alterations can be controlled to a reasonable level, such as in digital cameras and smartphones, flash memory has become the mass storage technology of choice. Indeed, since flash memory is not sensitive to physical shock (in contrast to magnetic and optic systems), it is now replacing other mass storage technologies in portable applications such as laptop computers.

Flash memory devices called **flash drives,** with capacities of hundreds of GBs, are available for general mass storage applications. These units are packaged in ever smaller plastic cases with a removable cap on one end to protect the unit's electrical connector when the drive is offline. The high capacity of these portable units as well as the fact that they are easily connected to and disconnected from a computer make them ideal for portable data storage. However, the vulnerability of their tiny storage chambers dictates that they are not as reliable as optical disks for truly long-term applications.

Larger flash memory devices called **SSDs (solid-state disks)** are explicitly designed to take the place of magnetic hard disks. SSDs compare favorably to hard disks in their resilience to vibrations and physical shock, their quiet operation (due to no moving parts), and their lower access times. SSDs remain more expensive than hard disks of comparable size and thus are still considered a high-end option when buying a computer. SSD sectors suffer from the more limited lifetime of all flash memory technologies, but the use of **wear-leveling** techniques can reduce the impact of this by relocating frequently altered data blocks to fresh locations on the drive.

Another application of flash technology is found in **SD (Secure Digital) memory cards** (or just SD Card). These provide up to two GBs of storage and are packaged in a plastic rigged wafer about the size a postage stamp (SD cards are also available in smaller mini and micro sizes), **SDHC (High Capacity)** memory cards can provide up to 32 GBs and the next generation **SDXC (Extended Capacity) memory cards** may exceed a TB. Given their compact physical size, these cards conveniently slip into slots of small electronic devices. Thus, they are ideal for digital cameras, smartphones, music players, car navigation systems, and a host of other electronic appliances.

Questions & Exercises

1. What is gained by increasing the rotation speed of a disk or CD?
2. When recording data on a multiple-disk storage system, should we fill a complete disk surface before starting on another surface, or should we first fill an entire cylinder before starting on another cylinder?
3. Why should the data in a reservation system that is constantly being updated be stored on a magnetic disk instead of a CD or DVD?

4. What factors allow CD, DVD, and Blu-ray disks all to be read by the same drive?
5. What advantage do flash drives have over the other mass storage systems introduced in this section?
6. What advantages continue to make magnetic hard disk drives competitive?

1.4 Representing Information as Bit Patterns

Having considered techniques for storing bits, we now consider how information can be encoded as bit patterns. Our study focuses on popular methods for encoding text, numerical data, images, and sound. Each of these systems has repercussions that are often visible to a typical computer user. Our goal is to understand enough about these techniques so that we can recognize their consequences for what they are.

Representing Text

Information in the form of text is normally represented by means of a code in which each of the different symbols in the text (such as the letters of the alphabet and punctuation marks) is assigned a unique bit pattern. The text is then represented as a long string of bits in which the successive patterns represent the successive symbols in the original text.

In the 1940s and 1950s, many such codes were designed and used in connection with different pieces of equipment, producing a corresponding proliferation of communication problems. To alleviate this situation, the **American National Standards Institute** (**ANSI,** pronounced "AN–see") adopted the **American Standard Code for Information Interchange** (**ASCII,** pronounced "AS–kee"). This code uses bit patterns of length seven to represent the upper- and lowercase letters of the English alphabet, punctuation symbols, the digits 0 through 9, and certain control information such as line feeds, carriage returns, and tabs. ASCII is extended to an eight-bit-per-symbol format by adding a 0 at the most significant end of each of the seven-bit patterns. This technique not only produces a code in which each pattern fits conveniently into a typical byte-size memory cell but also provides 128 additional bit patterns (those obtained by assigning the extra bit the value 1) that can be used to represent symbols beyond the English alphabet and associated punctuation.

A portion of ASCII in its eight-bit-per-symbol format is shown in Appendix A. By referring to this appendix, we can decode the bit pattern

01001000 01100101 01101100 01101100 01101111 00101110

as the message "Hello." as demonstrated in Figure 1.11.

The **International Organization for Standardization** (also known as **ISO,** in reference to the Greek word *isos,* meaning equal) has developed a number of extensions to ASCII, each of which was designed to accommodate a major language group. For example, one standard provides the symbols needed to express the text of most Western European languages. Included in its 128 additional patterns are symbols for the British pound and the German vowels ä, ö, and ü.

Figure 1.11 The message "Hello." in ASCII or UTF-8 encoding

01001000	01100101	01101100	01101100	01101111	00101110
H	e	l	l	o	.

The ISO-extended ASCII standards made tremendous headway toward supporting all of the world's multilingual communication; however, two major obstacles surfaced. First, the number of extra bit patterns available in extended ASCII is simply insufficient to accommodate the alphabet of many Asian and some East-ern European languages. Second, because a given document was constrained to using symbols in just the one selected standard, documents containing text of languages from disparate language groups could not be supported. Both proved to be a significant detriment to international use. To address this deficiency, **Unicode** was developed through the cooperation of several of the leading manufacturers of hardware and software and has rapidly gained the support of the computing community. This code uses a unique pattern of up to 21 bits to represent each symbol. When the Unicode character set is combined with the **Unicode Transformation Format 8-bit (UTF-8)** encoding standard, the original ASCII characters can still be represented with 8 bits, while the thousands of additional characters from such languages as Chinese, Japanese, and Hebrew can be represented by 16 bits. Beyond the characters required for all of the world's commonly used languages, UTF-8 uses 24- or 32-bit patterns to represent more obscure Unicode symbols, leaving ample room for future expansion.

A file consisting of a long sequence of symbols encoded using ASCII or Unicode is often called a **text file.** It is important to distinguish between simple text files that are manipulated by utility programs called **text editors** (or often simply editors) and the more elaborate files produced by **word processors** such as Microsoft's Word. Both consist of textual material. However, a text file contains only a character-by-character encoding of the text, whereas a file produced by a word processor contains numerous proprietary codes representing changes in fonts, alignment information, and other parameters.

Representing Numeric Values

Storing information in terms of encoded characters is inefficient when the information being recorded is purely numeric. To see why, consider the problem of storing the value 25. If we insist on storing it as encoded symbols in ASCII using one byte per symbol, we need a total of 16 bits. Moreover, the largest number we could store using 16 bits is 99. However, as we will shortly see, by using **binary notation** we can store any integer in the range from 0 to 65535 in these 16 bits. Thus, binary notation (or variations of it) is used extensively for encoded numeric data for computer storage.

Binary notation is a way of representing numeric values using only the digits 0 and 1 rather than the digits 0, 1, 2, 3, 4, 5, 6, 7, 8, and 9 as in the traditional decimal, or base 10, system. We will study the binary system more thoroughly in Section 1.5. For now, all we need is an elementary understanding of the system. For this purpose consider an old-fashioned car odometer whose display wheels

The American National Standards Institute

The American National Standards Institute (ANSI) was founded in 1918 by a small consortium of engineering societies and government agencies as a nonprofit federation to coordinate the development of voluntary standards in the private sector. Today, ANSI membership includes more than 1300 businesses, professional organizations, trade associations, and government agencies. ANSI is headquartered in New York and represents the United States as a member body in the ISO. The website for the American National Standards Institute is at http://www.ansi.org.

Similar organizations in other countries include Standards Australia (Australia), Standards Council of Canada (Canada), China State Bureau of Quality and Technical Supervision (China), Deutsches Institut für Normung (Germany), Japanese Industrial Standards Committee (Japan), Dirección General de Normas (Mexico), State Committee of the Russian Federation for Standardization and Metrology (Russia), Swiss Association for Standardization (Switzerland), and British Standards Institution (United Kingdom).

contain only the digits 0 and 1 rather than the traditional digits 0 through 9. The odometer starts with a reading of all 0s, and as the car is driven for the first few miles, the rightmost wheel rotates from a 0 to a 1. Then, as that 1 rotates back to a 0, it causes a 1 to appear to its left, producing the pattern 10. The 0 on the right then rotates to a 1, producing 11. Now the rightmost wheel rotates from 1 back to 0, causing the 1 to its left to rotate to a 0 as well. This in turn causes another 1 to appear in the third column, producing the pattern 100. In short, as we drive the car we see the following sequence of odometer readings:

0000
0001
0010
0011
0100
0101
0110
0111
1000

This sequence consists of the binary representations of the integers zero through eight. Although tedious, we could extend this counting technique to discover that the bit pattern consisting of 16 1s represents the value 65535, which confirms our claim that any integer in the range from 0 to 65535 can be encoded using 16 bits.

Due to this efficiency, it is common to store numeric information in a form of binary notation rather than in encoded symbols. We say "a form of binary notation" because the straightforward binary system just described is only the basis for several numeric storage techniques used within machines. Some of these variations of the binary system are discussed later in this chapter. For now, we merely note that a system called **two's complement** notation (see Section 1.6) is common for storing whole numbers because it provides a convenient method for representing negative numbers as well as positive. For representing numbers with fractional parts such as 4-1/2 or 3/4, another technique, called **floating-point notation** (see Section 1.7), is used.

Representing Images

One means of representing an image is to interpret the image as a collection of dots, each of which is called a **pixel,** short for "picture element." The appearance of each pixel is then encoded and the entire image is represented as a collection of these encoded pixels. Such a collection is called a **bit map.** This approach is popular because many display devices, such as printers and display screens, operate on the pixel concept. In turn, images in bit map form are easily formatted for display.

The method of encoding the pixels in a bit map varies among applications. In the case of a simple black-and-white image, each pixel can be represented by a single bit whose value depends on whether the corresponding pixel is black or white. This is the approach used by most facsimile machines. For more elaborate black-and-white photographs, each pixel can be represented by a collection of bits (usually eight), which allows a variety of shades of grayness to be represented. In the case of color images, each pixel is encoded by more complex system. Two approaches are common. In one, which we will call RGB encoding, each pixel is represented as three color components—a red component, a green component, and a blue component—corresponding to the three primary colors of light. One byte is normally used to represent the intensity of each color component. In turn, three bytes of storage are required to represent a single pixel in the original image.

An alternative to simple RGB encoding is to use a "brightness" component and two color components. In this case the "brightness" component, which is called the pixel's luminance, is essentially the sum of the red, green, and blue components. (Actually, it is considered to be the amount of white light in the pixel, but these details need not concern us here.) The other two components, called the blue chrominance and the red chrominance, are determined by computing the difference between the pixel's luminance and the amount of blue or red light, respectively, in the pixel. Together these three components contain the information required to reproduce the pixel.

The popularity of encoding images using luminance and chrominance components originated in the field of color television broadcast because this approach provided a means of encoding color images that was also compatible with older black-and-white television receivers. Indeed, a gray-scale version of an image can be produced by using only the luminance components of the encoded color image.

ISO—The International Organization for Standardization

The International Organization for Standardization (more commonly called ISO) was established in 1947 as a worldwide federation of standardization bodies, one from each country. Today, it is headquartered in Geneva, Switzerland, and has more than 100 member bodies as well as numerous correspondent members. (A correspondent member is usually a standardization body from a country that does not have a nationally recognized standardization body. Such members cannot participate directly in the development of standards but are kept informed of ISO activities.) ISO maintains a website at http://www.iso.org.

A disadvantage of representing images as bit maps is that an image cannot be rescaled easily to any arbitrary size. Essentially, the only way to enlarge the image is to make the pixels bigger, which leads to a grainy appearance. (This is the technique called "digital zoom" used in digital cameras as opposed to "optical zoom" that is obtained by adjusting the camera lens.)

An alternate way of representing images that avoids this scaling problem is to describe the image as a collection of geometric structures, such as lines and curves, that can be encoded using techniques of analytic geometry. Such a description allows the device that ultimately displays the image to decide how the geometric structures should be displayed rather than insisting that the device reproduce a particular pixel pattern. This is the approach used to produce the scalable fonts that are available via today's word processing systems. For example, TrueType (developed by Microsoft and Apple) is a system for geometrically describing text symbols. Likewise, PostScript (developed by Adobe Systems) provides a means of describing characters as well as more general pictorial data. This geometric means of representing images is also popular in **computer-aided design (CAD)** systems in which drawings of three-dimensional objects are displayed and manipulated on computer display screens.

The distinction between representing an image in the form of geometric structures as opposed to bit maps is evident to users of many drawing software systems (such as Microsoft's Paint utility) that allow the user to draw pictures consisting of pre-established shapes such as rectangles, ovals, and elementary curves. The user simply selects the desired geometric shape from a menu and then directs the drawing of that shape via a mouse. During the drawing process, the software maintains a geometric description of the shape being drawn. As directions are given by the mouse, the internal geometric representation is modified, reconverted to bit map form, and displayed. This allows for easy scaling and shaping of the image. Once the drawing process is complete, however, the underlying geometric description is discarded and only the bit map is preserved, meaning that additional alterations require a tedious pixel-by-pixel modification process. On the other hand, some drawing systems preserve the description as geometric shapes that can be modified later. With these systems, the shapes can be easily resized, maintaining a crisp display at any dimension.

Representing Sound

The most generic method of encoding audio information for computer storage and manipulation is to sample the amplitude of the sound wave at regular intervals and record the series of values obtained. For instance, the series 0, 1.5, 2.0, 1.5, 2.0, 3.0, 4.0, 3.0, 0 would represent a sound wave that rises in amplitude, falls briefly, rises to a higher level, and then drops back to 0 (Figure 1.12). This technique, using a sample rate of 8000 samples per second, has been used for years in long-distance voice telephone communication. The voice at one end of the communication is encoded as numeric values representing the amplitude of the voice every eight-thousandth of a second. These numeric values are then transmitted over the communication line to the receiving end, where they are used to reproduce the sound of the voice.

Although 8000 samples per second may seem to be a rapid rate, it is not sufficient for high-fidelity music recordings. To obtain the quality sound reproduction obtained by today's musical CDs, a sample rate of 44,100 samples per second

Figure 1.12 The sound wave represented by the sequence 0, 1.5, 2.0, 1.5, 2.0, 3.0, 4.0, 3.0, 0

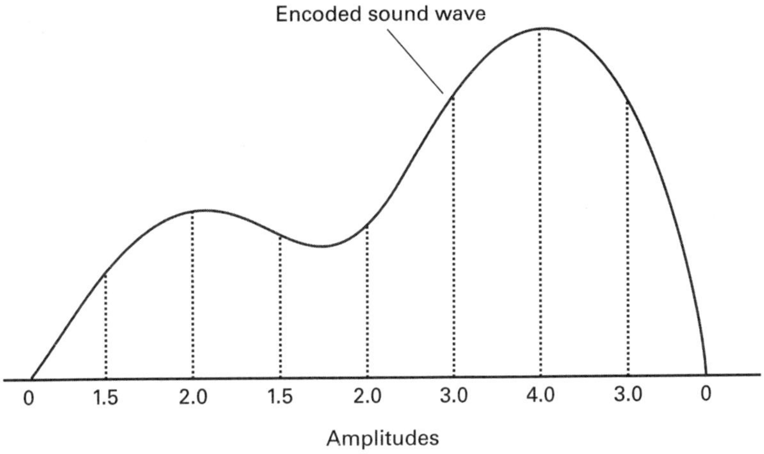

is used. The data obtained from each sample are represented in 16 bits (32 bits for stereo recordings). Consequently, each second of music recorded in stereo requires more than a million bits.

An alternative encoding system known as Musical Instrument Digital Interface (MIDI, pronounced "MID–ee") is widely used in the music synthesizers found in electronic keyboards, for video game sound, and for sound effects accompanying websites. By encoding directions for producing music on a synthesizer rather than encoding the sound itself, MIDI avoids the large storage requirements of the sampling technique. More precisely, MIDI encodes what instrument is to play which note for what duration of time, which means that a clarinet playing the note D for two seconds can be encoding in three bytes rather than more than two million bits when sampled at a rate of 44,100 samples per second.

In short, MIDI can be thought of as a way of encoding the sheet music read by a performer rather than the performance itself, and in turn, a MIDI "recording" can sound significantly different when performed on different synthesizers.

Questions & Exercises

1. Here is a message encoded in ASCII using 8 bits per symbol. What does it say? (See Appendix A)

   01000011 01101111 01101101 01110000 01110101 01110100 01100101 01110010 00100000 01010011 01100011 01101001 01100101 01101110 01100011 01100101

2. In the ASCII code, what is the relationship between the codes for an uppercase letter and the same letter in lowercase? (*See* Appendix A.)

3. Encode these sentences in ASCII:

   a. "Stop!" Cheryl shouted.
   b. Does 2 + 3 = 5?

4. Describe a device from everyday life that can be in either of two states, such as a flag on a flagpole that is either up or down. Assign the symbol 1 to one of the states and 0 to the other, and show how the ASCII representation for the letter b would appear when stored with such bits.

5. Convert each of the following binary representations to its equivalent base 10 form:

   a. 0101
   b. 1001
   c. 1011
   d. 0110
   e. 10000
   f. 10010

6. Convert each of the following base 10 representations to its equivalent binary form:

   a. 6
   b. 13
   c. 11
   d. 18
   e. 27
   f. 4

7. What is the largest numeric value that could be represented with three bytes if each digit were encoded using one ASCII pattern per byte? What if binary notation were used?

8. An alternative to hexadecimal notation for representing bit patterns is **dotted decimal notation** in which each byte in the pattern is represented by its base 10 equivalent. In turn, these byte representations are separated by periods. For example, 12.5 represents the pattern 0000110000000101 (the byte 00001100 is represented by 12, and 00000101 is represented by 5), and the pattern 100010000001000000000111 is represented by 136.16.7. Represent each of the following bit patterns in dotted decimal notation.

   a. 0000111100001111
   b. 001100110000000010000000
   c. 0000101010100000

9. What is an advantage of representing images via geometric structures as opposed to bit maps? What about bit map techniques as opposed to geometric structures?

10. Suppose a stereo recording of one hour of music is encoded using a sample rate of 44,100 samples per second as discussed in the text. How does the size of the encoded version compare to the storage capacity of a CD?

1.5 The Binary System

In Section 1.4 we saw that binary notation is a means of representing numeric values using only the digits 0 and 1 rather than the 10 digits 0 through 9 that are used in the more common base 10 notational system. It is time now to look at binary notation more thoroughly.

Binary Notation

Recall that in the base 10 system, each position in a representation is associated with a quantity. In the representation 375, the 5 is in the position associated with the quantity one, the 7 is in the position associated with ten, and the 3 is in the position associated with the quantity one hundred (Figure 1.13a). Each quantity is 10 times that of the quantity to its right. The value represented by the entire expression is obtained by multiplying the value of each digit by the quantity associated with that digit's position and then adding those products. To illustrate, the pattern 375 represents $(3 \times \text{hundred}) + (7 \times \text{ten}) + (5 \times \text{one})$, which, in more technical notation, is $(3 \times 10^2) + (7 \times 10^1) + (5 \times 10^0)$.

The position of each digit in binary notation is also associated with a quantity, except that the quantity associated with each position is twice the quantity associated with the position to its right. More precisely, the rightmost digit in a binary representation is associated with the quantity one (2^0), the next position to the left is associated with two (2^1), the next is associated with four (2^2), the next with eight (23), and so on. For example, in the binary representation 1011, the rightmost 1 is in the position associated with the quantity one, the 1 next to it is in the position associated with two, the 0 is in the position associated with four, and the leftmost 1 is in the position associated with eight (Figure 1.13b).

To extract the value represented by a binary representation, we follow the same procedure as in base 10—we multiply the value of each digit by the quantity associated with its position and add the results. For example, the value represented by 100101 is 37, as shown in Figure 1.14. Note that since binary notation uses only the digits 0 and 1, this multiply-and-add process reduces merely to adding the quantities associated with the positions occupied by 1s. Thus the binary pattern 1011 represents the value eleven, because the 1s are found in the positions associated with the quantities one, two, and eight.

In Section 1.4 we learned how to count in binary notation, which allowed us to encode small integers. For finding binary representations of large values, you may prefer the approach described by the algorithm in Figure 1.15. Let us apply this algorithm to the value thirteen (Figure 1.16). We first divide thirteen by two, obtaining a quotient of six and a remainder of one. Since the quotient was not zero, Step 2 tells us to divide the quotient (six) by two, obtaining a new quotient of three and a remainder of zero. The newest quotient is still not zero, so we divide it by two, obtaining a quotient of one and a remainder of one. Once again, we divide the newest quotient (one) by two, this time obtaining a quotient of zero and a remainder of one. Since we have now acquired a quotient of zero, we move on to Step 3, where we learn that the binary representation of the original value (thirteen) is 1101, obtained from the list of remainders.

Figure 1.13 The base 10 and binary systems

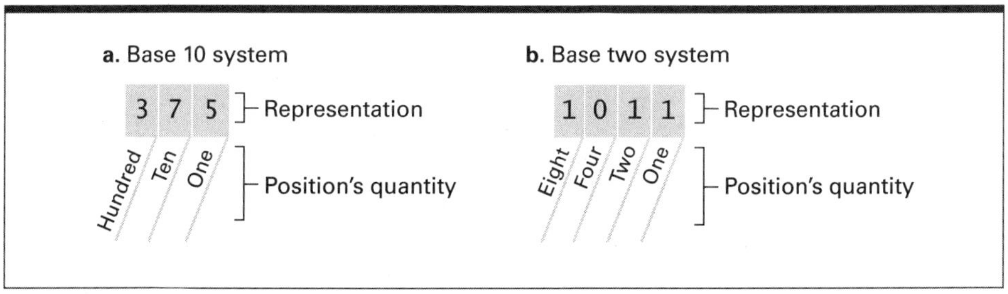

Figure 1.14 Decoding the binary representation 100101

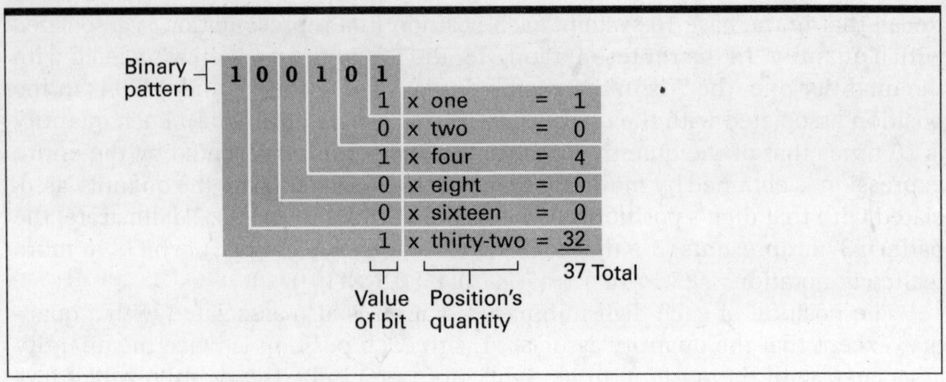

Figure 1.15 An algorithm for finding the binary representation of a positive integer

Step 1. Divide the value by two and record the remainder.

Step 2. As long as the quotient obtained is not zero, continue to divide the newest quotient by two and record the remainder.

Step 3. Now that a quotient of zero has been obtained, the binary representation of the original value consists of the remainders listed from right to left in the order they were recorded.

Figure 1.16 Applying the algorithm in Figure 1.15 to obtain the binary representation of thirteen

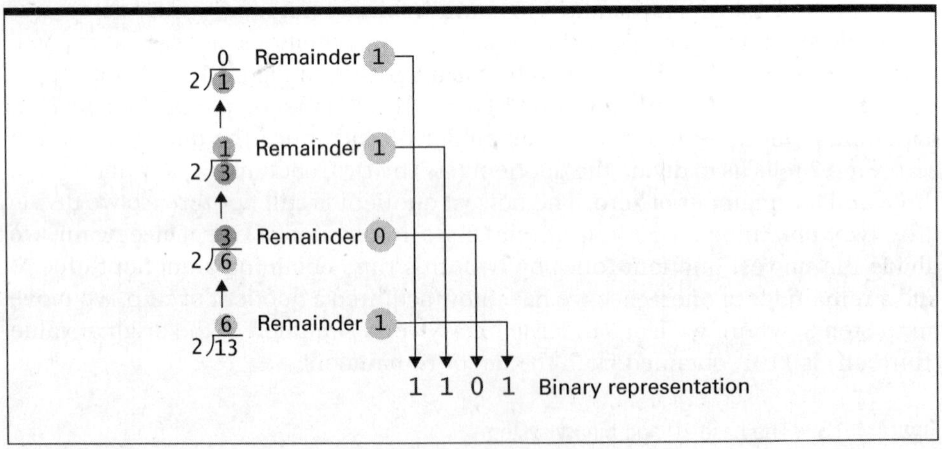

Binary Addition

To understand the process of adding two integers that are represented in binary, let us first recall the process of adding values that are represented in traditional base 10 notation. Consider, for example, the following problem:

$$\begin{array}{r} 58 \\ +\ 27 \\ \hline \end{array}$$

We begin by adding the 8 and the 7 in the rightmost column to obtain the sum 15. We record the 5 at the bottom of that column and carry the 1 to the next column, producing

$$\begin{array}{r} 1 \\ 58 \\ +\ 27 \\ \hline 5 \end{array}$$

We now add the 5 and 2 in the next column along with the 1 that was carried to obtain the sum 8, which we record at the bottom of the column. The result is as follows:

$$\begin{array}{r} 58 \\ +\ 27 \\ \hline 85 \end{array}$$

In short, the procedure is to progress from right to left as we add the digits in each column, write the least significant digit of that sum under the column, and carry the more significant digit of the sum (if there is one) to the next column.

To add two integers represented in binary notation, we follow the same procedure except that all sums are computed using the addition facts shown in Figure 1.17 rather than the traditional base 10 facts that you learned in elementary school. For example, to solve the problem

$$\begin{array}{r} 111010 \\ +\ 11011 \\ \hline \end{array}$$

we begin by adding the rightmost 0 and 1; we obtain 1, which we write below the column. Now we add the 1 and 1 from the next column, obtaining 10. We write the 0 from this 10 under the column and carry the 1 to the top of the next column. At this point, our solution looks like this:

$$\begin{array}{r} 1 \\ 111010 \\ +\ 11011 \\ \hline 01 \end{array}$$

We add the 1, 0, and 0 in the next column, obtain 1, and write the 1 under this column. The 1 and 1 from the next column total 10; we write the 0 under the column and carry the 1 to the next column. Now our solution looks like this:

$$\begin{array}{r} 1 \\ 111010 \\ +\ 11011 \\ \hline 0101 \end{array}$$

Figure 1.17 The binary addition facts

$$\begin{array}{r} 0 \\ +0 \\ \hline 0 \end{array} \quad \begin{array}{r} 1 \\ +0 \\ \hline 1 \end{array} \quad \begin{array}{r} 0 \\ +1 \\ \hline 1 \end{array} \quad \begin{array}{r} 1 \\ +1 \\ \hline 10 \end{array}$$

The 1, 1, and 1 in the next column total 11 (binary notation for the value three); we write the low-order 1 under the column and carry the other 1 to the top of the next column. We add that 1 to the 1 already in that column to obtain 10. Again, we record the low-order 0 and carry the 1 to the next column. We now have

```
 1
  111010
+  11011
  010101
```

The only entry in the next column is the 1 that we carried from the previous column so we record it in the answer. Our final solution is this:

```
  111010
+  11011
 1010101
```

Fractions in Binary

To extend binary notation to accommodate fractional values, we use a **radix point** in the same role as the decimal point in decimal notation. That is, the digits to the left of the point represent the integer part (whole part) of the value and are interpreted as in the binary system discussed previously. The digits to its right represent the fractional part of the value and are interpreted in a manner similar to the other bits, except their positions are assigned fractional quantities. That is, the first position to the right of the radix is assigned the quantity 1/2 (which is 2^{-1}), the next position the quantity 1/4 (which is 2^{-2}), the next 1/8 (which is 2^{-3}), and so on. Note that this is merely a continuation of the rule stated previously: Each position is assigned a quantity twice the size of the one to its right. With these quantities assigned to the bit positions, decoding a binary representation containing a radix point requires the same procedure as used without a radix point. More precisely, we multiply each bit value by the quantity assigned to that bit's position in the representation. To illustrate, the binary representation 101.101 decodes to 5-5/8, as shown in Figure 1.18.

For addition, the techniques applied in the base 10 system are also applicable in binary. That is, to add two binary representations having radix points, we

Figure 1.18 Decoding the binary representation 101.101

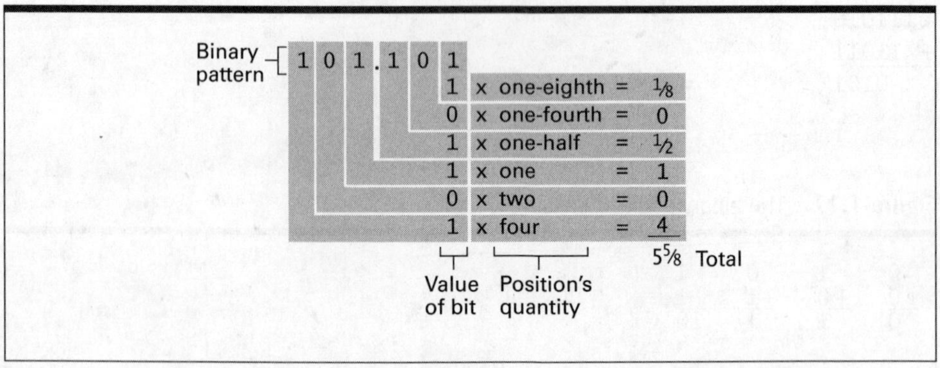

Analog versus Digital

Prior to the twenty-first century, many researchers debated the pros and cons of digital versus analog technology. In a digital system, a value is encoded as a series of digits and then stored using several devices, each representing one of the digits. In an analog system, each value is stored in a single device that can represent any value within a continuous range.

Let us compare the two approaches using buckets of water as the storage devices. To simulate a digital system, we could agree to let an empty bucket represent the digit 0 and a full bucket represent the digit 1. Then we could store a numeric value in a row of buckets using floating-point notation (see Section 1.7). In contrast, we could simulate an analog system by partially filling a single bucket to the point at which the water level represented the numeric value being represented. At first glance, the analog system may appear to be more accurate since it would not suffer from the truncation errors inherent in the digital system (again see Section 1.7). However, any movement of the bucket in the analog system could cause errors in detecting the water level, whereas a significant amount of sloshing would have to occur in the digital system before the distinction between a full bucket and an empty bucket would be blurred. Thus the digital system would be less sensitive to error than the analog system. This robustness is a major reason why many applications that were originally based on analog technology (such as telephone communication, audio recordings, and television) are shifting to digital technology.

merely align the radix points and apply the same addition process as before. For example, 10.011 added to 100.11 produces 111.001, as shown here:

```
   10.011
+ 100.110
  111.001
```

Questions & Exercises

1. Convert each of the following binary representations to its equivalent base 10 form:

   a. 101010 b. 100001 c. 10111 d. 0110 e. 11111

2. Convert each of the following base 10 representations to its equivalent binary form:

   a. 32 b. 64 c. 96 d. 15 e. 27

3. Convert each of the following binary representations to its equivalent base 10 form:

   a. 11.01 b. 101.111 c. 10.1 d. 110.011 e. 0.101

4. Express the following values in binary notation:

   a. $4\frac{1}{2}$ b. $2\frac{3}{4}$ c. $1\frac{1}{8}$ d. $\frac{5}{16}$ e. $5\frac{5}{8}$

5. Perform the following additions in binary notation:

a.	b.	c.	d.
11011 +1100	1010.001 + 1.101	11111 + 0001	111.11 + 00.01

1.6 Storing Integers

Mathematicians have long been interested in numeric notational systems, and many of their ideas have turned out to be very compatible with the design of digital circuitry. In this section we consider two of these notational systems, two's complement notation and excess notation, which are used for representing integer values in computing equipment. These systems are based on the binary system but have additional properties that make them more compatible with computer design. With these advantages, however, come disadvantages as well. Our goal is to understand these properties and how they affect computer usage.

Two's Complement Notation

The most popular system for representing integers within today's computers is **two's complement** notation. This system uses a fixed number of bits to represent each of the values in the system. In today's equipment, it is common to use a two's complement system in which each value is represented by a pattern of 32 bits. Such a large system allows a wide range of numbers to be represented but is awkward for demonstration purposes. Thus, to study the properties of two's complement systems, we will concentrate on smaller systems.

Figure 1.19 shows two complete two's complement systems—one based on bit patterns of length three, the other based on bit patterns of length four. Such a system is constructed by starting with a string of 0s of the appropriate length and then counting in binary until the pattern consisting of a single 0 followed by 1s is reached. These patterns represent the values 0, 1, 2, 3, ... The patterns representing negative values are obtained by starting with a string of 1s of the appropriate length and then counting backward in binary until the pattern consisting of a single 1 followed by 0s is reached. These patterns represent the values −1, −2, −3, ... (If counting backward in binary is difficult for you, merely start at the very bottom of the table with the pattern consisting of a single 1 followed by 0s, and count up to the pattern consisting of all 1s.)

Note that in a two's complement system, the leftmost bit of a bit pattern indicates the sign of the value represented. Thus, the leftmost bit is often called the **sign bit.** In a two's complement system, negative values are represented by the patterns whose sign bits are 1; nonnegative values are represented by patterns whose sign bits are 0.

In a two's complement system, there is a convenient relationship between the patterns representing positive and negative values of the same magnitude. They are identical when read from right to left, up to and including the first 1. From there on, the patterns are complements of one another. (The **complement** of a pattern is the pattern obtained by changing all the 0s to 1s and all the 1s to 0s; 0110 and 1001 are complements.) For example, in the 4-bit system in Figure 1.19

Figure 1.19 Two's complement notation systems

a. Using patterns of length three

Bit pattern	Value represented
011	3
010	2
001	1
000	0
111	-1
110	-2
101	-3
100	-4

b. Using patterns of length four

Bit pattern	Value represented
0111	7
0110	6
0101	5
0100	4
0011	3
0010	2
0001	1
0000	0
1111	-1
1110	-2
1101	-3
1100	-4
1011	-5
1010	-6
1001	-7
1000	-8

the patterns representing 2 and −2 both end with 10, but the pattern representing 2 begins with 00, whereas the pattern representing −2 begins with 11. This observation leads to an algorithm for converting back and forth between bit patterns representing positive and negative values of the same magnitude. We merely copy the original pattern from right to left until a 1 has been copied, then we complement the remaining bits as they are transferred to the final bit pattern (Figure 1.20).

Understanding these basic properties of two's complement systems also leads to an algorithm for decoding two's complement representations. If the pattern

Figure 1.20 Encoding the value—6 in two's complement notation using 4 bits

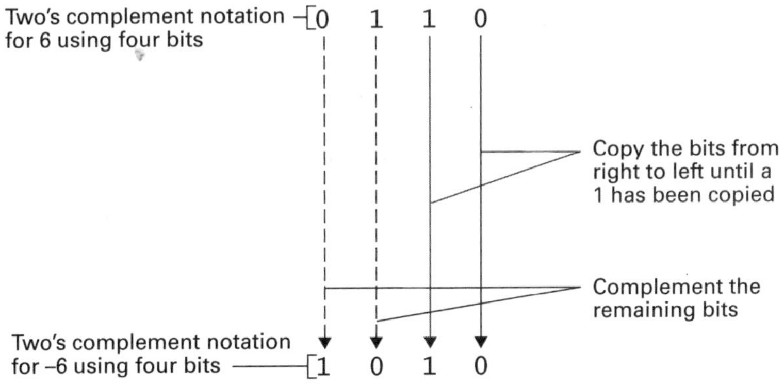

to be decoded has a sign bit of 0, we need merely read the value as though the pattern were a binary representation. For example, 0110 represents the value 6, because 110 is binary for 6. If the pattern to be decoded has a sign bit of 1, we know the value represented is negative, and all that remains is to find the magnitude of the value. We do this by applying the "copy and complement" procedure in Figure 1.20 and then decoding the pattern obtained as though it were a straightforward binary representation. For example, to decode the pattern 1010, we first recognize that since the sign bit is 1, the value represented is negative. Hence, we apply the "copy and complement" procedure to obtain the pattern 0110, recognize that this is the binary representation for 6, and conclude that the original pattern represents −6.

Addition in Two's Complement Notation To add values represented in two's complement notation, we apply the same algorithm that we used for binary addition, except that all bit patterns, including the answer, are the same length. This means that when adding in a two's complement system, any extra bit generated on the left of the answer by a final carry must be truncated. Thus "adding" 0101 and 0010 produces 0111, and "adding" 0111 and 1011 results in 0010 (0111 + 1011 = 10010, which is truncated to 0010).

With this understanding, consider the three addition problems in Figure 1.21. In each case, we have translated the problem into two's complement notation (using bit patterns of length four), performed the addition process previously described, and decoded the result back into our usual base 10 notation.

Observe that the third problem in Figure 1.21 involves the addition of a positive number to a negative number, which demonstrates a major benefit of two's complement notation: Addition of any combination of signed numbers can be accomplished using the same algorithm and thus the same circuitry. This is in stark contrast to how humans traditionally perform arithmetic computations. Whereas elementary school children are first taught to add and later taught to subtract, a machine using two's complement notation needs to know only how to add.

Figure 1.21 Addition problems converted to two's complement notation

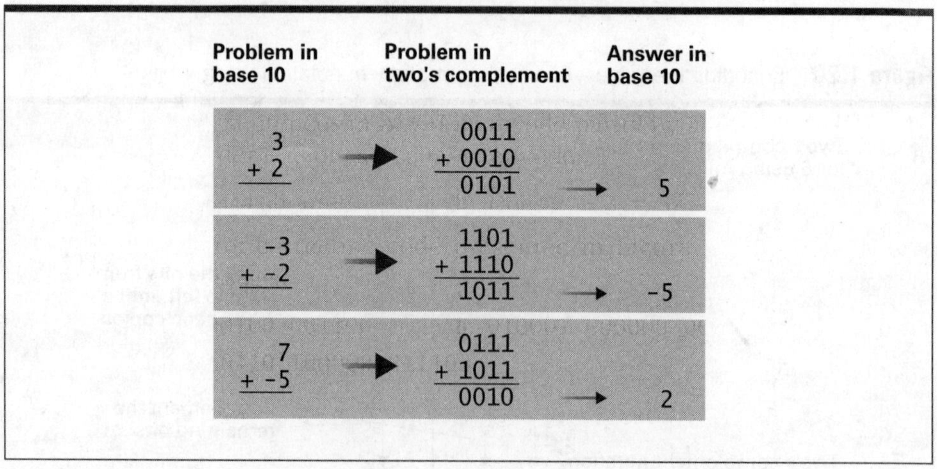

For example, the subtraction problem 7 − 5 is the same as the addition problem 7 + (−5). Consequently, if a machine were asked to subtract 5 (stored as 0101) from 7 (stored as 0111), it would first change the 5 to −5 (represented as 1011) and then perform the addition process of 0111 + 1011 to obtain 0010, which represents 2, as follows:

7		0111		0111		
-5	→	- 0101	→	+ 1011		
				0010	→	2

We see, then, that when two's complement notation is used to represent numeric values, a circuit for addition combined with a circuit for negating a value is sufficient for solving both addition and subtraction problems. (Such circuits are shown and explained in Appendix B.)

The Problem of Overflow One problem we have avoided in the preceding examples is that in any two's complement system there is a limit to the size of the values that can be represented. When using two's complement with patterns of 4 bits, the largest positive integer that can be represented is 7, and the most negative integer is −8. In particular, the value 9 cannot be represented, which means that we cannot hope to obtain the correct answer to the problem 5 + 4. In fact, the result would appear as −7. This phenomenon is called **overflow.** That is, overflow is the problem that occurs when a computation produces a value that falls outside the range of values that can be represented. When using two's complement notation, this might occur when adding two positive values or when adding two negative values. In either case, the condition can be detected by checking the sign bit of the answer. An overflow is indicated if the addition of two positive values results in the pattern for a negative value or if the sum of two negative values appears to be positive.

Of course, because most computers use two's complement systems with longer bit patterns than we have used in our examples, larger values can be manipulated without causing an overflow. Today, it is common to use patterns of 32 bits for storing values in two's complement notation, allowing for positive values as large as 2,147,483,647 to accumulate before overflow occurs. If still larger values are needed, longer bit patterns can be used or perhaps the units of measure can be changed. For instance, finding a solution in terms of miles instead of inches results in smaller numbers being used and might still provide the accuracy required.

The point is that computers can make mistakes. So, the person using the machine must be aware of the dangers involved. One problem is that computer programmers and users become complacent and ignore the fact that small values can accumulate to produce large numbers. For example, in the past it was common to use patterns of 16 bits for representing values in two's complement notation, which meant that overflow would occur when values of $2^{15} = 32{,}768$ or larger were reached. On September 19, 1989, a hospital computer system malfunctioned after years of reliable service. Close inspection revealed that this date was 32,768 days after January 1, 1900, and the machine was programmed to compute dates based on that starting date. Thus, because of overflow, September 19, 1989, produced a negative value—a phenomenon the computer's program was not designed to handle.

Excess Notation

Another method of representing integer values is **excess notation.** As is the case with two's complement notation, each of the values in an excess notation system is represented by a bit pattern of the same length. To establish an excess system, we first select the pattern length to be used, then write down all the different bit patterns of that length in the order they would appear if we were counting in binary. Next, we observe that the first pattern with a 1 as its most significant bit appears approximately halfway through the list. We pick this pattern to represent zero; the patterns following this are used to represent 1, 2, 3, . . .; and the patterns preceding it are used for −1, −2, −3, ... The resulting code, when using patterns of length four, is shown in Figure 1.22. There we see that the value 5 is represented by the pattern 1101 and −5 is represented by 0011. (Note that one difference between an excess system and a two's complement system is that the sign bits are reversed.)

The system represented in Figure 1.22 is known as excess eight notation. To understand why, first interpret each of the patterns in the code using the traditional binary system and then compare these results to the values represented in the excess notation. In each case, you will find that the binary interpretation exceeds the excess notation interpretation by the value 8. For example, the pattern 1100 in binary notation represents the value 12, but in our excess system it represents 4; 0000 in binary notation represents 0, but in the excess system it represents negative 8. In a similar manner, an excess system based on patterns of length five would be called excess 16 notation, because the pattern 10000, for instance, would be used to represent zero rather than representing its usual value of 16. Likewise, you may want to confirm that the three-bit excess system would be known as excess four notation (Figure 1.23).

Figure 1.22 An excess eight conversion table

Bit pattern	Value represented
1111	7
1110	6
1101	5
1100	4
1011	3
1010	2
1001	1
1000	0
0111	-1
0110	-2
0101	-3
0100	-4
0011	-5
0010	-6
0001	-7
0000	-8

Figure 1.23 An excess notation system using bit patterns of length three

Bit pattern	Value represented
111	3
110	2
101	1
100	0
011	-1
010	-2
001	-3
000	-4

Questions & Exercises

1. Convert each of the following two's complement representations to its equivalent base 10 form:

   a. 00011 b. 01111 c. 11100
   d. 11010 e. 00000 f. 10000

2. Convert each of the following base 10 representations to its equivalent two's complement form using patterns of 8 bits:

   a. 6 b. −6 c. −17
   d. 13 e. −1 f. 0

3. Suppose the following bit patterns represent values stored in two's complement notation. Find the two's complement representation of the negative of each value:

   a. 00000001 b. 01010101 c. 11111100
   d. 11111110 e. 00000000 f. 01111111

4. Suppose a machine stores numbers in two's complement notation. What are the largest and smallest numbers that can be stored if the machine uses bit patterns of the following lengths?

   a. four b. six c. eight

5. In the following problems, each bit pattern represents a value stored in two's complement notation. Find the answer to each problem in two's complement notation by performing the addition process described in the text. Then check your work by translating the problem and your answer into base 10 notation.

   a. 0101 + 0010 b. 0011 + 0001 c. 0101 + 1010
   d. 1110 + 0011 e. 1010 + 1110

6. Solve each of the following problems in two's complement notation, but this time watch for overflow and indicate which answers are incorrect because of this phenomenon.

   a. 0100 + 0011 b. 0101 + 0110 c. 1010 + 1010
   d. 1010 + 0111 e. 0111 + 0001

7. Translate each of the following problems from base 10 notation into two's complement notation using bit patterns of length four, then convert each problem to an equivalent addition problem (as a machine might do), and perform the addition. Check your answers by converting them back to base 10 notation.

   a. $6 - (-1)$ b. $3 - (-2)$ c. $4 - 6$
   d. $2 - (-4)$ e. $1 - 5$

8. Can overflow ever occur when values are added in two's complement notation with one value positive and the other negative? Explain your answer.

9. Convert each of the following excess eight representations to its equivalent base 10 form without referring to the table in the text:

   a. 1110 b. 0111 c. 1000
   d. 0010 e. 0000 f. 1001

10. Convert each of the following base 10 representations to its equivalent excess eight form without referring to the table in the text:

    a. 5 b. −5 c. 3
    d. 0 e. 7 f. −8

11. Can the value 9 be represented in excess eight notation? What about representing 6 in excess four notation? Explain your answer.

1.7 Storing Fractions

In contrast to the storage of integers, the storage of a value with a fractional part requires that we store not only the pattern of 0s and 1s representing its binary representation but also the position of the radix point. A popular way of doing this is based on scientific notation and is called **floating-point** notation.

Floating-Point Notation

Let us explain floating-point notation with an example using only one byte of storage. Although machines normally use much longer patterns, this 8-bit format is representative of actual systems and serves to demonstrate the important concepts without the clutter of long bit patterns.

We first designate the high-order bit of the byte as the sign bit. Once again, a 0 in the sign bit will mean that the value stored is nonnegative, and a 1 will mean that the value is negative. Next, we divide the remaining 7 bits of the byte into two groups, or fields: the **exponent field** and the **mantissa field.** Let us designate the 3 bits following the sign bit as the exponent field and the remaining 4 bits as the mantissa field. Figure 1.24 illustrates how the byte is divided.

We can explain the meaning of the fields by considering the following example. Suppose a byte consists of the bit pattern 01101011. Analyzing this pattern with the preceding format, we see that the sign bit is 0, the exponent is 110, and the mantissa is 1011. To decode the byte, we first extract the mantissa and place a radix point on its left side, obtaining

```
.1011
```

Next, we extract the contents of the exponent field (110) and interpret it as an integer stored using the 3-bit excess method (see again Figure 1.24). Thus the pattern in the exponent field in our example represents a positive 2. This tells us to move the radix in our solution to the right by 2 bits. (A negative exponent would mean to move the radix to the left.) Consequently, we obtain

```
10.11
```

which is the binary representation for $2\frac{3}{4}$. (Recall the representation of binary fractions from Figure 1.18.) Next, we note that the sign bit in our example is 0; the value represented is thus nonnegative. We conclude that the byte 01101011 represents $2\frac{3}{4}$. Had the pattern been 11101011 (which is the same as before except for the sign bit), the value represented would have been $2\frac{3}{4}$.

As another example, consider the byte 00111100. We extract the mantissa to obtain

```
.1100
```

and move the radix 1 bit to the left, since the exponent field (011) represents the value -1. We therefore have

```
.01100
```

which represents 3/8. Since the sign bit in the original pattern is 0, the value stored is nonnegative. We conclude that the pattern 00111100 represents $\frac{3}{8}$.

To store a value using floating-point notation, we reverse the preceding process. For example, to encode $1\frac{1}{8}$, first we express it in binary notation and obtain 1.001. Next, we copy the bit pattern into the mantissa field from left to right, starting with the leftmost 1 in the binary representation. At this point, the byte looks like this:

```
_ _ _ _ 1 0 0 1
```

Figure 1.24 Floating-point notation components

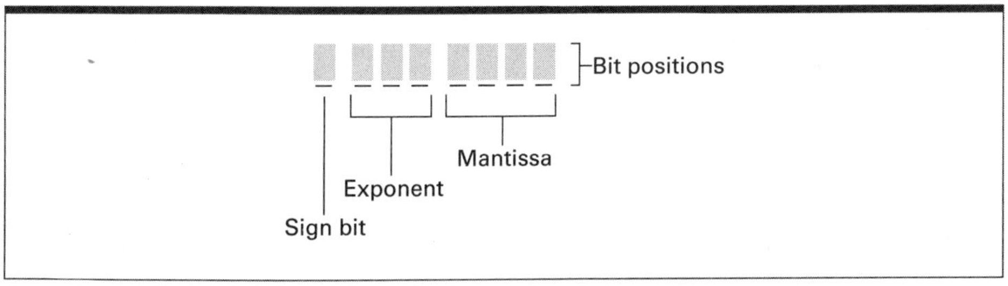

We must now fill in the exponent field. To this end, we imagine the contents of the mantissa field with a radix point at its left and determine the number of bits and the direction the radix must be moved to obtain the original binary number. In our example, we see that the radix in .1001 must be moved 1 bit to the right to obtain 1.001. The exponent should therefore be a positive one, so we place 101 (which is positive one in excess four notation as shown in Figure 1.23) in the exponent field. Finally, we fill the sign bit with 0 because the value being stored is nonnegative. The finished byte looks like this:

0 1 0 1 1 0 0 1

There is a subtle point you may have missed when filling in the mantissa field. The rule is to copy the bit pattern appearing in the binary representation from left to right, starting with the leftmost 1. To clarify, consider the process of storing the value $\frac{3}{8}$, which is .011 in binary notation. In this case the mantissa will be

_ _ _ _ 1 1 0 0

It will not be

_ _ _ _ 0 1 1 0

This is because we fill in the mantissa field starting with the leftmost 1 that appears in the binary representation. Representations that conform to this rule are said to be in **normalized form.**

Using normalized form eliminates the possibility of multiple representations for the same value. For example, both 00111100 and 01000110 would decode to the value $\frac{3}{8}$, but only the first pattern is in normalized form. Complying with normalized form also means that the representation for all nonzero values will have a mantissa that starts with 1. The value zero, however, is a special case; its floating-point representation is a bit pattern of all 0s.

Truncation Errors

Let us consider the annoying problem that occurs if we try to store the value $2\frac{5}{8}$ with our one-byte floating-point system. We first write $2\frac{5}{8}$ in binary, which gives us 10.101. But when we copy this into the mantissa field, we run out of room, and the rightmost 1 (which represents the last $\frac{1}{8}$) is lost (Figure 1.25). If we ignore this problem for now and continue by filling in the exponent field and the sign bit, we end up with the bit pattern 01101010, which represents $2\frac{1}{2}$ instead of $2\frac{5}{8}$. What has occurred is called a **truncation error,** or **round-off error**—meaning that part of the value being stored is lost because the mantissa field is not large enough.

The significance of such errors can be reduced by using a longer mantissa field. In fact, most computers manufactured today use at least 32 bits for storing values in floating-point notation instead of the 8 bits we have used here. This also allows for a longer exponent field at the same time. Even with these longer formats, however, there are still times when more accuracy is required.

Another source of truncation errors is a phenomenon that you are already accustomed to in base 10 notation: the problem of nonterminating expansions, such as those found when trying to express $\frac{1}{3}$ in decimal form. Some values cannot be accurately expressed regardless of how many digits we use. The difference between our traditional base 10 notation and binary notation is that more values have nonterminating representations in binary than in decimal notation. For example, the value 1/10 is nonterminating when expressed in binary. Imagine the problems this might cause the unwary person using floating-point notation to

Figure 1.25 Encoding the value 2⅝

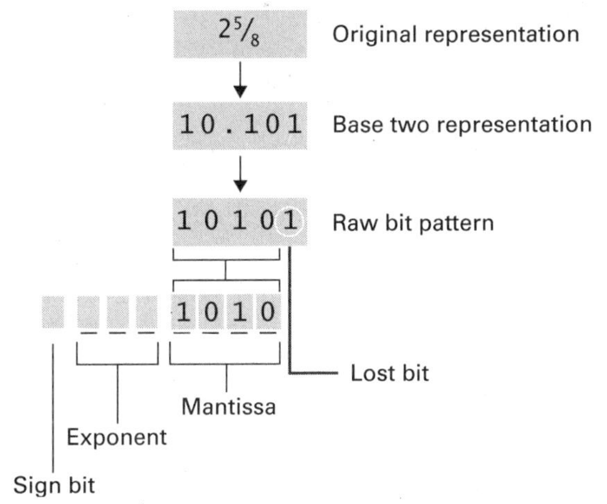

store and manipulate dollars and cents. In particular, if the dollar is used as the unit of measure, the value of a dime could not be stored accurately. A solution in this case is to manipulate the data in units of pennies so that all values are integers that can be accurately stored using a method such as two's complement.

Truncation errors and their related problems are an everyday concern for people working in the area of numerical analysis. This branch of mathematics deals with the problems involved when doing actual computations that are often massive and require significant accuracy.

The following is an example that would warm the heart of any numerical analyst. Suppose we are asked to add the following three values using our one-byte floating-point notation defined previously:

$2^1/_2 + {}^1/_8 + {}^1/_8$

Single Precision Floating Point

The floating-point notation introduced in this chapter (Section 1.7) is far too simplistic to be used in an actual computer. After all, with just 8 bits, only 256 numbers out of the set of all real numbers can be expressed. Our discussion has used 8 bits to keep the examples simple, yet still cover the important underlying concepts.

Many of today's computers support a 32-bit form of this notation called **Single Precision Floating Point.** This format uses 1 bit for the sign, 8 bits for the exponent (in an excess notation), and 23 bits for the mantissa. Thus, single precision floating point is capable of expressing very large numbers (order of 10^{38}) down to very small numbers (order of 10^{-37}) with the precision of 7 decimal digits. That is to say, the first 7 digits of a given decimal number can be stored with very good accuracy (a small amount of error may still be present). Any digits passed the first 7 will certainly be lost by truncation error (although the magnitude of the number is retained).

Another form, called **Double Precision Floating Point,** uses 64 bits and provides a precision of 15 decimal digits.

If we add the values in the order listed, we first add $2\frac{1}{2}$ to $\frac{1}{8}$ and obtain $2\frac{5}{8}$, which in binary is 10.101. Unfortunately, because this value cannot be stored accurately (as seen previously), the result of our first step ends up being stored as $2\frac{1}{2}$ (which is the same as one of the values we were adding). The next step is to add this result to the last 1/8. Here again a truncation error occurs, and our final result turns out to be the incorrect answer $2\frac{1}{2}$.

Now let us add the values in the opposite order. We first add $\frac{1}{8}$ to $\frac{1}{8}$ to obtain $\frac{1}{4}$. In binary this is .01; so the result of our first step is stored in a byte as 00111000, which is accurate. We now add this $\frac{1}{4}$ to the next value in the list, $2\frac{1}{2}$, and obtain $2\frac{3}{4}$, which we can accurately store in a byte as 01101011. The result this time is the correct answer.

To summarize, in adding numeric values represented in floating-point notation, the order in which they are added can be important. The problem is that if a very large number is added to a very small number, the small number may be truncated. Thus, the general rule for adding multiple values is to add the smaller values together first, in hopes that they will accumulate to a value that is significant when added to the larger values. This was the phenomenon experienced in the preceding example.

Designers of today's commercial software packages do a good job of shielding the uneducated user from problems such as this. In a typical spreadsheet system, correct answers will be obtained unless the values being added differ in size by a factor of 10^{16} or more. Thus, if you found it necessary to add one to the value

```
10,000,000,000,000,000
```

you might get the answer

```
10,000,000,000,000,000
```

rather than

```
10,000,000,000,000,001
```

Such problems are significant in applications (such as navigational systems) in which minor errors can be compounded in additional computations and ultimately produce significant consequences, but for the typical PC user the degree of accuracy offered by most commercial software is sufficient.

Questions & Exercises

1. Decode the following bit patterns using the floating-point format discussed in the text:

   a. 01001010 **b.** 01101101 **c.** 00111001 **d.** 11011100 **e.** 10101011

2. Encode the following values into the floating-point format discussed in the text. Indicate the occurrence of truncation errors.

   a. $2\frac{3}{4}$ **b.** $5\frac{1}{4}$ **c.** $\frac{3}{4}$ **d.** $-3\frac{1}{2}$ **e.** $-4\frac{3}{8}$

3. In terms of the floating-point format discussed in the text, which of the patterns 01001001 and 00111101 represents the larger value? Describe a simple procedure for determining which of two patterns represents the larger value.
4. When using the floating-point format discussed in the text, what is the largest value that can be represented? What is the smallest positive value that can be represented?

1.8 Data and Programming

While humans have devised the data representations and basic operations that comprise modern computers, few people are very good at working with computers directly at this level. People prefer to reason about computational problems at a higher level of abstraction, and they rely on the computer to handle the lowest levels of detail. A *programming language* is a computer system created to allow humans to precisely express algorithms to the computer using a higher level of abstraction.

In the twentieth century, programming computers was considered to be the province of a few highly trained experts; to be sure, there remain many problems in computing that require the attention of experienced computer scientists and software engineers. However, in the twenty-first century, as computers and computing have become increasingly intertwined in every aspect of our modern lives, it has grown steadily more difficult to identify career fields that do not require at least some degree of programming skill. Indeed, some have identified programming or *coding* to be the next foundational pillar of modern literacy, alongside reading, writing, and arithmetic.

In this section, and in programming supplement sections in subsequent chapters, we look at how a programming language reflects the main ideas of the chapter and allows humans to more easily solve problems involving computation.

Getting Started with Python

Python is a programming language that was created by Guido van Rossum in the late 1980s. Today it is one of the top ten most-used languages and remains popular in developing web applications, in scientific computation, and as an introductory language for students. Organizations that use Python range from Google to NASA, DropBox to Industrial Light & Magic, and across the spectrum of casual, scientific, and artistic computer users. Python emphasizes readability and includes elements of the imperative, object-oriented, and functional programming paradigms, which will be explored in Chapter 6.

The software for editing and running programs written in Python is freely available from `www.python.org`, as are many other resources for getting started. The Python language has evolved and continues to evolve over time. All of the examples in this book will use a version of the language called Python 3. Earlier versions of Python are capable of running very similar programs, but there have been many minor changes, such as punctuation, since Python 2.

Python is an *interpreted language,* which for beginners means that Python instructions can be typed into an interactive prompt or can be stored in a plain text file (called a "script") and run later. In the examples below, either mode can be used, but exercise and chapter review problems will generally ask for a Python script.

Hello Python

By longstanding tradition, the first program described in many programming language introductions is "Hello, World." This simple program outputs a nominal greeting, demonstrating how a particular language produces a result, and also how a language represents text. In Python[1], we write this program as

```
print('Hello, World!')
```

Type this statement into Python's interactive interpreter, or save it as a Python script and execute it. In either case, the result should be:

```
Hello, World!
```

Python parrots the text between the quotation marks back to the user.

There are several aspects to note even in this simple Python script. First, `print` is a built-in function, a predefined operation that Python scripts can use to produce *output,* a result of the program that will be made visible to the user. The print is followed by opening and closing parentheses; what comes between those parentheses is the value to be printed.

Second, Python can denote strings of text using single quotation marks. The quotation marks in front of the capital `H` and after the exclamation point denote the beginning and end of a string of characters that will be treated as a value in Python.

Programming languages carry out their instructions very precisely. If a user makes subtle changes to the message between the starting and finishing quotation marks within the print statement, the resultant printed text will change accordingly. Take a moment to try different capitalizations, punctuation, and even different words within the print statement to see that this is so.

Variables

Python allows the user to name values for later use, an important abstraction when constructing compact, understandable scripts. These named storage locations are termed *variables,* analogous to the mathematical variables often seen in algebra courses. Consider the slightly enhanced version of Hello World below:

```
message = 'Hello, World!'
print(message)
```

In this script, the first line is an *assignment statement.* The use of the = can be misleading to beginners, who are accustomed to the algebraic usage of the equal sign. This assignment statement should be read, "variable **message** is assigned

[1]This Python code is for version 3 of the language, which will be referred to only as "Python" for the remainder of the book. Earlier versions of Python do not always require the opening and closing parentheses.

the string value 'Hello, World!'". In general, an assignment statement will have a variable name on the left side of the equal sign and a value to the right.

Python is a *dynamically typed* language, which means that our script need not establish ahead of time that there will be a variable called message, or what type of value should be stored in message. In the script, it is sufficient to state that our text string will be assigned to message, and then to refer to that variable message in the subsequent print statement.

The naming of variables is largely up to the user in Python. Python's simple rules are that variable names must begin with an alphabet letter and may consist of an arbitrary number of letters, digits, and the underscore character, _. While a variable named m may be sufficient for a two-line example script, experienced programmers strive to give meaningful, descriptive variable names in their scripts.

Python variable names are *case-sensitive,* meaning that capitalization matters. A variable named size is treated as distinct from variables named Size or SIZE. A small number of *keywords,* names that are reserved for special meaning in Python, cannot be used as variable names. You can view this list by accessing the built-in Python help system.

```
help('keywords')
```

Variables can be used to store all of the types of values that Python is able to represent.

```
my_integer = 5
my_floating_point = 26.2
my_Boolean = True
my_string = 'characters'
```

Observe that the types of values we see here correspond directly to the representations covered earlier in this chapter: Boolean trues and falses (Section 1.1), text (Section 1.4), integers (Section 1.6), and floating point numbers (Section 1.7). With additional Python code (beyond the scope of our simple introduction in this text) we could store image and sound data (Section 1.4) with Python variables, as well.

Python expresses hexadecimal values using a 0x prefix, as in

```
my_integer = 0xFF
print(my_integer)
```

Specifying a value in hexadecimal does not alter the representation of that value in the computer's memory, which stores integer values as a collection of ones and zeros regardless of the numerical base used in the programmer's reasoning. Hexadecimal notation remains a shortcut for humans, used in situations where that representation may aid in understanding the script. The print statement above thus prints 255, the base 10 interpretation of hexadecimal 0xFF, because that is the default behavior for print. More complex adjustments to the print statement can be used to output values in other representations, but we confine our discussion here to the more familiar base 10.

Unicode characters, including those beyond the ubiquitous ASCII subset, can be included directly in strings when the text editor supports them,

```
print('₹1000')            # Prints ₹1000, one thousand Indian Rupees
```

or can be specified using four hexadecimal digits following a '\u' prefix.

```
print('\u00A31000')       # Prints £1000, one thousand British
                          # Pounds Sterling
```

The portion of the string '\u00A3' encodes the Unicode representation of the British pound symbol. The '1000' follows immediately so that there will be no space between the currency symbol and the amount in the final output: £1000.

These example statements introduce another language feature, in addition to Unicode text strings. The # symbol denotes the beginning of a *comment,* a human-readable notation to the Python code that will be ignored by the computer when executed. Experienced programmers use comments in their code to explain difficult segments of the algorithm, include history or authorship information, or just to note where a human should pay attention when reading the code. All of the characters to the right of the # until the end of the line are ignored by Python.

Operators and Expressions

Python's built-in operators allow values to be manipulated and combined in a variety of familiar ways.

```
print(3 + 4)         # Prints "7", which is 3 plus 4.
print(5 - 6)         # Prints "-1", which is 5 minus 6
print(7 * 8)         # Prints "56", which is 7 times 8
print(45 / 4)        # Prints "11.25", which is 45 divided by 4
print(2 ** 10)       # Prints "1024", which is 2 to the 10th power
```

When an operation such as forty-five divided by four produces a non-integer result, such as 11.25, Python implicitly switches to a floating-point representation. When purely integer answers are desired, a different set of operators can be used.

```
print(45 // 4)       # Prints "11", which is 45 integer divided by 4
print(45 % 4)        # Prints "1", because 4 * 11 + 1 = 45
```

The double slash signifies the *integer floor division* operator, while the percentage symbol signifies the *modulus,* or remainder operator. Taken together, we can read these calculations as, "four goes into forty-five eleven times, with a remainder of one." In the earlier example, we used ** to signify exponentiation, which can be somewhat surprising given that the caret symbol, ^, is often used for this purpose in typewritten text and even some other programming languages. In Python, the caret operator belongs to the group of *bitwise Boolean operations,* which will be discussed in the next chapter.

String values also can be combined and manipulated in some intuitive ways.

```
s = 'hello' + 'world'
t = s * 4

print(t)     # Prints "helloworldhelloworldhelloworldhelloworld"
```

The plus operator *concatenates* string values, while the multiplication operator *replicates* string values.

The multiple meanings of some of the built-in operators can lead to confusion. This script will produce an error:

```
print('USD$' + 1000)     # TypeError: Can't convert 'int' to str implicitly
```

The error indicates that the string concatenation operator doesn't know what to do when the second operand is not also a string. Fortunately, Python provides functions that allow values to be converted from one type of representation to another. The `int()` function will convert a floating-point value back to an integer representation, discarding the fractional part. It will also convert a string of text digits into an integer representation, provided that the string correctly spells out a valid number. Likewise, the `str()` function can be used to convert numeric representations into UTF-8 encoded text strings. Thus, the following modification to the `print` statement above corrects the error.

```
print('USD$' + str(1000))     # Prints "USD$1000"
```

Currency Conversion

The complete Python script example below demonstrates many of the concepts introduced in this section. Given a set number of U.S. dollars, the script produces monetary conversions to four other currencies.

```
# A converter for international currency exchange.
USD_to_GBP = 0.66   # Today's rate, US dollars to British Pounds
USD_to_EUR = 0.77   # Today's rate, US dollars to Euros
USD_to_JPY = 99.18  # Today's rate, US dollars to Japanese Yen
USD_to_INR = 59.52  # Today's rate, US dollars to Indian Rupees

GBP_sign    = '\u00A3' # Unicode values for non-ASCII currency symbols.
EUR_sign    = '\u20AC'
JPY_sign    = '\u00A5'
INR_sign    = '\u20B9'


dollars     = 1000 # The number of dollars to convert


pounds      = dollars * USD_to_GBP    # Conversion calculations
euros       = dollars * USD_to_EUR
yen         = dollars * USD_to_JPY
rupees      = dollars * USD_to_INR


print('Today, $' + str(dollars))    # Printing the results
print('converts to ' + GBP_sign + str(pounds))
```

```
print('converts to ' + EUR_sign + str(euros))
print('converts to ' + JPY_sign + str(yen))
print('converts to ' + INR_sign + str(rupees))
```

When executed, this script outputs the following:

```
Today, $1000
converts to £660.0
converts to €770.0
converts to ¥99180.0
converts to ₹59520.0
```

Debugging

Programming languages are not very forgiving for beginners, and a great deal of time learning to write software can be spent trying to find **bugs,** or errors in the code. There are three major classes of bug that we create in software: **syntax errors** (mistakes in the symbols that have been typed), **semantic errors** (mistakes in the meaning of the program), and **runtime errors** (mistakes that occur when the program is executed.)

Syntax errors are the most common for novices and include simple errors such as forgetting one of the quote marks at the beginning or ending of a text string, failing to close open parentheses, or misspelling the function name `print`. The Python interpreter will generally try to point these errors out when it encounters them, displaying an offending line number and a description of the problem. With some practice, a beginner can quickly learn to recognize and interpret common error cases. As examples:

```
print(5 + )
SyntaxError: invalid syntax
```

This expression is missing a value between the addition operator and the closing parenthesis.

```
print(5.e)
SyntaxError: invalid token
```

Python expects digits to follow the decimal point, not a letter.

```
pront(5)
NameError: name 'pront' is not defined
```

Like calling someone by the wrong name, misspelling the name of a known function or variable can result in confusion and embarrassment.

Semantic errors are flaws in the algorithm, or flaws in the way the algorithm is expressed in a language. Examples might include using the wrong variable name in a calculation or getting the order of arithmetic operations wrong in a complex expression. Python follows the standard rules for operator precedence, so in an expression like `total_pay = 40 + extra_hours * pay_rate`, the multiplication will be performed before the addition, incorrectly calculating the total pay. (Unless your pay rate happens to be $1/hour.) Use parenthesis to properly specify the order of operations in complex expressions, thereby avoiding both semantic errors and code that may be harder to understand (e.g., `total_pay = (40 + extra_hours) * pay_rate`).

Finally, runtime errors at this level might include unintentionally dividing by zero or using a variable before you have defined it. Python reads statements from top to bottom; it and must see an assignment statement to a variable before that variable is used in an expression.

Testing is an integral part of writing Python scripts—or really any kind of program—effectively. Run your script frequently as you write it, perhaps as often as after you complete each line of code. This allows syntax errors to be identified and fixed early and helps focus the author's attention on what should be happening at each step of the script.

Questions & Exercises

1. What makes Python an *interpreted* programming language?
2. Write Python statements that print the following:
   a. The words "Computer Science Rocks", followed by an exclamation point
   b. The number 42
   c. An approximation of the value of Pi to 4 decimal places
3. Write Python statements to make the following assignments to variables:
   a. The word "programmer" to a variable called, `rockstar`
   b. The number of seconds in an hour to a variable called `seconds_per_hour`
   c. The average temperature of the human body to a variable called `bodyTemp`
4. Write a Python statement that given an existing variable called `bodyTemp` in degrees Fahrenheit stores the equivalent temperature in degrees Celsius to a new variable called `metricBodyTemp`.

1.9 Data Compression

For the purpose of storing or transferring data, it is often helpful (and sometimes mandatory) to reduce the size of the data involved while retaining the underlying information. The technique for accomplishing this is called **data compression.** We begin this section by considering some generic data compression methods and then look at some approaches designed for specific applications.

Generic Data Compression Techniques

Data compression schemes fall into two categories. Some are **lossless,** others are **lossy.** Lossless schemes are those that do not lose information in the compression process. Lossy schemes are those that may lead to the loss of information. Lossy techniques often provide more compression than lossless ones and are therefore popular in settings in which minor errors can be tolerated, as in the case of images and audio.

In cases where the data being compressed consist of long sequences of the same value, the compression technique called **run-length encoding,** which is a lossless method, is popular. It is the process of replacing sequences of identical data elements with a code indicating the element that is repeated and the number of times it occurs in the sequence. For example, less space is required to indicate that a bit pattern consists of 253 ones, followed by 118 zeros, followed by 87 ones than to actually list all 458 bits.

Another lossless data compression technique is **frequency-dependent encoding,** a system in which the length of the bit pattern used to represent a data item is inversely related to the frequency of the item's use. Such codes are examples of variable-length codes, meaning that items are represented by patterns of different lengths. David Huffman is credited with discovering an algorithm that is commonly used for developing frequency-dependent codes, and it is common practice to refer to codes developed in this manner as **Huffman codes.** In turn, most frequency-dependent codes in use today are Huffman codes.

As an example of frequency-dependent encoding, consider the task of encoded English language text. In the English language the letters *e, t, a,* and i are used more frequently than the letters *z, q,* and *x*. So, when constructing a code for text in the English language, space can be saved by using short bit patterns to represent the former letters and longer bit patterns to represent the latter ones. The result would be a code in which English text would have shorter representations than would be obtained with uniform-length codes.

In some cases, the stream of data to be compressed consists of units, each of which differs only slightly from the preceding one. An example would be consecutive frames of a motion picture. In these cases, techniques using **relative encoding,** also known as **differential encoding,** are helpful. These techniques record the differences between consecutive data units rather than entire units; that is, each unit is encoded in terms of its relationship to the previous unit. Relative encoding can be implemented in either lossless or lossy form depending on whether the differences between consecutive data units are encoded precisely or approximated.

Still other popular compression systems are based on **dictionary encoding** techniques. Here the term *dictionary* refers to a collection of building blocks from which the message being compressed is constructed, and the message itself is encoded as a sequence of references to the dictionary. We normally think of dictionary encoding systems as lossless systems, but as we will see in our discussion of image compression, there are times when the entries in the dictionary are only approximations of the correct data elements, resulting in a lossy compression system.

Dictionary encoding can be used by word processors to compress text documents because the dictionaries already contained in these processors for the purpose of spell checking make excellent compression dictionaries. In particular, an entire word can be encoded as a single reference to this dictionary rather than as a sequence of individual characters encoded using a system such as UTF-8. A typical dictionary in a word processor contains approximately 25,000 entries, which means an individual entry can be identified by an integer in the range of 0 to 24,999. This means that a particular entry in the dictionary can be identified by a pattern of only 15 bits. In contrast, if the word being referenced consisted of six letters, its character-by-character encoding would require 48 bits using UTF-8.

A variation of dictionary encoding is **adaptive dictionary encoding** (also known as dynamic dictionary encoding). In an adaptive dictionary encoding system, the dictionary is allowed to change during the encoding process. A popular example is **Lempel-Ziv-Welsh (LZW) encoding** (named after its creators, Abraham Lempel, Jacob Ziv, and Terry Welsh). To encode a message using LZW, one starts with a dictionary containing the basic building blocks from which the message is constructed, but as larger units are found in the message, they are added to the dictionary—meaning that future occurrences of those units can be encoded as single, rather than multiple, dictionary references. For example, when encoding English text, one could start with a dictionary containing individual characters, digits, and punctuation marks. But as words in the message are identified, they could be added to the dictionary. Thus, the dictionary would grow as the message is encoded, and as the dictionary grows, more words (or recurring patterns of words) in the message could be encoded as single references to the dictionary.

The result would be a message encoded in terms of a rather large dictionary that is unique to that particular message. But this large dictionary would not have to be present to decode the message. Only the original small dictionary would be needed. Indeed, the decoding process could begin with the same small dictionary with which the encoding process started. Then, as the decoding process continues, it would encounter the same units found during the encoding process, and thus be able to add them to the dictionary for future reference just as in the encoding process.

To clarify, consider applying LZW encoding to the message

xyx xyx xyx xyx

starting with a dictionary with three entries, the first being *x*, the second being y, and the third being a space. We would begin by encoding *xyx* as 121, meaning that the message starts with the pattern consisting of the first dictionary entry, followed by the second, followed by the first. Then the space is encoded to produce 1213. But, having reached a space, we know that the preceding string of characters forms a word, and so we add the pattern *xyx* to the dictionary as the fourth entry. Continuing in this manner, the entire message would be encoded as 121343434.

If we were now asked to decode this message, starting with the original three-entry dictionary, we would begin by decoding the initial string 1213 as *xyx* followed by a space. At this point we would recognize that the string *xyx* forms a word and add it to the dictionary as the fourth entry, just as we did during the encoding process. We would then continue decoding the message by recognizing that the 4 in the message refers to this new fourth entry and decode it as the word *xyx*, producing the pattern

xyx xyx

Continuing in this manner we would ultimately decode the string 121343434 as

xyx xyx xyx xyx

which is the original message.

Compressing Images

In Section 1.4, we saw how images are encoded using bit map techniques. Unfortunately, the bit maps produced are often very large. In turn, numerous compression schemes have been developed specifically for image representations.

One system known as **GIF** (short for **Graphic Interchange Format** and pronounced "Giff" by some and "Jiff" by others) is a dictionary encoding system that was developed by CompuServe. It approaches the compression problem by reducing the number of colors that can be assigned to a pixel to only 256. The red-green-blue combination for each of these colors is encoded using three bytes, and these 256 encodings are stored in a table (a dictionary) called the palette. Each pixel in an image can then be represented by a single byte whose value indicates which of the 256 palette entries represents the pixel's color. (Recall that a single byte can contain any one of 256 different bit patterns.) Note that GIF is a lossy compression system when applied to arbitrary images because the colors in the palette may not be identical to the colors in the original image.

GIF can obtain additional compression by extending this simple dictionary system to an adaptive dictionary system using LZW techniques. In particular, as patterns of pixels are encountered during the encoding process, they are added to the dictionary so that future occurrences of these patterns can be encoded more efficiently. Thus, the final dictionary consists of the original palette and a collection of pixel patterns.

One of the colors in a GIF palette is normally assigned the value "transparent," which means that the background is allowed to show through each region assigned that "color." This option, combined with the relative simplicity of the GIF system, makes GIF a logical choice in simple animation applications in which multiple images must move around on a computer screen. On the other hand, its ability to encode only 256 colors renders it unsuitable for applications in which higher precision is required, as in the field of photography.

Another popular compression system for images is **JPEG** (pronounced "JAY-peg"). It is a standard developed by the **Joint Photographic Experts Group** (hence the standard's name) within ISO. JPEG has proved to be an effective standard for compressing color photographs and is widely used in the photography industry, as witnessed by the fact that most digital cameras use JPEG as their default compression technique.

The JPEG standard actually encompasses several methods of image compression, each with its own goals. In those situations that require the utmost in precision, JPEG provides a lossless mode. However, JPEG's lossless mode does not produce high levels of compression when compared to other JPEG options. Moreover, other JPEG options have proven very successful, meaning that JPEG's lossless mode is rarely used. Instead, the option known as JPEG's baseline standard (also known as JPEG's lossy sequential mode) has become the standard of choice in many applications.

Image compression using the JPEG baseline standard requires a sequence of steps, some of which are designed to take advantage of a human eye's limitations. In particular, the human eye is more sensitive to changes in brightness than to changes in color. So, starting from an image that is encoded in terms of luminance and chrominance components, the first step is to average the chrominance values over two-by-two pixel squares. This reduces the size of the chrominance information by a factor of four while preserving all the original brightness information. The result is a significant degree of compression without a noticeable loss of image quality.

The next step is to divide the image into eight-by-eight pixel blocks and to compress the information in each block as a unit. This is done by applying a mathematical technique known as the discrete cosine transform, whose details need not concern us here. The important point is that this transformation converts the original eight-by-eight block into another block whose entries reflect how the pixels in the original block relate to each other rather than the actual pixel values. Within this new block, values below a predetermined threshold are then replaced by zeros, reflecting the fact that the changes represented by these values are too subtle to be detected by the human eye. For example, if the original block contained a checkerboard pattern, the new block might reflect a uniform average color. (A typical eight-by-eight pixel block would represent a very small square within the image so the human eye would not identify the checkerboard appearance anyway.)

At this point, more traditional run-length encoding, relative encoding, and variable-length encoding techniques are applied to obtain additional compression. All together, JPEG's baseline standard normally compresses color images by a factor of at least 10, and often by as much as 30, without noticeable loss of quality.

Still another data compression system associated with images is **TIFF** (short for **Tagged Image File Format**). However, the most popular use of TIFF is not as a means of data compression but instead as a standardized format for storing photographs along with related information such as date, time, and camera settings. In this context, the image itself is normally stored as red, green, and blue pixel components without compression.

The TIFF collection of standards does include data compression techniques, most of which are designed for compressing images of text documents in facsimile applications. These use variations of run-length encoding to take advantage of the fact that text documents consist of long strings of white pixels. The color image compression option included in the TIFF standards is based on techniques similar to those used by GIF and are therefore not widely used in the photography community.

Compressing Audio and Video

The most commonly used standards for encoding and compressing audio and video were developed by the **Motion Picture Experts Group (MPEG)** under the leadership of ISO. In turn, these standards themselves are called MPEG.

MPEG encompasses a variety of standards for different applications. For example, the demands for high definition television (HDTV) broadcast are distinct from those for video conferencing, in which the broadcast signal must find its way over a variety of communication paths that may have limited capabilities. Both of these applications differ from that of storing video in such a manner that sections can be replayed or skipped over.

The techniques employed by MPEG are well beyond the scope of this text, but in general, video compression techniques are based on video being constructed as a sequence of pictures in much the same way that motion pictures are recorded on film. To compress such sequences, only some of the pictures, called I-frames, are encoded in their entirety. The pictures between the I-frames are encoded using relative encoding techniques. That is, rather than encode the entire picture, only its distinctions from the prior image are recorded. The I-frames themselves are usually compressed with techniques similar to JPEG.

The best known system for compressing audio is **MP3,** which was developed within the MPEG standards. In fact, the acronym *MP3* is short for

MPEG layer 3. Among other compression techniques, MP3 takes advantage of the properties of the human ear, removing those details that the human ear cannot perceive. One such property, called **temporal masking,** is that for a short period after a loud sound, the human ear cannot detect softer sounds that would otherwise be audible. Another, called **frequency masking,** is that a sound at one frequency tends to mask softer sounds at nearby frequencies. By taking advantage of such characteristics, MP3 can be used to obtain significant compression of audio while maintaining near CD quality sound.

Using MPEG and MP3 compression techniques, video cameras are able to record as much as an hour's worth of video within 128MB of storage, and portable music players can store as many as 400 popular songs in a single GB. But, in contrast to the goals of compression in other settings, the goal of compressing audio and video is not necessarily to save storage space. Just as important is the goal of obtaining encodings that allow information to be transmitted over today's communication systems fast enough to provide timely presentation. If each video frame required a MB of storage and the frames had to be transmitted over a communication path that could relay only one KB per second, there would be no hope of successful video conferencing. Thus, in addition to the quality of reproduction allowed, audio and video compression systems are often judged by the transmission speeds required for timely data communication. These speeds are normally measured in **bits per second (bps).** Common units include **Kbps** (kilo-bps, equal to one thousand bps), **Mbps** (mega-bps, equal to one million bps), and **Gbps** (giga-bps, equal to one billion bps). Using MPEG techniques, video presentations can be successfully relayed over communication paths that provide transfer rates of 40 Mbps. MP3 recordings generally require transfer rates of no more than 64 Kbps.

Questions & Exercises

1. List four generic compression techniques.
2. What would be the encoded version of the message

   `xyx yxxxy xyx yxxxy yxxxy`

   if LZW compression, starting with the dictionary containing *x*, *y*, and a space (as described in the text), were used?
3. Why would GIF be better than JPEG when encoding color cartoons?
4. Suppose you were part of a team designing a spacecraft that will travel to other planets and send back photographs. Would it be a good idea to compress the photographs using GIF or JPEG's baseline standard to reduce the resources required to store and transmit the images?
5. What characteristic of the human eye does JPEG's baseline standard exploit?
6. What characteristic of the human ear does MP3 exploit?
7. Identify a troubling phenomenon that is common when encoding numeric information, images, and sound as bit patterns.

1.10 Communication Errors

When information is transferred back and forth among the various parts of a computer, or transmitted from the earth to the moon and back, or, for that matter, merely left in storage, a chance exists that the bit pattern ultimately retrieved may not be identical to the original one. Particles of dirt or grease on a magnetic recording surface or a malfunctioning circuit may cause data to be incorrectly recorded or read. Static on a transmission path may corrupt portions of the data. In the case of some technologies, normal background radiation can alter patterns stored in a machine's main memory.

To resolve such problems, a variety of encoding techniques have been developed to allow the detection and even the correction of errors. Today, because these techniques are largely built into the internal components of a computer system, they are not apparent to the personnel using the machine. Nonetheless, their presence is important and represents a significant contribution to scientific research. It is fitting, therefore, that we investigate some of these techniques that lie behind the reliability of today's equipment.

Parity Bits

A simple method of detecting errors is based on the principle that if each bit pattern being manipulated has an odd number of 1s and a pattern with an even number of 1s is encountered, an error must have occurred. To use this principle, we need an encoding system in which each pattern contains an odd number of 1s. This is easily obtained by first adding an additional bit, called a **parity bit,** to each pattern in an encoding system already available (perhaps at the high-order end). In each case, we assign the value 1 or 0 to this new bit so that the entire resulting pattern has an odd number of 1s. Once our encoding system has been modified in this way, a pattern with an even number of 1s indicates that an error has occurred and that the pattern being manipulated is incorrect.

Figure 1.26 demonstrates how parity bits could be added to the ASCII codes for the letters A and F. Note that the code for A becomes 101000001 (parity bit 1) and the ASCII for F becomes 001000110 (parity bit 0). Although the original 8-bit pattern for A has an even number of 1s and the original 8-bit pattern for F has an odd number of 1s, both the 9-bit patterns have an odd number of 1s. If this technique were applied to all the 8-bit ASCII patterns, we would obtain a 9-bit encoding system in which an error would be indicated by any 9-bit pattern with an even number of 1s.

Figure 1.26 The ASCII codes for the letters A and F adjusted for odd parity

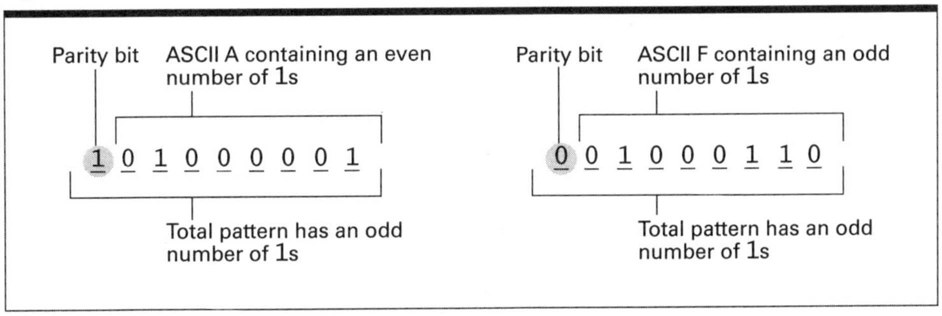

The parity system just described is called **odd parity,** because we designed our system so that each correct pattern contains an odd number of 1s. Another technique is called **even parity.** In an even parity system, each pattern is designed to contain an even number of 1s, and thus an error is signaled by the occurrence of a pattern with an odd number of 1s.

Today it is not unusual to find parity bits being used in a computer's main memory. Although we envision these machines as having memory cells of 8-bit capacity, in reality each has a capacity of 9 bits, 1 bit of which is used as a parity bit. Each time an 8-bit pattern is given to the memory circuitry for storage, the circuitry adds a parity bit and stores the resulting 9-bit pattern. When the pattern is later retrieved, the circuitry checks the parity of the 9-bit pattern. If this does not indicate an error, then the memory removes the parity bit and confidently returns the remaining 8-bit pattern. Otherwise, the memory returns the 8 data bits with a warning that the pattern being returned may not be the same pattern that was originally entrusted to memory.

The straightforward use of parity bits is simple, but it has its limitations. If a pattern originally has an odd number of 1s and suffers two errors, it will still have an odd number of 1s, and thus the parity system will not detect the errors. In fact, straightforward applications of parity bits fail to detect any even number of errors within a pattern.

One means of minimizing this problem is sometimes applied to long bit patterns, such as the string of bits recorded in a sector on a magnetic disk. In this case the pattern is accompanied by a collection of parity bits making up a **checkbyte.** Each bit within the checkbyte is a parity bit associated with a particular collection of bits scattered throughout the pattern. For instance, one parity bit may be associated with every eighth bit in the pattern starting with the first bit, while another may be associated with every eighth bit starting with the second bit. In this manner, a collection of errors concentrated in one area of the original pattern is more likely to be detected, since it will be in the scope of several parity bits. Variations of this checkbyte concept lead to error detection schemes known as **checksums** and **cyclic redundancy checks (CRC).**

Error-Correcting Codes

Although the use of a parity bit allows the detection of an error, it does not provide the information needed to correct the error. Many people are surprised that **error-correcting codes** can be designed so that errors can be not only detected but also corrected. After all, intuition says that we cannot correct errors in a received message unless we already know the information in the message. However, a simple code with such a corrective property is presented in Figure 1.27.

To understand how this code works, we first define the term **Hamming distance,** which is named after R. W. Hamming, who pioneered the search for error-correcting codes after becoming frustrated with the lack of reliability of the early relay machines of the 1940s. The Hamming distance between two bit patterns is the number of bits in which the patterns differ. For example, the Hamming distance between the patterns representing A and B in the code in Figure 1.27 is four, and the Hamming distance between B and C is three. The

Figure 1.27 An error-correcting code

Symbol	Code
A	000000
B	001111
C	010011
D	011100
E	100110
F	101001
G	110101
H	111010

important feature of the code in Figure 1.27 is that any two patterns are separated by a Hamming distance of at least three.

If a single bit is modified in a pattern from Figure 1.27, the error can be detected since the result will not be a legal pattern. (We must change at least 3 bits in any pattern before it will look like another legal pattern.) Moreover, we can also figure out what the original pattern was. After all, the modified pattern will be a Hamming distance of only one from its original form but at least two from any of the other legal patterns.

Thus, to decode a message that was originally encoded using Figure 1.27, we simply compare each received pattern with the patterns in the code until we find one that is within a distance of one from the received pattern. We consider this to be the correct symbol for decoding. For example, if we received the bit pattern 010100 and compared this pattern to the patterns in the code, we would obtain the table in Figure 1.28. Thus, we would conclude that the character transmitted must have been a D because this is the closest match.

Figure 1.28 Decoding the pattern 010100 using the code in Figure 1.27

Character	Code	Pattern received	Distance between received pattern and code
A	0 0 0 0 0 0	0 **1** 0 **1** 0 0	2
B	0 0 1 1 1 1	0 **1** 0 1 **0** **0**	4
C	0 1 0 0 1 1	0 1 0 **1** **0** **0**	3
D	0 1 1 1 0 0	0 1 **0** 1 0 0	**1** — Smallest distance
E	1 0 0 1 1 0	**0** **1** 0 1 **0** 0	3
F	1 0 1 0 0 1	**0** **1** **0** **1** 0 **0**	5
G	1 1 0 1 0 1	**0** 1 0 1 0 **0**	2
H	1 1 1 0 1 0	**0** 1 **0** **1** **0** 0	4

You will observe that using this technique with the code in Figure 1.27 actually allows us to detect up to two errors per pattern and to correct one error. If we designed the code so that each pattern was a Hamming distance of at least five from each of the others, we would be able to detect up to four errors per pattern and correct up to two. Of course, the design of efficient codes associated with large Hamming distances is not a straightforward task. In fact, it constitutes a part of the branch of mathematics called algebraic coding theory, which is a subject within the fields of linear algebra and matrix theory.

Error-correcting techniques are used extensively to increase the reliability of computing equipment. For example, they are often used in high-capacity magnetic disk drives to reduce the possibility that flaws in the magnetic surface will corrupt data. Moreover, a major distinction between the original CD format used for audio disks and the later format used for computer data storage is in the degree of error correction involved. CD-DA format incorporates error-correcting features that reduce the error rate to only one error for two CDs. This is quite adequate for audio recordings, but a company using CDs to supply software to customers would find that flaws in 50 percent of the disks would be intolerable. Thus, additional error-correcting features are employed in CDs used for data storage, reducing the probability of error to one in 20,000 disks.

Questions & Exercises

1. The following bytes were originally encoded using odd parity. In which of them do you know that an error has occurred?

   a. 100101101 b. 100000001 c. 000000000
   d. 111000000 e. 011111111

2. Could errors have occurred in a byte from question 1 without your knowing it? Explain your answer.
3. How would your answers to questions 1 and 2 change if you were told that even parity had been used instead of odd?
4. Encode these sentences in ASCII using odd parity by adding a parity bit at the high-order end of each character code:

   a. "Stop!" Cheryl shouted. b. Does 2 + 3 = 5?

5. Using the error-correcting code presented in Figure 1.27, decode the following messages:

   a. 001111 100100 001100 b. 010001 000000 001011
   c. 011010 110110 100000 011100

6. Construct a code for the characters A, B, C, and D using bit patterns of length five so that the Hamming distance between any two patterns is at least three.

Chapter Review Problems

(Asterisked problems are associated with optional sections.)

1. Determine the output of each of the following circuits, assuming that the upper input is 1 and the lower input is 0. What would be the output when upper input is 0 and the lower input is 1?

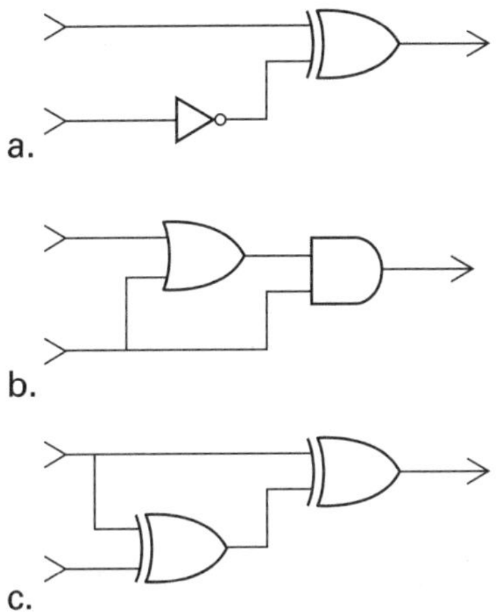

2. a. What Boolean operation does the circuit compute?

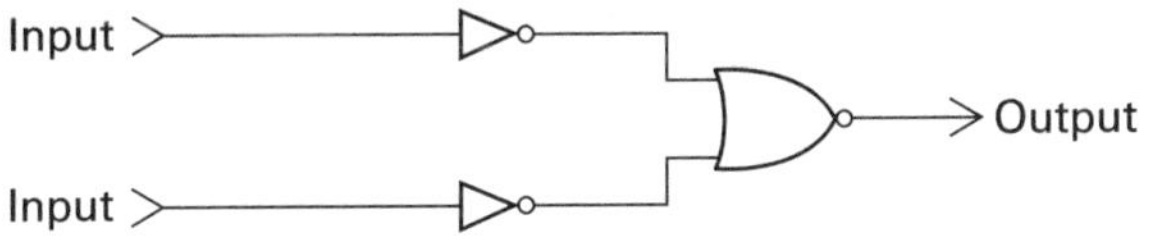

b. What Boolean operation does the circuit compute?

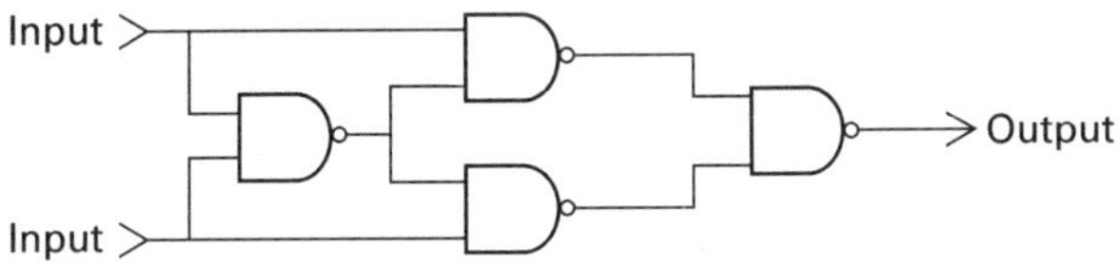

***3.** a. If we were to purchase a flip-flop circuit from an electronic component store, we may find that it has an additional input called *flip*. When this input changes from a 0 to 1, the output flips state (if it was 0 it is now 1 and vice versa). However, when the flip input changes from 1 to a 0, nothing happens. Even though we may not know the details of the circuitry needed to accomplish this behavior, we could still use this device as an abstract tool in other circuits. Consider the circuitry using two of the following flip-flops. If a pulse were sent on the circuit's input, the bottom flip-flop would change state. However, the second flip-flop would not change, since its input (received from the output of the NOT gate) went from a 1 to a 0. As a result, this circuit would now produce the outputs 0 and 1. A second pulse would flip the state of both flip-flops, producing an output of 1 and 0. What would be the output after a third pulse? After a fourth pulse?

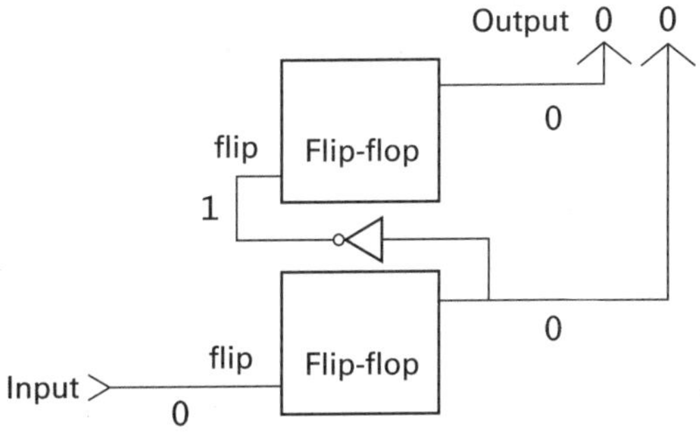

b. It is often necessary to coordinate activities of various components within a computer. This is accomplished by connecting a pulsating signal (called a clock) to circuitry similar to part a. Additional gates (as shown) send signals in a coordinated fashion to other connected circuits. On studying this circuit, you should be able to confirm that on the 1st, 5th, 9th . . . pulses of the clock, a 1 will be sent on output A. On what pulses of the clock will a 1 be sent on output B? On what pulses of the clock will a 1 be sent on output C? On which output is a 1 sent on the 4th pulse of the clock?

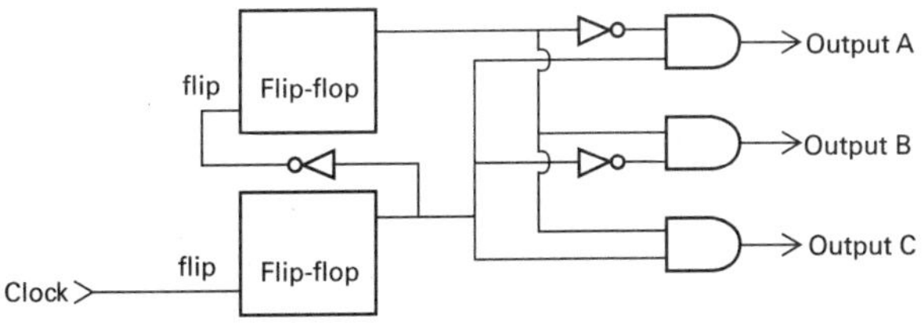

4. Assume that both of the inputs in the following circuit are 1. Describe what would happen if the upper input were temporarily changed to 0. Describe what would happen if the lower input were temporarily changed to 0. Redraw the circuit using NAND gates.

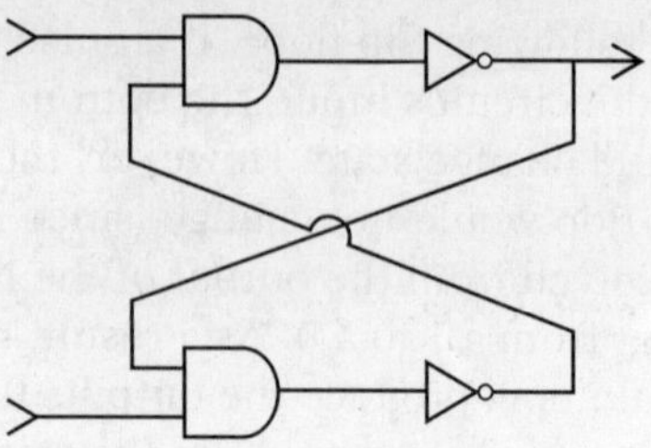

5. The following table represents the addresses and contents (using hexadecimal notation) of some cells in a machine's main memory. Starting with this memory arrangement, follow the sequence of instructions and record the final contents of each of these memory cells:

Address	Contents
00	AB
01	53
02	D6
03	02

Step 1. Move the contents of the cell whose address is 03 to the cell at address 00.

Step 2. Move the value 01 into the cell at address 02.

Step 3. Move the value stored at address 01 into the cell at address 03.

6. How many cells can be in a computer's main memory if each cell's address can be represented by two hexadecimal digits? What if four hexadecimal digits are used?

7. What bit patterns are represented by the following hexadecimal notations?

a. 8A9 b. DCB c. EF3
d. A01 e. C99

8. What is the value of the least significant bit in the bit patterns represented by the following hexadecimal notations?

a. 9A b. 90
c. 1B d. 6E

9. Express the following bit patterns in hexadecimal notation:

a. 10110100101101001011
b. 000111100001
c. 1111111011011011

10. Suppose a digital camera has a storage capacity of 500MB. How many black-and-white photographs could be stored in the camera if each consisted of 512 pixels per row and 512 pixels per column if each pixel required one bit of storage?

11. Suppose an image is represented on a display screen by a square array containing 256 columns and 256 rows of pixels. If for each pixel, 3 bytes are required to encode the color and 8 bits to encode the intensity, how many byte-size memory cells are required to hold the entire picture?

12. a. What are the advantages, if any, of using zoned-bit recording?

b. What is the difference between seek time and access time?

13. Suppose that you want to create a backup of your entire data which is around 10GB. Would it be reasonable to use DVDs for the purpose of creating this backup? What about BDs (Blu-ray Disks)?

14. If each sector on a magnetic disk can store 512 bytes of data, how many sectors are required to store two pages of integers (perhaps 10 lines of 100 integers in each page) if every integer is represented by using four bytes?

15. How many bytes of storage space would be required to store a 20-page document containing details of employees, in which each page contains 100 records and every record is of 200 characters, if two byte Unicode characters were used?

16. In zoned-bit recording, why does the rate of data transfer vary, depending on the portion of the disk being used?

17. What is the average access time for a hard disk which has a rotation delay of 10 milliseconds and a seek time of 9 milliseconds?

18. Suppose a disk storage system consists of 5 platters with 10 tracks on each side and

8 sectors in each track. What is the capacity of the system? Assume every sector contains 512 bytes and data can be stored on both surfaces of each platter.

19. Here is a message in ASCII. What does it say?
01000011 01101111 01101101 01110000 01110101 01110100 01100101 01110010 00100000 01010011 01100011 01101001 01100101 01101110 01100011 01100101 00100001

20. The following two messages are encoded in ASCII using one byte per character and then represented in hexadecimal notation. Are both the messages same?

436F6D7075746572 436F6D7075736572

21. Encode the following sentences in ASCII using one byte per character.
a. Is 1 byte = 8 bits?
b. Yes, a byte contains 8 bits!

22. Combine the two sentences of the previous problem and express it in hexadecimal notation.

23. List the hexadecimal representations of the integers from 20 to 27.

24. a. Write the number 100 by representing 1 and 0 in ASCII.
b. Write the number 255 in binary representation.

25. What values have binary representations in which only one of the bits is 1? List the binary representations for the smallest six values with this property.

***26.** Convert each of the following hexadecimal representations to binary representation and then to its equivalent base 10 representation:

a. A b. 14 c. 1E
d. 28 e. 32 f. 3C
g. 46 h. 65 i. CA
j. 12F k. 194 l. 1F9

***27.** Convert each of the following base 10 representations to its equivalent binary representation:

a. 110 b. 99 c. 72
d. 81 e. 36

***28.** Convert each of the following excess 32 representations to its equivalent base 10 representation:

a. 011111 b. 100110 c. 111000
d. 000101 e. 010101

***29.** Convert each of the following base 10 representations to its equivalent excess sixteen representation:

a. −12 b. 0 c. 10
d. −8 e. 9

***30.** Convert each of the following two's complement representations to its equivalent base 10 representation:

a. 010101 b. 101010 c. 110110
d. 011011 e. 111001

***31.** Convert each of the following base 10 representations to its equivalent two's complement representation in which each value is represented in 8 bits:

a. −27 b. 3 c. 21
d. 8 e. −18

***32.** Perform each of the following additions assuming the bit strings represent values in two's complement notation. Identify each case in which the answer is incorrect because of overflow.

a. 00101 + 01000 b. 11111 + 00001
c. 01111 + 00001 d. 10111 + 11010
e. 11111 + 11111 f. 00111 + 01100

***33.** Solve each of the following problems by translating the values into two's complement notation (using patterns of 5 bits), converting any subtraction problem to an equivalent addition problem, and performing that addition. Check your work by converting your answer to base 10 notation. (Watch out for overflow.)

a. 5 + 1 b. 5 − 1 c. 12 − 5
d. 8 − 7 e. 12 + 5 f. 5 − 11

***34.** Convert each of the following binary representations into its equivalent base 10 representation:

a. 11.11 b. 100.0101 c. 0.1101
d. 1.0 e. 10.01

***35.** Express each of the following values in binary notation:

a. $5\frac{3}{4}$ b. $15\frac{15}{16}$ c. $5\frac{3}{8}$
d. $1\frac{1}{4}$ e. $6\frac{5}{8}$

***36.** Decode the following bit patterns using the floating-point format described in Figure 1.24:

a. 01011001 b. 11001000
c. 10101100 d. 00111001

***37.** Encode the following values using the 8-bit floating-point format described in Figure 1.24. Indicate each case in which a truncation error occurs.

a. $-7\frac{1}{2}$ b. $\frac{1}{2}$ c. $-3\frac{3}{4}$
d. $\frac{7}{32}$ e. $\frac{31}{32}$

***38.** Assuming you are not restricted to using normalized form, list all the bit patterns that could be used to represent the value 3/8 using the floating-point format described in Figure 1.24.

***39.** What is the best approximation to the square root of 2 that can be expressed in the 8-bit floating-point format described in Figure 1.24? What value is actually obtained if this approximation is squared by a machine using this floating-point format?

***40.** What is the best approximation to the value one-tenth that can be represented using the 8-bit floating-point format described in Figure 1.24?

***41.** Explain how errors can occur when measurements using the metric system are recorded in floating-point notation. For example, what if 110 cm was recorded in units of meters?

***42.** One of the bit patterns 01011 and 11011 represents a value stored in excess 16 notation and the other represents the same value stored in two's complement notation.

a. What can be determined about this common value?
b. What is the relationship between a pattern representing a value stored in two's complement notation and the pattern representing the same value stored in excess notation when both systems use the same bit pattern length?

***43.** The three bit patterns 10000010, 01101000, and 00000010 are representations of the same value in two's complement, excess, and the 8-bit floating-point format presented in Figure 1.24, but not necessarily in that order. What is the common value, and which pattern is in which notation?

***44.** Which of the following values cannot be represented accurately in the floating-point format introduced in Figure 1.24?

a. $6\frac{1}{2}$ b. $\frac{13}{16}$ c. 9
d. $\frac{17}{32}$ e. $\frac{15}{16}$

***45.** If you changed the length of the bit strings being used to represent integers in binary from 4 bits to 6 bits, what change would be made in the value of the largest integer you could represent? What if you were using two's complement notation?

***46.** What would be the hexadecimal representation of the largest memory address in a memory consisting of 4MB if each cell had a one-byte capacity?

***47.** What would be the encoded version of the message

`xxy yyx xxy xxy yyx`

if LZW compression, starting with the dictionary containing x, y, and a space (as described in Section 1.8), were used?

***48.** The following message was compressed using LZW compression with a dictionary whose first, second, and third entries are x, y, and space, respectively. What is the decompressed message?

`22123113431213536`

***49.** If the message

`xxy yyx xxy xxyy`

were compressed using LZW with a starting dictionary whose first, second, and third entries were x, y, and space, respectively, what would be the entries in the final dictionary?

***50.** As we will learn in the next chapter, one means of transmitting bits over traditional telephone systems is to convert the bit patterns into sound, transfer the sound over the telephone lines, and then convert the sound back into bit patterns. Such techniques are limited to transfer rates of 57.6 Kbps. Is this sufficient for teleconferencing if the video is compressed using MPEG?

***51.** Encode the following sentences in ASCII using even parity by adding a parity bit at the high-order end of each character code:

a. Does 100/5 = 20?
b. The total cost is $7.25.

***52.** The following message was originally transmitted with odd parity in each short bit string. In which strings have errors definitely occurred?

11001 11011 10110 00000 11111 10001 10101 00100 01110

***53.** Suppose a 24-bit code is generated by representing each symbol by three consecutive copies of its ASCII representation (for example, the symbol A is represented by the bit string 010000010100000101000001). What error-correcting properties does this new code have?

***54.** Using the error-correcting code described in Figure 1.28, decode the following words:
a. 111010 110110
b. 101000 100110 001100
c. 011101 000110 000000 010100
d. 010010 001000 001110 101111 000000 110111 100110
e. 010011 000000 101001 100110

***55.** International currency exchange rates change frequently. Investigate current exchange rates, and update the currency converter script from Section 1.8 accordingly.

***56.** Find another currency not already included in the currency converter from Section 1.8. Acquire its current conversion rate and find its Unicode currency symbol on the web. Extend the script to convert this new currency.

***57.** If your web browser and text editor properly support Unicode and UTF-8, copy/paste the actual international currency symbols into the converter script of Section 1.8, in place of the cumbersome codes like, '\u00A3'. (If your software has trouble handling Unicode, you may get strange symbols in your text editor when you try to do this.)

***58.** The currency converter script of Section 1.8 uses the variable `dollars` to store the amount of money to be converted before performing each of the multiplications. This made the script one line longer than simply typing the integer quantity 1000 directly into each of the multiplication calculations. Why is it advantageous to create this extra variable ahead of time?

***59.** Write and test a Python script that given a number of bytes outputs the equivalent number of kilobytes, megabytes, gigabytes, and terabytes. Write and test a complementary script that given a number of terabytes outputs the equivalent number of GB, MB, KB, and bytes.

***60.** Write and test a Python script that given a number of minutes and seconds for a recording calculates the number of bits used to encode uncompressed, CD-quality stereo audio data of that length. (Review Section 1.4 for the necessary parameters and equations.)

***61.** Identify the error(s) in this Python script.

```
days_per_week = 7
weeks_per_year = 52
days_per_year = days_per_week **
                weeks_per_year
PRINT(days_per_year)
```

Social Issues

The following questions are intended as a guide to the ethical/social/legal issues associated with the field of computing. The goal is not merely to answer these questions. You should also consider why you answered as you did and whether your justifications are consistent from one question to the next.

1. A truncation error has occurred in a critical situation, causing extensive damage and loss of life. Who is liable, if anyone? The designer of the hardware? The designer of the software? The programmer who actually wrote that part of the program? The person who decided to use the software in that particular application? What if the software had been corrected by the company that originally developed it, but that update had not been purchased and applied in the critical application? What if the software had been pirated?

2. Is it acceptable for an individual to ignore the possibility of truncation errors and their consequences when developing his or her own applications?
3. Was it ethical to develop software in the 1970s using only two digits to represent the year (such as using 76 to represent the year 1976), ignoring the fact that the software would be flawed as the turn of the century approached? Is it ethical today to use only three digits to represent the year (such as 982 for 1982 and 015 for 2015)? What about using only four digits?
4. Many argue that encoding information often dilutes or otherwise distorts the information, since it essentially forces the information to be quantified. They argue that a questionnaire in which subjects are required to record their opinions by responding within a scale from one to five is inherently flawed. To what extent is information quantifiable? Can the pros and cons of different locations for a waste disposal plant be quantified? Is the debate over nuclear power and nuclear waste quantifiable? Is it dangerous to base decisions on averages and other statistical analysis? Is it ethical for news agencies to report polling results without including the exact wording of the questions? Is it possible to quantify the value of a human life? Is it acceptable for a company to stop investing in the improvement of a product, even though additional investment could lower the possibility of a fatality relating to the product's use?
5. Should there be a distinction in the rights to collect and disseminate data depending on the form of the data? That is, should the right to collect and disseminate photographs, audio, or video be the same as the right to collect and disseminate text?
6. Whether intentional or not, a report submitted by a journalist usually reflects that journalist's bias. Often by changing only a few words, a story can be given either a positive or negative connotation. (Compare, "The majority of those surveyed opposed the referendum." to "A significant portion of those surveyed supported the referendum.") Is there a difference between altering a story (by leaving out certain points or carefully selecting words) and altering a photograph?
7. Suppose that the use of a data compression system results in the loss of subtle but significant items of information. What liability issues might be raised? How should they be resolved?

Additional Reading

Drew, M., and Z. Li. *Fundamentals of Multimedia.* Upper Saddle River, NJ: Prentice-Hall, 2004.

Halsall, F. *Multimedia Communications.* Boston, MA: Addison-Wesley, 2001.

Hamacher, V. C., Z. G. Vranesic, and S. G. Zaky. *Computer Organization,* 5th ed. New York: McGraw-Hill, 2002.

Knuth, D. E. *The Art of Computer Programming,* Vol. 2, 3rd ed. Boston, MA: Addison-Wesley, 1998.

Long, B. *Complete Digital Photography,* 3rd ed. Hingham, MA: Charles River Media, 2005.

Miano, J. *Compressed Image File Formats.* New York: ACM Press, 1999.

Petzold, C. *CODE: The Hidden Language of Computer Hardware and Software.* Redman, WA: Microsoft Press, 2000.

Salomon, D. *Data Compression: The Complete Reference,* 4th ed. New York: Springer, 2007.

Sayood, K. *Introduction to Data Compression,* 3rd ed. San Francisco, CA: Morgan Kaufmann, 2005.

CHAPTER

Data Manipulation 2

In this chapter we will learn how a computer manipulates data and communicates with peripheral devices such as printers and keyboards. In doing so, we will explore the basics of computer architecture and learn how computers are programmed by means of encoded instructions, called machine language instructions.

**Asterisks indicate suggestions for optional sections.*

In Chapter 1 we studied topics relating to the storage of data inside a computer. In this chapter we will see how a computer manipulates that data. This manipulation consists of moving data from one location to another as well as performing operations such as arithmetic calculations, text editing, and image manipulation. We begin by extending our understanding of computer architecture beyond that of data storage systems.

2.1 Computer Architecture

The circuitry in a computer that controls the manipulation of data is called the **central processing unit,** or **CPU** (often referred to as merely the processor). In the machines of the mid-twentieth century, CPUs were large units comprised of perhaps several racks of electronic circuitry that reflected the significance of the unit. However, technology has shrunk these devices drastically. The CPUs found in today's desktop computers and notebooks are packaged as small flat squares (approximately two inches by two inches) whose connecting pins plug into a socket mounted on the machine's main circuit board (called the **motherboard**). In smartphones, mini-notebooks, and other **Mobile Internet Devices (MID),** CPUs are around half the size of a postage stamp. Due to their small size, these processors are called **microprocessors.**

CPU Basics

A CPU consists of three parts (Figure 2.1): the **arithmetic/logic unit,** which contains the circuitry that performs operations on data (such as addition and subtraction); the **control unit,** which contains the circuitry for coordinating the machine's activities; and the **register unit,** which contains data storage cells (similar to main memory cells), called **registers,** that are used for temporary storage of information within the CPU.

Some of the registers within the register unit are considered **general-purpose registers,** whereas others are **special-purpose registers.** We will discuss some of the special-purpose registers in Section 2.3. For now, we are concerned only with the general-purpose registers.

Figure 2.1 CPU and main memory connected via a bus

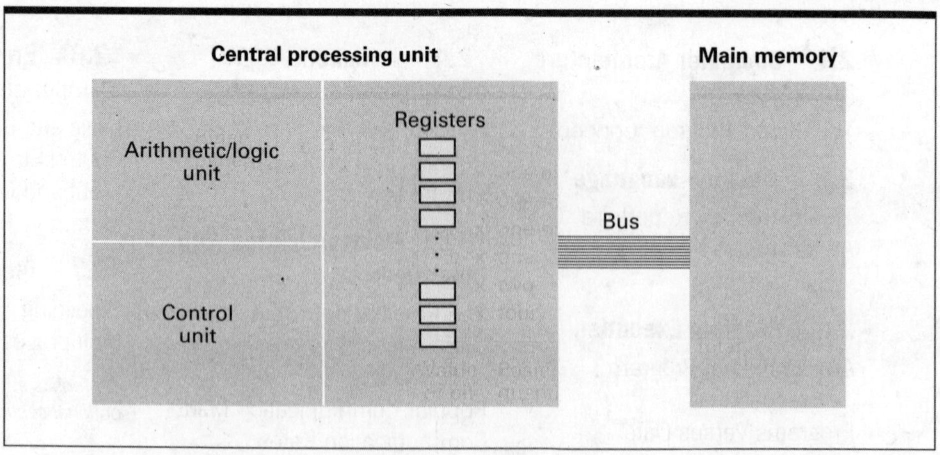

General-purpose registers serve as temporary holding places for data being manipulated by the CPU. These registers hold the inputs to the arithmetic/logic unit's circuitry and provide storage space for results produced by that unit. To perform an operation on data stored in main memory, the control unit transfers the data from memory into the general-purpose registers, informs the arithmetic/logic unit which registers hold the data, activates the appropriate circuitry within the arithmetic/logic unit, and tells the arithmetic/logic unit which register should receive the result.

For the purpose of transferring bit patterns, a machine's CPU and main memory are connected by a collection of wires called a **bus** (see again Figure 2.1). Through this bus, the CPU extracts (reads) data from main memory by supplying the address of the pertinent memory cell along with an electronic signal telling the memory circuitry that it is supposed to retrieve the data in the indicated cell. In a similar manner, the CPU places (writes) data in memory by providing the address of the destination cell and the data to be stored together with the appropriate electronic signal telling main memory that it is supposed to store the data being sent to it.

Based on this design, the task of adding two values stored in main memory involves more than the mere execution of the addition operation. The data must be transferred from main memory to registers within the CPU, the values must be added with the result being placed in a register, and the result must then be stored in a memory cell. The entire process is summarized by the five steps listed in Figure 2.2.

The Stored-Program Concept

Early computers were not known for their flexibility—the steps that each device executed were built into the control unit as a part of the machine. To gain more flexibility, some of the early electronic computers were designed so that the CPU could be conveniently rewired. This flexibility was accomplished by means of a pegboard arrangement similar to old telephone switchboards in which the ends of jumper wires were plugged into holes.

Figure 2.2 Adding values stored in memory

Step 1. Get one of the values to be added from memory and place it in a register.

Step 2. Get the other value to be added from memory and place it in another register.

Step 3. Activate the addition circuitry with the registers used in Steps 1 and 2 as inputs and another register designated to hold the result.

Step 4. Store the result in memory.

Step 5. Stop.

Cache Memory

It is instructive to compare the memory facilities within a computer in relation to their functionality. Registers are used to hold the data immediately applicable to the operation at hand; main memory is used to hold data that will be needed in the near future; and mass storage is used to hold data that will likely not be needed in the immediate future. Many machines are designed with an additional memory level, called cache memory. **Cache memory** is a portion (perhaps several hundred KB) of high-speed memory located within the CPU itself. In this special memory area, the machine attempts to keep a copy of that portion of main memory that is of current interest. In this setting, data transfers that normally would be made between registers and main memory are made between registers and cache memory. Any changes made to cache memory are then transferred collectively to main memory at a more opportune time. The result is a CPU that can execute its machine cycle more rapidly because it is not delayed by main memory communication.

A breakthrough (credited, apparently incorrectly, to John von Neumann) came with the realization that a program, just like data, can be encoded and stored in main memory. If the control unit is designed to extract the program from memory, decode the instructions, and execute them, the program that the machine follows can be changed merely by changing the contents of the computer's memory instead of rewiring the CPU.

The idea of storing a computer's program in its main memory is called the **stored-program concept** and has become the standard approach used today—so standard, in fact, that it seems obvious. What made it difficult originally was that everyone thought of programs and data as different entities: Data were stored in memory; programs were part of the CPU. The result was a prime example of not seeing the forest for the trees. It is easy to be caught in such ruts, and the development of computer science might still be in many of them today without our knowing it. Indeed, part of the excitement of the science is that new insights are constantly opening doors to new theories and applications.

Questions & Exercises

1. What sequence of events do you think would be required to move the contents of one memory cell in a computer to another memory cell?
2. What information must the CPU supply to the main memory circuitry to write a value into a memory cell?
3. Mass storage, main memory, and general-purpose registers are all storage systems. What is the difference in their use?

2.2 Machine Language

To apply the stored-program concept, CPUs are designed to recognize instructions encoded as bit patterns. This collection of instructions along with the encoding system is called the **machine language.** An instruction expressed in this language is called a machine-level instruction or, more commonly, a **machine instruction.**

The Instruction Repertoire

The list of machine instructions that a typical CPU must be able to decode and execute is quite short. In fact, once a machine can perform certain elementary but well-chosen tasks, adding more features does not increase the machine's theoretical capabilities. In other words, beyond a certain point, additional features may increase such things as convenience but add nothing to the machine's fundamental capabilities.

The degree to which machine designs should take advantage of this fact has led to two philosophies of CPU architecture. One is that a CPU should be designed to execute a minimal set of machine instructions. This approach leads to what is called a **reduced instruction set computer (RISC).** The argument in favor of RISC architecture is that such a machine is efficient, fast, and less expensive to manufacture. On the other hand, others argue in favor of CPUs with the ability to execute a large number of complex instructions, even though many of them are technically redundant. The result of this approach is known as a **complex instruction set computer (CISC).** The argument in favor of CISC architecture is that the more complex CPU can better cope with the ever-increasing complexities

Who Invented What?

Awarding a single individual credit for an invention is always a dubious undertaking. Thomas Edison is credited with inventing the incandescent lamp, but other researchers were developing similar lamps, and in a sense Edison was lucky to be the one to obtain the patent. The Wright brothers are credited with inventing the airplane, but they were competing with and benefited from the work of many contemporaries, all of whom were preempted to some degree by Leonardo da Vinci, who toyed with the idea of flying machines in the fifteenth century. Even Leonardo's designs were apparently based on earlier ideas. Of course, in these cases the designated inventor still has legitimate claims to the credit bestowed. In other cases, history seems to have awarded credit inappropriately—an example is the stored-program concept. Without a doubt, John von Neumann was a brilliant scientist who deserves credit for numerous contributions. But one of the contributions for which popular history has chosen to credit him, the stored-program concept, was apparently developed by researchers led by J. P. Eckert at the Moore School of Electrical Engineering at the University of Pennsylvania. John von Neumann was merely the first to publish work reporting the idea and thus computing lore has selected him as the inventor.

of today's software. With CISC, programs can exploit a powerful rich set of instructions, many of which would require a multi-instruction sequence in a RISC design.

In the 1990s and into the millennium, commercially available CISC and RISC processors were actively competing for dominance in desktop computing. Intel processors, used in PCs, are examples of CISC architecture; PowerPC processors (developed by an alliance between Apple, IBM, and Motorola) are examples of RISC architecture and were used in the Apple Macintosh. As time progressed, the manufacturing cost of CISC was drastically reduced; thus Intel's processors (or their equivalent from AMD—Advanced Micro Devices, Inc.) are now found in virtually all desktop and laptop computers (even Apple is now building computers based on Intel products).

While CISC secured its place in desktop computers, it has an insatiable thirst for electrical power. In contrast, the company Advanced RISC Machine (ARM) has designed a RISC architecture specifically for low power consumption. (Advanced RISC Machine was originally Acorn Computers and is now ARM Holdings.) Thus, ARM-based processors, manufactured by a host of vendors including Qualcomm and Texas Instruments, are readily found in game controllers, digital TVs, navigation systems, automotive modules, cellular telephones, smartphones, and other consumer electronics.

Regardless of the choice between RISC and CISC, a machine's instructions can be categorized into three groupings: (1) the data transfer group, (2) the arithmetic/logic group, and (3) the control group.

Data Transfer The data transfer group consists of instructions that request the movement of data from one location to another. Steps 1, 2, and 4 in Figure 2.2 fall into this category. We should note that using terms such as *transfer* or *move* to identify this group of instructions is actually a misnomer. It is rare that the data being transferred is erased from its original location. The process involved in a transfer instruction is more like copying the data rather than moving it. Thus terms such as *copy* or *clone* better describe the actions of this group of instructions.

While on the subject of terminology, we should mention that special terms are used when referring to the transfer of data between the CPU and main memory. A request to fill a general-purpose register with the contents of a memory cell is

Variable-Length Instructions

To simplify explanations in the text, the machine language used for examples in this chapter (and described in Appendix C) uses a fixed size (two bytes) for all instructions. Thus, to fetch an instruction, the CPU always retrieves the contents of two consecutive memory cells and increments its program counter by two. This consistency streamlines the task of fetching instructions and is characteristic of RISC machines. CISC machines, however, have machine languages whose instructions vary in length. Today's Intel processors, for example, have instructions that range from single-byte instructions to multiple-byte instructions whose length depends on the exact use of the instruction. CPUs with such machine languages determine the length of the incoming instruction by the instruction's op-code. That is, the CPU first fetches the op-code of the instruction and then, based on the bit pattern received, knows how many more bytes to fetch from memory to obtain the rest of the instruction.

commonly referred to as a LOAD instruction; conversely, a request to transfer the contents of a register to a memory cell is called a STORE instruction. In Figure 2.2, Steps 1 and 2 are LOAD instructions, and Step 4 is a STORE instruction.

An important group of instructions within the data transfer category consists of the commands for communicating with devices outside the CPU-main memory context (printers, keyboards, display screens, disk drives, etc.). Since these instructions handle the input/output (I/O) activities of the machine, they are called **I/O instructions** and are sometimes considered as a category in their own right. On the other hand, Section 2.5 describes how these I/O activities can be handled by the same instructions that request data transfers between the CPU and main memory. Thus, we shall consider the I/O instructions to be a part of the data transfer group.

Arithmetic/Logic The arithmetic/logic group consists of the instructions that tell the control unit to request an activity within the arithmetic/logic unit. Step 3 in Figure 2.2 falls into this group. As its name suggests, the arithmetic/logic unit is capable of performing operations other than the basic arithmetic operations. Some of these additional operations are the Boolean operations AND, OR, and XOR, introduced in Chapter 1, which we will discuss in more detail later in this chapter.

Another collection of operations available within most arithmetic/logic units allows the contents of registers to be moved to the right or the left within the register. These operations are known as either SHIFT or ROTATE operations, depending on whether the bits that "fall off the end" of the register are merely discarded (SHIFT) or are used to fill the holes left at the other end (ROTATE).

Control The control group consists of those instructions that direct the execution of the program rather than the manipulation of data. Step 5 in Figure 2.2 falls into this category, although it is an extremely elementary example. This group contains many of the more interesting instructions in a machine's repertoire, such as the family of JUMP (or BRANCH) instructions used to direct the CPU to execute an instruction other than the next one in the list. These JUMP instructions appear in two varieties: **unconditional jumps** and **conditional jumps.** An example of the former would be the instruction "Skip to Step 5"; an example of the latter would be, "If the value obtained is 0, then skip to Step 5." The distinction is that a conditional jump results in a "change of venue" only if a certain condition is satisfied. As an example, the sequence of instructions in Figure 2.3 represents an algorithm for dividing two values where Step 3 is a conditional jump that protects against the possibility of division by zero.

An Illustrative Machine Language

Let us now consider how the instructions of a typical computer are encoded. The machine that we will use for our discussion is described in Appendix C and summarized in Figure 2.4. It has 16 general-purpose registers and 256 main memory cells, each with a capacity of 8 bits. For referencing purposes, we label the registers with the values 0 through 15 and address the memory cells with the values 0 through 255. For convenience we think of these labels and addresses as values represented in base two and compress the resulting bit patterns using hexadecimal notation. Thus, the registers are labeled 0 through F, and the memory cells are addressed 00 through FF.

Figure 2.3 Dividing values stored in memory

Step 1. LOAD a register with a value from memory.

Step 2. LOAD another register with another value from memory.

Step 3. If this second value is zero, JUMP to Step 6.

Step 4. Divide the contents of the first register by the second register and leave the result in a third register.

Step 5. STORE the contents of the third register in memory.

Step 6. STOP.

The encoded version of a machine instruction consists of two parts: the **op-code** (short for operation code) field and the **operand** field. The bit pattern appearing in the op-code field indicates which of the elementary operations, such as STORE, SHIFT, XOR, and JUMP, is requested by the instruction. The bit patterns found in the operand field provide more detailed information about the operation specified by the op-code. For example, in the case of a STORE operation, the information in the operand field indicates which register contains the data to be stored and which memory cell is to receive the data.

The entire machine language of our illustrative machine (Appendix C) consists of only twelve basic instructions. Each of these instructions is encoded using a total of 16 bits, represented by four hexadecimal digits (Figure 2.5). The op-code for each instruction consists of the first 4 bits or, equivalently, the first hexadecimal digit. Note (Appendix C) that these op-codes are represented by the hexadecimal digits 1 through C. In particular, the table in Appendix C

Figure 2.4 The architecture of the machine described in Appendix C

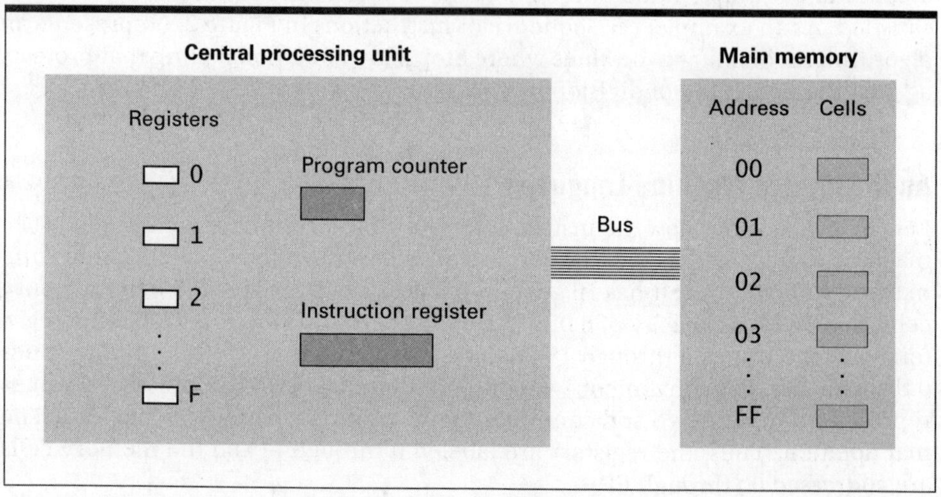

Figure 2.5 The composition of an instruction for the machine in Appendix C

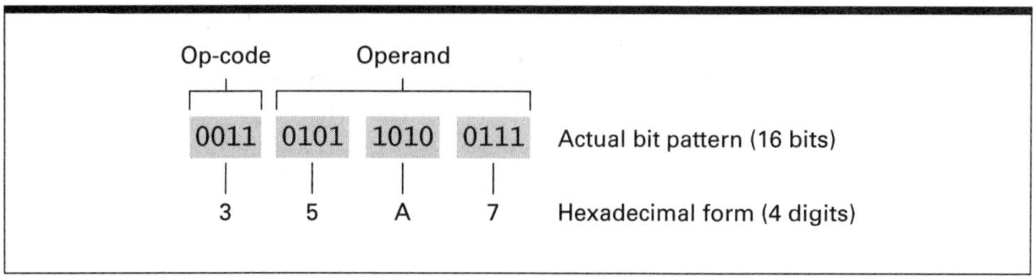

shows us that an instruction beginning with the hexadecimal digit 3 refers to a STORE instruction, and an instruction beginning with hexadecimal A refers to a ROTATE instruction.

The operand field of each instruction in our illustrative machine consists of three hexadecimal digits (12 bits), and in each case (except for the HALT instruction, which needs no further refinement) clarifies the general instruction given by the op-code. For example (Figure 2.6), if the first hexadecimal digit of an instruction were 3 (the op-code for storing the contents of a register), the next hexadecimal digit of the instruction would indicate which register is to be stored, and the last two hexadecimal digits would indicate which memory cell is to receive the data. Thus the instruction 35A7 (hexadecimal) translates to the statement "STORE the bit pattern found in register 5 in the memory cell whose address is A7." (Note how the use of hexadecimal notation simplifies our discussion. In reality, the instruction 35A7 is the bit pattern 0011010110100111.)

The instruction 35A7 also provides an explicit example of why main memory capacities are measured in powers of two. Because 8 bits in the instruction are reserved for specifying the memory cell utilized by this instruction, it is possible to reference exactly 2^8 different memory cells. It behooves us therefore to build main memory with this many cells—addressed from 0 to 255. If main memory had more cells, we would not be able to write instructions that distinguished between them; if main memory had fewer cells, we would be able to write instructions that referenced nonexisting cells.

Figure 2.6 Decoding the instruction 35A7

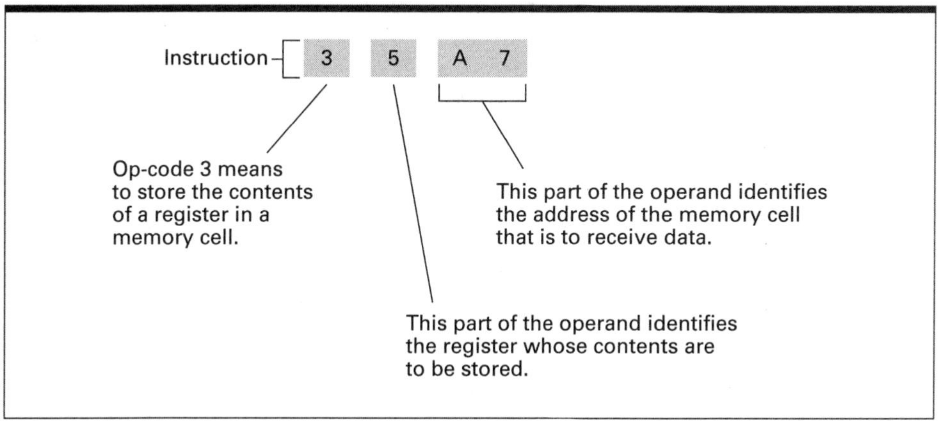

As another example of how the operand field is used to clarify the general instruction given by an op-code, consider an instruction with the op-code 7 (hexadecimal), which requests that the contents of two registers be ORed. (We will see what it means to OR two registers in Section 2.4. For now we are interested merely in how instructions are encoded.) In this case, the next hexadecimal digit indicates the register in which the result should be placed, while the last two hexadecimal digits indicate which two registers are to be ORed. Thus the instruction 70C5 translates to the statement "OR the contents of register C with the contents of register 5 and leave the result in register 0."

A subtle distinction exists between our machine's two LOAD instructions. Here we see that the op-code 1 (hexadecimal) identifies an instruction that loads a register with the contents of a memory cell, whereas the op-code 2 (hexadecimal) identifies an instruction that loads a register with a particular value. The difference is that the operand field in an instruction of the first type contains an address, whereas in the second type the operand field contains the actual bit pattern to be loaded.

Note that the machine has two ADD instructions: one for adding two's complement representations and one for adding floating-point representations. This distinction is a consequence of the fact that adding bit patterns that represent values encoded in two's complement notation requires different activities within the arithmetic/logic unit from adding values encoded in floating-point notation. We close this section with Figure 2.7, which contains an encoded version of the instructions in Figure 2.2. We have assumed that the values to be added are stored in two's complement notation at memory addresses 6C and 6D and the sum is to be placed in the memory cell at address 6E.

Figure 2.7 An encoded version of the instructions in Figure 2.2

Encoded instructions	Translation
156C	Load register 5 with the bit pattern found in the memory cell at address 6C.
166D	Load register 6 with the bit pattern found in the memory cell at address 6D.
5056	Add the contents of register 5 and 6 as though they were two's complement representation and leave the result in register 0.
306E	Store the contents of register 0 in the memory cell at address 6E.
C000	Halt.

Questions & Exercises

1. Why might the term *move* be considered an incorrect name for the operation of moving data from one location in a machine to another?
2. In the text, JUMP instructions were expressed by identifying the destination explicitly by stating the name (or step number) of the destination within the JUMP instruction (for example, "Jump to Step 6"). A drawback of this technique is that if an instruction name (number) is later changed, we must be sure to find all jumps to that instruction and change that name also. Describe another way of expressing a JUMP instruction so that the name of the destination is not explicitly stated.
3. Is the instruction "If 0 equals 0, then jump to Step 7" a conditional or unconditional jump? Explain your answer.
4. Write the example program in Figure 2.7 in actual bit patterns.
5. The following are instructions written in the machine language described in Appendix C. Rewrite them in English.

   a. 368A **b.** BADE **c.** 803C **d.** 40F4
6. What is the difference between the instructions 15AB and 25AB in the machine language of Appendix C?
7. Here are some instructions in English. Translate each of them into the machine language of Appendix C.
   - **a.** LOAD register number 3 with the hexadecimal value 56.
   - **b.** ROTATE register number 5 three bits to the right.
   - **c.** AND the contents of register A with the contents of register 5 and leave the result in register 0.

2.3 Program Execution

A computer follows a program stored in its memory by copying the instructions from memory into the CPU as needed. Once in the CPU, each instruction is decoded and obeyed. The order in which the instructions are fetched from memory corresponds to the order in which the instructions are stored in memory unless otherwise altered by a JUMP instruction.

To understand how the overall execution process takes place, it is necessary to consider two of the special purpose registers within the CPU: the **instruction register** and the **program counter** (see again Figure 2.4). The instruction register is used to hold the instruction being executed. The program counter contains the address of the next instruction to be executed, thereby serving as the machine's way of keeping track of where it is in the program.

The CPU performs its job by continually repeating an algorithm that guides it through a three-step process known as the **machine cycle.** The steps in the machine cycle are fetch, decode, and execute (Figure 2.8). During the fetch step, the CPU requests that main memory provide it with the instruction that is stored at the address indicated by the program counter. Since each instruction in our machine is two bytes long, this fetch process involves retrieving the contents of two memory cells from main memory. The CPU places the instruction received from memory in its instruction register and then increments the program counter by two so that the counter contains the address of the next instruction stored in memory. Thus the program counter will be ready for the next fetch.

With the instruction now in the instruction register, the CPU decodes the instruction, which involves breaking the operand field into its proper components based on the instruction's op-code.

The CPU then executes the instruction by activating the appropriate circuitry to perform the requested task. For example, if the instruction is a load from memory, the CPU sends the appropriate signals to main memory, waits for main memory to send the data, and then places the data in the requested register. If the instruction is for an arithmetic operation, the CPU activates the appropriate circuitry in the arithmetic/logic unit with the correct registers as inputs and waits for the arithmetic/logic unit to compute the answer and place it in the appropriate register.

Once the instruction in the instruction register has been executed, the CPU again begins the machine cycle with the fetch step. Observe that since the program counter was incremented at the end of the previous fetch, it again provides the CPU with the correct address.

A somewhat special case is the execution of a JUMP instruction. Consider, for example, the instruction B258 (Figure 2.9), which means "JUMP to the instruction at address 58 (hexadecimal) if the contents of register 2 is the same as that of register 0." In this case, the execute step of the machine cycle begins with the comparison of registers 2 and 0. If they contain different bit patterns, the execute

Figure 2.8 The machine cycle

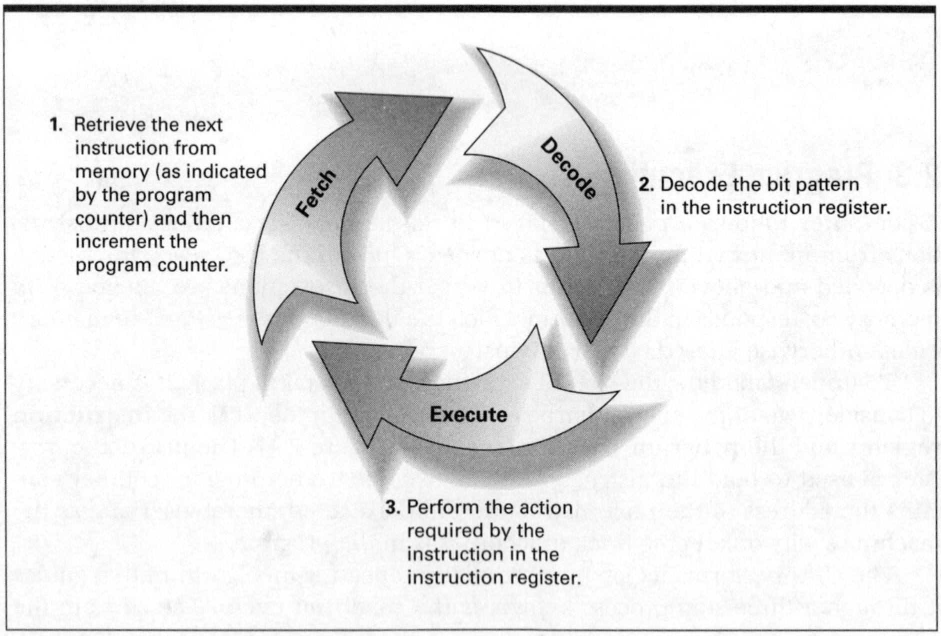

Comparing Computer Power

When shopping for a personal computer, you will find that clock speeds are often used to compare machines. A computer's **clock** is a circuit, called an oscillator, that generates pulses that are used to coordinate the machine's activities—the faster this oscillating circuit generates pulses, the faster the machine performs its machine cycle. Clock speeds are measured in hertz (abbreviated as Hz) with one Hz equal to one cycle (or pulse) per second. Typical clock speeds in desktop computers are in the range of a few hundred MHz (older models) to several GHz. (MHz is short for megahertz, which is a million Hz. GHz is short for gigahertz, which is 1000 MHz.)

Unfortunately, different CPU designs might perform different amounts of work in one clock cycle, and thus clock speed alone fails to be relevant in comparing machines with different CPUs. If you are comparing a machine based on an Intel processor to one based on ARM, it would be more meaningful to compare performance by means of **benchmarking,** which is the process of comparing the performance of different machines when executing the same program, known as a benchmark. By selecting benchmarks representing different types of applications, you get meaningful comparisons for various market segments.

step terminates and the next machine cycle begins. If, however, the contents of these registers are equal, the machine places the value 58 (hexadecimal) in its program counter during the execute step. In this case, then, the next fetch step finds 58 in the program counter, so the instruction at that address will be the next instruction to be fetched and executed.

Note that if the instruction had been B058, then the decision of whether the program counter should be changed would depend on whether the contents of register 0 was equal to that of register 0. But these are the same registers and thus must have equal content. In turn, any instruction of the form B0XY will cause a jump to be executed to the memory location XY regardless of the contents of register 0.

Figure 2.9 Decoding the instruction B258

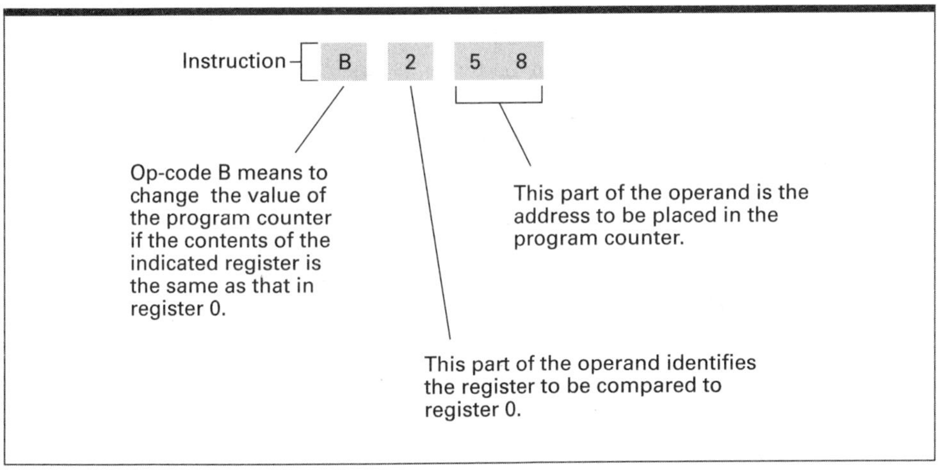

An Example of Program Execution

Let us follow the machine cycle applied to the program presented in Figure 2.7, which retrieves two values from main memory, computes their sum, and stores that total in a main memory cell. We first need to put the program somewhere in memory. For our example, suppose the program is stored in consecutive addresses, starting at address A0 (hexadecimal). With the program stored in this manner, we can cause the machine to execute it by placing the address (A0) of the first instruction in the program counter and starting the machine (Figure 2.10).

The CPU begins the fetch step of the machine cycle by extracting the instruction stored in main memory at location A0 and placing this instruction (156C) in its instruction register (Figure 2.11a). Notice that, in our machine, instructions are 16 bits (two bytes) long. Thus the entire instruction to be fetched occupies the memory cells at both address A0 and A1. The CPU is designed to take this into account so it retrieves the contents of both cells and places the bit patterns received in the instruction register, which is 16 bits long. The CPU then adds two to the program counter so that this register contains the address of the next instruction (Figure 2.11b). At the end of the fetch step of the first machine cycle, the program counter and instruction register contain the following data:

```
Program Counter: A2
Instruction Register: 156C
```

Next, the CPU analyzes the instruction in its instruction register and concludes that it is to load register 5 with the contents of the memory cell at address 6C. This load activity is performed during the execution step of the machine cycle, and the CPU then begins the next cycle.

This cycle begins by fetching the instruction 166D from the two memory cells starting at address A2. The CPU places this instruction in the instruction register

Figure 2.10 The program from Figure 2.7 stored in main memory ready for execution

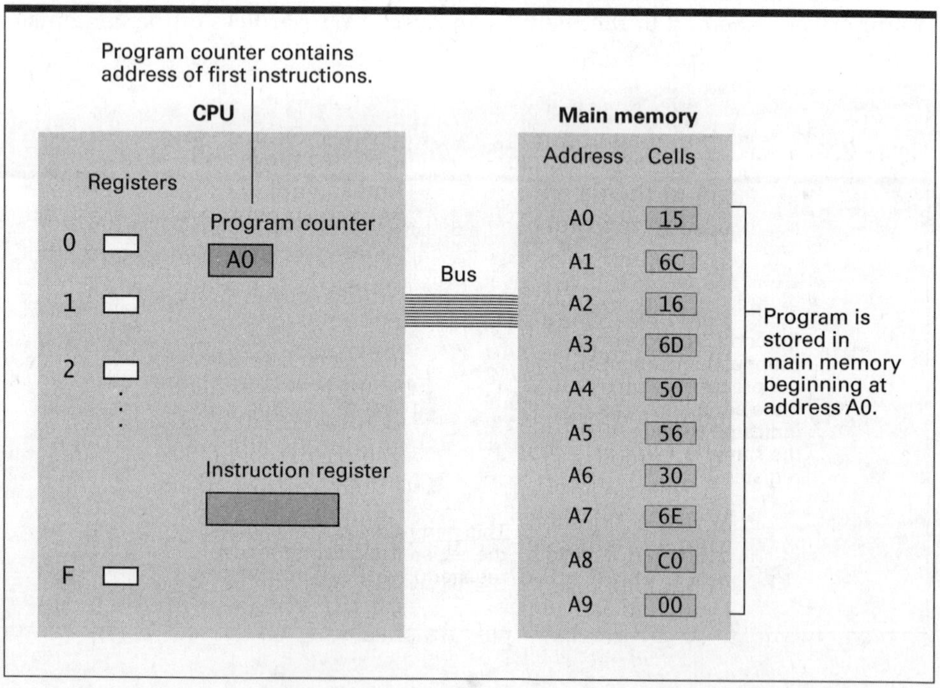

Figure 2.11 Performing the fetch step of the machine cycle

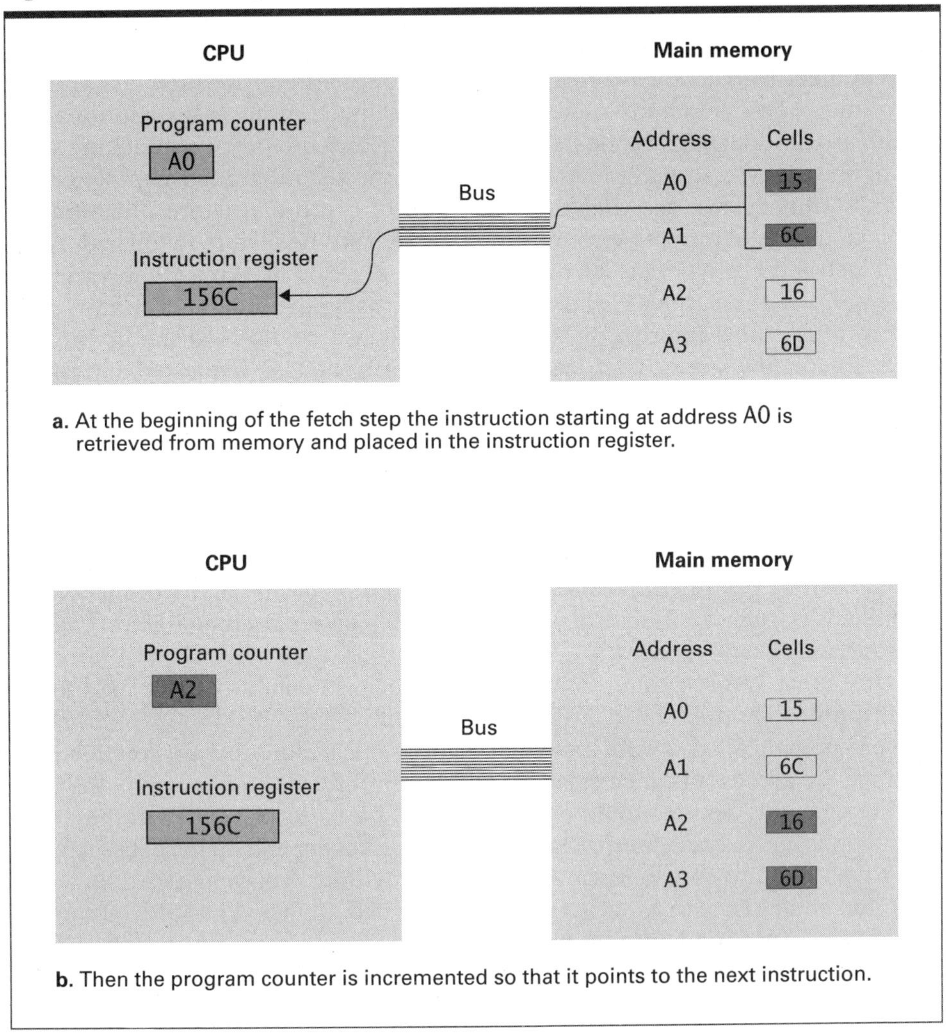

a. At the beginning of the fetch step the instruction starting at address A0 is retrieved from memory and placed in the instruction register.

b. Then the program counter is incremented so that it points to the next instruction.

and increments the program counter to A4. The values in the program counter and instruction register therefore become the following:

```
Program Counter: A4
Instruction Register: 166D
```

Now the CPU decodes the instruction 166D and determines that it is to load register 6 with the contents of memory address 6D. It then executes the instruction. It is at this time that register 6 is actually loaded.

Since the program counter now contains A4, the CPU extracts the next instruction starting at this address. The result is that 5056 is placed in the instruction register, and the program counter is incremented to A6. The CPU now decodes the contents of its instruction register and executes it by activating the two's complement addition circuitry with inputs being registers 5 and 6.

During this execution step, the arithmetic/logic unit performs the requested addition, leaves the result in register 0 (as requested by the control unit), and reports to the control unit that it has finished. The CPU then begins another machine cycle. Once again, with the aid of the program counter, it fetches the next instruction (306E) from the two memory cells starting at memory location A6 and increments the program counter to A8. This instruction is then decoded and executed. At this point, the sum is placed in memory location 6E.

The next instruction is fetched starting from memory location A8, and the program counter is incremented to AA. The contents of the instruction register (C000) are now decoded as the halt instruction. Consequently, the machine stops during the execute step of the machine cycle, and the program is completed.

In summary, we see that the execution of a program stored in memory involves the same process you and I might use if we needed to follow a detailed list of instructions. Whereas we might keep our place by marking the instructions as we perform them, the CPU keeps its place by using the program counter. After determining which instruction to execute next, we would read the instruction and extract its meaning. Then, we would perform the task requested and return to the list for the next instruction in the same manner that the CPU executes the instruction in its instruction register and then continues with another fetch.

Programs Versus Data

Many programs can be stored simultaneously in a computer's main memory, as long as they occupy different locations. Which program will be run when the machine is started can then be determined merely by setting the program counter appropriately.

One must keep in mind, however, that because data are also contained in main memory and encoded in terms of 0s and 1s, the machine alone has no way of knowing what is data and what is program. If the program counter were assigned the address of data instead of the address of the desired program, the CPU, not knowing any better, would extract the data bit patterns as though they were instructions and execute them. The final result would depend on the data involved.

We should not conclude, however, that providing programs and data with a common appearance in a machine's memory is bad. In fact, it has proved a useful attribute because it allows one program to manipulate other programs (or even itself) the same as it would data. Imagine, for example, a program that modifies itself in response to its interaction with its environment and thus exhibits the ability to learn, or perhaps a program that writes and executes other programs in order to solve problems presented to it.

Questions & Exercises

1. Suppose the memory cells from addresses 00 to 05 in the machine described in Appendix C contain the (hexadecimal) bit patterns given in the following table:

Address	Contents
00	14
01	02
02	34
03	17
04	C0
05	00

If we start the machine with its program counter containing 00, what bit pattern is in the memory cell whose address is hexadecimal 17 when the machine halts?

2. Suppose the memory cells at addresses B0 to B8 in the machine described in Appendix C contain the (hexadecimal) bit patterns given in the following table:

Address	Contents
B0	13
B1	B8
B2	A3
B3	02
B4	33
B5	B8
B6	C0
B7	00
B8	0F

a. If the program counter starts at B0, what bit pattern is in register number 3 after the first instruction has been executed?

b. What bit pattern is in memory cell B8 when the halt instruction is executed?

3. Suppose the memory cells at addresses A4 to B1 in the machine described in Appendix C contain the (hexadecimal) bit patterns given in the following table:

Address	Contents
A4	20
A5	00
A6	21
A7	03
A8	22
A9	01
AA	B1
AB	B0
AC	50
AD	02
AE	B0
AF	AA
B0	C0
B1	00

When answering the following questions, assume that the machine is started with its program counter containing A4.

a. What is in register 0 the first time the instruction at address AA is executed?

b. What is in register 0 the second time the instruction at address AA is executed?

c. How many times is the instruction at address AA executed before the machine halts?

4. Suppose the memory cells at addresses F0 to F9 in the machine described in Appendix C contain the (hexadecimal) bit patterns described in the following table:

Address	Contents
F0	20
F1	C0
F2	30
F3	F8
F4	20
F5	00
F6	30
F7	F9
F8	FF
F9	FF

If we start the machine with its program counter containing F0, what does the machine do when it reaches the instruction at address F8?

2.4 Arithmetic/Logic Instructions

As indicated earlier, the arithmetic/logic group of instructions consists of instructions requesting arithmetic, logic, and shift operations. In this section, we look at these operations more closely.

Logic Operations

We introduced the logic operations AND, OR, and XOR (exclusive or, often pronounced, "ex-or") in Chapter 1 as operations that combine two input bits to produce a single output bit. These operations can be extended to **bitwise operations** that combine two strings of bits to produce a single output string by applying the basic operation to individual columns. For example, the result of ANDing the patterns 10011010 and 11001001 results in

```
    10011010
AND 11001001
    10001000
```

where we have merely written the result of ANDing the two bits in each column at the bottom of the column. Likewise, ORing and XORing these patterns would produce

```
   10011010          10011010
OR 11001001      XOR 11001001
   11011011          01010011
```

One of the major uses of the AND operation is for placing 0s in one part of a bit pattern while not disturbing the other part. There are many applications for this in practice, such as filtering certain colors out of a digital image represented in the RGB format, as described in the previous chapter. Consider, for example, what happens if the byte 00001111 is the first operand of an AND operation.

Without knowing the contents of the second operand, we still can conclude that the four most significant bits of the result will be 0s. Moreover, the four least significant bits of the result will be a copy of that part of the second operand, as shown in the following example:

```
    00001111
AND 10101010
    00001010
```

This use of the AND operation is an example of the process called **masking.** Here one operand, called a **mask,** determines which part of the other operand will affect the result. In the case of the AND operation, masking produces a result that is a partial replica of one of the operands, with 0s occupying the nonduplicated positions. One trivial use of the AND operation in this context would be to mask off all of the bits associated with the red component of the pixels in an image, leaving only the blue and green components. This transformation is frequently available as an option in image manipulation software.

AND operations are useful when manipulating other types of **bit map** besides images, whenever a string of bits is used in which each bit represents the presence or absence of a particular object. As a non-graphical example, a string of 52 bits, in which each bit is associated with a particular playing card, can be used to represent a poker hand by assigning 1s to those five bits associated with the cards in the hand and 0s to all the others. Likewise, a bit map of 52 bits, of which thirteen are 1s, can be used to represent a hand of bridge, or a bit map of 32 bits can be used to represent which of thirty-two ice cream flavors are available.

Suppose, then, that the eight bits in a memory cell are being used as a bit map, and we want to find out whether the object associated with the third bit from the high-order end is present. We merely need to AND the entire byte with the mask 00100000, which produces a byte of all 0s if and only if the third bit from the high-order end of the bit map is itself 0. A program can then act accordingly by following the AND operation with a conditional branch instruction. Moreover, if the third bit from the high-order end of the bit map is a 1, and we want to change it to a 0 without disturbing the other bits, we can AND the bit map with the mask 11011111 and then store the result in place of the original bit map.

Where the AND operation can be used to duplicate a part of a bit string while placing 0s in the nonduplicated part, the OR operation can be used to duplicate a part of a string while putting 1s in the nonduplicated part. For this we again use a mask, but this time we indicate the bit positions to be duplicated with 0s and use 1s to indicate the nonduplicated positions. For example, ORing any byte with 11110000 produces a result with 1s in its most significant four bits while its remaining bits are a copy of the least significant four bits of the other operand, as demonstrated by the following example:

```
   11110000
OR 10101010
   11111010
```

Consequently, whereas the mask 11011111 can be used with the AND operation to force a 0 in the third bit from the high-order end of a byte, the mask 00100000 can be used with the OR operation to force a 1 in that position.

A major use of the XOR operation is in forming the complement of a bit string. XORing any byte with a mask of all 1s produces the complement of the byte. For example, note the relationship between the second operand and the result in the following example:

```
    11111111
XOR 10101010
    01010101
```

The XOR operation can be used to invert all of the bits of an RGB bitmap image, resulting in an "inverted" color image in which light colors have been replaced by dark colors, and vice versa.

In the machine language described in Appendix C, op-codes 7, 8, and 9 are used for the logic operations OR, AND, and XOR, respectively. Each requests that the corresponding logic operation be performed between the contents of two designated registers and that the result be placed in another designated register. For example, the instruction 7ABC requests that the result of ORing the contents of registers B and C be placed in register A.

Rotation and Shift Operations

The operations in the class of rotation and shift operations provide a means for moving bits within a register and are often used in solving alignment problems. These operations are classified by the direction of motion (right or left) and whether the process is circular. Within these classification guidelines are numerous variations with mixed terminology. Let us take a quick look at the ideas involved.

Consider a register containing a byte of bits. If we shift its contents one bit to the right, we imagine the rightmost bit falling off the edge and a hole appearing at the leftmost end. What happens with this extra bit and the hole is the distinguishing feature among the various shift operations. One technique is to place the bit that fell off the right end in the hole at the left end. The result is a **circular shift,** also called a **rotation.** Thus, if we perform a right circular shift on a byte-size bit pattern eight times, we obtain the same bit pattern we started with.

Another technique is to discard the bit that falls off the edge and always fill the hole with a 0. The term **logical shift** is often used to refer to these operations. Such shifts to the left can be used for multiplying two's complement representations by two. After all, shifting binary digits to the left corresponds to multiplication by two, just as a similar shift of decimal digits corresponds to multiplication by ten. Moreover, division by two can be accomplished by shifting the binary string to the right. In either shift, care must be taken to preserve the sign bit when using certain notational systems. Thus, we often find right shifts that always fill the hole (which occurs at the sign bit position) with its original value. Shifts that leave the sign bit unchanged are sometimes called **arithmetic shifts.**

Among the variety of shift and rotate instructions possible, the machine language described in Appendix C contains only a right circular shift, designated by op-code A. In this case the first hexadecimal digit in the operand specifies the register to be rotated, and the rest of the operand specifies the number of bits to be rotated. Thus the instruction A501 means "Rotate the contents of register

5 to the right by 1 bit." In particular, if register 5 originally contained the bit pattern 65 (hexadecimal), then it would contain B2 after this instruction is executed (Figure 2.12). (You may wish to experiment with how other shift and rotate instructions can be produced with combinations of the instructions provided in the machine language of Appendix C. For example, since a register is eight bits long, a right circular shift of three bits produces the same result as a left circular shift of five bits.)

Arithmetic Operations

Although we have already mentioned the arithmetic operations of add, subtract, multiply, and divide, a few loose ends should still be connected. First, we have already seen that subtraction can be simulated by means of addition and negation. Moreover, multiplication is merely repeated addition and division is repeated subtraction. (Six divided by two is three because three twos can be subtracted from six.) For this reason, some small CPUs are designed with only the add or perhaps only the add and subtract instructions.

We should also mention that numerous variations exist for each arithmetic operation. We have already alluded to this in relation to the add operations available on our machine in Appendix C. In the case of addition, for example, if the values to be added are stored in two's complement notation, the addition process must be performed as a straightforward column by column addition. However, if the operands are stored as floating-point values, the addition process must extract the mantissa of each, shift them right or left according to the exponent fields, check the sign bits, perform the addition, and translate the result into floating-point notation. Thus, although both operations are considered addition, the action of the machine is not the same.

Figure 2.12 Rotating the bit pattern 65 (hexadecimal) one bit to the right

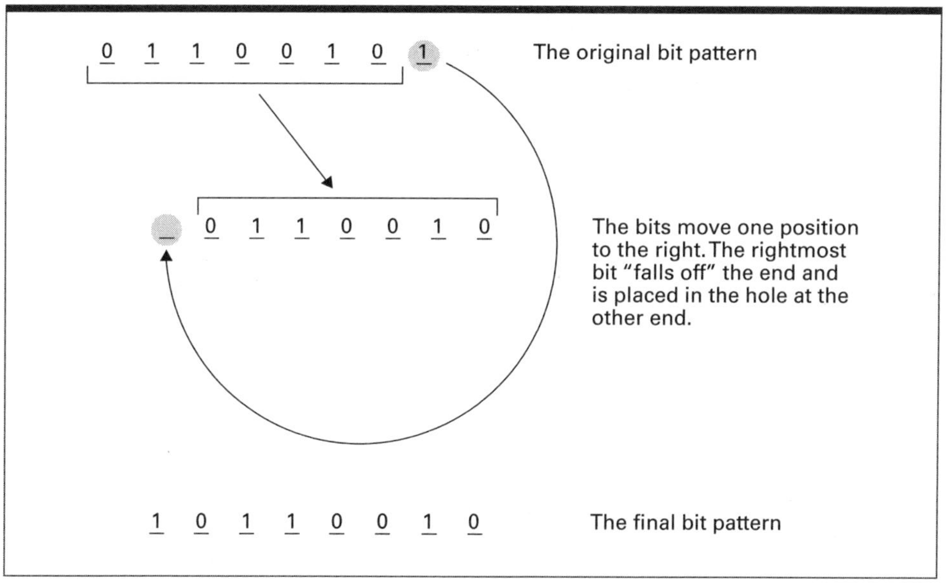

Questions & Exercises

1. Perform the indicated operations.

a. 01001011 AND 10101011	b. 100000011 AND 11101100	c. 11111111 AND 00101101
d. 01001011 OR 10101011	e. 10000011 OR 11101100	f. 11111111 OR 00101101
g. 01001011 XOR 10101011	h. 100000011 XOR 11101100	i. 11111111 XOR 00101101

2. Suppose you want to isolate the middle four bits of a byte by placing 0s in the other four bits without disturbing the middle four bits. What mask must you use together with what operation?

3. Suppose you want to complement the four middle bits of a byte while leaving the other four bits undisturbed. What mask must you use together with what operation?

4. a. Suppose you XOR the first two bits of a string of bits and then continue down the string by successively XORing each result with the next bit in the string. How is your result related to the number of 1s appearing in the string?
   b. How does this problem relate to determining what the appropriate parity bit should be when encoding a message?

5. It is often convenient to use a logical operation in place of a numeric one. For example, the logical operation AND combines two bits in the same manner as multiplication. Which logical operation is almost the same as adding two bits, and what goes wrong in this case?

6. What logical operation together with what mask can you use to change ASCII codes of lowercase letters to uppercase? What about uppercase to lowercase?

7. What is the result of performing a three-bit right circular shift on the following bit strings:

   a. 01101010 b. 00001111 c. 01111111

8. What is the result of performing a one-bit left circular shift on the following bytes represented in hexadecimal notation? Give your answer in hexadecimal form.

   a. AB b. 5C c. B7 d. 35

9. A right circular shift of three bits on a string of eight bits is equivalent to a left circular shift of how many bits?

10. What bit pattern represents the sum of 01101010 and 11001100 if the patterns represent values stored in two's complement notation? What if the

patterns represent values stored in the floating-point format discussed in Chapter 1?

11. Using the machine language of Appendix C, write a program that places a 1 in the most significant bit of the memory cell whose address is A7 without modifying the remaining bits in the cell.

12. Using the machine language of Appendix C, write a program that copies the middle four bits from memory cell E0 into the least significant four bits of memory cell E1, while placing 0s in the most significant four bits of the cell at location E1.

2.5 Communicating with Other Devices

Main memory and the CPU form the core of a computer. In this section, we investigate how this core, which we will refer to as the computer, communicates with peripheral devices such as mass storage systems, printers, keyboards, mice, display screens, digital cameras, and even other computers.

The Role of Controllers

Communication between a computer and other devices is normally handled through an intermediary apparatus known as a **controller.** In the case of a personal computer, a controller may consist of circuitry permanently mounted on the computer's motherboard or, for flexibility, it may take the form of a circuit board that plugs into a slot on the motherboard. In either case, the controller connects via cables to peripheral devices within the computer case or perhaps to a connector, called a **port,** on the back of the computer where external devices can be attached. These controllers are sometimes small computers themselves, each with its own memory circuitry and simple CPU that performs a program directing the activities of the controller.

A controller translates messages and data back and forth between forms compatible with the internal characteristics of the computer and those of the peripheral device to which it is attached. Originally, each controller was designed for a particular type of device; thus, purchasing a new peripheral device often required the purchase of a new controller as well.

Recently, steps have been taken within the personal computer arena to develop standards, such as the **universal serial bus (USB)** and **FireWire,** by which a single controller is able to handle a variety of devices. For example, a single USB controller can be used as the interface between a computer and any collection of USB-compatible devices. The list of devices on the market today that can communicate with a USB controller includes mice, printers, scanners, mass storage devices, digital cameras, and smartphones.

Each controller communicates with the computer itself by means of connections to the same bus that connects the computer's CPU and main memory (Figure 2.13). From this position it is able to monitor the signals being sent between the CPU and main memory as well as to inject its own signals onto the bus.

Figure 2.13 Controllers attached to a machine's bus

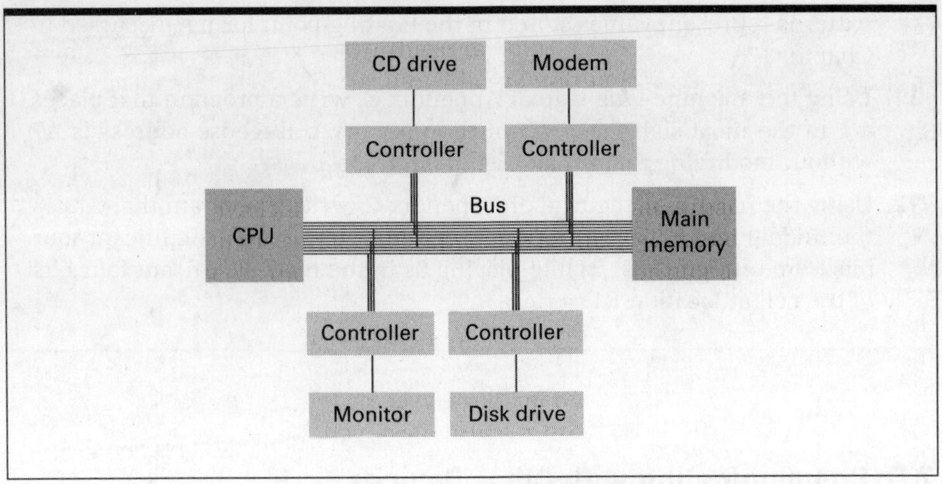

With this arrangement, the CPU is able to communicate with the controllers attached to the bus in the same manner that it communicates with main memory. To send a bit pattern to a controller, the bit pattern is first constructed in one of the CPU's general-purpose registers. Then an instruction similar to a STORE instruction is executed by the CPU to "store" the bit pattern in the controller. Likewise, to receive a bit pattern from a controller, an instruction similar to a LOAD instruction is used.

In some computer designs the transfer of data to and from controllers is directed by the same LOAD and STORE op-codes that are already provided for communication with main memory. In these cases, each controller is designed to respond to references to a unique set of addresses while main memory is designed to ignore references to these locations. Thus when the CPU sends a message on the bus to store a bit pattern at a memory location that is assigned to a controller, the bit pattern is actually "stored" in the controller rather than main memory. Likewise, if the CPU tries to read data from such a memory location, as in a LOAD instruction, it will receive a bit pattern from the controller rather than from memory. Such a communication system is called **memory-mapped I/O** because the computer's input/output devices appear to be in various memory locations (Figure 2.14).

An alternative to memory-mapped I/O is to provide special op-codes in the machine language to direct transfers to and from controllers. Instructions with these op-codes are called I/O instructions. As an example, if the language

Figure 2.14 A conceptual representation of memory-mapped I/O

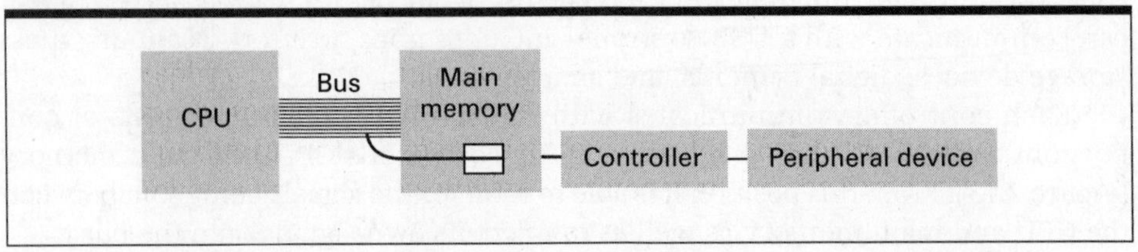

described in Appendix C followed this approach, it might include an instruction such as F5A3 to mean "STORE the contents of register 5 in the controller identified by the bit pattern A3."

Direct Memory Access

Since a controller is attached to a computer's bus, it can carry on its own communication with main memory during those nanoseconds in which the CPU is not using the bus. This ability of a controller to access main memory is known as **direct memory access (DMA),** and it is a significant asset to a computer's performance. For instance, to retrieve data from a sector of a disk, the CPU can send requests encoded as bit patterns to the controller attached to the disk asking the controller to read the sector and place the data in a specified area of main memory. The CPU can then continue with other tasks while the controller performs the read operation and deposits the data in main memory via DMA. Thus two activities will be performed at the same time. The CPU will be executing a program and the controller will be overseeing the transfer of data between the disk and main memory. In this manner, the computing resources of the CPU are not wasted during the relatively slow data transfer.

The use of DMA also has the detrimental effect of complicating the communication taking place over a computer's bus. Bit patterns must move between the CPU and main memory, between the CPU and each controller, and between each controller and main memory. Coordination of all this activity on the bus is a major design issue. Even with excellent designs, the central bus can become an impediment as the CPU and the controllers compete for bus access. This impediment

USB and FireWire

The universal serial bus (USB) and FireWire are standardized serial communication systems that simplify the process of adding new peripheral devices to a personal computer. USB was developed under the lead of Intel. The development of FireWire was led by Apple. In both cases the underlying theme is for a single controller to provide external ports at which a variety of peripheral devices can be attached. In this setting, the controller translates the internal signal characteristics of the computer to the appropriate USB or FireWire standard signals. In turn, each device connected to the controller converts its internal idiosyncrasies to the same USB or FireWire standard, allowing communication with the controller. The result is that attaching a new device to a PC does not require the insertion of a new controller. Instead, one merely plugs any USB compatible device into a USB port or a FireWire compatible device into a FireWire port.

Of the two, FireWire provides a faster transfer rate, but the lower cost of USB 2.0 technology has made it the leader in the lower-cost mass market arena. A new, faster version of the USB standard, version 3.0, has also begun to appear on the market. USB-compatible devices on the market today include mice, keyboards, printers, scanners, digital cameras, smartphones, and mass storage systems designed for backup applications. FireWire applications tend to focus on devices that require higher transfer rates such as video recorders and online mass storage systems.

is known as the **von Neumann bottleneck** because it is a consequence of the underlying **von Neumann architecture** in which a CPU fetches its instructions from memory over a central bus.

Handshaking

The transfer of data between two computer components is rarely a one-way affair. Even though we may think of a printer as a device that receives data, the truth is that a printer also sends data back to the computer. After all, a computer can produce and send characters to a printer much faster than the printer can print them. If a computer blindly sent data to a printer, the printer would quickly fall behind, resulting in lost data. Thus a process such as printing a document involves a constant two-way dialogue, known as **handshaking,** in which the computer and the peripheral device exchange information about the device's status and coordinate their activities.

Handshaking often involves a **status word,** which is a bit pattern that is generated by the peripheral device and sent to the controller. The status word is a bit map in which the bits reflect the conditions of the device. For example, in the case of a printer, the value of the least significant bit of the status word may indicate whether the printer is out of paper, while the next bit may indicate whether the printer is ready for additional data. Still another bit may be used to indicate the presence of a paper jam. Depending on the system, the controller may respond to this status information itself or make it available to the CPU. In either case, the status word provides the mechanism by which communication with a peripheral device can be coordinated.

Popular Communication Media

Communication between computing devices is handled over two types of paths: parallel and serial. These terms refer to the manner in which signals are transferred with respect to each other. In the case of **parallel communication,** several signals are transferred at the same time, each on a separate "line." Such a technique is capable of transferring data rapidly but requires a relatively complex communication path. Examples include a computer's internal bus where multiple wires are used to allow large blocks of data and other signals to be transferred simultaneously.

In contrast, **serial communication** is based on transferring signals one after the other over a single line. Thus serial communication requires a simpler data path than parallel communication, which is the reason for its popularity. USB and FireWire, which offer relatively high-speed data transfer over short distances of only a few meters, are examples of serial communication systems. For slightly longer distances (within a home or office building), serial communication over Ethernet connections (Section 4.1), either by wire or radio broadcast, are popular.

For communication over greater distances, traditional voice telephone lines dominated the personal computer arena for many years. These communication paths, consisting of a single wire over which tones are transferred one after the other, are inherently serial systems. The transfer of digital data over these lines is accomplished by first converting bit patterns into audible tones by means of a **modem** (short for *modulator-demodulator*), transferring these tones serially over the telephone system, and then converting the tones back into bits by another modem at the destination.

For faster long-distance communication over traditional telephone lines, telephone companies offer a service known as **DSL (Digital Subscriber Line),** which takes advantage of the fact that existing telephone lines are capable of handling a wider frequency range than that used by traditional voice communication. More precisely, DSL uses frequencies above the audible range to transfer digital data while leaving the lower-frequency spectrum for voice communication. Although DSL has been highly successful, telephone companies are rapidly upgrading their systems to fiber-optic lines, which support digital communication more readily than traditional telephone lines.

Cable modems are a competing technology that modulate and demodulate bit patterns to be transmitted over cable television systems. Many cable providers now make use of both fiber-optic lines and traditional coaxial cable to provide both high definition television signals and computer network access.

Satellite links via high-frequency radio broadcast make computer network access possible even in some remote locations far from high speed telephone and cable television networks.

Communication Rates

The rate at which bits are transferred from one computing component to another is measured in **bits per second (bps).** Common units include **Kbps** (kilo-bps, equal to one thousand bps), **Mbps** (mega-bps, equal to one million bps), and **Gbps** (giga-bps, equal to one billion bps). (Note the distinction between bits and bytes—that is, 8 Kbps is equal to 1 KB per second. In abbreviations, a lowercase b usually means *bit* whereas an uppercase B means *byte.*)

For short distance communication, USB 2.0 and FireWire provide transfer rates of several hundred Mbps, which is sufficient for most multimedia applications. This, combined with their convenience and relatively low cost, is why they are popular for communication between home computers and local peripherals such as printers, external disk drives, and cameras.

By combining **multiplexing** (the encoding or interweaving of data so that a single communication path serves the purpose of multiple paths) and data compression techniques, traditional voice telephone systems were able to support transfer rates of 57.6 Kbps. This falls short of the needs of today's multimedia and Internet applications, such as high definition video streaming from sites like Netflix or YouTube. To play MP3 music recordings requires a transfer rate of about 64 Kbps, and to play even low quality video clips requires transfer rates measured in units of Mbps. This is why alternatives such as DSL, cable, and satellite links, which provide transfer rates well into the Mbps range, have replaced traditional audio telephone systems. (For example, DSL offers transfer rates on the order of 54 Mbps.)

The maximum rate available in a particular setting depends on the type of the communication path and the technology used in its implementation. This maximum rate is often loosely equated to the communication path's **bandwidth,** although the term *bandwidth* also has connotations of capacity rather than transfer rate. That is, to say that a communication path has a high bandwidth (or provides **broadband** service) means that the communication path has the ability to transfer bits at a high rate as well as the capacity to carry large amounts of information simultaneously.

Questions & Exercises

1. Assume that the machine described in Appendix C uses memory-mapped I/O and that the address B5 is the location within the printer port to which data to be printed should be sent.
   a. If register 7 contains the ASCII code for the letter A, what machine language instruction should be used to cause that letter to be printed at the printer?
   b. If the machine executes a million instructions per second, how many times can this character be sent to the printer in one second?
   c. If the printer is capable of printing five traditional pages of text per minute, will it be able to keep up with the characters being sent to it in (b)?
2. Suppose that the hard disk on your personal computer rotates at 3000 revolutions a minute, that each track contains 16 sectors, and that each sector contains 1024 bytes. Approximately what communication rate is required between the disk drive and the disk controller if the controller is going to receive bits from the disk drive as they are read from the spinning disk?
3. Estimate how long it would take to transfer a 300-page novel encoded in 16-bit Unicode characters at a transfer rate of 54 Mbps.

2.6 Programming Data Manipulation

One of the essential features of computer programming languages such as Python is that they shield users from the tedious details of working with the lowest levels of the machine. Having just completed much of a chapter on the lowest levels of data manipulation in computer processors, it is instructive to review some of the major details that Python scripts shield the programmer from needing to worry about.

As we will explore in greater detail in Chapter 6, high-level programming language statements are mapped down to low-level machine instructions in order to be executed. A single Python statement might map to a single machine instruction, or to many tens or even hundreds of machine instructions, depending on the complexity of the statement and the efficiency of the machine language. Different implementations of the Python language interpreter, in concert with other elements of the computer's operating system software, take care of this mapping process for each particular computer processor. As a result, the Python programmer does not need to know whether she is executing her Python script on a RISC processor or a CISC processor.

We can recognize many Python operations that correspond closely to the basic machine instructions for modern computers or for the simple machine described in Appendix C. Addition of Python integers and floating-point numbers clearly resembles the ADD op-codes of our simple machine. Assigning values to variables surely involves the LOAD, STORE, and MOVE op-codes in some arrangement. Python shields us from worrying about which processor registers are in use, but leverages the op-codes of the machine to carry out our instructions. We cannot see the instruction register, program counter, or memory cell addresses, but the Python script executes sequentially, one statement after the other, in the same way as the simple machine language programs.

Logic and Shift Operations

Logic and shift operations can be executed on any kind of numerical data, but because they often deal with individual bits of data, it is easiest to illustrate these operations with binary values. Just as Python uses the `0x` prefix to specify values in hexadecimal, the `0b` prefix can be used to specify values in binary[1].

```
x    = 0b00110011
mask = 0b00001111
```

Note that this is effectively no different from assigning `x` the value 51, (which is 110011 in binary), or `0x33` (which is 51 expressed in hexadecimal), or from assigning `mask` the value 15, (which is 1111 in binary), or `0x0F` (15 in hexadecimal). The representation we use to spell out the integer value in the Python assignment statement does not change how it is represented in the computer, only how human readers understand it.

Built-in Python operators exist for each of the bitwise logical operators described in Section 2.4.

```
print(0b00000101 ^ 0b00000100)      # Prints 5 XOR 4, which is 1
print(0b00000101 | 0b00000100)      # Prints 5 OR  4, which is 5
print(0b00000101 & 0b00000100)      # Prints 5 AND 4, which is 4
```

As a result, we can replicate each of the example problems of Section 2.4 as Python code.

```
                                    #         10011010
print(0b10011010 & 0b11001001)      #     AND 11001001
                                    #         10001000

                                    #         10011010
print(0b10011010 | 0b11001001)      #     OR  11001001
                                    #         11011011

                                    #         10011010
print(0b10011010 ^ 0b11001001)      #     XOR 11001001
                                    #         01010011
```

For all of these examples, Python will print the result in its default output representation, which is base-10. If the user would also like the output to be displayed in binary notation, a built-in function exists to convert any integer value into the string of zero and one characters for the corresponding binary representation.

---

[1]This syntax is another recent addition to the evolving Python language. Make sure that you are using at least Python 3 to replicate these examples.

```
print(bin(0b10011010 & 0b11001001))    # Prints "0b10001000"
print(bin(0b10011010 | 0b11001001))    # Prints "0b11011011"
print(bin(0b10011010 ^ 0b11001001))    # Prints "0b1010011"
```

Because newer versions of Python can use an arbitrary number of digits for representing numbers, leading zeros are not printed. Thus, the third line above prints only seven digits, rather than eight.

Python's built-in operators for performing logical shift operations consist of dual greater-than and less-than symbols, visually suggesting the direction of shift. The operand on the right of the operator indicates the number of bit positions to shift.

```
print(0b00111100 >> 2)    # Prints  "15", which is 0b00001111
print(0b00111100 << 2)    # Prints "240", which is 0b11110000
```

In addition to shifting bit masks left or right, bit shift operators are also an efficient way to multiply (left shift) or divide (right shift) by powers of 2.

Control Structures

The control group of machine language instructions presented earlier in this chapter affords us a mechanism for jumping from one part of a program to another. In higher-level languages like Python, this enables what are called **control structures,** syntax patterns that allow us to express algorithms more powerfully. One example of this is the `if`-statement, which allows a segment of code to be conditionally skipped if a Boolean value in the script is not true.

```
if (water_temp > 140):
  print('Bath water too hot!')
```

Intuitively, this Python snippet will be mapped to machine instructions that make the comparison between the `water_temp` variable and the integer value 140, probably both previously loaded into registers. A conditional jump instruction will skip over the machine instructions for the `print()` built-in if the `water_temp` value was not 140 or larger.

Another control structure is the looping construct `while`, which allows a segment of code to be executed multiple times, often subject to some condition.

```
while (n < 10):
  print(n)
  n = n + 1
```

Assuming the variable `n` starts with a value less than 10, this loop will continue printing and incrementing `n` until it becomes greater than or equal to 10.

We will spend more time examining these and other control structures in Chapter 5 and beyond. For now, we focus on a mechanism that allows us to jump to another part of the program, carry out a desired task, and then return to the program point we came from.

Functions We have already seen three built-in Python operations that do not follow the same syntactic form as the arithmetic and logic operators. The `print()`, str() and bin() operations are invoked using given names instead of symbols, and also involve parentheses wrapped around their operands.

Both of these are examples of a Python language feature called **functions.** The term *function* in mathematics is often used to describe algebraic relationships, such as "$f(x) = x^2 + 3x + 4$." Upon seeing such a function definition, we understand that in subsequent lines the expression "f(5)" is taken to mean that the value 5 should be plugged in wherever the parameter x occurs in the expression defining f(). Thus, $f(5) = 5^2 + 3*5 + 4 = 25 + 15 + 4 = 44$. Programming language functions are quite similar in that they allow us to use a name for a series of operations that should be performed on the given parameter or parameters. Due to the way that this language feature is mapped to lower level machine languages, the appearance of a function in an expression or statement is known as a **function call,** or sometimes **calling** a function.

The occurrences of print() and bin() in the examples above are two such function calls; they indicate that the Python interpreter will go execute the definition of the named function, and then return to continue with its work. The syntax is to follow the name of the function immediately with an opening parenthesis, and then to give the function **argument value** that will be plugged in for the parameter when the function definition is evaluated, followed by a closing parenthesis. It is important to match opening and closing parentheses—not doing so will cause a Python syntax error and is a common mistake for beginners.

From now on, we will follow the convention of including the parentheses when talking about Python functions, such as print(), so as to clearly denote them as distinct from variables or other items.

Functions come in many varieties beyond what we have already seen. Some functions take more than one argument, such as the max() function:

```
x = 1034
y = 1056
z = 2078
biggest = max(x, y, z)
print(biggest)                    # Prints "2078"
```

Multiple arguments are separated by commas within the parentheses. Some functions **return** a value, which is to say that the function call itself can appear as part of a more complex expression, or as the right-hand side of an assignment statement. These are sometimes called **fruitful functions.** This is the case for both max() (as above) and bin(), which takes an integer value as an argument and returns the corresponding string of zeros and ones. Other functions do not return a value, and usually are used as standalone statements, as is the case for print(). Functions that do not return a value are sometimes called **void functions,** or **procedures,** although Python makes no distinction in its syntax rules. It makes no sense to assign the result of a void function to a variable, as in

```
x = print('hello world!')     # x is assigned None
```

although this is not an error in Python, per se, and is subtly different from not assigning a value to x at all.

Each of the functions we have seen so far is one of the few dozen built-in functions that Python knows about, but there are extensive libraries of additional functions that a more advanced script can refer to. The Python library modules contain many useful functions that may not normally be required, but that can be called upon when needed.

```
# Calculates the hypotenuse of a right triangle
import math

sideA = 3.0
sideB = 4.0
# Calculate third side via Pythagorean Theorem
hypotenuse = math.sqrt(sideA**2 + sideB**2)

print(hypotenuse)
```

In this example, the `import` statement forewarns the Python interpreter that the script refers to the library called "`math`," which happens to be one of the standard set of library modules that Python comes equipped with. The `sqrt()` function defined within the `math` library module provides the square root of the argument, which in this case was the expression of `sideA` squared plus `sideB` squared. Note that the library function call includes both the module name ("`math`") and the function name ("`sqrt`"), joined by a period.

The Python `math` module includes dozens of useful mathematical functions, including logorithmic, trigonometric, and hyperbolic functions, as well as some familiar constant values such as `math.pi`.

Beyond the built-in and library module functions, Python provides syntax for a script to define its own functions. We will define a few very simple examples at the end of this section, and explore more elaborate variations in a later chapter.

Input and Output

The previous example snippets and scripts have used the built-in Python `print()` function to output results. Many programming languages provide similar mechanisms for achieving input and output, providing programmers with a convenient abstraction to move data in or out of the computer processor. In fact, these I/O built-ins communicate with the hardware controllers and peripheral devices discussed in the previous section.

None of our example scripts thus far have required any input from the user. Simple user input can be accomplished with the built-in Python `input()` function.

```
echo = input('Please enter a string to echo: ')
print(echo * 3)
```

The `input()` function takes as an optional argument a prompt string to present to the user when waiting for input. When run, this script will pause after displaying "`Please enter a string to echo: `", and wait for the user to type something. When the user hits the enter key, the script assigns the string of characters typed (not including the enter key,) to the variable `echo`. The second line of the script then outputs the string repeated three times. (Recall that the * operator replicates string operands.)

Armed with the ability to acquire input, let's rewrite our hypotenuse script to prompt a user for the side lengths rather than hardcode the values into assignment statements.

```
# Calculates the hypotenuse of a right triangle
import math

# Inputting the side lengths, first try
sideA = input('Length of side A? ')
sideB = input('Length of side B? ')
# Calculate third side via Pythagorean Theorem
hypotenuse = math.sqrt(sideA**2 + sideB**2)

print(hypotenuse)
```

When run, this script prompts the user with, "`Length of side A? `", and awaits input. Let us suppose that the user types "3" and enter. The script prompts the user with "`Length of side B? `", and awaits input. Let us suppose that the user types "4" and enter. At this point, the Python interpreter aborts the script, printing out:

```
hypotenuse = math.sqrt(sideA**2 + sideB**2)
TypeError: unsupported operand type(s) for ** or pow(): 'str' and 'int'
```

This type of error can be easy to create in a dynamically typed language like Python. Our hypotenuse calculation, which worked in the earlier version of the script, now causes an error when the values have been read as input from the user instead. The problem is indeed a "`TypeError`," stemming from the fact that Python no longer knows how to take the square of variable `sideA`, because `sideA` is now a character string in this version of the script, rather than an integer as before. The problem comes not from the line that calculates the hypotenuse, but from earlier in the script, when the values of `sideA` and `sideB` are returned from `input()`. This, too, is common when encountering errors with programming languages. The Python interpreter attempts to provide the line of script responsible for the problem, but the real culprit is actually earlier in the script.

In the string echoing snippet above, it was clear that the value assigned to `echo` should be the string of characters typed in by the user. The `input()` function behaves in the same way in the hypotenuse program, even though the programmer's intent is now to enter integer values. The representation of the ASCII- or UTF-8-encoded string "4" differs from the two's complement representation of the integer 4, and the Python script must explicitly make the conversion from one representation to the other before proceeding to calculations with integers.

Fortunately, another built-in function provides the capability. The `int()` function attempts to convert its argument into an integer representation. If it cannot, an appropriate error message is produced.

There are at least three places that we can use the `int()` function to remove the bug in this script. We can call it before even assigning the result of `input()` to the variable. We can add new lines of script that are only for calling the conversion function. Or, we can make the conversion just before squaring the variable within the call to the `math.sqrt()` function. The revised script below uses the first option; the other two are left as an exercise for the reader.

```
# Calculates the hypotenuse of a right triangle
import math
```

```
# Inputting the side lengths, with integer conversion
sideA = int(input('Length of side A? '))
sideB = int(input('Length of side B? '))
# Calculate third side via Pythagorean Theorem
hypotenuse = math.sqrt(sideA**2 + sideB**2)

print(hypotenuse)
```

The revised script operates as intended and can be used for many right triangles without having to edit the script, as in the pre-input version.

As a final note, the `int()` function performs its conversion by carefully examining the string argument and interpreting it as a number. If the input string is a number, but not an integer, as for example, "3.14," the `int()` function discards the fractional portion and returns only the integer value. This operation is a truncation and will not "round up" as a human might expect. Similar conversion functions exist in Python for all of the other standard value types.

Marathon Training Assistant

The complete Python script below demonstrates many of the concepts introduced in this section. As the popularity of recreational distance running has increased, many participants find themselves pursuing complex training schedules to prepare their bodies for the rigors of running a marathon. This script assists a runner who wishes to calculate how long her training workout will take, based upon the distance and pace she wishes to run. Given a *pace* (number of minutes and seconds to run a single mile), and a total mileage, this script calculates the projected elapsed time to run the workout, as well as a user-friendly speed calculation in miles per hour. Figure 2.15 gives some example data points; in each row, given the first three columns as input, the last three columns would be the expected results. Note that different implementations of Python may print a different number of decimal places from Figure 2.15 for speed values that don't work out to round numbers.

Figure 2.15 Example marathon training data

Time Per Mile				Total Elapsed Time	
Minutes	Seconds	Miles	Speed (mph)	Minutes	Seconds
9	14	5	6.49819494584	46	10
8	0	3	7.5	24	0
7	45	6	7.74193548387	46	30
7	25	1	8.08988764044	7	25

```
# Marathon training assistant.
import math

# This function converts a number of minutes and seconds into just seconds.
def total_seconds(min, sec):
  return min * 60 + sec

# This function calculates a speed in miles per hour given
# a time (in seconds) to run a single mile.
def speed(time):
  return 3600 / time

# Prompt user for pace and mileage.
pace_minutes = int(input('Minutes per mile? '))
pace_seconds = int(input('Seconds per mile? '))
miles = int(input('Total miles? '))

# Calculate and print speed.
mph = speed(total_seconds(pace_minutes, pace_seconds))
print('Your speed is')
print(mph)

# Calculate elapsed time for planned workout.
total = miles * total_seconds(pace_minutes, pace_seconds)
elapsed_minutes = total // 60
elapsed_seconds = total % 60

print('Your total elapsed time is')
print(elapsed_minutes)
print(elapsed_seconds)
```

The script above uses both built-in functions—`input()`, `int()`, and `print()`—as well as user-defined functions—`speed()` and `total_seconds()`. The keyword `def` precedes a user function definition and is followed by the name for the function and a list of parameters to be provided when the function is called. The indented line that follows is called the **body** of a function and expresses the steps that define the function. In a later chapter, we will see examples of functions with more than one statement in their body. The keyword `return` highlights the expression that will be calculated to find the result of the function.

The user-defined functions are defined at the top of the script, but are not actually invoked until the script reaches the lines where they are called as part of a larger expression. Note also the way in which function calls are stacked in this script. The results of the calls to `input()` are immediately passed as arguments to the `int()` function, and the result of the `int()` function is then assigned to a variable. Similarly, the result of `total_seconds()` is immediately passed as an argument to the `speed()` function, whose result is then assigned to the variable `mph`. In each of these cases, it would be permissible to make the function calls one at a time, assign the result to a new variable, and then call the next function that relies on the first result. However, this more compact form is more succinct and does not require a proliferation of temporary variables to hold intermediate results of the calculation.

Given inputs of 7 minutes and 45 seconds per mile, for 6 miles, this script outputs:

```
Your speed is
7.74193548387
Your total elapsed time is
46
30
```

The format of this output remains quite primitive. It lacks proper units (`7.74193548387 mph`, and `46 minutes, 30 seconds`), prints an inappropriate number of decimal places for a simple calculation, and breaks lines in too many places. Cleaner output is left as an exercise for the reader.

Questions & Exercises

1. The hypotenuse example script truncates the sides to integers, but outputs a floating-point number. Why? Adapt the script to output an integer.
2. Adapt the hypotenuse script to use floating-point numbers as input, without truncating them. Which is more appropriate, the integer version from the previous question, or the floating-point version?
3. The Python built-in function `str()` will convert a numerical argument into a character string representation, and the `'+'` can be used to concatenate strings together. Use these to modify the marathon script to produce cleaner output, for example:

```
Your speed is 7.74193548387 mph
Your total elapsed time is 46 minutes, 30 seconds
```

4. Use the Python built-in `bin()` to write a script that reads a base-10 integers as input and outputs the corresponding binary representation of that integer in ones and zeros.
5. The XOR operation is often used both for efficiently calculating checksums (see Section 1.9) and encryption (see Section 4.5). Write a simple Python script that reads in a number and outputs that number XORed with a pattern of ones and zeros, such as 0x55555555. The same script will "encrypt" a number into a seemingly unrelated number, but when run again and given the encrypted number as input will return the original number.
6. Explore some of the error conditions that you can create with unexpected inputs to the example scripts from this section. What happens if you enter all zeros for the hypotenuse script or the marathon script? What about negative numbers? Strings of characters instead of numbers?

2.7 Other Architectures

To broaden our perspective, let us consider some alternatives to the traditional machine architecture we have discussed so far.

Pipelining

Electric pulses travel through a wire no faster than the speed of light. Since light travels approximately 1 foot in a nanosecond (one billionth of a second), it requires at least 2 nanoseconds for the CPU to fetch an instruction from a memory cell that is 1 foot away. (The read request must be sent to memory, requiring at least 1 nanosecond, and the instruction must be sent back to the CPU, requiring at least another nanosecond.) Consequently, to fetch and execute an instruction in such a machine requires several nanoseconds—which means that increasing the execution speed of a machine ultimately becomes a miniaturization problem.

However, increasing execution speed is not the only way to improve a computer's performance. The real goal is to improve the machine's **throughput,** which refers to the total amount of work the machine can accomplish in a given amount of time.

An example of how a computer's throughput can be increased without requiring an increase in execution speed involves **pipelining,** which is the technique of allowing the steps in the machine cycle to overlap. In particular, while one instruction is being executed, the next instruction can be fetched, which means that more than one instruction can be in "the pipe" at any one time, each at a different stage of being processed. In turn, the total throughput of the machine is increased even though the time required to fetch and execute each individual instruction remains the same. (Of course, when a JUMP instruction is reached, any gain that would have been obtained by prefetching is not realized because the instructions in "the pipe" are not the ones needed after all.)

Modern machine designs push the pipelining concept beyond our simple example. They are often capable of fetching several instructions at the same time and actually executing more than one instruction at a time when those instructions do not rely on each other.

The Multi-Core CPU

As technology provides ways of placing more and more circuitry on a silicon chip, the physical distinction between a computer's components diminishes. For instance, a single chip might contain a CPU and main memory. This is an example of the "system-on-a-chip (SoC)" approach in which the goal is to provide a complete apparatus in a single device that can be used as an abstract tool in higher level designs. In other cases, multiple copies of the same circuit are provided within a single device. This latter tactic originally appeared in the form of chips containing several independent gates or perhaps multiple flip-flops. Today's state of the art allows for more than one entire CPU to be placed on a single chip. This is the underlying architecture of devices known as multi-core CPUs, which consist of two or more CPUs residing on the same chip along with shared cache memory. (Multi-core CPUs containing two processing units are typically called dual-core CPUs.) Such devices simplify the construction of MIMD systems and are readily available for use in home computers.

Multiprocessor Machines

Pipelining can be viewed as a first step toward **parallel processing,** which is the performance of several activities at the same time. However, true parallel processing requires more than one processing unit, resulting in computers known as multiprocessor or **multi-core** machines.

Most computers today are designed with this idea in mind. One strategy is to attach several processing units, each resembling the CPU in a single-processor machine, to the same main memory. In this configuration, the processors can proceed independently yet coordinate their efforts by leaving messages to one another in the common memory cells. For instance, when one processor is faced with a large task, it can store a program for part of that task in the common memory and then request another processor to execute it. The result is a machine in which different instruction sequences are performed on different sets of data, which is called a **MIMD** (**multiple-instruction stream, multiple-data stream**) architecture, as opposed to the more traditional **SISD** (**single-instruction stream, single-data stream**) architecture.

A variation of multiple-processor architecture is to link the processors together so that they execute the same sequence of instructions in unison, each with its own set of data. This leads to a **SIMD** (**single-instruction stream, multiple-data stream**) architecture. Such machines are useful in applications in which the same task must be applied to each set of similar items within a large block of data. Another approach to parallel processing is to construct large computers as conglomerates of smaller machines, each with its own memory and CPU. Within such an architecture, each of the small machines is coupled to its neighbors so that tasks assigned to the whole system can be divided among the individual machines. Thus if a task assigned to one of the internal machines can be broken into independent subtasks, that machine can ask its neighbors to perform these subtasks concurrently. The original task can then be completed in much less time than would be required by a single-processor machine.

Questions & Exercises

1. Referring back to question 3 of Section 2.3, if the machine used the pipeline technique discussed in the text, what will be in "the pipe" when the instruction at address AA is executed? Under what conditions would pipelining not prove beneficial at this point in the program?
2. What conflicts must be resolved in running the program in question 4 of Section 2.3 on a pipeline machine?
3. Suppose there were two "central" processing units attached to the same memory and executing different programs. Furthermore, suppose that one of these processors needs to add one to the contents of a memory cell at roughly the same time that the other needs to subtract one from the same cell. (The net effect should be that the cell ends up with the same value with which it started.)
   a. Describe a sequence in which these activities would result in the cell ending up with a value one less than its starting value.
   b. Describe a sequence in which these activities would result in the cell ending up with a value one greater than its starting value.

Chapter Review Problems

(Asterisked problems are associated with optional sections.)

1. a. In what way are general-purpose registers and main memory cells similar?
   b. In what way do general-purpose registers and main memory cells differ?
2. Answer the following questions in terms of the machine language described in Appendix C.
   a. Write the instruction 2304 (hexadecimal) as a string of 16 bits.
   b. Write the op-code of the instruction B2A5 (hexadecimal) as a string of 4 bits.
   c. Write the operand field of the instruction B2A5 (hexadecimal) as a string of 12 bits.
3. Suppose a block of data is stored in the memory cells of the machine described in Appendix C from address 98 to A2, inclusive. How many memory cells are in this block? List their addresses.
4. What is the value of the program counter in the machine described in Appendix C immediately after executing the instruction B0CD?
5. Suppose the memory cells at addresses 00 through 05 in the machine described in Appendix C contain the following bit patterns:

Address	Contents
00	22
01	11
02	32
03	02
04	C0
05	00

   Assuming that the program counter initially contained 00, record the contents of the program counter, instruction register, and memory cell at address 02 at the end of each fetch phase of the machine cycle until the machine halts.
6. Suppose three values x, y, and z are stored in a machine's memory. Describe the sequence of events (loading registers from memory, saving values in memory, and so on) that leads to the computation of x + y + z. How about (2x) + y?
7. The following are instructions written in the machine language described in Appendix C. Translate them into English.

   a. 7123 b. 40E1 c. A304
   d. B100 e. 2BCD
8. Suppose a machine language is designed with an op-code field of 4 bits. How many different instruction types can the language contain? What if the op-code field is increased to 6 bits?
9. Translate the following instructions from English into the machine language described in Appendix C.
   a. LOAD register 6 with the hexadecimal value 77.
   b. LOAD register 7 with the contents of memory cell 77.
   c. JUMP to the instruction at memory location 24 if the contents of register 0 equals the value in register A.
   d. ROTATE register 4 three bits to the right.
   e. AND the contents of registers E and 2 leaving the result in register 1.
10. Rewrite the program in Figure 2.7 assuming that the values to be added are encoded using floating-point notation rather than two's complement notation.
11. Classify each of the following instructions (in the machine language of Appendix C) in terms of whether its execution changes the contents of the memory cell at location 3B, retrieves the contents of the memory cell at location 3C, or is independent of the contents of the memory cell at location 3C.
   a. 353C b. 253C c. 153C
   d. 3C3C e. 403C
12. Suppose the memory cells at addresses 00 through 03 in the machine described in Appendix C contain the following bit patterns:

Address	Contents
00	26
01	55
02	C0
03	00

   a. Translate the first instruction into English.
   b. If the machine is started with its program counter containing 00, what bit pattern is in register 6 when the machine halts?

13. Suppose the memory cells at addresses 00 through 02 in the machine described in Appendix C contain the following bit patterns:

Address	Contents
00	12
01	21
02	34

a. What would be the first instruction executed if we started the machine with its program counter containing 00?
b. What would be the first instruction executed if we started the machine with its program counter containing 01?

14. Suppose the memory cells at addresses 00 through 05 in the machine described in Appendix C contain the following bit patterns:

Address	Contents
00	12
01	02
02	32
03	42
04	C0
05	00

When answering the following questions, assume that the machine starts with its program counter equal to 00.
a. Translate the instructions that are executed into English.
b. What bit pattern is in the memory cell at address 42 when the machine halts?
c. What bit pattern is in the program counter when the machine halts?

15. Suppose the memory cells at addresses 00 through 09 in the machine described in Appendix C contain the following bit patterns:

Address	Contents
00	1C
01	03
02	2B
03	03
04	5A
05	BC
06	3A
07	00
08	C0
09	00

Assume that the machine starts with its program counter containing 00.
a. What will be in the memory cell at address 00 when the machine halts?
b. What bit pattern will be in the program counter when the machine halts?

16. Suppose the memory cells at addresses 00 through 07 in the machine described in Appendix C contain the following bit patterns:

Address	Contents
00	2B
01	07
02	3B
03	06
04	C0
05	00
06	00
07	23

a. List the addresses of the memory cells that contain the program that will be executed if we start the machine with its program counter containing 00.
b. List the addresses of the memory cells that are used to hold data.

17. Suppose the memory cells at addresses 00 through 0D in the machine described in Appendix C contain the following bit patterns:

Address	Contents
00	20
01	04
02	21
03	01
04	40
05	12
06	51
07	12
08	B1
09	0C
0A	B0
0B	06
0C	C0
0D	00

Assume that the machine starts with its program counter containing 00.
a. What bit pattern will be in register 0 when the machine halts?

b. What bit pattern will be in register 1 when the machine halts?
c. What bit pattern is in the program counter when the machine halts?

18. Suppose the memory cells at addresses F0 through FD in the machine described in Appendix C contain the following (hexadecimal) bit patterns:

Address	Contents
F0	20
F1	00
F2	22
F3	02
F4	23
F5	04
F6	B3
F7	FC
F8	50
F9	02
FA	B0
FB	F6
FC	C0
FD	00

If we start the machine with its program counter containing F0, what is the value in register 0 when the machine finally executes the halt instruction at location FC?

19. If the machine in Appendix C executes an instruction every microsecond (a millionth of a second), how long does it take to complete the program in Problem 18?

20. Suppose the memory cells at addresses 20 through 28 in the machine described in Appendix C contain the following bit patterns:

Address	Contents
20	12
21	20
22	32
23	30
24	B0
25	21
26	24
27	C0
28	00

Assume that the machine starts with its program counter containing 20.
a. What bit patterns will be in registers 0, 1, and 2 when the machine halts?
b. What bit pattern will be in the memory cell at address 30 when the machine halts?
c. What bit pattern will be in the memory cell at address B0 when the machine halts?

21. Suppose the memory cells at addresses AF through B1 in the machine described in Appendix C contain the following bit patterns:

Address	Contents
AF	B0
B0	B0
B1	AF

What would happen if we started the machine with its program counter containing AF?

22. Suppose the memory cells at addresses 00 through 05 in the machine described in Appendix C contain the following (hexadecimal) bit patterns:

Address	Contents
00	25
01	B0
02	35
03	04
04	C0
05	00

If we start the machine with its program counter containing 00, when does the machine halt?

23. In each of the following cases, write a short program in the machine language described in Appendix C to perform the requested activities. Assume that each of your programs is placed in memory starting at address 00.
a. Move the value at memory location D8 to memory location B3.
b. Interchange the values stored at memory locations D8 and B3.
c. If the value stored in memory location 44 is 00, then place the value 01 in memory location 46; otherwise, put the value FF in memory location 46.

24. A game that used to be popular among computer hobbyists is core wars—a variation of battleship. (The term *core* originates from an early memory technology in which 0s and 1s were represented as magnetic fields in little rings of magnetic material. The rings were called cores.) The game is played between two opposing programs, each stored in different locations of the same computer's memory. The computer is assumed to alternate between the two programs, executing an instruction from one followed by an instruction from the other. The goal of each program is to cause the other to malfunction by writing extraneous data on top of it; however, neither program knows the location of the other.

a. Write a program in the machine language of Appendix C that approaches the game in a defensive manner by being as small as possible.

b. Write a program in the language of Appendix C that tries to avoid any attacks from the opposing program by moving to different locations. More precisely, beginning at location 00, write a program that will copy itself to location 70 and then jump to location 70.

c. Extend the program in (b) to continue relocating to new memory locations. In particular, make your program move to location 70, then to E0 (= 70 + 70) then to 60 (= 70 + 70 + 70) etc.

25. Write a program in the machine language of Appendix C to compute the sum of floating-point values stored at memory locations A0, A1, A2, and A3. Your program should store the total at memory location A4.

26. Suppose the memory cells at addresses 00 through 05 in the machine described in Appendix C contain the following (hexadecimal) bit patterns:

Address	Contents
00	20
01	C0
02	30
03	04
04	00
05	00

What happens if we start the machine with its program counter containing 00?

27. What happens if the memory cells at addresses 08 and 09 of the machine described in Appendix C contain the bit patterns B0 and 08, respectively, and the machine is started with its program counter containing the value 08?

28. Suppose the following program, written in the machine language of Appendix C, is stored in main memory beginning at address 30 (hexadecimal). What task will the program perform when executed?

```
2003
2101
2200
2310
1400
3410
5221
5331
3239
333B
B248
B038
C000
```

29. Summarize the steps involved when the machine described in Appendix C performs an instruction with op-code B. Express your answer as a set of directions as though you were telling the CPU what to do.

***30.** Summarize the steps involved when the machine described in Appendix C performs an instruction with op-code 5. Express your answer as a set of directions as though you were telling the CPU what to do.

***31.** Summarize the steps involved when the machine described in Appendix C performs an instruction with op-code 6. Express your answer as a set of directions as though you were telling the CPU what to do.

***32.** Suppose the registers 4 and 5 in the machine described in Appendix C contain the bit patterns 3A and C8, respectively. What bit pattern is left in register 0 after executing each of the following instructions:

a. 5045 b. 6045 c. 7045
d. 8045 e. 9045

*33. Using the machine language described in Appendix C, write programs to perform each of the following tasks:
  a. Copy the bit pattern stored in memory location 44 into memory location AA.
  b. Change the least significant 4 bits in the memory cell at location 34 to 0s while leaving the other bits unchanged.
  c. Copy the least significant 4 bits from memory location A5 into the least significant 4 bits of location A6 while leaving the other bits at location A6 unchanged.
  d. Copy the least significant 4 bits from memory location A5 into the most significant 4 bits of A5. (Thus, the first 4 bits in A5 will be the same as the last 4 bits.)

*34. Perform the indicated operations:

```
a.     111001        b.     000101
   AND 101001           AND 101010

c.     001110        d.     111011
   AND 010101           AND 110111

e.     111001        f.     010100
   OR  101001           OR  101010

g.     000100        h.     101010
   OR  010101           OR  110101

i.     111001        j.     000111
   XOR 101001           XOR 101010

k.     010000        l.     111111
   XOR 010101           XOR 110101
```

*35. Identify both the mask and the logical operation needed to accomplish each of the following objectives:
  a. Put 1s in the upper 4 bits of an 8-bit pattern without disturbing the other bits.
  b. Complement the most significant bit of an 8-bit pattern without changing the other bits.
  c. Complement a pattern of 8 bits.
  d. Put a 0 in the least significant bit of an 8-bit pattern without disturbing the other bits.
  e. Put 1s in all but the most significant bit of an 8-bit pattern without disturbing the most significant bit.
  f. Filter out all of the green color component from an RGB bitmap image pixel in which the middle 8 bits of a 24-bit pattern store the green information.
  g. Invert all of the bits in a 24-bit RGB bitmap pixel.
  h. Set all the bits in a 24-bit RGB bitmap pixel to 1, indicating the color "white".

*36. Write and test short Python scripts to implement each of the parts of the previous question.

*37. Identify a logical operation (along with a corresponding mask) that, when applied to an input string of 8 bits, produces an output string of all 0s if and only if the input string is 10000001.

*38. Write and test a short Python script to implement the previous question.

*39. Describe a sequence of logical operations (along with their corresponding masks) that, when applied to an input string of 8 bits, produces an output byte of all 0s if the input string both begins and ends with 1s. Otherwise, the output should contain at least one 1.

*40. Write and test a short Python script to implement the previous question.

*41. What would be the result of performing a 4-bit left circular shift on the following bit patterns?
  a. 10101 b. 11110000 c. 001
  d. 101000 e. 00001

*42. What would be the result of performing a 2-bit right circular shift on the following bytes represented in hexadecimal notation (give your answers in hexadecimal notation)?
  a. 3F b. 0D
  c. FF d. 77

*43. a. What single instruction in the machine language of Appendix C could be used to accomplish a 5-bit right circular shift of register B?
  b. What single instruction in the machine language of Appendix C could be used to accomplish a 2-bit left circular shift of register B?

*44. Write a program in the machine language of Appendix C that reverses the contents of the memory cell at address 8C. (That is, the final bit pattern at address 8C when read from left to right should agree with the original pattern when read from right to left.)

*45. Write a program in the machine language of Appendix C that subtracts the value stored at A1 from the value stored at address A2 and places the result at address A0. Assume that the values are encoded in two's complement notation.

*46. High definition video can be delivered at a rate of 30 frames per second (fps) where each frame has a resolution of 1920 x 1080 pixels using 24 bits per pixel. Can an uncompressed video stream of this format be sent over a USB 1.1 serial port? USB 2.0 serial port? USB 3.0 serial port? (Note: The maximum speeds of USB 1.1, USB 2.0, and USB 3.0 serial ports are 12Mbps, 480Mbps, and 5Gbps respectively.)

*47. Suppose a person is typing forty words per minute at a keyboard. (A word is considered to be five characters.) If a machine executes 500 instructions every microsecond (millionth of a second), how many instructions does the machine execute during the time between the typing of two consecutive characters?

*48. How many bits per second must a keyboard transmit to keep up with a typist typing forty words per minute? (Assume each character is encoded in ASCII and each word consists of six characters.)

*49. Suppose the machine described in Appendix C communicates with a printer using the technique of memory-mapped I/O. Suppose also that address FF is used to send characters to the printer, and address FE is used to receive information about the printer's status. In particular, suppose the least significant bit at the address FE indicates whether the printer is ready to receive another character (with a 0 indicating "not ready" and a 1 indicating "ready"). Starting at address 00, write a machine language routine that waits until the printer is ready for another character and then sends the character represented by the bit pattern in register 5 to the printer.

*50. Write a program in the machine language described in Appendix C that places 0s in all the memory cells from address A0 through C0 but is small enough to fit in the memory cells from address 00 through 13 (hexadecimal).

*51. Suppose a machine has 200 GB of storage space available on a hard disk and receives data over a broadband connection at the rate of 15 Mbps. At this rate, how long will it take to fill the available storage space?

*52. Suppose a satellite system is being used to receive a serial data stream at 250 Kbps. If a burst of atmospheric interference lasts 6.96 seconds, how many data bits will be affected?

*53. Suppose you are given 32 processors, each capable of finding the sum of two multidigit numbers in a millionth of a second. Describe how parallel processing techniques can be applied to find the sum of 64 numbers in only six-millionths of a second. How much time does a single processor require to find this same sum?

*54. Summarize the difference between a CISC architecture and a RISC architecture.

*55. Identify two approaches to increasing throughput.

*56. Describe how the average of a collection of numbers can be computed more rapidly with a multiprocessor machine than a single processor machine.

*57. Write and test a Python script that reads in a floating-point radius of a circle and outputs the circumference and area of the circle.

*58. Write and test a Python script that reads in a character string and an integer and outputs the character string repeated the number of times given by the integer.

*59. Write and test a Python script that reads in two floating-point side lengths of a right triangle and outputs the hypotenuse length, perimeter, and area.

Social Issues

The following questions are intended as a guide to the ethical/social/legal issues associated with the field of computing. The goal is not merely to answer these questions. You should also consider why you answered as you did and whether your justifications are consistent from one question to the next.

1. Suppose a computer manufacturer develops a new machine architecture. To what extent should the company be allowed to own that architecture? What policy would be best for society?
2. In a sense, the year 1923 marked the birth of what many now call *planned obsolescence*. This was the year that General Motors, led by Alfred Sloan, introduced the automobile industry to the concept of model years. The idea was to increase sales by changing styling rather than necessarily introducing a better automobile. Sloan is quoted as saying, "We want to make you dissatisfied with your current car so you will buy a new one." To what extent is this marketing ploy used today in the computer industry?
3. We often think in terms of how computer technology has changed our society. Many argue, however, that this technology has often kept changes from occurring by allowing old systems to survive and, in some cases, become more entrenched. For example, would a central government's role in society have survived without computer technology? To what extent would centralized authority be present today had computer technology not been available? To what extent would we be better or worse off without computer technology?
4. Is it ethical for an individual to take the attitude that he or she does not need to know anything about the internal details of a machine because someone else will build it, maintain it, and fix any problems that arise? Does your answer depend on whether the machine is a computer, automobile, nuclear power plant, or toaster?
5. Suppose a manufacturer produces a computer chip and later discovers a flaw in its design. Suppose further that the manufacturer corrects the flaw in future production but decides to keep the original flaw a secret and does not recall the chips already shipped, reasoning that none of the chips already in use are being used in an application in which the flaw will have consequences. Is anyone hurt by the manufacturer's decision? Is the manufacturer's decision justified if no one is hurt and the decision keeps the manufacturer from losing money and possibly having to lay off employees?
6. Does advancing technology provide cures for heart disease or is it a source of a sedentary life style that contributes to heart disease?
7. It is easy to imagine financial or navigational disasters that may occur as the result of arithmetic errors due to overflow and truncation problems. What consequences could result from errors in image storage systems due to loss of image details (perhaps in fields such as reconnaissance or medical diagnosis)?
8. ARM Holdings is a small company that designs the processors for a wide variety of consumer electronic devices. It does not manufacture any of the processors; instead the designs are licensed to semiconductor vendors (such as Qualcomm, Samsung, and Texas Instruments) who pay a royalty for each unit produced. This business model spreads the high cost of research and

development of computer processors across the entire consumer electronic market. Today, over 95 percent of all cellular phones (not just smartphones), over 40 percent of all digital cameras, and 25 percent of digital TVs use an ARM processor. Furthermore, ARM processors are found in mini-notebooks, MP3 players, game controllers, electronic book readers, navigation systems, and the list goes on. Given this, do you consider this company to be a monopoly? Why or why not? Because consumer devices play an ever-increasing role in today's society, is the dependency on this little-known company good, or does it raise concerns?

Additional Reading

Carpinelli, J. D. *Computer Systems Organization and Architecture.* Boston, MA: Addison-Wesley, 2001.

Comer, D. E. *Essentials of Computer Architecture.* Upper Saddle River, NJ: Prentice-Hall, 2005.

Dandamudi, S P. *Guide to RISC Processors for Programmers and Engineers.* New York: Springer, 2005.

Furber, S. *ARM System-on-Chip Architecture,* 2nd ed. Boston, MA: Addison Wesley, 2000.

Hamacher, V. C., Z. G. Vranesic, and S. G. Zaky. *Computer Organization,* 5th ed. New York: McGraw-Hill, 2002.

Knuth, D. E. *The Art of Computer Programming, Vol. 1,* 3rd ed. Boston, MA: Addison-Wesley, 1998.

Murdocca, M. J., and V. P. Heuring. *Computer Architecture and Organization: An Integrated Approach.* New York: Wiley, 2007.

Stallings, W. *Computer Organization and Architecture,* 9th ed. Upper Saddle River, NJ: Prentice-Hall, 2012.

Tanenbaum, A. S. *Structured Computer Organization,* 6th ed. Upper Saddle River, NJ: Prentice-Hall, 2012.

CHAPTER 3

Operating Systems

In this chapter we study operating systems, which are software packages that coordinate a computer's internal activities as well as oversee its communication with the outside world. It is a computer's operating system that transforms the computer hardware into a useful tool. Our goal is to understand what operating systems do and how they do it. Such a background is central to being an enlightened computer user.

**Asterisks indicate suggestions for optional sections.*

An **operating system** is the software that controls the overall operation of a computer. It provides the means by which a user can store and retrieve files, provides the interface by which a user can request the execution of programs, and provides the environment necessary to execute the programs requested.

Perhaps the best known example of an operating system is Windows, which is provided in numerous versions by Microsoft and widely used in the PC arena. Another well-established example is UNIX, which is a popular choice for larger computer systems as well as PCs. In fact, UNIX is the core of two other popular operating systems: Mac OS, which is the operating system provided by Apple for its range of Mac machines, and Solaris, which was developed by Sun Microsystems (now owned by Oracle). Still another example of an operating system found on both large and small machines is Linux, which was originally developed noncommercially by computer enthusiasts and is now available through many commercial sources, including IBM.

For casual computer users, the differences between operating systems are largely cosmetic. For computing professionals, different operating systems can represent major changes in the tools they work with or the philosophy they follow in disseminating and maintaining their work. Nevertheless, at their core all mainstream operating systems address the same kinds of problems that computing experts have faced for more than half a century.

3.1 The History of Operating Systems

Today's operating systems are large, complex software packages that have grown from humble beginnings. The computers of the 1940s and 1950s were not very flexible or efficient. Machines occupied entire rooms. Program execution required significant preparation of equipment in terms of mounting magnetic tapes, placing punched cards in card readers, setting switches, and so on. The execution of each program, called a **job,** was handled as an isolated activity—the machine was prepared for executing the program, the program was executed, and then all the tapes, punched cards, etc. had to be retrieved before the next program preparation could begin. When several users needed to share a machine, sign-up sheets were provided so that users could reserve the machine for blocks of time. During the time period allocated to a user, the machine was totally under that user's control. The session usually began with program setup, followed by short periods of program execution. It was often completed in a hurried effort to do just one more thing ("It will only take a minute") while the next user was impatiently starting to set up.

In such an environment, operating systems began as systems for simplifying program setup and for streamlining the transition between jobs. One early development was the separation of users and equipment, which eliminated the physical transition of people in and out of the computer room. For this purpose a computer operator was hired to operate the machine. Anyone wanting a program run was required to submit it, along with any required data and special directions about the program's requirements, to the operator and return later for the results. The operator, in turn, loaded these materials into the machine's mass storage where a program called the operating system could read and execute them one at a time. This was the beginning of **batch processing**—the execution of jobs by collecting them in a single batch, then executing them without further interaction with the user.

In batch processing systems, the jobs residing in mass storage wait for execution in a **job queue** (Figure 3.1). A **queue** is a storage organization in which objects (in this case, jobs) are ordered in **first-in, first-out** (abbreviated FIFO and pronounced "FI-foe") fashion. That is, the objects are removed from the queue in the order in which they arrived. In reality, most job queues do not rigorously follow the FIFO structure, since most operating systems provide for consideration of job priorities. As a result, a job waiting in the job queue can be bumped by a higher-priority job.

In early batch-processing systems, each job was accompanied by a set of instructions explaining the steps required to prepare the machine for that particular job. These instructions were encoded, using a system known as a job control language (JCL), and stored with the job in the job queue. When the job was selected for execution, the operating system printed these instructions at a printer where they could be read and followed by the computer operator. This communication between the operating system and the computer operator is still seen today, as witnessed by PC operating systems that report such errors as "network not available" and "printer not responding."

A major drawback to using a computer operator as an intermediary between a computer and its users is that the users have no interaction with their jobs once they are submitted to the operator. This approach is acceptable for some applications, such as payroll processing, in which the data and all processing decisions are established in advance. However, it is not acceptable when the user must interact with a program during its execution. Examples include reservation systems in which reservations and cancellations must be reported as they occur; word processing systems in which documents are developed in a dynamic write and rewrite manner; and computer games in which interaction with the machine is the central feature of the game.

To accommodate these needs, new operating systems were developed that allowed a program being executed to carry on a dialogue with the user through remote terminals—a feature known as **interactive processing** (Figure 3.2). (A terminal consisted of little more than an electronic typewriter by which the user could type input and read the computer's response that was printed on paper. Today terminals have evolved into more sophisticated devices called workstations and even into complete PCs that can function as stand-alone computers when desired.)

Figure 3.1 Batch processing

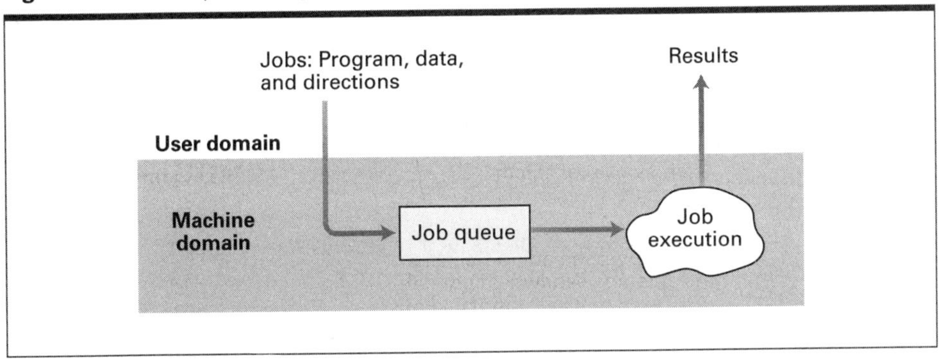

Figure 3.2 Interactive processing

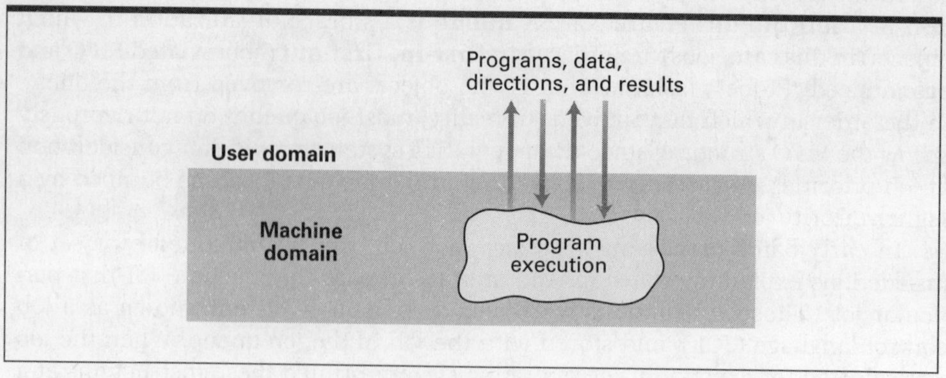

Paramount to successful interactive processing is that the actions of the computer be sufficiently fast to coordinate with the needs of the user rather than forcing the user to conform to the machine's timetable. (The task of processing payroll can be scheduled to conform to the amount of time required by the computer, but using a word processor would be frustrating if the machine did not respond promptly as characters are typed.) In a sense, the computer is forced to execute tasks under a deadline, a process that became known as **real-time processing** in which the actions performed are said to occur in real-time. That is, to say that a computer performs a task in real time means that the computer performs the task in accordance with deadlines in its (external real-world) environment.

If interactive systems had been required to serve only one user at a time, real-time processing would have been no problem. But computers in the 1960s and 1970s were expensive, so each machine had to serve more than one user. In turn, it was common for several users, working at remote terminals, to seek interactive service from a machine at the same time, and real-time considerations presented obstacles. If the operating system insisted on executing only one job at a time, only one user would receive satisfactory real-time service.

The solution to this problem was to design operating systems that provided service to multiple users at the same time: a feature called **time-sharing.** One means of implementing time-sharing is to apply the technique called **multiprogramming** in which time is divided into intervals and then the execution of each job is restricted to only one interval at a time. At the end of each interval, the current job is temporarily set aside and another is allowed to execute during the next interval. By rapidly shuffling the jobs back and forth in this manner, the illusion of several jobs executing simultaneously is created. Depending on the types of jobs being executed, early time-sharing systems were able to provide acceptable real-time processing to as many as 30 users simultaneously. Today, multiprogramming techniques are used in single-user as well as multiuser systems, although in the former the result is usually called **multitasking.** That is, time-sharing refers to multiple users sharing access to a common computer, whereas multitasking refers to one user executing numerous tasks simultaneously.

With the development of multiuser, time-sharing operating systems, a typical computer installation was configured as a large central computer connected to numerous workstations. From these workstations, users could communicate directly with the computer from outside the computer room rather than submitting requests to a computer operator. Commonly used programs were stored in the machine's mass storage devices, and operating systems were designed to execute these programs as requested from the workstations. In turn, the role of a computer operator as an intermediary between the users and the computer begins to fade.

Today, the existence of a computer operator has essentially disappeared, especially in the arena of personal computers where the computer user assumes all of the responsibilities of computer operation. Even most large computer installations run essentially unattended. Indeed, the job of computer operator has given way to that of a system administrator who manages the computer system—obtaining and overseeing the installation of new equipment and software, enforcing local regulations such as the issuing of new accounts and establishing mass storage space limits for the various users, and coordinating efforts to resolve problems that arise in the system—rather than operating the machines in a hands-on manner.

In short, operating systems have grown from simple programs that retrieved and executed programs one at a time into complex systems that coordinate time-sharing, maintain programs and data files in the machine's mass storage devices, and respond directly to requests from the computer's users.

But the evolution of operating systems continues. The development of multiprocessor machines has led to operating systems that provide time-sharing/multitasking capabilities by assigning different tasks to different processors as well as by sharing the time of each single processor. These operating systems must wrestle with such problems as **load balancing** (dynamically allocating tasks to the various processors so that all processors are used efficiently) as well as **scaling** (breaking tasks into a number of subtasks compatible with the number of processors available).

Moreover, the advent of computer networks in which numerous machines are connected over great distances has led to the creation of software systems to coordinate the network's activities. Thus the field of networking (which we will study in Chapter 4) is in many ways an extension of the subject of operating systems—the goal being to manage resources across many users on many machines rather than a single, isolated computer.

What's in a Smartphone?

As cell phones have become more powerful, it has become possible for them to offer services well beyond simply processing voice calls. A typical **smartphone** can now be used to text message, browse the Web, provide directions, view multimedia content—in short, it can be used to provide many of the same services as a traditional PC. As such, smartphones require full-fledged operating systems, not only to manage the limited resources of the smartphone hardware, but also to provide features that support the rapidly expanding collection of smartphone application software. The battle for dominance in the smartphone operating system market place promises to be fierce and will likely be settled on the basis of which system can provide the most imaginative features at the best price. Competitors in the smartphone operating system arena include Apple's iPhone OS, Research In Motion's BlackBerry OS, Microsoft's Windows Phone, Nokia's Symbian OS, and Google's Android.

Still another direction of research in operating systems focuses on devices that are dedicated to specific tasks such as medical devices, vehicle electronics, home appliances, cell phones, or other hand-held computers. The computer systems found in these devices are known as **embedded systems.** Embedded operating systems are often expected to conserve battery power, meet demanding real-time deadlines, or operate continuously with little or no human oversight. Successes in this endeavor are marked by systems such as VxWORKS, developed by Wind River Systems and used in the Mars Exploration Rovers named Spirit and Opportunity; Windows CE (also known as Pocket PC) developed by Microsoft; and Palm OS developed by PalmSource, Inc., especially for use in hand-held devices.

Questions & Exercises

1. Identify examples of queues. In each case, indicate any situations that violate the FIFO structure.
2. Which of the following activities require real-time processing?
   a. Printing mailing labels
   b. Playing a computer game
   c. Displaying numbers on a smartphone screen as they are dialed
   d. Executing a program that predicts the state of next year's economy
   e. Playing an MP3 recording
3. What is the difference between embedded systems and PCs?
4. What is the difference between time-sharing and multitasking?

3.2 Operating System Architecture

To understand the composition of a typical operating system, we first consider the complete spectrum of software found within a typical computer system. Then we will concentrate on the operating system itself.

A Software Survey

We approach our survey of the software found on a typical computer system by presenting a scheme for classifying software. Such classification schemes invariably place similar software units in different classes in the same manner as the assignment of time zones dictates that nearby communities must set their clocks an hour apart even though there is no significant difference between the occurrence of sunrise and sunset. Moreover, in the case of software classification, the dynamics of the subject and the lack of a definitive authority lead to contradictory terminology. For example, users of Microsoft's Windows operating systems will find groups of programs called "Accessories" and "Administrative Tools" that include software from what we will call the application and utility classes. The following taxonomy should therefore be viewed as a means of gaining a foothold in an extensive, dynamic subject rather than as a statement of universally accepted fact.

Let us begin by dividing a machine's software into two broad categories: **application software** and **system software** (Figure 3.3). Application software consists of the programs for performing tasks particular to the machine's utilization. A machine used to maintain the inventory for a manufacturing company will contain different application software from that found on a machine used by an electrical engineer. Examples of application software include spreadsheets, database systems, desktop publishing systems, accounting systems, program development software, and games.

In contrast to application software, system software performs those tasks that are common to computer systems in general. In a sense, the system software provides the infrastructure that the application software requires, in much the same manner as a nation's infrastructure (government, roads, utilities, financial institutions, etc.) provides the foundation on which its citizens rely for their individual lifestyles.

Within the class of system software are two categories: One is the operating system itself and the other consists of software units collectively known as **utility software.** The majority of an installation's utility software consists of programs for performing activities that are fundamental to computer installations but not included in the operating system. In a sense, utility software consists of software units that extend (or perhaps customize) the capabilities of the operating system. For example, the ability to format a magnetic disk or to copy a file from a magnetic disk to a CD is often not implemented within the operating system itself but instead is provided by means of a utility program. Other instances of utility software include software to compress and decompress data, software for playing multimedia presentations, and software for handling network communication.

Implementing certain activities as utility software allows system software to be customized to the needs of a particular installation more easily than if they were included in the operating system. Indeed, it is common to find companies or

Figure 3.3 Software classification

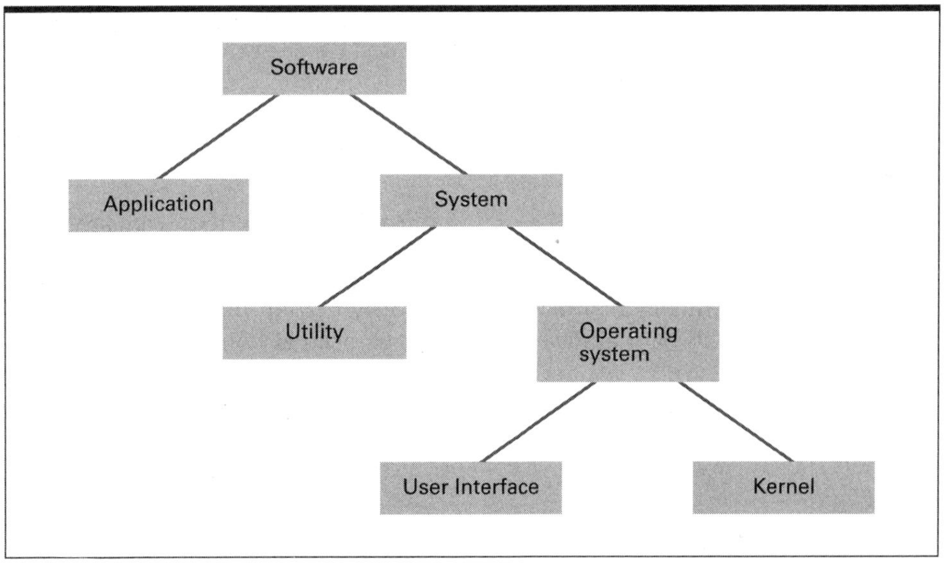

Linux

For the computer enthusiast who wants to experiment with the internal components of an operating system, there is Linux. Linux is an operating system originally designed by Linus Torvalds while a student at the University of Helsinki. It is a nonproprietary product and available, along with its source code (see Chapter 6) and documentation, without charge. Because it is freely available in source code form, it has become popular among computer hobbyists, students of operating systems, and programmers in general. Moreover, Linux is recognized as one of the more reliable operating systems available today. For this reason, several companies now package and market versions of Linux in an easily usable form, and these products are now challenging the long-established commercial operating systems on the market. You can learn more about Linux from the website at www.linux.org.

individuals who have modified, or added to, the utility software that was originally provided with their machine's operating system.

Unfortunately, the distinction between application software and utility software can be vague. From our point of view, the difference is whether the package is part of the computer's "software infrastructure." Thus a new application may evolve to the status of a utility if it becomes a fundamental tool. When still a research project, software for communicating over the Internet was considered application software; today such tools are fundamental to most PC usage and would therefore be classified as utility software.

The distinction between utility software and the operating system is equally vague. In particular, antitrust lawsuits in the United States and Europe have been founded on questions regarding whether units such as browsers and media players are components of Microsoft's operating systems or utilities that Microsoft has included merely to squash competition.

Components of an Operating System

Let us focus now on components that are within the domain of an operating system. In order to perform the actions requested by the computer's users, an operating system must be able to communicate with those users. The portion of an operating system that handles this communication is often called the **user interface.** Older user interfaces, called **shells,** communicated with users through textual messages using a keyboard and monitor screen. More modern systems perform this task by means of a **graphical user interface (GUI**—pronounced "GOO–ee") in which objects to be manipulated, such as files and programs, are represented pictorially on the display as icons. These systems allow users to issue commands by using one of several common input devices. For example, a computer mouse, with one or more buttons, can be used to click or drag icons on the screen. In place of a mouse, special-purpose pointing devices or styluses are often used by graphic artists or on several types of handheld devices. More recently, advances in fine-grained touch screens allow users to manipulate icons directly with their fingers. Whereas today's GUIs use two-dimensional image projection systems, three-dimensional interfaces that allow human users to communicate with computers by means of 3D projection systems, tactile sensory devices, and surround sound audio reproduction systems are subjects of current research.

Although an operating system's user interface plays an important role in establishing a machine's functionality, this framework merely acts as an intermediary between the computer's user and the real heart of the operating system (Figure 3.4). This distinction between the user interface and the internal parts of the operating system is emphasized by the fact that some operating systems allow a user to select among different interfaces to obtain the most comfortable interaction for that particular user. Users of the UNIX operating system, for example, can select among a variety of shells including the Bourne shell, the C shell, and the Korn shell, as well as a GUI called X11. The earliest versions of Microsoft Windows were a GUI application program that could be loaded from the MS-DOS operating system's command shell. The DOS cmd.exe shell can still be found as a utility program in the latest versions of Windows, although this interface is almost never required by casual users. Similarly, Apple's OS X retains a Terminal utility shell that hearkens back to that system's UNIX ancestors.

An important component within today's GUI shells is the **window manager,** which allocates blocks of space on the screen, called windows, and keeps track of which application is associated with each window. When an application wants to display something on the screen, it notifies the window manager, and the window manager places the desired image in the window assigned to the application. In turn, when a mouse button is clicked, it is the window manager that computes the mouse's location on the screen and notifies the appropriate application of the mouse action. Window managers are responsible for what is generally called the "style" of a GUI, and most managers offer a range of configurable choices. Linux users even have a range of choices for a window manager, with popular choices including KDE and Gnome.

In contrast to an operating system's user interface, the internal part of an operating system is called the **kernel.** An operating system's kernel contains those software components that perform the very basic functions required by the computer installation. One such unit is the **file manager,** whose job is to coordinate the use of the machine's mass storage facilities. More precisely, the file manager maintains records of all the files stored in mass storage, including where

Figure 3.4 The user interface acts as an intermediary between users and the operating system's kernel

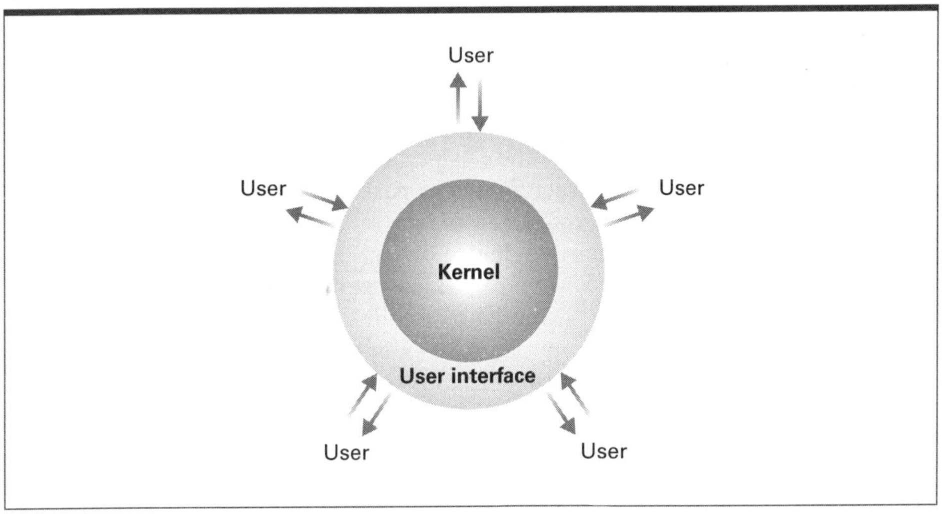

each file is located, which users are allowed to access the various files, and which portions of mass storage are available for new files or extensions to existing files. These records are kept on the individual storage medium containing the related files so that each time the medium is placed online, the file manager can retrieve them and thus know what is stored on that particular medium.

For the convenience of the machine's users, most file managers allow files to be grouped into a bundle called a **directory** or **folder.** This approach allows a user to organize his or her files according to their purposes by placing related files in the same directory. Moreover, by allowing directories to contain other directories, called subdirectories, a hierarchical organization can be constructed. For example, a user may create a directory called `MyRecords` that contains subdirectories called `FinancialRecords`, `MedicalRecords`, and `HouseHoldRecords`. Within each of these subdirectories could be files that fall within that particular category. (Users of a Windows operating system can ask the file manager to display the current collection of folders by executing the utility program Windows Explorer.)

A chain of directories within directories is called a **directory path.** Paths are often expressed by listing the directories along the path separated by slashes. For instance, `animals/prehistoric/dinosaurs` would represent the path starting at the directory named `animals`, passing through its subdirectory named `prehistoric`, and terminating in the sub-subdirectory `dinosaurs`. (For Windows users the slashes in such a path expression are reversed as in `animals\prehistoric\dinosaurs`.)

Any access to a file by other software units is obtained at the discretion of the file manager. The procedure begins by requesting that the file manager grant access to the file through a procedure known as opening the file. If the file manager approves the requested access, it provides the information needed to find and to manipulate the file.

Another component of the kernel consists of a collection of **device drivers,** which are the software units that communicate with the controllers (or at times, directly with peripheral devices) to carry out operations on the peripheral devices attached to the machine. Each device driver is uniquely designed for its particular type of device (such as a printer, disk drive, or monitor) and translates generic requests into the more technical steps required by the device assigned to that driver. For example, a device driver for a printer contains the software for reading and decoding that particular printer's status word as well as all the other handshaking details. Thus, other software components do not have to deal with those technicalities in order to print a file. Instead, the other components can merely rely on the device driver software to print the file, and let the device driver take care of the details. In this manner, the design of the other software units can be independent of the unique characteristics of particular devices. The result is a generic operating system that can be customized for particular peripheral devices by merely installing the appropriate device drivers.

Still another component of an operating system's kernel is the **memory manager,** which is charged with the task of coordinating the machine's use of main memory. Such duties are minimal in an environment in which a computer is asked to perform only one task at a time. In these cases, the program for performing the current task is placed at a predetermined location in main memory, executed, and then replaced by the program for performing the next task. However, in multiuser or multitasking environments in which the computer is asked to address many needs at the same time, the duties of the memory manager are extensive. In these cases, many programs and blocks of data must reside in main memory concurrently. Thus, the memory manager must find and assign memory space for these needs and ensure that the actions of each program are restricted to the program's allotted space. Moreover, as the needs of different activities come and go, the memory manager must keep track of those memory areas no longer occupied.

The task of the memory manager is complicated further when the total main memory space required exceeds the space actually available in the computer. In this case the memory manager may create the illusion of additional memory space by rotating programs and data back and forth between main memory and mass storage (a technique called **paging**). Suppose, for example, that a main memory of 8GB is required but the computer only has 4GB. To create the illusion of the larger memory space, the memory manager reserves 4GB of storage space on a magnetic disk. There it records the bit patterns that would be stored in main memory if main memory had an actual capacity of 8GB. This data is divided into uniform sized units called **pages,** which are typically a few KB in size. Then the memory manager shuffles these pages back and forth between main memory and mass storage so that the pages that are needed at any given time are actually present in the 4GB of main memory. The result is that the computer is able to function as though it actually had 8GB of main memory. This large "fictional" memory space created by paging is called **virtual memory.**

Two additional components within the kernel of an operating system are the **scheduler** and **dispatcher,** which we will study in the next section. For now we merely note that in a multiprogramming system the scheduler determines which activities are to be considered for execution, and the dispatcher controls the allocation of time to these activities.

Getting It Started

We have seen that an operating system provides the software infrastructure required by other software units, but we have not considered how the operating system gets started. This is accomplished through a procedure known as

Firmware

In addition to the boot loader, a PC's ROM contains a collection of software routines for performing fundamental input/output activities such as receiving information from the keyboard, displaying messages on the computer screen, and reading data from mass storage. Being stored in nonvolatile memory such as FlashROM, this software is not immutably etched into the silicon of the machine—the hardware—but is also not as readily changeable as the rest of the programs in mass storage—the software. The term **firmware** was coined to describe this middle ground. Firmware routines can be used by the boot loader to perform I/O activities before the operating system becomes functional. For example, they are used to communicate with the computer user before the boot process actually begins and to report errors during booting. Widely used firmware systems include the BIOS (Basic Input/Output System) long used in PCs, the newer EFI (Extensible Firmware Interface), Sun's Open Firmware (now a product of Oracle), and the CFE (Common Firmware Environment) used in many embedded devices.

boot strapping (often shortened to **booting**) that is performed by a computer each time it is turned on. It is this procedure that transfers the operating system from mass storage (where it is permanently stored) into main memory (which is essentially empty when the machine is first turned on). To understand the boot strap process and the reason it is necessary, we begin by considering the machine's CPU.

A CPU is designed so that its program counter starts with a particular predetermined address each time the CPU is turned on. It is at this location that the CPU expects to find the beginning of the program to be executed. Conceptually, then, all that is needed is to store the operating system at this location. However, for technical reasons, a computer's main memory is typically constructed from volatile technologies—meaning that the memory loses the data stored in it when the computer is turned off. Thus, the contents of main memory must be replenished each time the computer is restarted.

In short, we need a program (preferably the operating system) to be present in main memory when the computer is first turned on, but the computer's volatile memory is erased each time the machine is turned off. To resolve this dilemma, a small portion of a computer's main memory where the CPU expects to find its initial program is constructed from special nonvolatile memory cells. Such memory is known as **read-only memory (ROM)** because its contents can be read but not altered. As an analogy, you can think of storing bit patterns in ROM as blowing tiny fuses (some blown open—ones—and some blown closed—zeros), although the technology used is more advanced. More precisely, most ROM in today's PCs is constructed with flash memory technology (which means that it is not strictly ROM because it can be altered under special circumstances).

In a general-purpose computer, a program called the **boot loader** is permanently stored in the machine's ROM. This, then, is the program that is initially executed when the machine is turned on. The instructions in the boot loader direct the CPU to transfer the operating system from a predetermined location into the volatile area of main memory (Figure 3.5). Modern boot loaders can copy an operating system into main memory from a variety of locations. For example, in embedded systems, such as smartphones, the operating system is copied from special flash (nonvolatile) memory; in the case of small workstations at large companies or universities, the operating system may be copied from a distant machine over a network. Once the operating system has been placed in main memory, the boot loader directs the CPU to execute a jump instruction to that area of memory. At this point, the operating system takes over and begins controlling the machine's activities. The overall process of executing the boot loader and thus starting the operating system is called **booting** the computer.

You may ask why desktop computers are not provided with enough ROM to hold the entire operating system so that booting from mass storage would not be necessary. While this is feasible for embedded systems with small operating systems, devoting large blocks of main memory in general-purpose computers to nonvolatile storage is not efficient with today's technology. Moreover, computer operating systems undergo frequent updates in order to maintain security and keep abreast of new and improved device drivers for the latest hardware. While it is possible to update operating systems and boot loaders stored in ROM (often

Figure 3.5 The booting process

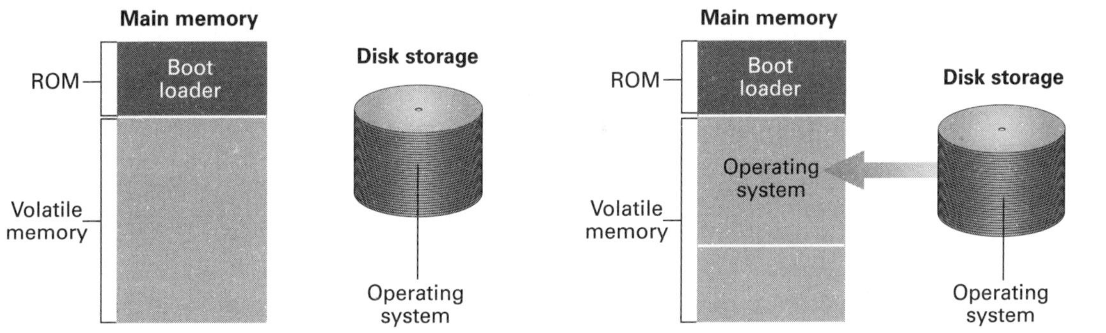

Step 1: Machine starts by executing the boot loader program already in memory. Operating system is stored in mass storage.

Step 2: Boot loader program directs the transfer of the operating system into main memory and then transfers control to it.

called a **firmware update**), the technological limits make mass storage the most common choice for more traditional computer systems.

In closing we should point out that understanding the boot process as well as the distinctions between an operating system, utility software, and application software allows us to comprehend the overall methodology under which most general-purpose computer systems operate. When such a machine is first turned on, the boot loader loads and activates the operating system. The user then makes requests to the operating system regarding the utility or application programs to be executed. As each utility or application is terminated, the user is put back in touch with the operating system, at which time the user can make additional requests. Learning to use such a system is therefore a two-layered process. In addition to learning the details of the specific utility or application desired, one must learn enough about the machine's operating system to navigate among the applications.

Questions & Exercises

1. List the components of a typical operating system and summarize the role of each in a single phrase.
2. What is the difference between application software and utility software?
3. What is virtual memory?
4. Summarize the booting procedure.

3.3 Coordinating the Machine's Activities

In this section we consider how an operating system coordinates the execution of application software, utility software, and units within the operating system itself. We begin with the concept of a process.

The Concept of a Process

One of the most fundamental concepts of modern operating systems is the distinction between a program and the activity of executing a program. The former is a static set of directions, whereas the latter is a dynamic activity whose properties change as time progresses. (This distinction is analogous to a piece of sheet music, sitting inert in a book on the shelf, versus a musician performing that piece by taking actions that the sheet music describes.) The activity of executing a program under the control of the operating system is known as a **process.** Associated with a process is the current status of the activity, called the **process state.** This state includes the current position in the program being executed (the value of the program counter) as well as the values in the other CPU registers and the associated memory cells. Roughly speaking, the process state is a snapshot of the machine at a particular time. At different times during the execution of a program (at different times in a process) different snapshots (different process states) will be observed.

Unlike a musician, who normally tries to play only one musical piece at a time, typical time-sharing/multitasking computers are running many processes, all competing for the computer's resources. It is the task of the operating system to manage these processes so that each process has the resources (peripheral devices, space in main memory, access to files, and access to a CPU) that it needs, that independent processes do not interfere with one another, and that processes that need to exchange information are able to do so.

Process Administration

The tasks associated with coordinating the execution of processes are handled by the scheduler and dispatcher within the operating system's kernel. The scheduler maintains a record of the processes present in the computer system, introduces new processes to this pool, and removes completed processes from the pool. Thus when a user requests the execution of an application, it is the scheduler that adds the execution of that application to the pool of current processes.

To keep track of all the processes, the scheduler maintains a block of information in main memory called the **process table.** Each time the execution of a program is requested, the scheduler creates a new entry for that process in the process table. This entry contains such information as the memory area assigned to the process (obtained from the memory manager), the priority of the process, and whether the process is ready or waiting. A process is **ready** if it is in a state in which its progress can continue; it is **waiting** if its progress is currently delayed until some external event occurs, such as the completion of a mass storage operation, the pressing of a key at the keyboard, or the arrival of a message from another process.

The dispatcher is the component of the kernel that oversees the execution of the scheduled processes. In a time-sharing/multitasking system this task is accomplished by **multiprogramming**; that is, dividing time into short segments, each called a **time slice** (typically measured in milliseconds or microseconds), and then switching the CPU's attention among the processes as each is allowed to execute for one time slice (Figure 3.6). The procedure of changing from one process to another is called a **process switch** (or a **context switch**).

Each time the dispatcher awards a time slice to a process, it initiates a timer circuit that will indicate the end of the slice by generating a signal called an **interrupt.** The CPU reacts to this interrupt signal in much the same way that you react when interrupted from a task. You stop what you are doing, record where you are in the task (so that you will be able to return at a later time), and take care of the interrupting entity. When the CPU receives an interrupt signal, it completes its current machine cycle, saves its position in the current process, and begins executing a program, called an **interrupt handler,** which is stored at a predetermined location in main memory. This interrupt handler is a part of the dispatcher, and it describes how the dispatcher should respond to the interrupt signal.

Thus, the effect of the interrupt signal is to preempt the current process and transfer control back to the dispatcher. At this point, the dispatcher selects the process from the process table that has the highest priority among the ready processes (as determined by the scheduler), restarts the timer circuit, and allows the selected process to begin its time slice.

Paramount to the success of a multiprogramming system is the ability to stop, and later restart, a process. If you are interrupted while reading a book, your ability to continue reading at a later time depends on your ability to remember your location in the book as well as the information that you had accumulated to that point. In short, you must be able to re-create the environment that was present immediately prior to the interruption.

In the case of a process, the environment that must be re-created is the process's state, which as already mentioned, includes the value of the program counter as well as the contents of the registers and pertinent memory cells. CPUs designed for multiprogramming systems incorporate the task of saving this information as part of the CPU's reaction to the interrupt signal. These CPUs

Figure 3.6 Multiprogramming between process A and process B

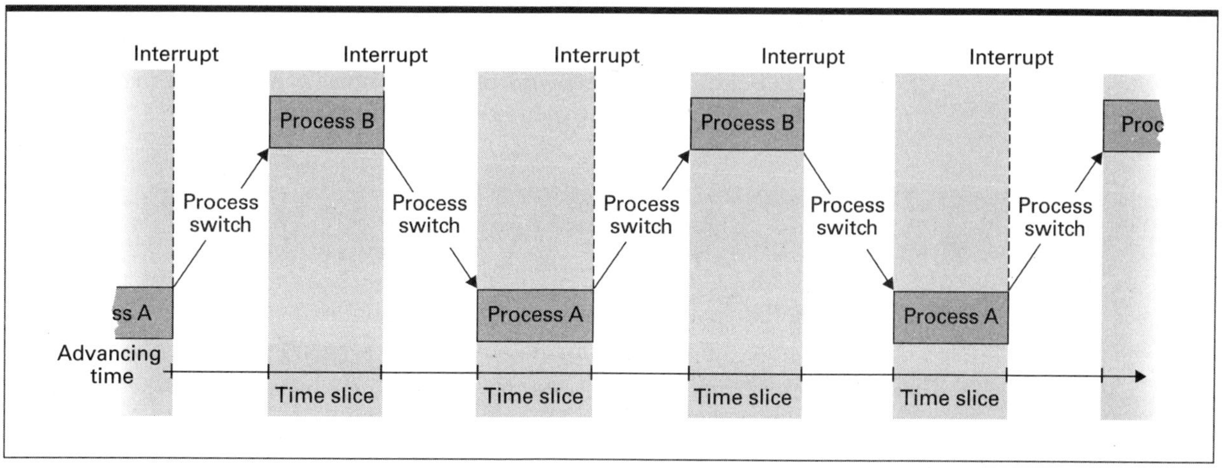

Interrupts

The use of interrupts for terminating time slices, as described in the text, is only one of many applications of a computer's interrupt system. There are many situations in which an interrupt signal is generated, each with its own interrupt routine. Indeed, interrupts provide an important tool for coordinating a computer's actions with its environment. For example, both clicking a mouse and pressing a key on the keyboard generate interrupt signals that cause the CPU to set aside its current activity and address the cause of the interrupt.

To manage the task of recognizing and responding to incoming interrupts, the various interrupt signals are assigned priorities so that the more important tasks can be taken care of first. The highest priority interrupt is usually associated with a power failure. Such an interrupt signal is generated if the computer's power is unexpectedly disrupted. The associated interrupt routine directs the CPU through a series of "housekeeping" chores during the milliseconds before the voltage level drops below an operational level.

also tend to have machine-language instructions for reloading a previously saved state. Such features simplify the task of the dispatcher when performing a process switch and exemplify how the design of modern CPUs is influenced by the needs of today's operating systems.

In closing, we should note that the use of multiprogramming has been found to increase the overall efficiency of a machine. This is somewhat counterintuitive since the shuffling of processes required by multiprogramming introduces an overhead. However, without multiprogramming each process runs to completion before the next process begins, meaning that the time that a process is waiting for peripheral devices to complete tasks or for a user to make the next request is wasted. Multiprogramming allows this lost time to be given to another process. For example, if a process executes an I/O request, such as a request to retrieve data from a magnetic disk, the scheduler will update the process table to reflect that the process is waiting for an external event. In turn, the dispatcher will cease to award time slices to that process. Later (perhaps several hundred milliseconds), when the I/O request has been completed, the scheduler will update the process table to show that the process is ready, and thus that process will again compete for time slices. In short, progress on other tasks will be made while the I/O request is being performed, and thus the entire collection of tasks will be completed in less time than if executed in a sequential manner.

Questions & Exercises

1. Summarize the difference between a program and a process.
2. Summarize the steps performed by the CPU when an interrupt occurs.
3. In a multiprogramming system, how can high-priority processes be allowed to run faster than others?

4. If each time slice in a multiprogramming system is 50 milliseconds and each context switch requires at most a microsecond, how many processes can the machine service in a single second?
5. If each process uses its complete time slice in the machine in question 4, what fraction of the machine's time is spent actually performing processes? What would this fraction be if each process executed an I/O request after only a microsecond of its time slice?

3.4 Handling Competition Among Processes

An important task of an operating system is the allocation of the machine's resources to the processes in the system. Here we are using the term *resource* in a broad sense, including the machine's peripheral devices as well as features within the machine itself. The file manager allocates access to files as well and allocates mass storage space for the construction of new files; the memory manager allocates memory space; the scheduler allocates space in the process table; and the dispatcher allocates time slices. As with many problems in computer systems, this allocation task may appear simple at first glance. Below the surface, however, lie several subtleties that can lead to malfunctions in a poorly designed system. Remember, a machine does not think for itself; it merely follows directions. Thus, to construct reliable operating systems, we must develop algorithms that cover every possible contingency, regardless of how minuscule it may appear.

Semaphores

Let us consider a time-sharing/multitasking operating system controlling the activities of a computer with a single printer. If a process needs to print its results, it must request that the operating system give it access to the printer's device driver. At this point, the operating system must decide whether to grant this request, depending on whether the printer is already being used by another process. If it is not, the operating system should grant the request and allow the process to continue; otherwise, the operating system should deny the request and

Microsoft's Task Manager

You can gain insight to some of the internal activity of a Microsoft Windows operating system by executing the utility program called Task Manager. (Press the Ctrl, Alt, and Delete keys simultaneously.) In particular, by selecting the Processes tab in the Task Manager window, you can view the process table. Here is an experiment you can perform: Look at the process table before you activate any application program. (You may be surprised that so many processes are already in the table. These are necessary for the system's basic operation.) Now activate an application and confirm that an additional process has entered the table. You will also be able to see how much memory space was allocated to the process.

perhaps classify the process as a waiting process until the printer becomes available. After all, if two processes were given simultaneous access to the computer's printer, the results would be worthless to both.

To control access to the printer, the operating system must keep track of whether the printer has been allocated. One approach to this task would be to use a flag, which in this context refers to a bit in memory whose states are often referred to as *set* and *clear*, rather than 1 and 0. A clear flag (value 0) indicates that the printer is available and a set flag (value 1) indicates that the printer is currently allocated. On the surface, this approach seems well-founded. The operating system merely checks the flag each time a request for printer access is made. If it is clear, the request is granted and the operating system sets the flag. If the flag is set, the operating system makes the requesting process wait. Each time a process finishes with the printer, the operating system either allocates the printer to a waiting process or, if no process is waiting, merely clears the flag.

However, this simple flag system has a problem. The task of testing and possibly setting the flag may require several machine instructions. (The value of the flag must be retrieved from main memory, manipulated within the CPU, and finally stored back in memory.) It is therefore possible for a task to be interrupted after a clear flag has been detected but before the flag has been set. In particular, suppose the printer is currently available, and a process requests use of it. The flag is retrieved from main memory and found to be clear, indicating that the printer is available. However, at this point, the process is interrupted and another process begins its time slice. It too requests the use of the printer. Again, the flag is retrieved from main memory and found still clear because the previous process was interrupted before the operating system had time to set the flag in main memory. Consequently, the operating system allows the second process to begin using the printer. Later, the original process resumes execution where it left off, which is immediately after the operating system found the flag to be clear. Thus the operating system continues by setting the flag in main memory and granting the original process access to the printer. Two processes are now using the same printer.

The solution to this problem is to insist that the task of testing and possibly setting the flag be completed without interruption. One approach is to use the interrupt disable and interrupt enable instructions provided in most machine languages. When executed, an interrupt disable instruction causes future interrupts to be blocked, whereas an interrupt enable instruction causes the CPU to resume responding to interrupt signals. Thus, if the operating system starts the flag-testing routine with a disable interrupt instruction and ends it with an enable interrupt instruction, no other activity can interrupt the routine once it starts.

Another approach is to use the **test-and-set** instruction that is available in many machine languages. This instruction directs the CPU to retrieve the value of a flag, note the value received, and then set the flag—all within a single machine instruction. The advantage here is that because the CPU always completes an instruction before recognizing an interrupt, the task of testing and setting the flag cannot be split when it is implemented as a single instruction.

A properly implemented flag, as just described, is called a **semaphore,** in reference to the railroad signals used to control access to sections of track. In fact, semaphores are used in software systems in much the same way as they are in railway systems. Corresponding to the section of track that can contain only one train at a time is a sequence of instructions that should be executed by only one process at a time. Such a sequence of instructions is called a **critical region.** The requirement that only one process at a time be allowed to execute a critical region is known as **mutual exclusion.** In summary, a common way of obtaining mutual exclusion to a critical region is to guard the critical region with a semaphore. To enter the critical region, a process must find the semaphore clear and then set the semaphore before entering the critical region; then upon exiting the critical region, the process must clear the semaphore. If the semaphore is found in its set state, the process trying to enter the critical region must wait until the semaphore has been cleared.

Deadlock

Another problem that can arise during resource allocation is **deadlock,** the condition in which two or more processes are blocked from progressing because each is waiting for a resource that is allocated to another. For example, one process may have access to the computer's printer but be waiting for access to the computer's CD player, while another process has access to the CD player but is waiting for the printer. Another example occurs in systems in which processes are allowed to create new processes (an action called **forking** in the UNIX vernacular) to perform subtasks. If the scheduler has no space left in the process table and each process in the system must create an additional process before it can complete its task, then no process can continue. Such conditions, as in other settings (Figure 3.7), can severely degrade a system's performance.

Analysis of deadlock has revealed that it cannot occur unless all three of the following conditions are satisfied:

1. There is competition for nonsharable resources.
2. The resources are requested on a partial basis; that is, having received some resources, a process will return later to request more.
3. Once a resource has been allocated, it cannot be forcibly retrieved.

Figure 3.7 A deadlock resulting from competition for nonsharable railroad intersections

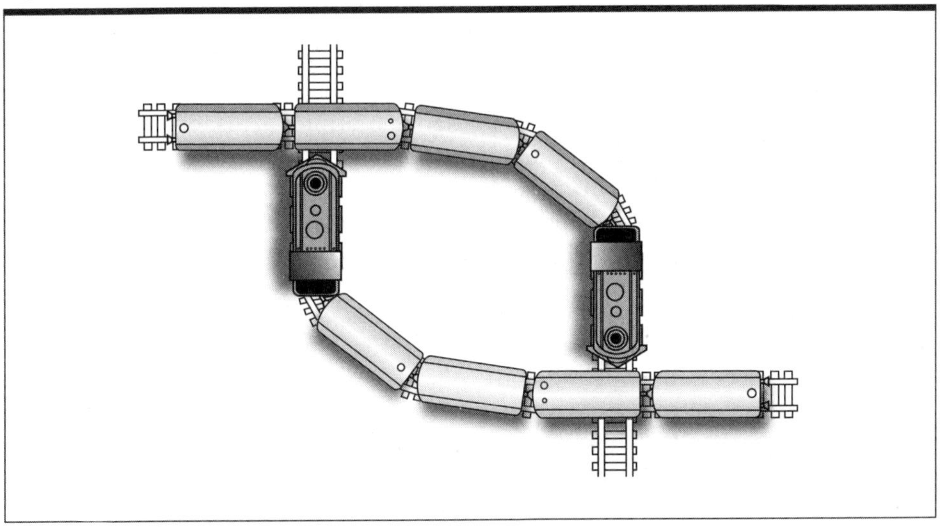

Python and Operating Systems

When a Python script is executed by a user, the operating system launches a new process to run the script. Such scripts are often applications, although they can also be considered utility software if they extend or customize the capabilities of the system. Python scripts interact with components of the operating system to accomplish their work, such as the file manager for reading and writing files, or the GUI or shell for providing user interactions. The Python module "os" provides a variety of predefined, system-agnostic functions for accessing common operating system features, such as forking new Python processes, or executing other utility or application programs.

The point of isolating these conditions is that the deadlock problem can be removed by attacking any one of the three. Techniques that attack the third condition fall into the category known as deadlock detection and correction schemes. In these cases, the occurrence of deadlock is considered so remote that no effort is made to avoid the problem. Instead, the approach is to detect it should it occur and then correct it by forcibly retrieving some of the allocated resources. Our example of a full process table might fall in this class. If deadlock should occur due to a full table, routines within the operating system (or perhaps a human administrator using his or her powers as "super user") can remove (the technical term is **kill**) some of the processes. This releases space in the process table, breaking the deadlock and allowing the remaining processes to continue their tasks.

Techniques that attack the first two conditions are known as deadlock avoidance schemes. One, for example, attacks the second condition by requiring each process to request all its resources at one time. Another scheme attacks the first condition, not by removing the competition directly but by converting nonsharable resources into sharable ones. For example, suppose the resource in question is a printer and a variety of processes require its use. Each time a process requests the printer, the operating system could grant the request. However, instead of connecting the process to the printer's device driver, the operating system would connect it to a device driver that stores the information to be printed in mass storage rather than sending it to the printer. Thus each process, thinking it has access to the printer, could execute in its normal way. Later, when the printer is available, the operating system could transfer the data from mass storage to the printer. In this manner, the operating system would make the nonsharable resource appear sharable by creating the illusion of more than one printer. This technique of holding data for output at a later but more convenient time is called **spooling.**

We have introduced spooling as a technique for granting several processes access to a common resource—a theme that has many variations. For example, a file manager could grant several processes access to the same file if the processes are merely reading data from the file, but conflicts can occur if more than one process tries to alter a file at the same time. Thus, a file manager may allocate file access according to the needs of the processes, allowing several processes to have read access but allowing only one to have write access. Other systems may divide the file into pieces so that different processes can alter different parts of the file concurrently. Each of these techniques, however, has subtleties that must be resolved to obtain a reliable system. How, for example, should those processes with only read access to a file be notified when a process with write access alters the file?

Multi-Core Operating Systems

Traditional time-sharing/multitasking systems give the illusion of executing many processes at once by switching rapidly between time slices faster than a human can perceive. Modern systems continue to multitask in this way, but in addition, the latest multi-core CPUs are genuinely capable of running two, four, or many more processes simultaneously. Unlike a group of single-core computers working together, a multi-core machine contains multiple independent processors (in this case called cores) that share the computer's peripherals, memory, and other resources. For a multi-core operating system, this means that the dispatcher and scheduler must consider which processes to execute on each core. With different processes running on different cores, handling competition among processes becomes more challenging because disabling interrupts on all cores whenever one needs to enter a critical region would be highly inefficient. Computer science has many active research areas related to building operating system mechanisms better suited to the new multi-core world.

Questions & Exercises

1. Suppose process A and process B are sharing time on the same machine, and each needs the same nonsharable resource for short periods of time. (For example, each process may be printing a series of independent, short reports.) Each process may then repeatedly acquire the resource, release it, and later request it again. What is a drawback to controlling access to the resource in the following manner:

   Begin by assigning a flag the value 0. If process A requests the resource and the flag is 0, grant the request. Otherwise, make process A wait. If process B requests the resource and the flag is 1, grant the request. Otherwise, make process B wait. Each time process A finishes with the resource, change the flag to 1. Each time process B finishes with the resource, change the flag to 0.

2. Suppose a two-lane road converges to one lane to pass through a tunnel. To coordinate the use of the tunnel, the following signal system has been installed:

   A car entering either end of the tunnel causes red lights above the tunnel entrances to be turned on. As the car exits the tunnel, the lights are turned off. If an approaching car finds a red light on, it waits until the light is turned off before entering the tunnel.

   What is the flaw in this system?

3. Suppose the following solutions have been proposed for removing the deadlock that occurs on a single-lane bridge when two cars meet. Identify which condition for deadlock given in the text is removed by each solution.

   a. Do not let a car onto the bridge until the bridge is empty.
   b. If cars meet, make one of them back up.
   c. Add a second lane to the bridge.

4. Suppose we represent each process in a multiprogramming system with a dot and draw an arrow from one dot to another if the process represented by the first dot is waiting for a (nonsharable) resource being used by the second. Mathematicians call the resulting picture a **directed graph.** What property of the directed graph is equivalent to deadlock in the system?

3.5 Security

Since the operating system oversees the activities in a computer, it is natural for it to play a vital role in maintaining security as well. In the broad sense, this responsibility manifests itself in multiple forms, one of which is reliability. If a flaw in the file manager causes the loss of part of a file, then the file was not secure. If a defect in the dispatcher leads to a system failure (often called a system crash) causing the loss of an hour's worth of typing, we would argue that our work was not secure. Thus the security of a computer system requires a well-designed, dependable operating system.

The development of reliable software is not a subject that is restricted to operating systems. It permeates the entire software development spectrum and constitutes the field of computer science known as software engineering, which we will study in Chapter 7. In this section, then, we focus on security problems that are more closely related to the specifics of operating systems.

Attacks from the Outside

An important task performed by operating systems is to protect the computer's resources from access by unauthorized personnel. In the case of computers used by multiple people, this is usually approached by means of establishing "accounts" for the various authorized users—an account being essentially a record within the operating system containing such entries as the user's name, password, and privileges to be granted to that user. The operating system can then use this information during each **login** procedure (a sequence of transactions in which the user establishes initial contact with a computer's operating system) to control access to the system.

Accounts are established by a person known as the **super user** or the **administrator.** This person gains highly privileged access to the operating system by identifying him- or herself as the administrator (usually by name and password) during the login procedure. Once this contact is established, the administrator can alter settings within the operating system, modify critical software packages, adjust the privileges granted to other users, and perform a variety of other maintenance activities that are denied normal users.

From this "lofty perch," the administrator is also able to monitor activity within the computer system in an effort to detect destructive behavior, whether malicious or accidental. To assist in this regard, numerous software utilities, called **auditing software,** have been developed that record and then analyze the activities taking place within the computer system. In particular, auditing software may expose a flood of attempts to login using incorrect passwords, indicating that an unauthorized user may be trying to gain access to the computer.

Auditing software may also identify activities within a user's account that do not conform to that user's past behavior, which may indicate that an unauthorized user has gained access to that account. (It is unlikely that a user who traditionally uses only word processing and spreadsheet software will suddenly begin to access highly technical software applications or try to execute utility packages that lie outside that user's privileges.)

Another culprit that auditing systems are designed to detect is the presence of **sniffing software**, which is software that, when left running on a computer, records activities and later reports them to a would-be intruder. An old, well-known example is a program that simulates the operating system's login procedure. Such a program can be used to trick authorized users into thinking they are communicating with the operating system, whereas they are actually supplying their names and passwords to an impostor.

With all the technical complexities associated with computer security, it is surprising to many that one of the major obstacles to the security of computer systems is the carelessness of the users themselves. They select passwords that are relatively easy to guess (such as names and dates), they share their passwords with friends, they fail to change their passwords on a timely basis, they subject offline mass storage devices to potential degradation by transferring them back and forth between machines, and they import unapproved software into the system that might subvert the system's security. For problems like these, most institutions with large computer installations adopt and enforce policies that catalog the requirements and responsibilities of the users.

Attacks from Within

Once an intruder (or perhaps an authorized user with malicious intent) gains access to a computer system, the next step is usually to explore, looking for information of interest or for places to insert destructive software. This is a straightforward process if the prowler has gained access to the administrator's account, which is why the administrator's password is closely guarded. If, however, access is through a general user's account, it becomes necessary to trick the operating system into allowing the intruder to reach beyond the privileges granted to that user. For example, the intruder may try to trick the memory manager into allowing a process to access main memory cells outside its allotted area, or the prowler may try to trick the file manager into retrieving files whose access should be denied.

Today's CPUs are enhanced with features that are designed to foil such attempts. As an example, consider the need to restrict a process to the area of main memory assigned to it by the memory manager. Without such restrictions, a process could erase the operating system from main memory and take control of the computer itself. To counter such attempts, CPUs designed for multiprogramming systems typically contain special-purpose registers in which the operating system can store the upper and lower limits of a process's allotted memory area. Then, while performing the process, the CPU compares each memory reference to these registers to ensure that the reference is within the designated limits. If the reference is found to be outside the process's designated area, the CPU automatically transfers control back to the operating system (by performing an interrupt sequence) so that the operating system can take appropriate action.

Embedded in this illustration is a subtle but significant problem. Without further security features, a process could still gain access to memory cells outside of its designated area merely by changing the special-purpose registers that contain its memory limits. That is, a process that wanted access to additional memory could merely increase the value in the register containing the upper memory limit and then proceed to use the additional memory space without approval from the operating system.

To protect against such actions, CPUs for multiprogramming systems are designed to operate in one of two **privilege levels**; we will call one "privileged mode," the other we will call "nonprivileged mode." When in privileged mode, the CPU is able to execute all the instructions in its machine language. However, when in nonprivileged mode, the list of acceptable instructions is limited. The instructions that are available only in privileged mode are called **privileged instructions.** (Typical examples of privileged instructions include instructions that change the contents of memory limit registers and instructions that change the current privilege mode of the CPU.) An attempt to execute a privileged instruction when the CPU is in nonprivileged mode causes an interrupt. This interrupt converts the CPU to privileged mode and transfers control to an interrupt handler within the operating system.

When first turned on, the CPU is in privileged mode. Thus, when the operating system starts at the end of the boot process, all instructions are executable. However, each time the operating system allows a process to start a time slice, it switches the CPU to nonprivileged mode by executing a "change privilege mode" instruction. In turn, the operating system will be notified if the process attempts to execute a privileged instruction, and thus the operating system will be in position to maintain the integrity of the computer system.

Privileged instructions and the control of privilege levels is the major tool available to operating systems for maintaining security. However, the use of these tools is a complex component of an operating system's design, and errors continue to be found in current systems. A single flaw in privilege level control can open the door to disaster from malicious programmers or from inadvertent programming errors. If a process is allowed to alter the timer that controls the system's multiprogramming system, that process can extend its time slice and dominate the machine. If a process is allowed to access peripheral devices directly, then it can read files without supervision by the system's file manager. If a process is allowed to access memory cells outside its allotted area, it can read and even alter data being used by other processes. Thus, maintaining security continues to be an important task of an administrator as well as a goal in operating system design.

Questions & Exercises

1. Give some examples of poor choices for passwords and explain why they would be poor choices.
2. Processors in Intel's Pentium series provide for four privilege levels. Why would the designers of CPUs decide to provide four levels rather than three or five?
3. If a process in a multiprogramming system could access memory cells outside its allotted area, how could it gain control of the machine?

Chapter Review Problems

(Asterisked problems are associated with optional sections.)

1. List four activities of a typical operating system.
2. What led to the development of the interactive operating system?
3. Suppose three items R, S, and T are placed in a queue in that order. Then one item is removed from the queue before a fourth item, X, is placed in the queue. Then one item is removed from the queue, the items Y and Z are placed in the queue, and then the queue is emptied by removing one item at a time. List all the items in the order in which they were removed.
4. What is the significance of the window manager in current GUI shells?
5. What is a real-time operating system?
6. If you have a PC, identify some situations in which you can take advantage of its multitasking capabilities.
7. On the basis of a computer system with which you are familiar, identify two units of application software and two units of utility software. Then explain why you classified them as you did.
8. a. What is the role of the user interface of an operating system?
   b. What is the role of the kernel of an operating system?
9. What is the use of the process table in program execution?
10. Give some examples of functions that are provided by the Python module "os".
11. What is the Linux or UNIX command for creating new processes?
12. What is the difference between a process that is ready and a process that is waiting?
13. What is the difference between virtual memory and main memory?
14. Suppose a computer contained 512MB (MiB) of main memory, and an operating system needed to create a virtual memory of twice that size using pages of 2KB (KiB). How many pages would be required?
15. What complications could arise in a time-sharing/multitasking system if two processes require access to the same file at the same time? Are there cases in which the file manager should grant such requests? Are there cases in which the file manager should deny such requests?
16. How is firmware different from hardware and software? What do you mean by a firmware update?
17. Define load balancing and scaling in the context of multiprocessor architectures.
18. What is a context switch?
19. What are the flaws of privilege level control?
20. If you have a PC, record the sequence activities that you can observe when you turn it on. Then determine what messages appear on the computer screen before the booting process actually begins. What software writes these messages?
21. Suppose a multiprogramming operating system allocated time slices of 10 milliseconds and the machine executed an average of five instructions per nanosecond. How many instructions could be executed in a single time slice?
22. If a typist types 60 words per minute (where a word is considered five characters), how much time would pass between typing each character? If a multiprogramming operating system allocated time slices in 10 millisecond units and we ignore the time required for process switches, how many time slices could be allocated between characters being typed?
23. Suppose a multiprogramming operating system is allotting time slices of 50 milliseconds. If it normally takes 8 milliseconds to position a disk's read/write head over the desired track and another 17 milliseconds for the desired data to rotate around to the read/write head, how much of a program's time slice can be spent waiting for a read operation from a disk to take place? If the machine is capable of executing 10 instructions each nanosecond,

how many instructions can be executed during this waiting period? (This is why when a process performs an operation with a peripheral device, a multiprogramming system terminates that process's time slice and allows another process to run while the first process is waiting for the services of the peripheral device.)

24. What is the drawback of using the set and clear flag system while allocating devices?

25. A process is said to be I/O-bound if it requires a lot of I/O operations, whereas a process that consists of mostly computations within the CPU/memory system is said to be compute-bound. If both a compute-bound process and an I/O-bound process are waiting for a time slice, which should be given priority? Why?

26. Would greater throughput be achieved by a system running two processes in a multiprogramming environment if both processes were I/O-bound (refer to problem 25) or if one were I/O-bound and the other were compute-bound? Why?

27. Write a set of directions that tells an operating system's dispatcher what to do when a process's time slice is over.

28. What are the various functions of the memory manager in an operating system?

29. Identify a situation in a multiprogramming system in which a process does not consume the entire time slice allocated to it.

30. What is meant by an interrupt handler in multiprogramming systems and what is its significance?

31. Answer each of the following in terms of an operating system that you use:
  a. How do you ask the operating system to copy a file from one location to another?
  b. How do you ask the operating system to show you the directory on a disk?
  c. How do you ask the operating system to execute a program?

32. Answer each of the following in terms of an operating system that you use:
  a. How does the operating system restrict access to only those who are approved users?
  b. How do you ask the operating system to show you what processes are currently in the process table?
  c. How do you tell the operating system that you do not want other users of the machine to have access to your files?

***33.** Explain an important use for the test-and-set instruction found in many machine languages. Why is it important for the entire test-and-set process to be implemented as a single instruction?

***34.** A banker with only $100,000 loans $50,000 to each of two customers. Later, both customers return with the story that before they can repay their loans they must each borrow another $10,000 to complete the business deals in which their previous loans are involved. The banker resolves this deadlock by borrowing the additional funds from another source and passing on this loan (with an increase in the interest rate) to the two customers. Which of the three conditions for deadlock has the banker removed?

***35.** Students who want to enroll in Model Railroading II at the local university are required to obtain permission from the instructor and pay a laboratory fee. The two requirements are fulfilled independently in either order and at different locations on campus. Enrollment is limited to 20 students; this limit is maintained by both the instructor, who will grant permission to only 20 students, and the financial office, which will allow only 20 students to pay the laboratory fee. Suppose that this registration system has resulted in 19 students having successfully registered for the course, but with the final space being claimed by two students—one who has only obtained permission from the instructor and another who has only paid the fee. Which requirement for deadlock is removed by each of the following solutions to the problem?
  a. Both students are allowed in the course.
  b. The class size is reduced to 19, so neither of the two students is allowed to register for the course.
  c. The competing students are both denied entry to the class and a third student is given the twentieth space.
  d. It is decided that the only requirement for entry into the course is the payment of the fee. Thus the student who has paid the fee gets into the course, and entry is denied to the other student.

***36.** Since each area on a computer's display can be used by only one process at a time (otherwise the image on the screen would be unreadable), these areas are nonsharable resources that are allocated by the window manager. Which of the three conditions necessary for deadlock does the window manager remove in order to avoid deadlock?

***37.** Suppose each nonsharable resource in a computer system is classified as a level 1, level 2, or level 3 resource. Moreover, suppose each process in the system is required to request the resources it needs according to this classification. That is, it must request all the required level 1 resources at once before requesting any level 2 resources. Once it receives the level 1 resources, it can request all the required level 2 resources, and so on. Can deadlock occur in such a system? Why or why not?

***38.** Each of two robot arms is programmed to lift assemblies from a conveyor belt, test them for tolerances, and place them in one of two bins depending on the results of the test. The assemblies arrive one at a time with a sufficient interval between them. To keep both arms from trying to grab the same assembly, the computers controlling the arms share a common memory cell. If an arm is available as an assembly approaches, its controlling computer reads the value of the common cell. If the value is nonzero, the arm lets the assembly pass. Otherwise, the controlling computer places a nonzero value in the memory cell, directs the arm to pick up the assembly, and places the value 0 back into the memory cell after the action is complete. What sequence of events could lead to a tug-of-war between the two arms?

***39.** Why is disabling the interrupts in a multicore operating system not considered to be an efficient approach?

***40.** A process that is waiting for a time slice is said to suffer **starvation** if it is never given a time slice.

a. The pavement in the middle of an intersection can be considered as a nonsharable resource for which cars approaching the intersection compete. A traffic light rather than an operating system is used to control the allocation of the resource. If the light is able to sense the amount of traffic arriving from each direction and is programmed to give the green light to the heavier traffic, the lighter traffic might suffer from starvation. How is starvation avoided?

b. In what sense can a process starve if the dispatcher always assigns time slices according to a priority system in which the priority of each process remains fixed? (Hint: What is the priority of the process that just completed its time slice in comparison to the processes that are waiting, and consequently which routine gets the next time slice?) How, would you guess, do many operating systems avoid this problem?

***41.** Why can't special-purpose registers restrict a process in its allotted memory area? Explain your answer.

***42.** The following is the "dining philosophers" problem that was originally proposed by E. W. Dijkstra and is now a part of computer science folklore. Five philosophers are sitting at a round table. In front of each is a plate of spaghetti. There are five forks on the table, one between each plate. Each philosopher wants to alternate between thinking and eating. To eat, a philosopher requires possession of both the forks that are adjacent to the philosopher's plate. Identify the possibilities of deadlock and starvation (see problem 40) that are present in the dining philosophers' problem.

***43.** What problem arises as the lengths of the time slices in a multiprogramming system are made shorter and shorter? What about as they become longer and longer?

***44.** When is it preferable to use the deadlock prevention scheme, the deadlock avoidance scheme, and the deadlock detection and recovery scheme? Can you provide scenarios where more than one of these schemes can be used?

45. Identity two activities that can be performed by an operating system's administrator but not by a typical user.

46. How is the read action different from the write action when multiple processes access the same file?

47. Suppose a password consisted of a string of nine characters from the English alphabet

(26 characters). If each possible password could be tested in a millisecond, how long would it take to test all possible passwords?

48. Why are CPUs that are designed for multitasking operating systems capable of operating at different privilege levels?

49. How are privileged instructions handled in nonprivileged mode?

50. Identify three ways in which a process could challenge the security of a computer system if not prevented from doing so by the operating system.

51. What are the conditions that lead to a deadlock?

52. What are the policies that a user should follow to manage login passwords?

53. Give appropriate examples of auditing software and sniffing software.

54. How is security relevant in current operating systems?

55. How is the booting process different in embedded systems from traditional systems?

Social Issues

The following questions are intended as a guide to the ethical/social/legal issues associated with the field of computing. The goal is not merely to answer these questions. You should also consider why you answered as you did and whether your justifications are consistent from one question to the next.

1. Suppose you are using a multiuser operating system that allows you to view the names of the files belonging to other users as well as to view the contents of those files that are not otherwise protected. Would viewing such information without permission be similar to wandering through someone's unlocked home without permission, or would it be more like reading materials placed in a common lounge such as a physician's waiting room?

2. When you have access to a multiuser computer system, what responsibilities do you have when selecting your password?

3. If a flaw in an operating system's security allows a malicious programmer to gain unauthorized access to sensitive data, to what extent should the developer of the operating system be held responsible?

4. Is it your responsibility to lock your house in such a way that intruders cannot get in, or is it the public's responsibility to stay out of your house unless invited? Is it the responsibility of an operating system to guard access to a computer and its contents, or is it the responsibility of hackers to leave the machine alone?

5. In *Walden,* Henry David Thoreau argues that we have become tools of our tools; that is, instead of benefiting from the tools that we have, we spend our time obtaining and maintaining our tools. To what extent is this true with regard to computing? For example, if you own a personal computer, how much time do you spend earning the money to pay for it, learning how to use its operating system, learning how to use its utility and application software, maintaining it, and downloading upgrades to its software in comparison to the amount of time you spend benefiting from it? When you use it, is your time well spent? Are you more socially active with or without a personal computer?

Additional Reading

Bishop, M. *Introduction to Computer Security*. Boston, MA: Addison-Wesley, 2005.

Craig, B. *Cyberlaw: The Law of the Internet and Information Technology*. Upper Saddle River, NJ: Prentice-Hall, 2012.

Davis, W. S., and T. M. Rajkumar. *Operating Systems: A Systematic View,* 6th ed. Boston, MA: Addison-Wesley, 2005.

Deitel, H. M., P. J. Deitel, and D. R. Choffnes. *Operating Systems,* 3rd ed. Upper Saddle River, NJ: Prentice-Hall, 2005.

Silberschatz, A., P. B. Galvin, and G. Gagne. *Operating System Concepts,* 9th ed., New York: Wiley, 2012.

Stallings, W. *Operating Systems,* 8th ed. Upper Saddle River, NJ: Prentice-Hall, 2014.

Tanenbaum, A. S. *Modern Operating Systems,* 3rd ed. Upper Saddle River, NJ: Prentice-Hall, 2008.

CHAPTER 4

Networking and the Internet

In this chapter we discuss the area of computer science known as networking, which encompasses the study of how computers can be linked together to share information and resources. Our study will include the construction and operation of networks, applications of networks, and security issues. A prominent topic will be a particular worldwide network of networks known as the Internet.

**Asterisks indicate suggestions for optional sections.*

The need to share information and resources among different computers has led to linked computer systems, called **networks,** in which computers are connected so that data can be transferred from machine to machine. In these networks, computer users can exchange messages and share resources—such as printing capabilities, software packages, and data storage facilities—that are scattered throughout the system. The underlying software required to support such applications has grown from simple utility packages into an expanding system of network software that provides a sophisticated network-wide infrastructure. In a sense, network software is evolving into a network-wide operating system. In this chapter we will explore this expanding field of computer science.

4.1 Network Fundamentals

We begin our study of networks by introducing a variety of basic networking concepts.

Network Classifications

A computer network is often classified as being either a **personal area network (PAN),** a **local area network (LAN),** a **metropolitan area network (MAN),** or a **wide area network (WAN).** A PAN is normally used for short-range communications—typically less than a few meters—such as between a wireless headset and a smartphone or between a wireless mouse and its PC. In contrast, a LAN normally consists of a collection of computers in a single building or building complex. For example, the computers on a university campus or those in a manufacturing plant might be connected by a LAN. A MAN is a network of intermediate size, such as one spanning a local community. Finally, a WAN links machines over a greater distance—perhaps in neighboring cities or on opposite sides of the world.

Another means of classifying networks is based on whether the network's internal operation is based on designs that are in the public domain or on innovations owned and controlled by a particular entity such as an individual or a corporation. A network of the former type is called an **open** network; a network of the latter type is called a **closed,** or sometimes a **proprietary,** network. Open network designs are freely circulated and often grow in popularity to the point that they ultimately prevail over proprietary approaches whose applications are restricted by license fees and contract conditions.

The Internet (a popular worldwide network of networks that we will study in this chapter) is an open system. In particular, communication throughout the Internet is governed by an open collection of standards known as the TCP/IP protocol suite, which is the subject of Section 4.4. Anyone is free to use these standards without paying fees or signing license agreements. In contrast, a company such as Novell Inc. might develop proprietary systems for which it chooses to maintain ownership rights, allowing the company to draw income from selling or leasing these products.

Still another way of classifying networks is based on the topology of the network, which refers to the pattern in which the machines are connected. Two of the more popular topologies are the bus, in which the machines are all connected to a common communication line called a bus (Figure 4.1a), and the star, in which one machine serves as a central focal point to which all the others are

Figure 4.1 Two popular network topologies

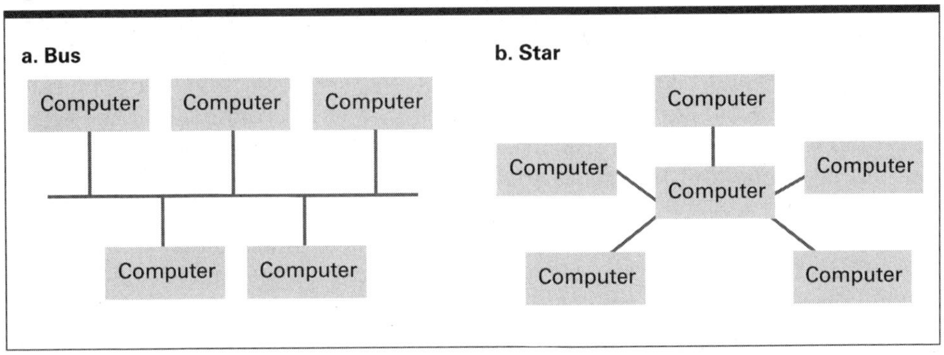

connected (Figure 4.1b). The bus topology was popularized in the 1990s when it was implemented under a set of standards known as Ethernet, and Ethernet networks remain one of the most popular networking systems in use today.

The star topology has roots as far back as the 1970s. It evolved from the paradigm of a large central computer serving many users. As the simple terminals employed by these users grew into small computers themselves, a star network emerged. Today, the star configuration is popular in wireless networks where communication is conducted by means of radio broadcast and the central machine, called the **access point (AP),** serves as a focal point around which all communication is coordinated.

The difference between a bus network and a star network is not always obvious by the physical arrangement of equipment. The distinction is whether the machines in the network envision themselves as communicating directly with each other over a common bus or indirectly through an intermediary central machine. For instance, a bus network might not appear as a long bus from which computers are connected over short links as depicted in Figure 4.1. Instead, it may have a very short bus with long links to the individual machines, meaning that the network would look more like a star. Indeed, sometimes a bus network is created by running links from each computer to a central location where they are connected to a device called a **hub.** This hub is little more than a very short bus. All it does is relay any signal it receives (with perhaps some amplification) back out to all the machines connected to it. The result is a network that looks like a star network although it operates like a bus network.

Protocols

For a network to function reliably, it is important to establish rules by which activities are conducted. Such rules are called **protocols.** By developing and adopting protocol standards, vendors are able to build products for network applications that are compatible with products from other vendors. Thus, the development of protocol standards is an indispensable process in the development of networking technologies.

As an introduction to the protocol concept, let us consider the problem of coordinating the transmission of messages among computers in a network. Without rules governing this communication, all the computers might insist on transmitting messages at the same time or fail to assist other machines when that assistance is required.

In a bus network based on the Ethernet standards, the right to transmit messages is controlled by the protocol known as **Carrier Sense, Multiple Access with Collision Detection (CSMA/CD).** This protocol dictates that each message be broadcast to all the machines on the bus (Figure 4.2). Each machine monitors all the messages but keeps only those addressed to itself. To transmit a message, a machine waits until the bus is silent, and at this time it begins transmitting while continuing to monitor the bus. If another machine also begins transmitting, both machines detect the clash and pause for a brief, independently random period of time before trying to transmit again. The result is a system similar to that used by a small group of people in a conversation. If two people start to talk at once, they both stop. The difference is that people might go through a series such as, "I'm sorry, what were you going to say?", "No, no. You go first," whereas under the CSMA/CD protocol each machine merely tries again later.

Note that CSMA/CD is not compatible with wireless star networks in which all machines communicate through a central AP. This is because a machine may be unable to detect that its transmissions are colliding with those of another. For example, the machine may not hear the other because its own signal drowns out that of the other machine. Another cause might be that the signals from the different machines are blocked from each other by objects or distance even though they can all communicate with the central AP (a condition known as the **hidden terminal problem,** Figure 4.3). The result is that wireless networks adopt the policy of trying to avoid collisions rather than trying to detect them. Such policies are classified as **Carrier Sense, Multiple Access with Collision Avoidance (CSMA/CA),** many of which are standardized by IEEE (see the sidebar "Institute of Electrical and Electronics Engineers" in Chapter 7) within the protocols defined in IEEE 802.11 and commonly referred to as **WiFi.** We emphasize that collision avoidance protocols are designed to avoid collisions and may not eliminate them completely. When collisions do occur, messages must be retransmitted.

The most common approach to collision avoidance is based on giving advantage to machines that have already been waiting for an opportunity to transmit. The protocol used is similar to Ethernet's CSMA/CD. The basic difference is that when a machine first needs to transmit a message and finds the communication channel silent, it does not start transmitting immediately. Instead, it waits for a short period of time and then starts transmitting only if the channel has remained silent throughout that period. If a busy channel is experienced during this process, the machine waits for a randomly determined period before trying again. Once this period is exhausted, the machine is allowed to claim a silent channel

Figure 4.2 Communication over a bus network

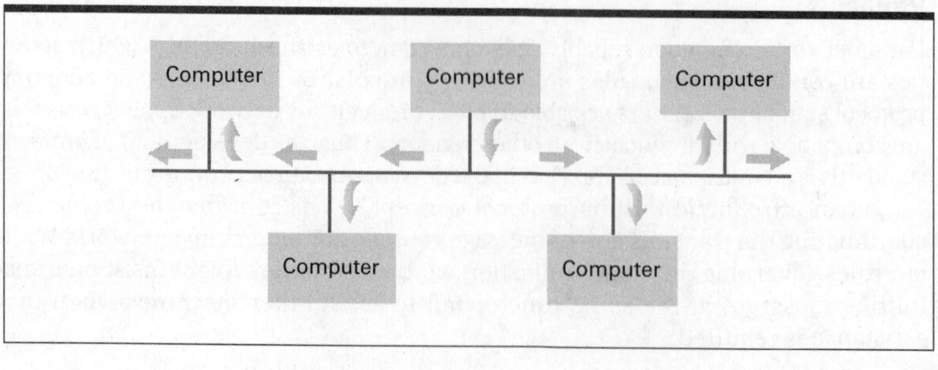

Figure 4.3 The hidden terminal problem

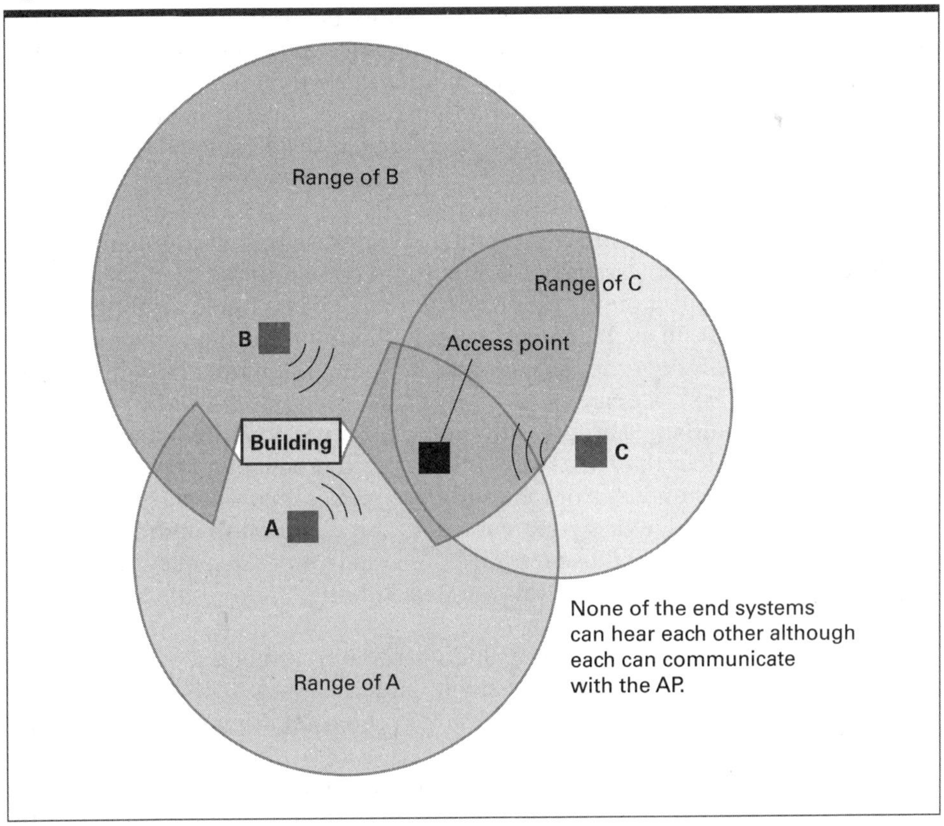

without hesitation. This means that collisions between "newcomers" and those that have already been waiting are avoided because a "newcomer" is not allowed to claim a silent channel until any machine that has been waiting is given the opportunity to start.

This protocol, however, does not solve the hidden terminal problem. After all, any protocol based on distinguishing between a silent or busy channel requires that each individual station be able to hear all the others. To solve this problem, some WiFi networks require that each machine send a short "request" message to the AP and wait until the AP acknowledges that request before transmitting an entire message. If the AP is busy because it is dealing with a "hidden terminal," it will ignore the request, and the requesting machine will know to wait. Otherwise, the AP will acknowledge the request, and the machine will know that it is safe to transmit. Note that all the machines in the network will hear all acknowledgments sent from the AP and thus have a good idea of whether the AP is busy at any given time, even though they may not be able to hear the transmissions taking place.

Combining Networks

Sometimes it is necessary to connect existing networks to form an extended communication system. This can be done by connecting the networks to form a larger version of the same "type" of network. For example, in the case of bus networks based on the Ethernet protocols, it is often possible to connect the buses to form a single long bus. This is done by means of different devices known as repeaters, bridges, and switches, the distinctions of which are subtle yet informative. The simplest of these is the **repeater,** which is little more than a device that passes signals back and forth between the two original buses (usually with some form of amplification) without considering the meaning of the signals (Figure 4.4a).

A **bridge** is similar to, but more complex than, a repeater. Like a repeater, it connects two buses, but it does not necessarily pass all messages across the connection. Instead, it looks at the destination address that accompanies each message and forwards a message across the connection only when that message is destined for a computer on the other side. Thus, two machines residing on the same side of a bridge can exchange messages without interfering with communication taking place on the other side. A bridge produces a more efficient system than that produced by a repeater.

A **switch** is essentially a bridge with multiple connections, allowing it to connect several buses rather than just two. Thus, a switch produces a network consisting of several buses extending from the switch as spokes on a wheel (Figure 4.4b). As in the case of a bridge, a switch considers the destination addresses of all messages and forwards only those messages destined for other spokes. Moreover, each message that is forwarded is relayed only into the appropriate spoke, thus minimizing the traffic in each spoke.

It is important to note that when networks are connected via repeaters, bridges, and switches, the result is a single large network. The entire system operates in the same manner (using the same protocols) as each of the original smaller networks.

Sometimes, however, the networks to be connected have incompatible characteristics. For instance, the characteristics of a WiFi network are not readily compatible with an Ethernet network. In these cases the networks must be connected in a manner that builds a network of networks, known as an **internet,** in

Figure 4.4 Building a large bus network from smaller ones

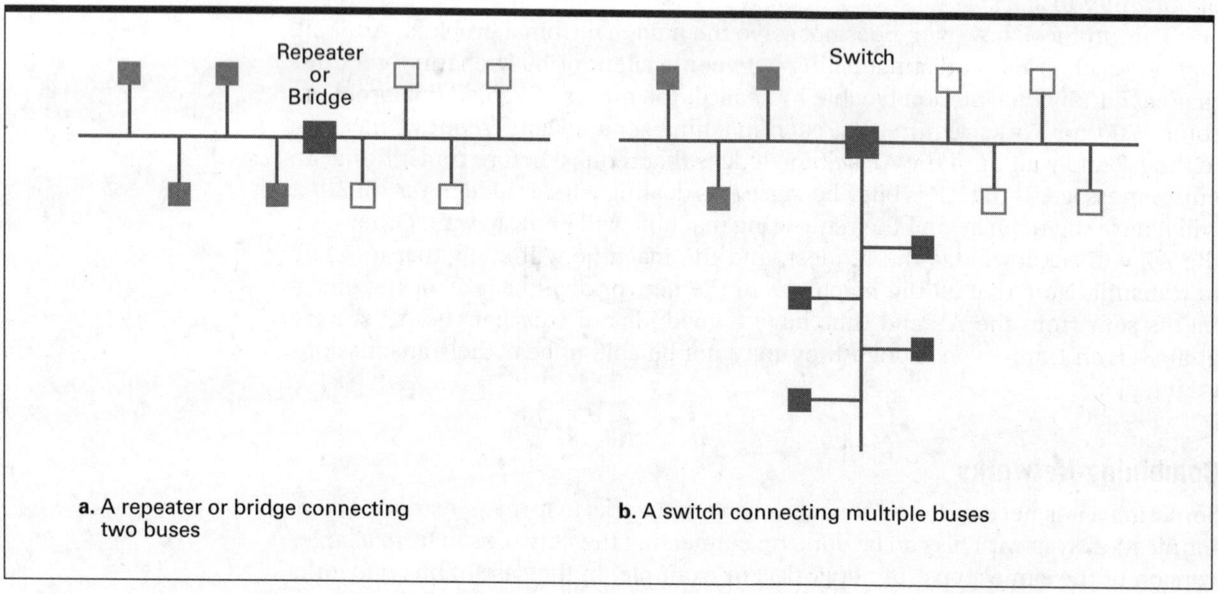

which the original networks maintain their individuality and continue to function as autonomous networks. (Note that the generic term *internet* is distinct from *the Internet*. The Internet, written with an uppercase *I*, refers to a particular, worldwide internet that we will study in later sections of this chapter. There are many other examples of internets. Indeed, traditional telephone communication was handled by worldwide internet systems well before the Internet was popularized.)

The connection between networks to form an internet is handled by devices known as **routers,** which are special purpose computers used for forwarding messages. Note that the task of a router is different from that of repeaters, bridges, and switches in that routers provide links between networks while allowing each network to maintain its unique internal characteristics. As an example, Figure 4.5 depicts two WiFi star networks and an Ethernet bus network connected by routers. When a machine in one of the WiFi networks wants to send a message to a machine in the Ethernet network, it first sends the message to the AP in its network. From there, the AP sends the message to its associated router, and this router forwards the message to the router at the Ethernet. There the message is given to a machine on the bus, and that machine then forwards the message to its final destination in the Ethernet.

The reason that routers are so named is that their purpose is to forward messages in their proper directions. This forwarding process is based on an internet-wide addressing system in which all the devices in an internet (including the machines in the original networks and the routers) are assigned unique addresses. (Thus, each machine in one of the original networks has two addresses: its original "local" address within its own network and its internet address.) A machine wanting to send a message to a machine in a distant network attaches the internet address of the destination to the message and directs the message to its local router. From there it is forwarded in the proper direction. For this forwarding

Figure 4.5 Routers connecting two WiFi networks and an Ethernet network to form an internet

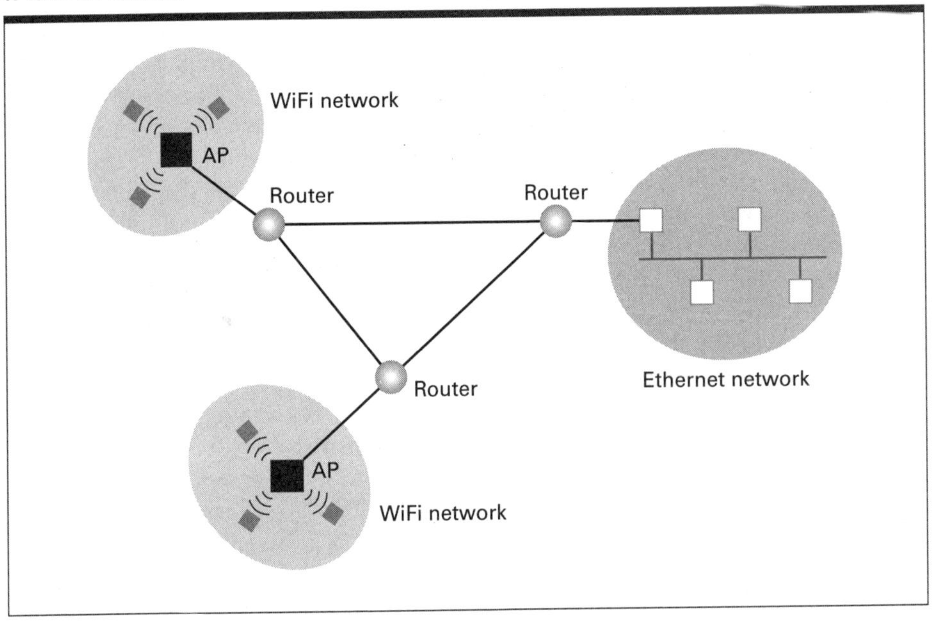

purpose, each router maintains a **forwarding table** that contains the router's knowledge about the direction in which messages should be sent depending on their destination addresses.

The "point" at which one network is linked to an internet is often called a **gateway** because it serves as a passageway between the network and the outside world. Gateways can be found in a variety of forms, and thus the term is used rather loosely. In many cases a network's gateway is merely the router through which it communicates with the rest of the internet. In other cases the term *gateway* may be used to refer to more than just a router. For example, in most residential WiFi networks that are connected to the Internet, the term *gateway* refers collectively to both the network's AP and the router connected to the AP because these two devices are normally packaged in a single unit.

Methods of Process Communication

The various activities (or processes) executing on the different computers within a network (or even executing on the same machine via time-sharing/multitasking) must often communicate with each other to coordinate their actions and to perform their designated tasks. Such communication between processes is called **interprocess communication.**

A popular convention used for interprocess communication is the **client/server** model. This model defines the basic roles played by the processes as either a **client,** which makes requests of other processes, or a **server,** which satisfies the requests made by clients.

An early application of the client/server model appeared in networks connecting all the computers in a cluster of offices. In this situation, a single, high-quality printer was attached to the network where it was available to all the machines in the network. In this case the printer played the role of a server (often called a **print server**), and the other machines were programmed to play the role of clients that sent print requests to the print server.

Another early application of the client/server model was used to reduce the cost of magnetic disk storage while also removing the need for duplicate copies of records. Here one machine in a network was equipped with a high-capacity mass storage system (usually a magnetic disk) that contained all of an organization's records. Other machines on the network then requested access to the records as they needed them. Thus the machine that actually contained the records played the role of a server (called a **file server**), and the other machines played the role of clients that requested access to the files that were stored at the file server.

Today the client/server model is used extensively in network applications, as we will see later in this chapter. However, the client/server model is not the only means of interprocess communication. Another model is the **peer-to-peer** (often abbreviated **P2P**) model. Whereas the client/server model involves one process (the server) providing a service to numerous others (clients), the peer-to-peer model involves processes that provide service to and receive service from each other (Figure 4.6). Moreover, whereas a server must execute continuously so that it is prepared to serve its clients at any time, the peer-to-peer model usually involves processes that execute on a temporary basis. For example, applications of the peer-to-peer model include instant messaging in which people carry on a written conversation over the Internet as well as situations in which people play competitive interactive games.

Figure 4.6 The client/server model compared to the peer-to-peer model

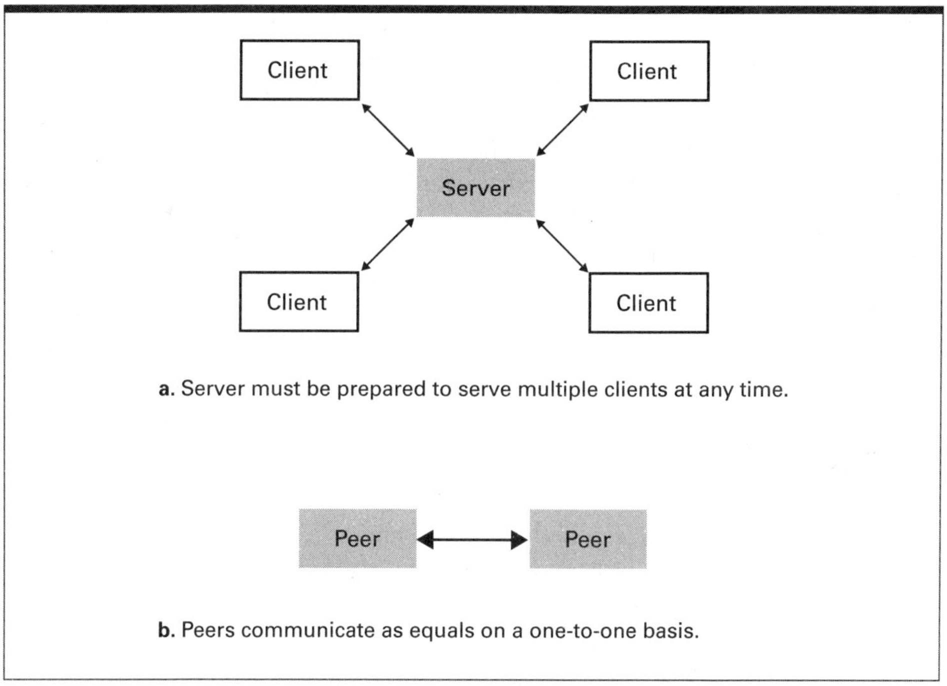

The peer-to-peer model is also a popular means of distributing files such as music recordings and motion pictures via the Internet. In this case, one peer may receive a file from another and then provide that file to other peers. The collection of peers participating in such a distribution is sometimes called a swarm. The swarm approach to file distribution is in contrast to earlier approaches that applied the client/server model by establishing a central distribution center (the server) from which clients downloaded files (or at least found sources for those files).

One reason that the P2P model is replacing the client/server model for file sharing is that it distributes the service task over many peers rather than concentrating it at one server. This lack of a centralized base of operation leads to a more efficient system. Unfortunately, another reason for the popularity of file distribution systems based on the P2P model is that, in cases of questionable legality, the lack of a central server makes legal efforts to enforce copyright laws more difficult. There are numerous cases, however, in which individuals have discovered that "difficult" does not mean "impossible" and have found themselves faced with significant liabilities due to copyright infringement violations.

You might often read or hear the term *peer-to-peer network*, which is an example of how misuse of terminology can evolve when technical terms are adopted by the nontechnical community. The term *peer-to-peer* refers to a system by which two processes communicate over a network (or internet). It is not a property of the network (or internet). A process might use the peer-to-peer model to communicate with another process and later use the client/server model to communicate with another process over the same network. Thus, it would be more accurate to speak of communicating by means of the peer-to-peer model rather than communicating over a peer-to-peer network.

Distributed Systems

With the success of networking technology, interaction between computers via networks has become common and multifaceted. Many modern software systems, such as global information retrieval systems, company-wide accounting and inventory systems, computer games, and even the software that controls a network's infrastructure itself are designed as **distributed systems,** meaning that they consist of software units that execute as processes on different computers.

Early distributed systems were developed independently from scratch. But today, research is revealing a common infrastructure running throughout these systems, including such things as communication and security systems. In turn, efforts have been made to produce prefabricated systems that provide this basic infrastructure and therefore allow distributed applications to be constructed by merely developing the part of the system that is unique to the application.

Several types of distributed computing systems are now common. **Cluster computing** describes a distributed system in which many independent computers work closely together to provide computation or services comparable to a much larger machine. The cost of these individual machines, plus the high-speed network to connect them, can be less than a higher-priced supercomputer, but with higher reliability and lower maintenance costs. Such distributed systems are used to provide **high-availability**—because it is more likely that at least one member of the cluster will be able to answer a request, even if other cluster members break down or are unavailable—and **load-balancing**—because the workload can be shifted automatically from members of the cluster that have too much to do to those that may have too little. **Grid computing** refers to distributed systems that are more loosely coupled than clusters but that still work together to accomplish large tasks. Grid computing can involve specialized software to make it easier to distribute data and algorithms to the machines participating in a grid. Examples include University of Wisconsin's Condor system, or Berkeley's Open Infrastructure for Network Computing (BOINC). Both of these systems are often installed on computers that are used for other purposes, such as PCs at work or at home, that can then volunteer computing power to the grid when the machine is not otherwise being used. Enabled by the growing connectivity of the Internet, this type of voluntary, distributed grid computing has enabled millions of home PCs to work on enormously complex mathematical and scientific problems. **Cloud computing,** whereby huge pools of shared computers on the network can be allocated for use by clients as needed, is the latest trend in distributed systems. Much as the spread of metropolitan electrical grids in the early twentieth century eliminated the need for individual factories and businesses to maintain their own generators, the Internet is making it possible for entities to entrust their data and computations to "the Cloud," which in this case refers to the enormous computing resources already available on the network. Services such as Amazon's Elastic Compute Cloud allow clients to rent virtual computers by the hour, without concern for where the computer hardware is actually located. Google Drive and Google Apps allow users to collaborate on information or build Web services without needing to know how many computers are working on the problem or where the relevant data are stored. Cloud computing services provide reasonable guarantees of reliability and scalability, but also raise concerns about privacy and security in a world where we may no longer know who owns and operates the computers that we use.

Questions & Exercises

1. What is an open network?
2. Summarize the distinction between a bridge and a switch.
3. What is a router?
4. Identify some relationships in society that conform to the client/server model.
5. Identify some protocols used in society.
6. Summarize the distinction between cluster computing and grid computing.

4.2 The Internet

The most notable example of an internet is the **Internet** (note the uppercase I), which originated from research projects going back to the early 1960s. The goal was to develop the ability to link a variety of computer networks so that they could function as a connected system that would not be disrupted by local disasters. Much of this work was sponsored by the U.S. government through the Defense Advanced Research Projects Agency (DARPA—pronounced "DAR–pa"). Over the years, the development of the Internet shifted from a government-sponsored project to an academic research project, and today it is largely a commercial undertaking that links a worldwide combination of PANs, LANs, MANs, and WANs involving millions of computers.

Internet Architecture

As we have already mentioned, the Internet is a collection of connected networks. In general, these networks are constructed and maintained by organizations called **Internet Service Providers (ISPs).** It is also customary to use the term ISP in reference to the networks themselves. Thus, we will speak of connecting to an ISP, when what we really mean is connecting to the network provided by an ISP.

The system of networks operated by the ISPs can be classified in a hierarchy according to the role they play in the overall Internet structure (Figure 4.7). At the top of this hierarchy are relatively few **tier-1 ISPs** that consist of very high-speed, high-capacity, international WANs. These networks are thought of as the backbone of the Internet. They are typically operated by large companies that are in the communications business. An example would be a company that originated as a traditional telephone company and has expanded its scope into providing other communication services.

Connecting to the tier-1 ISPs are the **tier-2 ISPs** that tend to be more regional in scope and less potent in their capabilities. (The distinction between the tier-1 and tier-2 ISPs is often a matter of opinion.) Again, these networks tend to be operated by companies in the communications business.

Tier-1 and tier-2 ISPs are essentially networks of routers that collectively provide the Internet's communication infrastructure. As such, they can be

Figure 4.7 Internet composition

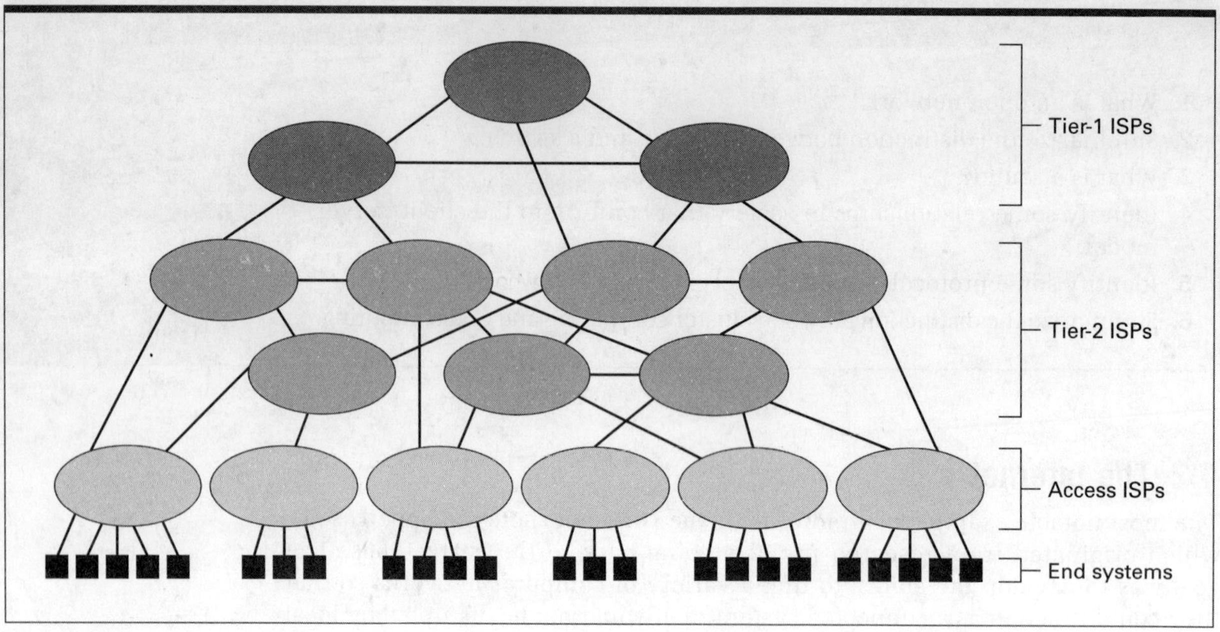

thought of as the core of the Internet. Access to this core is usually provided by an intermediary called an **access** or **tier-3 ISP.** An access ISP is essentially an independent internet, sometimes called an **intranet,** operated by a single authority that is in the business of supplying Internet access to individual homes and businesses. Examples include cable and telephone companies that charge for their service as well as organizations such as universities or corporations that take it upon themselves to provide Internet access to individuals within their organizations.

The devices that individual users connect to the access ISPs are known as **end systems** or **hosts.** These end systems may be laptops or PCs, but increasingly range over a multitude of other devices including telephones, video cameras, automobiles, and home appliances. After all, the Internet is essentially a communications system, and thus any device that would benefit from communicating with other devices is a potential end system.

The technology by which end systems connect to larger networks is also varied. Perhaps the fastest growing are wireless connections based on WiFi technology. The strategy is to connect the AP to an access ISP and thus provide Internet access through that ISP to end systems within the AP's broadcast range. The area within the AP or group of APs' range is often called a **hot spot,** particularly when the network access is publicly available or free. Hot spots can be found in individual residences, hotel and office buildings, small businesses, parks, and in some cases span entire cities. A similar technology is used by the cellular telephone industry where hot spots are known as cells and the "routers" generating the cells are coordinated to provide continuous service as an end system moves from one cell to another.

Internet2

Now that the Internet has shifted from a research project to a household commodity, the research community has moved on to a project called Internet2. Internet2 is intended as an academic-only system and involves numerous universities working in partnership with industry and government. The goal is to conduct research in internet applications requiring high bandwidth communication, such as remote access and control of costly state-of-the-art equipment such as telescopes and medical diagnostic devices. An example of current research involves remote surgery performed by robot hands that mimic the hands of a distant surgeon who views the patient by video. You can learn more about Internet2 at http://www.internet2.org.

Other popular techniques for connecting to access ISP's use telephone lines or cable/satellite systems. These technologies may be used to provide direct connection to an end system or to a customer's router to which multiple end systems are connected. This latter tactic is popular for individual residences where a local hot spot is created by a router/AP connected to an access ISP by means of existing cable or telephone lines.

Telephone, cable television, and satellite wide area networks of the twentieth century were designed to carry analog communications, such as the human voice or pre-digital television signals. Modern networks can be designed to carry digital data directly between computers, but older, analog network infrastructure still comprises a significant portion of the Internet. Issues arising from these legacy analog linkages are often referred to collectively as the **last mile problem.** The main arteries of WANs, MANs, and many LANs are relatively easy to modernize with high-speed digital technology such as fiber optics, but it can be far costlier to replace the existing copper telephone lines and coaxial cables that connect these arteries to each individual home or office. Thus, information that originated on the Internet continents away from an end system may spend almost its entire trip on high-speed digital connections, only to traverse the "last mile" to the end system over a slow, century-old analog phone line. As alluded to in Chapter 2, several clever schemes have been developed to extend these legacy analog links to accommodate transmission of digital data. DSL modems, cable modems, satellite uplinks, and even direct fiber-optic connections to the home are used to bring broadband Internet access to end users.

Internet Addressing

As we learned in Section 4.1, an internet needs an internet-wide addressing system that assigns a unique identifying address to each computer in the system. In the Internet these addresses are known as **IP addresses.** (The term *IP* refers to "Internet Protocol," which is a term we will learn more about in Section 4.4.) Originally, each IP address was a pattern of 32 bits, but to provide a larger set of addresses, the process of converting to 128-bit addresses is currently underway (see the discussion of IPv6 in Section 4.4). Blocks of consecutively numbered IP addresses are awarded to ISPs by the **Internet Corporation for Assigned Names and Numbers (ICANN),** which is a nonprofit corporation established to coordinate the Internet's operation. The ISPs are then allowed to allocate the addresses within their awarded blocks to machines within their region of authority. Thus, machines throughout the Internet are assigned unique IP addresses.

IP addresses are traditionally written in **dotted decimal notation** in which the bytes of the address are separated by periods and each byte is expressed as an integer represented in traditional base 10 notation. For example, using dotted decimal notation, the pattern 5.2 would represent the two-byte bit pattern 0000010100000010, which consists of the byte 00000101 (represented by 5) followed by the byte 00000010 (represented by 2), and the pattern 17.12.25 would represent the three-byte bit pattern consisting of the byte 00010001 (which is 17 written in binary notation), followed by the byte 00001100 (12 written in binary), followed by the byte 00011001 (25 written in binary). In summary, a 32-bit IP address might appear as 192.207.177.133 when expressed in dotted decimal notation.

Addresses in bit-pattern form (even when compressed using dotted decimal notation) are rarely conducive to human consumption. For this reason the Internet has an alternative addressing system in which machines are identified by mnemonic names. This addressing system is based on the concept of a **domain,** which can be thought of as a "region" of the Internet operated by a single authority such as a university, club, company, or government agency. (The word region is in quotations here because, as we will soon see, such a region may not correspond to a physical area of the Internet.) Each domain must be registered with ICANN—a process handled by companies, called **registrars,** that have been assigned this role by ICANN. As a part of this registration process, the domain is assigned a mnemonic **domain name,** which is unique among all the domain names throughout the Internet. Domain names are often descriptive of the organization registering the domain, which enhances their utility for humans.

As an example, the domain name of Marquette University is `mu.edu`. Note the suffix following the period. It is used to reflect the domain's classification, which in this case is "educational" as indicated by the `edu` suffix. These suffixes are called **top-level domains (TLDs).** Other TLDs include `com` for commercial institutions, `gov` for U.S. government institutions, `org` for nonprofit organizations, `museum` for museums, `info` for unrestricted use, and `net`, which was originally intended for ISPs but is now used on a much broader scale. In addition to these general TLDs, there are also two-letter TLDs for specific countries (called **country-code TLDs**) such as `au` for Australia and `ca` for Canada.

Once a domain's mnemonic name is registered, the organization that registered the name is free to extend the name to obtain mnemonic identifiers for individual items within the domain. For example, an individual host within Marquette University may be identified as `eagle.mu.edu`. Note that domain names are extended to the left and separated by a period. In some cases multiple extensions, called **subdomains,** are used as a means of organizing the names within a domain. These subdomains often represent different networks within the domain's jurisdiction. For example, if Yoyodyne Corporation was assigned the domain name `yoyodyne.com`, then an individual computer at Yoyodyne might have a name such as `overthruster.propulsion.yoyodyne.com`, meaning that the computer `overthruster` is in the subdomain `propulsion` within the domain `yoyodyne` within the TLD `com`. (We should emphasize that the dotted notation used in mnemonic addresses is not related to the dotted decimal notation used to represent addresses in bit pattern form.)

Although mnemonic addresses are convenient for humans, messages are always transferred over the Internet by means of IP addresses. Thus, if a human wants to send a message to a distant machine and identifies the destination by means of a mnemonic address, the software being used must be able to convert that address into an IP address before transmitting the message. This conversion is performed with the aid of numerous servers, called **name servers,** that are essentially directories that provide address translation services to clients. Collectively, these name servers are used as an Internet-wide directory system known as the **domain name system (DNS).** The process of using DNS to perform a translation is called a **DNS lookup.**

Thus, for a machine to be accessible by means of a mnemonic domain name, that name must be represented in a name server within the DNS. In those cases in which the entity establishing the domain has the resources, it can establish and maintain its own name server containing all the names within that domain. Indeed, this is the model on which the domain system was originally based. Each registered domain represented a physical region of the Internet that was operated by a local authority such as a company, university, or government agency. This authority was essentially an access ISP that provided Internet access to its members by means of its own intranet that was linked to the Internet. As part of this system, the organization maintained its own name server that provided translation services for all the names used within its domain.

This model is still common today. However, many individuals or small organizations want to establish a domain presence on the Internet without committing the resources necessary to support it. For example, it might be beneficial for a local chess club to have a presence on the Internet as `KingsandQueens.org`, but the club would likely not have the resources to establish its own network, maintain a link from this network to the Internet, and implement its own name server. In this case, the club can contract with an access ISP to create the appearance of a registered domain using the resources already established by the ISP. Typically, the club, perhaps with the assistance of the ISP, registers the name chosen by the club and contracts with the ISP to have that name included in the ISP's name server. This means that all DNS lookups regarding the new domain name will be directed to the ISP's name server, from which the proper translation will be obtained. In this way, many registered domains can reside within a single ISP, each often occupying only a small portion of a single computer.

Internet Applications

In the earlier days of the Internet, most applications were separate, simple programs that each followed a network protocol. A newsreader application contacted servers using the **Network News Transfer Protocol (NNTP),** an application for listing and copying files across the network implemented the **File Transfer Protocol (FTP),** or an application for accessing another computer from a great distance used the **Telnet** protocol, or later the **Secure Shell (SSH)** protocol. As webservers and browsers have become more sophisticated, more and more of these traditional network applications have come to be handled by webpages via the powerful **Hyper Text Transfer Protocol (HTTP).** Nevertheless, when examining a network protocol for an Internet application for the first time, it behooves us to begin with a few simpler examples before moving on to HTTP in the next section.

Electronic Mail A wide variety of systems now exist for exchanging messages between end users over the network; instant messaging (IM), browser-based online chatting, Twitter-based "tweets", and the Facebook "wall" are but a few. One of the oldest and most enduring uses of the Internet is the electronic mail system, or **email** for short. While many users now rely on their browser or a sophisticated application like Microsoft's Outlook, Apple's Mail, or Mozilla's Thunderbird to read and compose their email, the actual transmission of email messages from one computer to another on the Internet remains the domain of basic network protocols like SMTP.

SMTP (Simple Mail Transfer Protocol) defines a way that two computers on the network may interact when transmitting an email message from one host to the other. Consider the example case of a **mail server** `mail.skaro.gov` sending an email from end user "`dalek`" to end user "`doctor`" in the domain `tardis.edu`. First, a mail handling process on `mail.skaro.gov` contacts the mail server process on `mail.tardis.edu`. To accomplish this, it uses DNS, another network protocol, to map the human-readable destination domain name to the proper mail server name, and then to its IP address. This is not unlike looking up the phone number of an acquaintance before dialing. Similarly, when the server process at the other end answers, the protocol states that it must identify itself to the caller. The transcript of their SMTP exchange might look something like this:

```
1  220 mail.tardis.edu SMTP Sendmail Gallifrey-1.0; Fri, 23
     Aug 2413 14:34:10
2  HELO mail.skaro.gov
3  250 mail.tardis.edu Hello mail.skaro.gov, pleased to meet you
4  MAIL From: dalek@skaro.gov
5  250 2.1.0 dalek@skaro.gov... Sender ok
6  RCPT To: doctor@tardis.edu
7  250 2.1.5 doctor@tardis.edu... Recipient ok
8  DATA
9  354 Enter mail, end with "." on a line by itself
10 Subject: Extermination.
11
12 EXTERMINATE!
13 Regards, Dalek
14 .
15 250 2.0.0 r7NJYAEl028071 Message accepted for delivery
16 QUIT
17 221 2.0.0 mail.tardis.edu closing connection
```

In line 1, the remote mail server process answers the caller by announcing its name, the protocol it speaks, and other optional information, such as the version of protocol, and the date and time. In line 2, the sending mail server process introduces itself. In line 3, the remote server acknowledges the name of the sending server.

Most Internet protocols are not necessarily transmitted in ASCII characters so easily interpreted by a human. To be sure, the quaint politeness of "`pleased to meet you`" in line 3 is neither appreciated by the software on either end of this connection, nor essential to SMTP's proper function. However, this is actual behavior built into one popular SMTP mail server, held over from the early days of the Internet when human operators frequently needed to review SMTP transcripts to debug incompatibilities between mail servers. Untold millions of these exchanges occur on the network each day, known only to the software agents that transport email across the Internet.

In the simplest case, the remote mail server will take `mail.skaro.gov` at its word in line 2, accepting that the sending server is the machine named `mail` from the domain `skaro.gov`. SMTP is an example of a protocol originally built on trust that has subsequently been abused by spammers and other Internet miscreants. Modern mail servers must use extended versions of SMTP or their equivalent to help ensure that email is transmitted securely. We discuss concerns about network security in greater detail in the final segment of this chapter.

Returning to the transcript, in line 4 the sending server announces that it has a mail message to deliver, and identifies the sending user. In line 5, the remote server acknowledges that it will receive mail from this user at this domain. In line 6, the sending server announces the recipient on the remote server. In line 7, the remote server acknowledges that it will receive email destined for that user. In line 8, the sending server dispenses with the introductions, and announces that it is ready to send the `DATA`, the actual body of the e-mail message. In line 8, the remote server acknowledges (with code 354, in accordance with the SMTP protocol) that it is ready to receive the body of the message and includes a helpful human-readable instruction on how to conclude the message transfer.

In lines 10 through 14, the sending server conveys the text of the email message to be delivered. The remote server acknowledges acceptance in line 15, and in line 17 acknowledges the sending server's `QUIT` announcement from line 16.

The technical documents describing SMTP define each of the allowed steps in a conversation such as the transcript above. The keywords `HELO`, `MAIL`, `RCPT`, `DATA`, and `QUIT` are each precisely defined in terms of how they will be sent, what options can accompany them, and how they should be interpreted. Similarly, the remote server's numeric response codes for acknowledgment are enumerated and defined. Software designers use a protocol description to develop algorithms that will correctly implement sending and receiving email over the network.

Other protocols come into play for other aspects of transporting email. Because SMTP was initially designed for transferring text messages encoded with ASCII, additional protocols such as **MIME (Multipurpose Internet Mail Extensions)** have been developed to convert non-ASCII data to SMTP compatible form.

There are two popular protocols that may be used for accessing email that has arrived and accumulated at a user's mail server. These are **POP3 (Post Office Protocol version 3)** and **IMAP (Internet Mail Access Protocol).** POP3 (pronounced "pop-THREE") is the simpler of the two. Using POP3, a user transfers (downloads) messages to his or her local computer where they can be read, stored in various folders, edited, and otherwise manipulated as the user desires. This is done on the user's local machine using the local machine's mass storage.

IMAP (pronounced "EYE-map") allows a user to store and manipulate messages and related materials on the same machine as the mail server. In this manner, a user who must access his or her email from different computers can maintain records at the mail server that are then accessible from any remote computer to which the user may have access.

VoIP As an example of a more recent Internet application, consider **VoIP (Voice over Internet Protocol)** in which the Internet infrastructure is used to provide voice communication similar to that of traditional telephone systems. In its simplest form, VoIP consists of two processes on different machines transferring audio data via the P2P model—a process that in itself presents no significant problems. However, tasks such as initiating and receiving calls, linking VoIP with traditional telephone systems, and providing services such as emergency 911 communication are issues that extend beyond traditional Internet applications. Moreover, governments that own their country's traditional telephone companies view VoIP as a threat and have either taxed it heavily or outlawed it completely.

Existing VoIP systems come in four different forms that are competing for popularity. VoIP **soft phones** consist of P2P software that allows two or more PCs to share a call with no more special hardware than a speaker and a microphone. An example of a VoIP soft phone system is Skype, which also provides its clients with links to the traditional telephone communication system. One drawback to Skype is that it is a proprietary system, and thus much of its operational structure is not publicly known. This means that Skype users must trust the integrity of the Skype software without third-party verification. For instance, to receive calls, a Skype user must leave his or her PC connected to the Internet and available to the Skype system, which means that some of the PC's resources may be used to support other Skype communications without the PC owner's awareness—a feature that has generated some resistance.

A second form of VoIP consists of **analog telephone adapters,** which are devices that allow a user to connect his or her traditional telephone to phone service provided by an access ISP. This choice is frequently bundled with traditional Internet service and/or digital television service.

The third type of VoIP comes in the form of embedded VoIP phones, which are devices that replace a traditional telephone with an equivalent handset connected directly to a TCP/IP network. Embedded VoIP phones are becoming increasingly common for large organizations, many of whom are replacing their traditional internal copper wire telephone systems with VoIP over Ethernet to reduce costs and enhance features.

Finally, the current generation of smartphones use wireless VoIP technology. That is, earlier generations of wireless phones only communicated with the telephone company's network using that company's protocols. Access to the Internet was obtained by gateways between the company's network and the Internet, at which point signals were converted to the TCP/IP system. However, the 4G phone network is an IP-based network throughout, which means a 4G telephone is essentially just another broadband-connected host computer on the global Internet.

Internet Multimedia Streaming An enormous portion of current Internet traffic is used for transporting audio and video across the Internet in real-time, known as **streaming.** Netflix streamed more than 4 billion hours of programming to end users in the first three months of 2013 alone. Combined with YouTube,

The Generations of Wireless Telephones

Mobile phone technology has evolved rapidly since the first simple, handheld electronic units were introduced in the 1980s. An entirely new wave of phone technology has emerged roughly every 10 years since that time, leading up to our current complex, multifunction smartphones. The first generation wireless telephone network transmitted analog voice signals through the air, much like traditional telephones but without the copper wire running into the wall. In retrospect, we call these early phones "1G," or first generation. The second generation used digital signals to encode voice, providing more effective use of the airwaves, and the transmission of other kinds of digital data, like text messaging. The third generation ("**3G**") phone network provided higher data rates, allowing for mobile video calls and other bandwidth-intensive activities. The **4G** network provides even higher data rates and a fully packet-switched IP network, which has allowed smartphones to enjoy the connectivity and flexibility previously available only to broadband-enabled PCs.

these two services will consume more than half of the bandwidth of the Internet in 2014.

On the surface, Internet streaming may not seem to require special consideration. For example, one might guess that an Internet radio station could merely establish a server that would send program messages to each of the clients who requested them. This technique is known as **N-unicast.** (More precisely, *unicast* refers to one sender sending messages to one receiver, whereas *N-unicast* refers to a single sender involved with multiple unicasts.) The N-unicast approach has been applied but has the drawback of placing a substantial burden on the station's server as well as on the server's immediate Internet neighbors. Indeed, N-unicast forces the server to send individual messages to each of its clients on a real-time basis, and all these messages must be forwarded by the server's neighbors.

Most alternatives to N-unicast represent attempts to alleviate this problem. One applies the P2P model in a manner reminiscent of file-sharing systems. That is, once a peer has received data, it begins to distribute that data to those peers that are still waiting, meaning that much of the distribution problem is transferred from the data's source to the peers.

Another alternative, called **multicast,** transfers the distribution problem to the Internet routers. Using multicast, a server transmits a message to multiple clients by means of a single address and relies on the routers in the Internet to recognize the significance of that address and to produce and forward copies of the message to the appropriate destinations. Note then that applications relying on multicast require that the functionality of the Internet routers be expanded beyond their original duties. Multicast support has been implemented in small networks, but has yet to expand to the global Internet.

More importantly, most applications in this category are now **on-demand streaming,** in which the end user expects to view or listen to media at an arbitrary time of his or her choosing. This is quite a different problem from the Internet radio station example, because each end user expects to be able to start, pause, or rewind content at his or her own pace. In this case, N-unicast and multicast technologies are of little help. Each on-demand stream is effectively unicast from a media server that stores the content to the end user that wishes to retrieve it.

In order for this type of streaming to scale to thousands or even millions of simultaneous users, each with his or her own personal stream, replication of the content to many distinct servers is essential. Large-scale streaming services make use of **content delivery networks (CDNs),** groups of servers distributed strategically around the Internet that specialize in streaming copies of content to nearby end users in their network "neighborhood." In many cases, CDN machines may reside in an access ISP network, allowing customers of that access ISP to stream copies of multimedia content at high speed from a nearby server that is much closer in the network than the streaming service's central server machines. A networking technology called **anycast,** which enables an end user to automatically connect to the closest server out of a defined group of servers, helps to make CDNs practical.

Internet streaming of high-definition, on-demand video has permeated far more than traditional PCs. A broad class of embedded devices such as televisions, DVD/Blu-ray players, smartphones, and game consoles connect directly to the TCP/IP network to select viewable content from a multitude of both free and subscription servers.

Questions & Exercises

1. What is the purpose of tier-1 and tier-2 ISPs? What is the purpose of access ISPs?
2. What is DNS?
3. What bit pattern is represented by 3.6.9 in dotted decimal notation? Express the bit pattern 0001010100011100 using dotted decimal notation.
4. In what way is the structure of a mnemonic address of a computer on the Internet (such as `overthruster.propulsion.yoyodyne.com`) similar to a traditional postal address? Does this same structure occur in IP addresses?
5. Name three types of servers found on the Internet and tell what each does.
6. What aspects of network communication are described by a protocol?
7. In what way do the P2P and multicast approaches to Internet radio broadcast differ from N-unicast?
8. What criteria should one consider when choosing one of the four types of VoIP?

4.3 The World Wide Web

The World Wide Web had its origins in the work of Tim Berners-Lee who realized the potential of combining internet technology with the concept of linked-documents, called **hypertext.** His first software for implementing the Web was released in December, 1990. While this early prototype did not yet support multimedia data, it included the key components of what we now recognize as the World Wide Web: a hypertext document format for embedding **hyperlinks** to other documents; a protocol for transferring hypertext across the network, and a server process that supplied hypertext pages upon request. From this humble beginning, the Web quickly grew to support images, audio and video, and by the mid-1990s had become the dominant application powering the growth of the Internet.

Web Implementation

Software packages that allow users to access hypertext on the Internet fall into one of two categories: **browsers** and **webservers.** A browser resides on the user's computer and is charged with the tasks of obtaining materials requested by the user and presenting these materials to the user in an organized manner. Common Internet browsers include Firefox, Safari, and Internet Explorer. The webserver resides on a computer containing hypertext documents to be accessed. Its task is to provide access to the documents under its control as requested by clients (browsers). Hypertext documents are normally transferred between browsers and webservers using a protocol known as the Hypertext Transfer Protocol (HTTP).

In order to locate and retrieve documents on the Web, each document is given a unique address called a **Uniform Resource Locator (URL).** Each URL contains the information needed by a browser to contact the proper server and request the desired document. Thus to view a webpage, a person first provides his or her browser with the URL of the desired document and then instructs the browser to retrieve and display the document.

A typical URL is presented in Figure 4.8. It consists of four segments: the protocol to use to communicate with the server controlling access to the document, the mnemonic address of the machine containing the server, the directory path needed for the server to find the directory containing the document, and the name of the document itself. In short, the URL in Figure 4.8 tells a browser to contact the webserver on the computer known as `eagle.mu.edu` using the protocol `HTTP` and to retrieve the document named `Julius_Caesar.html` found within the subdirectory `Shakespeare` within the directory called `authors`.

Sometimes a URL might not explicitly contain all the segments shown in Figure 4.8. For example, if the server does not need to follow a directory path

Figure 4.8 A typical URL

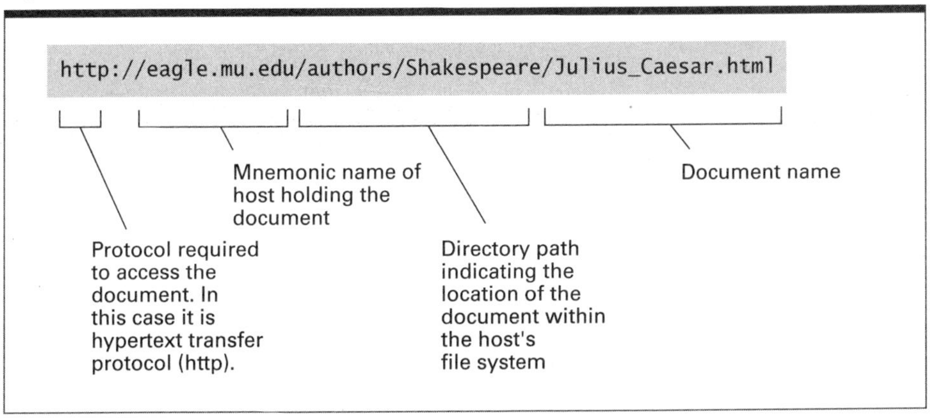

to reach the document, no directory path will appear in the URL. Moreover, sometimes a URL will consist of only a protocol and the mnemonic address of a computer. In these cases, the webserver at that computer will return a predetermined document, typically called a home page, that usually describes the information available at that website. Such shortened URLs provide a simple means of contacting organizations. For example, the URL `http://www.google.com` will lead to the home page of Google, which contains hyperlinks to the services, products, and documents relating to the company.

To further simplify locating websites, many browsers assume that the HTTP protocol should be used if no protocol is identified. These browsers correctly retrieve the Google home page when given the "URL" consisting merely of `www.google.com`.

HTML

A traditional hypertext document is similar to a text file because its text is encoded character by character using a system such as ASCII or Unicode. The distinction is that a hypertext document also contains special symbols, called **tags,** that describe how the document should appear on a display screen, what multimedia resources (such as images) should accompany the document, and which items within the document are linked to other documents. This system of tags is known as **Hypertext Markup Language (HTML).**

Thus, it is in terms of HTML that an author of a webpage describes the information that a browser needs in order to present the page on the user's screen and to find any related documents referenced by the current page. The process is analogous to adding typesetting directions to a plain typed text (perhaps using a red pen) so that a typesetter will know how the material should appear in its final form. In the case of hypertext, the red markings are replaced by HTML tags, and a browser ultimately plays the role of the typesetter, reading the HTML tags to learn how the text is to be presented on the computer screen.

The HTML-encoded version (called the **source** version) of an extremely simple webpage is shown in Figure 4.9a. Note that the tags are delineated by the symbols < and >. The HTML source document consists of two sections—a head (surrounded by the `<head>` and `</head>` tags) and a body (surrounded by the `<body>` and `</body>` tags). The distinction between the head and body of a webpage is similar to that of the head and body of an interoffice memo. In both cases, the head contains preliminary information about the document (date, subject,

The World Wide Web Consortium

The World Wide Web Consortium (W3C) was formed in 1994 to promote the World Wide Web by developing protocol standards (known as W3C standards). W3C is headquartered at CERN, the high-energy particle physics laboratory in Geneva, Switzerland. CERN is where the original HTML markup language was developed as well as the HTTP protocol for transferring HTML documents over the Internet. Today W3C is the source of many standards (including standards for XML and numerous multimedia applications) that lead to compatibility over a wide range of Internet products. You can learn more about W3C via its website at http://www.w3c.org.

etc. in the case of a memo). The body contains the meat of the document, which in the case of a webpage is the material to be presented on the computer screen when the page is displayed.

The head of the webpage displayed in Figure 4.9a contains only the title of the document (surrounded by "title" tags). This title is only for documentation purposes; it is not part of the page that is to be displayed on the computer screen. The material that is displayed on the screen is contained in the body of the document.

The first entry in the body of the document in Figure 4.9a is a level-one heading (surrounded by the <h1> and </h1> tags) containing the text "My Web Page." Being a level-one heading means that the browser should display this text prominently on the screen. The next entry in the body is a paragraph of text (surrounded by the <p> and </p> tags) containing the text "Click here for another page." Figure 4.9b shows the page as it would be presented on a computer screen by a browser.

In its present form, the page in Figure 4.9 is not fully functional in the sense that nothing will happen when the viewer clicks on the word *here*,

Figure 4.9 A simple webpage

a. The page encoded using HTML.

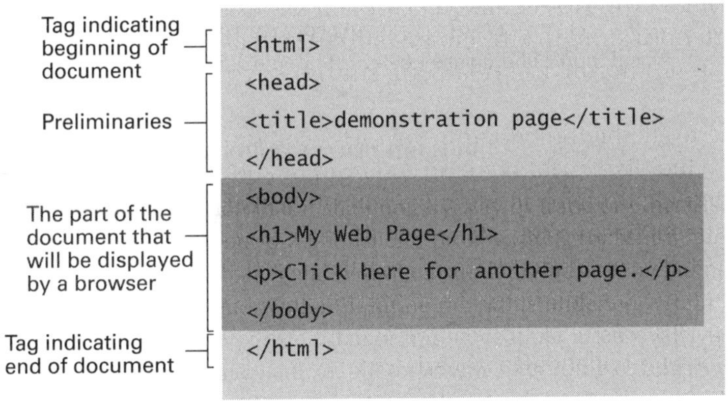

b. The page as it would appear on a computer screen.

even though the page implies that doing so will cause the browser to display another page. To cause the appropriate action, we must link the word *here* to another document.

Let us suppose that, when the word *here* is clicked, we want the browser to retrieve and display the page at the URL `http://crafty.com/demo.html`. To do so, we must first surround the word *here* in the source version of the page with the tags `<a>` and `</a>`, which are called anchor tags. Inside the opening anchor tag we insert the parameter

```
href = http://crafty.com/demo.html
```

(as shown in Figure 4.10a) indicating that the hypertext reference (`href`) associated with the tag is the URL following the equal sign (`http://crafty.com/demo.html`). Having added the anchor tags, the webpage will now appear on a computer screen as shown in Figure 4.10b. Note that this is identical to Figure 4.9b except that the word *here* is highlighted by color indicating that it is a link to another webpage. Clicking on such highlighted terms will cause the browser to retrieve and display the associated webpage. Thus, it is by means of anchor tags that webpages are linked to each other.

Finally, we should indicate how an image could be included in our simple webpage. For this purpose, let us suppose that a JPEG encoding of the image we want to include is stored as the file named `OurPic.jpg` in the directory `Images` at `Images.com` and is available via the webserver at that location. Under these conditions, we can tell a browser to display the image at the top of the webpage by inserting the image tag `<img src = "http://Images.com/Images/OurPic.jpg">` immediately after the `<body>` tag in the HTML source document. This tells the browser that the image named `OurPic.jpg` should be displayed at the beginning of the document. (The term `src` is short for "source," meaning that the information following the equal sign indicates the source of the image to be displayed.) When the browser finds this tag, it will send a message to the HTTP server at `Images.com` requesting the image called `OurPic.jpg` and then display the image appropriately.

If we moved the image `tag` to the end of the document just before the `</body>` tag, then the browser would display the image at the bottom of the webpage. There are, of course, more sophisticated techniques for positioning an image on a webpage, but these need not concern us now.

XML

HTML is essentially a notational system by which a text document along with the document's appearance can be encoded as a simple text file. In a similar manner we can also encode nontextual material as text files—an example being sheet music. At first glance the pattern of staffs, measure bars, and notes in which music is traditionally represented does not conform to the character-by-character format dictated by text files. However, we can overcome this problem by developing an alternative notation system. More precisely, we could agree to represent the start of a staff by `<staff clef = "treble">`, the end of the staff by `</staff>`, a time signature with the form `<time> 2/4 </time>`, the beginning and ending of a measure by `<measure>` and `</measure>`, respectively, a

Figure 4.10 An enhanced simple webpage

a. The page encoded using HTML.

```
<html>
<head>
<title>demonstration page</title>
</head>
<body>
<h1>My Web Page</h1>
<p>Click
   <a href="http://crafty.com/demo.html">
   here
   </a>
   for another page.</p>
</body>
</html>
```

Anchor tag containing parameter — `<a href="http://crafty.com/demo.html">`

Closing anchor tag — `</a>`

b. The page as it would appear on a computer screen.

note such as an eighth note on C as `<notes> egth C </notes>`, and so on. Then the text

```
<staff clef = "treble"> <key>C minor</key>
<time> 2/4 </time>
<measure> <rest> egth </rest> <notes> egth G,
egth G, egth G </notes></measure>
<measure> <notes> hlf E </notes></measure>
</staff>
```

could be used to encode the music shown in Figure 4.11. Using such notation, sheet music could be encoded, modified, stored, and transferred over the Internet as text files. Moreover, software could be written to present the contents of such files in the form of traditional sheet music or even to play the music on a synthesizer.

Figure 4.11 The first two bars of Beethoven's Fifth Symphony

Note that our sheet music encoding system encompasses the same style used by HTML. We chose to delineate the tags that identify components by the symbols `<` and `>`. We chose to indicate the beginning and end of structures (such as a staff, string of notes, or measure) by tags of the same name—the ending tag being designated by a slash (a `<measure>` was terminated with the tag `</measure>`). And we chose to indicate special attributes within tags by expressions such as `clef = "treble"`. This same style could also be used to develop systems for representing other formats such as mathematical expressions and graphics.

The **eXtensible Markup Language (XML)** is a standardized style (similar to that of our music example) for designing notational systems for representing data as text files. (Actually, XML is a simplified derivative of an older set of standards called the Standard Generalized Markup Language, better known as SGML.) Following the XML standard, notational systems called **markup languages** have been developed for representing mathematics, multimedia presentations, and music. In fact, HTML is the markup language based on the XML standard that was developed for representing webpages. (Actually, the original version of HTML was developed before the XML standard was solidified, and therefore some features of HTML do not strictly conform to XML. That is why you might see references to XHTML, which is the version of HTML that rigorously adheres to XML.)

XML provides a good example of how standards are designed to have wide-ranging applications. Rather than designing individual, unrelated markup languages for encoding various types of documents, the approach represented by XML is to develop a standard for markup languages in general. With this standard, markup languages can be developed for various applications. Markup languages developed in this manner possess a uniformity that allows them to be combined to obtain markup languages for complex applications such as text documents that contain segments of sheet music and mathematical expressions.

Finally, we should note that XML allows the development of new markup languages that differ from HTML in that they emphasize semantics rather than appearance. For example, with HTML the ingredients in a recipe can be marked so that they appear as a list in which each ingredient is positioned on a separate line. But if we used semantic-oriented tags, ingredients in a recipe could be marked ...dients (perhaps using the tags `<ingredient>` and `</ingredient>`) rather ...rely items in a list. The difference is subtle but important. The seman- ...oach would allow **search engines** (websites that assist users in locating ...aterial pertaining to a subject of interest) to identify recipes that contain ...not contain certain ingredients, which would be a substantial improvement the current state of the art in which only recipes that do or do not contain ...ain words can be isolated. More precisely, if semantic tags are used, a search ...gine can identify recipes for lasagna that do not contain spinach, whereas ...similar search based merely on word content would skip over a recipe that started with the statement "This lasagna does not contain spinach." In turn, by using an Internet-wide standard for marking documents according to semantics rather than appearance, a World Wide *Semantic* Web, rather than the World Wide *Syntactic* Web we have today, would be created.

Client-Side and Server-Side Activities

Consider now the steps that would be required for a browser to retrieve the simple webpage shown in Figure 4.10 and display it on the browser's computer screen. First, playing the role of a client, the browser would use the information in a URL (perhaps obtained from the person using the browser) to contact the webserver controlling access to the page and ask that a copy of the page be transferred to it. The server would respond by sending the text document displayed in Figure 4.10a to the browser. The browser would then interpret the HTML tags in the document to determine how the page should be displayed and present the document on its computer screen accordingly. The user of the browser would see an image like that depicted in Figure 4.10b. If the user then clicked the mouse over the word *here*, the browser would use the URL in the associated anchor tag to contact the appropriate server to obtain and display another webpage. In summary, the process consists of the browser merely fetching and displaying webpages as directed by the user.

But what if we wanted a webpage involving animation or one that allows a customer to fill out an order form and submit the order? These needs would require additional activity by either the browser or the webserver. Such activities are called **client-side** activities if they are performed by a client (such as a browser) or **server-side** activities if they are performed by a server (such as a webserver).

As an example, suppose a travel agent wanted customers to be able to identify desired destinations and dates of travel, at which time the agent would present the customer with a customized webpage containing only the information pertinent to that customer's needs. In this case the travel agent's website would first provide a webpage that presents a customer with the available destinations. On the basis of this information, the customer would specify the destinations of interest and desired dates of travel (a client-side activity). This information would then be transferred back to the agent's server where it would be used to construct the appropriate customized webpage (a server-side activity), which would then be sent to the customer's browser.

Another example occurs when using the services of a search engine. In this case a user at the client specifies a topic of interest (a client-side activity), which is then transferred to the search engine where a customized webpage identifying documents of possible interest is constructed (a server-side activity) and sent back to the client. Still another example occurs in the case of Web mail—an increasingly popular means by which computer users are able to access their email by means of Web browsers. In this case, the webserver is an intermediary between the client and the client's mail server. Essentially, the webserver builds webpages that contain information from the mail server (a server-side activity) and sends those pages to the client where the client's browser displays them (a client-side activity). Conversely, the browser allows the user to create messages (a client-side activity) and sends that information to the webserver, which then forwards the messages to the mail server (a server-side activity) for mailing.

There are numerous systems for performing client- and server-side activities, each competing with the others for prominence. An early and still popular means of controlling client-side activities is to include programs written in the language JavaScript (developed by Netscape Communications, Inc.) within the HTML source document for the webpage. From there a browser can extract the programs and follow them as needed. Another approach (developed by Sun Microsystems) is to first transfer a webpage to a browser and then transfer additional program units called applets (written in the language Java) to the browser as requested within the HTML source document. Still another approach is the system Flash (developed by Macromedia) by which extensive multimedia client-side presentations can be implemented.

An early means of controlling server-side activities was to use a set of standards called CGI (Common Gateway Interface) by which clients could request the execution of programs stored at a server. A variation of this approach (developed by Sun Microsystems) is to allow clients to cause program units called servlets to be executed at the server side. A simplified version of the servlet approach is applicable when the requested server-side activity is the construction of a customized webpage, as in our travel agent example. In this case webpage templates called JavaServer Pages (JSP) are stored at the webserver and completed using information received from a client. A similar approach is used by Microsoft, where the templates from which customized webpages are constructed are called Active Server Pages (ASP). In contrast to these proprietary systems, PHP (originally standing for Personal Home Page but now considered to mean PHP Hypertext Preprocessor) is an open source system for implementing server-side functionality.

Finally, we would be remiss if we did not recognize the security and ethical problems that arise from allowing clients and servers to execute programs on the other's machine. The fact that webservers routinely transfer programs to clients where they are executed leads to ethical questions on the server side and security questions on the client side. If the client blindly executes any program sent to it by a webserver, it opens itself to malicious activities by the server. Likewise, the fact that clients can cause programs to be executed at the server leads to ethical questions on the client side and security questions on the server side. If the server blindly executes any program sent to it by a client, security breaches and potential damage at the server could result.

Questions & Exercises

1. What is a URL? What is a browser?
2. What is a markup language?
3. What is the difference between HTML and XML?
4. What is the purpose of each of the following HTML tags?
   a. `<html>`
   b. `<head>`
   c. `</p>`
   d. `</a>`
5. To what do the terms *client side* and *server side* refer?

4.4 Internet Protocols

In this section we investigate how messages are transferred over the Internet. This transfer process requires the cooperation of all the computers in the system, and therefore software for controlling this process resides on every computer in the Internet. We begin by studying the overall structure of this software.

The Layered Approach to Internet Software

A principal task of networking software is to provide the infrastructure required for transferring messages from one machine to another. In the Internet, this message-passing activity is accomplished by means of a hierarchy of software units, which perform tasks analogous to those that would be performed if you were to send a gift in a package from the West Coast of the United States to a friend on the East Coast (Figure 4.12). You would first wrap the gift as a package and write the appropriate address on the outside of the package. Then, you would take the package to a shipping company such as the U.S. Postal Service. The shipping company might place the package along with others in a large container and deliver the container to an airline, whose services it has contracted. The airline would place the container in an aircraft and transfer it to the destination city, perhaps with intermediate stops along the way. At the final destination, the airline would remove the container from the aircraft and give it to the shipping company's office at the destination. In turn, the shipping company would take your package out of the container and deliver it to the addressee.

In short, the transportation of the gift would be carried out by a three-level hierarchy: (1) the user level (consisting of you and your friend), (2) the shipping company, and (3) the airline. Each level uses the next lower level as an abstract tool. (You are not concerned with the details of the shipping company, and the shipping company is not concerned with the internal operations of the airline.) Each level in the hierarchy has representatives at both the origin and the

Figure 4.12 Package-shipping example

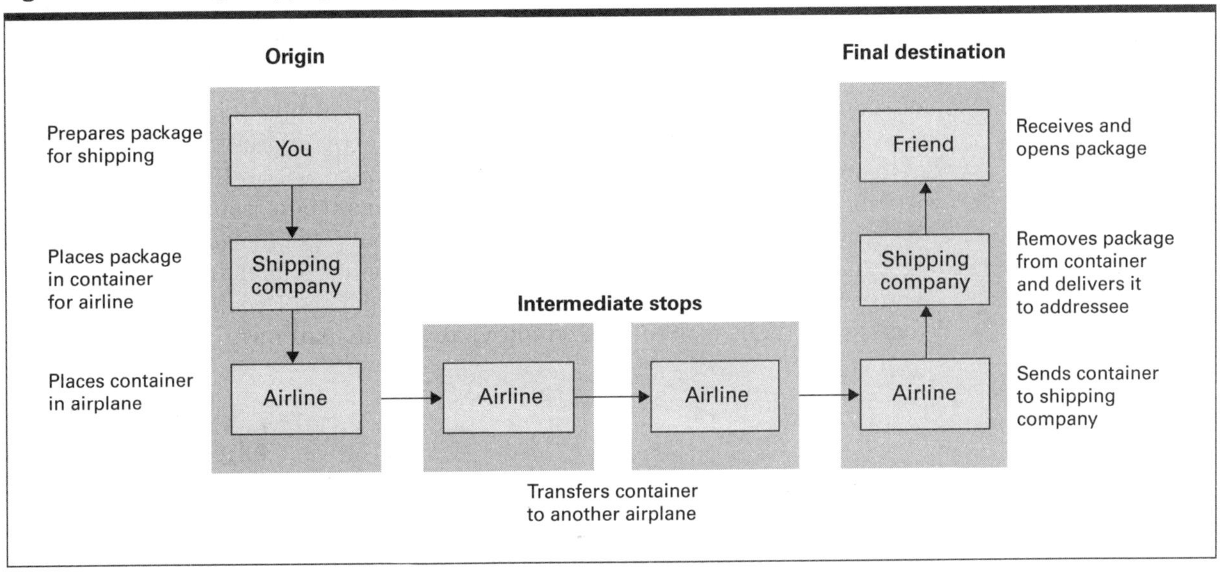

destination, with the representatives at the destination tending to do the reverse of their counterparts at the origin.

Such is the case with software for controlling communication over the Internet, except that the Internet software has four layers rather than three, each consisting of a collection of software routines rather than people and businesses. The four layers are known as the **application layer,** the **transport layer,** the **network layer,** and the **link layer** (Figure 4.13). A message typically originates in the application layer. From there it is passed down through the transport and network layers as it is prepared for transmission, and finally it is transmitted by the link layer. The message is received by the link layer at the destination and passed back up the hierarchy until it is delivered to the application layer at the message's destination.

Let us investigate this process more thoroughly by tracing a message as it finds its way through the system (Figure 4.14). We begin our journey with the application layer.

The application layer consists of those software units such as clients and servers that use Internet communication to carry out their tasks. Although the names are similar, this layer is not restricted to software in the application classification presented in Section 3.2, but also includes many utility packages. For example, software for transferring files using FTP or for providing remote login capabilities using SSH have become so common that they are normally considered utility software.

The application layer uses the transport layer to send and receive messages over the Internet in much the same way that you would use a shipping company to send and receive packages. Just as it is your responsibility to provide an address compatible with the specifications of the shipping company, it is the application layer's responsibility to provide an address that is compatible with the Internet infrastructure. To fulfill this need, the application layer may use the services of the name servers within the Internet to translate mnemonic addresses used by humans into Internet-compatible IP addresses.

Figure 4.13 The Internet software layers

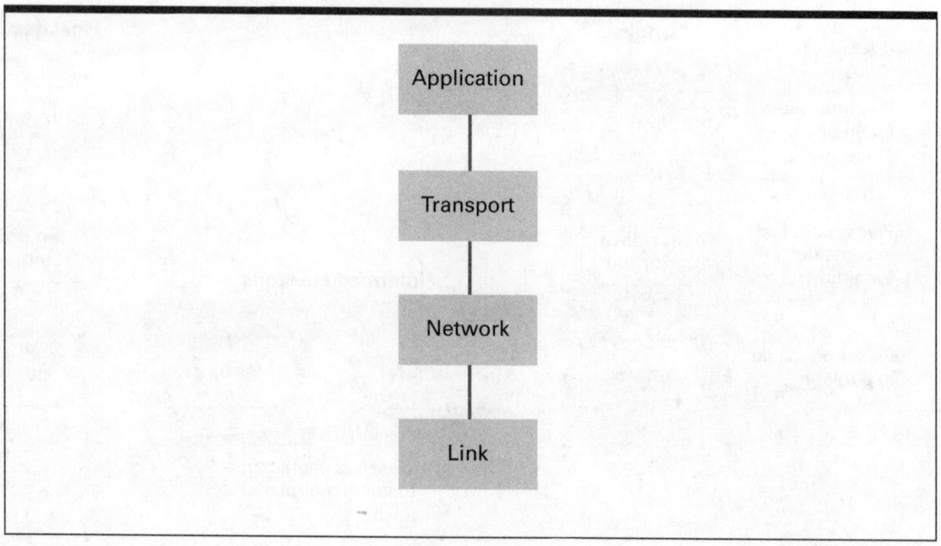

Figure 4.14 Following a message through the Internet

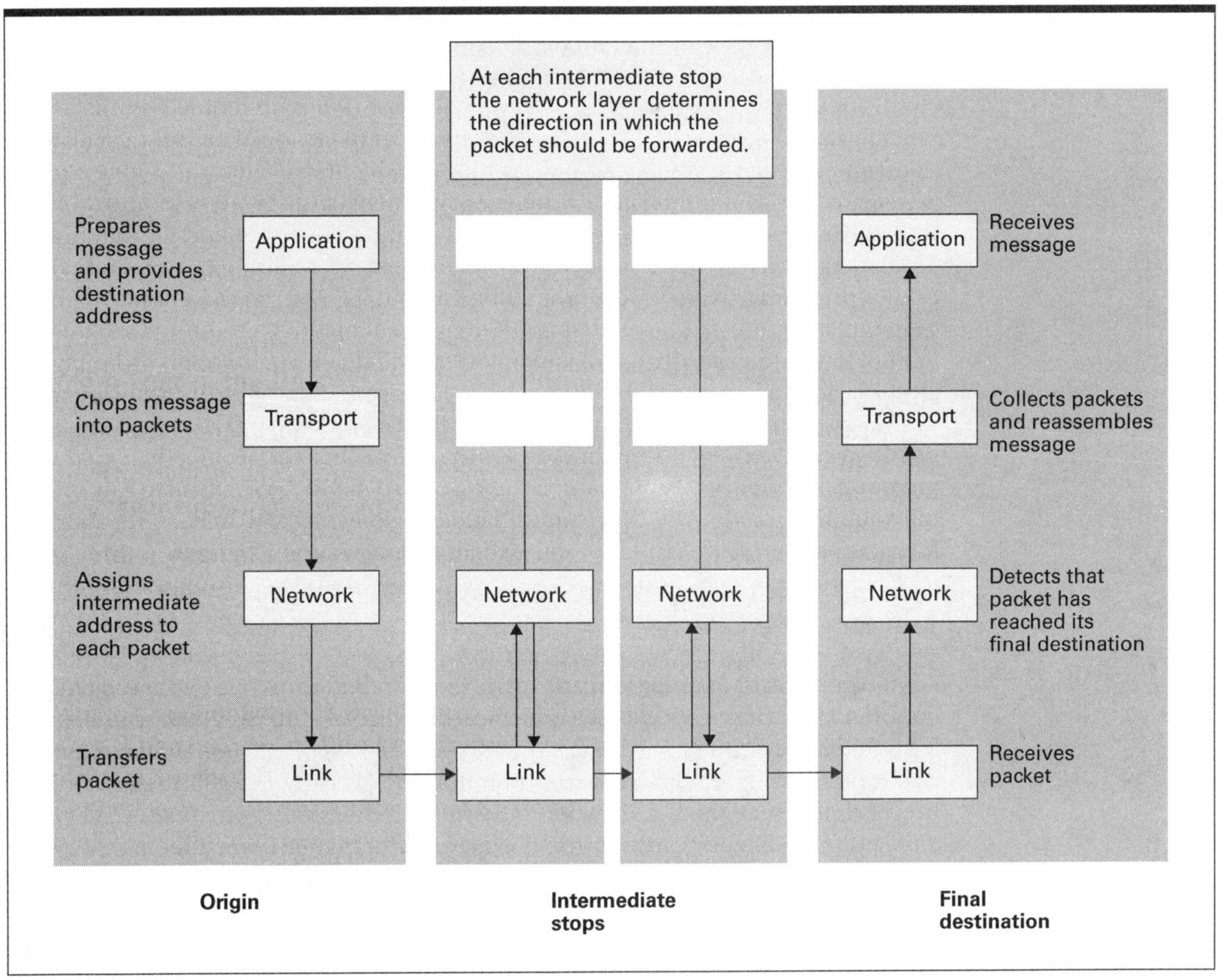

An important task of the transport layer is to accept messages from the application layer and to ensure that the messages are properly formatted for transmission over the Internet. Toward this latter goal, the transport layer divides long messages into small segments, which are transmitted over the Internet as individual units. This division is necessary because a single long message can obstruct the flow of other messages at the Internet routers where numerous messages cross paths. Indeed, small segments of messages can interweave at these points, whereas a long message forces others to wait while it passes (much like cars waiting for a long train to pass at a railroad crossing).

The transport layer adds sequence numbers to the small segments it produces so that the segments can be reassembled at the message's destination. Then it hands these segments, known as **packets,** to the network layer. From this point, the packets are treated as individual, unrelated messages until they reach the transport layer at their final destination. It is quite possible for the packets related to a common message to follow different paths through the Internet.

It is the network layer's job to decide in which direction a packet should be sent at each step along the packet's path through the Internet. In fact, the combination of the network layer and the link layer below it constitutes the software residing on the Internet routers. The network layer is in charge of maintaining the router's forwarding table and using that table to determine the direction in which to forward packets. The link layer at the router is in charge of receiving and transmitting the packets.

Thus, when the network layer at a packet's origin receives the packet from the transport layer, it uses its forwarding table to determine where the packet should be sent to get it started on its journey. Having determined the proper direction, the network layer hands the packet to the link layer for actual transmission.

The link layer has the responsibility of transferring the packet. Thus the link layer must deal with the communication details particular to the individual network in which the computer resides. For instance, if that network is an Ethernet, the link layer applies CSMA/CD. If the network is a WiFi network, the link layer applies CSMA/CA.

When a packet is transmitted, it is received by the link layer at the other end of the connection. There, the link layer hands the packet up to its network layer where the packet's final destination is compared to the network layer's forwarding table to determine the direction of the packet's next step. With this decision made, the network layer returns the packet to the link layer to be forwarded along its way. In this manner each packet hops from machine to machine on its way to its final destination.

Note that only the link and network layers are involved at the intermediate stops during this journey (see again Figure 4.14), and thus these are the only layers present on routers, as previously noted. Moreover, to minimize the delay at each of these intermediate "stops," the forwarding role of the network layer within a router is closely integrated with the link layer. In turn, the time required for a modern router to forward a packet is measured in millionths of a second.

At a packet's final destination, it is the network layer that recognizes that the packet's journey is complete. In that case the network layer hands the packet to its transport layer rather than forwarding it. As the transport layer receives packets from the network layer, it extracts the underlying message segments and reconstructs the original message according to the sequence numbers that were provided by the transport layer at the message's origin. Once the message is assembled, the transport layer hands it to the appropriate unit within the application layer—thus completing the message transmission process.

Determining which unit within the application layer should receive an incoming message is an important task of the transport layer. This is handled by assigning unique **port numbers** (not related to the I/O ports discussed in Chapter 2) to the various units and requiring that the appropriate port number be appended to a message's address before starting the message on its journey. Then, once the message is received by the transport layer at the destination, the transport layer merely hands the message to the application layer software at the designated port number.

Users of the Internet rarely need to be concerned with port numbers because the common applications have universally accepted port numbers. For example, if a Web browser is asked to retrieve the document whose URL is `http://www.zoo.org/animals/frog.html`, the browser assumes that it should contact the HTTP server at `www.zoo.org` via port number 80. Likewise, when sending email, an SMTP client assumes that it should communicate with the SMTP mail server through port number 25.

In summary, communication over the Internet involves the interaction of four layers of software. The application layer deals with messages from the application's point of view. The transport layer converts these messages into segments that are compatible with the Internet and reassembles messages that are received before delivering them to the appropriate application. The network layer deals with directing the segments through the Internet. The link layer handles the actual transmission of segments from one machine to another. With all this activity, it is somewhat amazing that the response time of the Internet is measured in milliseconds, so that many transactions appear to take place instantaneously.

The TCP/IP Protocol Suite

The demand for open networks has generated a need for published standards by which manufacturers can supply equipment and software that function properly with products from other vendors. One standard that has resulted is the **Open System Interconnection (OSI)** reference model, produced by the International Organization for Standardization. This standard is based on a seven-level hierarchy as opposed to the four-level hierarchy we have just described. It is an often-quoted model because it carries the authority of an international organization, but it has been slow to replace the four-level point of view, mainly because it was established after the four-level hierarchy had already become the de facto standard for the Internet.

The TCP/IP protocol suite is a collection of protocol standards used by the Internet to implement the four-level communication hierarchy. Actually, the **Transmission Control Protocol (TCP)** and the **Internet Protocol (IP)** are the names of only two of the protocols in this vast collection—so the fact that the entire collection is referred to as the TCP/IP protocol suite is rather misleading. More precisely, TCP defines a version of the transport layer. We say a *version* because the TCP/IP protocol suite provides for more than one way of implementing the transport layer; one of the other options is defined by the **User Datagram Protocol (UDP).** This diversity is analogous to the fact that when shipping a package, you have a choice of different shipping companies, each of which offers the same basic service but with its own unique characteristics. Thus, depending on the particular quality of service required, a unit within the application layer might choose to send data via a TCP or UDP version of the transport layer (Figure 4.15).

There are several differences between TCP and UDP. One is that before sending a message as requested by the application layer, a transport layer based on TCP sends its own message to the transport layer at the destination telling it that a message is about to be sent. It then waits for this message to be acknowledged before starting to send the application layer's message. In this manner, a TCP transport layer is said to establish a connection before sending a message. A transport layer based on UDP does not establish such a connection prior to sending a message. It merely sends the message to the address it was given and forgets about it. For all it knows, the destination computer might not even be operational. For this reason, UDP is called a connectionless protocol.

Another difference between TCP and UDP is that TCP transport layers at the origin and destination work together by means of acknowledgments and packet retransmissions to assure that all segments of a message are successfully transferred to the destination. For this reason TCP is called a reliable protocol, whereas UDP, which does not offer such retransmission services, is said to be an unreliable protocol.

Figure 4.15 Choosing between TCP and UDP

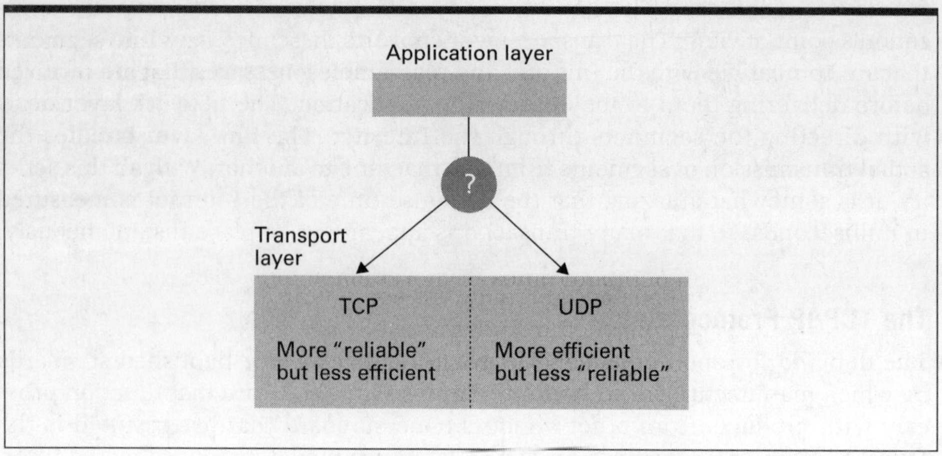

Still another distinction between TCP and UDP is that TCP provides for both **flow control,** meaning that a TCP transport layer at a message's origin can reduce the rate at which it transmits segments to keep from overwhelming its counterpart at the destination, as well as **congestion control,** meaning that a TCP transport layer at a message's origin can adjust its transmission rate to alleviate congestion between it and the message's destination.

All this does not mean that UDP is a poor choice. After all, a transport layer based on UDP is more streamlined than a layer based on TCP, and thus if an application is prepared to handle the potential consequences of UDP, that option might be the better choice. For example, the efficiency of UDP makes it the protocol of choice for DNS lookups and VoIP. However, because email is less time sensitive, mail servers use TCP to transfer email.

IP is the Internet's standard for implementing the tasks assigned to the network layer. We have already observed that this task consists of **forwarding,** which involves relaying packets through the Internet, and **routing,** which involves updating the layer's forwarding table to reflect changing conditions. For instance, a router may malfunction, meaning that traffic should no longer be forwarded in its direction, or a section of the Internet may become congested, meaning that traffic should be routed around the blockage. Much of the IP standard associated with routing deals with the protocols used for communication among neighboring network layers as they interchange routing information.

An interesting feature associated with forwarding is that each time an IP network layer at a message's origin prepares a packet, it appends a value called a **hop count,** or time to live, to that packet. This value is a limit to the number of times the packet should be forwarded as it tries to find its way through the Internet. Each time an IP network layer forwards a packet, it decrements that packet's hop count by one. With this information, the network layer can protect the Internet from packets circling endlessly within the system. Although the Internet continues to grow on a daily basis, an initial hop count of 64 remains more than sufficient to allow a packet to find its way through the maze of routers within today's ISPs.

For years a version of IP known as IPv4 (IP version four) has been used for implementing the network layer within the Internet. However, the Internet is rapidly outgrowing the 32-bit internet addressing system dictated by IPv4. To solve this problem as well as to implement other improvements such as multicast, a new version of IP known as IPv6, which uses internet addresses consisting of 128 bits, has been established. The process of converting from IPv4 to IPv6 is currently underway—this is the conversion that was alluded to in our introduction of Internet addresses in Section 4.2—and it is expected that the use of 32-bit addresses within the Internet will be extinct by 2025.

Questions & Exercises

1. What layers of the Internet software hierarchy are not needed at a router?
2. What are some differences between a transport layer based on the TCP protocol and another based on the UDP protocol?
3. How does the transport layer determine which unit with the application layer should receive an incoming message?
4. What keeps a computer on the Internet from recording copies of all the messages passing through it?

4.5 Security

When a computer is connected to a network, it becomes subject to unauthorized access and vandalism. In this section we address topics associated with these problems.

Forms of Attack

There are numerous ways that a computer system and its contents can be attacked via network connections. Many of these incorporate the use of malicious software (collectively called **malware**). Such software might be transferred to, and executed on, the computer itself, or it might attack the computer from a distance. Examples of software that is transferred to, and executed on, the computer under

The Computer Emergency Response Team

In November 1988 a worm released into the Internet caused significant disruption of service. Consequently, the U.S. Defense Advanced Research Projects Agency (DARPA—pronounced "DAR–pa") formed the Computer Emergency Response Team (CERT—pronounced "SERT"), located at the CERT Coordination Center at Carnegie-Mellon University. The CERT is the Internet's security "watchdog." Among its duties are the investigation of security problems, the issuance of security alerts, and the implementation of public awareness campaigns to improve Internet security. The CERT Coordination Center maintains a website at http://www.cert.org where it posts notices of its activities.

attack include viruses, worms, Trojan horses, and spyware, whose names reflect the primary characteristic of the software.

A **virus** is software that infects a computer by inserting itself into programs that already reside in the machine. Then, when the "host" program is executed, the virus is also executed. When executed, many viruses do little more than try to transfer themselves to other programs within the computer. Some viruses, however, perform devastating actions such as degrading portions of the operating system, erasing large blocks of mass storage, or otherwise corrupting data and other programs.

A **worm** is an autonomous program that transfers itself through a network, taking up residence in computers and forwarding copies of itself to other computers. As in the case of a virus, a worm can be designed merely to replicate itself or to perform more extreme vandalism. A characteristic consequence of a worm is an explosion of the worm's replicated copies that degrades the performance of legitimate applications and can ultimately overload an entire network or internet.

A **Trojan horse** is a program that enters a computer system disguised as a desirable program, such as a game or useful utility package, that is willingly imported by the victim. Once in the computer, however, the Trojan horse performs additional activities that might have harmful effects. Sometimes these additional activities start immediately. In other instances, the Trojan horse might lie dormant until triggered by a specific event such as the occurrence of a preselected date. Trojan horses often arrive in the form of attachments to enticing email messages. When the attachment is opened (that is, when the recipient asks to view the attachment), the misdeeds of the Trojan horse are activated. Thus, email attachments from unknown sources should never be opened.

Another form of malicious software is **spyware** (sometimes called **sniffing** software), which is software that collects information about activities at the computer on which it resides and reports that information back to the instigator of the attack. Some companies use spyware as a means of building customer profiles, and in this context, it has questionable ethical merit. In other cases, spyware is used for blatantly malicious purposes such as recording the symbol sequences typed at the computer's keyboard in search of passwords or credit card numbers.

As opposed to obtaining information secretly by sniffing via spyware, **phishing** is a technique of obtaining information explicitly by simply asking for it. The term *phishing* is a play on the word *fishing* because the process involved is to cast numerous "lines" in hopes that someone will "take the bait." Phishing is often carried out via email, and in this form, it is little more than an old telephone con. The perpetrator sends email messages posing as a financial institution, a government bureau, or perhaps a law enforcement agency. The email asks the potential victim for information that is supposedly needed for legitimate purposes. However, the information obtained is used by the perpetrator for hostile purposes.

In contrast to suffering from such internal infections as viruses and spyware, a computer in a network can also be attacked by software being executed on other computers in the system. An example is a **denial of service (DoS)** attack, which is the process of overloading a computer with messages. Denial of service attacks have been launched against large commercial webservers on the Internet to disrupt the company's business and in some cases have brought the company's commercial activity to a halt.

A denial of service attack requires the generation of a large number of messages over a brief period of time. To accomplish this, an attacker usually plants software on numerous unsuspecting computers that will generate messages when a signal is given. Then, when the signal is given, all of these computers (sometimes called a **botnet**) swamp the target with messages. Inherent, then, in denial of service attacks is the availability of unsuspecting computers to use as accomplices. This is why all PC users are discouraged from leaving their computers connected to the Internet when not in use. It has been estimated that once a PC is connected to the Internet, at least one intruder will attempt to exploit its existence within 20 minutes. In turn, an unprotected PC represents a significant threat to the integrity of the Internet.

Another problem associated with an abundance of unwanted messages is the proliferation of unwanted junk email, called **spam.** However, unlike a denial of service attack, the volume of spam is rarely sufficient to overwhelm the computer system. Instead, the effect of spam is to overwhelm the person receiving the spam. This problem is compounded by the fact that, as we have already seen, spam is a widely adopted medium for phishing and instigating Trojan horses that might spread viruses and other detrimental software.

Protection and Cures

The old adage "an ounce of prevention is worth a pound of cure" is certainly true in the context of controlling vandalism over network connections. A primary prevention technique is to filter traffic passing through a point in the network, usually with a program called a **firewall.** For instance, a firewall might be installed at the gateway of an organization's intranet to filter messages passing in and out of the region. Such firewalls might be designed to block outgoing messages with certain destination addresses or to block incoming messages from origins that are known to be sources of trouble. This latter function is a tool for terminating a denial of service attack because it provides a means of blocking traffic from the attacking computers. Another common role of a firewall at a gateway is to block all incoming messages that have origin addresses within the region accessed through the gateway because such a message would indicate that an outsider is pretending to be a member of the inside region. Masquerading as a party other than one's self is known as **spoofing.**

Firewalls are also used to protect individual computers rather than entire networks or domains. For example, if a computer is not being used as a webserver, a name server, or an email server, then a firewall should be installed at that computer to block all incoming traffic addressed to such applications. Indeed, one way an intruder might gain entry to a computer is by establishing contact through a "hole" left by a nonexistent server. In particular, one method for retrieving information gathered by spyware is to establish a clandestine server on the infected computer by which malicious clients can retrieve the spyware's findings. A properly installed firewall could block the messages from these malicious clients.

Some variations of firewalls are designed for specific purposes—an example being **spam filters,** which are firewalls designed to block unwanted email. Many spam filters use rather sophisticated techniques to distinguish between desirable email and spam. Some learn to make this distinction via a training process in which the user identifies items of spam until the filter acquires enough examples to make decisions on its own. These filters are examples of how a variety of subject areas (probability theory, artificial intelligence, etc.) can jointly contribute to developments in other fields.

Another preventative tool that has filtering connotations is the **proxy server.** A proxy server is a software unit that acts as an intermediary between a client and a server with the goal of shielding the client from adverse actions of the server. Without a proxy server, a client communicates directly with a server, meaning that the server has an opportunity to learn a certain amount about the client. Over time, as many clients within an organization's intranet deal with a distant server, that server can collect a multitude of information about the intranet's internal structure—information that can later be used for malicious activity. To counter this, an organization can establish a proxy server for a particular kind of service (FTP, HTTP, telnet, etc.). Then, each time a client within the intranet tries to contact a server of that type, the client is actually placed in contact with the proxy server. In turn, the proxy server, playing the role of a client, contacts the actual server. From then on the proxy server plays the role of an intermediary between the actual client and the actual server by relaying messages back and forth. The first advantage of this arrangement is that the actual server has no way of knowing that the proxy server is not the true client, and in fact, it is never aware of the actual client's existence. In turn, the actual server has no way of learning about the intranet's internal features. The second advantage is that the proxy server is in position to filter all the messages sent from the server to the client. For example, an FTP proxy server could check all incoming files for the presence of known viruses and block all infected files.

Still another tool for preventing problems in a network environment is auditing software that is similar to the auditing software we learned about in our discussion on operating system security (Section 3.5). Using network auditing software, a system administrator can detect a sudden increase in message traffic at various locations within the administrator's realm, monitor the activities of the system's firewalls, and analyze the pattern of requests being made by the individual computers in order to detect irregularities. In effect, auditing software is an administrator's primary tool for identifying problems before they grow out of control.

Another means of defense against invasions via network connections is software called **antivirus software,** which is used to detect and remove the presence of known viruses and other infections. (Actually, antivirus software represents a broad class of software products, each designed to detect and remove a specific type of infection. For example, whereas many products specialize in virus control, others specialize in spyware protection.) It is important for users of these packages to understand that, just as in the case of biological systems, new computer infections are constantly coming on the scene that require updated vaccines. Thus, antivirus software must be routinely maintained by downloading updates from the software's vendor. Even this, however, does not guarantee the safety of a computer. After all, a new virus must first infect some computers before it is discovered and a vaccine is produced. Thus, a wise computer user never opens email attachments from unfamiliar sources, does not download software without first confirming its reliability, does not respond to pop-up adds, and does not leave a PC connected to the Internet when such connection is not necessary.

Encryption

In some cases the purpose of network vandalism is to disrupt the system (as in denial of service attacks), but in other cases the ultimate goal is to gain access to information. The traditional means of protecting information is to control its access through the use of passwords. However, passwords can be compromised and are of little value when data are transferred over networks and internets where messages are relayed by unknown entities. In these cases encryption can be used so that even if the data fall into unscrupulous hands, the encoded information will remain confidential. Today, many traditional Internet applications have been altered to incorporate encryption techniques, producing what are called "secure versions" of the applications.

A prime example is the secure version of HTTP, known as **HTTPS,** which is used by most financial institutions to provide customers with secure Internet access to their accounts. The backbone of HTTPS is the protocol system known as **Secure Sockets Layer (SSL),** which was originally developed by Netscape to provide secure communication links between Web clients and servers. Most browsers indicate the use of SSL by displaying a tiny padlock icon on the computer screen. (Some use the presence or absence of the icon to indicate whether SSL is being used; others display the padlock in either the locked or unlocked position.)

One of the more fascinating topics in the field of encryption is **public-key encryption,** which involves techniques by which encryption systems are designed so that having knowledge about how messages are encrypted does not allow one to decrypt messages. This characteristic is somewhat counterintuitive. After all, intuition would suggest that if a person knows how messages are encrypted, then that person should be able to reverse the encryption process and thus decrypt messages. But public-key encryption systems defy this intuitive logic.

A public-key encryption system involves the use of two values called keys. One key, known as the **public key,** is used to encrypt messages; the other key, known as the **private key,** is required to decrypt messages. To use the system, the public key is first distributed to those who might need to send messages to a particular destination. The private key is held in confidence at this destination. Then, the originator of a message can encrypt the message using the public key and send the message to its destination with assurance that its contents are safe, even if it is handled by intermediaries who also know the public key. Indeed, the only party that can decrypt the message is the party at the message's destination who holds the private key. Thus if Bob creates a public-key encryption system and gives both Alice and Carol the public key, then both Alice and Carol can encrypt messages to Bob, but they cannot spy on the other's communication. Indeed, if Carol intercepts a message from Alice, she cannot decrypt it even though she knows how Alice encrypted it (Figure 4.16).

There are, of course, subtle problems lurking within public-key systems. One is to ensure that the public key being used is, in fact, the proper key for the destination party. For example, if you are communicating with your bank, you want to be sure that the public key you are using for encryption is the one for the bank and not an impostor. If an impostor presents itself as the bank (an example of spoofing) and gives you its public key, the messages you encrypt and send to the "bank" would be meaningful to the impostor and not your bank. Thus, the task of associating public keys with correct parties is significant.

One approach to resolving this problem is to establish trusted Internet sites, called **certificate authorities,** whose task is to maintain accurate lists of parties and their public keys. These authorities, acting as servers, then provide reliable public-key information to their clients in packages known as **certificates.** A certificate is a package containing a party's name and that party's public key.

Figure 4.16 Public key encryption

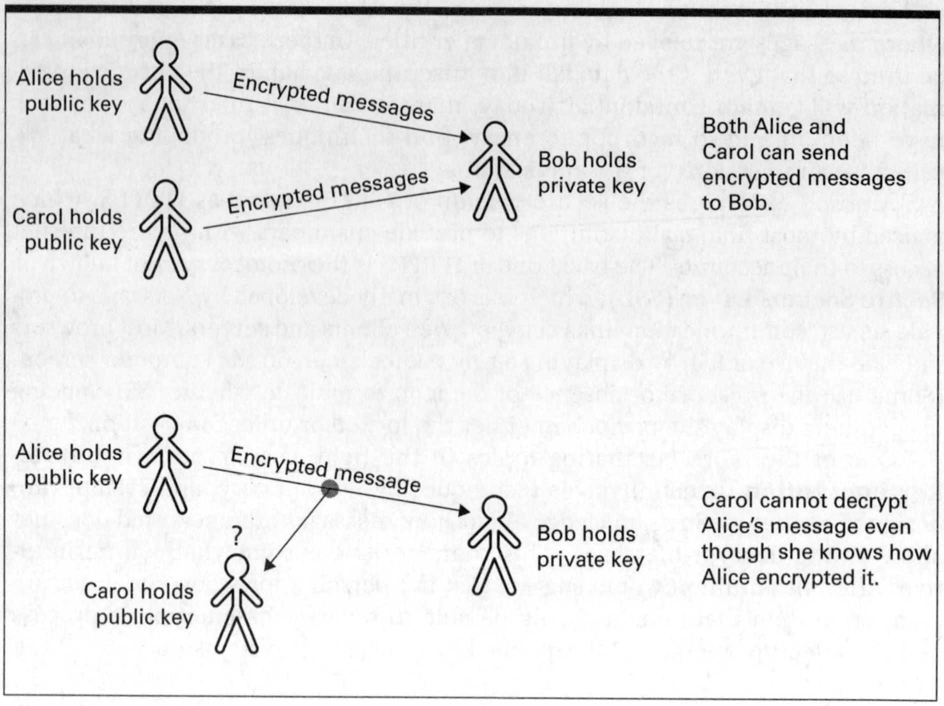

Many commercial certificate authorities are now available on the Internet, although it is also common for organizations to maintain their own certificate authorities in order to maintain tighter control over the security of the organization's communication.

Finally, we should comment on the role public-key encryption systems play in solving problems of **authentication**—making sure that the author of a message is, in fact, the party it claims to be. The critical point here is that, in some public-key encryption systems, the roles of the encryption and decryption keys can be reversed. That is, text can be encrypted with the private key, and because only one party has access to that key, any text that is so encrypted must have originated from that party. In this manner, the holder of the private key can produce a bit pattern, called a **digital signature,** that only that party knows how to produce. By attaching that signature to a message, the sender can mark the message as being authentic. A digital signature can be as simple as the encrypted version of the message itself. All the sender must do is encrypt the message being transmitted using his or her private key (the key typically used for decrypting). When the message is received, the receiver uses the sender's public key to decrypt the signature. The message that is revealed is guaranteed to be authentic because only the holder of the private key could have produced the encrypted version.

We will return to the topic of public-key encryption at the end of Chapter 12, as an example of a complex computer algorithm.

Legal Approaches to Network Security

Another way of enhancing the security of computer networking systems is to apply legal remedies. There are, however, two obstacles to this approach. The first is that making an action illegal does not preclude the action. All it does is provide a legal recourse. The second is that the international nature of networking means that obtaining recourse is often very difficult. What is illegal in one country might be legal in another. Ultimately, enhancing network security by legal means is an international project, and thus must be handled by international legal bodies—a potential player would be the International Court of Justice in The Hague.

Having made these disclaimers, we must admit that, although less than perfect, legal forces still have a tremendous influence, and thus it behooves us to explore some of the legal steps that are being taken to resolve conflicts in the networking arena. For this purpose, we use examples from the federal laws of the United States. Similar examples could be drawn from other government bodies such as the European Union.

We begin with the proliferation of malware. In the United States this problem is addressed by the Computer Fraud and Abuse Act, which was first passed in 1984, although it has been amended several times. It is under this act that most cases involving the introduction of worms and viruses have been prosecuted. In short, the act requires proof that the defendant knowingly caused the transmission of a program or data that intentionally caused damage. The Computer Fraud and Abuse Act also covers cases involving the theft of information. In particular, the act outlaws obtaining anything of value via the unauthorized access of a computer. Courts have tended to assign a broad interpretation to the phrase "anything of value," and thus the Computer Fraud and Abuse Act has been applied to more than the theft of information. For instance, courts have ruled that the mere use of a computer might constitute "anything of value."

The right of privacy is another, and perhaps the most controversial, networking issue facing the legal community. Questions involving an employer's right to monitor the communications of employees and the extent to which an Internet service provider is authorized to access the information being communicated by its clients have been given considerable thought. In the United States, many of these questions are addressed by the Electronic Communication Privacy Act (ECPA) of 1986, which has its origins in legislation to control wiretapping. Although the act is lengthy, its intent is captured in a few short excerpts. In particular, it states that

> Except as otherwise specifically provided in this chapter any person who intentionally intercepts, endeavors to intercept, or procures any other person to intercept or endeavor to intercept, any wire, oral, or electronic communication . . . shall be punished as provided in subsection (4) or shall be subject to suit as provided in subsection (5).

and

> . . . any person or entity providing an electronic communication service to the public shall not intentionally divulge the contents of any communication . . . on that service to any person or entity other than an addressee or intended recipient of such communication or an agent of such addressee or intended recipient.

In brief, the ECPA confirms an individual's right to private communication—it is illegal for an Internet service provider to release information about the communication of its clients, and it is illegal for unauthorized personnel to eavesdrop on another's communication. But the ECPA leaves room for debate. For example, the question regarding the rights of an employer to monitor the communication of employees becomes a question of authorization, which courts have tended to grant to employers when the communication is carried out using the employer's equipment.

Moreover, the act goes on to give some government agencies authority to monitor electronic communications under certain restrictions. These provisions have been the source of much debate. For example, in 2000 the FBI revealed the existence of its system, called Carnivore, that reports on the communication of all subscribers of an Internet service provider rather than just a court-designated target, and in 2001 in response to the terrorist attack on the World Trade Center, congress passed the controversial USA PATRIOT (Uniting and Strengthening America by Providing Appropriate Tools Required to Intercept and Obstruct Terrorism) Act that modified the restrictions under which government agencies must operate. In 2013, it was subsequently revealed that these laws had been interpreted to authorize the collection of vast amounts of telephone and Internet usage data on ordinary Americans indiscriminately.

In addition to the legal and ethical controversies raised by these developments, providing monitoring rights raises some technical problems that are more pertinent to our study. One is that to provide these capabilities, a communication system must be constructed and programmed so that communications can be monitored. To establish such capabilities was the goal of the Communications Assistance for Law Enforcement Act (CALEA). It requires telecommunication carriers to modify their equipment to accommodate law enforcement taps—a requirement that has been complex and expensive to meet.

Another controversial issue involves the clash between the government's right to monitor communications and the public's right to use encryption. If the messages being monitored are well encrypted, then tapping the communication is of limited value to law enforcement agencies. Governments in the United States, Canada, and Europe are considering systems that would require the registration of ciphering keys, but such demands are being fought by corporations. After all, due to corporate espionage it is understandable that requiring the registration of ciphering keys would make many law-abiding corporations, as well as citizens, uncomfortable. How secure can the registration system be?

Finally, as a means of recognizing the scope of legal issues surrounding the Internet, we cite the Anticybersquatting Consumer Protection Act of 1999 that is designed to protect organizations from impostors who might otherwise establish look-alike domain names (a practice known as cybersquatting). The act prohibits the use of domain names that are identical or confusingly similar to another's trademark or "common law trademark." One effect is that although the act does not outlaw domain name speculation (the process of registering potentially desirable domain names and later selling the rights to that name), it limits the practice to generic domain names. Thus, a domain name speculator might legally register a generic name such as `GreatUsedCars.com` but might not be able to claim rights to the name `BigAlUsedCars.com` if Big Al is already in the used car business. Such distinctions are often the subject of debate in lawsuits based on the Anticybersquatting Consumer Protection Act.

Questions & Exercises

1. What is *phishing*? How are computers secured against it?
2. What distinction is there between the types of firewalls that can be placed at a domain's gateway as opposed to an individual host within the domain?

3. Technically, the term *data* refers to representations of information, whereas *information* refers to the underlying meaning. Does the use of passwords protect data or information? Does the use of encryption protect data or information?
4. What advantage does public-key encryption have over more traditional encryption techniques?
5. What problems are associated with legal attempts to protect against network security problems?

Chapter Review Problems

(Asterisked problems are associated with optional sections.)

1. What is a protocol? Identify three protocols introduced in this chapter and describe the purpose of each.
2. What is interprocess communication?
3. What is meant by an intranet?
4. Describe the three types of ISP tiers.
5. What is the difference between a bus network and a star network?
6. What happens when two nodes using the CSMA/CD, encounter collision in the network?
7. Can collisions be completely eliminated by using the CSMA/CA like collision avoidance protocols?
8. What is the last mile problem? Describe a technique for solving it.
9. How does a hub differ from a switch?
10. How does a router differ from such devices as repeaters, bridges, and switches?
11. State the distinction between the client-server model and the P2P model.
12. What is the difference between congestion control and flow control?
13. Using 32-bit Internet addresses was originally thought to provide ample room for expansion, but that conjecture is not proving to be accurate. IPv6 uses 128-bit addressing. Will that prove to be adequate? Justify your answer. (For example, you might compare the number of possible addresses to the population of the world.)
14. Encode each of the following bit patterns using dotted decimal notation.
    a. 000001010001001000100011
    b. 1000000000100000
    c. 0011000000011000
15. What bit pattern is represented by each of the following dotted decimal patterns?
    a. 0.0
    b. 26.19.1
    c. 8.12.20.13
16. Suppose the address of an end system on the Internet is quoted as 134.48.4.122. What is the 32-bit address in hexadecimal notation?
17. What is on-demand streaming?
18. If a computer's mnemonic Internet address is `batman.batcave.metropolis.gov` what might you conjecture about the structure of the domain containing the machine?
19. Explain the components of the email address `kermit@animals.com`
20. In the context of VoIP, what is the difference between an analog telephone adapter and an embedded phone?
21. What is the role of a name server?
22. What is the distinction between routing and forwarding?
23. Define each of the following:
    a. Cloud computing
    b. Hot spot
    c. Top-level domains
    d. Secure Shell

24. Define each of the following:
a. Content delivery networks
b. Anycast
c. Markup languages

25. Many "lay users" of the Internet interchange the terms *Internet* and *World Wide Web*. To what do each of the terms correctly refer?

26. When viewing a simple webpage, ask your browser to display the source version of the document. Then identify the basic structure of the document. In particular, identify the head and the body of the document and list some of the statements you find in each.

27. State the difference between sniffing and phishing.

28. Modify the HTML document below so that the word "Rover" is linked to the document whose URL is `http://animals.org/pets/dogs.html`.

```
<html>
<head>
<title>Example</title>
</head>
<body>
<h1> My Pet Dog</h1>
<p>My dog's name is Rover.</p>
</body>
</html>
```

29. Draw a sketch showing how the following HTML document would appear when displayed on a computer screen.

```
<html>
<head>
<title>Example</title>
</head>
<body>
<h1> My Pet Dog</h1>
<img src = "Rover.jpg">
</body>
</html>
```

30. Using the informal XML style presented in the text, design a markup language for representing simple algebraic expressions as text files.

31. Using the informal XML style presented in the text, design a set of tags that a word processor might use for marking the underlying text. For example, how would a word processor indicate what text should be bold, italic, underlined, and so on?

32. Using the informal XML style presented in the text, design a set of tags that could be used to mark motion picture reviews according to the way the text items should appear on a printed page. Then design a set of tags that could be used to mark the reviews according to the meaning of the items in the text.

33. Using the informal XML style presented in the text, design a set of tags that could be used to mark articles about sporting events according to the way the text items should appear on a printed page. Then design a set of tags that could be used to mark the articles according to the meaning of the items in the text.

34. Identify the components of the following URL and describe the meaning of each.
`http://lifeforms.com/animals/moviestars/kermit.html`

35. Identify the components of each of the following abbreviated URLs.
a. `http://www.farmtools.org/windmills.html`
b. `http://castles.org/`
c. `www.coolstuff.com`

36. How would the action of a browser differ if you asked it to "find the document" at the URL `http://stargazer.universe.org` as opposed to `https://stargazer.universe.org`?

37. Give two examples of client-side activities on the Web. Give two examples of server-side activities on the Web.

***38.** What is the TCP/IP protocol suite?

***39.** In a network based on the bus topology, the bus is a nonsharable resource for which the machines must compete in order to transmit messages. How is deadlock (see the optional Section 3.4) controlled in this context?

***40.** List the four layers in the Internet software hierarchy and identify a task performed by each layer.

***41.** Why does the transport layer chop large messages into small packets?

*42. When an application asks the transport layer to use TCP to transmit a message, what additional messages will be sent by the transport layer in order to fulfill the application layer's request?

*43. In what way could TCP be considered a better protocol for implementing the transport layer than UDP? In what way could UDP be considered better than TCP?

*44. What does it mean to say that the TCP is a connection-oriented protocol?

*45. At what layer in the TCP/IP protocol hierarchy could a firewall be placed to filter incoming traffic by means of
   a. Message content
   b. Source address
   c. Type of application

46. Suppose you wanted to establish a firewall to filter out email messages containing certain terms and phrases. Would this firewall be placed at your domain's gateway or at the domain's mail server? Explain your answer.

47. What is SSL and what are its benefits?

48. What is the significance of using spam filters?

49. What is the significance of certificate authorities in public-key encryption?

50. In what sense does the global nature of the Internet limit legal solutions to Internet problems?

Social Issues

The following questions are intended as a guide to the ethical/social/legal issues associated with the field of computing. The goal is not merely to answer these questions. You should also consider why you answered as you did and whether your justifications are consistent from one question to the next.

1. The ability to connect computers via networks has popularized the concept of working at home. What are some pros and cons of this movement? Will it affect the consumption of natural resources? Will it strengthen families? Will it reduce "office politics"? Will those who work at home have the same career advancement opportunities as those who work on site? Will community ties be weakened? Will reduced personal contact with peers have a positive or negative effect?
2. Ordering merchandise over the Internet is becoming an alternative to "hands-on" shopping. What effect will such a shift in shopping habits have on communities? What about shopping malls? What about small shops, such as bookstores and clothing stores, in which you like to browse without buying? To what extent is buying at the lowest possible price good or bad? Is there any moral obligation to pay more for an item in order to support a local business? Is it ethical to compare products at a local store and then order your selection at a lower price via the Internet? What are the long-term consequences of such behavior?
3. To what extent should a government control its citizens' access to the Internet (or any international network)? What about issues that involve national security? What are some security issues that might occur?
4. Electronic bulletin boards allow users of networks to post messages (often anonymously) and read messages posted by others. Should the manager of such a bulletin board be held responsible for its contents? Should a telephone company be held responsible for the contents of telephone conversations?

Should the manager of a grocery store be held responsible for the contents of a community bulletin board located in the store?

5. Should the use of the Internet be monitored? Should it be regulated? If so, by whom and to what extent?
6. How much time do you spend using the Internet? Is that time well spent? Has Internet access altered your social activities? Do you find it easier to talk to people via the Internet than in person?
7. When you buy a software package for a personal computer, the developer usually asks you to register with the developer so that you can be notified of future upgrades. This registration process is increasingly being handled via the Internet. You are usually asked to give such things as your name, address, and perhaps how you learned of the product, and then the developer's software automatically transfers this data to the developer. What ethical issues would be raised if the developer designed the registration software so that it sent additional information to the developer during the registration process? For example, the software might scan the contents of your system and report the other software packages found.
8. When you visit a website, that site has the capability of recording data, called cookies, on your computer indicating that you have visited that site. These cookies can then be used to identify return visitors and to record their previous activities so that future visits to the site can be handled more efficiently. The cookies on your computer also provide a record of the sites you have visited. Should a website have the capability to record cookies on your computer? Should a website be allowed to record cookies on your computer without your knowledge? What are possible benefits of cookies? What problems could arise from the use of cookies?
9. If corporations are required to register their encryption keys with a government agency, will they be safe?
10. In general, etiquette tells us to avoid calling a friend at his or her place of work for personal or social matters such as making arrangements for a weekend outing. Likewise, most of us would hesitate to call a customer at his or her home to describe a new product. In a similar manner, we mail wedding invitations to the guests' residences, whereas we mail announcements of business conferences to the attendees' work addresses. Is it proper to send personal email to a friend via the mail server at the friend's place of employment?
11. Suppose a PC owner leaves the PC connected to the Internet where it ultimately is used by another party to implement a denial of service attack. To what extent should the PC owner be liable? Does your answer depend on whether the owner installed proper firewalls?
12. Is it ethical for companies that produce candy or toys to provide games on their company websites that entertain children while promoting the company's products? What if the game is designed to collect information from the children? What are the boundaries between entertaining, advertising, and exploitation?

Additional Reading

Antoniou, G., P. Groth, F. van Harmelem and R. Hoekstra. *A Semantic Web Primer*, 3rd ed. Cambridge, MA: MIT Press, 2012.

Bishop, M. *Introduction to Computer Security*. Boston, MA: Addison-Wesley, 2005.

Comer, D. E. *Computer Networks and Internets*, 6th ed. Upper Saddle River, NJ: Prentice-Hall, 2014.

Comer, D. E. *Internetworking with TCP/IP, Vol. 1*, 6th ed. Upper Saddle River, NJ: Prentice-Hall, 2013.

Goldfarb, C. F., and P. Prescod. *The XML Handbook*, 5th ed. Upper Saddle River, NJ: Prentice-Hall, 2004.

Halsal, F. *Computer Networking and the Internet*, 5th ed. Boston, MA: Addison-Wesley, 2005.

Harrington, J. L. *Network Security: A Practical Approach*. San Francisco, CA: Morgan Kaufmann, 2005.

Kurose, J. F., and K. W. Ross. *Computer Networking: A Top Down Approach Featuring the Internet*, 6th ed. Boston, MA: Addison-Wesley, 2012.

Peterson, L. L., and B. S. Davie. *Computer Networks: A Systems Approach*, 5th ed. San Francisco, CA: Morgan Kaufmann, 2011.

Rosenoer, J. *CyberLaw: The Law of the Internet*. New York: Springer, 1997.

Spinello, R. A., and H. T. Tavani. *Readings in CyberEthics*, 2nd ed. Sudbury, MA: Jones and Bartlett, 2004.

Stallings, W. *Cryptography and Network Security*, 5th ed. Upper Saddle River, NJ: Prentice-Hall, 2010.

Stevens, W. R. *TCP/IP Illustrated, Vol. 1*. Boston, MA: Addison-Wesley, 1994.

CHAPTER 5

Algorithms

In the introductory chapter we learned that the central theme of computer science is the study of algorithms. It is time now for us to focus on this core topic. Our goal is to explore enough of this foundational material so that we can truly understand and appreciate the science of computing.

We have seen that before a computer can perform a task, it must be given an algorithm telling it precisely what to do; consequently, the study of algorithms is the cornerstone of computer science. In this chapter we introduce many of the fundamental concepts of this study, including the issues of algorithm discovery and representation as well as the major control concepts of iteration and recursion. In so doing we also present a few well-known algorithms for searching and sorting. We begin by reviewing the concept of an algorithm.

5.1 The Concept of an Algorithm

In the introductory chapter we informally defined an algorithm as a set of steps that define how a task is performed. In this section we look more closely at this fundamental concept.

An Informal Review

We have encountered a multitude of algorithms in our study. We have found algorithms for converting numeric representations from one form to another, detecting and correcting errors in data, compressing and decompressing data files, controlling multiprogramming in a multitasking environment, and many more. Moreover, we have seen that the machine cycle that is followed by a CPU is nothing more than the simple algorithm

```
As long as the halt instruction has not been executed continue to
execute the following steps:
  a. Fetch an instruction.
  b. Decode the instruction.
  c. Execute the instruction.
```

As demonstrated by the algorithm describing a magic trick in Figure 0.1, algorithms are not restricted to technical activities. Indeed, they underlie even such mundane activities as shelling peas:

```
Obtain a basket of unshelled peas and an empty bowl. As long as
there are unshelled peas in the basket continue to execute the
following steps:
  a. Take a pea from the basket.
  b. Break open the pea pod.
  c. Dump the peas from the pod into the bowl.
  d. Discard the pod.
```

In fact, many researchers believe that every activity of the human mind, including imagination, creativity, and decision making, is actually the result of algorithm execution—a conjecture we will revisit in our study of artificial intelligence (Chapter 11).

But before we proceed further, let us consider the formal definition of an algorithm.

The Formal Definition of an Algorithm

Informal, loosely defined concepts are acceptable and common in everyday life, but a science must be based on well-defined terminology. Consider, then, the formal definition of an algorithm stated in Figure 5.1.

Figure 5.1 The definition of an algorithm

An algorithm is an ordered set of unambiguous, executable steps that defines a terminating process.

Note that the definition requires that the set of steps in an algorithm be ordered. This means that the steps in an algorithm must have a well-established structure in terms of the order of their execution. This does not mean, however, that the steps must be executed in a sequence consisting of a first step, followed by a second, and so on. Some algorithms, known as parallel algorithms, contain more than one sequence of steps, each designed to be executed by different processors in a multiprocessor machine. In such cases the overall algorithm does not possess a single thread of steps that conforms to the first-step, second-step scenario. Instead, the algorithm's structure is that of multiple threads that branch and reconnect as different processors perform different parts of the overall task. (We will revisit this concept in Chapter 6.) Other examples include algorithms executed by circuits such as the flip-flop in Chapter 1, in which each gate performs a single step of the overall algorithm. Here the steps are ordered by cause and effect, as the action of each gate propagates throughout the circuit.

Next, consider the requirement that an algorithm must consist of executable steps. To appreciate this condition, consider the instruction

```
Make a list of all the positive integers
```

which would be impossible to perform because there are infinitely many positive integers. Thus any set of instructions involving this instruction would not be an algorithm. Computer scientists use the term *effective* to capture the concept of being executable. That is, to say that a step is effective means that it is doable.

Another requirement imposed by the definition in Figure 5.1 is that the steps in an algorithm be unambiguous. This means that during execution of an algorithm, the information in the state of the process must be sufficient to determine uniquely and completely the actions required by each step. In other words, the execution of each step in an algorithm does not require creative skills. Rather, it requires only the ability to follow directions. (In Chapter 12 we will learn that "algorithms," called nondeterministic algorithms, that do not conform to this restriction are an important topic of research.)

The definition in Figure 5.1 also requires that an algorithm define a terminating process, which means that the execution of an algorithm must lead to an end. The origin of this requirement is in theoretical computer science, where the goal is to answer such questions as "What are the ultimate limitations of algorithms and machines?" Here computer science seeks to distinguish between problems whose answers can be obtained algorithmically and problems whose answers lie beyond the capabilities of algorithmic systems. In this context, a line is drawn between processes that culminate with an answer and those that merely proceed forever without producing a result.

There are, however, meaningful applications for nonterminating processes, including monitoring the vital signs of a hospital patient and maintaining an aircraft's altitude in flight. Some would argue that these applications involve merely the repetition of algorithms, each of which reaches an end and then automatically repeats. Others would counter that such arguments are simply attempts to cling to an overly restrictive formal definition. In any case, the result is that the term *algorithm* is often used in applied, or informal, settings in reference to sets of steps that do not necessarily define terminating processes. An example is the long-division "algorithm" that does not define a terminating process for dividing 1 by 3. Technically, such instances represent misuses of the term.

The Abstract Nature of Algorithms

It is important to emphasize the distinction between an algorithm and its representation—a distinction that is analogous to that between a story and a book. A story is abstract, or conceptual, in nature; a book is a physical representation of a story. If a book is translated into another language or republished in a different format, it is merely the representation of the story that changes—the story itself remains the same.

In the same manner, an algorithm is abstract and distinct from its representation. A single algorithm can be represented in many ways. As an example, the algorithm for converting temperature readings from Celsius to Fahrenheit is traditionally represented as the algebraic formula

$$F = (9/5)C + 32$$

But it could be represented by the instruction

Multiply the temperature reading in Celsius by 9/5
and then add 32 to the product

or even in the form of an electronic circuit. In each case the underlying algorithm is the same; only the representations differ.

The distinction between an algorithm and its representation presents a problem when we try to communicate algorithms. A common example involves the level of detail at which an algorithm must be described. Among meteorologists, the instruction "Convert the Celsius reading to its Fahrenheit equivalent" suffices, but a layperson, requiring a more detailed description, might argue that the instruction is ambiguous. The problem, however, is not with the underlying algorithm but that the algorithm is not represented in enough detail for the layperson. In the next section we will see how the concept of primitives can be used to eliminate such ambiguity problems in an algorithm's representation.

Finally, while on the subject of algorithms and their representations, we should clarify the distinction between two other related concepts—programs and processes. A *program* is a representation of an algorithm. (Here we are using the term *algorithm* in its less formal sense in that many programs are representations of nonterminating "algorithms.") In fact, within the computing community the term *program* usually refers to a formal representation of an algorithm designed for computer application. We defined a *process* in Chapter 3 to be the activity of executing a program. Note, however, that to execute a program is to execute the algorithm represented by the program, so a process could equivalently be defined as the activity of executing an algorithm. We conclude that programs, algorithms, and processes are distinct, yet related, entities. A program is the representation of an algorithm, whereas a process is the activity of executing an algorithm.

Questions & Exercises

1. Summarize the distinctions between a process, an algorithm, and a program.
2. Give some examples of algorithms with which you are familiar. Are they really algorithms in the precise sense?
3. Identify some points of vagueness in our informal definition of an algorithm introduced in Section 0.1 of the introductory chapter.
4. In what sense do the steps described by the following list of instructions fail to constitute an algorithm?

   Step 1. Take a coin out of your pocket and put it on the table.

   Step 2. Return to Step 1.

5.2 Algorithm Representation

In this section we consider issues relating to an algorithm's representation. Our goal is to introduce the basic concepts of primitives and pseudocode as well as to establish a representation system for our own use.

Primitives

The representation of an algorithm requires some form of language. In the case of humans this might be a traditional natural language (English, Spanish, Russian, Japanese) or perhaps the language of pictures, as demonstrated in Figure 5.2, which describes an algorithm for folding a bird from a square piece of paper. Often, however, such natural channels of communication lead to misunderstandings, sometimes because the terminology used has more than one meaning. (The sentence, "Visiting grandchildren can be nerve-racking," could mean either that the grandchildren cause problems when they come to visit or that going to see them is problematic.) Problems also arise over misunderstandings regarding the level of detail required. Few readers could successfully fold a bird from the directions given in Figure 5.2, yet a student of origami would probably have little difficulty. In short, communication problems arise when the language used for an algorithm's representation is not precisely defined or when information is not given in adequate detail.

Computer science approaches these problems by establishing a well-defined set of building blocks from which algorithm representations can be constructed. Such a building block is called a **primitive.** Assigning precise definitions to these primitives removes many problems of ambiguity, and requiring algorithms to be described in terms of these primitives establishes a uniform level of detail. A collection of primitives along with a collection of rules stating how the primitives can be combined to represent more complex ideas constitutes a **programming language.**

Each primitive has its own syntax and semantics. Syntax refers to the primitive's symbolic representation; semantics refers to the meaning of the primitive. The syntax of *air* consists of three symbols, whereas the semantics is a gaseous substance that surrounds the world. As an example, Figure 5.3 presents some of the primitives used in origami.

Figure 5.2 Folding a bird from a square piece of paper

To obtain a collection of primitives to use in representing algorithms for computer execution, we could turn to the individual instructions that the machine is designed to execute. If an algorithm is expressed at this level of detail, we will certainly have a program suitable for machine execution. However, expressing algorithms at this level is tedious, and so one normally uses a collection of "higher-level" primitives, each being an abstract tool constructed from the lower-level primitives provided in the machine's language. The result is a formal programming language in which algorithms can be expressed at a conceptually higher level than in machine language. We will discuss such programming languages in the next chapter.

Pseudocode

For now, we forgo the introduction of a formal programming language in favor of a less formal, more intuitive notational system known as pseudocode. In general, a **pseudocode** is a notational system in which ideas can be expressed informally during the algorithm development process.

Figure 5.3 Origami primitives

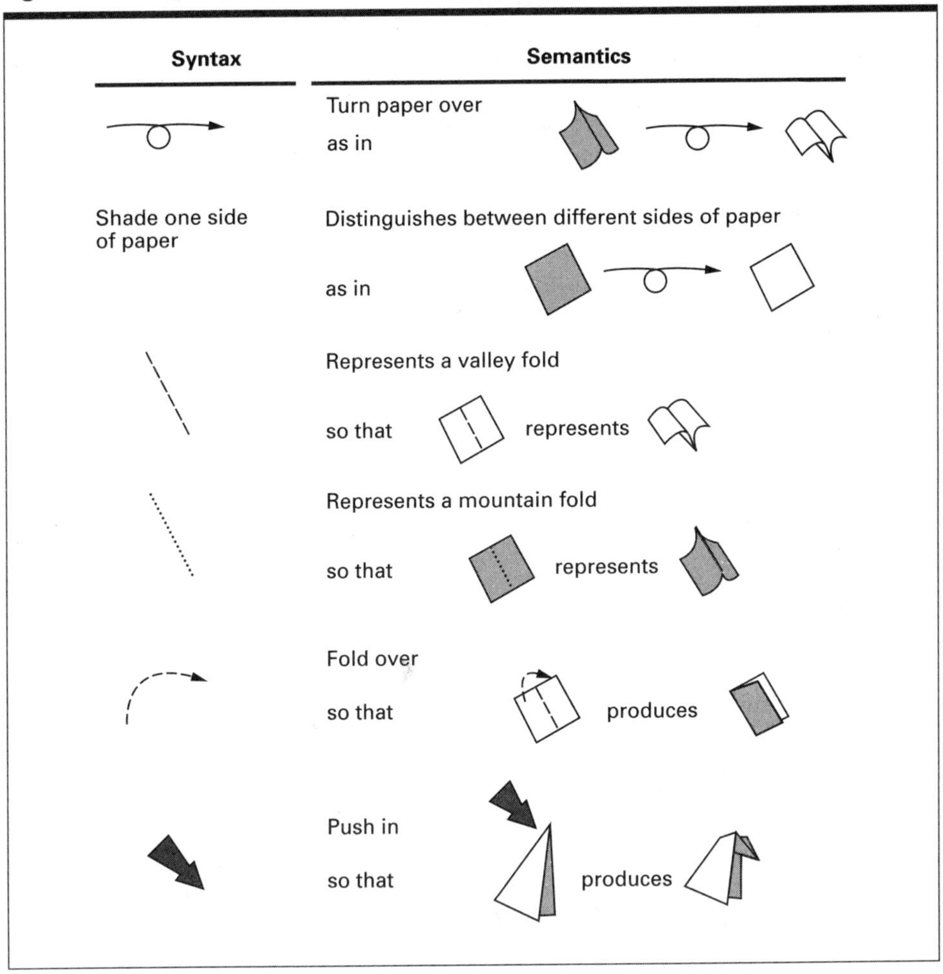

One way to obtain a pseudocode is simply to loosen the rules of a formal programming language, borrowing the syntax-semantic structures of the language, intermixed with less formal constucts. There are many such pseudocode variants, because there are many programming languages in existence. Two particularly popular choices are loose versions of the languages Algol and Pascal, largely because these were widely used in textbooks and academic papers for decades. More recently, pseudocode reminiscent of the Java and C languages has proliferated, again because most programmers will have at least a reading knowledge of these languages. Regardless of where a pseudocode borrows its syntax from, one essential property is required for it to serve its purpose in expressing algorithms: A pseudocode must have a consistent, concise notation for representing recurring semantic structures. For our purposes, we will use a Python-like syntax to express pseudocode throughout the remainder of the book. Some of our pseudocode semantic structures will borrow from language constructs presented in previous chapters, while others will look ahead to constructs to be formally covered in future chapters.

One such recurring semantic structure is the saving of a computed value. For example, if we have computed the sum of our checking and savings account

Algorithm Representation During Algorithm Design

The task of designing a complex algorithm requires that the designer keep track of numerous interrelated concepts—a requirement that can exceed the capabilities of the human mind. Thus the designer of complex algorithms needs a way to record and recall portions of an evolving algorithm as his or her concentration requires.

During the 1950s and 1960s, flowcharts (by which algorithms are represented by geometric shapes connected by arrows) were the state-of-the-art design tool. However, flowcharts often became tangled webs of crisscrossing arrows that made understanding the structure of the underlying algorithm difficult. Thus the use of flowcharts as design tools has given way to other representation techniques. An example is the pseudocode used in this text, by which algorithms are represented with well-defined textual structures. Flowcharts are still beneficial when the goal is presentation rather than design. For example, Figures 5.8 and 5.9 apply flowchart notation to demonstrate the algorithmic structure represented by popular control statements.

The search for better design notations is a continuing process. In Chapter 7 we will see that the trend is to use graphical techniques to assist in the global design of large software systems, while pseudocode remains popular for designing the smaller procedural components within a system.

balances, we may want to save the result so we can refer to it later. In such cases we will use the form

```
name = expression
```

where `name` is the name by which we will refer to the result and `expression` describes the computation whose result is to be saved. This pseudocode structure directly follows the equivalent Python **assignment statement,** which we introduced in Chapter 1 for storing a value into a Python variable. For example, the statement

```
RemainingFunds = CheckingBalance + SavingsBalance
```

is an assignment statement that assigns the sum of `CheckingBalance` and `SavingsBalance` to the name `RemainingFunds`. Thus, the term `RemainingFunds` can be used in future statements to refer to that sum.

Another recurring semantic structure is the selection of one of two possible activities depending on the truth or falseness of some condition. Examples include:

> If the gross domestic product has increased, buy common stock; otherwise, sell common stock.
>
> Buy common stock if the gross domestic product has increased and sell it otherwise.
>
> Buy or sell common stock depending on whether the gross domestic product has increased or decreased, respectively.

Each of these statements could be rewritten to conform to the structure

```
if (condition):
  activity
else:
  activity
```

From Pseudocode to Python

Our pseudocode in this chapter closely mirrors actual Python syntax for the `if` and `while` structures, as well as function definition and calling syntax.

```
if (condition):
  activity
else:
  activity
```

Our pseudocode `if` and `while` structures can be converted to Python simply by being more precise with the **condition** and **activity** portions. For example, rather than the English phrase, "sales have decreased" as a condition, we would need a proper Python comparison expression, such as

```
if (sales_current < sales_previous):
```

where the sales variables had already been assigned in previous lines of the script. Similarly, informal English sentences or phrases used as the **activity** in our pseudocode would need to be replaced with Python statements and expressions such as those we have already seen in earlier chapters.

How can you tell the difference between pseudocode and actual Python code in this book? As a rule, real Python code uses operators (like "<", "=", or "+") to string together multiple named variables into more complex expressions, or commas to separate a list of parameters being sent to a function. Articles like "the" and "a," or prepositions like "from" appear in pseudocode. We use periods at the end of sentences in pseudocode; Python statements do not have punctuation at the end.

where we have used the keywords `if` and `else` to announce the different substructures within the main structure and have used colons and indentation to delineate the boundaries of these substructures. The **condition** and the `else` will always be followed immediately by a colon. The corresponding **activity** will be indented. If an **activity** consists of multiple steps, they will all be similarly indented. By adopting this syntactic structure for our pseudocode, we acquire a uniform way in which to express this common semantic structure. Thus, whereas the statement

> Depending on whether the year is a leap year, divide the total by 366 or 365, respectively

might possess a more creative literary style, we will consistently opt for the straightforward

```
if (year is leap year):
  daily total = total / 366
else:
  daily total = total / 365
```

We also adopt the shorter syntax

```
if (condition):
  Activity
```

for those cases not involving an `else` activity. Using this notation, the statement

> Should it be the case that sales have decreased, lower the price by 5%.

will be reduced to

```
if (sales have decreased):
  lower the price by 5%
```

Still another common semantic structure is the repeated execution of a statement or sequence of statements as long as some condition remains true. Informal examples include

> As long as there are tickets to sell, continue selling tickets.

and

> While there are tickets to sell, keep selling tickets.

For such cases, we adopt the uniform pattern

```
while (condition):
  Activity
```

for our pseudocode. In short, such a statement means to check the `condition` and, if it is true, perform the `activity` and return to check the `condition` again. If, however, the `condition` is found to be false, move on to the next instruction following the `while` structure. Thus both of the preceding statements are reduced to

```
while (tickets remain to be sold):
  sell a ticket
```

In many programming languages, indentation often enhances the readability of a program. In Python, and thus also in our Python-derived pseudocode, indentation is essential to the notation. For example, in the statement

```
if (not raining):
  if (temperature == hot):
    go swimming
  else:
    play golf
else:
  watch television
```

indentation tells us that the question of whether `temperature` equals `hot` will not even be asked unless it is `not raining`. Note the use of double equal signs, "==" to differentiate between assignment (=) and comparison (==). The question about the temperature is **nested** inside the if-statement, and is, in effect, the activity to be performed if the outer if-statement condition holds true. Similarly, indentation tells us that `else: play golf` belongs to the inner if-statement, rather than to the outer if-statement. Thus we will adopt the use of indentation in our pseudocode.

We want to use our pseudocode to describe activities that can be used as abstract tools in other applications. Computer science has a variety of terms for such program units, including subprogram, subroutine, procedure, method, and function, each with its own variation of meaning. We will follow Python convention, using the term **function** for our pseudocode and using the Python keyword def to announce the title by which the pseudocode unit will be known. More precisely, we will begin a pseudocode unit with a statement of the form

```
def name():
```

where name is the particular name of the unit. We will then follow this introductory statement with the statements that define the unit's action. For example, Figure 5.4 is a pseudocode representation of a function called Greetings that prints the message "Hello" three times.

When the task performed by a function is required elsewhere in our pseudocode, we will merely request it by name. For example, if two functions were named ProcessLoan and RejectApplication, then we could request their services within an if-else structure by writing

```
if (. . . ):
  ProcessLoan()
else:
  RejectApplication()
```

which would result in the execution of the function ProcessLoan if the tested condition were true or in the execution of RejectApplication if the condition were false.

If functions are to be used in different situations, they should be designed to be as generic as possible. A function for sorting lists of names should be designed to sort any list—not a particular list—so it should be written in such a way that the list to be sorted is not specified in the function itself. Instead, the list should be referred to by a generic name within the function's representation.

In our pseudocode, we will adopt the convention of listing these generic names (which are called **parameters**) in parentheses on the same line on which we identify the function's name. In particular, a function named Sort, which is designed to sort any list of names, would begin with the statement

```
def Sort (List):
```

Later in the representation where a reference to the list being sorted is required, the generic name List would be used. In turn, when the services of Sort are required, we will identify which list is to be substituted for List in the function Sort. Thus we will write something such as

```
Sort(the organization's membership list)
```

and

```
Sort(the wedding guest list)
```

depending on our needs.

Figure 5.4 The function Greetings in pseudocode

```
def Greetings():
  Count = 3
  while (Count > 0):
    print('Hello')
    Count = Count - 1
```

Naming Items in Programs

In a natural language, items often have multiword names such as "cost of producing a widget" or "estimated arrival time." Experience has shown that use of such multiword names in the representation of an algorithm can complicate the algorithm's description. It is better to have each item identified by a single contiguous block of text. Over the years many techniques have been used to compress multiple words into a single lexical unit to obtain descriptive names for items in programs. One is to use underlines to connect words, producing names such as `estimated_arrival_time`. Another is to use uppercase letters to help a reader comprehend a compressed multiword name. For example, one could start each word with an uppercase letter to obtain names such as `EstimatedArrivalTime`. This technique is called **Pascal casing,** because it was popularized by users of the Pascal programming language. A variation of Pascal casing is called **camel casing,** which is identical to Pascal casing except that the first letter remains in lowercase as in `estimatedArrivalTime`. In this text we lean toward Pascal casing, but the choice is largely a matter of taste.

Questions & Exercises

1. A primitive in one context might turn out to be a composite of primitives in another. For instance, our `while` statement is a primitive in our pseudocode, yet it is ultimately implemented as a composite of machine-language instructions. Give two examples of this phenomenon in a non-computer setting.
2. In what sense is the construction of functions the construction of primitives?
3. The Euclidean algorithm finds the greatest common divisor of two positive integers X and Y by the following process:

   As long as the value of neither X nor Y is zero, assign the larger the remainder of dividing the larger by the smaller. The greatest common divisor, if it exists, will be the remaining non-zero value.

   Express this algorithm in our pseudocode.
4. Describe a collection of primitives that are used in a subject other than computer programming.

5.3 Algorithm Discovery

The development of a program consists of two activities—discovering the underlying algorithm and representing that algorithm as a program. Up to this point we have been concerned with the issues of algorithm representation without considering the question of how algorithms are discovered in the first place. Yet algorithm discovery is usually the more challenging step in the software development process. After all, discovering an algorithm to solve a problem requires finding a method of solving that problem. Thus, to understand how algorithms are discovered is to understand the problem-solving process.

The Art of Problem Solving

The techniques of problem solving and the need to learn more about them are not unique to computer science but rather are topics pertinent to almost any field. The close association between the process of algorithm discovery and that of general problem solving has caused computer scientists to join with those of other disciplines in the search for better problem-solving techniques. Ultimately, one would like to reduce the process of problem solving to an algorithm in itself, but this has been shown to be impossible. (This is a result of the material in Chapter 12, where we will show that there are problems that do not have algorithmic solutions.) Thus the ability to solve problems remains more of an artistic skill to be developed than a precise science to be learned.

As evidence of the elusive, artistic nature of problem solving, the following loosely defined problem-solving phases presented by the mathematician G. Polya in 1945 remain the basic principles on which many attempts to teach problem-solving skills are based today.

Phase 1. Understand the problem.

Phase 2. Devise a plan for solving the problem.

Phase 3. Carry out the plan.

Phase 4. Evaluate the solution for accuracy and for its potential as a tool for solving other problems.

Translated into the context of program development, these phases become

Phase 1. Understand the problem.

Phase 2. Get an idea of how an algorithmic function might solve the problem.

Phase 3. Formulate the algorithm and represent it as a program.

Phase 4. Evaluate the program for accuracy and for its potential as a tool for solving other problems.

Having presented Polya's list, we should emphasize that these phases are not steps to be followed when trying to solve a problem but rather phases that will be completed sometime during the solution process. The key word here is *followed*. You do not solve problems by following. Rather, to solve a problem, you must take the initiative and lead. If you approach the task of solving a problem in the frame of mind depicted by "Now I've finished Phase 1, it's time to move on to Phase 2," you are not likely to be successful. However, if you become involved with the problem and ultimately solve it, you most likely can look back at what you did and realize that you performed Polya's phases.

Another important observation is that Polya's phases are not necessarily completed in sequence. Successful problem solvers often start formulating strategies for solving a problem (Phase 2) before the problem itself is entirely understood (Phase 1). Then, if these strategies fail (during Phases 3 or 4), the potential problem solver gains a deeper understanding of the intricacies of the problem and, with this deeper understanding, can return to form other and hopefully more successful strategies.

Keep in mind that we are discussing how problems are solved—not how we would like them to be solved. Ideally, we would like to eliminate the waste inherent in the trial-and-error process just described. In the case of developing large software systems, discovering a misunderstanding as late as Phase 4 can represent a tremendous loss in resources. Avoiding such catastrophes is a major goal of software engineers (Chapter 7), who have traditionally insisted on a thorough understanding of a problem before proceeding with a solution. One could argue, however, that a true understanding of a problem is not obtained until a solution has been found. The mere fact that a problem is unsolved implies a lack of understanding. To insist on a complete understanding of the problem before proposing any solutions is therefore somewhat idealistic.

As an example, consider the following problem:

> Person A is charged with the task of determining the ages of person B's three children. B tells A that the product of the children's ages is 36. After considering this clue, A replies that another clue is required, so B tells A the sum of the children's ages. Again, A replies that another clue is needed, so B tells A that the oldest child plays the piano. After hearing this clue, A tells B the ages of the three children.
>
> How old are the three children?

At first glance the last clue seems to be totally unrelated to the problem, yet it is apparently this clue that allows A to finally determine the ages of the children. How can this be? Let us proceed by formulating a plan of attack and following this plan, even though we still have many questions about the problem. Our plan will be to trace the steps described by the problem statement while keeping track of the information available to person A as the story progresses.

The first clue given A is that the product of the children's ages is 36. This means that the triple representing the three ages is one of those listed in Figure 5.5(a). The next clue is the sum of the desired triple. We are not told what this sum is, but we are told that this information is not enough for A to isolate the correct triple; therefore the desired triple must be one whose sum appears at least twice in the table of Figure 5.5(b). But the only triples appearing in Figure 5.5(b) with identical sums are (1,6,6) and (2,2,9), both of which produce the sum 13. This is the information available to A at the time the last clue is given. It is at this point that we finally understand the significance of the last clue. It has nothing to do with playing the piano; rather it is the fact that there is an oldest child. This rules out the triple (1,6,6) and thus allows us to conclude that the children's ages are 2, 2, and 9.

In this case, then, it is not until we attempt to implement our plan for solving the problem (Phase 3) that we gain a complete understanding of the problem (Phase 1). Had we insisted on completing Phase 1 before proceeding, we would probably never have found the children's ages. Such irregularities in the problem-solving process are fundamental to the difficulties in developing systematic approaches to problem solving.

Figure 5.5 Analyzing the possibilities

a. Triples whose product is 36		b. Sums of triples from part (a)	
(1,1,36)	(1,6,6)	1 + 1 + 36 = 38	1 + 6 + 6 = 13
(1,2,18)	(2,2,9)	1 + 2 + 18 = 21	2 + 2 + 9 = 13
(1,3,12)	(2,3,6)	1 + 3 + 12 = 16	2 + 3 + 6 = 11
(1,4,9)	(3,3,4)	1 + 4 + 9 = 14	3 + 3 + 4 = 10

Another irregularity is the mysterious inspiration that might come to a potential problem solver who, having worked on a problem without apparent success, at a later time suddenly sees the solution while doing another task. This phenomenon was identified by H. von Helmholtz as early as 1896 and was discussed by the mathematician Henri Poincaré in a lecture before the Psychological Society in Paris. There, Poincaré described his experiences of realizing the solution to a problem he had worked on after he had set it aside and begun other projects. The phenomenon reflects a process in which a subconscious part of the mind appears to continue working and, if successful, forces the solution into the conscious mind. Today, the period between conscious work on a problem and the sudden inspiration is known as an incubation period, and its understanding remains a goal of current research.

Getting a Foot in the Door

We have been discussing problem solving from a somewhat philosophical point of view while avoiding a direct confrontation with the question of how we should go about trying to solve a problem. There are, of course, numerous problem-solving approaches, each of which can be successful in certain settings. We will identify some of them shortly. For now, we note that there seems to be a common thread running through these techniques, which simply stated is "get your foot in the door." As an example, let us consider the following simple problem:

> Before A, B, C, and D ran a race they made the following predictions:
>
> A predicted that B would win.
> B predicted that D would be last.
> C predicted that A would be third.
> D predicted that A's prediction would be correct.
>
> Only one of these predictions was true, and this was the prediction made by the winner. In what order did A, B, C, and D finish the race?

After reading the problem and analyzing the data, it should not take long to realize that since the predictions of A and D were equivalent and only one prediction was true, the predictions of both A and D must be false. Thus neither A nor D were winners. At this point we have our foot in the door, and obtaining the complete solution to our problem is merely a matter of extending our knowledge from here. If A's prediction was false, then B did not win either. The only remaining choice for the winner is C. Thus, C won the race, and C's prediction was true. Consequently, we know that A came in third. That means that the finishing order was either CBAD or CDAB. But the former is ruled out because B's prediction must be false. Therefore the finishing order was CDAB.

Of course, being told to get our foot in the door is not the same as being told how to do it. Obtaining this toehold, as well as realizing how to expand this initial thrust into a complete solution to the problem, requires creative input from the would-be problem solver. There are, however, several general approaches that have been proposed by Polya and others for how one might go about getting a foot in the door. One is to try working the problem backward. For instance, if the problem is to find a way of producing a particular output from a given input, one might start with that output and attempt to back up to the given input. This approach is typical of people trying to discover the bird-folding algorithm in the previous section. They tend to unfold a completed bird in an attempt to see how it is constructed.

Another general problem-solving approach is to look for a related problem that is either easier to solve or has been solved before and then try to apply its solution to the current problem. This technique is of particular value in the context of program development. Generally, program development is not the process of solving a particular instance of a problem but rather of finding a general algorithm that can be used to solve all instances of the problem. More precisely, if we were faced with the task of developing a program for alphabetizing lists of names, our task would not be to sort a particular list but to find a general algorithm that could be used to sort any list of names. Thus, although the instructions

```
Interchange the names David and Alice.
Move the name Carol to the position between Alice and David.
Move the name Bob to the position between Alice and Carol.
```

correctly sort the list David, Alice, Carol, and Bob, they do not constitute the general-purpose algorithm we desire. What we need is an algorithm that can sort this list as well as other lists we might encounter. This is not to say that our solution for sorting a particular list is totally worthless in our search for a general-purpose algorithm. We might, for instance, get our foot in the door by considering such special cases in an attempt to find general principles that can in turn be used to develop the desired general-purpose algorithm. In this case, then, our solution is obtained by the technique of solving a collection of related problems.

Still another approach to getting a foot in the door is to apply **stepwise refinement,** which is essentially the technique of not trying to conquer an entire task (in all its detail) at once. Rather, stepwise refinement proposes that one first view the problem at hand in terms of several subproblems. The idea is that by breaking the original problem into subproblems, one is able to approach the overall solution in terms of steps, each of which is easier to solve than the entire original problem. In turn, stepwise refinement proposes that these steps be decomposed into smaller steps and these smaller steps be broken into still smaller ones until the entire problem has been reduced to a collection of easily solved subproblems.

In this light, stepwise refinement is a **top-down methodology** in that it progresses from the general to the specific. In contrast, a **bottom-up methodology** progresses from the specific to the general. Although contrasting in theory, the two approaches often complement each other in creative problem solving. The decomposition of a problem proposed by the top-down methodology of stepwise refinement is often guided by the problem solver's intuition, which might be working in a bottom-up mode.

The top-down methodology of stepwise refinement is essentially an organizational tool whose problem-solving attributes are consequences of this organization. It has long been an important design methodology in the data processing community, where the development of large software systems encompasses a significant organizational component. But, as we will learn in Chapter 7, large software systems are increasingly being constructed by combining prefabricated components—an approach that is inherently bottom-up. Thus, both top-down and bottom-up methodologies remain important tools in computer science.

The importance of maintaining such a broad perspective is exemplified by the fact that bringing preconceived notions and preselected tools to the problem-solving task can sometimes mask a problem's simplicity. The ages-of-the-children problem discussed earlier in this section is an excellent example of this phenomenon. Students of algebra invariably approach the problem as a system of simultaneous equations, an approach that leads to a dead end and often traps the would-be problem solver into believing that the information given is not sufficient to solve the problem.

Another example is the following:

> As you step from a pier into a boat, your hat falls into the water, unbeknownst to you. The river is flowing at 2.5 miles per hour so your hat begins to float downstream. In the meantime, you begin traveling upstream in the boat at a speed of 4.75 miles per hour relative to the water. After 10 minutes you realize that your hat is missing, turn the boat around, and begin to chase your hat down the river. How long will it take to catch up with your hat?

Most algebra students as well as calculator enthusiasts approach this problem by first determining how far upstream the boat will have traveled in 10 minutes as well as how far downstream the hat will have traveled during that same time. Then, they determine how long it will take for the boat to travel downstream to this position. But, when the boat reaches this position, the hat will have floated farther downstream. Thus, the problem solver either begins to apply techniques of calculus or becomes trapped in a cycle of computing where the hat will be each time the boat goes to where the hat was.

The problem is much simpler than this, however. The trick is to resist the urge to begin writing formulas and making calculations. Instead, we need to put these skills aside and adjust our perspective. The entire problem takes place in the river. The fact that the water is moving in relation to the shore is irrelevant. Think of the same problem posed on a large conveyor belt instead of a river. First, solve the problem with the conveyor belt at rest. If you place your hat at your feet while standing on the belt and then walk away from your hat for 10 minutes, it will take 10 minutes to return to your hat. Now turn on the conveyor belt. This means that the scenery will begin to move past the belt, but, because you are on the belt, this does not change your relationship to the belt or your hat. It will still take 10 minutes to return to your hat.

We conclude that algorithm discovery remains a challenging art that must be developed over a period of time rather than taught as a subject consisting of well-defined methodologies. Indeed, to train a potential problem solver to follow certain methodologies is to quash those creative skills that should instead be nurtured.

Questions & Exercises

1. **a.** Find an algorithm for solving the following problem: Given a positive integer n, find the list of positive integers whose product is the largest among all the lists of positive integers whose sum is n. For example, if n is 4, the desired list is 2, 2 because 2×2 is larger than $1 \times 1 \times 1 \times 1$, $2 \times 1 \times 1$, and 3×1. If n is 5, the desired list is 2, 3.

   b. What is the desired list if $n = 2001$?

   c. Explain how you got your foot in the door.

2. a. Suppose we are given a checkerboard consisting of 2^n rows and 2^n columns of squares, for some positive integer n, and a box of L-shaped tiles, each of which can cover exactly three squares on the board. If any single square is cut out of the board, can we cover the remaining board with tiles such that tiles do not overlap or hang off the edge of the board?

   b. Explain how your solution to (a) can be used to show that $2^{2n} - 1$ is divisible by 3 for all positive integers n.

   c. How are (a) and (b) related to Polya's phases of problem solving?

3. Decode the following message, then explain how you got your foot in the door. *Pdeo eo pda yknnayp wjosan.*

4. Would you be following a top-down methodology if you attempted to solve a picture puzzle merely by pouring the pieces out on a table and trying to piece them together? Would your answer change if you looked at the puzzle box to see what the entire picture was supposed to look like?

5.4 Iterative Structures

Our goal now is to study some of the repetitive structures used in describing algorithmic processes. In this section we discuss **iterative structures** in which a collection of instructions is repeated in a looping manner. In the next section we will introduce the technique of recursion. As a side effect, we will introduce some popular algorithms—the sequential search, the binary search, and the insertion sort. We begin by introducing the sequential search algorithm.

The Sequential Search Algorithm

Consider the problem of searching within a list for the occurrence of a particular target value. We want to develop an algorithm that determines whether that value is in the list. If the value is in the list, we consider the search a success; otherwise we consider it a failure. We assume that the list is sorted according to some rule for ordering its entries. For example, if the list is a list of names, we assume the names appear in alphabetical order, or if the list consists of numeric values, we assume its entries appear in order of increasing magnitude.

To get our foot in the door, we imagine how we might search a guest list of perhaps 20 entries for a particular name. In this setting we might scan the list from its beginning, comparing each entry with the target name. If we find the target name, the search terminates as a success. However, if we reach the end of the list without finding the target value, our search terminates as a failure. In fact, if we reach a name greater than (alphabetically) the target name without finding the target, our search terminates as a failure. (Remember, the list is arranged in alphabetical order, so reaching a name greater than the target name indicates that the target does not appear in the list.) In summary, our rough idea is to continue searching down the list as long as there are more names to be investigated and the target name is greater than the name currently being considered.

In our pseudocode, this process can be represented as

```
Select the first entry in the list as TestEntry.
while (TargetValue > TestEntry and entries remain):
  Select the next entry in the list as TestEntry.
```

Upon terminating this `while` structure, one of two conditions will be true: Either the target value has been found or the target value is not in the list. In either case we can detect a successful search by comparing the test entry to the target value. If they are equal, the search has been successful. Thus we add the statement

```
if (TargetValue == TestEntry):
  Declare the search a success.
else:
  Declare the search a failure.
```

to the end of our pseudocode routine.

Finally, we observe that the first statement in our routine, which selects the first entry in the list as the test entry, is based on the assumption that the list in question contains at least one entry. We might reason that this is a safe guess, but just to be sure, we can position our routine as the else option of the statement

```
if (List is empty):
  Declare search a failure.
else:
  . . .
```

This produces the function shown in Figure 5.6. Note that this function can be used from within other functions by using statements such as

```
Search() the passenger list using Darrel Baker as the target value.
```

to find out if Darrel Baker is a passenger and

```
Search() the list of ingredients using nutmeg as the target value.
```

to find out if nutmeg appears in the list of ingredients.

Figure 5.6 The sequential search algorithm in pseudocode

```
def Search(List, TargetValue):
  if (List is empty):
    Declare search a failure.
  else:
    Select the first entry in List to be TestEntry.
    while (TargetValue > TestEntry and
        there remain entries to be considered):
      Select the next entry in List as TestEntry.
    if (TargetValue == TestEntry):
      Declare search a success.
    else:
      Declare search a failure.
```

In summary, the algorithm represented by Figure 5.6 considers the entries in the sequential order in which they occur in the list. For this reason, the algorithm is called the **sequential search** algorithm. Because of its simplicity, it is often used for short lists or when other concerns dictate its use. However, in the case of long lists, sequential searches are not as efficient as other techniques (as we shall soon see).

Loop Control

The repetitive use of an instruction or sequence of instructions is an important algorithmic concept. One method of implementing such repetition is the iterative structure known as the **loop,** in which a collection of instructions, called the **body** of the loop, is executed in a repetitive fashion under the direction of some control process. A typical example is found in the sequential search algorithm represented in Figure 5.6. Here we use a `while` statement to control the repetition of the single statement `Select the next entry in List as the TestEntry`. Indeed, the `while` statement

```
while (condition):
  Body
```

exemplifies the concept of a loop structure in that its execution traces the cyclic pattern

```
check the condition.
execute the body.
check the condition.
execute the body.
      .
      .
      .
check the condition.
```

until the condition fails.

As a general rule, the use of a loop structure produces a higher degree of flexibility than would be obtained merely by explicitly writing the body several times. For example, to execute the statement

```
Add a drop of sulfuric acid.
```

three times, we could write:

```
Add a drop of sulfuric acid.
Add a drop of sulfuric acid.
Add a drop of sulfuric acid.
```

But we cannot produce a similar sequence that is equivalent to the loop structure

```
while (the pH level is greater than 4):
  add a drop of sulfuric acid
```

because we do not know in advance how many drops of acid will be required.

Let us now take a closer look at the composition of loop control. You might be tempted to view this part of a loop structure as having minor importance. After all, it is typically the body of the loop that actually performs the task at hand (for example, adding drops of acid)—the control activities appear merely as the overhead involved because we chose to execute the body in a repetitive fashion. However, experience has shown that the control of a loop is the more error-prone part of the structure and therefore deserves our attention.

The control of a loop consists of the three activities initialize, test, and modify (Figure 5.7), with the presence of each being required for successful loop control. The test activity has the obligation of causing the termination of the looping process by watching for a condition that indicates termination should take place. This condition is known as the **termination condition.** It is for the purpose of this test activity that we provide a condition within each `while` statement of our pseudocode. In the case of the `while` statement, however, the condition stated is the condition under which the body of the loop should be executed—the termination condition is the negation of the condition appearing in the `while` structure. Thus, in the statement

```
while (the pH level is greater than 4):
  add a drop of sulfuric acid
```

the termination condition is "the pH level is *not* greater than 4," and in the `while` statement of Figure 5.6, the termination condition could be stated as

```
(TargetValue <= TestEntry) or (there are no more entries to be considered)
```

The other two activities in the loop control ensure that the termination condition will ultimately occur. The initialization step establishes a starting condition, and the modification step moves this condition toward the termination condition. For instance, in Figure 5.6, initialization takes place in the statement preceding the `while` statement, where the current test entry is established as the first list entry. The modification step in this case is actually accomplished within the loop body, where our position of interest (identified by the test entry) is moved toward the end of the list. Thus, having executed the initialization step, repeated application of the modification step results in the termination condition being reached. (Either we will reach a test entry that is greater than or equal to the target value or we ultimately reach the end of the list.)

We should emphasize that the initialization and modification steps must lead to the appropriate termination condition. This characteristic is critical for proper loop control, and thus one should always double-check for its presence when designing a loop structure. Failure to make such an evaluation can

Figure 5.7 Components of repetitive control

Initialize:	Establish an initial state that will be modified toward the termination condition
Test:	Compare the current state to the termination condition and terminate the repetition if equal
Modify:	Change the state in such a way that it moves toward the termination condition

lead to errors even in the simplest cases. A typical example is found in the statements

```
Number = 1
while (Number != 6):
  Number = Number + 2
```

Note the use of the Python "`!=`" operator, which we read as, "not equal". Here the termination condition is "`Number == 6`." But the value of `Number` is initialized at 1 and then incremented by 2 in the modification step. Thus, as the loop cycles, the values assigned to `Number` will be 1, 3, 5, 7, 9, and so on, but never the value 6. As a result, this loop will never terminate.

The order in which the components of loop control are executed can have subtle consequences. In fact, there are two common loop structures that differ merely in this regard. The first is exemplified by our pseudocode statement

```
while (condition):
  Activity
```

whose semantics are represented in Figure 5.8 in the form of a **flowchart.** (Such charts use various shapes to represent individual steps and use arrows to indicate the order of the steps. The distinction between the shapes indicates the type of action involved in the associated step. A diamond indicates a decision and a rectangle indicates an arbitrary statement or sequence of statements.) Note that the test for termination in the while structure occurs before the loop's body is executed.

In contrast, the structure in Figure 5.9 requests that the body of the loop be executed before the test for termination is performed. In this case, the loop's body is always performed at least once, whereas in the `while` structure, the body is never executed if the termination condition is satisfied the first time it is tested.

Python does not have a built-in structure for this second kind of loop, although it is easy enough to build an equivalent using the existing `while` structure with an `if`-statement and a `break` at the end of the loop body. For our pseudocode,

Figure 5.8 The while loop structure

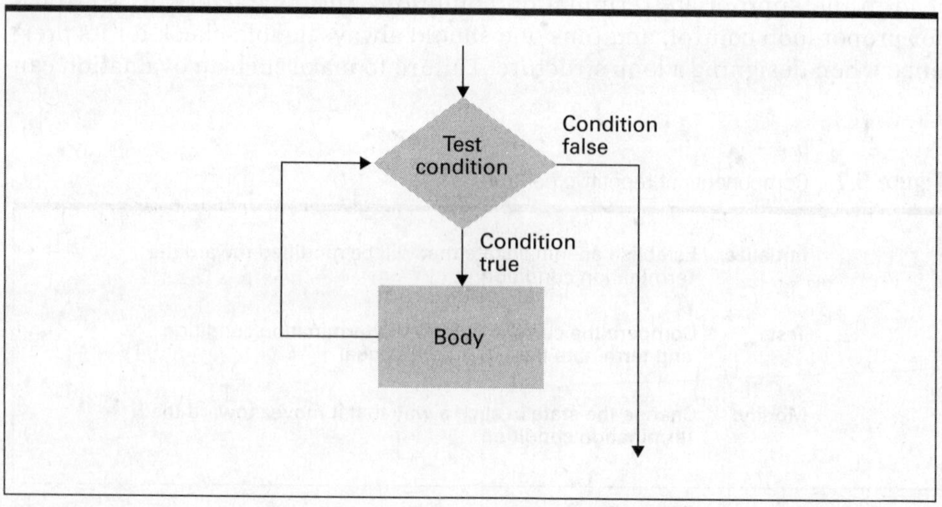

Figure 5.9 The repeat loop structure

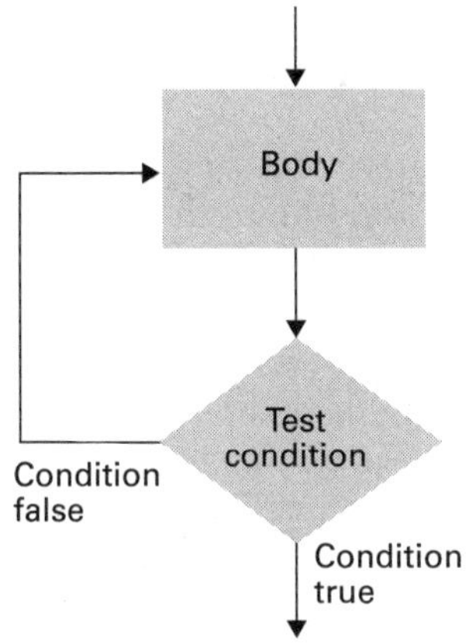

we will borrow keywords that exists in several other languages, using the syntactic form

```
repeat:
  activity
  until (condition)
```

to represent the structure shown in Figure 5.9. Thus, the statement

```
repeat:
  take a coin from your pocket
  until (there are no coins in your pocket)
```

assumes there is a coin in your pocket at the beginning, but

```
while (there is a coin in your pocket):
  take a coin from your pocket
```

does not.

Following the terminology of our pseudocode, we will usually refer to these structures as the `while` loop structure or the **`repeat`** loop structure. In a more generic context you might hear the `while` loop structure referred to as a **pretest loop** (since the test for termination is performed before the body is executed) and the **`repeat`** loop structure referred to as a **posttest loop** (since the test for termination is performed after the body is executed).

While many algorithms require careful consideration of the initialization, test, and modify activities when controlling loops, others follow some very common patterns. Particularly when working with lists of data, the most common pattern is to start with the first element in a list and consider each element in the list until the end is reached. Returning briefly to our sequential search example, we saw the pattern similar to

```
Select the first entry in the list
while (there remain entries to be considered):
  . . .
  Select the next entry in the list
```

Because this structure occurs so frequently in algorithms, we will use the syntactic form

```
for Item in List:
  . . .
```

to describe a loop that iterates through each element of a list. Notice that this pseudocode primitive is effectively one level of abstraction higher than the `while` structure, because we can accomplish the same effect with separate initialize, modify, and test structures, but this version more succinctly conveys the meaning of the loop without unnecessary detail.

Each time through the body of this `for` loop structure, the value `Item` will become the next element in `List`. The termination condition of this loop is implicitly when the end of `List` is reached. As an example, to total up the numbers in a list we could use

```
Sum = 0
for Number in List:
  Sum = Sum + Number
```

This type of loop is often called a **for-each** loop in languages other than Python and is a special case of the pretest loop. The `for` structure is best suited to situations in which the algorithm will perform the same steps on each element in a list, and it is not necessary to separately keep track of a loop counting variable.

The Insertion Sort Algorithm

As an additional example of using iterative structures, let us consider the problem of sorting a list of names into alphabetical order. But before proceeding, we should identify the constraints under which we will work. Simply stated, our goal is to sort the list "within itself." In other words, we want to sort the list by shuffling its entries as opposed to moving the list to another location. Our situation is analogous to the problem of sorting a list whose entries are recorded on separate index cards spread out on a crowded desktop. We have cleared off enough space for the cards but are not allowed to push additional materials back to make more room. This restriction is typical in computer applications, not because the workspace within the machine is necessarily crowded like our desktop, but simply because we want to use the storage space available in an efficient manner.

Let us get a foot in the door by considering how we might sort the names on the desktop. Consider the list of names

Fred
Alex
Diana
Byron
Carol

One approach to sorting this list is to note that the sublist consisting of only the top name, Fred, is sorted but the sublist consisting of the top two names, Fred and Alex, is not. Thus we might pick up the card containing the name Alex, slide the name Fred down into the space where Alex was, and then place the name Alex in the hole at the top of the list, as represented by the first row in Figure 5.10. At this point our list would be

Alex
Fred
Diana
Byron
Carol

Now the top two names form a sorted sublist, but the top three do not. Thus we might pick up the third name, Diana, slide the name Fred down into the hole

Figure 5.10 Sorting the list Fred, Alex, Diana, Byron, and Carol alphabetically

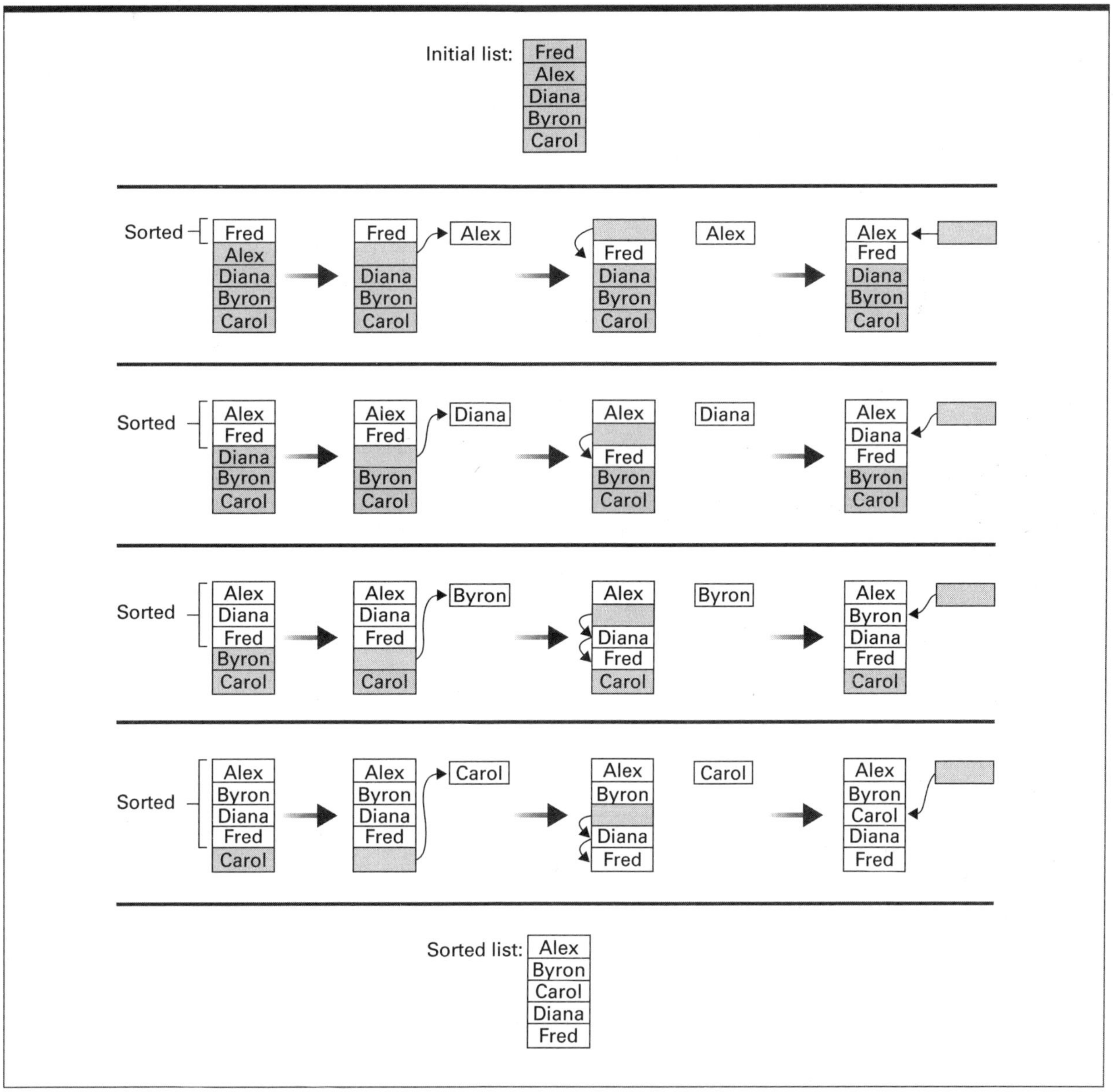

where Diana was, and then insert Diana in the hole left by Fred, as summarized in the second row of Figure 5.10. The top three entries in the list would now be sorted. Continuing in this fashion, we could obtain a list in which the top four entries are sorted by picking up the fourth name, Byron, sliding the names Fred and Diana down, and then inserting Byron in the hole (see the third row of Figure 5.10). Finally, we can complete the sorting process by picking up Carol, sliding Fred and Diana down, and then inserting Carol in the remaining hole (see the fourth row of Figure 5.10).

Having analyzed the process of sorting a particular list, our task now is to generalize this process to obtain an algorithm for sorting general lists. To this end, we observe that each row of Figure 5.10 represents the same general process: Pick up the first name in the unsorted portion of the list, slide the names greater than the extracted name down, and insert the extracted name back in the list where the hole appears. If we identify the extracted name as the pivot entry, this process can be expressed in our pseudocode as

```
Move the pivot entry to a temporary location leaving a hole in List
while (there is a name above the hole and
  that name is greater than the pivot):
  move the name above the hole down into the hole
    leaving a hole above the name
Move the pivot entry into the hole in List.
```

Iterative Structures in Music

Musicians were using and programming iterative structures centuries before computer scientists. Indeed, the structure of a song (being composed of multiple verses, each followed by the chorus) is exemplified by the `while` statement

```
while (there is a verse remaining):
  sing the next verse
  sing the chorus
```

Moreover, the notation

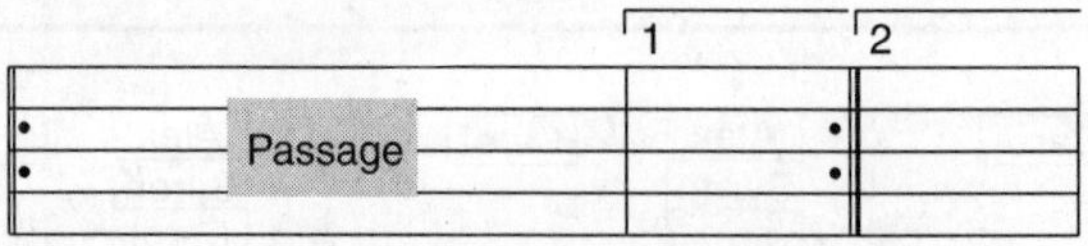

is merely a composer's way of expressing the structure

```
N = 1
while (N < 3):
  play the passage
  play the Nth ending
  N = N + 1
```

Next, we observe that this process should be executed repeatedly. To begin the sorting process, the pivot should be the second entry in the list and then, before each additional execution, the pivot selection should be one more entry down the list until the last entry has been positioned. That is, as the preceding routine is repeated, the initial position of the pivot entry should advance from the second entry to the third, then to the fourth, etc., until the routine has positioned the last entry in the list. Following this lead we can control the required repetition with the statements

```
N = 2
while (the value of N does not exceed the length of List):
  Select the Nth entry in List as the pivot entry
    .
    .
    .
  N = N + 1
```

where `N` represents the position to use for the pivot entry, `the length of List` refers to the number of entries in the list, and the dots indicate the location where the previous routine should be placed.

Our complete pseudocode program is shown in Figure 5.11. In short, the program sorts a list by repeatedly removing an entry and inserting it into its proper place. It is because of this repeated insertion process that the underlying algorithm is called the **insertion sort.**

Note that the structure of Figure 5.11 is that of a loop within a loop, the outer loop being expressed by the first `while` statement and the inner loop represented by the second `while` statement. Each execution of the body of the outer loop results in the inner loop being initialized and executed until its termination condition is obtained. Thus, a single execution of the outer loop's body will result in several executions of the inner loop's body.

The initialization component of the outer loop's control consists of establishing the initial value of `N` with the statement

```
N = 2
```

Figure 5.11 The insertion sort algorithm expressed in pseudocode

```
def Sort (List):
  N = 2
  while (the value of N does not exceed the length of List):
    Select the Nth entry in List as the pivot entry.
    Move the pivot entry to a temporary location leaving
      a hole in List.
    while (there is a name above the hole and that name
        is greater than the pivot):
      Move the name above the hole down into the hole
        leaving a hole above the name.
    Move the pivot entry into the hole in List.
    N = N + 1
```

The modification component is handled by incrementing the value of N at the end of the loop's body with the statement

```
N = N + 1
```

The termination condition occurs when the value of N exceeds the length of the list.

The inner loop's control is initialized by removing the pivot entry from the list and thus creating a hole. The loop's modification step is accomplished by moving entries down into the hole, thus causing the hole to move up. The termination condition consists of the hole being immediately below a name that is not greater than the pivot or of the hole reaching the top of the list.

Questions & Exercises

1. Modify the sequential search function in Figure 5.6 to allow for lists that are not sorted.
2. Convert the pseudocode routine

```
Z = 0
X = 1
while (X < 6):
  Z = Z + X
  X = X + 1
```

   to an equivalent routine using a `repeat` statement.
3. Some of the popular programming languages today use the syntax

```
while (. . . ) do (. . . )
```

   to represent a pretest loop and the syntax

```
do (. . . ) while (. . . )
```

   to represent a posttest loop. Although elegant in design, what problems could result from such similarities?
4. Suppose the insertion sort as presented in Figure 5.11 was applied to the list Gene, Cheryl, Alice, and Brenda. Describe the organization of the list at the end of each execution of the body of the outer `while` structure.
5. Why would we not want to change the phrase "greater than" in the `while` statement in Figure 5.11 to "greater than or equal to"?
6. A variation of the insertion sort algorithm is the **selection sort.** It begins by selecting the smallest entry in the list and moving it to the front. It then selects the smallest entry from the remaining entries in the list and moves it to the second position in the list. By repeatedly selecting the smallest entry from the remaining portion of the list and moving that entry forward, the sorted version of the list grows from the front of the list, while the back portion of the list consisting of the remaining unsorted entries shrinks. Use our pseudocode to express a function similar to that in Figure 5.11 for sorting a list using the selection sort algorithm.

7. Another well-known sorting algorithm is the **bubble sort.** It is based on the process of repeatedly comparing two adjacent names and interchanging them if they are not in the correct order relative to each other. Let us suppose that the list in question has n entries. The bubble sort would begin by comparing (and possibly interchanging) the entries in positions n and $n - 1$. Then, it would consider the entries in positions $n - 1$ and $n - 2$, and continue moving forward in the list until the first and second entries in the list had been compared (and possibly interchanged). Observe that this pass through the list will pull the smallest entry to the front of the list. Likewise, another such pass will ensure that the next to the smallest entry will be pulled to the second position in the list. Thus, by making a total of $n - 1$ passes through the list, the entire list will be sorted. (If one watches the algorithm at work, one sees the small entries bubble to the top of the list—an observation from which the algorithm gets its name.) Use our pseudocode to express a function similar to that in Figure 5.11 for sorting a list using the bubble sort algorithm.

5.5 Recursive Structures

Recursive structures provide an alternative to the loop paradigm for implementing the repetition of activities. Whereas a loop involves repeating a set of instructions in a manner in which the set is completed and then repeated, recursion involves repeating the set of instructions as a subtask of itself. As an analogy, consider the process of conducting telephone conversations with the call waiting feature. There, an incomplete telephone conversation is set aside while another incoming call is processed. The result is that two conversations take place. However, they are not performed one-after-the-other as in a loop structure, but instead one is performed within the other.

The Binary Search Algorithm

As a way of introducing recursion, let us again tackle the problem of searching to see whether a particular entry is in a sorted list, but this time we get our foot in the door by considering the procedure we follow when searching a dictionary. In this case we do not perform a sequential entry-by-entry or even a page-by-page procedure. Rather, we begin by opening the directory to a page in the area where we believe the target entry is located. If we are lucky, we will find the target value there; otherwise, we must continue searching. But at this point we will have narrowed our search considerably.

Of course, in the case of searching a dictionary, we have prior knowledge of where words are likely to be found. If we are looking for the word *somnambulism,* we would start by opening to the latter portion of the dictionary. In the case of generic lists, however, we do not have this advantage, so let us agree to always start our search with the "middle" entry in the list. Here we write the word *middle* in quotation marks because the list might have an even number of entries and thus no middle entry in the exact sense. In this case, let us agree that the "middle" entry refers to the first entry in the second half of the list.

If the middle entry in the list is the target value, we can declare the search a success. Otherwise, we can at least restrict the search process to the first or last half of the list depending on whether the target value is less than or greater than the entry we have considered. (Remember that the list is sorted.)

To search the remaining portion of the list, we could apply the sequential search, but instead let us apply the same approach to this portion of the list that we used for the whole list. That is, we select the middle entry in the remaining portion of the list as the next entry to consider. As before, if that entry is the target value, we are finished. Otherwise we can restrict our search to an even smaller portion of the list.

This approach to the searching process is summarized in Figure 5.12, where we consider the task of searching the list on the left of the figure for the entry John. We first consider the middle entry Harry. Since our target belongs after this entry, the search continues by considering the lower half of the original list. The middle of this sublist is found to be Larry. Since our target should precede Larry, we turn our attention to the first half of the current sublist. When we interrogate the middle of that secondary sublist, we find our target John and declare the search a success. In short, our strategy is to successively divide the list in question into smaller segments until the target is found or the search is narrowed to an empty segment.

We need to emphasize this last point. If the target value is not in the original list, our approach to searching the list will proceed by dividing the list into smaller segments until the segment under consideration is empty. At this point our algorithm should recognize that the search is a failure.

Figure 5.13 is a first draft of our thoughts using our pseudocode. It directs us to begin a search by testing to see if the list is empty. If so, we are told to report that the search is a failure. Otherwise, we are told to consider the middle entry in the list. If this entry is not the target value, we are told to search either the front half or the back half of the list. Both of these possibilities require a secondary search. It would be nice to perform these searches by calling on the services of

Figure 5.12 Applying our strategy to search a list for the entry John

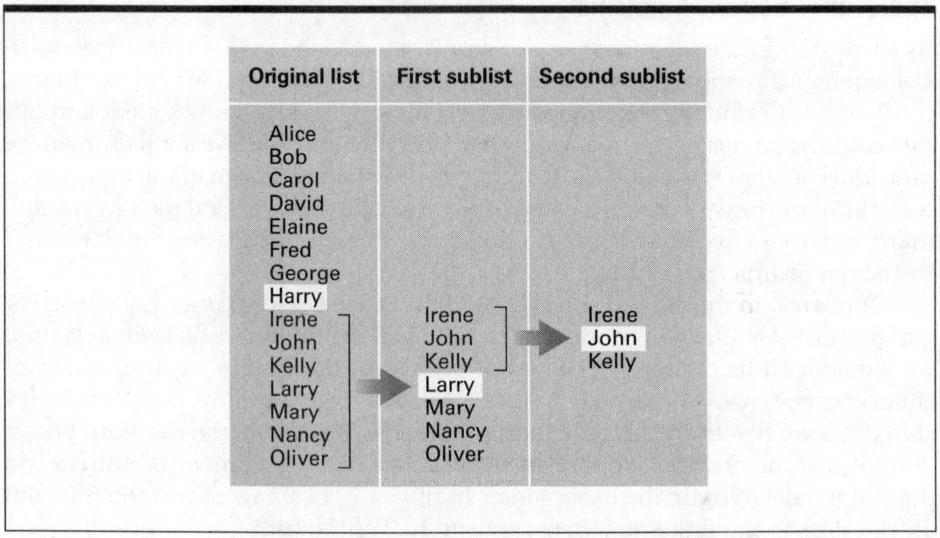

Figure 5.13 A first draft of the binary search technique

```
if (List is empty):
  Report that the search failed.
else:
  TestEntry = the "middle" entry in the List
  if (TargetValue == TestEntry):
    Report that the search succeeded.
  if (TargetValue < TestEntry):
    Search() the portion of List preceding TestEntry for TargetValue,
      and report the result of that search.
  if (TargetValue > TestEntry):
    Search() the portion of List following TestEntry for TargetValue,
      and report the result of that search.
```

an abstract tool. In particular, our approach is to apply a function named Search to carry out these secondary searches. To complete our program, therefore, we must provide such a function.

But this function should perform the same task that is expressed by the pseudocode we have already written. It should first check to see if the list it is given is empty, and if it is not, it should proceed by considering the middle entry of that list. Thus we can supply the function we need merely by identifying the current routine as being the function named `Search` and inserting references to that function where the secondary searches are required. The result is shown in Figure 5.14.

Note that this function contains a reference to itself. If we were following this function and came to the instruction

```
Search(. . . )
```

we would apply the same function to the smaller list that we were applying to the original one. If that search succeeded, we would return to declare our original search successful; if this secondary search failed, we would declare our original search a failure.

Searching and Sorting

The sequential and binary search algorithms are only two of many algorithms for performing the search process. Likewise, the insertion sort is only one of many sorting algorithms. Other classic algorithms for sorting include the merge sort (discussed in Chapter 12), the selection sort (question 6 in Section 5.4), the bubble sort (question 7 in Section 5.4), the quick sort (which applies a divide-and-conquer approach to the sorting process), and the heap sort (which uses a clever technique for finding the entries that should be moved forward in the list). You will find discussions of these algorithms in the books listed under Additional Reading at the end of this chapter.

Figure 5.14 The binary search algorithm in pseudocode

```
def Search(List, TargetValue):
  if (List is empty):
    Report that the search failed.
  else:
    TestEntry = the "middle" entry in List
    if (TargetValue == TestEntry):
      Report that the search succeeded.
    if (TargetValue < TestEntry):
      Sublist = portion of List preceding
        TestEntry
      Search(Sublist, TargetValue)
    if (TargetValue > TestEntry):
      Sublist = portion of List following
        TestEntry
      Search(Sublist, TargetValue)
```

To see how the function in Figure 5.14 performs its task, let us follow it as it searches the list Alice, Bill, Carol, David, Evelyn, Fred, and George, for the target value Bill. Our search begins by selecting David (the middle entry) as the test entry under consideration. Since the target value (Bill) is less than this test entry, we are instructed to apply the function `Search` to the list of entries preceding David—that is, the list Alice, Bill, and Carol. In so doing, we create a second copy of the search function and assign it to this secondary task.

We now have two copies of our search function being executed, as summarized in Figure 5.15. Progress in the original copy is temporarily suspended at the instruction

```
Search(Sublist, TargetValue)
```

while we apply the second copy to the task of searching the list Alice, Bill, and Carol. When we complete this secondary search, we will discard the second copy of the function, report its findings to the original copy, and continue progress in the original. In this way, the second copy of the function executes as a subordinate to the original, performing the task requested by the original module and then disappearing.

The secondary search selects Bill as its test entry because that is the middle entry in the list Alice, Bill, and Carol. Since this is the same as the target value, it declares its search to be a success and terminates.

At this point, we have completed the secondary search as requested by the original copy of the function, so we are able to continue the execution of that original copy. Here we are told that the result of the secondary search should be reported as the result of the original search. Thus we report that the original search has succeeded. Our process has correctly determined that Bill is a member of the list Alice, Bill, Carol, David, Evelyn, Fred, and George.

Let us now consider what happens if we ask the function in Figure 5.14 to search the list Alice, Carol, Evelyn, Fred, and George for the entry David. This time the original copy of the function selects Evelyn as its test entry and concludes that the target value must reside in the preceding portion of the list. It therefore

Figure 5.15 Recursively Searching

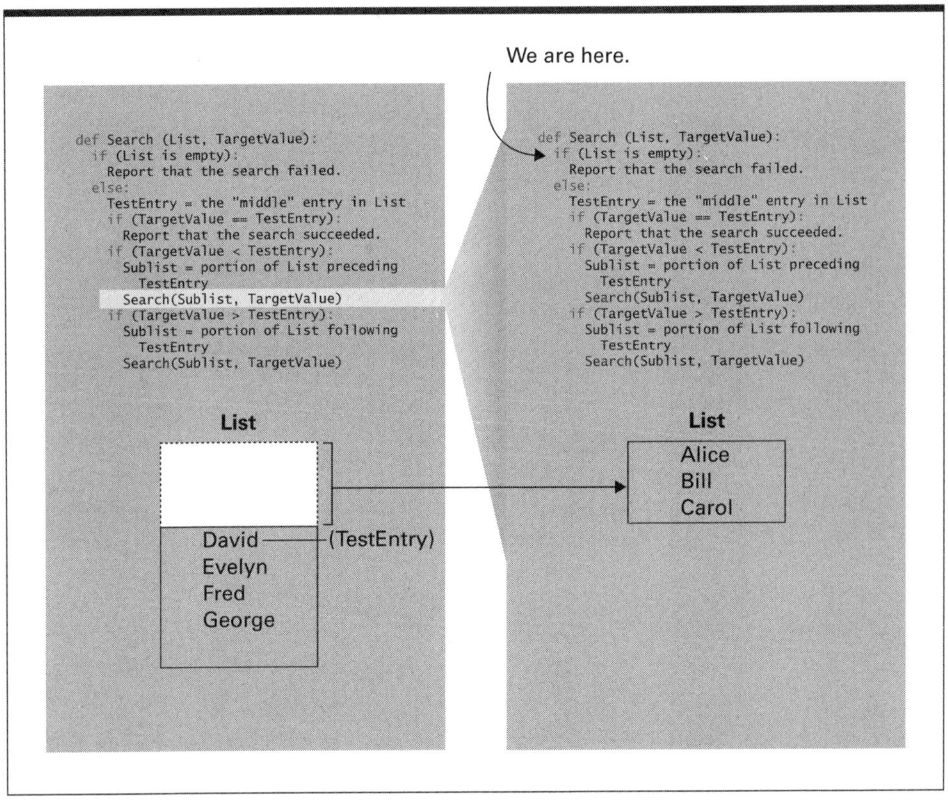

requests another copy of the function to search the list of entries appearing in front of Evelyn—that is, the two-entry list consisting of Alice and Carol. At this stage our situation is as represented in Figure 5.16.

The second copy of the function selects Carol as its current entry and concludes that the target value must lie in the latter portion of its list. It then requests a third copy of the function to search the list of names following Carol in the list Alice and Carol. This sublist is empty, so the third copy of the function has the task of searching the empty list for the target value David. Our situation at this point is represented by Figure 5.17. The original copy of the function is charged with the task of searching the list Alice, Carol, Evelyn, Fred, and George, with the test entry being Evelyn; the second copy is charged with searching the list Alice and Carol, with its test entry being Carol; and the third copy is about to begin searching the empty list.

Of course, the third copy of the function quickly declares its search to be a failure and terminates. The completion of the third copy's task allows the second copy to continue its task. It notes that the search it requested was unsuccessful, declares its own task to be a failure, and terminates. This report is what the original copy of the function has been waiting for, so it can now proceed. Since the search it requested failed, it declares its own search to have failed and terminates. Our routine has correctly concluded that David is not contained in the list Alice, Carol, Evelyn, Fred, and George.

In summary, if we were to look back at the previous examples, we could see that the process employed by the algorithm represented in Figure 5.14 is to

Figure 5.16 Second Recursive Search, First Snapshot

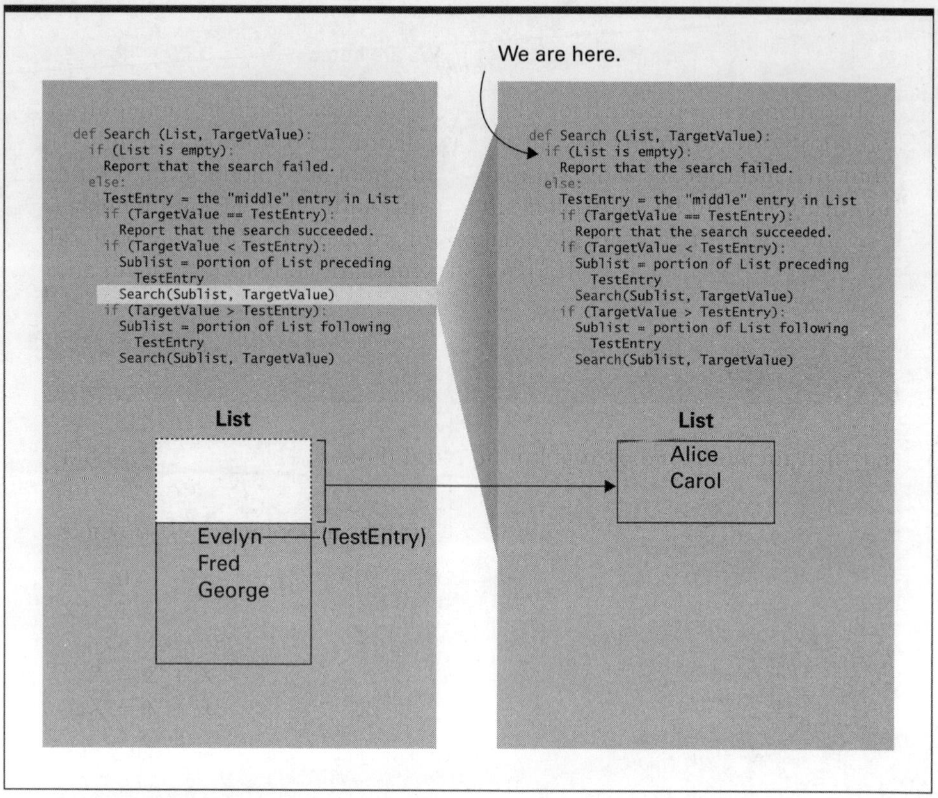

repeatedly divide the list in question into two smaller pieces in such a way that the remaining search can be restricted to only one of these pieces. This divide-by-two approach is the reason why the algorithm is known as the **binary search.**

Recursive Control

The binary search algorithm is similar to the sequential search in that each algorithm requests the execution of a repetitive process. However, the implementation of this repetition is significantly different. Whereas the sequential search involves a circular form of repetition, the binary search executes each stage of the repetition as a subtask of the previous stage. This technique is known as **recursion.**

As we have seen, the illusion created by the execution of a recursive function is the existence of multiple copies of the function, each of which is called an activation of the function. These activations are created dynamically in a telescoping manner and ultimately disappear as the algorithm advances. Of those activations existing at any given time, only one is actively progressing. The others are effectively in limbo, each waiting for another activation to terminate before it can continue.

Being a repetitive process, recursive systems are just as dependent on proper control as are loop structures. Just as in loop control, recursive systems are dependent on testing for a termination condition and on a design that ensures

Figure 5.17 Second Recursive Search, Second Snapshot

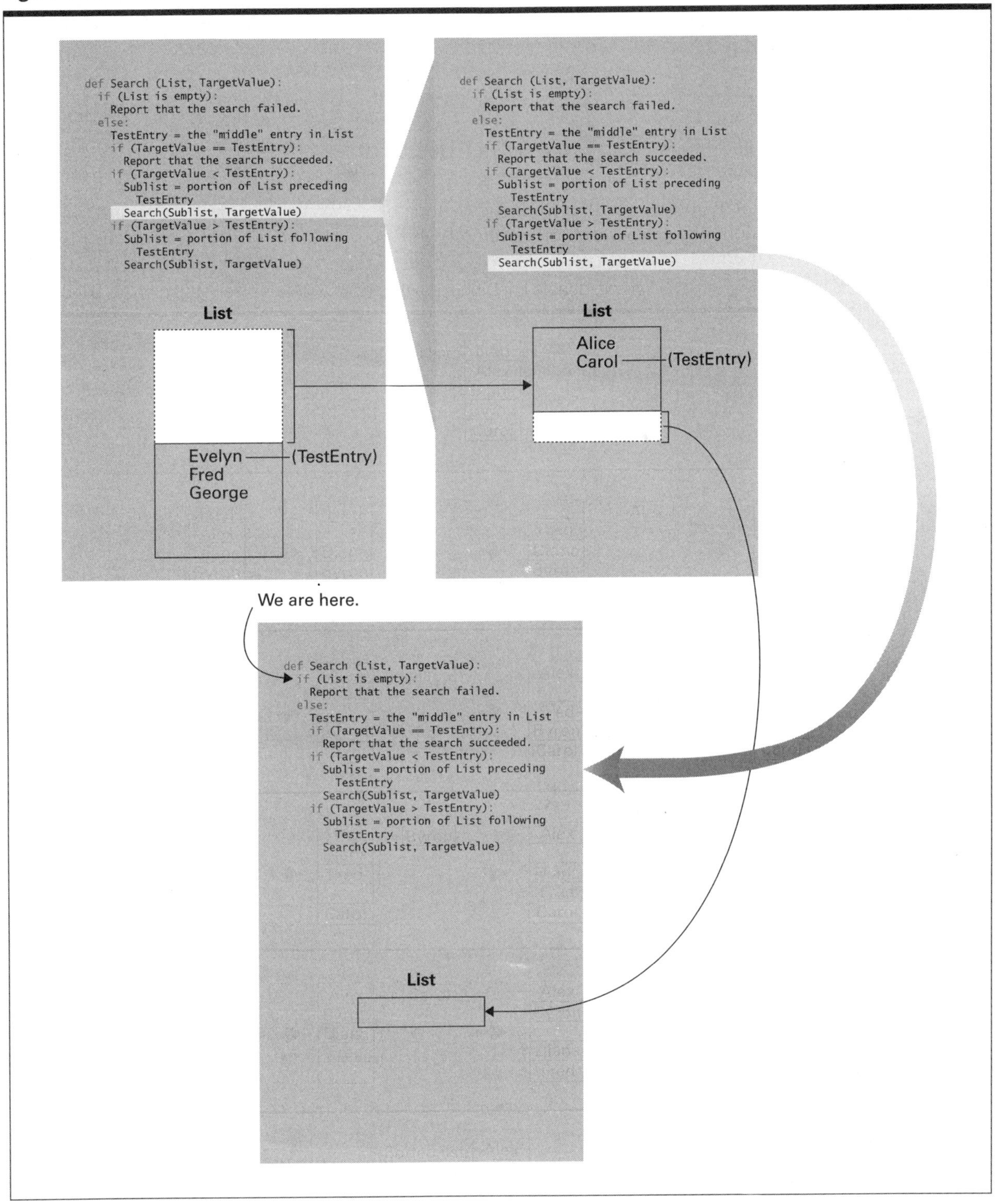

Recursive Structures in Art

The following recursive function can be applied to a rectangular canvas to produce drawings of the style of the Dutch painter Piet Mondrian (1872–1944), who produced paintings in which the rectangular canvas was divided into successively smaller rectangles. Try following the function yourself to produce drawings similar to the one shown. Begin by applying the function to a rectangle representing the canvas on which you are working. (If you are wondering whether the algorithm represented by this function is an algorithm according to the definition in Section 5.1, your suspicions are well-founded. It is, in fact, an example of a nondeterministic algorithm since there are places at which the person or machine following the function is asked to make "creative" decisions. Perhaps this is why Mondrian's results are considered art while ours are not.)

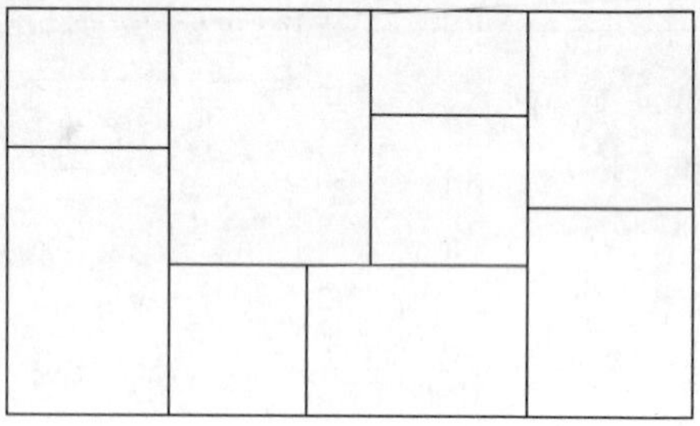

```
def Mondrian (Rectangle):
  if (the size of Rectangle is too large for your artistic taste):
     divide Rectangle into two smaller rectangles.
     apply the function Mondrian to one of the smaller rectangles.
     apply the function Mondrian to the other smaller rectangle.
```

this condition will be reached. In fact, proper recursive control involves the same three ingredients—initialization, modification, and test for termination—that are required in loop control.

In general, a recursive function is designed to test for the termination condition (often called the **base case** or **degenerative case**) before requesting further activations. If the termination condition is not met, the routine creates another activation of the function and assigns it the task of solving a revised problem that is closer to the termination condition than that assigned to the current activation. However, if the termination condition is met, a path is taken that causes the current activation to terminate without creating additional activations.

Let us see how the initialization and modification phases of repetitive control are implemented in our binary search function of Figure 5.14. In this case, the creation of additional activations is terminated once the target value is found or the task is reduced to that of searching an empty list. The process is initialized implicitly by being given an initial list and a target value. From this initial configuration the function modifies its assigned task to that of searching a smaller list. Since the original list is of finite length and each modification step reduces the length of the list in question, we are assured that the target value ultimately is found or the task is reduced to that of searching the empty list. We can therefore conclude that the repetitive process is guaranteed to cease.

Finally, since both loop and recursive control structures are ways to cause the repetition of a set of instructions, we might ask whether they are equivalent in power. That is, if an algorithm were designed using a loop structure, could another algorithm using only recursive techniques be designed that would solve the same problem and vice versa? Such questions are important in computer science because their answers ultimately tell us what features should be provided in a programming language in order to obtain the most powerful programming system possible. We will return to these ideas in Chapter 12 where we consider some of the more theoretical aspects of computer science and its mathematical foundations. With this background, we will then be able to prove the equivalence of iterative and recursive structures in Appendix E.

Questions & Exercises

1. What names are interrogated by the binary search (Figure 5.14) when searching for the name Joe in the list Alice, Brenda, Carol, Duane, Evelyn, Fred, George, Henry, Irene, Joe, Karl, Larry, Mary, Nancy, and Oliver?
2. What is the maximum number of entries that must be interrogated when applying the binary search to a list of 200 entries? What about a list of 100,000 entries?
3. What sequence of numbers would be printed by the following recursive function if we started it with N assigned the value 1?

```
def Exercise (N):
  print(N)
  if (N < 3):
    Exercise(N + 1)
  print(N)
```

4. What is the termination condition in the recursive function of question 3?

5.6 Efficiency and Correctness

In this section we introduce two topics that constitute important research areas within computer science. The first of these is algorithm efficiency, and the second is algorithm correctness.

Algorithm Efficiency

Even though today's machines are capable of executing millions or billions of instructions each second, efficiency remains a major concern in algorithm design. Often the choice between efficient and inefficient algorithms can make the difference between a practical solution to a problem and an impractical one.

Let us consider the problem of a university registrar faced with the task of retrieving and updating student records. Although the university has an actual enrollment of approximately 10,000 students during any one semester, its "current student" file contains the records of more than 30,000 students who are considered current in the sense that they have registered for at least one course in the past few years but have not completed a degree. For now, let us assume that these records are stored in the registrar's computer as a list ordered by student identification numbers. To find any student record, the registrar would therefore search this list for a particular identification number.

We have presented two algorithms for searching such a list: the sequential search and the binary search. Our question now is whether the choice between these two algorithms makes any difference in the case of the registrar. We consider the sequential search first.

Given a student identification number, the sequential search algorithm starts at the beginning of the list and compares the entries found to the identification number desired. Not knowing anything about the source of the target value, we cannot conclude how far into the list this search must go. We can say, though, that after many searches we expect the average depth of the searches to be halfway through the list; some will be shorter, but others will be longer. Thus, we estimate that over a period of time, the sequential search will investigate roughly 15,000 records per search. If retrieving and checking each record for its identification number requires 10 milliseconds (10 one-thousandths of a second), such a search would require an average of 150 seconds or 2.5 minutes—an unbearably long time for the registrar to wait for a student's record to appear on a computer screen. Even if the time required to retrieve and check each record were reduced to only 1 millisecond, the search would still require an average of 15 seconds, which is still a long time to wait.

In contrast, the binary search proceeds by comparing the target value to the middle entry in the list. If this is not the desired entry, then at least the remaining search is restricted to only half of the original list. Thus, after interrogating the middle entry in the list of 30,000 student records, the binary search has at most 15,000 records still to consider. After the second inquiry, at most 7,500 remain, and after the third retrieval, the list in question has dropped to no more than 3,750 entries. Continuing in this fashion, we see that the target record will be found after retrieving at most 15 entries from the list of 30,000 records. Thus, if each of these retrievals can be performed in 10 milliseconds, the process of searching for a particular record requires only 0.15 of a second—meaning that access to any particular student record will appear to be instantaneous from the registrar's point of view. We conclude that the choice between the sequential search algorithm and the binary search algorithm would have a significant impact in this application.

This example indicates the importance of the area of computer science known as algorithm analysis that encompasses the study of the resources, such as time or storage space, that algorithms require. A major application of such studies is the evaluation of the relative merits of alternative algorithms. Algorithm analysis often involves best-case, worst-case, and average-case scenarios. In our example, we performed an average-case analysis of the sequential search algorithm and a worst-case analysis of the binary search algorithm in order to estimate the time required to search through a list of 30,000 entries. In general such analysis is performed in a more generic context. That is, when considering algorithms for searching lists, we do not focus on a list of a particular length, but instead try to identify a formula that would indicate the algorithm's performance for lists of arbitrary lengths. It is not difficult to generalize our previous reasoning to lists of arbitrary lengths. In particular, when applied to a list with n entries, the sequential search algorithm will interrogate an average of $n/2$ entries, whereas the binary search algorithm will interrogate at most $log_2\, n$ entries in its worst-case scenario. ($log_2\, n$ represents the base two logarithm of n. Unless otherwise stated, computer scientists usually mean base two when talking about logorithms.)

Let us analyze the insertion sort algorithm (summarized in Figure 5.11) in a similar manner. Recall that this algorithm involves selecting a list entry, called the pivot entry, comparing this entry to those preceding it until the proper place for the pivot is found, and then inserting the pivot entry in this place. Since the activity of comparing two entries dominates the algorithm, our approach will be to count the number of such comparisons that are performed when sorting a list whose length is n.

The algorithm begins by selecting the second list entry to be the pivot. It then progresses by picking successive entries as the pivot until it has reached the end of the list. In the best possible case, each pivot is already in its proper place, and thus it needs to be compared to only a single entry before this is discovered. Thus, in the best case, applying the insertion sort to a list with n entries requires $n - 1$ comparisons. (The second entry is compared to one entry, the third entry to one entry, and so on.)

In contrast, the worst-case scenario is that each pivot must be compared to all the preceding entries before its proper location can be found. This occurs if the original list is in reverse order. In this case the first pivot (the second list entry) is compared to one entry, the second pivot (the third list entry) is compared to two entries, and so on (Figure 5.18). Thus the total number of comparisons when sorting a list of n entries is $1 + 2 + 3 + \ldots + (n - 1)$, which is equivalent to $(1/2)(n^2 - n)$. In particular, if the list contained 10 entries, the worst-case scenario of the insertion sort algorithm would require 45 comparisons.

Figure 5.18 Applying the insertion sort in a worst-case situation.

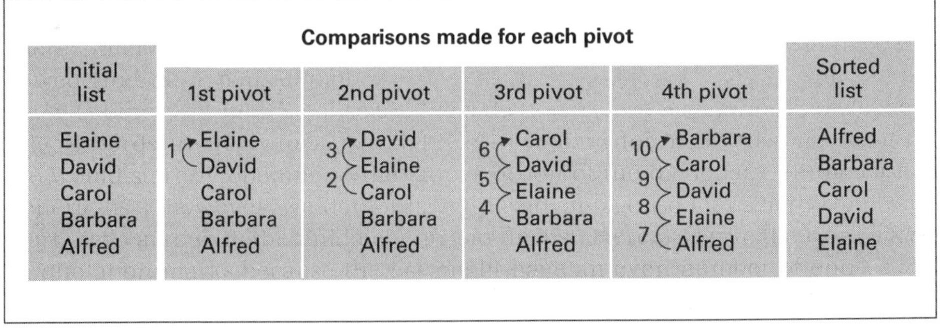

In the average case of the insertion sort, we would expect each pivot to be compared to half of the entries preceding it. This results in half as many comparisons as were performed in the worst case, or a total of $(^1/_4)(n^2 - n)$ comparisons to sort a list of n entries. If, for example, we use the insertion sort to sort a variety of lists of length 10, we expect the average number of comparisons per sort to be 22.5.

The significance of these results is that the number of comparisons made during the execution of the insertion sort algorithm gives an approximation of the amount of time required to execute the algorithm. Using this approximation, Figure 5.19 shows a graph indicating how the time required to execute the insertion sort algorithm increases as the length of the list increases. This graph is based on our worst-case analysis of the algorithm, where we concluded that sorting a list of length n would require at most $(^1/_2)(n^2 - n)$ comparisons between list entries. On the graph, we have marked several list lengths and indicated the time required in each case. Notice that as the list lengths increase by uniform increments, the time required to sort the list increases by increasingly greater amounts. Thus the algorithm becomes less efficient as the size of the list increases.

Let us apply a similar analysis to the binary search algorithm. Recall that we concluded that searching a list with n entries using this algorithm would require interrogating at most $log_2\ n$ entries, which again gives an approximation to the amount of time required to execute the algorithm for various list sizes. Figure 5.20 shows a graph based on this analysis on which we have again marked several list lengths of uniformly increasing size and identified the time required by the algorithm in each case. Note that the time required by the algorithm increases by decreasing increments. That is, the binary search algorithm becomes more efficient as the size of the list increases.

Figure 5.19 Graph of the worst-case analysis of the insertion sort algorithm

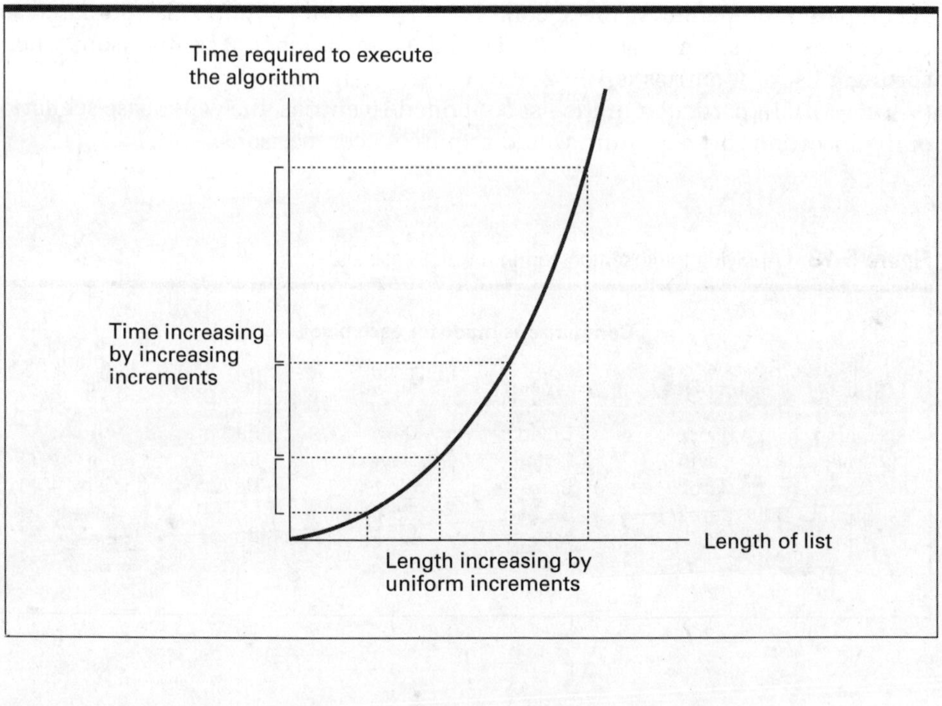

Figure 5.20 Graph of the worst-case analysis of the binary search algorithm

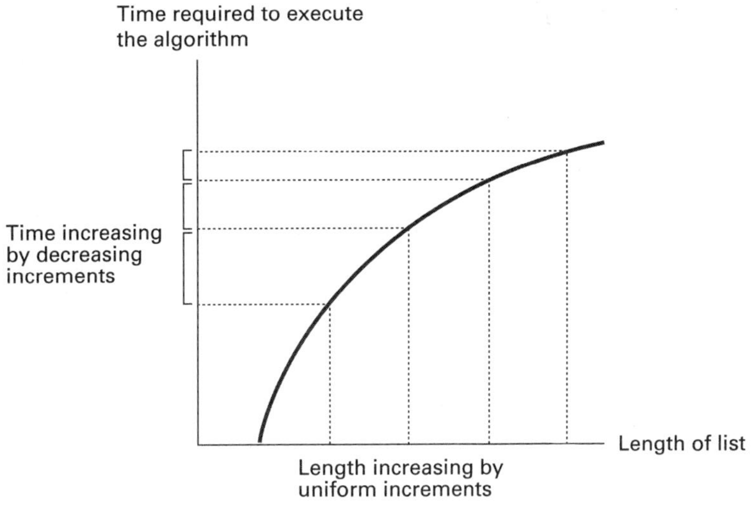

The distinguishing factor between Figures 5.19 and 5.20 is the general shape of the graphs involved. This general shape reveals how well an algorithm should be expected to perform for larger and larger inputs. Moreover, the general shape of a graph is determined by the type of the expression being represented rather than the specifics of the expression—all linear expressions produce a straight line; all quadratic expressions produce a parabolic curve; all logarithmic expressions produce the logarithmic shape shown in Figure 5.20. It is customary to identify a shape with the simplest expression that produces that shape. In particular, we identify the parabolic shape with the expression n^2 and the logarithmic shape with the expression $log_2\ n$.

Since the shape of the graph obtained by comparing the time required for an algorithm to perform its task to the size of the input data reflects the efficiency characteristics of the algorithm, it is common to classify algorithms according to the shapes of these graphs—normally based on the algorithm's worst-case analysis. The notation used to identify these classes is sometimes called **big-theta notation.** All algorithms whose graphs have the shape of a parabola, such as the insertion sort, are put in the class represented by $\Theta(n^2)$ (read "big theta of *n* squared"); all algorithms whose graphs have the shape of a logarithmic expression, such as the binary search, fall in the class represented by $\Theta(log_2\ n)$ (read "big theta of *log n*"). Knowing the class in which a particular algorithm falls allows us to predict its performance and to compare it against other algorithms that solve the same problem. Two algorithms in $\Theta(n^2)$ will exhibit similar changes in time requirements as the size of the inputs increases. Moreover, the time requirements of an algorithm in $\Theta(log_2\ n)$ will not expand as rapidly as that of an algorithm in $\Theta(n^2)$.

Software Verification

Recall that the fourth phase in Polya's analysis of problem solving (Section 5.3) is to evaluate the solution for accuracy and for its potential as a tool for solving other problems. The significance of the first part of this phase is exemplified by the following example:

> A traveler with a gold chain of seven links must stay in an isolated hotel for seven nights. The rent each night consists of one link from the chain. What is the fewest number of links that must be cut so that the traveler can pay the hotel one link of the chain each morning without paying for lodging in advance?

To solve this problem we first realize that not every link in the chain must be cut. If we cut only the second link, we could free both the first and second links from the other five. Following this insight, we are led to the solution of cutting only the second, fourth, and sixth links in the chain, a process that releases each link while cutting only three (Figure 5.21). Furthermore, any fewer cuts leaves two links connected, so we might conclude that the correct answer to our problem is three.

Upon reconsidering the problem, however, we might make the observation that when only the third link in the chain is cut, we obtain three pieces of chain of lengths one, two, and four (Figure 5.22). With these pieces we can proceed as follows:

First morning: Give the hotel the single link.
Second morning: Retrieve the single link and give the hotel the two-link piece.
Third morning: Give the hotel the single link.
Fourth morning: Retrieve the three links held by the hotel and give the hotel the four-link piece.
Fifth morning: Give the hotel the single link.
Sixth morning: Retrieve the single link and give the hotel the double-link piece.
Seventh morning: Give the hotel the single link.

Consequently, our first answer, which we thought was correct, is incorrect. How, then, can we be sure that our new solution is correct? We might argue as follows: Since a single link must be given to the hotel on the first morning, at least one link of the chain must be cut, and since our new solution requires only one cut, it must be optimal.

Translated into the programming environment, this example emphasizes the distinction between a program that is believed to be correct and a program that is

Figure 5.21 Separating the chain using only three cuts

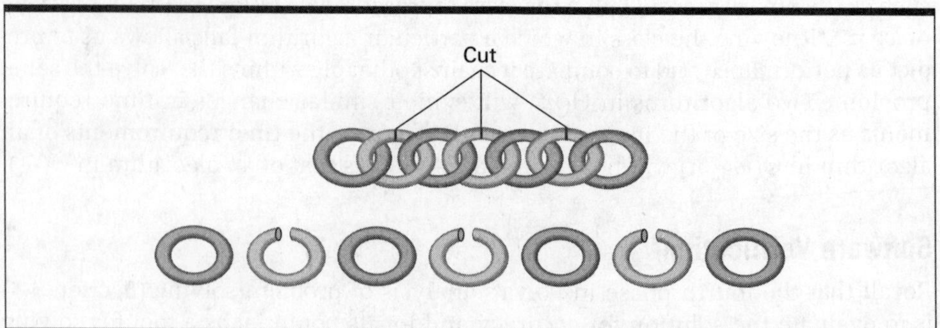

Figure 5.22 Solving the problem with only one cut

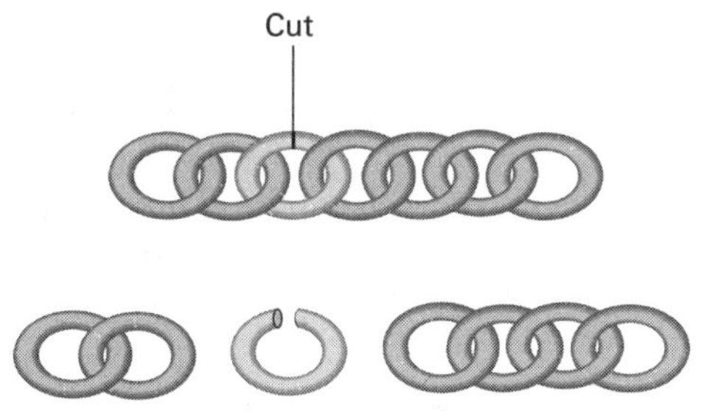

correct. The two are not necessarily the same. The data processing community is rich in horror stories involving software that although "known" to be correct, still failed at a critical moment because of some unforeseen situation. Verification of software is therefore an important undertaking, and the search for efficient verification techniques constitutes an active field of research in computer science.

A major line of research in this area attempts to apply the techniques of formal logic to prove the correctness of a program. That is, the goal is to apply formal logic to prove that the algorithm represented by a program does what it is intended to do. The underlying thesis is that by reducing the verification process to a formal procedure, one is protected from the inaccurate conclusions that might be associated with intuitive arguments, as was the case in the gold chain problem. Let us consider this approach to program verification in more detail.

Just as a formal mathematical proof is based on axioms (geometric proofs are often founded on the axioms of Euclidean geometry, whereas other proofs are based on the axioms of set theory), a formal proof of a program's correctness is based on the specifications under which the program was designed. To prove that a program correctly sorts lists of names, we are allowed to begin with the assumption that the program's input is a list of names, or if the program is designed to compute the average of one or more positive numbers, we assume that the input does, in fact, consist of one or more positive numbers. In short, a

Beyond Verification of Software

Verification problems, as discussed in the text, are not unique to software. Equally important is the problem of confirming that the hardware that executes a program is free of flaws. This involves the verification of circuit designs as well as machine construction. Again, the state of the art relies heavily on testing, which, as in the case of software, means that subtle errors can find their way into finished products. Records indicate that the Mark I, constructed at Harvard University in the 1940s, contained wiring errors that were not detected for many years. In the 1990s, a flaw was discovered in the floating- point portion of the early Pentium microprocessors that caused it to calculate the wrong answer when certain numbers were divided. In both of these cases, the error was detected before serious consequences developed.

proof of correctness begins with the assumption that certain conditions, called **preconditions,** are satisfied at the beginning of the program's execution.

The next step in a proof of correctness is to consider how the consequences of these preconditions propagate through the program. For this purpose, researchers have analyzed various program structures to determine how a statement, known to be true before the structure is executed, is affected by executing the structure. As a simple example, if a certain statement about the value of `Y` is known to hold prior to executing the instruction

```
X = Y
```

then that same statement can be made about `X` after the instruction has been executed. More precisely, if the value of `Y` is not 0 before the instruction is executed, then we can conclude that the value of `X` will not be 0 after the instruction is executed.

A slightly more involved example occurs in the case of an if-else structure such as

```
if (condition):
  instruction A
else:
  instruction B
```

Here, if some statement is known to hold before execution of the structure, then immediately before executing `instruction A`, we know that both that statement and the condition tested are true, whereas if `instruction B` is to be executed, we know the statement and the negation of the condition tested must hold.

Following rules such as these, a proof of correctness proceeds by identifying statements, called **assertions,** that can be established at various points in the program. The result is a collection of assertions, each being a consequence of the program's preconditions and the sequence of instructions that lead to the point in the program at which the assertion is established. If the assertion so established at the end of the program corresponds to the desired output specifications (which are called **postconditions**), we conclude that the program is correct.

As an example, consider the typical `while` loop structure represented in Figure 5.23. Suppose, as a consequence of the preconditions given at point A, we can establish that a particular assertion is true each time the test for termination is performed (point B) during the repetitive process. (An assertion at a point in a loop that is true every time that point in the loop is reached is known as a **loop invariant.**) Then, if the repetition ever terminates, execution moves to point C, where we can conclude that both the loop invariant and the termination condition hold. (The loop invariant still holds because the test for termination does not alter any values in the program, and the termination condition holds because otherwise the loop does not terminate.) If these combined statements imply the desired postconditions, our proof of correctness can be completed merely by showing that the initialization and modification components of the loop ultimately lead to the termination condition.

You should compare this analysis to our example of the insertion sort shown in Figure 5.11. The outer loop in that program is based on the loop invariant

> Each time the test for termination is performed, the entries in the list from position 1 through position $N - 1$ are sorted

Figure 5.23 The assertions associated with a typical while structure

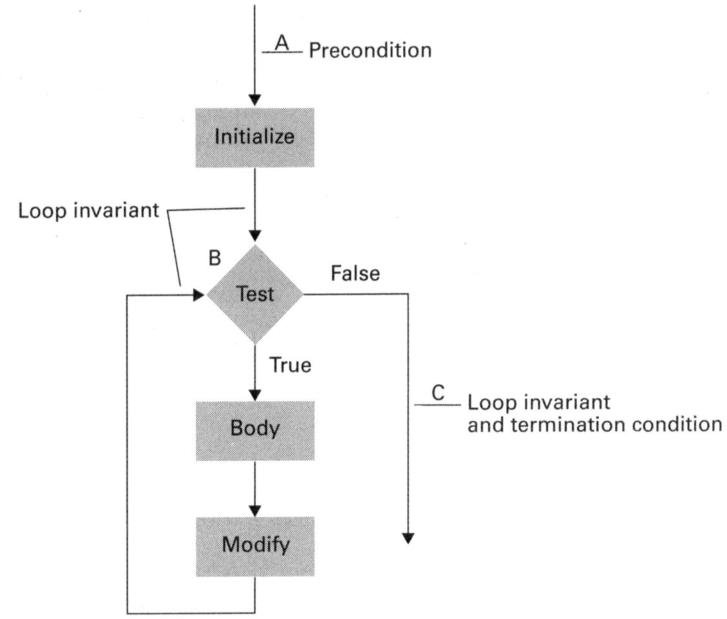

and the termination condition is

> The value of *N* is greater than the length of the list.

Thus, if the loop ever terminates, we know that both conditions must be satisfied, which implies that the entire list would be sorted.

Progress in the development of program verification techniques continues to be challenging. However, advancements are being made. One of the more significant is found in the programming language SPARK, which is closely related to the more popular language Ada. (Ada is one of the languages from which we will draw examples in the next chapter.) In addition to allowing programs to be expressed in a high-level form such as our pseudocode, SPARK gives programmers a means of including assertions such as preconditions, postconditions, and loop invariants within the program. Thus, a program written in SPARK contains not only the algorithm to be applied but also the information required for the application of formal proof-of-correctness techniques. To date, SPARK has been used successfully in numerous software development projects involving critical software applications, including secure software for the U.S. National Security Agency, internal control software used in Lockheed Martin's C130J Hercules aircraft, and critical rail transportation control systems.

In spite of successes such as SPARK, formal program verification techniques have not yet found widespread usage, and thus most of today's software is "verified" by testing—a process that is shaky at best. After all, verification by testing proves nothing more than that the program performs correctly for the cases under which it was tested. Any additional conclusions are merely projections. The errors contained in a program are often consequences of subtle oversights that are easily overlooked during testing as well as development. Consequently errors in a program, just as our error in the gold chain problem, can, and often do, go undetected, even though significant effort may be exerted to avoid it. A dramatic example occurred at AT&T: An error in the software controlling 114 switching stations went undetected from the software's installation in December 1989 until January 15, 1990, at which time a unique set of circumstances caused approximately five million calls to be unnecessarily blocked over a nine-hour period.

Questions & Exercises

1. Suppose we find that a machine programmed with our insertion sort algorithm requires an average of one second to sort a list of 100 names. How long do you estimate it takes to sort a list of 1,000 names? How about 10,000 names?
2. Give an example of an algorithm in each of the following classes: $\Theta(log_2 n)$, $\Theta(n)$, and $\Theta(n^2)$.
3. List the classes $\Theta(n^2)$, $\Theta(log_2 n)$, $\Theta(n)$, and $\Theta(n^3)$ in decreasing order of efficiency.
4. Consider the following problem and a proposed answer. Is the proposed answer correct? Why or why not?

   Problem:—Suppose a box contains three cards. One of three cards is painted black on both sides, one is painted red on both sides, and the third is painted red on one side and black on the other. One of the cards is drawn from the box, and you are allowed to see one side of it. What is the probability that the other side of the card is the same color as the side you see?

   Proposed answer:—One-half. Suppose the side of the card you can see is red. (The argument would be symmetric with this one if the side were black.) Only two cards among the three have a red side. Thus the card you see must be one of these two. One of these two cards is red on the other side, while the other is black. Thus the card you can see is just as likely to be red on the other side as it is to be black.
5. The following program segment is an attempt to compute the quotient (forgetting any remainder) of two positive integers (a dividend and a divisor) by counting the number of times the divisor can be subtracted from the dividend before what is left becomes less than the divisor. For instance, 7/3 should produce 2 because 3 can be subtracted from 7 twice. Is the program correct? Justify your answer.

```
Count = 0
Remainder = Dividend
repeat:
  Remainder = Remainder - Divisor
  Count = Count + 1
  until (Remainder < Divisor)
Quotient = Count.
```

6. The following program segment is designed to compute the product of two nonnegative integers X and Y by accumulating the sum of X copies of Y— that is, 3 times 4 is computed by accumulating the sum of three 4s. Is the program correct? Justify your answer.

```
Product = Y
Count = 1
while (Count < X):
  Product = Product + Y
  Count = Count + 1
```

7. Assuming the precondition that the value associated with N is a positive integer, establish a loop invariant that leads to the conclusion that if the following routine terminates, then Sum is assigned the value $0 + 1 + \ldots + N$.

```
Sum = 0
K = 0
while (K < N):
  K = K + 1
  Sum = Sum + K
```

Provide an argument to the effect that the routine does in fact terminate.

8. Suppose that both a program and the hardware that executes it have been formally verified to be accurate. Does this ensure accuracy?

Chapter Review Problems

(Asterisked problems are associated with optional sections.)

1. Give an example of a set of steps that conforms to the informal definition of an algorithm given in the opening paragraph of Section 5.1 but does not conform to the formal definition given in Figure 5.1.

2. Explain the distinction between an ambiguity in a proposed algorithm and an ambiguity in the representation of an algorithm.

3. Describe how the use of primitives helps remove ambiguities in an algorithm's representation.

4. Select a subject with which you are familiar and design a pseudocode for giving directions in that subject. In particular, describe the primitives you would use and the syntax you would use to represent them. (If you are having trouble thinking of a subject, try sports, arts, or crafts.)

5. Does the following program represent an algorithm in the strict sense? Why or why not?

```
Count = 0
while (Count != 5):
  Count = Count + 2
```

6. In what sense do the following three steps not constitute an algorithm?

Step 1: Draw a circle with center coordinates (2, 5) and radius 3.

Step 2: Draw a circle with center coordinates (6, 5) and radius 5.

Step 3: Draw a line segment whose endpoints are at the intersections of the previous two circles.

7. Rewrite the following program segment using a `repeat` structure rather than a `while` structure. Be sure the new version prints the same values as the original. Initialization:

```
num = 0
while (num < 50):
  if (num is Odd)
    print(num is Odd)
  num = num + 1
```

8. Rewrite the following program segment using a `while` structure rather than a `repeat` structure. Be sure the new version prints the same values as the original.

```
num = 100
repeat:
  print(num)
  num = num - 1
  until (num > 0)
```

9. What must be done to translate a posttest loop expressed in the form

```
repeat:
  (. . . )
  until (. . . )
```

into an equivalent posttest loop expressed in the form

```
do:
  (. . . )
  while (. . . )
```

10. Design an algorithm that, when given an arrangement of the digits 0, 1, 2, 3, 4, 5, 6, 7, 8, 9, rearranges the digits so that the new arrangement represents the next larger value that can be represented by these digits (or reports that no such rearrangement exists if no rearrangement produces a larger value). Thus 5647382901 would produce 5647382910.

11. Design an algorithm for finding all the factors of a positive integer. For example, in the case of the integer 12, your algorithm should report the values 1, 2, 3, 4, 6, and 12.

12. Design an algorithm for determining whether a particular year is a leap year. For example, the year 2000 was a leap year.

13. What is the difference between a formal programming language and a pseudocode?

14. What is the difference between syntax and semantics?

15. The following is an addition problem in traditional base 10 notation. Each letter represents a different digit. What digit does each letter represent? How did you get your foot in the door?

```
  SEND
+ MORE
 MONEY
```

16. The following is a multiplication problem in traditional base 10 notation. Each letter represents a different digit. What digit does each letter represent? How did you get your foot in the door?

```
   XY
 × YX
   XY
  YZ
  WVY
```

17. The following is a multiplication problem in binary notation. Each letter represents a unique binary digit. Which letter represents 1 and which represents 0? Design an algorithm for solving problems like this.

```
  XYYX
× X XY
 XYYXY
```

18. Four prospectors with only one lantern must walk through a mine shaft. At most, two prospectors can travel together and any prospector in the shaft must be with the lantern. The prospectors, named Andrews, Blake, Johnson, and Kelly, can walk through the shaft in one minute, two minutes, four minutes, and eight minutes, respectively. When two walk together they travel at the speed of the slower prospector. How can all four prospectors get through the mine shaft in only 15 minutes? After you have solved this problem, explain how you got your foot in the door.

19. Starting with a large wine glass and a small wine glass, fill the small glass with wine and then pour that wine into the large glass. Next, fill the small glass with water and pour

some of that water into the large glass. Mix the contents of the large glass, and then pour the mixture back into the small glass until the small glass is full. Will there be more water in the large glass than there is wine in the small glass? After you have solved this problem, explain how you got your foot in the door.

20. Two bees, named Romeo and Juliet, live in different hives but have met and fallen in love. On a windless spring morning, they simultaneously leave their respective hives to visit each other. Their routes meet at a point 50 meters from the closest hive, but they fail to see each other and continue on to their destinations. At their destinations, they spend the same amount of time to discover that the other is not home and begin their return trips. On their return trips, they meet at a point that is 20 meters from the closest hive. This time they see each other and have a picnic lunch before returning home. How far apart are the two hives? After you have solved this problem, explain how you got your foot in the door.

21. Design an algorithm that, given two strings of characters, tests whether the second string is same as the first string or not.

22. The following algorithm is designed to print the beginning of what is known as the Fibonacci sequence. Identify the body of the loop. Where is the initialization step for the loop control? The modification step? The test step? What list of numbers is produced?

```
Last = 0
Current = 1
while (Current < 100):
  print(Current)
  Temp = Last
  Last = Current
  Current = Last + Temp
```

23. What sequence of numbers is printed by the following algorithm if the input value is 1?

```
def CodeWrite (num):
  While (num < 100):
    for (i = 2; i <= num/2; ++i)
    if (num % i == 0) flag = 1;
    if (flag == 0) print (num);
    num ++;
```

24. Modify the function `CodeWrite` in the preceding problem so that perfect square values are printed.

25. What letters are interrogated by the binary search (Figure 5.14) if it is applied to the list A, B, C, D, E, F, G, H, I, J, K, L, M, N, O when searching for the value J? What about searching for the value Z?

26. After performing many sequential searches on a list of 6,000 entries, what would you expect to be the average number of times that the target value would have been compared to a list entry? What if the search algorithm was the binary search?

27. Identify the termination condition in each of the following iterative statements.

a.
```
while (Count < 5):
  . . .
```

b.
```
repeat:
  . . .
  until (Count == 1)
```

c.
```
while ((Count < 5) and (Total < 56)):
  . . .
```

28. Identify the body of the following loop structure and count the number of times it will be executed. What happens if the test is changed to read "(Count != 6)"?

```
Count = 1
while (Count != 7):
  print(Count)
  Count = Count + 3
```

29. What problems do you expect to arise if the following program is implemented on a computer? (Hint: Remember the problem of round-off errors associated with floating-point arithmetic.)

```
Count = one_tenth
repeat:
  print(Count)
  Count = Count + one_tenth
  until (Count == 1)
```

30. Design a recursive version of the Euclidean algorithm (question 3 of Section 5.2).

31. Suppose we apply both `Check1` and `Check2` (defined next) to the input value 1. What is the difference in the printed output of the two routines?

```
def Check1 (num):
  if (num % 2 == 0):
    print(num)
    Check1(num + 1)
def Check2(num):
  if (num % 2 == 1):
    print(num)
    Check2(num + 1)
```

32. Identify the important constituents of the control mechanism in the routines of the previous problem. In particular, what condition causes the process to terminate? Where is the state of the process modified toward this termination condition? Where is the state of the control process initialized?

33. Identify the termination condition in the following recursive function.

```
def XXX (N):
  if (N == 5):
    XXX(N + 1)
```

34. Call the function `CodeWrite` (defined below) with the value 100 and record the values that are printed.

```
def CodeWrite (N):
  if (N > 0):
    print(N)
    CodeWrite(N / 2)
  print(N + 1)
```

35. Call the function `MysteryPrint` (defined below) with the value 2 and record the values that are printed.

```
def MysteryPrint (N):
  if (N > 0):
    print(N)
    MysteryPrint(N - 2)
  else:
    print(N)
    if (N > -1):
      MysteryPrint(N + 1)
```

36. Design an algorithm to generate the sequence of positive integers (in increasing order) whose only prime divisors are 2 and 3; that is, your program should produce the sequence 2, 3, 4, 6, 8, 9, 12, 16, 18, 24, 27, ... Does your program represent an algorithm in the strict sense?

37. Answer the following questions in terms of the list: 19, 37, 53, 71, 96, 137, 289, 374, 559, 797, 979.

a. Which search algorithm (sequential or binary) will find the number 137 more quickly?
b. Which search algorithm (sequential or binary) will find the number 19 more quickly?
c. Which search algorithm (sequential or binary) will detect the absence of the number 99 more quickly?
d. Which search algorithm (sequential or binary) will detect the absence of the number 111 more quickly?
e. How many numbers will be interrogated when searching for the number 96 when using the sequential search? How many will be interrogated when using the binary search?

38. A positive integer is called an Armstrong number if the sum of the cubes of individual digits of the number is equal to that number itself. For example, the sum of cubes of individual digits of the number 153 is $1 * 1 * 1 + 5 * 5 * 5 + 3 * 3 * 3 = 153$. Hence, the number 153 is called an Armstrong number. Design an algorithm that checks whether a given number is an Armstrong number or not.

39. a. Suppose you must sort a list of ten integers in descending order, and you have already designed an algorithm that does this for six integers. Design an algorithm to sort ten integers by taking advantage of the previously designed algorithm.

b. Design a recursive algorithm to sort arbitrary lists of integers in descending order based on the technique used in (a).

40. The puzzle called the Towers of Hanoi consists of three pegs, one of which contains several rings stacked in order of descending diameter from bottom to top. The problem is to move the stack of rings to another peg. You are allowed to move only one ring at a time, and at no time is a ring to be placed on top of a smaller one. Observe that if the puzzle involved only one ring, it would be extremely easy. Moreover, when faced with the problem of moving several rings, if you could move all but the largest ring to another peg, the largest ring could then be placed on the third peg, and then the problem would be to move the remaining rings on top of it. Using this observation, develop a recursive algorithm for solving the Towers of Hanoi puzzle for an arbitrary number of rings.

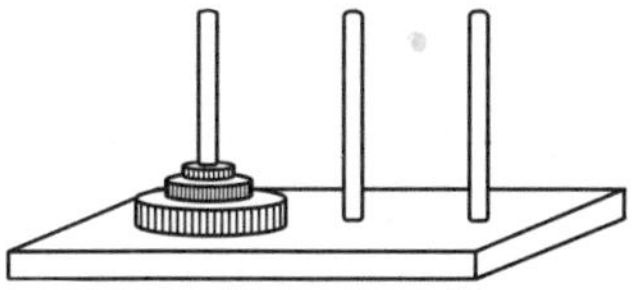

41. Another approach to solving the Towers of Hanoi puzzle (question 40) is to imagine the pegs arranged on a circular stand with a peg mounted at each of the positions of 4, 8, and 12 o'clock. The rings, which begin on one of the pegs, are numbered 1, 2, 3, and so on, starting with the smallest ring being 1. Odd-numbered rings, when on top of a stack, are allowed to move clockwise to the next peg; likewise, even-numbered rings are allowed to move counterclockwise (as long as that move does not place a ring on a smaller one). Under this restriction, always move the largest-numbered ring that can be moved. Based on this observation, develop a nonrecursive algorithm for solving the Towers of Hanoi puzzle.

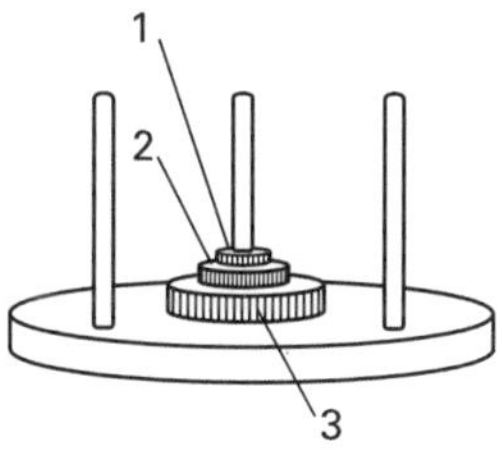

42. Develop two algorithms, one based on a loop structure and the other on a recursive structure, to print the daily salary of a worker who each day is paid twice the previous day's salary (starting with one penny for the first day's work) for a 30-day period. What problems relating to number storage are you likely to encounter if you implement your solutions on an actual machine?

43. Design an algorithm to find the square root of a positive number by starting with the number itself as the first guess and repeatedly producing a new guess from the previous one by averaging the previous guess with the result of dividing the original number by the previous guess. Analyze the control of this repetitive process. In particular, what condition should terminate the repetition?

44. Design an algorithm that lists all possible 4-digit integers made from digits 1 to 5 and are less than 5000.

45. Design an algorithm that, given a list of names, finds the longest name in the list. Use the `for` loop structure. Determine what your solution does if there are several "longest" names in the list. In particular, what would your algorithm do if all the names had the same length?

46. Design an algorithm that, given a list of nine or more names, sorts the list in alphabetical order and finds the name with the minimum number of characters.

47. Arrange the names Brenda, Doris, Raymond, Steve, Timothy, and William in an order that requires the least number of comparisons when sorted by the insertion sort algorithm (Figure 5.11).

48. What is the largest number of entries that are interrogated if the binary search algorithm (Figure 5.14) is applied to a list of 4,000 names? How does this compare to the sequential search (Figure 5.6)?

49. Use big-theta notation to classify the traditional grade school algorithms for addition and multiplication. That is, if asked to add two numbers each having n digits, how many individual additions must be performed? If requested to multiply two n-digit numbers, how many individual multiplications are required?

50. Sometimes a slight change in a problem can significantly alter the form of its solution. For example, find a simple algorithm for solving the following problem and classify it using big-theta notation:

> Divide a group of people into two disjoint subgroups (of arbitrary size) such that the difference in the total ages of the members of the two subgroups is as large as possible.

Now change the problem so that the desired difference is as small as possible and classify your approach to the problem.

51. From a given a list of 1000 integers from 1 to 1000, extract pairs of numbers whose product is 2424. How efficient is your approach to the problem?

52. Explain what will be the values of a and b if we call the function CodeWrite (defined below) with inputs 78 and 89.

```
def CodeWrite (a, b):
if (a > 0 and b > 0):
   a = a + b;
   a = a + b;
   a = a + b;
   print(a and b)
```

53. The following program segment is designed to compute the product of two nonnegative integers X and Y by accumulating the sum of X copies of Y; that is, 3 times 4 is computed by accumulating the sum of three 4s. Is the program segment correct? Explain your answer.

```
Product = 0
Count = 0
repeat:
   Product = Product + Y
   Count = Count + 1
   until (Count == X)
```

54. The following program segment is designed to report which of the positive integers X and Y is a divisor of the other. Is the program segment correct? Explain your answer.

```
if (X < Y)
if (Y % X == 0):
  print('X is Divisor of Y')
else if (X % Y == 0):
  print('Y is Divisor of X')
```

55. The following program segment is designed to find the smallest entry in a nonempty list of integers. Is it correct? Explain your answer.

```
TestValue = first list entry
CurrentEntry = first list entry
while (CurrentEntry is not the
      last entry):
  if (CurrentEntry < TestValue):
     TestValue = CurrentEntry
  CurrentEntry = the next list entry
```

56. a. Identify the preconditions for the sequential search as represented in Figure 5.6. Establish a loop invariant for the while structure in that program that, when combined with the termination condition, implies that upon termination of the loop, the algorithm will report success or failure correctly.

b. Give an argument showing that the while loop in Figure 5.6 does in fact terminate.

57. The following program segment is designed to calculate the factorial of a nonnegative number N using recursion. Is the program segment correct? Explain your answer. Modify this program segment to calculate the factorial without using recursion. Be sure that the output values do not change.

```
int fact (int N) {
if (N == 0)
return 1;
return N * fact (N - 1);
}
```

Social Issues

The following questions are intended as a guide to the ethical/social/legal issues associated with the field of computing. The goal is not merely to answer these questions. You should also consider why you answered as you did and whether your justifications are consistent from one question to the next.

1. Because it is currently impossible to verify completely the accuracy of complex programs, under what circumstances, if any, should the creator of a program be liable for errors?
2. Suppose you have an idea and develop it into a product that many people can use. Moreover, it has required a year of work and an investment of $50,000 to develop your idea into a form that is useful to the general public. In its

final form, however, the product can be used by most people without buying anything from you. What right do you have for compensation? Is it ethical to pirate computer software? What about music and motion pictures?

3. Suppose a software package is so expensive that it is totally out of your price range. Is it ethical to copy it for your own use? (After all, you are not cheating the supplier out of a sale because you would not have bought the package anyway.)
4. Ownership of rivers, forests, oceans, and so on has long been an issue of debate. In what sense should someone or some institution be given ownership of an algorithm?
5. Some people feel that new algorithms are discovered, whereas others feel that new algorithms are created. To which philosophy do you subscribe? Would the different points of view lead to different conclusions regarding ownership of algorithms and ownership rights?
6. Is it ethical to design an algorithm for performing an illegal act? Does it matter whether the algorithm is ever executed? Should the person who creates such an algorithm have ownership rights to that algorithm? If so, what should those rights be? Should algorithm ownership rights be dependent on the purpose of the algorithm? Is it ethical to advertise and circulate techniques for breaking security? Does it matter what is being broken into?
7. An author is paid for the motion picture rights to a novel even though the story is often altered in the film version. How much of a story has to change before it becomes a different story? What alterations must be made to an algorithm for it to become a different algorithm?
8. Educational software is now being marketed for children in the 18 months or younger age group. Proponents argue that such software provides sights and sounds that would otherwise not be available to many children. Opponents argue that it is a poor substitute for personal parent/child interaction. What is your opinion? Should you take any action based on your opinion without knowing more about the software? If so, what action?

Additional Reading

Aho, A. V., J. E. Hopcroft, and J. D. Ullman. *The Design and Analysis of Computer Algorithms.* Boston, MA: Addison-Wesley, 1974.

Baase, S., and A. Van Gelder. *Computer Algorithms: Introduction to Design and Analysis,* 3rd ed. Boston, MA: Addison-Wesley, 2000.

Barnes, J. *High Integrity Software: The SPARK Approach to Safety and Security.* Boston, MA: Addison-Wesley, 2003.

Gries, D. *The Science of Programming.* New York: Springer-Verlag, 1998.

Harbin, R. *Origami—the Art of Paper Folding.* London: Hodder Paperbacks, 1973.

Johnsonbaugh, R., and M. Schaefer. *Algorithms.* Upper Saddle River, NJ: Prentice-Hall, 2004.

Kleinberg, *Algorithm Design*, 2nd ed. Boston, MA: Addison-Wesley, 2014.

Knuth, D. E. *The Art of Computer Programming, Vol. 3,* 2nd ed. Boston, MA: Addison-Wesley, 1998.

Levitin, A. V. *Introduction to the Design and Analysis of Algorithms,* 3rd ed. Boston, MA: Addison-Wesley, 2011.

Polya, G. *How to Solve It.* Princeton, NJ: Princeton University Press, 1973.

Roberts, E. S. *Thinking Recursively.* New York: Wiley, 1986.

CHAPTER 6

Programming Languages

In this chapter we study programming languages. Our purpose is not to focus on a particular language, although we will continue to use examples from Python where appropriate. Rather it is to learn *about* programming languages. We want to appreciate the commonality as well as the diversity among programming languages and their associated methodologies.

**Asterisks indicate suggestions for optional sections.*

The development of complex software systems such as operating systems, network software, and the vast array of application software available today would likely be impossible if humans were forced to write programs in machine language. Dealing with the intricate detail associated with such languages while trying to organize complex systems would be a taxing experience, to say the least.

Consequently, many programming languages have been developed that allow algorithms to be expressed in a form that is both palatable to humans and easily convertible into machine language instructions. Our goal in this chapter is to explore the sphere of computer science that deals with the design and implementation of these languages.

6.1 Historical Perspective

We begin our study by tracing the historical development of programming languages.

Early Generations

As we learned in Chapter 2, programs for modern computers consist of sequences of instructions that are encoded as numeric digits. Such an encoding system is known as a machine language. Unfortunately, writing programs in a machine language is a tedious task that often leads to errors that must be located and corrected (a process known as **debugging**) before the job is finished.

In the 1940s, researchers simplified the programming process by developing notational systems by which instructions could be represented in mnemonic rather than numeric form. For example, the instruction

Move the contents of register 5 to register 6

would be expressed as

```
4056
```

using the machine language introduced in Chapter 2, whereas in a mnemonic system it might appear as

```
MOV R5, R6
```

As a more extensive example, the machine language routine

```
156C
166D
5056
306E
C000
```

which adds the contents of memory cells 6C and 6D and stores the result at location 6E (Figure 2.7 of Chapter 2) might be expressed as

```
LD R5,Price
LD R6,ShippingCharge
ADDI R0,R5 R6
ST R0,TotalCost
HLT
```

using mnemonics. (Here we have used `LD`, `ADDI`, `ST`, and `HLT` to represent *load, add, store,* and *halt.* Moreover, we have used the descriptive names `Price`, `ShippingCharge`, and `TotalCost` to refer to the memory cells at locations 6C, 6D, and 6E, respectively. Such descriptive names are often called program variables or **identifiers.**) Note that the mnemonic form, although still lacking, does a better job of representing the meaning of the routine than does the numeric form.

Once such a mnemonic system was established, programs called **assemblers** were developed to convert mnemonic expressions into machine language instructions. Thus, rather than being forced to develop a program directly in machine language, a human could develop a program in mnemonic form and then have it converted into machine language by means of an assembler.

A mnemonic system for representing programs is collectively called an **assembly language.** At the time assembly languages were first developed, they represented a giant step forward in the search for better programming techniques. In fact, assembly languages were so revolutionary that they became known as second-generation languages, the first generation being the machine languages themselves.

Although assembly languages have many advantages over their machine language counterparts, they still fall short of providing the ultimate programming environment. After all, the primitives used in an assembly language are essentially the same as those found in the corresponding machine language. The difference is simply in the syntax used to represent them. Thus a program written in an assembly language is inherently machine dependent—that is, the instructions within the program are expressed in terms of a particular machine's attributes. In turn, a program written in assembly language cannot be easily transported to another computer design because it must be rewritten to conform to the new computer's register configuration and instruction set.

Another disadvantage of an assembly language is that a programmer, although not required to code instructions in numeric form, is still forced to think in terms of the small, incremental steps of the machine's language. The situation is analogous to designing a house in terms of boards, nails, bricks, and so on. It is true that the actual construction of the house ultimately requires a description based on these elementary pieces, but the design process is easier if we think in terms of larger units such as rooms, windows, doors, and so on.

In short, the elementary primitives in which a product must ultimately be constructed are not necessarily the primitives that should be used during the product's design. The design process is better suited to the use of high-level primitives, each representing a concept associated with a major feature of the product. Once the design is complete, these primitives can be translated to lower-level concepts relating to the details of implementation.

Following this philosophy, computer scientists began developing programming languages that were more conducive to software development than were the low-level assembly languages. The result was the emergence of a third generation of programming languages that differed from previous generations in that their primitives were both higher level (in that they expressed instructions in larger increments) and **machine independent** (in that they did not rely on the characteristics of a particular machine). The best-known early examples are FORTRAN (FORmula TRANslator), which was developed for scientific and engineering applications, and COBOL (COmmon Business-Oriented Language), which was developed by the U.S. Navy for business applications.

In general, the approach to third-generation programming languages was to identify a collection of high-level primitives (in essentially the same spirit with which we developed our pseudocode in Chapter 5) in which software could be developed. Each of these primitives was designed so that it could be implemented as a sequence of the low-level primitives available in machine languages. For example, the statement

```
assign TotalCost the value Price + ShippingCharge
```

expresses a high-level activity without reference to how a particular machine should perform the task, yet it can be implemented by the sequence of machine instructions discussed earlier. Thus, our pseudocode structure

```
identifier = expression
```

is a potential high-level primitive.

Once this collection of high-level primitives had been identified, a program, called a **translator,** was written that translated programs expressed in these high-level primitives into machine-language programs. Such a translator was similar to the second-generation assemblers, except that it often had to compile several machine instructions into short sequences to simulate the activity requested by a single high-level primitive. Thus, these translation programs were often called **compilers.**

An alternative to translators, called **interpreters,** emerged as another means of implementing third-generation languages. These programs were similar to translators except that they executed the instructions as they were translated instead of recording the translated version for future use. That is, rather than producing a machine-language copy of a program that would be executed later, an interpreter actually executed a program from its high-level form.

As a side issue, we should note that the task of promoting third-generation programming languages was not as easy as might be imagined. The thought of writing programs in a form similar to a natural language was so revolutionary that many in managerial positions fought the notion at first. Grace Hopper, who is recognized as the developer of the first compiler, often told the story of demonstrating a translator for a third-generation language in which German terms, rather than English, were used. The point was that the programming language was constructed around a small set of primitives that could be expressed in a variety of natural languages with only simple modifications to the translator. But she was surprised to find that many in the audience were shocked that, in the years surrounding World War II, she would be teaching a computer to "understand" German. Today we know that understanding a natural language involves much, much more than responding to a few rigorously defined primitives. Indeed, **natural languages** (such as English, German, and Latin) are distinguished from **formal languages** (such as programming languages) in that the latter are precisely defined by grammars (Section 6.4), whereas the former evolved over time without formal grammatical analysis.

Machine Independence and Beyond

With the development of third-generation languages, the goal of machine independence was largely achieved. Since the statements in a third-generation language did not refer to the attributes of any particular machine, they could be

Cross-Platform Software

A typical application program must rely on the operating system to perform many of its tasks. It may require the services of the window manager to communicate with the computer user, or it may use the file manager to retrieve data from mass storage. Unfortunately, different operating systems dictate that requests for these services be made in different ways. Thus for programs to be transferred and executed across networks and internets involving different machine designs and different operating systems, the programs must be operating-system independent as well as machine independent. The term *cross-platform* is used to reflect this additional level of independence. That is, cross-platform software is software that is independent of an operating system's design as well as the machine's hardware design and is therefore executable throughout a network.

compiled as easily for one machine as for another. A program written in a third-generation language could theoretically be used on any machine simply by applying the appropriate compiler.

Reality, however, has not proven to be this simple. When a compiler is designed, particular characteristics of the underlying machine are sometimes reflected as conditions on the language being translated. For example, the different ways in which machines handle I/O operations have historically caused the "same" language to have different characteristics, or dialects, on different machines. Consequently, it is often necessary to make at least minor modifications to a program to move it from one machine to another.

Compounding this problem of portability is the lack of agreement in some cases as to what constitutes the correct definition of a particular language. To aid in this regard, the American National Standards Institute and the International Organization for Standardization have adopted and published standards for many of the popular languages. In other cases, informal standards have evolved because of the popularity of a certain dialect of a language and the desire of other compiler writers to produce compatible products. However, even in the case of highly standardized languages, compiler designers often provide features, sometimes called language extensions, that are not part of the standard version of the language. If a programmer takes advantage of these features, the program produced will not be compatible with environments using a compiler from a different vendor.

In the overall history of programming languages, the fact that third-generation languages fell short of true machine independence is actually of little significance for two reasons. First, they were close enough to being machine independent that software could be transported from one machine to another with relative ease. Second, the goal of machine independence turned out to be only a seed for more demanding goals. Indeed, the realization that machines could respond to such high-level statements as

```
assign TotalCost the value Price + ShippingCharge
```

led computer scientists to dream of programming environments that would allow humans to communicate with machines in terms of abstract concepts rather than forcing them to translate these concepts into machine-compatible form.

Moreover, computer scientists wanted machines that could perform much of the algorithm discovery process rather than just algorithm execution. The result has been an ever-expanding spectrum of programming languages that challenges a clear-cut classification in terms of generations.

Programming Paradigms

The generation approach to classifying programming languages is based on a linear scale (Figure 6.1) on which a language's position is determined by the degree to which the user of the language is freed from the world of computer gibberish and allowed to think in terms associated with the problem being solved. In reality, the development of programming languages has not progressed in this manner but has developed along different paths as alternative approaches to the programming process (called **programming paradigms**) have surfaced and been pursued. Consequently, the historical development of programming languages is better represented by a multiple-track diagram as shown in Figure 6.2, in which different paths resulting from different paradigms are shown to emerge and progress independently. In particular, the figure presents four paths representing the functional, object-oriented, imperative, and declarative paradigms, with various languages associated with each paradigm positioned in a manner that indicates their births relative to other languages. (It does not imply that one language necessarily evolved from a previous one.)

We should note that although the paradigms identified in Figure 6.2 are called *programming* paradigms, these alternatives have ramifications beyond the programming process. They represent fundamentally different approaches to building solutions to problems and therefore affect the entire software development process. In this sense, the term *programming paradigm* is a misnomer. A more realistic term would be *software development paradigm*.

The **imperative paradigm,** also known as the **procedural paradigm,** represents the traditional approach to the programming process. It is the paradigm on which Python and our pseudocode of Chapter 5 are based as well as the machine language discussed in Chapter 2. As the name suggests, the imperative paradigm defines the programming process to be the development of a sequence of commands that, when followed, manipulate data to produce the desired result. Thus the imperative paradigm tells us to approach the programming process by finding an algorithm to solve the problem at hand and then expressing that algorithm as a sequence of commands.

Figure 6.1 Generations of programming languages

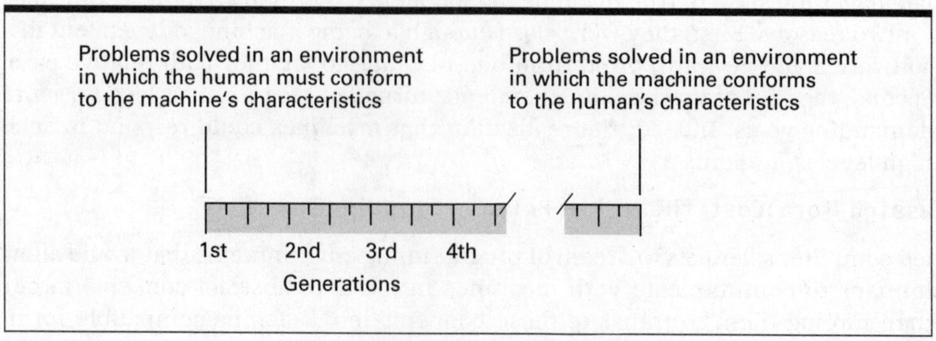

Figure 6.2 The evolution of programming paradigms

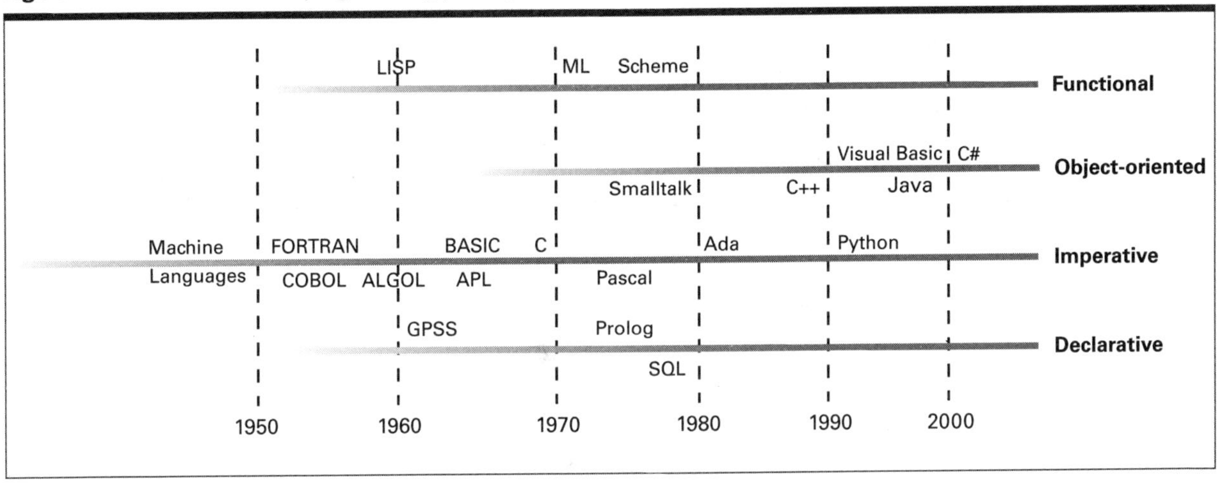

In contrast to the imperative paradigm is the **declarative paradigm,** which asks a programmer to describe the problem to be solved rather than an algorithm to be followed. More precisely, a declarative programming system applies a pre-established general-purpose problem-solving algorithm to solve problems presented to it. In such an environment the task of a programmer becomes that of developing a precise statement of the problem rather than of describing an algorithm for solving the problem.

A major obstacle in developing programming systems based on the declarative paradigm is the need for an underlying problem-solving algorithm. For this reason early declarative programming languages tended to be special-purpose in nature, designed for use in particular applications. For example, the declarative approach has been used for many years to simulate a system (political, economic, environmental, and so on) in order to test hypotheses or to obtain predictions. In these settings, the underlying algorithm is essentially the process of simulating the passage of time by repeatedly recomputing values of parameters (gross domestic product, trade deficit, and so on) based on the previously computed values. Thus, implementing a declarative language for such simulations requires that one first implement an algorithm that performs this repetitive function. Then the only task required of a programmer using the system is to describe the situation to be simulated. In this manner, a weather forecaster does not need to develop an algorithm for forecasting the weather but merely describes the current weather status, allowing the underlying simulation algorithm to produce weather predictions for the near future.

A tremendous boost was given to the declarative paradigm with the discovery that the subject of formal logic within mathematics provides a simple problem-solving algorithm suitable for use in a general-purpose declarative programming system. The result has been increased attention to the declarative paradigm and the emergence of **logic programming,** a subject discussed in Section 6.7.

Another programming paradigm is the **functional paradigm.** Under this paradigm a program is viewed as an entity that accepts inputs and produces outputs. Mathematicians refer to such entities as functions, which is the reason this approach is called the functional paradigm. Under this paradigm a program is constructed by connecting smaller predefined program units (predefined functions) so that each unit's outputs are used as another unit's inputs in such a way that the desired overall input-to-output relationship is obtained. In short, the programming process under the functional paradigm is that of building functions as nested complexes of simpler functions.

As an example, Figure 6.3 shows how a function for balancing your checkbook can be constructed from two simpler functions. One of these, called `Find_sum`, accepts values as its input and produces the sum of those values as its output. The other, called `Find_diff`, accepts two input values and computes their difference. The structure displayed in Figure 6.3 can be represented in the LISP programming language (a prominent functional programming language) by the expression

```
(Find_diff (Find_sum Old_balance Credits) (Find_sum Debits))
```

The nested structure of this expression (as indicated by parentheses) reflects the fact that the inputs to the function `Find_diff` are produced by two applications of `Find_sum`. The first application of `Find_sum` produces the result of adding all the `Credits` to the `Old_balance`. The second application of `Find_sum` computes the total of all `Debits`. Then, the function `Find_diff` uses these results to obtain the new checkbook balance.

To more fully understand the distinction between the functional and imperative paradigms, let us compare the functional program for balancing a checkbook to the following pseudocode program obtained by following the imperative paradigm:

```
Total_credits = sum of all Credits
Temp_balance = Old_balance + Total_credits
Total_debits = sum of all Debits
Balance = Temp_balance - Total_debits
```

Figure 6.3 A function for checkbook balancing constructed from simpler functions

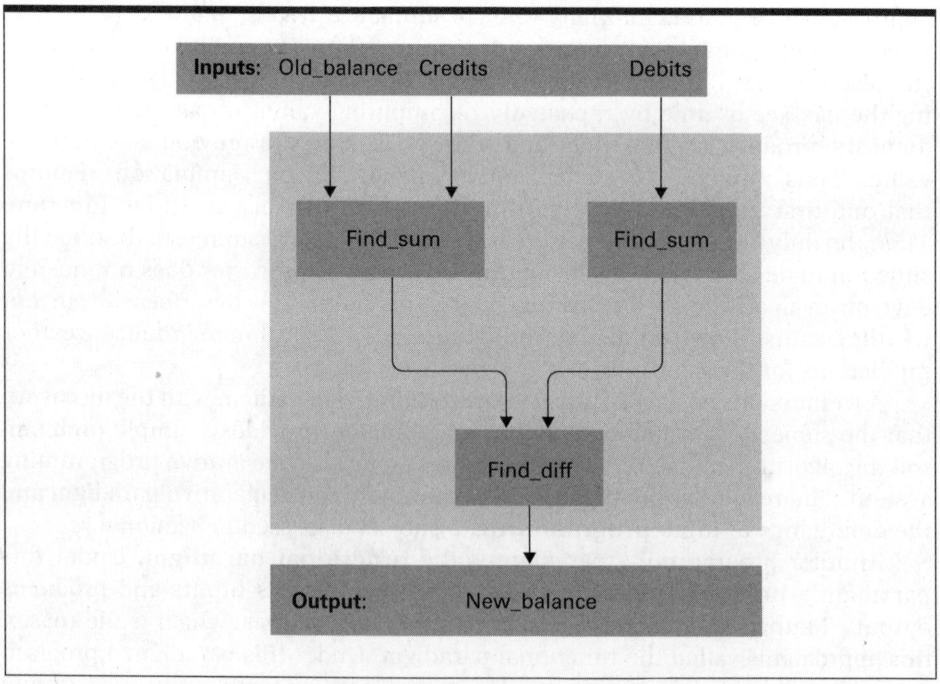

Note that this imperative program consists of multiple statements, each of which requests that a computation be performed and that the result be stored for later use. In contrast, the functional program consists of a single statement in which the result of each computation is immediately channeled into the next. In a sense, the imperative program is analogous to a collection of factories, each converting its raw materials into products that are stored in warehouses. From these warehouses, the products are later shipped to other factories as they are needed. But the functional program is analogous to a collection of factories that are coordinated so that each produces only those products that are ordered by other factories and then immediately ships those products to their destinations without intermediate storage. This efficiency is one of the benefits proclaimed by proponents of the functional paradigm.

Still another programming paradigm (and the most prominent one in today's software development) is the **object-oriented paradigm,** which is associated with the programming process called **object-oriented programming (OOP).** Following this paradigm, a software system is viewed as a collection of units, called **objects,** each of which is capable of performing the actions that are immediately related to itself as well as requesting actions of other objects. Together, these objects interact to solve the problem at hand.

As an example of the object-oriented approach at work, consider the task of developing a graphical user interface. In an object-oriented environment, the icons that appear on the screen would be implemented as objects. Each of these objects would encompass a collection of functions (called **methods** in the object-oriented vernacular) describing how that object is to respond to the occurrence of various events, such as being selected by a click of the mouse button or being dragged across the screen by the mouse. Thus the entire system would be constructed as a collection of objects, each of which knows how to respond to the events related to it.

To contrast the object-oriented paradigm with the imperative paradigm, consider a program involving a list of names. In the traditional imperative paradigm, this list would be merely a collection of data. Any program unit accessing the list would have to contain the algorithms for performing the required manipulations. In the object-oriented approach, however, the list would be constructed as an object that consisted of the list together with a collection of methods for manipulating the list. (This might include functions for inserting a new entry in the list, deleting an entry from the list, detecting if the list is empty, and sorting the list.) In turn, another program unit that needed to manipulate the list would not contain algorithms for performing the pertinent tasks. Instead, it would make use of the functions provided in the object. In a sense, rather than sorting the list as in the imperative paradigm, the program unit would ask the list to sort itself. Although we will discuss the object-oriented paradigm in more detail in Section 6.5, its significance in today's software development arena dictates that we include the concept of a class in this introduction. To this end, recall that an object can consist of data (such as a list of names) together with a collection of methods for performing activities (such as inserting new names in the list). These features must be described by statements in the written program. This description of the object's properties is called a **class.** Once a class has been constructed, it can be applied anytime an object with those characteristics is needed. Thus, several objects can be based on (that is, built from) the same class. Just like identical twins, these objects would be distinct entities but would have the same characteristics because they are constructed from the same template (the same class). (An object that is based on a particular class is said to be an **instance** of that class.)

It is because objects are well-defined units whose descriptions are isolated in reusable classes that the object-oriented paradigm has gained popularity. Indeed, proponents of object-oriented programming argue that the object-oriented paradigm provides a natural environment for the "building block" approach to software development. They envision software libraries of predefined classes from which new software systems can be constructed in the same way that many traditional products are constructed from off-the-shelf components. Building and expanding such libraries is an ongoing process, as we will learn in Chapter 7.

In closing, we should note that the methods within an object are essentially small imperative program units. This means that most programming languages based on the object-oriented paradigm contain many of the features found in imperative languages. For instance, the popular object-oriented language C++ was developed by adding object-oriented features to the imperative language known as C. Moreover, since Java and C# are derivatives of C++, they too have inherited this imperative core. In Sections 6.2 and 6.3 we will explore many of these imperative features, and in so doing, we will be discussing concepts that permeate a vast majority of today's object-oriented software. Then, in Section 6.5, we will consider features that are unique to the object-oriented paradigm.

Questions & Exercises

1. In what sense is a program in a third-generation language machine independent? In what sense is it still machine dependent?
2. What is the difference between an assembler and a compiler?
3. We can summarize the imperative programming paradigm by saying that it places emphasis on describing a process that leads to the solution of the problem at hand. Give a similar summary of the declarative, functional, and object-oriented paradigms.
4. In what sense are the third-generation programming languages at a higher level than the earlier generations?

6.2 Traditional Programming Concepts

In this section we consider some of the concepts found in imperative as well as object-oriented programming languages. For this purpose we will draw examples from the languages Ada, C, C++, C#, FORTRAN, and Java. Our goal is not to become entangled in the details of any particular language but merely to demonstrate how common language features appear in a variety of actual languages. Our collection of languages is therefore chosen to be representative of the landscape. C is a third-generation imperative language. C++ is an object-oriented language that was developed as an extension of the language C. Java and C# are object-oriented languages derived from C++. (Java was developed at Sun Microsystems, which was later purchased by Oracle, whereas C# is a product of Microsoft.) FORTRAN and Ada were originally designed as third-generation imperative languages although their newer versions have expanded to encompass most of the object-oriented paradigm. Appendix D contains a brief background of each of these languages.

Even though we are including object-oriented languages such as C++, Java, and C# among our example languages, we will approach this section as though we were writing a program in the imperative paradigm, because many units within an object-oriented program (such as the functions describing how an object should react to an outside stimulus) are essentially short imperative programs. Later, in Section 6.5, we will focus on features unique to the object-oriented paradigm.

Generally, a program consists of a collection of statements that tend to fall into three categories: declarative statements, imperative statements, and comments. **Declarative statements** define customized terminology that is used later in the program, such as the names used to reference data items; **imperative statements** describe steps in the underlying algorithms; and **comments** enhance the readability of a program by explaining its esoteric features in a more human-compatible form. Normally, an imperative program (or an imperative program unit within an object-oriented program) can be thought of as having the structure depicted in Figure 6.4. It begins with a collection of declarative statements describing the data to be manipulated by the program. This preliminary material is followed by imperative statements that describe the algorithm to be executed. Many languages now allow the declarative and imperative statements to be freely intermingled, but the conceptual distinction remains. Comment statements are dispersed as needed to clarify the program.

Following this lead, we approach our study of programming concepts by considering statement categories in the order in which we might encounter them in a program, beginning with concepts associated with declaration statements.

Variables and Data Types

As we learned in Section 1.8, high-level programming languages allow locations in main memory to be referenced by descriptive names rather than by numeric addresses. Such a name is known as a **variable,** in recognition of the fact that

Figure 6.4 The composition of a typical imperative program or program unit

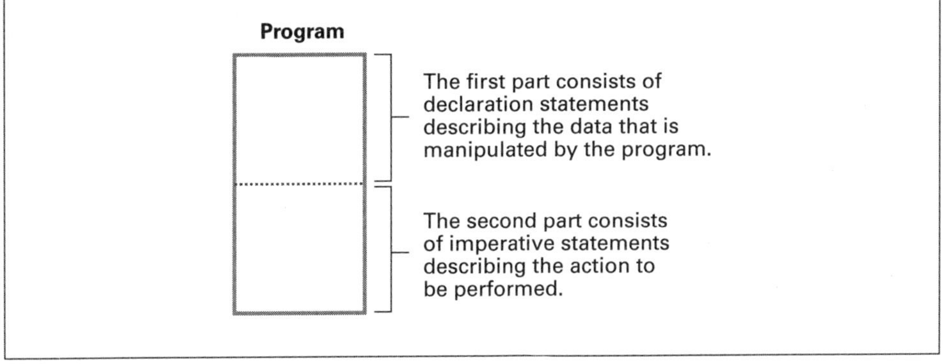

Scripting Languages

A subset of the imperative programming languages is the collection of languages known as **scripting languages.** These languages are typically used to perform administrative tasks rather than to develop complex programs. The expression of such a task is known as a **script,** which explains the term *scripting language.* For example, the administrator of a computer system might write a script to describe a sequence of record-keeping activities that should be performed every evening, or the user of a PC might write a script to direct the execution of a sequence of programs required to read pictures from a digital camera, index the pictures by date, and store copies of them in an archival storage system. The origin of scripting languages can be traced to the job control languages of the 1960s that were used to direct an operating system in the scheduling of batch processing jobs (see Section 3.1). Even today, many consider scripting languages to be languages for directing the execution of other programs, which is a rather restrictive view of current scripting languages. Examples of scripting languages include Perl and PHP, both of which are popular in controlling server-side Web applications (see Section 4.3), as well as VBScript, which is a dialect of Visual Basic that was developed by Microsoft and is used in Windows-specific situations.

by changing the value stored at the location, the value associated with the name changes as the program executes. Unlike Python, our example languages in this chapter require that variables be identified via a declarative statement prior to being used elsewhere in the program. These declarative statements also require that the programmer describe the type of data that will be stored at the memory location associated with the variable.

Such a type is known as a **data type** and encompasses both the manner in which the data item is encoded and the operations that can be performed on that data. For example, the type **integer** refers to numeric data consisting of whole numbers, probably stored using two's complement notation. Operations that can be performed on integer data include the traditional arithmetic operations and comparisons of relative size, such as determining whether one value is greater than another. The type **float** (sometimes called **real**) refers to numeric data that might contain values other than whole numbers, probably stored in floating-point notation. Operations performed on data of type float are similar to those performed on data of type integer. Recall, however, that the activity required for adding two items of type float differs from that for adding two items of type integer.

Suppose, then, that we wanted to use the variable `WeightLimit` in a program to refer to an area of main memory containing a numeric value encoded in two's complement notation. In the languages C, C++, Java, and C# we would declare our intention by inserting the statement

```
int WeightLimit;
```

toward the beginning of the program. This statement means "The name `WeightLimit` will be used later in the program to refer to a memory area containing a value stored in two's complement notation." Multiple variables of the same type can normally be declared in the same declaration statement. For example, the statement

```
int Height, Width;
```

would declare both `Height` and `Width` to be variables of type integer. Moreover, most languages allow a variable to be assigned an initial value when it is declared. Thus,

```
int WeightLimit = 100;
```

would not only declare `WeightLimit` to be a variable of type integer but also assign it the starting value 100. In contrast, dynamically typed languages like Python allow variables to be assigned without first declaring their type; such variables are checked for correct type later, when operations are performed upon them.

Other common data types include character and Boolean. The type character refers to data consisting of symbols, probably stored using ASCII or Unicode. Operations performed on such data include comparisons such as determining whether one symbol occurs before another in alphabetical order, testing to see whether one string of symbols appears inside another, and concatenating one string of symbols at the end of another to form one long string. The statement

```
char Letter, Digit;
```

could be used in the languages C, C++, C#, and Java to declare the variables `Letter` and `Digit` to be of type character.

The type **Boolean** refers to data items that can take on only the values true or false. Operations on data of type Boolean include inquiries as to whether the current value is true or false. For example, if the variable `LimitExceeded` was declared to be of type Boolean, then a statement of the form

```
if (LimitExceeded) then (...) else (...)
```

would be reasonable.

The data types that are included as primitives in a programming language, such as `int` for integer and `char` for character, are called **primitive data types.** As we have learned, the types integer, float, character, and Boolean are common primitives. Other data types that have not yet become widespread primitives include images, audio, video, and hypertext. However, types such as GIF, JPEG, and HTML might soon become as common as integer and float. Later (Sections 6.5 and Section 8.4) we will learn how the object-oriented paradigm enables a programmer to extend the repertoire of available data types beyond the primitive types provided in a language. Indeed, this ability is a celebrated trait of the object-oriented paradigm.

In summary, the following program segment, expressed in the language C and its derivatives C++, C#, and Java, declares the variables `Length` and `Width` to be of type `float`, the variables `Price`, `Tax`, and `Total` to be of type integer, and the variable `Symbol` to be of type character.

```
float Length, Width;
int   Price, Tax, Total;
char  Symbol;
```

In Section 6.4 we will see how a translator uses the knowledge that it gathers from such declaration statements to help it translate a program from a high-level language into machine language. For now, we note that such information can be used to identify errors. For example, if a translator found a statement requesting the addition of two variables that had been declared earlier to be of type Boolean, it should probably consider the statement to be in error and report this finding to the user.

Data Structure

In addition to data type, variables in a program are often associated with **data structure,** which is the conceptual shape or arrangement of data. For example, text is normally viewed as a long string of characters, whereas sales records might be envisioned as a rectangular table of numeric values, where each row represents the sales made by a particular employee and each column represents the sales made on a particular day.

One common data structure is the **array,** which is a block of elements of the same type such as a one-dimensional list, a two-dimensional table with rows and columns, or tables with higher dimensions. To establish such an array in a program, many programming languages require that the declaration statement declaring the name of the array also specify the length of each dimension of the array. For example, Figure 6.5 displays the conceptual structure declared by the statement

```
int Scores[2][9];
```

in the language C, which means "The variable Scores will be used in the following program unit to refer to a two-dimensional array of integers having two rows and nine columns." The same statement in FORTRAN would be written as

```
INTEGER Scores(2,9)
```

Once an array has been declared, it can be referenced elsewhere in the program by its name, or an individual element can be identified by means of integer values called **indices** that specify the row, column, and so on, desired. However, the range of these indices varies from language to language. For example, in C (and its derivatives C++, Java, and C#) indices start at 0, meaning that the entry in the second row and fourth column of the array called Scores (as declared above) would be referenced by Scores[1][3], and the entry in the first row and first column would be Scores[0][0]. In contrast, indices start at 1 in a FORTRAN program so the entry in the second row and fourth column would be referenced by Scores(2,4) (see again Figure 6.5).

In contrast to an array in which all data items are the same type, an **aggregate type** (also called a **structure,** a **record,** or sometimes a **heterogeneous array**)

Figure 6.5 A two-dimensional array with two rows and nine columns

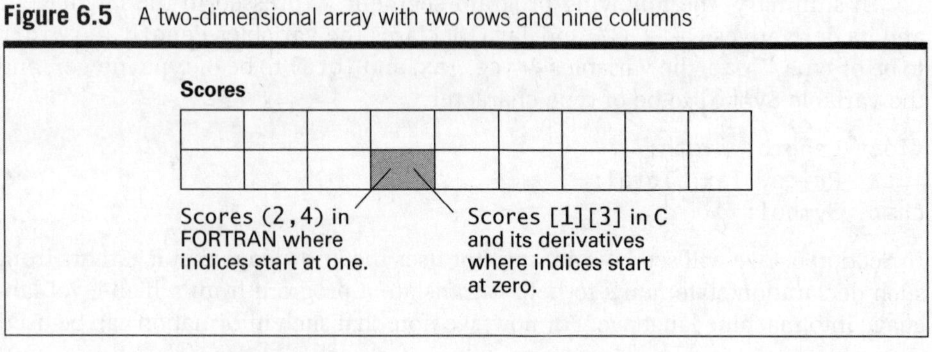

is a block of data in which different elements can have different types. For instance, a block of data referring to an employee might consist of an entry called `Name` of type character, an entry called `Age` of type integer, and an entry called `SkillRating` of type float. Such an aggregate type would be declared in C by the statement

```
struct { char  Name[25];
         int Age;
         float SkillRating;
       } Employee;
```

which says that the variable `Employee` is to refer to a structure (abbreviated `struct`) consisting of three components called `Name` (a string of 25 characters), `Age`, and `SkillRating` (Figure 6.6). Once such an aggregate has been declared, a programmer can use the structure name (`Employee`) to refer to the entire aggregate or can reference individual **fields** within the aggregate by means of the structure name followed by a period and the field name (such as `Employee.Age`).

In Chapter 8 we will see how conceptual constructs such as arrays are actually implemented inside a computer. In particular, we will learn that the data contained in an array might be scattered over a wide area of main memory or mass storage. This is why we refer to data structure as being the *conceptual* shape or arrangement of data. Indeed, the actual arrangement within the computer's storage system might be quite different from its conceptual arrangement.

Constants and Literals

Sometimes a fixed, predetermined value is used in a program. For example, a program for controlling air traffic in the vicinity of a particular airport might contain numerous references to that airport's altitude above sea level. When writing such a program, one can include this value, say 645 feet, literally each time it is required. Such an explicit appearance of a value is called a **literal.** The use of literals leads to program statements such as

```
EffectiveAlt = Altimeter + 645
```

where `EffectiveAlt` and `Altimeter` are assumed to be variables and 645 is a literal. Thus, this statement asks that the variable `EffectiveAlt` be assigned the result of adding 645 to the value assigned to the variable `Altimeter`.

Figure 6.6 The conceptual layout of the structure Employee

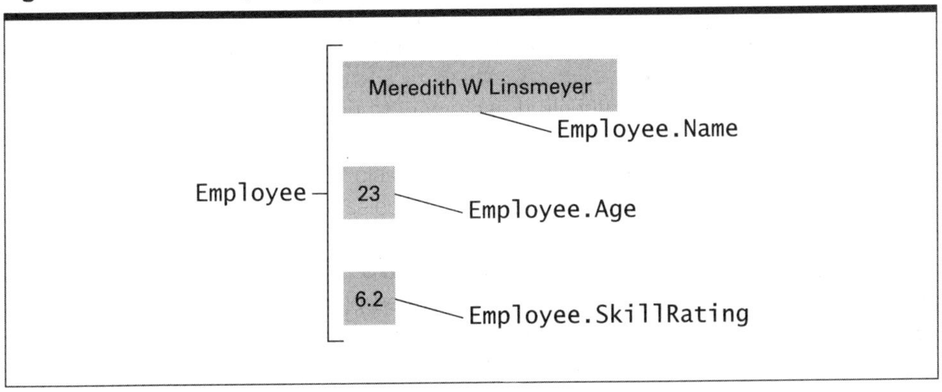

In most programming languages, literals consisting of text are delineated with single or double quotation marks to distinguish them from other program components. For instance, the statement

```
LastName = 'Smith'
```

might be used to assign the text "Smith" to the variable `LastName`, whereas the statement

```
LastName = Smith
```

would be used to assign the value of the variable `Smith` to the variable `LastName`.

Often, the use of literals is not good programming practice because literals can mask the meaning of the statements in which they appear. How, for instance, can a reader of the statement

```
EffectiveAlt = Altimeter + 645
```

know what the value 645 represents? Moreover, literals can complicate the task of modifying the program should it become necessary. If our air traffic program is moved to another airport, all references to the airport's altitude must be changed. If the literal 645 is used in each reference to that altitude, each such reference throughout the program must be located and changed. The problem is compounded if the literal 645 also occurs in reference to a quantity other than the airport's altitude. How do we know which occurrences of 645 to change and which to leave alone?

To solve these problems, programming languages allow descriptive names to be assigned to specific, nonchangeable values. Such a name is called a **constant.** As an example, in C++ and C#, the declarative statement

```
const int AirportAlt = 645;
```

associates the identifier `AirportAlt` with the fixed value 645 (which is considered to be of type integer). The similar concept in Java is expressed by

```
final int AirportAlt = 645;
```

Following such declarations, the descriptive name `AirportAlt` can be used in lieu of the literal 645. Using such a constant in our pseudocode, the statement

```
EffectiveAlt = Altimeter + 645
```

could be rewritten as

```
EffectiveAlt = Altimeter + AirportAlt
```

which better represents the meaning of the statement. Moreover, if such constants are used in place of literals and the program is moved to another airport whose altitude is 267 feet, then changing the single declarative statement in which the constant is defined is all that is needed to convert all references to the airport's altitude to the new value.

Assignment Statements

Once the special terminology to be used in a program (such as the variables and constants) has been declared, a programmer can begin to describe the algorithms involved. This is done by means of imperative statements. The most basic imperative statement is the **assignment statement,** which requests that a value be assigned to a variable (or more precisely, stored in the memory area identified by the variable). Such a statement normally takes the syntactic form of a variable, followed by a symbol representing the assignment operation, and then by an expression indicating the value to be assigned. The semantics of such a statement is that the expression is to be evaluated and the result stored as the value of the variable. For example, the statement

```
Z = X + Y;
```

in C, C++, C#, and Java requests that the sum of X and Y be assigned to the variable Z. The semicolon at the end of the line, which is used to separate statements in many imperative languages, is the only syntactic difference from an equivalent Python assignment statement. In some other languages (such as Ada) the equivalent statement would appear as

```
Z := X + Y;
```

Note that these statements differ only in the syntax of the assignment operator, which in C, C++, C#, and Java is merely an equal sign but in Ada is a colon followed by an equal sign. Perhaps a better notation for the assignment operator is found in APL, a language that was designed by Kenneth E. Iverson in 1962. (APL stands for A Programming Language.) It uses an arrow to represent assignment. Thus, the preceding assignment would be expressed as

```
Z ← X + Y
```

in APL. Unfortunately, the "←" symbol has historically not been available on most keyboards.

Much of the power of assignment statements comes from the scope of expressions that can appear on the right side of the statement. In general, any algebraic expression can be used, with the arithmetic operations of addition, subtraction, multiplication, and division typically represented by the symbols +, −, *, and /, respectively. In some languages (including Ada and Python, but not including C or Java), the combination ** is used to represent exponentiation, so the expression

```
x ** 2
```

represents x^2. Languages differ, however, in the manner in which algebraic expressions are interpreted. For example, the expression 2 * 4 + 6/2 could produce the value 14 if it is evaluated from right to left, or 7 if evaluated from left to right. These ambiguities are normally resolved by rules of **operator precedence,** meaning that certain operations are given precedence over others. The traditional rules of algebra dictate that multiplication and division have precedence over addition and subtraction. That is, multiplications and divisions are performed before additions and subtractions. Following this convention, the preceding expression would produce the value 11. In most languages, parentheses can be used to override the language's operator precedence. Thus 2 * (4 + 6)/2 would produce the value 10.

Many programming languages allow the use of one symbol to represent more than one operation. In these cases the meaning of the symbol is determined by the data type of the operands. For example, the symbol + traditionally indicates addition when its operands are numeric, but in some languages, such as Java and Python, the symbol indicates concatenation when its operands are character strings. That is, the result of the expression

```
'abra' + 'cadabra'
```

is *abracadabra.* Such multiple use of an operation symbol is called **overloading.** While many languages provide built-in overloading of a few common operators, others such as Ada, C++, and C# may allow programmers to define additional overloaded meanings or even add additional operators.

Control Statements

A **control statement** alters the execution sequence of the program. Of all the programming constructs, those from this group have probably received the most attention and generated the most controversy. The major villain is the simplest control statement of all, the `goto` statement. It provides a means of directing the execution sequence to another location that has been labeled for this purpose by a name or number. It is therefore nothing more than a direct application of the machine-level JUMP instruction. The problem with such a feature in a high-level programming language is that it allows programmers to write a rat's nest like

```
    goto 40
20  Evade()
    goto 70
40  if (KryptoniteLevel < LethalDose) then goto 60
    goto 20
60  RescueDamsel()
70  ...
```

when a single statement such as

```
if (KryptoniteLevel < LethalDose):
  RescueDamsel()
else:
  Evade()
```

does the job.

To avoid such complexities, modern languages are designed with control statements that allow an entire branching pattern to be expressed within a single lexical structure. The choice of which control statements to incorporate into a language is a design decision. The goal is to provide a language that not only allows algorithms to be expressed in a readable form but also assists the programmer in obtaining such readability. This is done by restricting the use of those features that have historically led to sloppy programming while encouraging the use of better-designed features. The result is the practice known as **structured programming,** which encompasses an organized design methodology combined with the appropriate use of the language's control statements. The idea is to produce a program that can be readily comprehended and shown to meet its specifications.

We have already met two popular branching structures in Chapter 5, represented by the `if-else` and `while` statements. These are present in almost all imperative, functional, or object-oriented languages. More precisely, the Python statements

```
if (condition):
  statementA
else:
  statementB
```

and

```
while (condition):
  body
```

Programming Language Cultures

As with natural languages, users of different programming languages tend to develop cultural differences and often debate the merits of their perspectives. Sometimes these differences are significant as, for instance, when different programming paradigms are involved. In other cases, the distinctions are subtle. For example, whereas Pascal distinguishes between procedures and functions (Section 6.3), C and Python programmers refer to both as functions. This is because a procedure in a Python program is declared in the same way as a function, but without defining a returned value. A similar example is that C++ programmers refer to a procedure within an object as a member function, whereas the generic term for this is method. This discrepancy can be traced to the fact that C++ was developed as an extension of C. Another cultural difference is that programs in Ada are normally typeset with reserved words in either uppercase or bold—a tradition that is not widely practiced by users of C, C++, C#, FORTRAN, or Java.

Although this book uses Python as an exemplar in most chapters, each specific example is presented in a form that is compatible with the style of the language involved. As you encounter these examples, you should keep in mind that they are presented as examples of how generic ideas appear in actual languages—not as a means of teaching the details of a particular language. Try to look at the forest rather than the trees.

would be written as

```
if (condition) statementA; else statementB;
```

and

```
while (condition) { body }
```

in C, C++, C#, and Java. Note that the fact that these statements are identical in all four languages is a consequence of the fact that C++, C#, and Java are object-oriented extensions of the imperative language C. In contrast, the corresponding statements would be written as

```
IF condition THEN
  statementA;
ELSE
  statementB;
END IF;
```

and

```
WHILE condition LOOP
  body
END LOOP;
```

in the language Ada.

Another common branching structure is often represented by a `switch` or `case` statement. It provides a means of selecting one statement sequence among several options, depending on the value assigned to a designated variable. For example, the statement

```
switch (variable) {
  case 'A': statementA; break;
  case 'B': statementB; break;
  case 'C': statementC; break;
  default: statementD;}
```

in C, C++, C#, and Java requests the execution of `statementA`, `statementB`, or `statementC` depending on whether the current value of `variable` is A, B, or C, respectively or the execution of `statementD` if the value of `variable` is something else. The same structure would be expressed as

```
CASE variable IS
  WHEN 'A'=> statementA;
  WHEN 'B'=> statementB;
  WHEN 'C'=> statementC;
  WHEN OTHERS=> statementD;
END CASE;
```

in Ada.

Still another common control structure, often called the `for` loop, is shown in Figure 6.7 along with its representation in C++, C#, and Java. This structure differs from the Python `for` structure introduced in Chapter 5. Instead of implicitly setting up the initialization, modification, and termination components for a loop that iterates through a list of data, the C family `for` structure explicitly incorporates initialization, modification, and termination of the loop in a single statement. Such a statement is convenient when the body of the loop is to be performed once for each value within a specific range. In particular, the statements in Figure 6.7 direct that the loop body be performed repeatedly—first with the value of `Count` being 1, then with the value of `Count` being 2, and again with the value of `Count`

Figure 6.7 The for loop structure and its representation in C++, C#, and Java

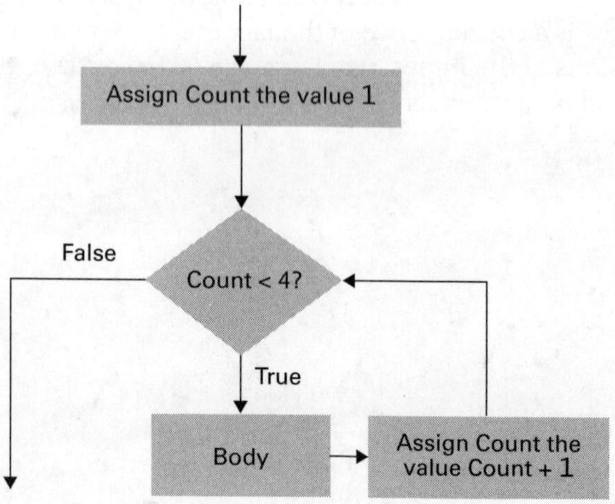


```
for (int Count = 1; Count < 4; Count++)
    body ;
```

being 3. Programming languages that incorporate both kinds of `for` structure may differentiate between them with syntax, such as `foreach` or `for...in`.

The point to be made from the examples we have cited is that common branching structures appear, with slight variations, throughout the gamut of imperative and object-oriented programming languages. A somewhat surprising result from theoretical computer science is that only a few of these structures are needed to ensure that a programming language provides a means of expressing a solution to any problem that has an algorithmic solution. We will investigate this claim in Chapter 12. For now, we merely point out that learning a programming language is not an endless task of learning different control statements. Most of the control structures found in today's programming languages are essentially variations of those we have identified here.

Comments

No matter how well a programming language is designed and how well the language's features are applied in a program, additional information is usually helpful or mandatory when a human tries to read and understand the program. For this reason, programming languages provide ways of inserting explanatory statements, called **comments,** within a program. These statements are ignored by a translator, and therefore their presence or absence does not affect the program from a machine's point of view. The machine-language version of the program produced by a translator will be the same with or without comments, but the information provided by these statements constitutes an important part of the program from a human's perspective. Without such documentation, large, complex programs can easily thwart the comprehension of a human programmer.

There are two common ways of inserting comments within a program. One is to surround the entire comment by special markers, one at the beginning of the comment and one at the end. The other is to mark only the beginning of the comment and allow the comment to occupy the remainder of the line to the right of the marker. We find examples of both these techniques in C++, C#, and Java. They allow comments to be bracketed by /* and */, but they also allow a comment to begin with // and extend through the remainder of the line.
Thus both

```
/* This is a comment. */
```

and

```
// This is a comment.
```

are valid comment statements.

A few words are in order about what constitutes a meaningful comment. Beginning programmers, when told to use comments for internal documentation, tend to follow a program statement such as

```
ApproachAngle = SlipAngle + HyperSpaceIncline;
```

with a comment such as "Calculate `ApproachAngle` by adding `HyperSpaceIncline` and `SlipAngle`." Such redundancy adds length rather than clarity to a program. The purpose of a comment is to explain the program, not to repeat it. A more appropriate comment in this case might be to explain why `ApproachAngle` is being calculated (if that is not obvious). For example, the comment, "`ApproachAngle` is used later to compute `ForceFieldJettisonVelocity` and is not needed after that," is more helpful than the previous one.

Additionally, comments that are scattered among a program's statements can sometimes hamper a human's ability to follow the program's flow and thus make it harder to comprehend the program than if no comments had been included. A good approach is to collect comments that relate to a single program unit in one place, perhaps at the beginning of the unit. This provides a central place where the reader of the program unit can look for explanations. It also provides a location in which the purpose and general characteristics of the program unit can be described. If this format is adopted for all program units, the entire program is given a degree of uniformity in which each unit consists of a block of explanatory statements followed by the formal presentation of the program unit. Such uniformity in a program enhances its readability.

Questions & Exercises

1. Why is the use of a constant considered better programming style than the use of a literal?
2. What is the difference between a declarative statement and an imperative statement?
3. List some common data types.
4. Identify some common control structures found in imperative and object-oriented programming languages.
5. What is the difference between an array and an aggregate type?

6.3 Procedural Units

In previous chapters we have seen advantages to dividing large programs into manageable units. In this section we focus on the concept of a function, which is the major technique for obtaining a modular representation of a program in an imperative language. As mentioned in Chapter 5, programming languages through the ages have used many terms for this essential concept: subprogram, subroutine, procedure, method, function, sometimes with subtle shades of different meaning. Among the strictly imperative languages, the term *function* has come to predominate, whereas in object-oriented languages, the term *method* is often preferred when programmers specify how objects should respond to various stimuli.

Functions

A **function,** in its generic sense, is a set of instructions for performing a task that can be used as an abstract tool by other program units. Control is transferred to the function at the time its services are required and then returned to the original

Figure 6.8 The flow of control involving a function

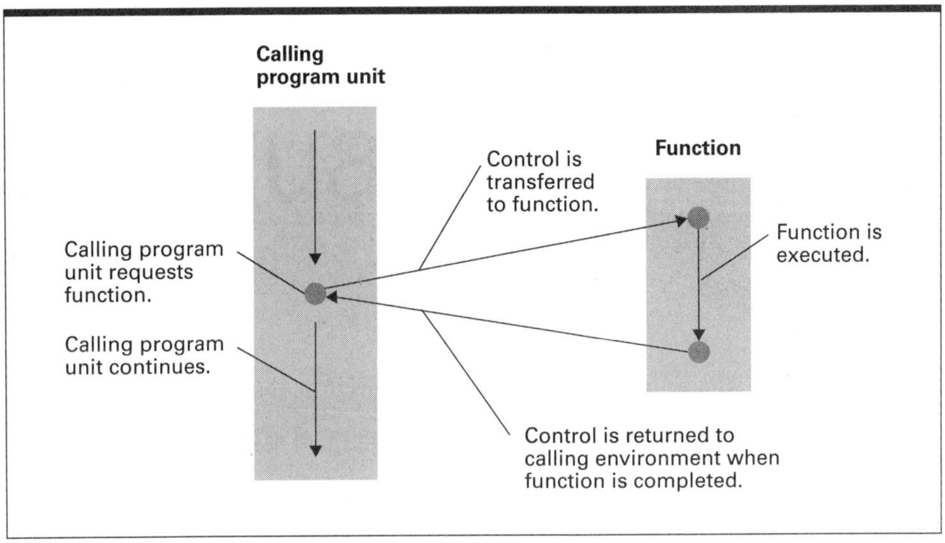

program unit after the function has finished (Figure 6.8). The process of transferring control to a function is often referred to as *calling* or *invoking* the function. We will refer to a program unit that requests the execution of a function as the *calling* unit.

As in our Python examples of Chapter 5, functions are usually written as individual program units. The unit begins with a statement, known as the function's **header,** that identifies, among other things, the name of the function. Following this header are the statements that define the function's details. These statements tend to be arranged in the same manner as those in a traditional imperative program, beginning with declaration statements that describe the variables used in the function followed by imperative statements that describe the steps to be performed when the function is executed.

As a general rule, a variable declared within a function is a **local variable,** meaning that it can be referenced only within that function. This eliminates any confusion that might occur if two functions, written independently, happen to use variables of the same name. (The portion of a program in which a variable can be referenced is called the **scope** of the variable. Thus, the scope of a local variable is the function in which it is declared. Variables whose scopes are not restricted to a particular part of a program are called **global variables.** Most programming languages provide a means of specifying whether a variable is to be local or global.)

Most modern programming languages allow functions to be called by merely stating the function's name. For example, if `GetNames`, `SortNames`, and `WriteNames` were the names of functions for acquiring, sorting, and printing a list of names, then a program to get, sort, and print the list could be written as

```
GetNames()
SortNames()
WriteNames()
```

Note that by assigning each function a name that indicates the action performed by the function, this condensed form appears as a sequence of commands that reflect the meaning of the program.

Parameters

Functions are often written using generic terms that are made specific when the function is applied. For example, Figure 5.11 of the preceding chapter is expressed in terms of a generic list rather than a specific list. In our pseudocode, we agreed to identify such generic terms within parentheses in the function's header. Thus the function in Figure 5.11 begins with the header

```
def Sort(List):
```

and then proceeds to describe the sorting process using the term `List` to refer to the list being sorted. If we want to apply the function to sort a wedding guest list, we need merely follow the directions in the function, assuming that the generic term `List` refers to the wedding guest list. If, however, we want to sort a membership list, we need merely interpret the generic term `List` as referring to the membership list.

Such generic terms within functions are called **parameters.** More precisely, the terms used within the function are called **formal parameters** and the precise meanings assigned to these formal parameters when the function is applied are called **actual parameters.** In a sense, the formal parameters represent slots in the function into which actual parameters are plugged when the function is requested.

As in Python, many programming languages require that, when defining a function, the formal parameters be listed in parentheses in the function's header. As another example, Figure 6.9 presents the definition of a function named `ProjectPopulation` as it might be written in the programming language C. The function expects to be given a specific yearly growth rate when it is called. Based on this rate, the function computes the projected population of a species, assuming an initial population of 100, for the next 10 years, and stores these values in a global array called `Population`.

Many programming languages also use parenthetical notation to identify the actual parameters when a function is called. That is, the statement requesting the execution of a function consists of the function name followed by a list of the actual parameters enclosed in parentheses. Thus, rather than a statement such as

```
Call ProjectPopulation() using a growth rate of 0.03
```

that we might use in pseudocode, the statement

```
ProjectPopulation(0.03);
```

would be used in a C program to call the function `ProjectPopulation` of Figure 6.9 using a growth rate of 0.03. The syntax is the same in Python, but without the trailing semicolon.

When more than one parameter is involved, the actual parameters are associated, entry by entry, with the formal parameters listed in the function's header—the first actual parameter is associated with the first formal parameter, and so on. Then, the values of the actual parameters are effectively transferred to their corresponding formal parameters, and the function is executed.

To emphasize this point, suppose the function `PrintCheck` was defined with a header such as

```
def PrintCheck(Payee, Amount):
```

Figure 6.9 The function ProjectPopulation written in the programming language C

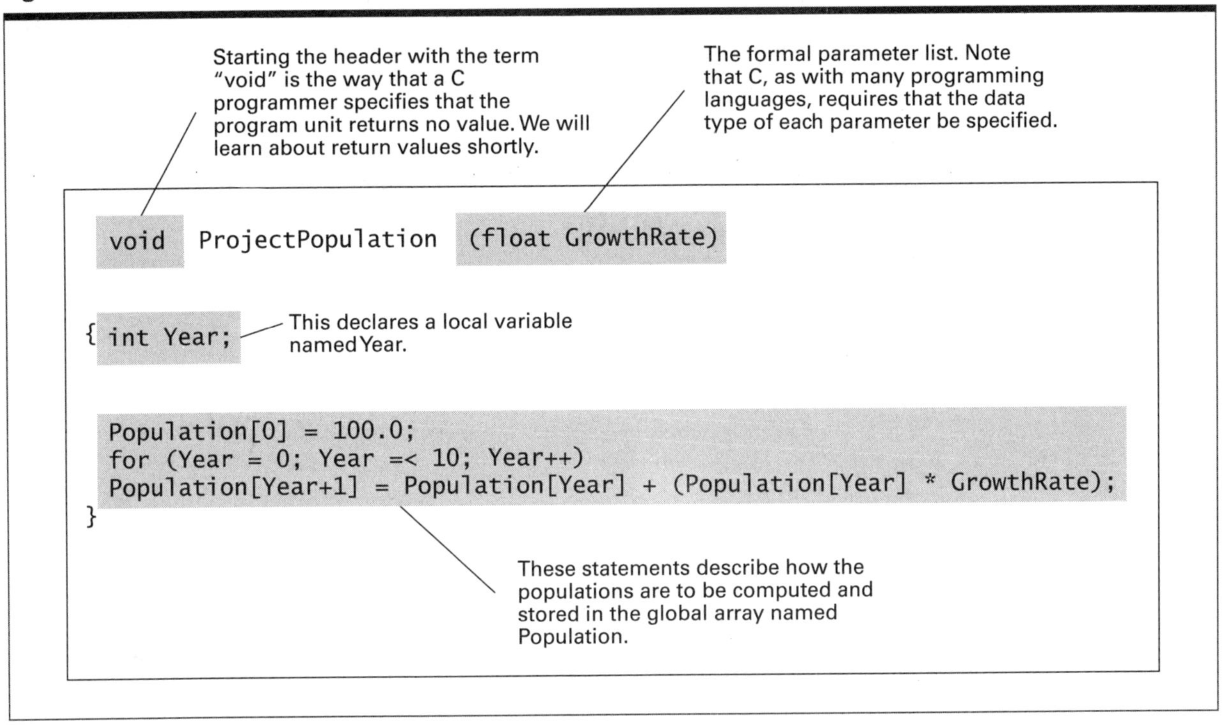

where **Payee** and **Amount** are formal parameters used within the function to refer to the person to whom the check is to be payable and the amount of the check, respectively. Then, calling the function with the statement

```
PrintCheck('John Doe', 150)
```

would cause the function to be executed with the formal parameter **Payee** being associated with the actual parameter John Doe and the formal parameter **Amount** being associated with the value 150. However, calling the function with the statement

```
PrintCheck(150, 'John Doe')
```

would cause the value 150 to be assigned to the formal parameter **Payee** and the name John Doe to be assigned to the formal parameter **Amount**, which would lead to erroneous results.

The task of transferring data between actual and formal parameters is handled in a variety of ways by different programming languages. In some languages a duplicate of the data represented by the actual parameters is produced and given to the function. Using this approach, any alterations to the data made by the function are reflected only in the duplicate—the data in the calling program unit are never changed. We often say that such parameters are **passed by value.** Note that passing parameters by value protects the data in the calling unit from being mistakenly altered by a poorly designed function. For example, if the calling unit passed an employee's name to a function, it might not want the function to change that name.

Unfortunately, passing parameters by value is inefficient when the parameters represent large blocks of data. A more efficient technique is to give the function direct access to the actual parameters by telling it the addresses of the actual parameters in the calling program unit. In this case we say that the parameters are **passed by reference.** Note that passing parameters by reference allows the function to modify the data residing in the calling environment. Such an approach would be desirable in the case of a function for sorting a list since the point of calling such a function would be to cause changes in the list.

As an example, let us suppose that the function Demo was defined as

```
def Demo (Formal):
  Formal = Formal + 1
```

Moreover, suppose that the variable Actual was assigned the value 5 and we called Demo with the statement

```
Demo(Actual)
```

Then, if parameters were passed by value, the change to Formal in the function would not be reflected in the variable Actual (Figure 6.10). But, if parameters were passed by reference, the value of Actual would be incremented by one (Figure 6.11).

Figure 6.10 Executing the function Demo and passing parameters by value

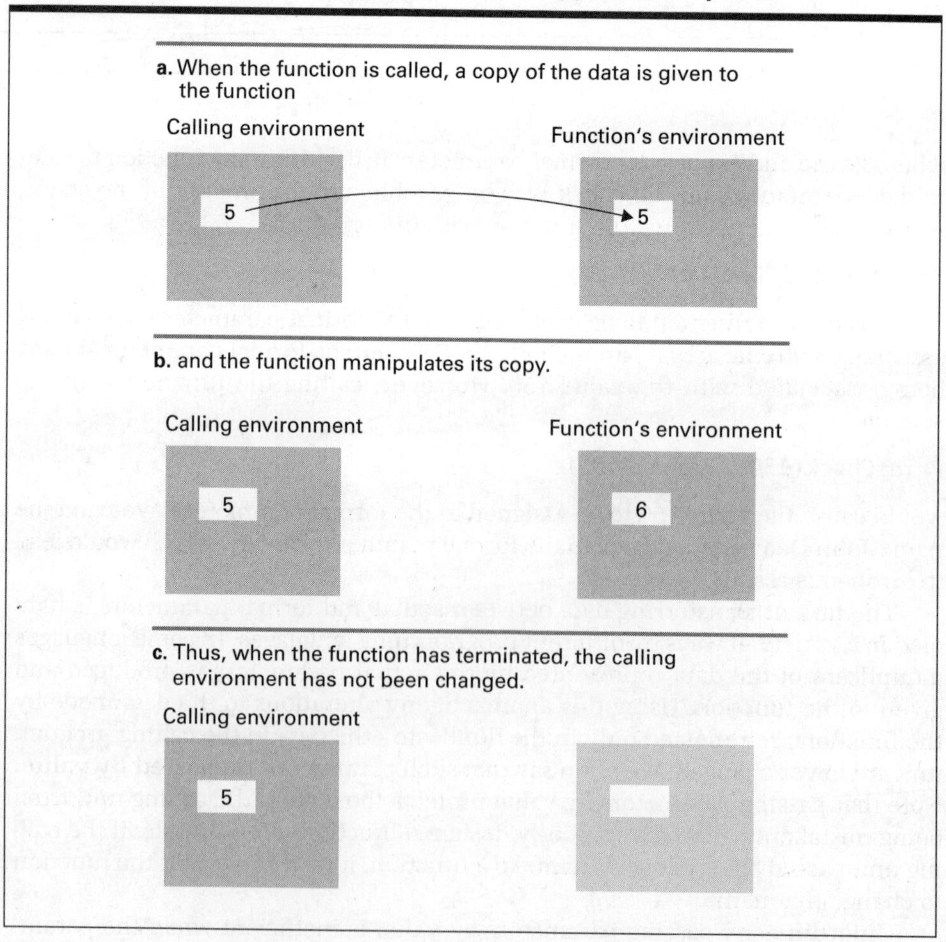

Figure 6.11 Executing the function Demo and passing parameters by reference

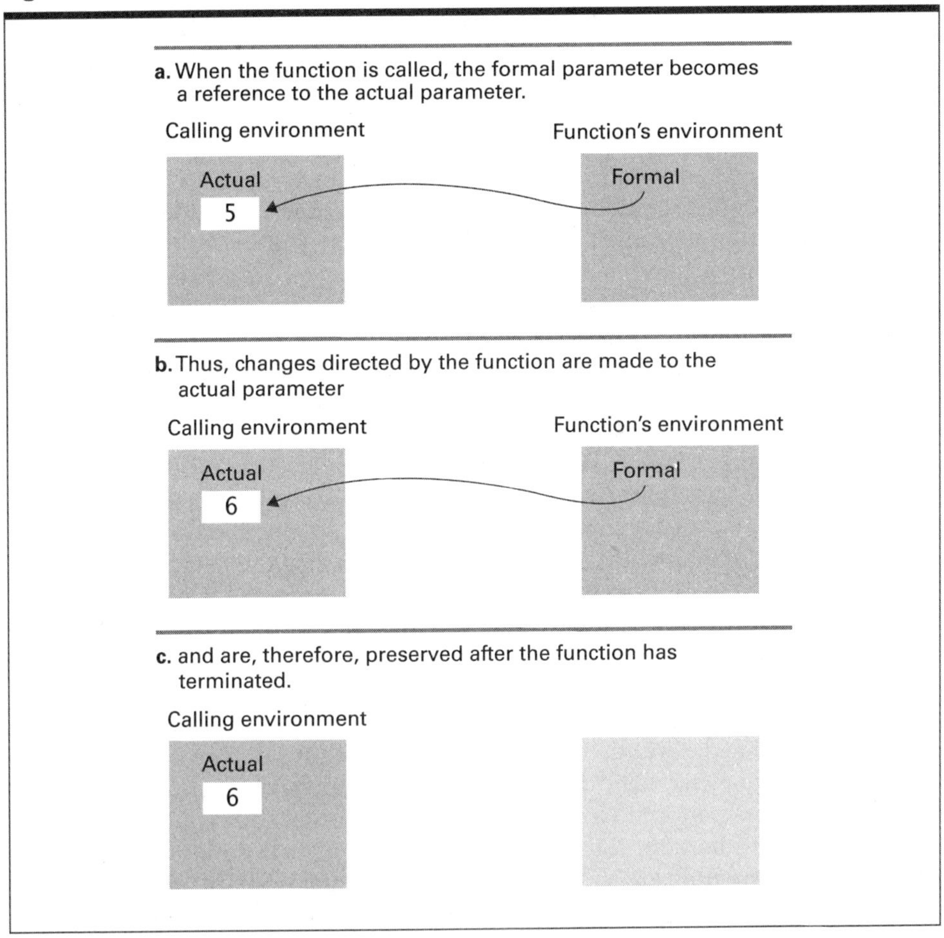

Visual Basic

Visual Basic is an object-oriented programming language that was developed by Microsoft as a tool by which users of Microsoft's Windows operating system could develop their own GUI applications. Actually, Visual Basic is more than a language—it is an entire software development package that allows a programmer to construct applications from predefined components (such as buttons, check boxes, text boxes, scroll bars, etc.) and to customize these components by describing how they should react to various events. In the case of a button, for example, the programmer would describe what should happen when that button is clicked. In Chapter 7 we will learn that this strategy of constructing software from predefined components represents the current trend in software development techniques.

The growing popularity of the Windows operating system combined with the convenience of the Visual Basic development package made the original Visual Basic a widely used programming language in the 1990s. Visual Basic successors, such as VB.NET, remain popular choices of language for rapid prototyping of software with graphical user interfaces.

Different programming languages provide different parameter-passing techniques, but in all cases the use of parameters allows a function to be written in a generic sense and applied to specific data at the appropriate time.

Fruitful Functions

Let us pause to consider a slight variation of the function concept that is found in many programming languages. At times the purpose of a function is to produce a value rather than perform an action. (Consider the subtle distinction between a function whose purpose is to estimate the number of widgets that will be sold as opposed to a function for playing a simple game—the emphasis in the former is to produce a value, the emphasis in the latter is to perform an action.) Indeed, the term *function* in computer science is derived from the mathematical concept of *function,* which by default is a relationship between a set of inputs and outputs. In this sense, all of the Python and pseudocode examples of functions we have defined thus far have been a special case of function, in which there is no output or returned value to be concerned about. (Technically, all functions in Python do return a value, and thus are suited to the use of the mathematical term *function*. Functions that do not include a `return` statement return the default value `None`.) In the family tree of programming languages, many terms have been used to differentiate these two different types of program unit. In the influential language Pascal, the term **procedure** was specifically used to refer to a subprogram that returned no value. C and Java use the keyword **void** to label functions or methods that return no value. Among Python programmers, the term **fruitful function** is sometimes used to differentiate functions that do specify a return a value. Regardless of the language-specific terms, most languages have names for the same idea— a program unit that transfers a value back to the calling program unit as "the value of the function." That is, as a consequence of executing the function, a value will be computed and sent back to the calling program unit. This value can then be stored in a variable for later reference or used immediately in a computation. For example, a C, C++, Java, or C# programmer might write

```
ProjectedJanSales = EstimatedSales(January);
```

to request that the variable `ProjectedJanSales` be assigned the result of applying the function `EstimatedSales` to determine how many widgets are expected to be sold in January. Or, the programmer might write

```
if (LastJanSales < EstimatedSales(January)) ...
else ...
```

to cause different actions to be performed depending on whether this January's sales are expected to be better than those of last January. Note that in the second case, the value computed by the function is used to determine which branch should be taken, but it is never stored.

Functions that return a value are defined within a program in much the same way as void functions. The difference is that a function header usually begins by specifying the data type of the value that is to be returned, and the function definition usually ends with a `return` statement in which the value to be returned is specified. Figure 6.12 presents a definition of a function named `CylinderVolume` as it might be written in the language C. (Actually, a C programmer would use a more succinct form, but we will use this somewhat verbose version for pedagogical reasons.) When called, the function receives specific values for the formal

Figure 6.12 The fruitful function CylinderVolume written in the programming language C

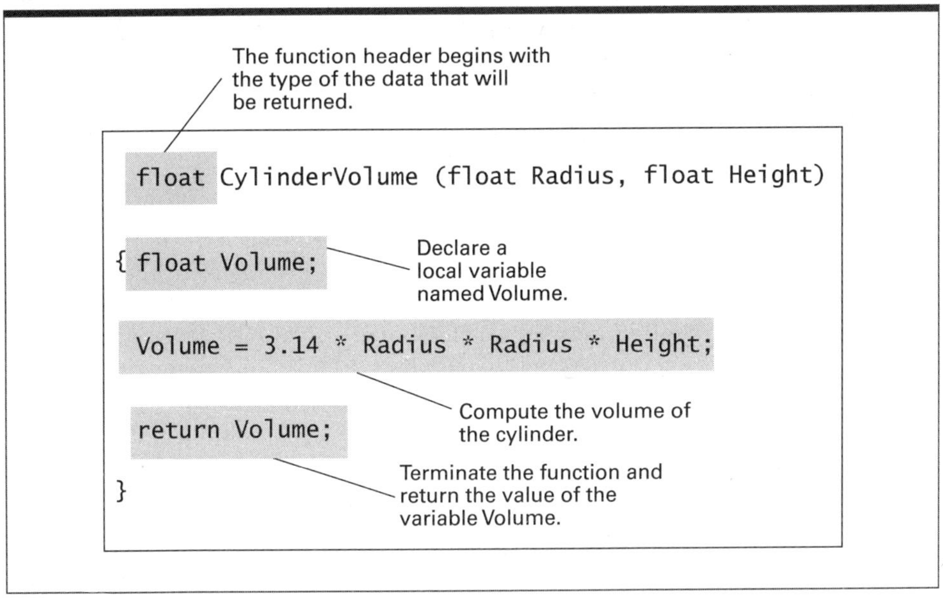

parameters **Radius** and **Height** and returns the result of computing the volume of a cylinder with those dimensions. Thus the function could be used elsewhere in the program in a statement such as

```
Cost = CostPerVolUnit * CylinderVolume(3.45, 12.7);
```

to determine the cost of the contents of a cylinder with radius 3.45 and height 12.7.

We have used several examples of built-in Python functions that return values in previous chapters, including the `input()` and `math.sqrt()` functions, but we have not defined one of our own. The Python version of the **CylinderVolume** function from Figure 6.12 would be

```
def CylinderVolume(Radius, Height):
  Volume = math.pi * Radius * Radius * Height
  return Volume
```

Event-Driven Software Systems

In the text, we have considered cases in which functions are activated as the result of statements elsewhere in the program that explicitly call the function. There are cases, however, in which functions are activated implicitly by the occurrence of an event. Examples are found in GUIs where the function that describes what should happen when a button is clicked is not activated by a call from another program unit, but instead is activated as the result of the button being clicked. Software systems in which functions are activated by events rather than explicit requests are called **event-driven** systems. In short, an event-driven software system consists of functions that describe what should happen as the result of various events. When the system is executed, these functions lie dormant until their respective event occurs—then they become active, perform their task, and return to dormancy.

Questions & Exercises

1. What is meant by the "scope" of a variable?
2. What is the difference between a function and a fruitful function?
3. Why do many programming languages implement I/O operations as if they were calls to functions?
4. What is the difference between a formal parameter and an actual parameter?
5. What is the difference between a function that passes parameters using call by reference and a function that uses call by value?

6.4 Language Implementation

In this section we investigate the process of converting a program written in a high-level language into a machine-executable form.

The Translation Process

The process of converting a program from one language to another is called **translation.** The program in its original form is the **source program**; the translated version is the **object program.** The translation process consists of three activities—lexical analysis, parsing, and code generation—that are performed by units in the translator known as the **lexical analyzer, parser,** and **code generator** (Figure 6.13).

Lexical analysis is the process of recognizing which strings of symbols from the source program represent a single entity, or **token.** For example, the three symbols 153 should not be interpreted as a 1, a 5, and a 3 but should be recognized as representing a single numeric value. Likewise, a word appearing in the program, although composed of individual symbols, should be interpreted as a single unit. Most humans perform lexical analysis with little conscious effort. When asked to read aloud, we pronounce words rather than individual characters.

Thus the lexical analyzer reads the source program symbol by symbol, identifying which groups of symbols represent tokens, and classifying those tokens according to whether they are numeric values, words, arithmetic operators, and so on. The lexical analyzer encodes each token with its classification and hands them to the parser. During this process, the lexical analyzer skips over all comment statements.

Figure 6.13 The translation process

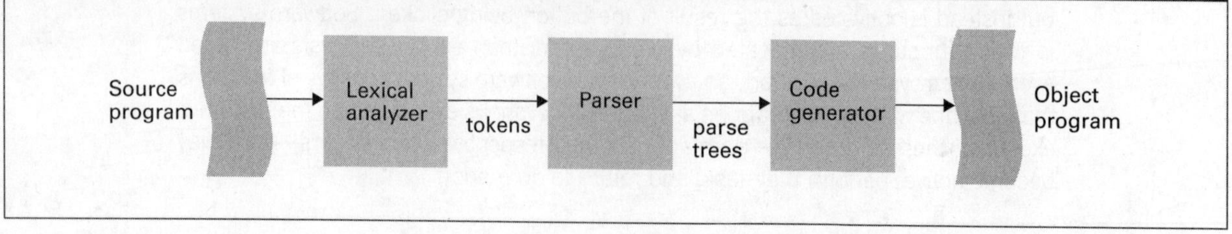

Thus the parser views the program in terms of lexical units (tokens) rather than individual symbols. It is the parser's job to group these units into statements. Indeed, parsing is the process of identifying the grammatical structure of the program and recognizing the role of each component. It is the technicalities of parsing that cause one to hesitate when reading the sentence

> The man the horse that won the race threw was not hurt.

(Try this one: "That that is is. That that is not is not. That that is not is not that that is."!)

To simplify the parsing process, early programming languages insisted that each program statement be positioned in a particular manner on the printed page. Such languages were known as **fixed-format** languages. Today, many programming languages are **free-format** languages, meaning that the positioning of statements is not critical. The advantage of free-format languages lies in a programmer's ability to organize the written program in a way that enhances readability from a human's point of view. In these cases it is common to use indentation to help a reader grasp the structure of a statement. Rather than writing

```
if Cost < CashOnHand then pay with cash else use credit card
```

a programmer might write

```
if Cost < CashOnHand
  then pay with cash
  else use credit card
```

For a machine to parse a program written in a free-format language, the syntax of the language must be designed so that the structure of a program can be identified regardless of the spacing used in the source program. To this end, most free-format languages use punctuation marks such as semicolons to mark the ends of statements, as well as **key words** such as `if`, `then`, and `else` to mark the beginning of individual phrases. These key words are often **reserved words,** meaning that they cannot be used by the programmer for other purposes within the program. Python is unusual in this respect, in that it has aspects of free-format languages, but strictly requires indentation to mark structure, rather than punctuation marks like semicolons and curly braces.

The parsing process is based on a set of rules that define the syntax of the programming language. Collectively, these rules are called a **grammar.** One way of expressing these rules is by means of **syntax diagrams,** which are pictorial representations of a language's grammatical structure. Figure 6.14 shows a syntax diagram of the if-else statement from Python in Chapter 5. This diagram indicates that an if-else structure begins with the word `if`, followed by a Boolean expression, followed by a colon, followed by Indented Statements. This combination might

Figure 6.14 A syntax diagram of Python's if-else statement

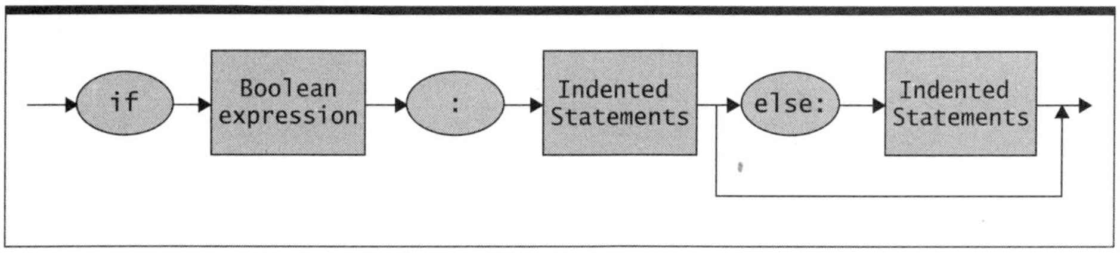

or might not be followed by the word `else`, a colon, and Indented Statements. Notice that terms that actually appear in an if-else statement are enclosed in ovals, whereas terms that require further description, such as *Boolean expression* and *Indented Statements,* are enclosed in rectangles. Terms that require further description (those in rectangles) are called **nonterminals;** terms that appear in ovals are called **terminals.** In a complete description of a language's syntax the nonterminals are described by additional diagrams.

As a more complete example, Figure 6.15 presents a set of syntax diagrams that describes the syntax of a structure called *Expression,* which is intended to be the structure of simple arithmetic expressions. The first diagram describes an *Expression* as consisting of a *Term* that might or might not be followed by either a + or − symbol followed by another *Expression.* The second diagram describes a *Term* as consisting of either a single *Factor* or a *Factor* followed by a × or ÷ symbol, followed by another *Term.* Finally, the last diagram describes a *Factor* as one of the symbols x, y, or z.

The manner in which a particular string conforms to a set of syntax diagrams can be represented in a pictorial form by a **parse tree,** as demonstrated in Figure 6.16, which presents a parse tree for the string

x+y×z

based on the set of diagrams in Figure 6.15. Note that the tree starts at the top with the nonterminal *Expression* and at each level shows how the nonterminals at that level are decomposed until the symbols in the string itself are obtained. In particular, the figure shows that (according to the first diagram in Figure 6.15) an

Figure 6.15 Syntax diagrams describing the structure of a simple algebraic expression

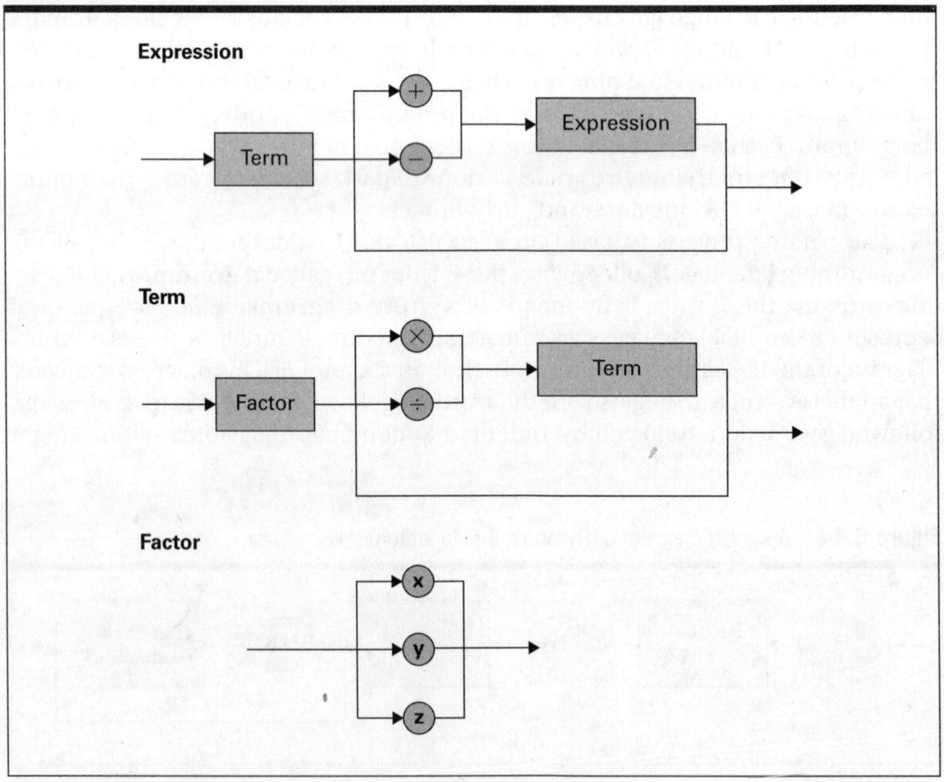

Figure 6.16 The parse tree for the string x + y × z based on the syntax diagrams in Figure 6.15

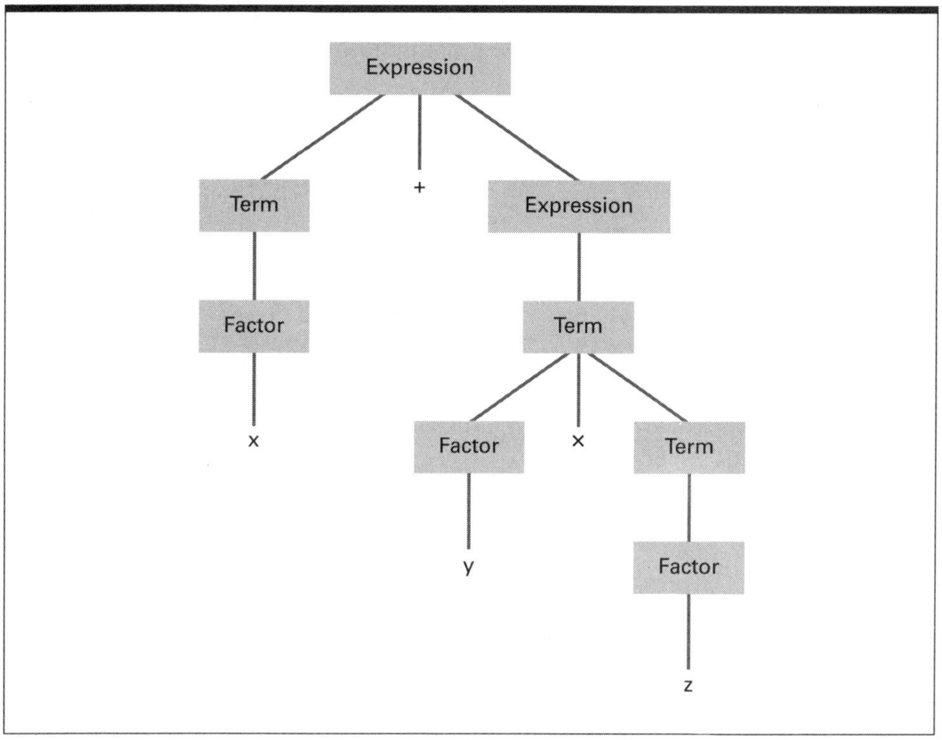

Expression can be decomposed as a *Term,* followed by the + symbol, followed by an *Expression.* In turn, the *Term* can be decomposed (using the second diagram in Figure 6.15) as a *Factor* (which turns out to be the symbol x), and the final *Expression* can be decomposed (using the third diagram in Figure 6.15) as a *Term* (which turns out to be y × z).

Implementation of Java and C#

In some cases, such as in the control of an animated Web page, software must be transferred over the Internet and executed on distant machines. If this software is supplied in source program form, additional delays will result at the destination because the software will have to be translated into the proper machine language before it is executed. However, supplying the software in machine-language form would mean that a different version of the software would have to be provided depending on the machine language used by the distant computer.

Sun Microsystems and Microsoft have resolved this problem by designing "universal machine languages" (called bytecode in the case of Java and .NET Common Intermediate Language in the case of C#) into which source programs can be translated. Although these languages are not really machine languages, they are designed to be quickly translatable. Thus if software written in Java or C# is translated into the appropriate "universal machine language," then it can be transferred to other machines in the Internet where it can be executed efficiently. In some cases this execution is performed by an interpreter. In other cases, it is quickly translated prior to execution, a process known as **just-in-time compilation.**

The process of parsing a program is essentially that of constructing a parse tree for the source program. Indeed, a parse tree represents the parser's interpretation of the program's grammatical composition. For this reason the syntax rules describing a program's grammatical structure must not allow two distinct parse trees for one string, since this would lead to ambiguities within the parser. A grammar that does allow two distinct parse trees for one string is said to be an **ambiguous grammar.**

Ambiguities in grammars can be quite subtle. In fact, the rule in Figure 6.14 contains such a flaw. It allows both the parse trees in Figure 6.17 for the single statement

```
if B1: if B2: S1 else: S2
```

Figure 6.17 Two distinct parse trees for the statement if B1: if B2: S1 else: S2

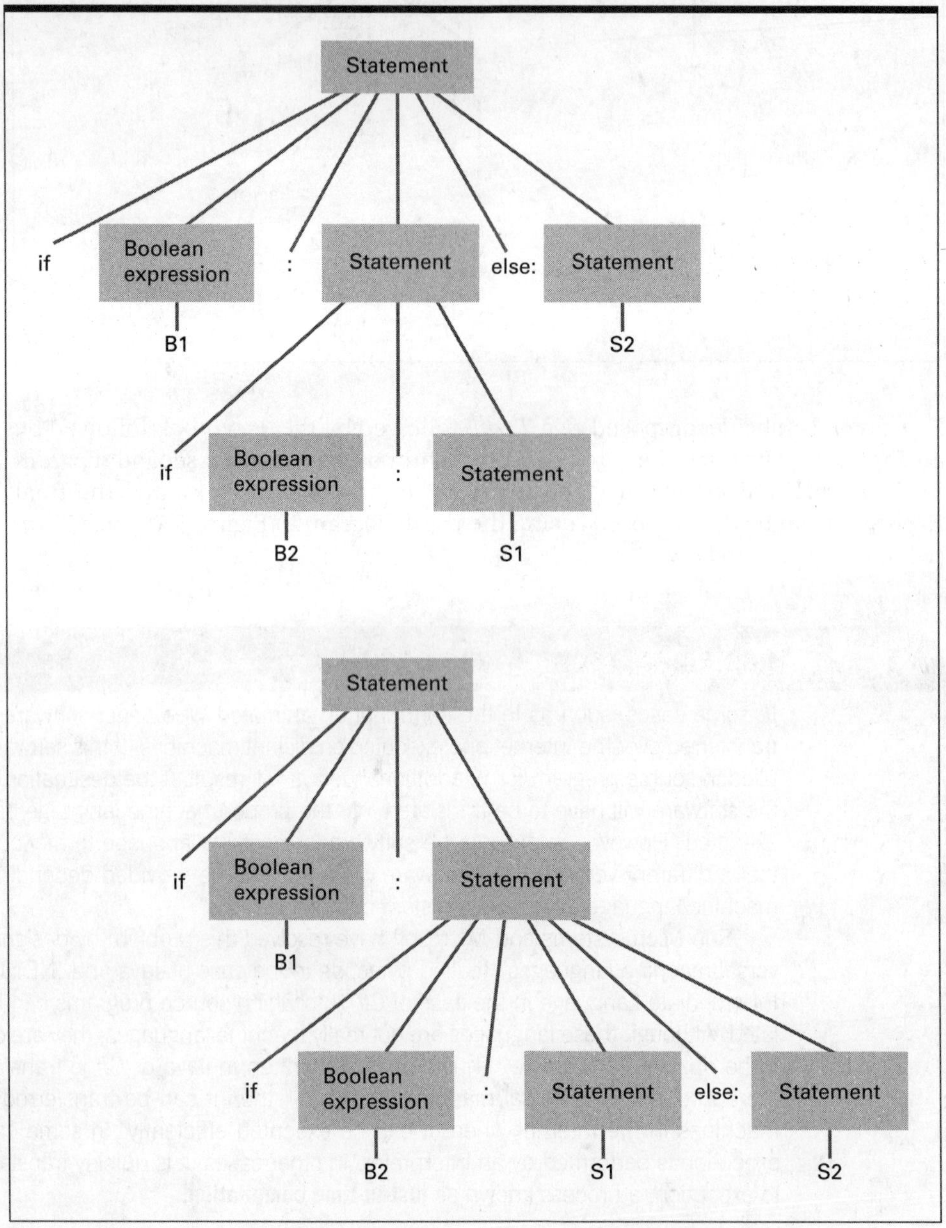

Note that these interpretations are significantly different. The first implies that statement *S2* is to execute if *B1* is false; the second implies that *S2* is to execute only if *B1* is true and *B2* is false.

The syntax definitions of formal programming languages are designed to avoid such ambiguities. In Python we avoid such problems by using indentation. In particular, we might write

```
if B1:
  if B2:
    S1
  else:
    S2
```

and

```
if B1:
  if B2:
    S1
else:
  S2
```

to distinguish between the two possible interpretations.

As a parser analyzes the grammatical structure of a program, it is able to identify individual statements and to distinguish between the declarative statements and imperative statements. As it recognizes the declarative statements, it records the information being declared in a table called the **symbol table.** Thus the symbol table contains such information as the names of the variables appearing in the program as well as what data types and data structures are associated with those variables. The parser then relies on this information when analyzing imperative statements such as

```
z = x + y
```

In particular, to determine the meaning of the symbol +, the parser must know the data type associated with x and y. If x is of type float and y is of type character, then adding x and y makes little sense and should be reported as an error. If x and y are both of type integer, then the parser will request that the code generator build a machine-language instruction using the machine's integer addition op-code; if both are of type float, the parser will request that floating-point addition op-code be used; or if both are of type character, the parser might request that the code generator build the sequence of machine- language instructions needed to perform the concatenation operation.

A somewhat special case arises if x is of type integer and y is of type float. Then the concept of addition is applicable but the values are not encoded in compatible forms. In this case the parser might choose to have the code generator build the instructions to convert one value to the other type and then perform the addition. Such implicit conversion between types is called **coercion.**

Coercion is frowned upon by many language designers, because implicit type conversion can alter the value of a data item, resulting in subtle program bugs. They argue that the need for coercion usually indicates a flaw in the program's design and therefore should not be accommodated by the parser. The result is that most modern languages are **strongly typed,** which means that all activities requested by a program must involve data of agreeable types. Some languages, such as Java, will allow coercion as long as it is a **type promotion,** meaning that it involves converting a low precision value to a higher precision value. Implicit coercions that might alter a value are reported as errors. In most cases a programmer can still request these type conversions by making an explicit **type cast,** which notifies the compiler that the programmer is aware that a type conversion will be applied.

The final activity in the translation process is **code generation,** which is the process of constructing the machine-language instructions to implement the statements recognized by the parser. This process involves numerous issues, one being that of producing efficient machine-language versions of programs. For example, consider the task of translating the two-statement sequence

```
x = y + z
w = x + z
```

If these statements are translated as individual statements, each would require that data be transferred from main memory into the CPU before the indicated addition takes place. However, efficiency can be gained by recognizing that once the first statement has been executed, the values of x and z will already be in the CPU's general-purpose registers and therefore need not be loaded from memory before performing the second addition. Implementing insights such as this is called **code optimization** and is an important task of the code generator.

Finally, we should note that the steps of lexical analysis, parsing, and code generation are not carried out in a strict sequential order. Instead, these activities are intertwined. The lexical analyzer begins by reading characters from the source program and identifying the first token. It hands this token to the parser. Each time the parser receives a token from the lexical analyzer, it analyzes the grammatical structure being read. At this point it might request another token from the lexical analyzer or, if the parser recognizes that a complete phrase or statement has been read, it calls on the code generator to produce the proper machine instructions. Each such request causes the code generator to build machine instructions that are added to the object program. In turn, the task of translating a program from one language to another conforms naturally to the object-oriented paradigm. The source program, lexical analyzer, parser, code generator, and object program are objects that interact by sending messages back and forth as each object goes about performing its task (Figure 6.18).

Figure 6.18 An object-oriented approach to the translation process

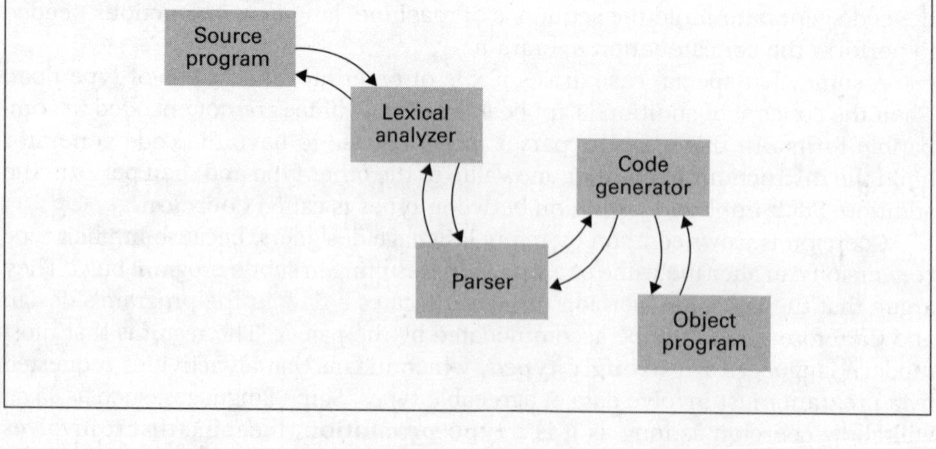

Software Development Packages

The software tools, such as editors and translators, used in the software development process are often grouped into a package that functions as one integrated software development system. Such a system would be classified as application software in the classification scheme of Section 3.2. By using this application package, a programmer gains ready access to an editor for writing programs, a translator for converting the programs into machine language, and a variety of debugging tools that allow the programmer to trace the execution of a malfunctioning program to discover where it goes astray.

The advantages of using such an integrated system are numerous. Perhaps the most obvious is that a programmer can move back and forth between the editor and debugging tools with ease as changes to the program are made and tested. Moreover, many software development packages allow related program units that are under development to be linked in such a way that access to related units is simplified. Some packages maintain records regarding which program units within a group of related units have been altered since the last benchmark was made. Such capabilities are quite advantageous in the development of large software systems in which many interrelated units are developed by different programmers.

On a smaller scale, the editors in software development packages are often customized to the programming language being used. Such an editor will usually provide automatic line indentation that is the de facto standard for the target language and in some cases might recognize and automatically complete key words after the programmer has typed only the first few characters. Moreover, the editor might highlight keywords within source programs (perhaps with color) so that they stand out, making the programs easier to read.

In the next chapter we will learn that software developers are increasingly searching for ways by which new software systems can be constructed from prefabricated blocks called components—leading to a new software development model called component architecture. Software development packages based on the component architecture model often use graphical interfaces in which components can be represented as icons on the display. In this setting a programmer (or component assembler) selects desired components with a mouse. A selected component can then be customized by means of the package's editor and then attached to other components by pointing and clicking with the mouse. Such packages represent a major step forward in the search for better software development tools.

Questions & Exercises

1. Describe the three major steps in the translation process.
2. What is a symbol table?
3. What is the difference between a terminal and a nonterminal?
4. Draw the parse tree for the expression

   $x \times y + x + z$

   based on the syntax diagrams in Figure 6.15.

5. Describe the strings that conform to the structure Chacha according to the following syntax diagrams.

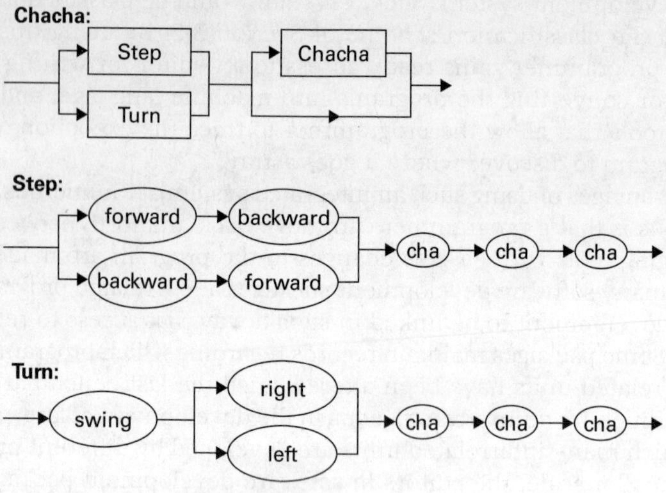

6. Like modern programming language editors, this text uses syntax coloring in an attempt to make code examples easier to read. How many colors have you seen? What does each color seem to mean?

6.5 Object-Oriented Programming

In Section 6.1 we learned that the object-oriented paradigm entails the development of active program units called **objects,** each of which contains functions describing how that object should respond to various stimuli. The object-oriented approach to a problem is to identify the objects involved and describe them as self-contained units. In turn, object-oriented programming languages provide statements for describing objects and their behavior. In this section we will introduce some of these statements as they appear in the languages C++, Java, and C#, which are three of the more prominent object-oriented languages used today.

Classes and Objects

Consider the task of developing a simple computer game in which the player must protect the Earth from falling meteors by shooting them with high-power lasers. Each laser contains a finite internal power source that is partially consumed each time the laser is fired. Once this source is depleted, the laser becomes useless. Each laser should be able to respond to the commands to aim farther to the right, aim farther to the left, and to fire its laser beam.

In the object-oriented paradigm, each laser in the computer game would be implemented as an object that contains a record of its remaining power as well as functions for modifying its aim and firing its laser beam. Since all the laser objects have the same properties, they can be described by means of a common template. In the object-oriented paradigm a template for a collection of objects is called a **class.**

In Chapter 8, we will explore the similarities between classes and data types. For now we simply note that a class describes the common characteristics of a collection of objects in much the same way as the concept of the primitive data type integer encompasses the common characteristics of such numbers as 1, 5, and 82. Once a programmer has included the description of a class in a program, that template can be used to construct and to manipulate objects of that "type" in much the same way that the primitive type integer allows the manipulation of "objects" of type integer.

In the languages C++, Java, and C# a class is described by a statement of the form

```
class Name
{
     .
     .
     .
}
```

where `Name` is the name by which the class can be referenced elsewhere in the program. It is within the braces that the properties of the class are described. In particular, a class named `LaserClass` describing the structure of a laser in our computer game is outlined in Figure 6.19. The class consists of the declaration of a variable named `RemainingPower` (of type integer) and three functions named `turnRight`, `turnLeft`, and `fire`. These functions describe the routines to be performed to accomplish the corresponding action. Thus any object that is constructed from this template will have these features: a variable called `RemainingPower` and three functions named `turnRight`, `turnLeft`, and `fire`.

A variable that resides within an object, such as `RemainingPower`, is called an **instance variable** and the functions within an object are called **methods** (or member functions in the C++ vernacular). Note that in Figure 6.19 the instance

Figure 6.19 The structure of a class describing a laser weapon in a computer game

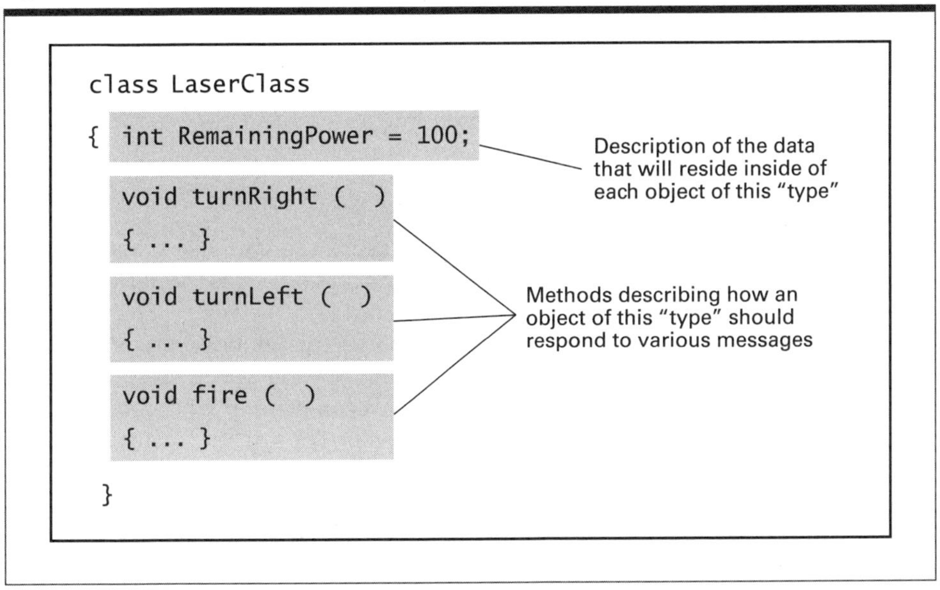

variable RemainingPower is described using a declaration statement similar to those discussed in Section 6.2 and the methods are described in a form reminiscent of functions as discussed in Section 6.3. After all, declarations of instance variables and descriptions of methods are basically imperative programming concepts.

Once we have described the class LaserClass in our game program, we can declare three variables Laser1, Laser2, and Laser3 to be of "type" LaserClass by a statement of the form

```
LaserClass Laser1, Laser2, Laser3;
```

Note that this is the same format as the statement

```
int x, y, z;
```

that would be used to declare three variables named x, y, and z of type integer, as we learned early in Section 6.2. Both consist of the name of a "type" followed by a list of the variables being declared. The difference is that the latter statement says that the variables x, y, and z will be used in the program to refer to items of type integer (which is a primitive type), whereas the former statement says the variables Laser1, Laser2, and Laser3 will be used in the program to refer to items of "type" LaserClass (which is a "type" defined within the program).

Once we have declared the variables Laser1, Laser2, and Laser3 to be of "type" LaserClass, we can assign them values. In this case the values must be objects that conform to the "type" LaserClass. These assignments can be made by assignment statements, but it is often convenient to assign starting values to the variables within the same declaration statements used to declare the variables. Such initial assignments are made automatically in the case of declarations in the language C++. That is, the statement

```
LaserClass Laser1, Laser2, Laser3;
```

not only establishes the variables Laser1, Laser2, and Laser3, but also creates three objects of "type" LaserClass, one as the value of each variable. In the languages Java and C#, such initial assignments are instigated in much the same way that initial assignments are made to variables of primitive types. In particular, whereas the statement

```
int x = 3;
```

not only declares x to be a variable of type integer but also assigns the variable the value 3, the statement

```
LaserClass Laser1 = new LaserClass();
```

declares the variable Laser1 to be of "type" LaserClass and also creates a new object using the LaserClass template and assigns that object as the starting value of Laser1.

At this point we should pause to emphasize the distinction between a class and an object. A class is a template from which objects are constructed. One class can be used to create numerous objects. We often refer to an object as an **instance** of the class from which it was constructed. Thus, in our computer game Laser1, Laser2, and Laser3 are variables whose values are instances of the class LaserClass.

After using declarative statements to create the variables Laser1, Laser2, and Laser3 and assign objects to them, we can continue our game program by writing imperative statements that activate the appropriate methods within these objects (in object-oriented vernacular, this is called sending messages to the objects). In particular, we could cause the object assigned to the variable `Laser1` to execute its `fire` method using the statement

```
Laser1.fire();
```

Or we could cause the object assigned to `Laser2` to execute its `turnLeft` method via the statement

```
Laser2.turnLeft();
```

These are actually little more than function calls. Indeed, the former statement is a call to the function (the method) `fire` inside the object assigned to the variable `Laser1`, and the latter statement is a call to the function `turnLeft` inside the object assigned to the variable `Laser2`.

At this stage our meteor game example has given us the background to grasp the overall structure of a typical object-oriented program (Figure 6.20). It will contain a variety of class descriptions similar to Figure 6.19, each describing the structure of one or more objects used in the program. In addition, the program will contain an imperative program segment (usually associated with the name "main") containing the sequence of steps to be performed initially when the program is executed. This segment will contain declaration statements similar to our laser declarations to establish the objects used in the program as well as imperative statements that call for the execution of methods within those objects.

Figure 6.20 The structure of a typical object-oriented program

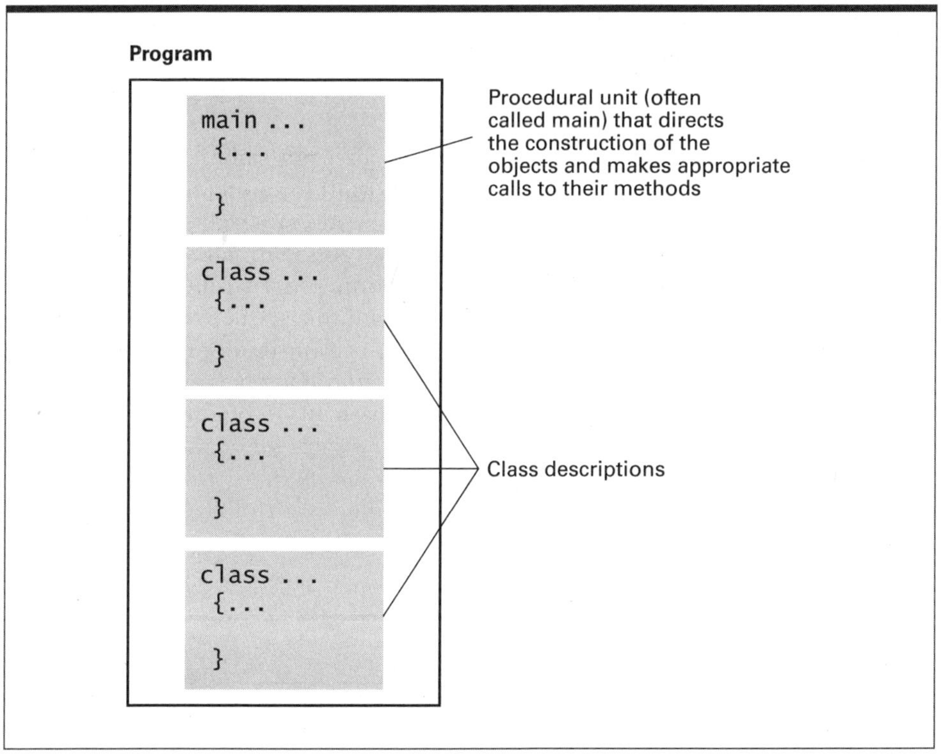

Constructors

When an object is constructed, often some customizing activities need to be performed. For example, in our meteor computer game we might want the different lasers to have different initial power settings, which would mean that the instance variables named `RemainingPower` within the various objects should be given different starting values. Such initialization needs are handled by defining special methods, called **constructors,** within the appropriate class. Constructors are executed automatically when an object is constructed from the class. A constructor is identified within a class definition by the fact that it is a method with the same name as the class.

Figure 6.21 presents an extension of the `LaserClass` definition originally shown in Figure 6.19. Note that it contains a constructor in the form of a method named `LaserClass`. This method assigns the instance variable `RemainingPower` the value it receives as its parameter. Thus, when an object is constructed from this class, this method will be executed, causing `RemainingPower` to be initialized at the appropriate setting.

The actual parameters to be used by a constructor are identified in a parameter list in the statement causing the creation of the object. Thus, based on the class definition in Figure 6.21, a C++, programmer would write

```
LaserClass Laser1(50), Laser2(100);
```

to create two objects of type `LaserClass`—one known as `Laser1` with an initial power reserve of 50, and the other known as `Laser2` with an initial power

Figure 6.21 A class with a constructor

```
class  LaserClass
{ int RemainingPower;

  LaserClass (InitialPower)
  { RemainingPower = InitialPower;
  }

  void turnRight ( )
  { ... }

  void turnLeft ( )
  { ... }

  void fire ( )
  { ... }

}
```

Constructor assigns a value to RemainingPower when an object is created.

reserve of 100. Java and C# programmers would accomplish the same task with the statements

```
LaserClass Laser1 = new LaserClass(50);
LaserClass Laser2 = new LaserClass(100);
```

Additional Features

Let us now suppose we want to enhance our meteor computer game so that a player who reaches a certain score will be rewarded by recharging some of the lasers to their original power setting. These lasers will have the same properties as the other lasers except that they will be rechargeable.

To simplify the description of objects with similar yet different characteristics, object-oriented languages allow one class to encompass the properties of another through a technique known as **inheritance.** As an example, suppose we were using Java to develop our game program. We could first use the class statement described previously to define a class called LaserClass that described those properties that are common to all lasers in the program. Then we could use the statement

```
class RechargeableLaser extends LaserClass
{
      .
      .
      .
}
```

to describe another class called RechargeableLaser. (C++ and C# programmers would merely replace the word extends with a colon.) Here the extends clause indicates that this class is to inherit the features of the class LaserClass as well as contain those features appearing within the braces. In our case, these braces would contain a new method (perhaps named recharge) that would describe the steps required to reset the instance variable RemainingPower to its original value. Once these classes were defined, we could use the statement

```
LaserClass Laser1, Laser2;
```

to declare Laser1 and Laser2 to be variables referring to traditional lasers, and use the statement

```
RechargeableLaser Laser3, Laser4;
```

to declare Laser3 and Laser4 to be variables referring to lasers having the additional properties described in the RechargeableLaser class.

The use of inheritance leads to the existence of a variety of objects with similar yet different characteristics, which in turn leads to a phenomenon reminiscent of overloading, which we met in Section 6.2. (Recall that overloading refers to the use of a single symbol, such as +, for representing different operations depending on the type of its operands.) Suppose that an object-oriented graphics package consists of a variety of objects, each representing a shape (circle, rectangle, triangle, and so on). A particular image might consist of a collection of these objects. Each object "knows" its size, location, and color as well as how to respond to messages telling it, for example, to move to a new location or to draw itself on the display. To draw an image, we merely send a "draw yourself" message to each object in the image. However, the routine used to draw an object varies according to the shape of the object—drawing a square is not the same process as drawing a circle. This customized interpretation of a message is known as **polymorphism;** the message is said to be polymorphic. Another characteristic associated with object-oriented programming is **encapsulation,** which refers to restricting access to an object's internal properties. To say that certain features of an object are *encapsulated* means that only the object itself is able to access them. Features that are encapsulated are said to be private. Features that are accessible from outside the object are said to be public.

As an example, let us return to our `LaserClass` originally outlined in Figure 6.19. Recall that it described an instance variable `RemainingPower` and three methods `turnRight`, `turnLeft`, and `fire`. These methods are to be accessed by other program units to cause an instance of `LaserClass` to perform the appropriate action. But the value of `RemainingPower` should only be altered by the instance's internal methods. No other program unit should be able to access this value directly. To enforce these rules we need merely designate `RemainingPower` as `private` and `turnRight`, `turnLeft`, and `fire` as `public` as shown in Figure 6.22. With these designations inserted, any attempt to access the value of `RemainingPower` from outside the object in which it resides will be identified as an error when the program is translated—forcing the programmer to correct the problem before proceeding.

Figure 6.22 Our LaserClass definition using encapsulation as it would appear in a Java or C# program

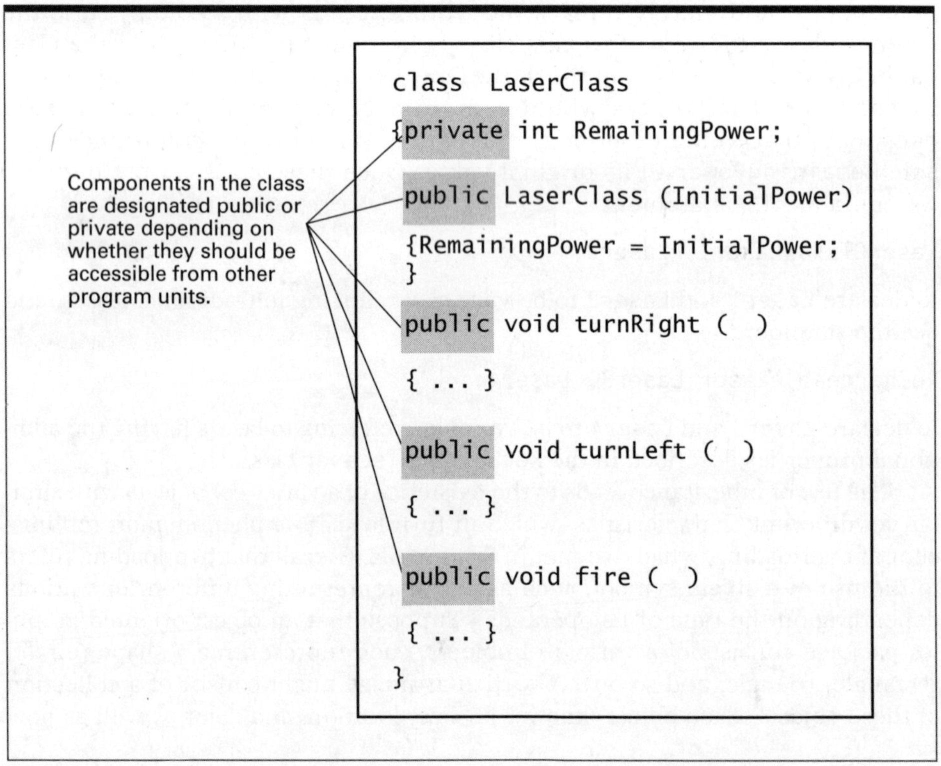

Questions & Exercises

1. What is the difference between an object and a class?
2. What classes of objects other than `LaserClass` might be found in the computer game example used in this section? What instance variables in addition to `RemainingPower` might be found in the class `LaserClass`?
3. Suppose the classes `PartTimeEmployee` and `FullTimeEmployee` inherited the properties of the class `Employee`. What are some features that you might expect to find in each class?
4. What is a constructor?
5. Why are some items within a class designated as `private`?

6.6 Programming Concurrent Activities

Suppose we were asked to design a program to produce animation for an action computer game involving multiple attacking enemy spaceships. One approach would be to design a single program that would control the entire animation screen. Such a program would be charged with drawing each of the spaceships, which (if the animation is to appear realistic) would mean that the program would have to keep up with the individual characteristics of numerous spacecraft. An alternate approach would be to design a program to control the animation of a single spaceship whose characteristics are determined by parameters assigned at the beginning of the program's execution. Then the animation could be constructed by creating multiple activations of this program, each with its own set of parameters. By executing these activations simultaneously, we could obtain the illusion of many individual spaceships streaking across the screen at the same time.

Such simultaneous execution of multiple activations is called **parallel processing** or **concurrent processing.** True parallel processing requires multiple CPU cores, one to execute each activation. When only one CPU is available, the illusion of parallel processing is obtained by allowing the activations to share the time of the single processor in a manner similar to that implemented by multiprogramming systems (Chapter 3).

Many modern computer applications are more easily solved in the context of parallel processing than in the more traditional context involving a single sequence of instructions. In turn, newer programming languages provide syntax for expressing the semantic structures involved in parallel computations. The design of such a language requires the identification of these semantic structures and the development of a syntax for representing them.

Each programming language tends to approach the parallel processing paradigm from its own point of view, resulting in different terminology. For example, what we have informally referred to as an *activation* is called a *task* in the Ada vernacular and a *thread* in Java. That is, in an Ada program, simultaneous actions are performed by creating multiple *tasks,* whereas in Java one creates multiple *threads.* In either case, the result is that multiple activities are generated and executed in much the same way as processes under the control of a multitasking operating system. We will adopt the Java terminology and refer to such "processes" as threads.

Perhaps the most basic action that must be expressed in a program involving parallel processing is that of creating new threads. If we want multiple activations of the spaceship program to be executed at the same time, we need a syntax for saying so. Such spawning of new threads is similar to that of requesting the execution of a traditional function. The difference is that, in the traditional setting, the program unit that requests the activation of a function does not progress any further until the requested function terminates (recall Figure 6.8), whereas in the parallel context the requesting program unit continues execution while the requested function performs its task (Figure 6.23). Thus to create multiple spaceships streaking across the screen, we would write a main program that simply generates multiple activations of the spaceship program, each provided with the parameters describing the distinguishing characteristics of that spaceship.

A more complex issue associated with parallel processing involves handling communication between threads. For instance, in our spaceship example, the threads representing the different spaceships might need to communicate their locations among themselves in order to coordinate their activities. In other cases one thread might need to wait until another reaches a certain point in its computation, or one thread might need to stop another one until the first has accomplished a particular task.

Such communication needs have long been a topic of study among computer scientists, and many newer programming languages reflect various approaches to thread interaction problems. As an example, let us consider the communication problems encountered when two threads manipulate the same data. (This example is presented in more detail in the optional Section 3.4.) If each of two threads that are executing concurrently need to add the value three to a common item of data, a method is needed to ensure that one thread is allowed to complete its transaction before the other is allowed to perform its task. Otherwise they could both start their individual computations with the same initial value, which would mean that the final result would be incremented by only three rather

Figure 6.23 Spawning threads

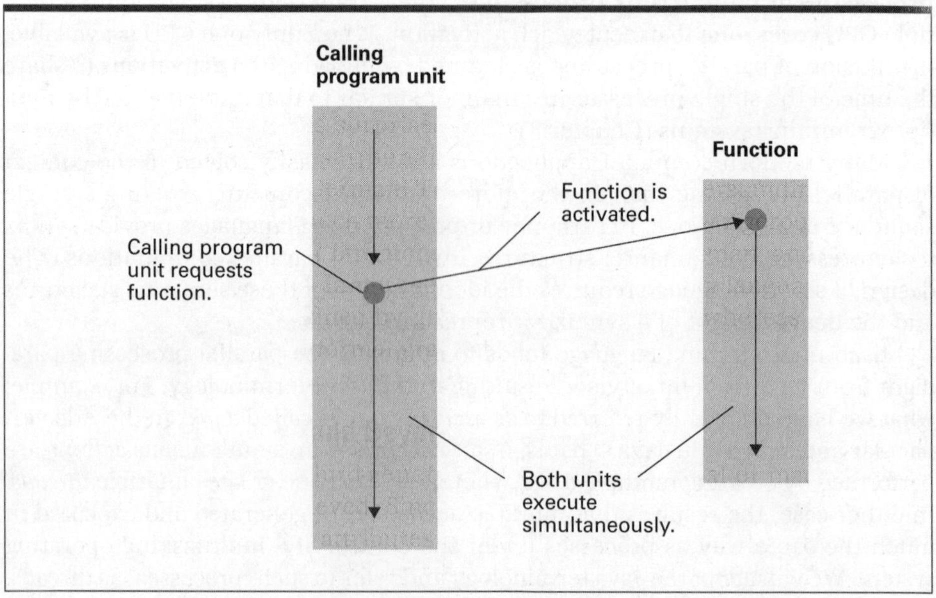

Programming Smartphones

Software for hand-held, mobile, and embedded devices is often developed using the same general-purpose programming languages that are used in other contexts. With a larger keyboard and extra patience, some smartphone applications can be written using the smartphone itself. However, in most cases smartphone software is developed on desktop computers using special software systems that provide tools for editing, translating, and testing smartphone software. Simple apps are often written in Java, C++, and C#. However, writing more complex apps or core system software may require additional support for concurrent and event-driven programming.

than six. Data that can be accessed by only one thread at a time is said to have mutually exclusive access.

One way to implement mutually exclusive access is to write the program units that describe the threads involved so that when a thread is using shared data, it blocks other threads from accessing that data until such access is safe. (This is the approach described in the optional Section 3.4, where we identified the portion of a process that accesses shared data as a critical region.) Experience has shown that this approach has the drawback of distributing the task of ensuring mutual exclusion throughout various parts of the program—each program unit accessing the data must be properly designed to enforce mutual exclusion, and thus a mistake in a single segment can corrupt the entire system. For this reason many argue that a better solution is to embody the data item with the ability to control access to itself. In short, instead of relying on the threads that access the data to guard against multiple access, the data item itself is assigned this responsibility. The result is that control of access is concentrated at a single point in the program rather than dispersed among many program units. A data item augmented with the ability to control access to itself is often called a **monitor.**

We conclude that the design of programming languages for parallel processing involves developing ways to express such things as the creation of threads, the pausing and restarting of threads, the identification of critical regions, and the composition of monitors.

In closing, we should note that although animation provides an interesting setting in which to explore the issues of parallel computing, it is only one of many fields that benefit from parallel processing techniques. Other areas include weather forecasting, air traffic control, simulation of complex systems (from nuclear reactions to pedestrian traffic), computer networking, and database maintenance.

Questions & Exercises

1. What are some properties that would be found in a programming language for concurrent processing that would not be found in a more traditional language?
2. Describe two methods for ensuring mutually exclusive access to data.
3. Identify some settings other than animation in which parallel computing is beneficial.

6.7 Declarative Programming

In Section 6.1 we claimed that formal logic provides a general problem-solving algorithm around which a declarative programming system can be constructed. In this section we investigate this claim by first introducing the rudiments of the algorithm and then taking a brief look at a declarative programming language based on it.

Logical Deduction

Suppose we know that either Kermit is on stage or Kermit is sick, and we are told that Kermit is not on stage. We could then conclude that Kermit must be sick. This is an example of a deductive-reasoning principle called **resolution.** Resolution is one of many techniques, called **inference rules,** for deriving a consequence from a collection of statements.

To better understand resolution, let us first agree to represent simple statements by single letters and to indicate the negation of a statement by the symbol ¬. For instance, we might represent the statement "Kermit is a prince" by A and "Miss Piggy is an actress" by B. Then, the expression

A OR B

would mean "Kermit is a prince or Miss Piggy is an actress" and

B AND ¬A

would mean "Miss Piggy is an actress and Kermit is not a prince." We will use an arrow to indicate "implies." For example, the expression

A→B

means "Kermit is a prince implies that Miss Piggy is an actress."

In its general form, the resolution principle states that from two statements of the form

P OR Q

and

R OR ¬Q

we can conclude the statement

P OR R

In this case we say that the two original statements resolve to form the third statement, which we call the **resolvent.** It is important to observe that the resolvent is a logical consequence of the original statements. That is, if the original statements are true, the resolvent must also be true. (If Q is true, then R must be true; but if Q is false, then P must be true. Thus regardless of the truth or falseness of Q, either P or R must be true.)

We will represent the resolution of two statements pictorially as shown in Figure 6.24, where we write the original statements with lines projecting down to their resolvent. Note that resolution can be applied only to pairs of statements that appear in **clause form**—that is, statements whose elementary components are connected by the Boolean operation OR. Thus

P OR Q

Figure 6.24 Resolving the statements (*P* OR ¬*Q*) and (*R* OR *Q*) to produce (*P* OR *R*)

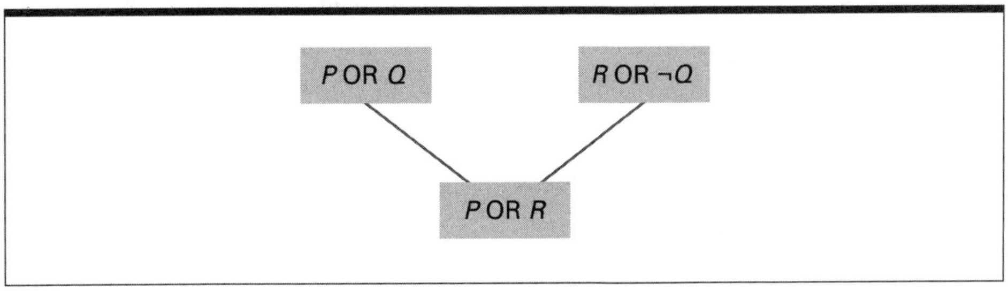

is in clause form, whereas

P→Q

is not. The fact that this potential problem poses no serious concern is a consequence of a theorem in mathematical logic that states that any statement expressed in the first-order predicate logic (a system for representing statements with extensive expressive powers) can be expressed in clause form. We will not pursue this important theorem here, but for future reference we observe that the statement

P→Q

is equivalent to the clause form statement

Q OR ¬P

A collection of statements is said to be **inconsistent** if it is impossible for all the statements to be true at the same time. In other words, an inconsistent collection of statements is a collection of statements that are self-contradictory. A simple example would be a collection containing the statement P as well as the statement ¬P. Logicians have shown that repeated resolution provides a systematic method of confirming the inconsistency of a set of inconsistent clauses. The rule is that if repeated application of resolution produces the empty clause (the result of resolving a clause of the form P with a clause of the form ¬P), then the original collection of statements must be inconsistent. As an example, Figure 6.25 demonstrates that the collection of statements

P OR Q
R OR ¬Q
¬R

¬P

is inconsistent.

Suppose now that we want to confirm that a collection of statements implies the statement P. To imply the statement P is the same as contradicting the statement ¬P. Thus, to demonstrate that the original collection of statements implies P, all we need to do is apply resolution to the original statements together with the statement ¬P until an empty clause occurs. Upon obtaining an empty clause, we can conclude that statement ¬P is inconsistent with the original statements, and thus the original statements must imply P.

Figure 6.25 Resolving the statements (P OR Q), (R OR $\neg Q$), $\neg R$, and $\neg P$

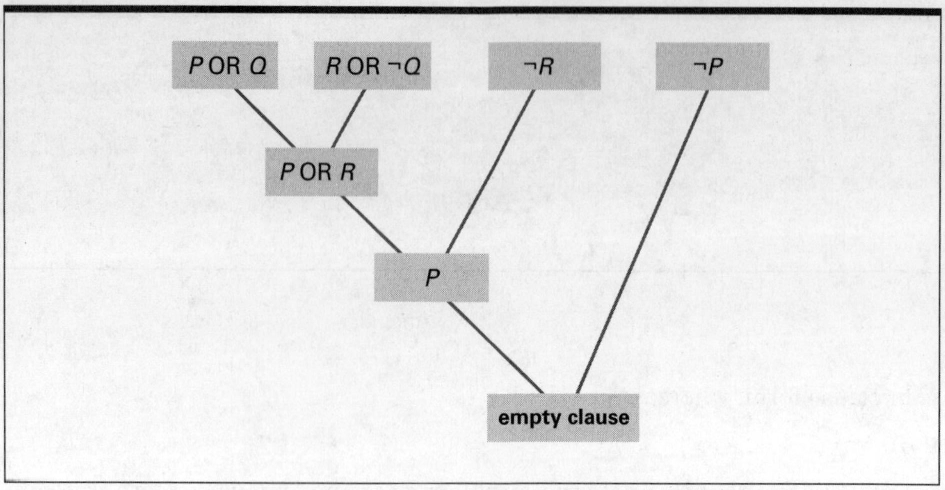

One final point remains before we are ready to apply resolution in an actual programming environment. Suppose we have the two statements

`(Mary is at X) → (Mary's lamb is at X)`

(where `X` represents any location) and

`Mary is at home`

In clause form the two statements become

`(Mary's lamb is at X) OR ¬(Mary is at X)`

and

`(Mary is at home)`

which at first glance do not have components that can be resolved. On the other hand, the components `(Mary is at home)` and `¬(Mary is at X)` are quite close to being opposites of each other. The problem is to recognize that `Mary is at X`, being a statement about locations in general, is a statement about *home* in particular. Thus a special case of the first statement from above is

`(Mary's lamb is at home) OR ¬(Mary is at home)`

which can be resolved with the statement

`(Mary is at home)`

to produce the statement

`(Mary's lamb is at home)`

The process of assigning values to variables (such as assigning the value *home* to `X`) so that resolution can be performed is called **unification.** It is this process that allows general statements to be applied to specific applications in a deduction system.

Prolog

The programming language Prolog (short for PROgramming in LOGic) is a declarative programming language whose underlying problem-solving algorithm is based on repeated resolution. Such languages are called **logic programming** languages. A program in Prolog consists of a collection of initial statements to which the underlying algorithm applies its deductive reasoning. The components from which these statements are constructed are called **predicates.** A predicate consists of a predicate identifier followed by a parenthetical statement listing the predicate's arguments. A single predicate represents a fact about its arguments, and its identifier is usually chosen to reflect this underlying semantics. Thus if we want to express the fact that Bill is Mary's parent, we can use the predicate form

```
parent(bill, mary)
```

Note that the arguments in this predicate start with lowercase letters, even though they represent proper nouns. This is because Prolog distinguishes arguments that are constants from arguments that are variables by insisting that constants begin with lowercase letters and variables begin with uppercase letters. (Here we have used the terminology of the Prolog culture where the term *constant* is used in place of the more generic term *literal.* More precisely, the term `bill` [note the lowercase] is used in Prolog to represent the literal that might be represented as `"Bill"` in a more generic notation. The term `Bill` [note the uppercase] is used in Prolog to refer to a variable.)

Statements in a Prolog program are either facts or rules, each of which is terminated by a period. A fact consists of a single predicate. For example, the fact that a turtle is faster than a snail could be represented by the Prolog statement

```
faster(turtle, snail).
```

and the fact that a rabbit is faster than a turtle could be represented by

```
faster(rabbit, turtle).
```

A Prolog rule is an "implies" statement. However, instead of writing such a statement in the form `X → Y`, a Prolog programmer writes "Y if X," except that the symbol `:-` (a colon followed by a dash) is used in place of the word *if.* Thus the rule "X is old implies X is wise" might be expressed by a logician as

```
old(X) → wise(X)
```

but would be expressed in Prolog as

```
wise(X) :- old(X).
```

As another example, the rule

```
(faster(X, Y) AND faster(Y, Z)) → faster(X, Z)
```

would be expressed in Prolog as

```
faster(X, Z) :- faster(X, Y), faster(Y, Z).
```

(The comma separating `faster(X, Y)` and `faster(Y, Z)` represents the conjunction AND.) Although rules such as these are not in clause form, they are allowed in Prolog because they can be easily converted into clause form.

Keep in mind that the Prolog system does not know the meaning of the predicates in a program; it simply manipulates the statements in a totally symbolic manner according to the resolution inference rule. Thus it is up to the programmer to describe all the pertinent features of a predicate in terms of facts and rules. In this light, Prolog facts tend to be used to identify specific instances of a predicate, whereas rules are used to describe general principles. This is the approach followed by the preceding statements regarding the predicate `faster`. The two facts describe particular instances of "fasterness" while the rule describes a general property. Note that the fact that a rabbit is faster than a snail, although not explicitly stated, is a consequence of the two facts combined with the rule.

When developing software using Prolog, the task of a programmer is to develop the collection of facts and rules that describe the information that is known. These facts and rules constitute the set of initial statements to be used in the deductive system. Once this collection of statements is established, conjectures (called goals in Prolog terminology) can be proposed to the system—usually by typing them at a computer's keyboard. When such a goal is presented to a Prolog system, the system applies resolution to try to confirm that the goal is a consequence of the initial statements. Based on our collection of statements describing the relationship faster, each of the goals

```
faster(turtle, snail).
faster(rabbit, turtle).
faster(rabbit, snail).
```

could be so confirmed because each is a logical consequence of the initial statements. The first two are identical to facts appearing in the initial statements, whereas the third requires a certain degree of deduction by the system.

More interesting examples are obtained if we provide goals whose arguments are variables rather than constants. In these cases Prolog tries to derive the goal from the initial statements while keeping track of the unifications required to do so. Then, if the goal is obtained, Prolog reports these unifications. For example, consider the goal

```
faster(W, snail).
```

In response to this, Prolog reports

```
faster(turtle, snail).
```

Indeed, this is a consequence of the initial statements and agrees with the goal via unification. Furthermore, if we asked Prolog to tell us more, it finds and reports the consequence

```
faster(rabbit, snail).
```

In contrast, we can ask Prolog to find instances of animals that are slower than a rabbit by proposing the goal

```
faster(rabbit, W).
```

In fact, if we started with the goal

```
faster(V, W).
```

Prolog would ultimately seek all the faster relationships that can be derived from the initial statements. This implies that a single Prolog program could be used to confirm that a particular animal is faster than another, to find those animals that are faster than a given animal, to find those animals that are slower than a given animal, or to find all faster relationships.

This potential versatility is one of the features that has captured the imagination of computer scientists. Unfortunately, when implemented in a Prolog system, the resolution procedure inherits limitations that are not present in its theoretical form, and thus Prolog programs can fail to live up to their anticipated flexibility. To understand what we mean, first note that the diagram in Figure 6.25 displays only those resolutions that are pertinent to the task at hand. There are other directions that the resolution process could pursue. For example, the leftmost and rightmost clauses could be resolved to produce the resolvent Q. Thus, in addition to the statements describing the basic facts and rules involved in an application, a Prolog program often must contain additional statements whose purpose is to guide the resolution process in the correct direction. For this reason actual Prolog programs may not capture the multiplicity of purpose suggested by our previous example.

Questions & Exercises

1. Which of the statements R, S, T, U, and V are logical consequences of the collection of statements (¬R OR T OR S), (¬S OR V), (¬V OR R), (U OR ¬S), (T OR U), and (S OR V)?
2. Is the following collection of statements consistent? Explain your answer.

   P OR Q OR R   ¬R OR Q   R OR ¬P   ¬Q
3. Complete the two rules at the end of the Prolog program below so that the predicate `mother(X, Y)` means "X is the mother of Y" and the predicate `father(X, Y)` means "X is the father of Y."

```
female(carol).
female(sue).
male(bill).
male(john).
parent(john, carol).
parent(sue, carol).
mother(X,Y) :-
father(X,Y) :-
```

4. In the context of the Prolog program in question 3, the following rule is intended to mean that X is Y's sibling if X and Y have a common parent.

```
sibling(X, Y) :- parent(Z, X), parent(Z, Y).
```

   What unexpected conclusion would this definition of the sibling relationship allow Prolog to make?

Chapter Review Problems

Asterisked problems are associated with optional sections.

1. What does it mean to say that a programming language is machine independent?

2. Translate the following Python program into the machine language described in Appendix C.

```
x = 0
while (x < 3):
  x = x + 1
```

3. Translate the statement

```
Halfway = Length + Width
```

into the machine language of Appendix C, assuming that `Length`, `Width`, and `Halfway` are all represented in floating-point notation.

4. Translate the high-level statement

```
if (X == 0):
  Z = Y + W
else:
  Z = Y + X
```

into the machine language of Appendix C, assuming that `W`, `X`, `Y`, and `Z` are all values represented in two's complement notation, each using one byte of memory.

5. Why was it necessary to identify the type of data associated with the variables in question 4 in order to translate the statements? Why do many high-level programming languages require the programmer to identify the type of each variable at the beginning of a program?

6. What are the different levels of programming languages?

7. Suppose the function *f* expects a string as its input and returns the same string as its output by removing the odd-positioned letters from the string. What is the result returned by function *f(f("programming"))*?

8. Suppose the function *f* expects two numeric values as its inputs and returns their addition as its output value, and *g* is a function that returns the subtraction of the two values given as its input. If *a* and *b* represent numeric values, what is the result returned by *f(f(a,b), g(a,b))*?

9. Suppose you are going to write an object-oriented program for calculating grades of students. What data should be stored inside the object representing a student's grades? To what messages should that object be able to respond? What are the different objects that might be used in the program?

10. Summarize the distinction between a machine language and an assembly language.

11. Design an assembly language for the machine described in Appendix C.

12. John Programmer argues that the ability to declare constants within a program is not necessary because variables can be used instead. For example, our example of `AirportAlt` in Section 6.2 could be handled by declaring `AirportAlt` to be a variable and then assigning it the required value at the beginning of the program. Why is this not as good as using a constant?

13. Summarize the distinction between the declaration and the definition of a variable.

14. Explain the differences between a local variable and a global variable.

15. a. What is operator precedence?
    b. Depending on operator precedence, what values could be associated with the expression $6 + 2 \times 3$?

16. Explain the advantages of code reuse.

17. What will be the output of the following C code? Explain your answer.

```
#define sqr(X)  X * X
main() {
int k = sqr (10 + 20);
   printf("%d", k);
}
```

18. Draw a flowchart representing the structure expressed by the following for statement.

```
for (int x = 2; x < 8; ++x)
{ . . . }
```

19. Translate the following `while` statement into an equivalent program segment using the Python `for` statement. Initialization: `x = 1`

```
while ( x! = 100)
{ x = x + 1 }
```

20. If you are familiar with written music, analyze musical notation as a programming language. What are the control structures? What is the syntax for inserting program comments? What music notation has semantics similar to the `for` statement in Figure 6.7?

21. Rewrite the following program segment using a `while` loop instead of a `for` loop.

```
for (i = 0; i<100; i++) {
if (i % 2 == 0)
{
   print(i)
}
}
```

22. Draw a flowchart representing the structure expressed by the following `if` and `else` conditional statements.

```
if (a > b) {
if (c > a) {
if (d > c) { print(d) }
}
} else if (b > a) {
if (c > b) {
if (d > c) { print(d) }
} }
```

23. Summarize the following rat's-nest routine with a single if-else statement:

```
    if X > 5 then goto 80
    X = X + 1
    goto 90
80  X = X + 2
90  stop
```

24. Summarize the basic control structures found in imperative and object-oriented programming languages for performing each of the following activities:

a. Determining which command should be executed next
b. Repeating a collection of commands
c. Changing a variable's value

25. Summarize the distinction between code generation and code optimization.

26. Suppose the variable `P` in a program is of type integer. What will be the output of the following two program statements?

```
P = 2.5 + 3.5
  print(P)
```

27. What does it mean to say that a programming language is strongly typed?

28. Can we return more than one value from a function? Explain your answer.

29. Suppose the Python function `Modify` is defined by

```
def Modify (Y):
  Y = 7
  print(Y)
```

If parameters are passed by value, what will be printed when the following program segment is executed? What if parameters are passed by reference?

```
X = 5
Modify(X)
print(X)
```

30. Suppose the Python function `Modify` is defined by

```
def Modify (Y):
  Y = 9
  print(X)
  print(Y)
```

Also suppose that `X` is a global variable. If parameters are passed by value, what will be printed when the following program segment is executed? What if parameters are passed by reference?

```
X = 5
Modify(X)
print(X)
```

31. Sometimes an actual parameter is passed to a function by producing a duplicate to be used by the function (as when the parameter is passed by value), but when the function is completed the value in the function's copy is transferred to the actual parameter before the calling function continues. In such cases the parameter is said to be passed by value-result. What would be printed by the program segment in question 30 if parameters were passed by value-result?

32. What is the main difference between passing parameters to a function by value and passing parameters to a function by address? Explain your answer with a proper example for each.

33. What ambiguity exists in the statement

```
P = 9/4 - 1
```

34. Suppose a small company has five employees and is planning to increase the number to six. Moreover, suppose one of the company's programs contained the following assignment statements.

```
DailySalary = TotalSal/5;
AvgSalary   = TotalSal/5;
DailySales  = TotalSales/5;
AvgSales    = TotalSales/5;
```

How would the task of updating the program be simplified if the program had originally been written using constants named `NumberOfEmp` and `WorkWeek` (both set to the value 5) so that the assignment statements could be expressed as

```
DailySalary = TotalSal/DaysWk;
AvgSalary   = TotalSal/NumEmpl;
DailySales  = TotalSales/DaysWk;
AvgSales    = TotalSales/NumEmpl;
```

35. a. What is the distinction between an assembly language and a third-generation programming language?
b. Give an example of each.

36. Draw a syntax diagram representing the structure of the Python nested `if-else` statement.

37. Design a set of syntax diagrams to describe the syntax of telephone numbers in your locality. For instance, in the United States telephone numbers consist of an area code, followed by a regional code, followed by a four-digit number such as (444) 555–1234.

38. Design a set of syntax diagrams to describe simple sentences in your native language.

39. Design a set of syntax diagrams to describe different ways of representing full names such as *firstname - middlename - lastname* or the reverse of it.

40. Design a set of syntax diagrams that describes the grammatical structure of "sentences" that consist of occurrences of the word *yes* followed by the same number of the word *no*. For example, "*yes yes no no*" would be such a sentence, whereas "*no yes,*" "*yes no no,*" and "*yes no yes*" would not.

41. Give an argument to the effect that a set of syntax diagrams cannot be designed that describes the grammatical structure of "sentences" that consist of occurrences of the word *yes,* followed by the same number of occurrences of the word *no,* followed by the same number of occurrences of the word *maybe.* For example, "*yes no maybe*" and "*yes yes no no maybe maybe*" would be such sentences, whereas "*yes maybe,*" "*yes no no maybe maybe,*" and "*maybe no*" would not.

42. Write a sentence describing the structure of a string as defined by the following syntax diagram. Then, draw the parse tree for the string *xxyxx.*

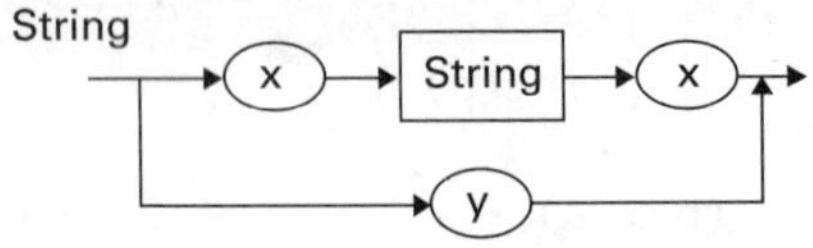

43. Add syntax diagrams to those in question 5 of Section 6.4 to obtain a set of diagrams that defines the structure Dance to be either a Chacha or a Waltz, where a Waltz consists of one or more copies of the pattern

forward diagonal close

or

backward diagonal close

44. Draw the parse tree for the expression $a \div d \times b \div c + a \div d \times b \div c$ based on the syntax diagrams in Figure 6.15.

45. What code optimization could be performed by a code generator when building the machine code representing the statement

```
if (X == 5):
  Z = X + 2
```

```
else:
  Z = X + 4
```

46. What will be the output of following code?

```
if (printf ("Hello")) {
  printf("World");
} else {
  printf("Hello");
}
```

47. Simplify the following program segment

```
while (Z < 10):
Z++;
```

48. In an object-oriented programming environment, how are types and classes similar? How are they different?

49. Describe how inheritance might be used to develop classes describing various types of sports.

50. What is the difference between the public and private parts of a class?

51. a. Give an example of a situation in which an instance variable should be private.
b. Give an example of a situation in which an instance variable should be public.
c. Give an example of a situation in which a method should be private.
d. Give an example of a situation in which a method should be public.

52. Describe some objects that might be found in a program for simulating the pedestrian traffic in a hotel lobby. Include explanations of the actions some of the objects should be able to perform.

***53.** What does the term *type cast* mean in the context of a programming language?

***54.** What is the difference between `while` and `do-while` loops in the context of a programming language?

***55.** Draw a diagram (similar to Figure 6.25) representing the resolutions needed to show that the collection of statements (Q OR ¬R), (T OR R), ¬P, (P OR ¬T), and (P OR ¬Q) are inconsistent.

***56.** Is the collection of statements ¬R, (T OR R), (P OR ¬Q), (Q OR ¬T), and (R OR ¬P) consistent? Explain your answer.

***57.** Extend the Prolog program outlined in questions 3 and 4 of Section 6.7 to include the additional family relationships of uncle, aunt, grandparent, and cousin. Also add a rule that defines `parents (X, Y, Z)` to mean that X and Y are Z's parents.

***58.** Assuming that the first statement in the following Prolog program is intended to mean "Alice likes sports," translate the last two statements of the program. Then, list all the things that, based on this program, Prolog would be able conclude that Alice likes. Explain your list.

```
likes(alice, sports).
likes(alice, music).
likes(carol, music).
likes(david, X) :- likes(X, sports).
likes(alice, X) :- likes(david, X).
```

***59.** What problem would be encountered if the following program segment was executed on a computer in which values are represented in the eight-bit floating-point format described in Section 1.7?

```
X = 0.01
while (X != 1.00):
  print(X)
  X = X + 0.01
```

Social Issues

The following questions are intended as a guide to the ethical/social/legal issues associated with the field of computing. The goal is not merely to answer these questions. You should also consider why you answered as you did and whether your justifications are consistent from one question to the next.

1. In general, copyright laws support ownership rights associated with the expression of an idea but not for the idea itself. As a result, a paragraph in a book is copyrightable but the ideas expressed in the paragraph are not. How should this right extend to source programs and the algorithms they express? To what extent should a person who knows the algorithms used in a commercial software package be allowed to write his or her own program expressing those same algorithms and market this version of the software?
2. By using a high-level programming language a programmer is able to express algorithms using words such as *if, else,* and *while.* To what extent does the computer understand the meaning of those words? Does the ability to respond correctly to the use of words imply an understanding of the words? How do you know when another person has understood what you said?
3. Should a person who develops a new and useful programming language have a right to profit from the use of that language? If so, how can that right be protected? To what extent can a language be owned? To what extent should a company have the right to own the creative, intellectual accomplishments of its employees?
4. With a deadline approaching, is it acceptable for a programmer to forgo documentation via comment statements to get a program running on time? (Beginning students are often surprised to learn how important documentation is considered among professional software developers.)
5. Much of the research in programming languages has been to develop languages that allow programmers to write programs that can be easily read and understood by humans. To what extent should a programmer be required to use such capabilities? That is, to what extent is it good enough for the program to perform correctly even though it is not well written from a human perspective?
6. Suppose an amateur programmer writes a program for his or her own use and in doing so is sloppy in the program's construction. The program does not use the programming language features that would make it more readable, it is not efficient, and it contains shortcuts that take advantage of the particular situation in which the programmer intends to use the program. Over time the programmer gives copies of the program to friends who want to use it themselves, and these friends give it to their friends. To what extent is the programmer liable for problems that might occur?
7. To what extent should a computer professional be knowledgeable in the various programming paradigms? Some companies insist that all software developed in that company be written in the same, predetermined programming language. Does your answer to the original question change if the professional works for such a company?

Additional Reading

Aho, A. V., M. S. Lam, R. Sethi, and J. D. Ullman. *Compilers: Principles, Techniques, and Tools*, 2nd ed. Boston, MA: Addison-Wesley, 2007.

Barnes, J. *Programming in Ada 2005*. Boston, MA: Addison-Wesley, 2006.

Clocksin, W. F., and C. S. Mellish. *Programming in Prolog,* 5th ed. New York: Springer-Verlag, 2013.

Friedman, D. P., and M. Felleisen. *The Little Schemer,* 4th ed. Cambridge, MA: MIT Press, 1995.

Hamburger, H., and D. Richards. *Logic and Language Models for Computer Science.* Upper Saddle River, NJ: Prentice-Hall, 2002.

Kernighan, B.W., and D.M. Ritchie. *The C Programming Language,* 2nd ed. Englewood Cliffs, NJ: Prentice Hall, 1988.

Metcalf, M., and J. Reid. *Fortran 90/95 Explained,* 2nd ed. Oxford, England: Oxford University Press, 1999.

Pratt, T. W., and M. V. Zelkowitz. *Programming Languages, Design and Implementation,* 4th ed. Upper Saddle River, NJ: Prentice-Hall, 2001.

Savitch, W., and K. Mock. *Absolute C+ +,* 5th ed. Boston, MA: Addison-Wesley, 2012.

Savitch, W., and K. Mock. *Absolute Java,* 5th ed. Boston, MA: Addison-Wesley, 2012.

Savitch, W. Problem Solving with C+ +, 8th ed. Boston, MA: Addison-Wesley, 2011.

Scott, M. L. *Programming Language Pragmatics,* 3rd ed. New York: Morgan Kaufmann, 2009.

Sebesta, R. W. *Concepts of Programming Languages,* 10th ed. Boston, MA: Addison Wesley, 2012.

Wu, C. T. *An Introduction to Object-Oriented Programming with Java,* 5th ed. Burr Ridge, IL: McGraw-Hill, 2009.

CHAPTER 7

Software Engineering

In this chapter we explore the problems that are encountered during the development of large, complex software systems. The subject is called *software engineering* because software development is an engineering process. The goal of researchers in software engineering is to find principles that guide the software development process and lead to efficient, reliable software products.

Software engineering is the branch of computer science that seeks principles to guide the development of large, complex software systems. The problems faced when developing such systems are more than enlarged versions of those problems faced when writing small programs. For instance, the development of such systems requires the efforts of more than one person over an extended period of time during which the requirements of the proposed system may be altered and the personnel assigned to the project may change. Consequently, software engineering includes topics such as personnel and project management that are more readily associated with business management than computer science. We, however, will focus on topics readily related to computer science.

7.1 The Software Engineering Discipline

To appreciate the problems involved in software engineering, it is helpful to select a large complex device (an automobile, a multistory office building, or perhaps a cathedral) and imagine being asked to design it and then to supervise its construction. How can you estimate the cost in time, money, and other resources to complete the project? How can you divide the project into manageable pieces? How can you ensure that the pieces produced are compatible? How can those working on the various pieces communicate? How can you measure progress? How can you cope with the wide range of detail (the selection of the doorknobs, the design of the gargoyles, the availability of blue glass for the stained glass windows, the strength of the pillars, the design of the duct work for the heating system)? Questions of the same scope must be answered during the development of a large software system.

Because engineering is a well-established field, you might think that there is a wealth of previously developed engineering techniques that can be useful in answering such questions. This reasoning is partially true, but it overlooks fundamental differences between the properties of software and those of other fields of engineering. These distinctions have challenged software engineering projects, leading to cost overruns, late delivery of products, and dissatisfied customers. In turn, identifying these distinctions has proven to be the first step in advancing the software engineering discipline.

One such distinction involves the ability to construct systems from generic prefabricated components. Traditional fields of engineering have long benefited from the ability to use "off-the-shelf" components as building blocks when constructing complex devices. The designer of a new automobile does not have to design a new engine or transmission but instead uses previously designed versions of these components. Software engineering, however, lags in this regard. In the past, previously designed software components were domain specific—that is, their internal design was based on a specific application—and thus their use as generic components was limited. The result is that complex software systems have historically been built from scratch. As we will see in this chapter, significant progress is being made in this regard, although more work remains to be done.

Another distinction between software engineering and other engineering disciplines is the lack of quantitative techniques, called **metrics,** for measuring the properties of software. For example, to project the cost of developing a software system, one would like to estimate the complexity of the proposed product, but methods for measuring the "complexity" of software are evasive. Similarly, evaluating the quality of a software product is challenging. In the case of mechanical devices, an important measure of quality is the mean time between failures, which is essentially a measurement of how well a device endures wear. Software, in contrast, does not wear out, so this method of measuring quality is not as applicable in software engineering.

The difficulties involved in measuring software properties in a quantitative manner is one of the reasons that software engineering has struggled to find a rigorous footing in the same sense as mechanical and electrical engineering. Whereas these latter subjects are founded on the established science of physics, software engineering continues to search for its roots.

Thus research in software engineering is currently progressing on two levels: Some researchers, sometimes called practitioners, work toward developing techniques for immediate application, whereas others, called theoreticians, search for underlying principles and theories on which more stable techniques can someday be constructed. Being based on a subjective foundation, many methodologies developed and promoted by practitioners in the past have been replaced by other approaches that may themselves become obsolete with time. Meanwhile, progress by theoreticians continues to be slow.

The need for progress by both practitioners and theoreticians is enormous. Our society has become addicted to computer systems and their associated software. Our economy, healthcare, government, law enforcement, transportation, and defense depend on large software systems. Yet there continue to be major problems with the reliability of these systems. Software errors have caused such disasters and near disasters as the rising moon being interpreted as a nuclear attack, a one-day loss of $5 million by the Bank of New York, the loss of space probes, radiation overdoses that have killed and paralyzed, and the simultaneous disruption of telephone communications over large regions.

This is not to say that the situation is all bleak. Much progress is being made in overcoming such problems as the lack of prefabricated components and metrics. Moreover, the application of computer technology to the software development process, resulting in what is called **computer-aided software engineering (CASE),** is continuing to streamline and otherwise simplify the software development process. CASE has led to the development of a variety of computerized systems, known as **CASE tools,** which include project planning systems (to assist in cost estimation, project scheduling, and personnel allocation), project management systems (to assist in monitoring the progress of the development project), documentation tools (to assist in writing and organizing documentation), prototyping and simulation systems (to assist in the development of prototypes), interface

Association for Computing Machinery

The Association for Computing Machinery (ACM) was founded in 1947 as an international scientific and educational organization dedicated to advancing the arts, sciences, and applications of information technology. It is headquartered in New York and includes numerous special interest groups (SIGs) focusing on such topics as computer architecture, artificial intelligence, biomedical computing, computers and society, computer science education, computer graphics, hypertext/hypermedia, operating systems, programming languages, simulation and modeling, and software engineering. The ACM's website is at `http://www.acm.org`. Its Code of Ethics and Professional Conduct can be found at `http://www.acm.org/constitution/code.html`.

design systems (to assist in the development of GUIs), and programming systems (to assist in writing and debugging programs). Some of these tools are little more than the word processors, spreadsheet software, and email communication systems that were originally developed for generic use and adopted by software engineers. Others are quite sophisticated packages designed primarily for the software engineering environment. Indeed, systems known as **integrated development environments (IDEs)** combine tools for developing software (editors, compilers, debugging tools, and so on) into a single, integrated package. Prime examples of such systems are those for developing applications for smartphones. These not only provide the programming tools necessary to write and debug the software but also provide simulators that, by means of graphical displays, allow a programmer to see how the software being developed would actually perform on a phone.

In addition to the efforts of researchers, professional and standardization organizations, including the ISO, the Association for Computing Machinery (ACM), and the Institute of Electrical and Electronics Engineers (IEEE), have joined the battle for improving the state of software engineering. These efforts range from adopting codes of professional conduct and ethics that enhance the professionalism of software developers and counter nonchalant attitudes toward each individual's responsibilities to establishing standards for measuring the quality of software development organizations and providing guidelines to help these organizations improve their standings.

In the remainder of this chapter we discuss some of the fundamental principles of software engineering (such as the software life cycle and modularity), look at some of the directions in which software engineering is moving (such as the identification and application of design patterns and the emergence of reusable software components), and witness the effects that the object-oriented paradigm has had on the field.

Questions & Exercises

1. Why would the number of lines in a program not be a good measure of the complexity of the program?
2. Suggest a metric for measuring software quality. What weaknesses does your metric have?
3. What technique can be used to determine how many errors are in a unit of software?
4. Identify two contexts in which the field of software engineering has been or currently is progressing toward improvements.

7.2 The Software Life Cycle

The most fundamental concept in software engineering is the software life cycle.

The Cycle as a Whole

The software life cycle is shown in Figure 7.1. This figure represents the fact that once software is developed, it enters a cycle of being used and maintained—a cycle that continues for the rest of the software's life. Such a pattern is common

Figure 7.1 The software life cycle

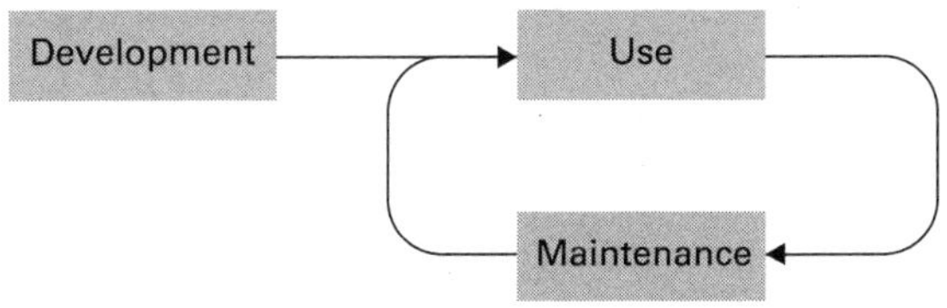

for many manufactured products as well. The difference is that, in the case of other products, the maintenance phase tends to be a repair process, whereas in the case of software, the maintenance phase tends to consist of correcting or updating. Indeed, software moves into the maintenance phase because errors are discovered, changes in the software's application occur that require corresponding changes in the software, or changes made during a previous modification are found to induce problems elsewhere in the software.

Regardless of why software enters the maintenance phase, the process requires that a person (often not the original author) study the underlying program and its documentation until the program, or at least the pertinent part of the program, is understood. Otherwise, any modification could introduce more problems than it solves. Acquiring this understanding can be a difficult task, even when the software is well-designed and documented. In fact, it is often within this phase that a piece of software is discarded under the pretense (too often true) that it is easier to develop a new system from scratch than to modify the existing package successfully.

Experience has shown that a little effort during the development of software can make a tremendous difference when modifications are required. For example, in our discussion of data description statements in Chapter 6 we saw how the use of constants rather than literals can greatly simplify future adjustments. In turn, most of the research in software engineering focuses on the development stage of the software life cycle, with the goal being to take advantage of this effort-versus-benefit leverage.

The Traditional Development Phase

The major steps in the traditional software development life cycle are requirements analysis, design, implementation, and testing (Figure 7.2).

Requirements Analysis The software life cycle begins with requirements analysis—the goal of which is to specify what services the proposed system will provide, to identify any conditions (time constraints, security, and so on) on those services, and to define how the outside world will interact with the system.

Requirements analysis involves significant input from the **stakeholders** (future users as well as those with other ties, such as legal or financial interests) of the proposed system. In fact, in cases where the ultimate user is an entity, such as a company or government agency, that intends to hire a software developer for the actual execution of the software project, requirements analysis may start by a feasibility study conducted solely by the user. In other cases, the software

Figure 7.2 The traditional development phase of the software life cycle

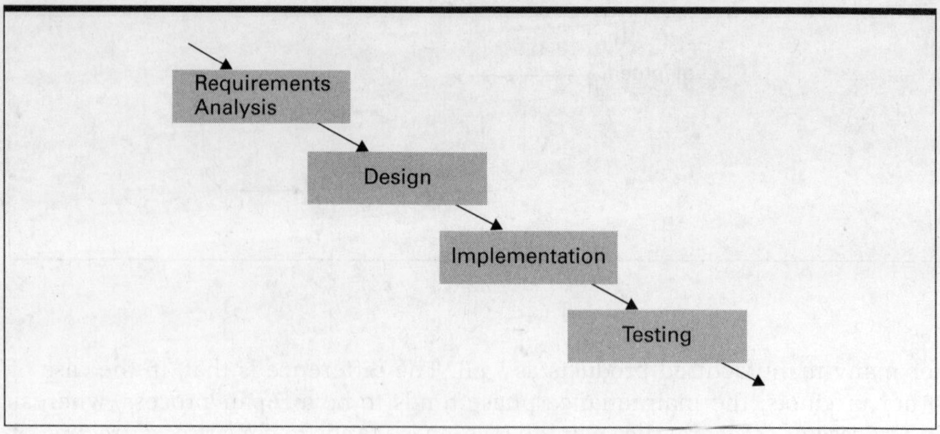

developer may be in the business of producing **commercial off-the-shelf (COTS)** software for the mass market, perhaps to be sold in retail stores or downloaded via the Internet. In this setting the user is a less precisely defined entity, and requirements analysis may begin with a market study by the software developer.

In any case, the requirements analysis process consists of compiling and analyzing the needs of the software user; negotiating with the project's stakeholders over trade-offs between wants, needs, costs, and feasibility; and finally developing a set of requirements that identify the features and services that the finished software system must have. These requirements are recorded in a document called a **software requirements specification.** In a sense, this document is a written agreement between all parties concerned, which is intended to guide the software's development and provide a means of resolving disputes that may arise later in the development process. The significance of the software requirements specification is demonstrated by the fact that professional organizations such as IEEE and large software clients such as the U.S. Department of Defense have adopted standards for its composition.

From the software developer's perspective, the software requirements specification should define a firm objective toward which the software's development can proceed. Too often, however, the document fails to provide this stability. Indeed, most practitioners in the software engineering field argue that poor communication and changing requirements are the major causes of cost overruns and late product delivery in the software engineering industry. Few customers would insist on major changes to a building's floor plan once the foundation has been constructed, but instances abound of organizations that have expanded, or otherwise altered, the desired capabilities of a software system well after the software's construction was underway. This may have been because a company decided that the system that was originally being developed for only a subsidiary should instead apply to the entire corporation or that advances in technology supplanted the capabilities available during the initial requirements analysis. In any case, software engineers have found that straightforward and frequent communication with the project's stakeholders is mandatory.

Design Whereas requirements analysis provides a description of the proposed software product, design involves creating a plan for the construction of the proposed system. In a sense, requirements analysis is about identifying the problem to be solved, while design is about developing a solution to the problem. From a layperson's perspective, requirements analysis is often equated with deciding *what* a software system is to do, whereas design is equated with deciding *how* the system will do it. Although this description is enlightening, many software engineers argue that it is flawed because, in actuality, there is a lot of *how* considered during requirements analysis and a lot of *what* considered during design.

It is in the design stage that the internal structure of the software system is established. The result of the design phase is a detailed description of the software system's structure that can be converted into programs.

If the project were to construct an office building rather than a software system, the design stage would consist of developing detailed structural plans for a building that meets the specified requirements. For example, such plans would include a collection of blueprints describing the proposed building at various levels of detail. It is from these documents that the actual building would be constructed. Techniques for developing these plans have evolved over many years and include standardized notational systems and numerous modeling and diagramming methodologies.

Likewise, diagramming and modeling play important roles in the design of software. However, the methodologies and notational systems used by software engineers are not as stable as they are in the architectural field. When compared to the well-established discipline of architecture, the practice of software engineering appears very dynamic as researchers struggle to find better approaches to the software development process. We will explore this shifting terrain in Section 7.3 and investigate some of the current notational systems and their associated diagramming/modeling methodologies in Section 7.5.

Implementation Implementation involves the actual writing of programs, creation of data files, and development of databases. It is at the implementation stage that we see the distinction between the tasks of a **software analyst** (sometimes

Institute of Electrical and Electronics Engineers

The Institute of Electrical and Electronics Engineers (IEEE, pronounced "i-triple-e") is an organization of electrical, electronics, and manufacturing engineers that was formed in 1963 as the result of merging the American Institute of Electrical Engineers (founded in 1884 by 25 electrical engineers, including Thomas Edison) and the Institute of Radio Engineers (founded in 1912). Today, IEEE's operation center is located in Piscataway, New Jersey. The Institute includes numerous technical societies such as the Aerospace and Electronic Systems Society, the Lasers and Electro-Optics Society, the Robotics and Automation Society, the Vehicular Technology Society, and the Computer Society. Among its activities, the IEEE is involved in the development of standards. As an example, IEEE's efforts led to the single-precision- floating point and double-precision floating-point standards (introduced in Chapter 1), which are used in most of today's computers.

You will find the IEEE's Web page at `http://www.ieee.org`, the IEEE Computer Society's Web page at `http://www.computer.org`, and the IEEE's Code of Ethics at `http://www.ieee.org/about/whatis/code.html`.

referred to as a system analyst) and a **programmer.** The former is a person involved with the entire development process, perhaps with an emphasis on the requirements analysis and design steps. The latter is a person involved primarily with the implementation step. In its narrowest interpretation, a programmer is charged with writing programs that implement the design produced by a software analyst. Having made this distinction, we should note again that there is no central authority controlling the use of terminology throughout the computing community. Many who carry the title of software analyst are essentially programmers, and many with the title programmer (or perhaps senior programmer) are actually software analysts in the full sense of the term. This blurring of terminology is founded in the fact that today the steps in the software development process are often intermingled, as we will soon see.

Testing In the traditional development phase of the past, testing was essentially equated with the process of debugging programs and confirming that the final software product was compatible with the software requirements specification. Today, however, this vision of testing is considered far too narrow. Programs are not the only artifacts that are tested during the software development process. Indeed, the result of each intermediate step in the entire development process should be "tested" for accuracy. Moreover, as we will see in Section 7.6, testing is now recognized as only one segment in the overall struggle for quality assurance, which is an objective that permeates the entire software life cycle. Thus, many software engineers argue that testing should no longer be viewed as a separate step in software development, but instead it, and its many manifestations, should be incorporated into the other steps, producing a three-step development process whose components might have names such as "requirements analysis *and confirmation,*" "design *and validation,*" and "implementation *and testing.*"

Unfortunately, even with modern quality assurance techniques, large software systems continue to contain errors, even after significant testing. Many of these errors may go undetected for the life of the system, but others may cause major malfunctions. The elimination of such errors is one of the goals of software engineering. The fact that they are still prevalent indicates that a lot of research remains to be done.

Questions & Exercises

1. How does the development stage of the software life cycle affect the maintenance stage?
2. Summarize each of the four stages (requirements analysis, design, implementation, and testing) within the development phase of the software life cycle.
3. What is the role of a software requirements specification?

7.3 Software Engineering Methodologies

Early approaches to software engineering insisted on performing requirements analysis, design, implementation, and testing in a strictly sequential manner. The belief was that too much was at risk during the development of a large software system to allow for variations. As a result, software engineers insisted that the entire requirements specification of the system be completed before beginning the design and, likewise, that the design be completed before beginning implementation. The result was a development process now referred to as the **waterfall model,** an analogy to the fact that the development process was allowed to flow in only one direction.

In recent years, software engineering techniques have changed to reflect the contradiction between the highly structured environment dictated by the waterfall model and the "free-wheeling," trial-and-error process that is often vital to creative problem solving. This is illustrated by the emergence of the **incremental model** for software development. Following this model, the desired software system is constructed in increments—the first being a simplified version of the final product with limited functionality. Once this version has been tested and perhaps evaluated by the future user, more features are added and tested in an incremental manner until the system is complete. For example, if the system being developed is a patient records system for a hospital, the first increment may incorporate only the ability to view patient records from a small sample of the entire record system. Once that version is operational, additional features, such as the ability to add and update records, would be added in a stepwise manner.

Another model that represents the shift away from strict adherence to the waterfall model is the **iterative model,** which is similar to, and in fact sometimes equated with, the incremental model, although the two are distinct. Whereas the incremental model carries the notion of *extending* each preliminary version of a product into a larger version, the iterative model encompasses the concept of *refining* each version. In reality, the incremental model involves an underlying iterative process, and the iterative model may incrementally add features.

A significant example of iterative techniques is the **rational unified process** (**RUP,** rhymes with "cup") that was created by the Rational Software Corporation, which is now a division of IBM. RUP is essentially a software development paradigm that redefines the steps in the development phase of the software life cycle and provides guidelines for performing those steps. These guidelines, along with CASE tools to support them, are marketed by IBM. Today, RUP is widely applied throughout the software industry. In fact, its popularity has led to the development of a nonproprietary version, called the **unified process,** that is available on a noncommercial basis.

Incremental and iterative models sometimes make use of the trend in software development toward **prototyping** in which incomplete versions of the proposed system, called prototypes, are built and evaluated. In the case of the incremental model these prototypes evolve into the complete, final system—a process known as **evolutionary prototyping.** In a more iterative situation, the prototypes may be discarded in favor of a fresh implementation of the final design. This approach is known as **throwaway prototyping.** An example that normally falls within this throwaway category is **rapid prototyping** in which a simple example of the proposed system is quickly constructed in the early stages of development. Such a prototype may consist of only a few screen images that give an indication of how the system will interact with its users and what capabilities it will have. The goal is not to produce a working version of the product but to obtain a demonstration tool that can be used to clarify communication between the parties involved in the software development process. For example, rapid prototypes have proved advantageous in clarifying system requirements during requirements analysis or as aids during sales presentations to potential clients.

A less formal incarnation of incremental and iterative ideas that has been used for years by computer enthusiasts/hobbyists is known as **open-source development.** This is the means by which much of today's free software is produced. Perhaps the most prominent example is the Linux operating system whose open-source development was originally led by Linus Torvalds. The open-source development of a software package proceeds as follows: A single author writes an initial version of the software (usually to fulfill his or her own needs) and posts the source code and its documentation on the Internet. From there it can be downloaded and used by others without charge. Because these other users have the source code and documentation, they are able to modify or enhance the software to fit their own needs or to correct errors that they find. They report these changes to the original author, who incorporates them into the posted version of the software, making this extended version available for further modifications. In practice, it is possible for a software package to evolve through several extensions in a single week.

Perhaps the most pronounced shift from the watcrfall model is represented by the collection of methodologies known as **agile methods,** each of which proposes early and quick implementation on an incremental basis, responsiveness to changing requirements, and a reduced emphasis on rigorous requirements analysis and design. One example of an agile method is **extreme programming (XP).** Following the XP model, software is developed by a team of less than a dozen individuals working in a communal work space where they freely share ideas and assist each other in the development project. The software is developed incrementally by means of repeated daily cycles of informal requirements analysis, designing, implementing, and testing. Thus, new expanded versions of the software package appear on a regular basis, each of which can be evaluated by the project's stakeholders and used to point toward further increments. In summary, agile methods are characterized by flexibility, which is in stark contrast to the waterfall model that conjures the image of managers and programmers working in individual offices while rigidly performing well-defined portions of the overall software development task.

The contrasts depicted by comparing the waterfall model and XP reveal the breadth of methodologies that are being applied to the software development process in the hopes of finding better ways to construct reliable software in an efficient manner. Research in the field is an ongoing process. Progress is being made, but much work remains to be done.

Questions & Exercises

1. Summarize the distinction between the traditional waterfall model of software development and the newer incremental and iterative paradigms.
2. Identify three development paradigms that represent the move away from strict adherence to the waterfall model.
3. What is the distinction between traditional evolutionary prototyping and open-source development?
4. What potential problems do you suspect could arise in terms of ownership rights of software developed via the open-source methodology?

7.4 Modularity

A key point in Section 7.2 is that to modify software one must understand the program or at least the pertinent parts of the program. Gaining such an understanding is often difficult enough in the case of small programs and would be close to impossible when dealing with large software systems if it were not for **modularity**—that is, the division of software into manageable units, generically called **modules,** each of which deals with only a part of the software's overall responsibility.

Modular Implementation

Modules come in a variety of forms. We have already seen (Chapters 5 and 6) that in the context of the imperative paradigm, modules appear as functions. In contrast, the object-oriented paradigm uses objects as the basic modular constituents. These distinctions are important because they determine the underlying goal during the initial software design process. Is the goal to represent the overall task as individual, manageable processes or to identify the objects in the system and understand how they interact?

To illustrate, let us consider how the process of developing a simple modular program to simulate a tennis game might progress in the imperative and the object-oriented paradigms. In the imperative paradigm we begin by considering the actions that must take place. Because each volley begins with a player serving the ball, we might start by considering a function named `Serve` that (based on the player's characteristics and perhaps a bit of probability) would compute the initial speed and direction of the ball. Next we would need to determine the path of the ball (Will it hit the net? Where will it bounce?). We might plan on placing these computations in another function named `ComputePath`. The next step might be to determine if the other player is able to return the ball, and if so we must compute the ball's new speed and direction. We might plan on placing these computations in a function named `Return`.

Continuing in this fashion, we might arrive at the modular structure depicted by the **structure chart** shown in Figure 7.3, in which functions are represented by rectangles and function dependencies (implemented by function calls) are represented by arrows. In particular, the chart indicates that the entire game is overseen by a function named `ControlGame`, and to perform its task, `ControlGame` calls on the services of the functions `Serve`, `Return`, `ComputePath`, and `UpdateScore`.

Figure 7.3 A simple structure chart

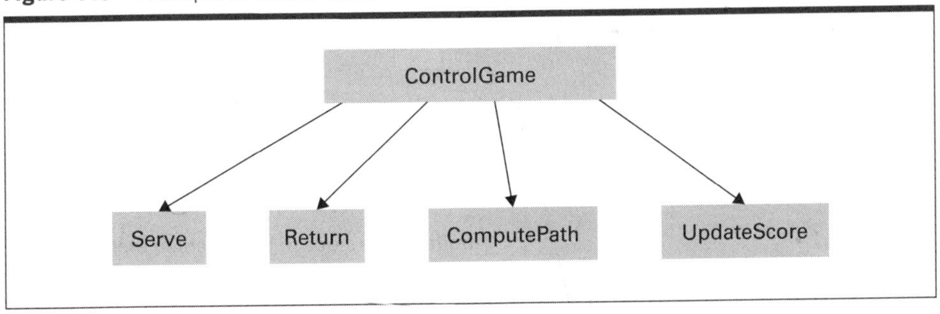

Note that the structure chart does not indicate how each function is to perform its task. Rather, it merely identifies the functions and indicates the dependencies among the functions. In reality, the function `ControlGame` might perform its task by first calling the `Serve` function, then repeatedly calling on the functions `ComputePath` and `Return` until one reports a miss, and finally calling on the services of `UpdateScore` before repeating the whole process by again calling on `Serve`.

At this stage we have obtained only a very simplistic outline of the desired program, but our point has already been made. In accordance with the imperative paradigm, we have been designing the program by considering the activities that must be performed and are therefore obtaining a design in which the modules are functions.

Let us now reconsider the program's design—this time in the context of the object-oriented paradigm. Our first thought might be that there are two players that we should represent by two objects: `PlayerA` and `PlayerB`. These objects will have the same functionality but different characteristics. (Both should be able to serve and return volleys but may do so with different skill and strength.) Thus, these objects will be instances of the same class. (Recall that in Chapter 6 we introduced the concept of a class: a template that defines the functions (called methods) and attributes (called instance variables) that are to be associated with each object.) This class, which we will call `PlayerClass`, will contain the methods `serve` and `return` that simulate the corresponding actions of the player. It will also contain attributes (such as `skill` and `endurance`) whose values reflect the player's characteristics. Our design so far is represented by the diagram in Figure 7.4. There we see that `PlayerA` and `PlayerB` are instances of the class `PlayerClass` and that this class contains the attributes `skill` and `endurance` as well as the methods `serve` and `returnVolley`. (Note that in Figure 7.4 we have underlined the names of objects to distinguish them from names of classes.)

Next we need an object to play the role of the official who determines whether the actions performed by the players are legal. For example, did the serve clear the net and land in the appropriate area of the court? For this purpose we might establish an object called `Judge` that contains the methods `evaluateServe` and `evaluateReturn`. If the `Judge` object determines a serve or return to be acceptable, play continues. Otherwise, the `Judge` sends a message to another object named `Score` to record the results accordingly.

Figure 7.4 The structure of PlayerClass and its instances

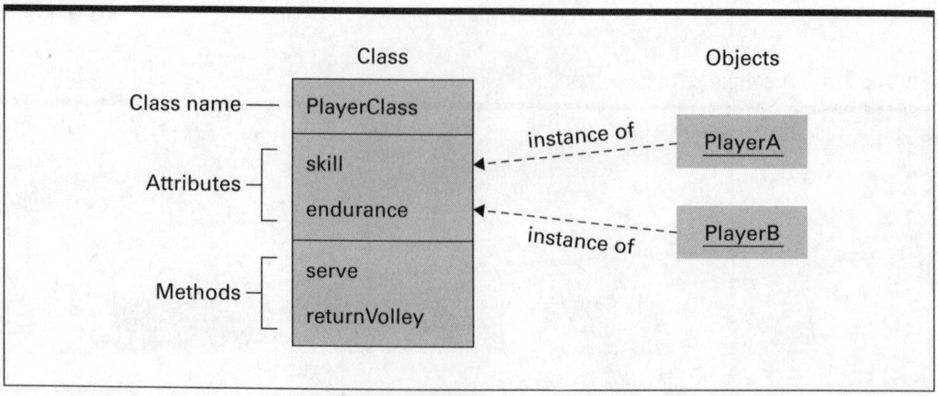

At this point the design for our tennis program consists of four objects: PlayerA, PlayerB, Judge, and Score. To clarify our design, consider the sequences of events that may occur during a volley as depicted in Figure 7.5 where we have represented the objects involved as rectangles. The figure is intended to present the communication between these objects as the result of calling the serve method within the object PlayerA. Events appear chronologically as we move down the figure. As depicted by the first horizontal arrow, PlayerA reports its serve to the object Judge by calling the method evaluateServe. The Judge then determines that the serve is good and asks PlayerB to return it by calling PlayerB's returnVolley method. The volley terminates when the Judge determines that PlayerA erred and asks the object Score to record the results.

As in the case of our imperative example, our object-oriented program is very simplistic at this stage. However, we have progressed enough to see how the object-oriented paradigm leads to a modular design in which fundamental components are objects.

Coupling

We have introduced modularity as a way of producing manageable software. The idea is that any future modification will likely apply to only a few of the modules, allowing the person making the modification to concentrate on that portion of the system rather than struggling with the entire package. This, of course, depends on the assumption that changes in one module will not unknowingly affect other modules in the system. Consequently, a goal when designing a modular system should be to maximize independence among modules or, in other words, to minimize the linkage between modules (known as intermodule **coupling**). Indeed, one metric that has been used to measure the complexity of a software system (and thus obtain a means of estimating the expense of maintaining the software) is to measure its intermodule coupling.

Intermodule coupling occurs in several forms. One is **control coupling,** which occurs when a module passes control of execution to another, as in a function call. The structure chart in Figure 7.3 represents the control coupling that exists between functions. In particular, the arrow from the module ControlGame

Figure 7.5 The interaction between objects resulting from PlayerA's serve

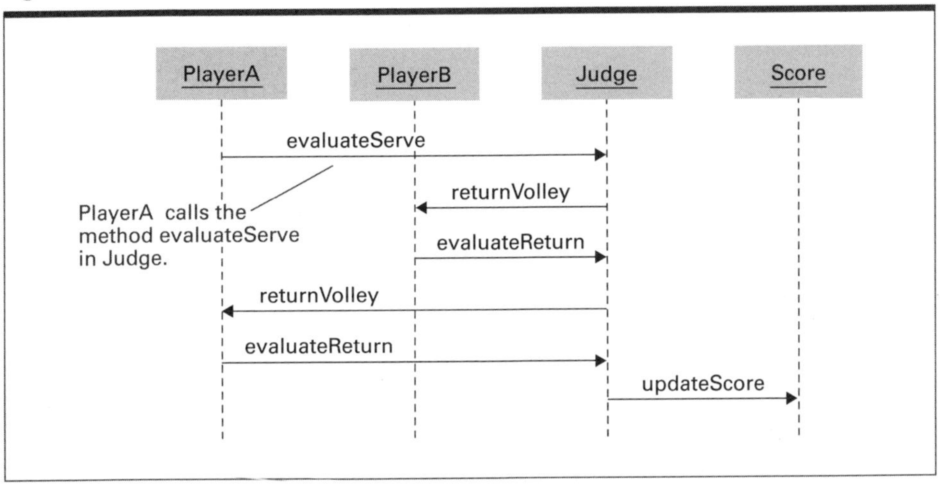

to Serve indicates that the former passes control to the latter. It is also control coupling that is represented in Figure 7.5, where the arrows trace the path of control as it is passed from object to object.

Another form of intermodule coupling is **data coupling,** which refers to the sharing of data between modules. If two modules interact with the same item of data, then modifications made to one module may affect the other, and modifications to the format of the data itself could have repercussions in both modules.

Data coupling between functions can occur in two forms. One is by explicitly passing data from one function to another in the form of parameters. Such coupling is represented in a structure chart by an arrow between the functions that is labeled to indicate the data being passed. The direction of the arrow indicates the direction in which the item is transferred. For example, Figure 7.6 is an extended version of Figure 7.3 in which we have indicated that the function ControlGame will tell the function Serve which player's characteristics are to be simulated when it calls Serve and that the function Serve will report the ball trajectory to ControlGame when Serve has completed its task.

Similar data coupling occurs between objects in an object-oriented design. For example, when PlayerA asks the object Judge to evaluate its serve (see Figure 7.5), it must pass the trajectory information to Judge. On the other hand, one of the benefits of the object-oriented paradigm is that it inherently tends to reduce data coupling between objects to a minimum. This is because the methods within an object tend to include all those functions that manipulate the object's internal data. For example, the object PlayerA will contain information regarding that player's characteristics as well as all the methods that require that information. In turn, there is no need to pass that information to other objects and thus interobject data coupling is minimized.

In contrast to passing data explicitly as parameters, data can be shared among modules implicitly in the form of **global data,** which are data items that are automatically available to all modules throughout the system, as opposed to local data items that are accessible only within a particular module unless explicitly passed to another. Most high-level languages provide ways of implementing both global and local data, but the use of global data should be employed with caution. The problem is that a person trying to modify a module that is dependent on global data may find it difficult to identify how the module in question interacts with other modules. In short, the use of global data can degrade the module's usefulness as an abstract tool.

Figure 7.6 A structure chart including data coupling

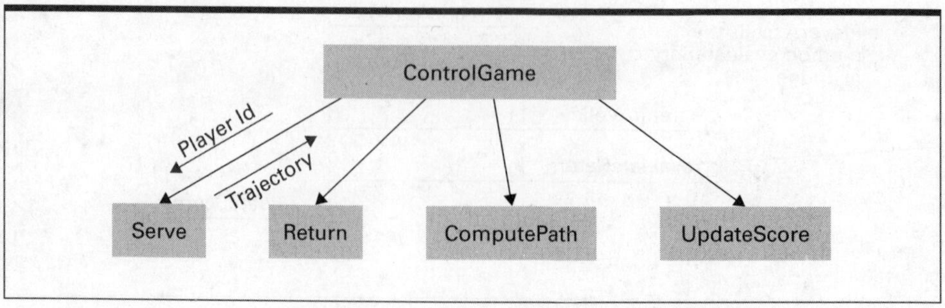

Cohesion

Just as important as minimizing the coupling between modules is maximizing the internal binding within each module. The term **cohesion** refers to this internal binding or, in other words, the degree of relatedness of a module's internal parts. To appreciate the importance of cohesion, we must look beyond the initial development of a system and consider the entire software life cycle. If it becomes necessary to make changes in a module, the existence of a variety of activities within it can confuse what would otherwise be a simple process. Thus, in addition to seeking low intermodule coupling, software designers strive for high intramodule cohesion.

A weak form of cohesion is known as **logical cohesion.** This is the cohesion within a module induced by the fact that its internal elements perform activities logically similar in nature. For example, consider a module that performs all of a system's communication with the outside world. The "glue" that holds such a module together is that all the activities within the module deal with communication. However, the topics of the communication can vary greatly. Some may deal with obtaining data, whereas others deal with reporting results.

A stronger form of cohesion is known as **functional cohesion,** which means that all the parts of the module are focused on the performance of a single activity. In an imperative design, functional cohesion can often be increased by isolating subtasks in other modules and then using these modules as abstract tools. This is demonstrated in our tennis simulation example (see again Figure 7.3) where the module `ControlGame` uses the other modules as abstract tools so that it can concentrate on overseeing the game rather than being distracted by the details of serving, returning, and maintaining the score.

In object-oriented designs, entire objects are usually only logically cohesive because the methods within an object often perform loosely related activities—the only common bond being that they are activities performed by the same object. For example, in our tennis simulation example, each player object contains methods for serving as well as returning the ball, which are significantly different activities. Such an object would therefore be only a logically cohesive module. However, software designers should strive to make each individual method within an object functionally cohesive. That is, even though the object in its entirety is only logically cohesive, each method within an object should perform only one functionally cohesive task (Figure 7.7).

Information Hiding

One of the cornerstones of good modular design is captured in the concept of **information hiding,** which refers to the restriction of information to a specific portion of a software system. Here the term *information* should be interpreted in a broad sense, including any knowledge about the structure and contents of a program unit. As such, it includes data, the type of data structures used, encoding systems, the internal compositional structure of a module, the logical structure of a procedural unit, and any other factors regarding the internal properties of a module.

The point of information hiding is to keep the actions of modules from having unnecessary dependencies or effects on other modules. Otherwise, the validity of a module may be compromised, perhaps by errors in the development of other modules or by misguided efforts during software maintenance. If, for example, a module does not restrict the use of its internal data from other modules, then that data may become corrupted by other modules. Or, if one module is designed

Figure 7.7 Logical and functional cohesion within an object

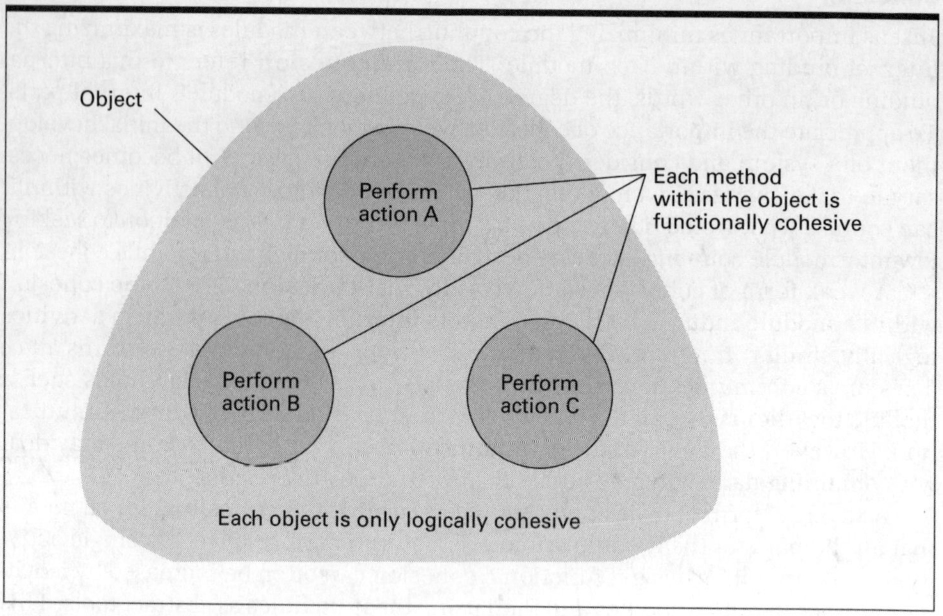

to take advantage of another's internal structure, it could malfunction later if that internal structure is altered.

It is important to note that information hiding has two incarnations—one as a design goal, the other as an implementation goal. A module should be designed so that other modules do not need access to its internal information, and a module should be implemented in a manner that reinforces its boundaries. Examples of the former are maximizing cohesion and minimizing coupling. Examples of the latter involve the use of local variables, applying encapsulation, and using well-defined control structures.

Finally we should note that information hiding is central to the theme of abstraction and the use of abstract tools. Indeed, the concept of an abstract tool is that of a "black box" whose interior features can be ignored by its user, allowing the user to concentrate on the larger application at hand. In this sense then, information hiding corresponds to the concept of sealing the abstract tool in much the same way as a tamperproof enclosure can be used to safeguard complex and potentially dangerous electronic equipment. Both protect their users from the dangers inside as well as protect their interiors from intrusion from their users.

Components

We have already mentioned that one obstacle in the field of software engineering is the lack of prefabricated "off-the-shelf" building blocks from which large software systems can be constructed. The modular approach to software development promises hope in this regard. In particular, the object-oriented programming paradigm is proving especially useful because objects form complete, self-contained units that have clearly defined interfaces with their environments. Once an object, or more correctly a class, has been designed to fulfill a certain role, it can be used to fulfill that role in any program requiring that service. Moreover, inheritance provides a means of refining prefabricated object definitions in those cases in which the definitions must be customized to conform to the needs of a specific application. It is not surprising, then, that the object-oriented programming languages C++, Java, and C# are accompanied by collections of prefabricated "templates" from which programmers can easily implement objects for performing certain roles. In particular, C++ is associated with the C++ Standard Template Library, the Java programming environment is accompanied by the Java Application Programmer Interface (API), and C# programmers have access to the .NET Framework Class Library.

The fact that objects and classes have the potential of providing prefabricated building blocks for software design does not mean that they are ideal. One problem is that they provide relatively small blocks from which to build. Thus, an object is actually a special case of the more general concept of a **component,** which is, by definition, a reusable unit of software. In practice, most components are based on the object-oriented paradigm and take the form of a collection of one or more objects that function as a self-contained unit.

Research in the development and use of components has led to the emerging field known as **component architecture** (also known as component-based software engineering) in which the traditional role of a programmer is replaced by a **component assembler** who constructs software systems from prefabricated components that, in many development environments, are displayed as icons in a graphical interface. Rather than be involved with the internal programming of the components, the methodology of a component assembler is to select pertinent components from collections of predefined components and then connect them, with minimal customization, to obtain the desired functionality. Indeed, a property of a well-designed component is that it can be extended to encompass features of a particular application without internal modifications.

An area where component architectures have found fertile ground is in smartphone systems. Due to the resource constraints of these devices, applications are actually a set of collaborating components, each of which provides some discrete

Software Engineering in the Real World

The following scenario is typical of the problems encountered by real-world software engineers. Company XYZ hires a software-engineering firm to develop and install a company-wide integrated software system to handle the company's data processing needs. As a part of the system produced by Company XYZ, a network of PCs is used to provide employees access to the company-wide system. Thus each employee finds a PC on his or her desk. Soon these PCs are used not only to access the new data management system but also as customizable tools with which each employee increases his or her productivity. For example, one employee may develop a spreadsheet program that streamlines that employee's tasks. Unfortunately, such customized applications may not be well designed or thoroughly tested and may involve features that are not completely understood by the employee. As the years go by, the use of these ad hoc applications becomes integrated into the company's internal business procedures. Moreover, the employees who developed these applications may be promoted, transferred, or quit the company, leaving others behind using a program they do not understand. The result is that what started out as a well-designed, coherent system can become dependent on a patchwork of poorly designed, undocumented, and error-prone applications.

function for the application. For example, each display screen within an application is usually a separate component. Behind the scenes, there may exist other service components to store and access information on a memory card, perform some continuous function (such as playing music), or access information over the Internet. Each of these components is individually started and stopped as needed to service the user efficiently; however, the application appears as a seamless series of displays and actions.

Aside from the motivation to limit the use of system resources, the component architecture of smartphones pays dividends in integration between applications. For example, Facebook (a well-known social networking system) when executed on a smartphone may use the components of the contacts application to add all Facebook friends as contacts. Furthermore, the telephony application (the one that handles the functions of the phone), may also access the contacts' components to lookup the caller of an incoming call. Thus, upon receiving a call from a Facebook friend, the friend's picture can be displayed on the phone's screen (along with his or her last Facebook post).

Questions & Exercises

1. How does a novel differ from an encyclopedia in terms of the degree of coupling between its units such as chapters, sections, or entries? What about cohesion?
2. A sporting event is often divided into units. For example, a baseball game is divided into innings and a tennis match is divided into sets. Analyze the coupling between such "modules." In what sense are such units cohesive?
3. Is the goal of maximizing cohesion compatible with minimizing coupling? That is, as cohesion increases, does coupling naturally tend to decrease?
4. Define coupling, cohesion, and information hiding.
5. Extend the structure chart in Figure 7.3 to include the data coupling between the modules `ControlGame` and `UpdateScore`.
6. Draw a diagram similar to that of Figure 7.5 to represent the sequence that would occur if `PlayerA`'s serve is ruled invalid.
7. What is the difference between a traditional programmer and a component assembler?
8. Assuming most smartphones have a number of personal organization applications (calendars, contacts, clocks, social networking, email systems, maps, etc.), what combinations of component functions would you find useful and interesting?

7.5 Tools of the Trade

In this section we investigate some of the modeling techniques and notational systems used during the analysis and design stages of software development. Several of these were developed during the years that the imperative paradigm dominated the software engineering discipline. Of these, some have found useful roles in the context of the object-oriented paradigm whereas others, such as the structure chart (see again Figure 7.3), are specific to the imperative paradigm. We begin by considering some of the techniques that have survived from their imperative roots and then move on to explore newer object-oriented tools as well as the expanding role of design patterns.

Some Old Friends

Although the imperative paradigm seeks to build software in terms of procedures or functions, a way of identifying those functions is to consider the data to be manipulated rather than the functions themselves. The theory is that by studying how data moves through a system, one identifies the points at which either data formats are altered or data paths merge and split. In turn, these are the locations at which processing occurs, and thus dataflow analysis leads to the identification of functions. A **dataflow diagram** is a means of representing the information gained from such dataflow studies. In a dataflow diagram, arrows represent data paths, ovals represent points at which data manipulation occurs, and rectangles represent data sources and stores. As an example, Figure 7.8 displays an elementary dataflow diagram representing a hospital's patient billing system. Note that the diagram shows that `Payments` (flowing from patients) and `PatientRecords` (flowing from the hospital's files) merge at the oval `ProcessPayments` from which `UpdatedRecords` flow back to the hospital's files.

Dataflow diagrams not only assist in identifying procedures during the design stage of software development, but they are also useful when trying to gain an understanding of the proposed system during the analysis stage. Indeed, constructing dataflow diagrams can serve as a means of improving communication between clients and software engineers (as the software engineer struggles to understand what the client wants and the client struggles to describe his or her expectations), and thus these diagrams continue to find applications even though the imperative paradigm has faded in popularity.

Another tool that has been used for years by software engineers is the **data dictionary,** which is a central repository of information about the data items appearing throughout a software system. This information includes the identifier used to reference each item, what constitutes valid entries in each item (Will the item always be numeric or perhaps always alphabetic? What will be the range of values that might be assigned to this item?), where the item is stored (Will the item be stored in a file or a database and, if so, which one?), and where the item is referenced in the software (Which modules will require the item's information?).

Figure 7.8 A simple dataflow diagram

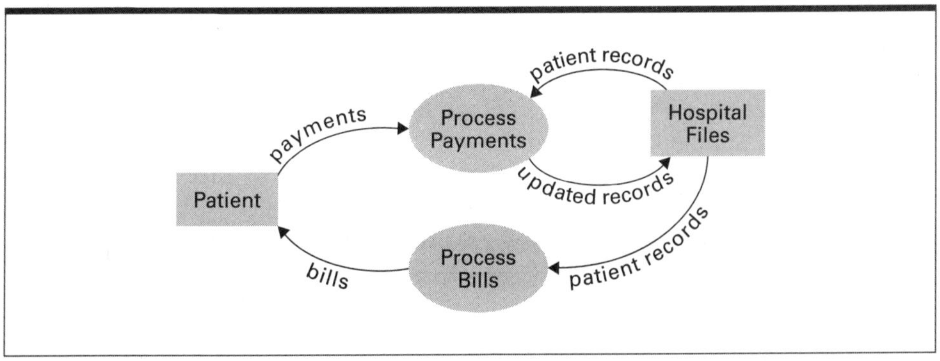

One goal of constructing a data dictionary is to improve communication between the stakeholders of a software system and the software engineer charged with the task of converting all of the stakeholder needs into a requirements specification. In this context the construction of a data dictionary helps ensure that the fact that part numbers are not really numeric will be revealed during the analysis stage rather than being discovered late in the design or implementation stages. Another goal associated with the data dictionary is to establish uniformity throughout the system. It is usually by means of constructing the dictionary that redundancies and contradictions surface. For example, the item referred to as `PartNumber` in the inventory records may be the same as the `PartId` in the sales records. Moreover, the personnel department may use the item `Name` to refer to an employee while inventory records may contain the term `Name` in reference to a part.

Unified Modeling Language

Dataflow diagrams and data dictionaries were tools in the software engineering arsenal well before the emergence of the object-oriented paradigm and have continued to find useful roles even though the imperative paradigm, for which they were originally developed, has faded in popularity. We turn now to the more modern collection of tools known as **Unified Modeling Language (UML)** that has been developed with the object-oriented paradigm in mind. The first tool that we consider within this collection, however, is useful regardless of the underlying paradigm because it attempts merely to capture the image of the proposed system from the user's point of view. This tool is the **use case diagram**—an example of which appears in Figure 7.9.

A use case diagram depicts the proposed system as a large rectangle in which interactions (called **use cases**) between the system and its users are represented as ovals and users of the system (called **actors**) are represented as stick figures (even though an actor may not be a person). Thus, the diagram in Figure 7.9 indicates that the proposed `Hospital Records System` will be used by both `Physicians` and `Nurses` to `Retrieve Medical Records`.

Whereas use case diagrams view a proposed software system from the outside, UML offers a variety of tools for representing the internal object-oriented design of a system. One of these is the **class diagram,** which is a notational system for representing the structure of classes and relationships between classes (called **associations** in UML vernacular). As an example, consider the relationships between physicians, patients, and hospital rooms. We assume that objects representing these entities are constructed from the classes `Physician`, `Patient`, and `Room`, respectively.

Figure 7.10 shows how the relationships among these classes could be represented in a UML class diagram. Classes are represented by rectangles and associations are represented by lines. Association lines may or may not be labeled. If they are labeled, a bold arrowhead can be used to indicate the direction in which the label should be read. For example, in Figure 7.10 the arrowhead following the label `cares for` indicates that a physician `cares for` a patient rather than a patient `cares for` a physician. Sometimes association lines are given two labels to provide terminology for reading the association in either direction. This is exemplified in Figure 7.10 in the association between the classes `Patient` and `Room`.

Figure 7.9 A simple use case diagram

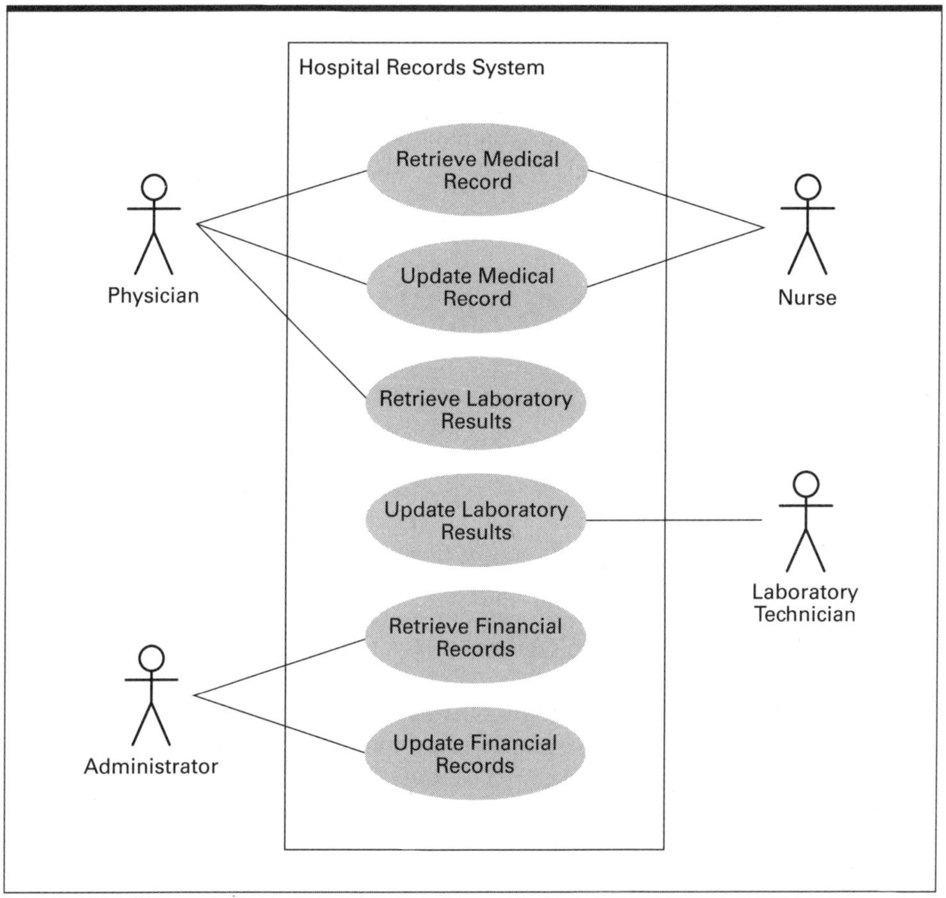

In addition to indicating associations between classes, a class diagram can also convey the multiplicities of those associations. That is, it can indicate how many instances of one class may be associated with instances of another. This information is recorded at the ends of the association lines. In particular, Figure 7.10 indicates that each patient can occupy one room and each room can host zero or one patient. (We are assuming that each room is a private room.) An asterisk is used to indicate an arbitrary nonnegative number. Thus, the asterisk in Figure 7.10 indicates that each physician may care for many patients, whereas the 1 at the physician end of the association means that each patient is cared for by only one physician. (Our design considers only the role of primary physicians.)

For the sake of completeness, we should note that association multiplicities occur in three basic forms: one-to-one relationships, one-to-many relationships,

Figure 7.10 A simple class diagram

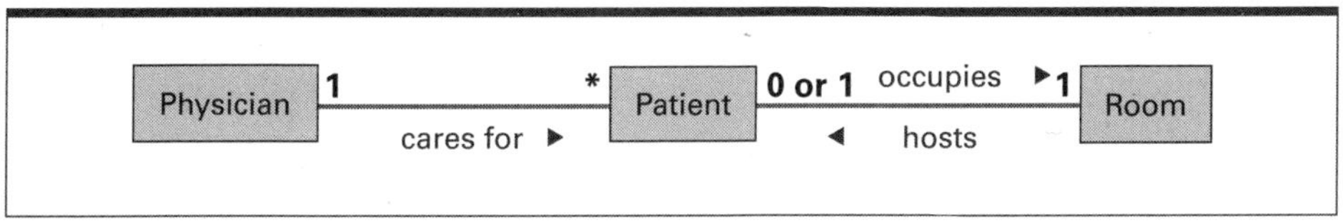

and many-to-many relationships as summarized in Figure 7.11. A **one-to-one relationship** is exemplified by the association between patients and occupied private rooms in that each patient is associated with only one room and each room is associated with only one patient. A **one-to-many relationship** is exemplified by the association between physicians and patients in that one physician is associated with many patients and each patient is associated with one (primary) physician. A **many-to-many relationship** would occur if we included consulting physicians in the physician–patient relationship. Then each physician could be associated with many patients and each patient could be associated with many physicians.

In an object-oriented design it is often the case that one class represents a more specific version of another. In those situations we say that the latter class is a generalization of the former. UML provides a special notation for representing generalizations. An example is given in Figure 7.12, which depicts the generalizations among the classes `MedicalRecord`, `SurgicalRecord`, and `OfficeVisitRecord`. There the associations between the classes are represented by arrows with hollow arrowheads, which is the UML notation for associations that are generalizations. Note that each class is represented by a rectangle containing the name, attributes, and methods of the class in the format introduced in Figure 7.4. This is UML's way of representing the internal characteristics of a class in a class diagram. The information portrayed in Figure 7.12 is that the class `MedicalRecord` is a generalization of the class `SurgicalRecord` as well as a generalization of `OfficeVisitRecord`. That is, the classes `SurgicalRecord` and `OfficeVisitRecord` contain all the features of the class `MedicalRecord` plus those features explicitly listed inside their appropriate rectangles. Thus, both the `SurgicalRecord` and the `OfficeVisitRecord` classes contain patient, doctor, and date of record, but the `SurgicalRecord` class also contains surgical procedure, hospital, discharge date, and the ability to discharge a patient, whereas the `OfficeVisitRecord` class contains symptoms and diagnosis. All three

Figure 7.11 One-to-one, one-to-many, and many-to-many relationships between entities of types X and Y

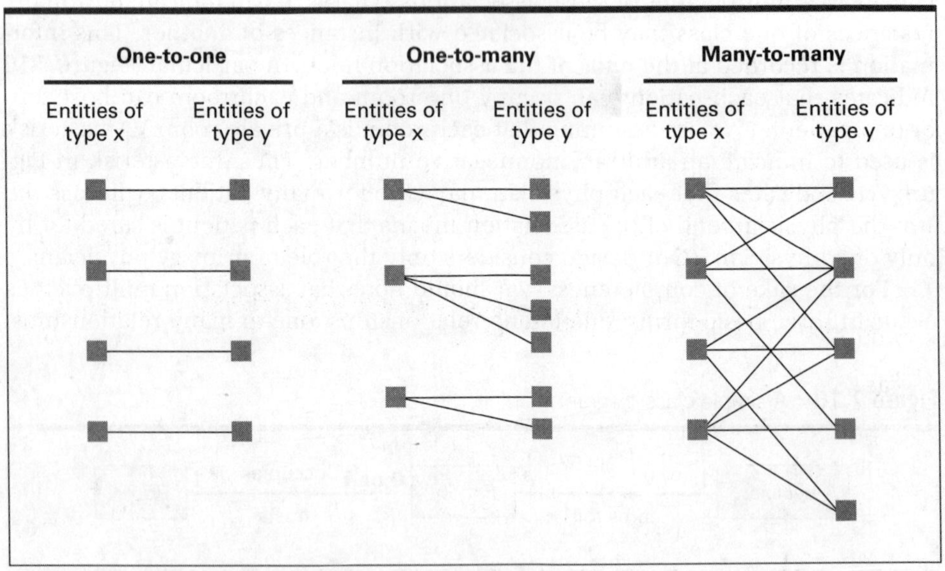

Figure 7.12 A class diagram depicting generalizations

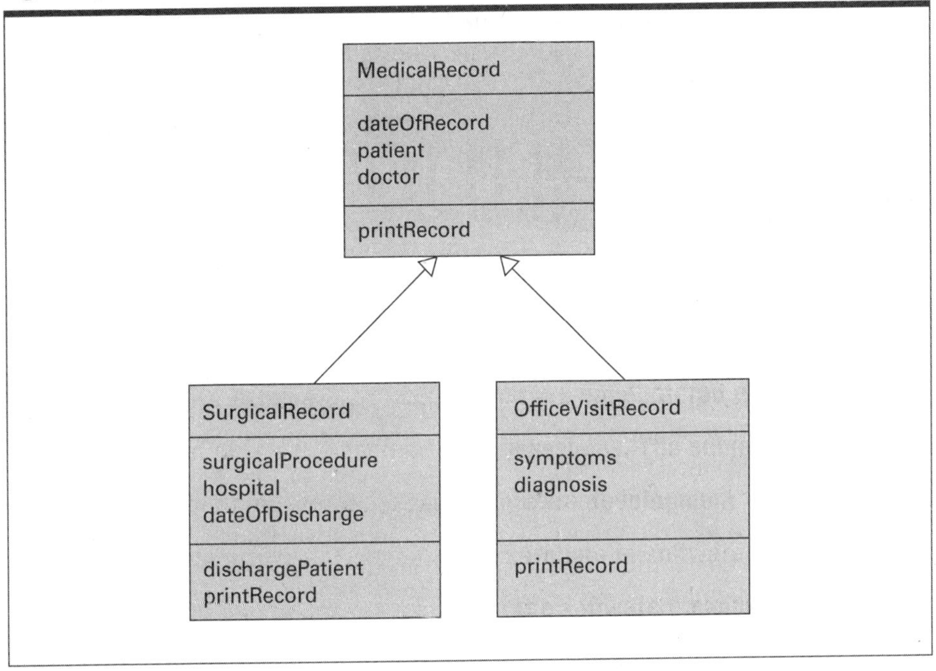

classes have the ability to print the medical record. The `printRecord` method in `SurgicalRecord` and `OfficeVisitRecord` are specializations of the `printRecord` method in `MedicalRecord`, each of which will print the information specific to its class.

Recall from Chapter 6 (Section 6.5) that a natural way of implementing generalizations in an object-oriented programming environment is to use inheritance. However, many software engineers caution that inheritance is not appropriate for all cases of generalization. The reason is that inheritance introduces a strong degree of coupling between the classes—a coupling that may not be desirable later in the software's life cycle. For example, because changes within a class are reflected automatically in all the classes that inherit from it, what may appear to be minor modifications during software maintenance can lead to unforeseen consequences. As an example, suppose a company opened a recreation facility for its employees, meaning that all people with membership in the recreation facility are employees. To develop a membership list for this facility, a programmer could use inheritance to construct a `RecreationMember` class from a previously defined `Employee` class. But, if the company later prospers and decides to open the recreation facility to dependents of employees or perhaps company retirees, then the embedded coupling between the `Employee` class and the `RecreationMember` class would have to be severed. Thus, inheritance should not be used merely for convenience. Instead, it should be restricted to those cases in which the generalization being implemented is immutable.

Class diagrams represent static features of a program's design. They do not represent sequences of events that occur during execution. To express such dynamic features, UML provides a variety of diagram types that are collectively known as **interaction diagrams.** One type of interaction diagram is the **sequence diagram** that depicts the communication between the individuals (such as actors, complete software components, or individual objects) that are involved in performing a task. These diagrams are similar to Figure 7.5 in that they represent the individuals by rectangles with dashed lines extending downward. Each rectangle together with its dashed line is called a **life line.** Communication between the individuals is represented by labeled arrows connecting the appropriate life line, where the label indicates the action being requested. These arrows appear chronologically as the diagram is read from top to bottom. The communication that occurs when an individual completes a requested task and returns control back to the requesting individual, as in the traditional return from a procedure, is represented by an unlabeled arrow pointing back to the original life line.

Thus, Figure 7.5 is essentially a sequence diagram. However, the syntax of Figure 7.5 alone has several shortcomings. One is that it does not allow us to capture the symmetry between the two players. We must draw a separate diagram to represent a volley starting with a serve from `PlayerB`, even though the interaction sequence is very similar to that when `PlayerA` serves. Moreover, whereas Figure 7.5 depicts only a specific volley, a general volley may extend indefinitely. Formal sequence diagrams have techniques for capturing these variations in a single diagram, and although we do not need to study these in detail, we should still take a brief look at the formal sequence diagram shown in Figure 7.13, which depicts a general volley based on our tennis game design.

Note also that Figure 7.13 demonstrates that an entire sequence diagram is enclosed in a rectangle (called a **frame**). In the upper left-hand corner of the frame is a pentagon containing the characters *sd* (meaning "sequence diagram")

Figure 7.13 A sequence diagram depicting a generic volley

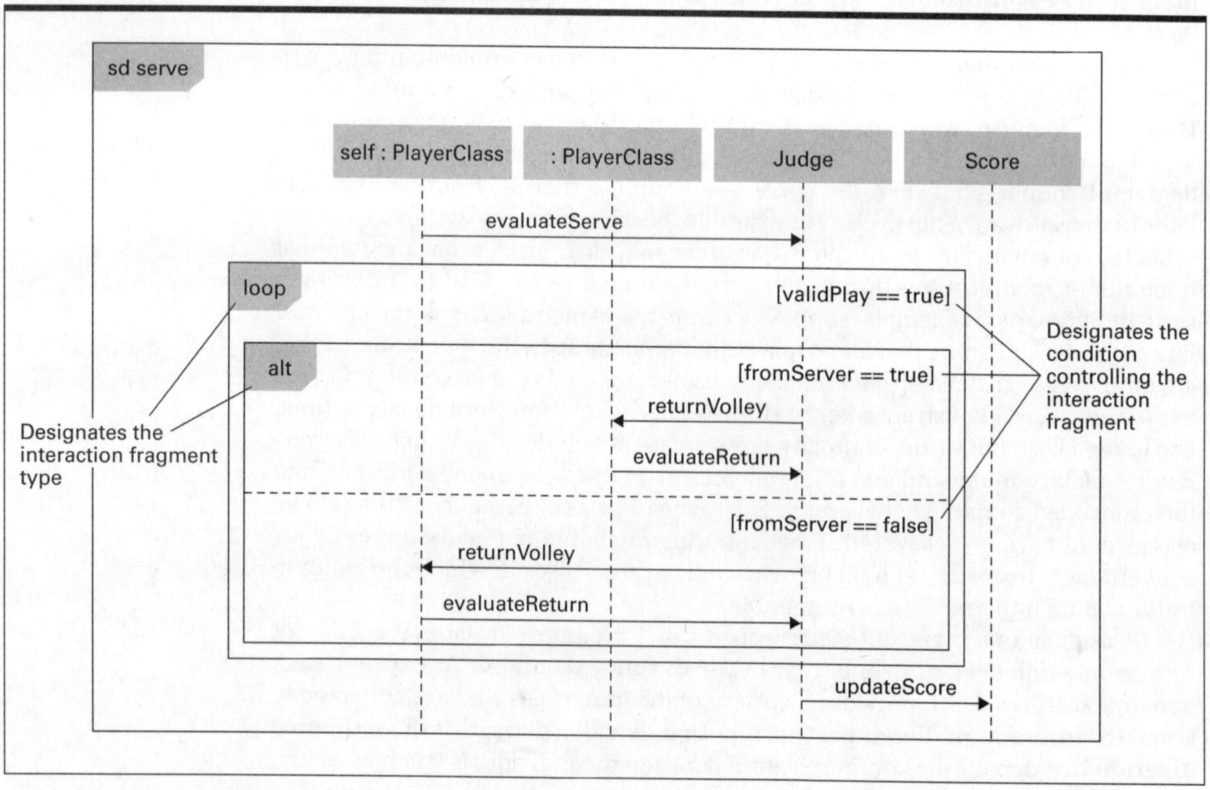

followed by an identifier. This identifier may be a name identifying the overall sequence or, as in Figure 7.13, the name of the method that is called to initiate the sequence. Note that in contrast to Figure 7.5, the rectangles representing the players in Figure 7.13 do not refer to specific players but merely indicate that they represent objects of the "type" `PlayerClass`. One of these is designated *self*, meaning that it is the one whose serve method is activated to initiate the sequence.

The other point to make regarding Figure 7.13 deals with the two inner rectangles. These are **interaction fragments,** which are used to represent alternative sequences within one diagram. Figure 7.13 contains two interaction fragments. One is labeled "loop," the other is labeled "alt." These are essentially the while and if-else structures that we first encountered in Python in Section 5.2. The "loop" interaction fragment indicates that the events within its boundaries are to be repeated as long as the `Judge` object determines that the value of `validPlay` is true. The "alt" interaction fragment indicates that one of its alternatives is to be performed depending on whether the value of `fromServer` is true or false.

Finally, although they are not a part of UML, it is appropriate at this point to introduce the role of **CRC (class-responsibility-collaboration) cards** because they play an important role in validating object-oriented designs. A CRC card is simply a card, such as an index card, on which the description of an object is written. The methodology of CRC cards is for the software designer to produce a card for each object in a proposed system and then to use the cards to represent the objects in a simulation of the system—perhaps on a desktop or via a "theatrical" experiment in which each member of the design team holds a card and plays the role of the object as described by that card. Such simulations (often called **structured walkthroughs**) have been found useful in identifying flaws in a design prior to the design's implementation.

Design Patterns

An increasingly powerful tool for software engineers is the growing collection of design patterns. A **design pattern** is a predeveloped model for solving a recurring problem in software design. For example, the Adapter pattern provides a solution to a problem that often occurs when constructing software from prefabricated modules. In particular, a prefabricated module may have the functionality needed to solve the problem at hand but may not have an interface that is compatible with the current application. In such cases the Adapter pattern provides a standard approach to "wrapping" that module inside another module that translates between the original module's interface and the outside world, thus allowing the original, prefabricated module to be used in the application.

Another well-established design pattern is the Decorator pattern. It provides a means of designing a system that performs different combinations of the same activities depending on the situation at the time. Such systems can lead to an explosion of options that, without careful design, can result in enormously complex software. However, the Decorator pattern provides a standardized way of implementing such systems that leads to a manageable solution.

The identification of recurring problems as well as the creation and cataloging of design patterns for solving them is an ongoing process in software engineering. The goal, however, is not merely to find solutions to design problems but to find high-quality solutions that provide flexibility later in the software life cycle. Thus, considerations of good design principles such as minimizing coupling and maximizing cohesion play an important role in the development of design patterns.

The results of progress in design pattern development are reflected in the library of tools provided in today's software development packages such as the Java programming environments provided by Oracle and the .NET Framework provided by Microsoft. Indeed, many of the templates found in these tool kits are essentially design pattern skeletons that lead to ready-made, high-quality solutions to design problems.

In closing, we should mention that the emergence of design patterns in software engineering is an example of how diverse fields can contribute to each other. The origins of design patterns lie in the research of Christopher Alexander in traditional architecture. His goal was to identify features that contribute to high-quality architectural designs for buildings or building complexes and then to develop design patterns that incorporated those features. Today, many of his ideas have been incorporated into software design and his work continues to be an inspiration for many software engineers.

Questions & Exercises

1. Draw a dataflow diagram representing the flow of data that occurs when a patron checks a book out of a library.
2. Draw a use case diagram of a library records system.
3. Draw a class diagram representing the relationship between travelers and the hotels in which they stay.
4. Draw a class diagram representing the fact that a person is a generalization of an employee. Include some attributes that might belong to each.
5. Convert Figure 7.5 into a complete sequence diagram.
6. What role in the software engineering process do design patterns play?

7.6 Quality Assurance

The proliferation of software malfunctions, cost overruns, and missed deadlines demands that methods of software quality control be improved. In this section we consider some of the directions being pursued in this endeavor.

The Scope of Quality Assurance

In the early years of computing, the problem of producing quality software focused on removing programming errors that occurred during implementation. Later in this section we will discuss the progress that has been made in this direction. However, today, the scope of software quality control extends far beyond the debugging process, with branches including the improvement of software engineering procedures, the development of training programs that in many cases lead to certification, and the establishment of standards on which sound software engineering can be based. In this regard, we have already noted the role of organizations such as ISO, IEEE, and ACM in improving professionalism and establishing standards for assessing quality control within software development companies. A specific example is the ISO 9000 series of standards, which address numerous industrial activities such as design, production, installation, and servicing. Another example is ISO/IEC 15504, which is a set of standards developed jointly by the ISO and the International Electrotechnical Commission (IEC).

Many major software contractors now require that the organizations they hire to develop software meet such standards. As a result, software development companies are establishing **software quality assurance (SQA)** groups, which are charged with overseeing and enforcing the quality control systems adopted by the organization. Thus, in the case of the traditional waterfall model, the SQA group would be charged with the task of approving the software requirements specification before the design stage began or approving the design and its related documents before implementation was initiated.

Several themes underlie today's quality control efforts. One is record keeping. It is paramount that each step in the development process be accurately documented for future reference. However, this goal conflicts with human nature. At issue is the temptation to make decisions or change decisions without updating the related documents. The result is the chance that records will be incorrect and hence their use at future stages will be misleading. Herein lies an important benefit of CASE tools. They make such tasks as redrawing diagrams and updating data dictionaries much easier than with manual methods. Consequently, updates are more likely to be made and the final documentation is more likely to be accurate. (This example is only one of many instances in which software engineering must cope with the faults of human nature. Others include the inevitable personality conflicts, jealousies, and ego clashes that arise when people work together.)

Another quality-oriented theme is the use of reviews in which various parties involved in a software development project meet to consider a specific topic. Reviews occur throughout the software development process, taking the form of requirements reviews, design reviews, and implementation reviews. They may appear as a prototype demonstration in the early stages of requirements analysis,

System Design Tragedies

The need for good design disciplines is exemplified by the problems encountered in the Therac-25, which was a computer-based electron-accelerator radiation-therapy system used by the medical community in the middle 1980s. Flaws in the machine's design contributed to six cases of radiation overdose—three of which resulted in death. The flaws included (1) a poor design for the machine's interface that allowed the operator to begin radiation before the machine had adjusted for the proper dosage, and (2) poor coordination between the design of the hardware and software that resulted in the absence of certain safety features.

In more recent cases, poor design has led to widespread power outages, severance of telephone service, major errors in financial transactions, loss of space probes, and disruption of the Internet. You can learn more about such problems through the Risks Forum at `http://catless.ncl.ac.uk/Risks`.

as a structured walkthrough among members of the software design team, or as coordination among programmers who are implementing related portions of the design. Such reviews, on a recurring basis, provide communication channels through which misunderstandings can be avoided and errors can be corrected before they grow into disasters. The significance of reviews is exemplified by the fact that they are specifically addressed in the IEEE Standard for Software Reviews, known as IEEE 1028.

Some reviews are pivotal in nature. An example is the review between representatives of a project's stakeholders and the software development team at which the final software requirements specification is approved. Indeed, this approval marks the end of the formal requirements analysis phase and is the basis on which the remaining development will progress. However, all reviews are significant, and for the sake of quality control, they should be documented as part of the ongoing record maintenance process.

Software Testing

Whereas software quality assurance is now recognized as a subject that permeates the entire development process, testing and verification of the programs themselves continues to be a topic of research. In Section 5.6 we discussed techniques for verifying the correctness of algorithms in a mathematically rigorous manner but concluded that most software today is "verified" by means of testing. Unfortunately, such testing is inexact at best. We cannot guarantee that a piece of software is correct via testing unless we run enough tests to exhaust all possible scenarios. But, even in simple programs, there may be billions of different paths that could potentially be traversed. Thus, testing all possible paths within a complex program is an impossible task.

On the other hand, software engineers have developed testing methodologies that improve the odds of revealing errors in software with a limited number of tests. One of these is based on the observation that errors in software tend to be clumped. That is, experience has shown that a small number of modules within a large software system tend to be more problematic than the rest. Thus, by identifying these modules and testing them more thoroughly, more of the system's errors can be discovered than if all modules were tested in a uniform, less-thorough manner. This is an instance of the proposition known as the **Pareto principle,** in reference to the economist and sociologist Vilfredo Pareto (1848 – 1923) who observed that a small part of Italy's population controlled most of Italy's wealth. In the field of software engineering, the Pareto principle states that results can often be increased most rapidly by applying efforts in a concentrated area.

Another software testing methodology, called **basis path testing,** is to develop a set of test data that insures that each instruction in the software is executed at least once. Techniques using an area of mathematics known as graph theory have been developed for identifying such sets of test data. Thus, although it may be impossible to ensure that every path through a software system is tested, it is possible to ensure that every statement within the system is executed at least once during the testing process.

Techniques based on the Pareto principle and basis path testing rely on knowledge of the internal composition of the software being tested. They therefore fall within the category called **glass-box testing**—meaning that the software tester is aware of the interior structure of the software and uses this knowledge when designing the test. In contrast is the category called **black-box testing,** which refers to tests that do not rely on knowledge of the software's interior composition. In short, black-box testing is performed from the user's point of view. In black-box testing, one is not concerned with how the software goes about its task but merely with whether the software performs correctly in terms of accuracy and timeliness.

An example of black-box testing is the technique, called **boundary value analysis,** that consists of identifying ranges of data, called **equivalence classes,** over which the software should perform in a similar manner and then testing the software on data close to the edge of those ranges. For example, if the software is supposed to accept input values within a specified range, then the software would be tested at the lowest and highest values in that range, or if the software is supposed to coordinate multiple activities, then the software would be tested on the largest possible collection of activities. The underlying theory is that by identifying equivalence classes, the number of test cases can be minimized because correct operation for a few examples within an equivalence class tends to validate the software for the entire class. Moreover, the best chance of identifying an error within a class is to use data at the class edges.

Another methodology that falls within the black-box category is **beta testing** in which a preliminary version of the software is given to a segment of the intended audience with the goal of learning how the software performs in real-life situations before the final version of the product is solidified and released to the market. (Similar testing performed at the developer's site is called **alpha testing.**) The advantages of beta testing extend far beyond the traditional discovery of errors. General customer feedback (both positive and negative) is obtained that may assist in refining market strategies. Moreover, early distribution of beta software assists other software developers in designing compatible products. For example, in the case of a new operating system for the PC market, the distribution of a beta version encourages the development of compatible utility software so that the final operating system ultimately appears on store shelves surrounded by companion products. Moreover, the existence of beta testing can generate a feeling of anticipation within the marketplace—an atmosphere that increases publicity and sales.

Questions & Exercises

1. What is the role of the SQA group within a software development organization?
2. In what ways does human nature work against quality assurance?
3. Identify two themes that are applied throughout the development process to enhance quality.
4. When testing software, is a successful test one that does or does not find errors?
5. What techniques would you propose using to identify the modules within a system that should receive more thorough testing than others?
6. What would be a good test to perform on a software package that was designed to sort a list of no more than 100 entries?

7.7 Documentation

A software system is of little use unless people can learn to use and maintain it. Hence, documentation is an important part of a final software package, and its development is, therefore, an important topic in software engineering.

Software documentation serves three purposes, leading to three categories of documentation: user documentation, system documentation, and technical documentation. The purpose of **user documentation** is to explain the features of the software and describe how to use them. It is intended to be read by the user of the software and is therefore expressed in the terminology of the application.

Today, user documentation is recognized as an important marketing tool. Good user documentation combined with a well-designed user interface makes a software package accessible and thus increases its sales. Recognizing this, many software developers hire technical writers to produce this part of their product, or they provide preliminary versions of their products to independent authors so that how-to books are available in book stores when the software is released to the public.

User documentation traditionally takes the form of a physical book or booklet, but in many cases the same information is included as part of the software itself. This allows a user to refer to the documentation while using the software. In this case the information may be broken into small units, sometimes called help packages, that may appear on the display screen automatically if the user dallies too long between commands.

The purpose of **system documentation** is to describe the software's internal composition so that the software can be maintained later in its life cycle. A major component of system documentation is the source version of all the programs in the system. It is important that these programs be presented in a readable format, which is why software engineers support the use of well-designed, high-level programming languages, the use of comment statements for annotating a program, and a modular design that allows each module to be presented as a coherent unit. In fact, most companies that produce software products have adopted conventions for their employees to follow when writing programs. These include indentation conventions for organizing a program on the written page; naming conventions that establish a distinction between names of different program constructs such as variables, constants, objects, and classes; and documentation conventions to ensure that all programs are sufficiently documented. Such conventions establish uniformity throughout a company's software, which ultimately simplifies the software maintenance process.

Another component of system documentation is a record of the design documents including the software requirements specification and records showing how these specifications were obtained during design. This information is useful during software maintenance because it indicates why the software was implemented as it was—information that reduces the chance that changes made during maintenance will disrupt the integrity of the system.

The purpose of **technical documentation** is to describe how a software system should be installed and serviced (such as adjusting operating parameters, installing updates, and reporting problems back to the software's developer). Technical documentation of software is analogous to the documentation provided to mechanics in the automobile industry. This documentation does not discuss how the car was designed and constructed (analogous to system documentation), nor does it explain how to drive the car and operate its heating/cooling system (analogous to user documentation). Instead, it describes how to service the car's components—for example, how to replace the transmission or how to track down an intermittent electrical problem.

The distinction between technical documentation and user documentation is blurred in the PC arena because the user is often the person who also installs and services the software. However, in multiuser environments, the distinction is sharper. Therefore, technical documentation is intended for the system administrator who is responsible for servicing all the software under his or her jurisdiction, allowing the users to access the software packages as abstract tools.

Questions & Exercises

1. In what forms can software be documented?
2. At what phase (or phases) in the software life cycle is system documentation prepared?
3. Which is more important, a program or its documentation?

7.8 The Human-Machine Interface

Recall from Section 7.2 that one of the tasks during requirements analysis is to define how the proposed software system will interact with its environment. In this section we consider topics associated with this interaction when it involves communicating with humans—a subject with profound significances. After all, humans should be allowed to use a software system as an abstract tool. This tool should be easy to apply and designed to minimize (ideally eliminate) communication errors between the system and its human users. This means that the system's interface should be designed for the convenience of humans rather than merely the expediency of the software system.

The importance of good interface design is further emphasized by the fact that a system's interface is likely to make a stronger impression on a user than any other system characteristic. After all, a human tends to view a system in terms of its usability, not in terms of how cleverly it performs its internal tasks. From a human's perspective, the choice between two competing systems is likely to be based on the systems' interfaces. Thus, the design of a system's interface can ultimately be the determining factor in the success or failure of a software engineering project.

For these reasons, the human-machine interface has become an important concern in the requirements stage of software development projects and is a growing subfield of software engineering. In fact, some would argue that the study of human-machine interfaces is an entire field in its own right.

A beneficiary of research in this field is the smartphone interface. In order to attain the goal of a convenient pocket-sized device, elements of the traditional human-machine interface (full-sized keyboard, mouse, scroll bars, menus) are being replaced with new approaches; such as gestures performed on a touch screen, voice commands, and virtual keyboards with advanced autocompletion of words and phrases. While these represent significant progress, most smartphone users would argue that there is plenty of room for further innovation.

Research in human-machine interface design draws heavily from the areas of engineering called **ergonomics,** which deals with designing systems that harmonize with the physical abilities of humans, and **cognetics,** which deals with designing systems that harmonize with the mental abilities of humans. Of the two, ergonomics is the better understood, largely because humans have been interacting physically with machines for centuries. Examples are found in ancient tools, weaponry, and transportation systems. Much of this history is self-evident; however, at times the application of ergonomics has been counterintuitive. An often-cited example is the design of the typewriter keyboard (now reincarnated as the computer keyboard) in which the keys were intentionally arranged to reduce a typist's speed so that the mechanical system of levers used in the early machines would not jam.

Mental interaction with machines, in contrast, is a relatively new phenomenon, and thus, it is cognetics that offers the higher potential for fruitful research and enlightening insights. Often the findings are interesting in their subtlety. For example, humans form habits—a trait that, on the surface, is good because it can increase efficiency. But, habits can also lead to errors, even when the design of an interface intentionally addresses the problem. Consider the process of a human asking a typical operating system to delete a file. To avoid unintentional deletions, most interfaces respond to such a request by asking the user to confirm the request—perhaps via a message such as, "Do you really want to delete this file?" At first glance, this confirmation requirement would seem to resolve any problem of unintentional deletions. However, after using the system for an extended period, a human develops the habit of automatically answering the question with "yes." Thus, the task of deleting a file ceases to be a two-step process consisting of a delete command followed by a thoughtful response to a question. Instead, it becomes a one-step "delete-yes" process, meaning that by the time the human realizes that an incorrect delete request has been submitted, the request has already been confirmed and the deletion has occurred.

The formation of habits may also cause problems when a human is required to use several application software packages. The interfaces of such packages may be similar yet different. Similar user actions may result in different system responses or similar system responses may require different user actions. In these cases habits developed in one application may lead to errors in the other applications.

Another human characteristic that concerns researchers in human-machine interface design is the narrowness of a human's attention, which tends to become more focused as the level of concentration increases. As a human becomes more engrossed in the task at hand, breaking that focus becomes more difficult. In 1972, a commercial aircraft crashed because the pilots became so absorbed with a landing gear problem (actually, with the process of changing the landing gear indicator light bulb) that they allowed the plane to fly into the ground, even though warnings were sounding in the cockpit.

Less critical examples appear routinely in PC interfaces. For example, a "Caps Lock" light is provided on most keyboards to indicate that the keyboard is in "Caps Lock" mode (i.e., the "Caps Lock" key has been pressed). However, if the key is accidentally pressed, a human rarely notices the status of the light until strange characters begin to appear on the display screen. Even then, the user often puzzles over the predicament for a while until realizing the cause of the problem. In a sense, this is not surprising—the light on the keyboard is not in the user's field of view. However, users often fail to notice indicators placed directly in their line of sight. For example, users can become so engaged in a task that they fail to observe changes in the appearance of the cursor on the display screen, even though their task involves watching the cursor.

Still another human characteristic that must be anticipated during interface design is the mind's limited capacity to deal with multiple facts simultaneously. In an article in *Psychological Review* in 1956, George A. Miller reported research indicating that the human mind is capable of dealing with only about seven details at once. Thus, it is important that an interface be designed to present all the relevant information when a decision is required rather than to rely on the human user's memory. In particular, it would be poor design to require that a human remember precise details from previous screen images. Moreover, if an interface requires extensive navigation among screen images, a human can get lost in the maze. Thus, the content and arrangement of screen images becomes an important design issue.

Although applications of ergonomics and cognetics give the field of human-machine interface design a unique flavor, the field also encompasses many of the more traditional topics of software engineering. In particular, the search for metrics is just as important in the field of interface design as it is in the more traditional areas of software engineering. Interface characteristics that have been subjected to measurement include the time required to learn an interface, the time required to perform tasks via the interface, the rate of user-interface errors, the degree to which a user retains proficiency with the interface after periods of nonuse, and even such subjective traits as the degree to which users like the interface.

The **GOMS** (rhymes with "Toms") model, originally introduced in 1954, is representative of the search for metrics in the field of human-machine interface design. The model's underlying methodology is to analyze tasks in terms of user goals (such as delete a word from a text), operators (such as click the mouse button), methods (such as double-click the mouse button and press the delete key), and selection rules (such as choose between two methods of accomplishing the same goal). This, in fact, is the origin of the acronym GOMS—goals, operators, methods, and selection rules. In short, GOMS is a methodology that allows the actions of a human using an interface to be analyzed as sequences of elementary steps (press a key, move the mouse, make a decision). The performance of each elementary step is assigned a precise time period, and thus, by adding the times assigned to the steps in a task, GOMS provides a means of comparing different proposed interfaces in terms of the time each would require when performing similar tasks.

Understanding the technical details of systems such as GOMS is not the purpose of our current study. The point in our case is that GOMS is founded on features of human behavior (moving hands, making decisions, and so on). In fact, the development of GOMS was originally considered a topic in psychology. Thus, GOMS reemphasizes the role that human characteristics play in the field of human-machine interface design, even in the topics that are carryovers from traditional software engineering.

The design of human-machine interfaces promises to be an active field of research in the foreseeable future. Many issues dealing with today's GUIs are yet unresolved, and a multitude of additional problems lurk in the use of three-dimensional interfaces that are now on the horizon. Indeed, because these interfaces promise to combine audio and tactile communication with three-dimensional vision, the scope of potential problems is enormous.

Questions & Exercises

1. a. Identify an application of ergonomics in the field of human-computer interface design.
   b. Identify an application of cognetics in the field of human-computer interface design.
2. A notable difference in the human-computer interface of a smartphone from that of a desktop computer are the techniques used to scroll a portion of the display. On a desktop, scroll is typically achieved by dragging the mouse on scrollbars displayed on the right and bottom sides of the scrolling region, or by using scroll wheels built into the mouse. On the other hand, scroll bars are often not used on a smartphone. (If used, they appear as thin lines to indicate what portion of the underlying display is currently visible.) Scrolling is thus achieved by the gesture of a sliding touch across the display screen.
   a. Based on ergonomics, what arguments can be made in support of this difference?
   b. Based on cognetics, what arguments can be made in support of this difference?
3. What distinguishes the field of human-machine interface design from the more traditional field of software engineering?
4. Identify three human characteristics that should be considered when designing a human-machine interface.

7.9 Software Ownership and Liability

Most would agree that a company or individual should be allowed to recoup, and profit from, the investment needed to develop quality software. Otherwise, it is unlikely that many would be willing to undertake the task of producing the software our society desires. In short, software developers need a level of ownership over the software they produce.

Legal efforts to provide such ownership fall under the category of **intellectual property** law, much of which is based on the well-established principles of copyright and patent law. Indeed, the purpose of a copyright or patent is to allow the developer of a product to release that product (or portions thereof) to intended parties while protecting his or her ownership rights. As such, the developer of a product (whether an individual or a corporation) will assert his or her ownership by including a copyright statement in all produced works; including requirement specifications, design documents, source code, test plans, and in some visible place within the final product. A copyright notice clearly identifies ownership, the personnel authorized to use the work, and other restrictions. Furthermore, the rights of the developer are formally expressed in legal terms in a **software license.**

A software license is a legal agreement between the owner and user of a software product that grants the user certain permissions to use the product without transferring ownership rights to the intellectual property. These agreements spell out, to a fine level of detail, the rights and obligations of both parties. Thus, it is important to carefully read and understand the terms of the software license before installing and using a software product.

While copyrights and software license agreements provide legal avenues to inhibit outright copying and unauthorized use of software, they are generally insufficient to prevent another party from independently developing a product with a nearly identical function. It is sad that over the years there have been many occasions where the developer of a truly revolutionary software product was unable to capitalize fully on his or her invention (two notable examples are spreadsheets and web browsers). In most of these cases, another company was successful in developing a competitive product that secured a dominant share of the market. A legal path to prevent this intrusion by a competitor is found in patent law.

Patent laws were established to allow an inventor to benefit commercially from an invention. To obtain a patent, the inventor must disclose the details of the invention and demonstrate that it is new, useful, and not obvious to others with similar backgrounds (a requirement that can be quite challenging for software). If a patent is granted, the inventor is given the right to prevent others from making, using, selling, or importing the invention for a limited period of time, which is typically 20 years from the date the patent application was filed.

One drawback to the use of patents is that the process to obtain a patent is expensive and time-consuming, often involving several years. During this time a software product could become obsolete, and until the patent is granted the applicant has only questionable authority to exclude others from appropriating the product.

The importance of recognizing copyrights, software licenses, and patents is paramount in the software engineering process. When developing a software product, software engineers often choose to incorporate software from other products, whether it be an entire product, subset of components, or even portions of source code downloaded over the Internet. However, failure to honor intellectual property rights during this process may lead to huge liabilities and consequences. For example, in 2004, a little-known company, NPT Inc., successfully won a lawsuit against Research In Motion (RIM—the makers of the BlackBerry smartphones) for patent infringement of a few key technologies embedded in RIM's email systems. The judgment included an injunction to suspend email services to all BlackBerry users in the United States! RIM eventually reached an agreement to pay NPT a total of $612.5 million, thereby averting a shutdown.

Finally, we should address the issue of liability. To protect themselves against liability, software developers often include disclaimers in the software licenses that state the limitations of their liability. Such statements as "In no event will Company X be liable for any damages arising out of the use of this software" are common. Courts, however, rarely recognize a disclaimer if the plaintiff can show negligence on the part of the defendant. Thus liability cases tend to focus on whether the defendant used a level of care compatible with the product being produced. A level of care that might be deemed acceptable in the case of developing a word processing system may be considered negligent when developing software to control a nuclear reactor. Consequently, one of the best defenses against software liability claims is to apply sound software engineering principles during the software's development, to use a level of care compatible with the software's application, and to produce and maintain records that validate these endeavors.

Questions & Exercises

1. What is the significance of a copyright notice in requirement specifications, design documents, source code, and the final product?
2. In what ways are copyright and patent laws designed to benefit society?
3. To what extent are disclaimers not recognized by the courts?

Chapter Review Problems

(Asterisked problems are associated with optional sections.)

1. Give an example of how efforts in the development of software can pay dividends later in software maintenance.
2. What is throwaway prototyping?
3. Explain how the lack of metrics for measuring certain software properties affects the software engineering discipline.
4. Would you expect a metric for measuring the complexity of a software system to be cumulative in the sense that the complexity of a complete system would be the sum of the complexities of its parts? Explain your answer.
5. Would you expect a metric for measuring the complexity of a software system to be commutative in the sense that the complexity of a complete system would be the same if it were originally developed with feature X and had feature Y added later or if it were originally developed with feature Y and had feature X added later? Explain your answer.
6. How does software engineering differ from other, more traditional fields of engineering such as electrical and mechanical engineering?
7. a. Identify a disadvantage of the traditional waterfall model for software development.
   b. Identify an advantage of the traditional waterfall model for software development.
8. Is open-source development a top-down or bottom-up methodology? Explain your answer.
9. Describe how the use of constants rather than literals can simplify software maintenance.
10. What is the difference between coupling and cohesion? Which should be minimized and which should be maximized? Why?
11. Select an object from everyday life and analyze its components in terms of functional or logical cohesion.
12. Contrast the coupling between two program units obtained by a simple `goto` statement with the coupling obtained by a function call.
13. In Chapter 6 we learned that parameters can be passed to functions by value or by reference. Which provides the more complex form of data coupling? Explain your answer.
14. What problems could arise during maintenance if a large software system were designed in such a way that all of its data elements were global?
15. In an object-oriented program, what does declaring an instance variable to be public or private indicate about data coupling? What would be the rationale behind a preference toward declaring instance variables as private?

*16. Identify a problem involving data coupling that can occur in the context of parallel processing.

17. Answer the following questions in relation to the accompanying structure chart:
    a. To which module does module Y return control?
    b. To which module does module Z return control?

c. Are modules W and X linked via control coupling?
d. Are modules W and X linked via data coupling?
e. What data is shared by both module W and module Y?
f. In what way are modules W and Z related?

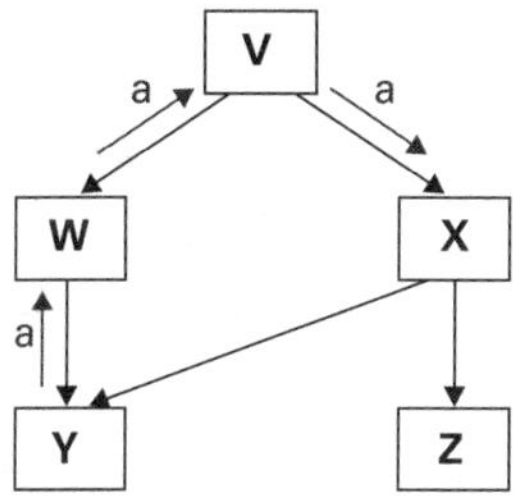

18. Using a structure chart, represent the procedural structure of a simple inventory/accounting system for a small store (perhaps a privately owned curio shop in a resort community). What modules in your system must be modified because of changes in sales tax laws? What modules would need to be changed if the decision is made to maintain a record of past customers so that advertising can be mailed to them?

19. Using a class diagram, design an object-oriented solution for the previous problem.

20. Draw a simple class diagram representing the relationships between magazine publishers, magazines, and subscribers. It is sufficient to depict only the class name within each box representing a class.

21. How is the relationship between the system and the user represented in a use case diagram?

22. Draw a simple use case diagram depicting the ways in which a traveler uses an airline reservation system.

23. Draw a sequence diagram representing the interaction sequence that would ensue when a utility company sends a bill to a customer.

24. Draw a simple dataflow diagram depicting the flow of data that occurs in an automated inventory system when a sale is made.

25. Contrast the information represented in a class diagram with that represented in a sequence diagram.

26. Provide at least two examples of a one-to-one relationship and a many-to-many relationship.

27. Give an example of a one-to-many relationship that is not mentioned in this chapter. Give an example of a many-to-many relationship that is not mentioned in this chapter.

28. Based on the information in Figure 7.10, imagine an interaction sequence that might occur between a physician and a patient during a visit with the patient. Draw a sequence diagram representing that sequence.

29. Draw a class diagram representing the relationships between the servers and customers in a restaurant.

30. Draw a class diagram representing the relationships between magazines, publishers of magazines, and subscribers to magazines. Include a set of instance variables and methods for each class.

31. Extend the sequence diagram in Figure 7.5 to show the interaction sequence that would occur if `PlayerA` successfully returns `PlayerB`'s volley, but `PlayerB` fails to return that volley.

32. Answer the following questions based on the accompanying class diagram that represents the associations between tools, their users, and their manufacturers.

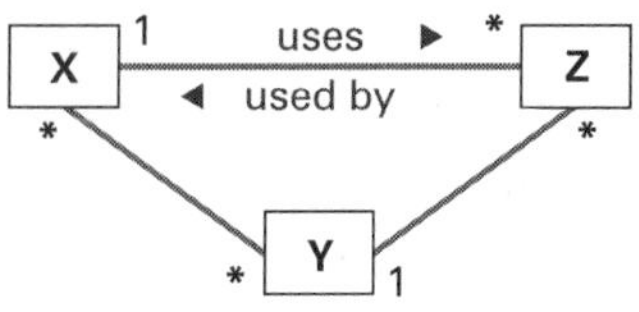

a. Which classes (X, Y, and Z) represent tools, users, and manufacturers? Justify your answer.
b. Can a tool be used by more than one user?
c. Can a tool be manufactured by more than one manufacturer?
d. Does each user use tools manufactured by many manufacturers?

33. In each of the following cases, identify whether the activity relates to a sequence diagram, a use case diagram, or a class diagram.
a. Represents the way in which users will interact with the system
b. Represents the relationship between classes in the system
c. Represents the manner in which objects will interact to accomplish a task

34. Answer the following questions based on the accompanying sequence diagram.

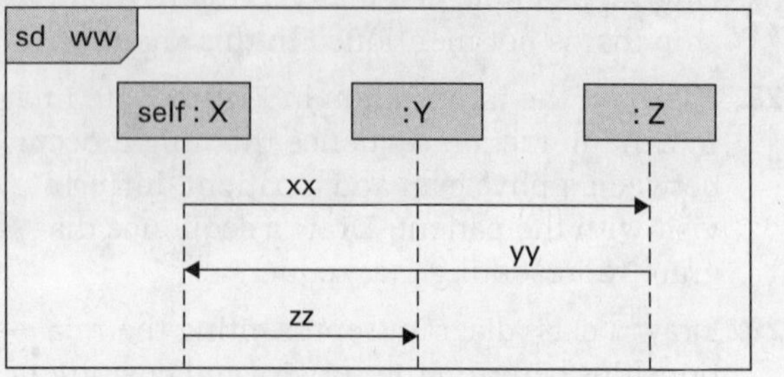

a. What class contains a method named ww?
b. What class contains a method named xx?
c. During the sequence, does the object of type Z ever communicate directly with the object of type Y?

35. Draw a sequence diagram indicating that object A calls the method bb in object B, B performs the requested action and returns control to A, and then A calls the method cc in object B.

36. Extend your solution to the previous problem to indicate that A calls the method bb only if the variable "continue" is true and continues calling bb as long as "continue" remains true after B returns control.

37. Draw a class diagram depicting the fact that the classes Truck and Automobile are generalizations of the class Vehicle.

38. Based on Figure 7.12, what additional instance variables would be contained in an object of type `SurgicalRecord`? Of type `OfficeVisitRecord`?

39. Explain why inheritance is not always the best way to implement class generalizations.

40. What is the significance of using the interaction diagrams provided by UML?

41. Summarize the process of software quality assurance (SQA).

42. To what extent are the control structures in a typical high-level programming language (`if-else`, `while`, and so on) small-scale design patterns?

43. Which of the following involve the Pareto principle? Explain your answers.
a. One obnoxious person can spoil the party for everyone.
b. Each radio station concentrates on a particular format such as hard rock music, classical music, or talk.
c. In an election, candidates are wise to focus their campaigns on the segment of the electorate that has voted in the past.

44. Do software engineers expect large software systems to be homogeneous or heterogeneous in error content? Explain your answer.

45. What is the difference between black-box testing and glass-box testing?

46. Give some analogies of black-box and glass-box testing that occur in fields other than software engineering.

47. How does open-source development differ from beta testing? (Consider glass-box testing versus black-box testing.)

48. Suppose that 100 errors were intentionally placed in a large software system before the system was subjected to final testing. Moreover, suppose that 200 errors were discovered and corrected during this final testing, of which 50 errors were from the group intentionally placed in the system. If the remaining 50 known errors are then corrected, how many unknown errors would you estimate are still in the system? Explain why.

49. What is boundary value analysis?

50. What is alpha testing and beta testing?

51. One difference between the human-computer interface of a smartphone and that of a desktop computer involves the technique used to alter the scale of an image on the display screen to obtain more or less detail (a process called "zooming"). On a desktop, zooming is typically achieved by dragging a slider that is separate from the area being displayed, or by using a menu or toolbar item. On a smartphone, zooming is performed by simultaneously touching the display screen with the thumb and index finger and then modifying the space between both touch points (a process called "double touch— spread" to "zoom in" or "double touch—pinch" to "zoom out").
a. Based on ergonomics, what arguments can be made in support of this difference?
b. Based on cognetics, what arguments can be made in support of this difference?

52. In what way do traditional copyright laws fail to safeguard the investments of software developers?

53. In what ways can a software developer be unsuccessful in obtaining a patent?

Social Issues

The following questions are intended as a guide to the ethical/social/legal issues associated with the field of computing. The goal is not merely to answer these questions. You should also consider why you answered as you did and whether your justifications are consistent from one question to the next.

1. a. Mary Analyst has been assigned the task of implementing a system with which medical records will be stored on a computer that is connected to a large network. In her opinion the design for the system's security is flawed but her concerns have been overruled for financial reasons. She has been told to proceed with the project using the security system that she feels is inadequate. What should she do? Why?

b. Suppose that Mary Analyst implemented the system as she was told, and now she is aware that the medical records are being observed by unauthorized personnel. What should she do? To what extent is she liable for the breach of security?

c. Suppose that instead of obeying her employer, Mary Analyst refuses to proceed with the system and blows the whistle by making the flawed design public, resulting in a financial hardship for the company and the loss of many innocent employees' jobs. Were Mary Analyst's actions correct? What if it turns out that, being only a part of the overall team, Mary Analyst was unaware that sincere efforts were being made elsewhere within the company to develop a valid security system that would be applied to the system on which Mary was working? How does this change your judgment of Mary's actions? (Remember, Mary's view of the situation is the same as before.)

2. When large software systems are developed by many people, how should liabilities be assigned? Is there a hierarchy of responsibility? Are there degrees of liability?

3. We have seen that large, complex software systems are often developed by many individuals, few of which may have a complete picture of the entire project. Is it ethically proper for an employee to contribute to a project without full knowledge of its function?

4. To what extent is someone responsible for how his or her accomplishments are ultimately applied by others?

5. In the relationship between a computer professional and a client, is it the professional's responsibility to implement the client's desires or to direct the client's desires? What if the professional foresees that a client's desires could lead to unethical consequences? For example, the client may wish to cut corners for the sake of efficiency, but the professional may foresee a potential source of erroneous data or misuse of the system if those shortcuts are taken. If the client insists, is the professional free of responsibility?

6. What happens if technology begins to advance so rapidly that new inventions are superseded before the inventor has time to profit from the invention? Is profit necessary to motivate inventors? How does the success of open-source development relate to your answer? Is free quality software a sustainable reality?
7. Is the computer revolution contributing to, or helping to solve, the world's energy problems? What about other large-scale problems such as hunger and poverty?
8. Will advances in technology continue indefinitely? What, if anything, would reverse society's dependency on technology? What would be the result of a society that continues to advance technology indefinitely?
9. If you had a time machine, in which period of history would you like to live? Are there current technologies that you would like to take with you? Can one technology be separated from another? Is it realistic to protest against global warming yet accept modern medical treatment?
10. Many applications on a smartphone automatically integrate with services provided by other applications. This integration may share information entered to one application with another. What are the benefits of this integration? Are there any concerns with "too much" integration?

Additional Reading

Alexander, C., S. Ishikawa, and M. Silverstein. *A Pattern Language.* New York: Oxford University Press, 1977.

Beck, K. *Extreme Programming Explained: Embrace Change,* 2nd ed. Boston, MA: Addison-Wesley, 2004.

Bowman, D. A., E. Kruijff, J. J. LaViola, Jr., and I. Poupyrev. *3D User Interfaces Theory and Practice.* Boston, MA: Addison-Wesley, 2005.

Braude, E. *Software Design: From Programming to Architecture.* New York: Wiley, 2004.

Bruegge, B., and A. Dutoit. *Object-Oriented Software Engineering Using UML, Patterns, and Java,* 3rd ed. Boston, MA: Addison-Wesley, 2010.

Cockburn, A. *Agile Software Development: The Cooperative Game,* 2nd ed. Boston, MA: Addison-Wesley, 2006.

Fox, C. *Introduction to Software Engineering Design: Processes, Principles and Patterns with UML2.* Boston, MA: Addison-Wesley, 2007.

Gamma, E., R. Helm, R. Johnson, and J. Vlissides. *Design Patterns: Elements of Reusable Object-Oriented Software.* Boston, MA: Addison-Wesley, 1995.

Maurer, P. M. *Component-Level Programming.* Upper Saddle River, NJ: Prentice Hall, 2003.

Pfleeger, S. L., and J. M. Atlee. *Software Engineering: Theory and Practice,* 4th ed. Upper Saddle River, NJ: Prentice-Hall, 2010.

Pilone, D., and N. Pitman. *UML 2.0 in a Nutshell.* Cambridge, MA: O'Reilly Media, 2005.

Pressman, R. S., and B. Maxim. *Software Engineering: A Practitioner's Approach,* 8th ed. New York: McGraw-Hill, 2014.

Schach, S. R. *Classical and Object-Oriented Software Engineering,* 8th ed. New York: McGraw-Hill, 2010.

Shalloway, A., and J. R. Trott. *Design Patterns Explained,* 2nd ed. Boston, MA: Addison-Wesley, 2005.

Shneiderman, B., C. Plaisant, M. Cohen, and S. Jacobs. *Designing the User Interface: Strategies for Effective Human-Computer Interaction,* 5th ed. Boston, MA: Addison-Wesley, 2009.

Sommerville, I. *Software Engineering,* 9th ed. Boston, MA: Addison-Wesley, 2010.

CHAPTER 8

Data Abstractions

In this chapter we investigate how data arrangements other than the cell-by-cell organization provided by a computer's main memory can be simulated—a subject known as data structures. The goal is to allow the data's user to access collections of data as abstract tools rather than force the user to think in terms of the computer's main memory organization. Our study will show how the desire to construct such abstract tools leads to the concept of objects and object-oriented programming.

**Asterisks indicate suggestions for optional sections.*

We introduced the concept of data structure in Chapter 6, where we learned that high-level programming languages provide techniques by which programmers can express algorithms as though the data being manipulated were stored in ways other than the cell-by-cell arrangement provided by a computer's main memory. We also learned that the data structures supported by a programming language are known as primitive structures. In this chapter we will explore techniques by which data structures other than a language's primitive structures can be constructed and manipulated—a study that will lead us from traditional data structures to the object-oriented paradigm. An underlying theme throughout this progression is the construction of abstract tools.

8.1 Basic Data Structures

We begin our study by introducing some basic data structures that will serve as examples in future sections.

Arrays and Aggregates

In Section 6.2, we learned about the data structures known as arrays and aggregate types. Recall that an **array** is a "rectangular" block of data whose entries are of the same type. The simplest form of array is the one-dimensional array, a single row of elements with each position identified by an index. A one-dimensional array with 26 elements could be used to store the number of times each alphabet letter occurs in a page of text, for example. A two-dimensional array consists of multiple rows and columns in which positions are identified by pairs of indices—the first index identifies the row associated with the position, the second index identifies the column. An example would be a rectangular array of numbers representing the monthly sales made by members of a sales force—the entries across each row representing the monthly sales made by a particular member and the entries down each column representing the sales by each member for a particular month. Thus, the entry in the third row and first column would represent the sales made by the third salesperson in January.

In contrast to an array, recall that an **aggregate type** is a block of data items that might be of different types and sizes. The items within the block are usually called **fields.** An example of an aggregate type would be the block of data relating to a single employee, the fields of which might be the employee's name (an array of type character), age (of type integer), and skill rating (of type float). Fields in an aggregate type are usually accessed by field name, rather than by a numerical index number.

Lists, Stacks, and Queues

Another basic data structure is a **list,** which is a collection whose entries are arranged sequentially (Figure 8.1a). The beginning of a list is called the **head** of the list. The other end of a list is called the **tail.**

Almost any collection of data can be envisioned as a list. For example, text can be envisioned as a list of symbols, a two-dimensional array can be envisioned as a list of rows, and music recorded on a CD can be envisioned as a list of sounds. More traditional examples include guest lists, shopping lists, class enrollment lists, and inventory lists. Activities associated with a list vary depending on the situation.

Figure 8.1 Lists, stacks, and queues

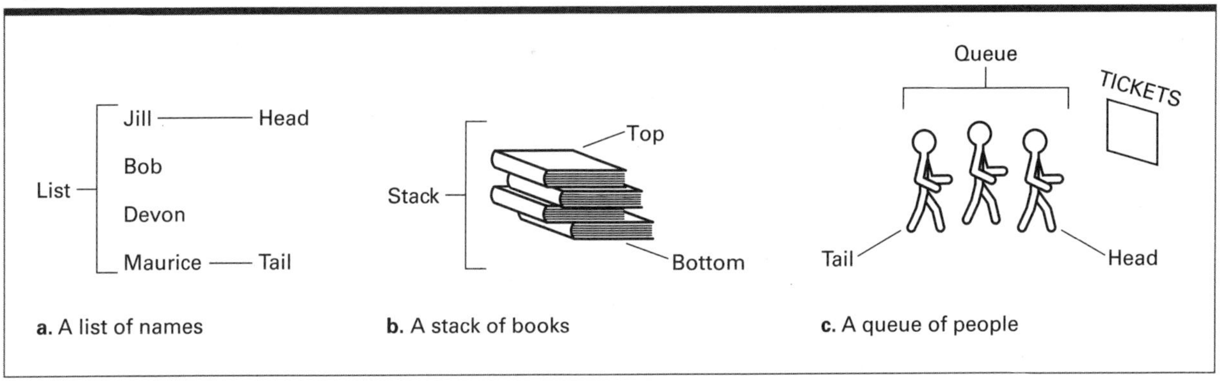

In some cases we may need to remove entries from a list, add new entries to a list, "process" the entries in a list one at a time, change the arrangement of the entries in a list, or perhaps search to see if a particular item is in a list. We will investigate such operations later in this chapter.

By restricting the manner in which the entries of a list are accessed, we obtain two special types of lists known as stacks and queues. A **stack** is a list in which entries are inserted and removed only at the head. An example is a stack of books where physical restrictions dictate that all additions and deletions occur at the top (Figure 8.1b). Following colloquial terminology, the head of a stack is called the **top** of the stack. The tail of a stack is called its **bottom** or **base.** Inserting a new entry at the top of a stack is called **pushing** an entry. Removing an entry from the top of a stack is called **popping** an entry. Note that the last entry placed on a stack will always be the first entry removed—an observation that leads to a stack being known as a **last-in, first-out,** or **LIFO** (pronounced "LIE-foe") structure.

This LIFO characteristic means that a stack is ideal for storing items that must be retrieved in the reverse order from which they were stored, and thus a stack is often used as the underpinning of backtracking activities. (The term **backtracking** refers to the process of backing out of a system in the opposite order from which the system was entered. A classic example is the process of retracing one's steps in order to find one's way out of a forest.) For instance, consider the underlying structure required to support a recursive process. As each new activation is started, the previous activation must be set aside. Moreover, as each activation is completed, the last activation that was set aside must be retrieved. Thus, if the activations are pushed on a stack as they are set aside, then the proper activation will be on the top of the stack each time an activation needs to be retrieved.

A **queue** is a list in which the entries are removed only at the head and new entries are inserted only at the tail. An example is a line, or queue, of people waiting to buy tickets at a theater (Figure 8.1c)—the person at the head of the queue is served while new arrivals step to the rear (or tail) of the queue. We have already met the queue structure in Chapter 3 where we saw that a batch processing operating system stores the jobs waiting to be executed in a queue called the job queue. There we also learned that a queue is a **first-in, first-out,** or **FIFO** (pronounced "FIE-foe") structure, meaning that the entries are removed from a queue in the order in which they were stored.

Queues are often used as the underlying structure of a buffer, introduced in Chapter 1,which is a storage area for the temporary placement of data being transferred from one location to another. As the items of data arrive at the buffer, they are placed at the tail of the queue. Then, when it comes time to forward items to their final destination, they are forwarded in the order in which they appear at the head of the queue. Thus, items are forwarded in the same order in which they arrived.

Trees

A **tree** is a collection whose entries have a hierarchical organization similar to that of an organization chart of a typical company (Figure 8.2). The president is represented at the top, with lines branching down to the vice presidents, who are followed by regional managers, and so on. To this intuitive definition of a tree structure we impose one additional constraint, which (in terms of an organization chart) is that no individual in the company reports to two different superiors. That is, different branches of the organization do not merge at a lower level. (We have already seen examples of trees in Chapter 6 where they appeared in the form of parse trees.)

Each position in a tree is called a **node** (Figure 8.3). The node at the top is called the **root node** (if we turned the drawing upside down, this node would represent the base or root of the tree). The nodes at the other extreme are called **terminal nodes** (or sometimes **leaf nodes**). We often refer to the number of nodes in the longest path from the root to a leaf as the **depth** of the tree. In other words, the depth of a tree is the number of horizontal layers within it.

At times we refer to tree structures as though each node gives birth to those nodes immediately below it. In this sense, we often speak of a node's ancestors or descendants. We refer to its immediate descendants as its **children** and its immediate ancestor as its **parent.** Moreover, we speak of nodes with the same parent as being **siblings.** A tree in which each parent has no more than two children is called a **binary tree.**

If we select any node in a tree, we find that that node together with the nodes below it also have the structure of a tree. We call these smaller structures **subtrees.** Thus, each child node is the root of a subtree below the child's parent. Each such subtree is called a **branch** from the parent. In a binary tree, we often speak of a node's left branch or right branch in reference to the way the tree is displayed.

Figure 8.2 An example of an organization chart

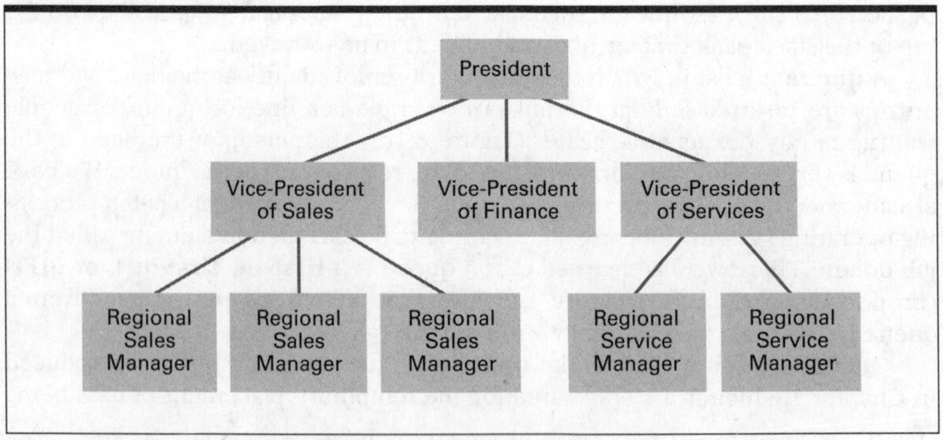

Figure 8.3 Tree terminology

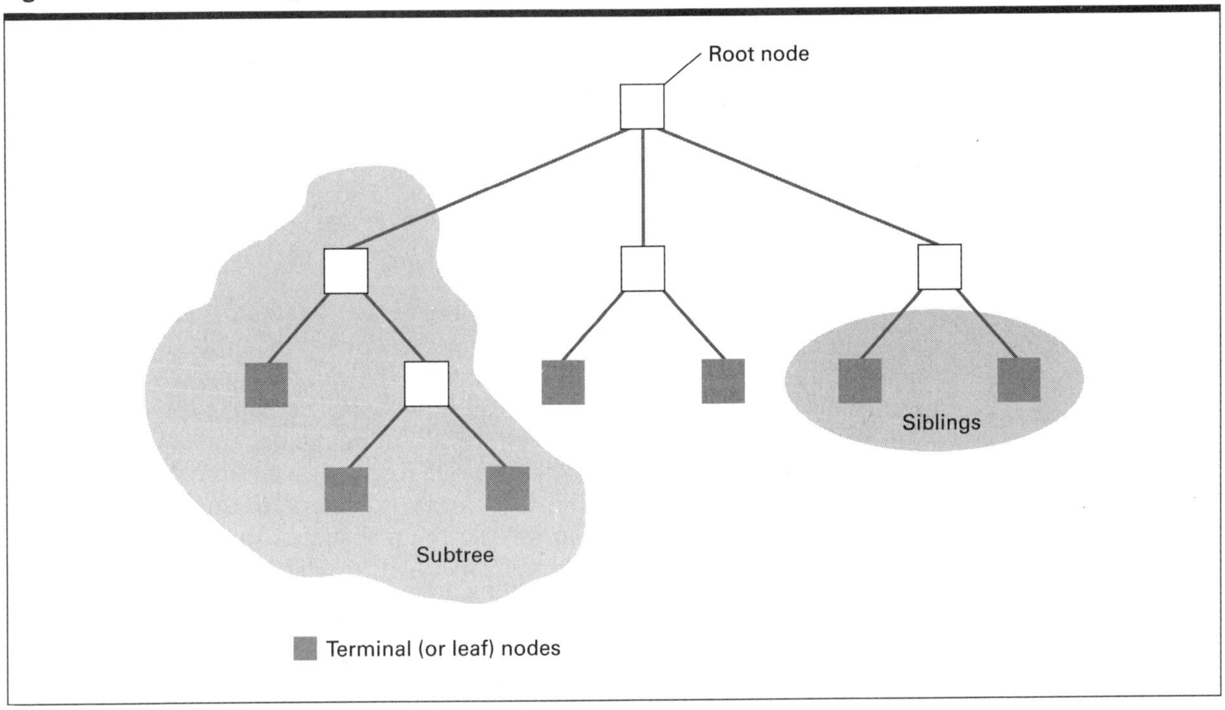

Questions & Exercises

1. Give examples (outside of computer science) of each of the following structures: list, stack, queue, and tree.
2. Summarize the distinction between lists, stacks, and queues.
3. Suppose the letter A is pushed onto an empty stack, followed by the letters B and C, in that order. Then suppose that a letter is popped off the stack and the letters D and E are pushed on. List the letters that would be on the stack in the order they would appear from top to bottom. If a letter is popped off the stack, which letter will be retrieved?
4. Suppose the letter A is placed in an empty queue, followed by the letters B and C, in that order. Then suppose that a letter is removed from the queue and the letters D and E are inserted. List the letters that would be in the queue in the order they would appear from head to tail. If a letter is now removed from the queue, which letter will it be?
5. Suppose a tree has four nodes A, B, C, and D. If A and C are siblings and D's parent is A, which nodes are leaf nodes? Which node is the root?

8.2 Related Concepts

In this section we isolate three topics that are closely associated with the subject of data structures: abstraction, the distinction between static and dynamic structures, and the concept of a pointer.

Abstraction Again

The structures presented in the previous section are often associated with data. However, a computer's main memory is not organized as arrays, lists, stacks, queues, and trees but is instead organized as a sequence of addressable memory cells. Thus, all other structures must be simulated. How this simulation is accomplished is the subject of this chapter. For now we merely point out that organizations such as arrays, lists, stacks, queues, and trees are abstract tools that are created so that users of the data can be shielded from the details of actual data storage and can be allowed to access information as though it were stored in a more convenient form.

The term *user* in this context does not necessarily refer to a human. Instead, the meaning of the word depends on our perspective at the time. If we are thinking in terms of a person using a PC to maintain bowling league records, then the user is a human. In this case, the application software (perhaps a spreadsheet software package) would be responsible for presenting the data in an abstract form convenient to the human—most likely as an array. If we are thinking in terms of a server on the Internet, then the user might be a client. In this case, the server would be responsible for presenting data in an abstract form convenient to the client. If we are thinking in terms of the modular structure of a program, then the user would be any module requiring access to the data. In this case, the module containing the data would be responsible for presenting the data in an abstract form convenient to the other modules. In each of these scenarios, the common thread is that the user has the privilege of accessing data as an abstract tool.

Static Versus Dynamic Structures

An important distinction in constructing abstract data structures is whether the structure being simulated is static or dynamic, that is, whether the shape or size of the structure changes over time. For example, if the abstract tool is a list of names, it is important to consider whether the list will remain a fixed size throughout its existence or expand and shrink as names are added and deleted.

As a general rule, static structures are more easily managed than dynamic ones. If a structure is static, we need merely to provide a means of accessing the various data items in the structure and perhaps a means of changing the values at designated locations. But, if the structure is dynamic, we must also deal with the problems of adding and deleting entries as well as finding the memory space required by a growing data structure. In the case of a poorly designed structure, adding a single new entry could result in a massive rearrangement of the structure, and excessive growth could dictate that the entire structure be transferred to another memory area where more space is available.

Pointers

Recall that the various cells in a machine's main memory are identified by numeric addresses. Being numeric values, these addresses themselves can be encoded and stored in memory cells. A **pointer** is a storage area that contains such an encoded address. In the case of data structures, pointers are used to record the location where data items are stored. For example, if we must repeatedly move an item of data from one location to another, we might designate a fixed location to serve as a pointer. Then, each time we move the item, we can

Figure 8.4 Novels arranged by title but linked according to authorship

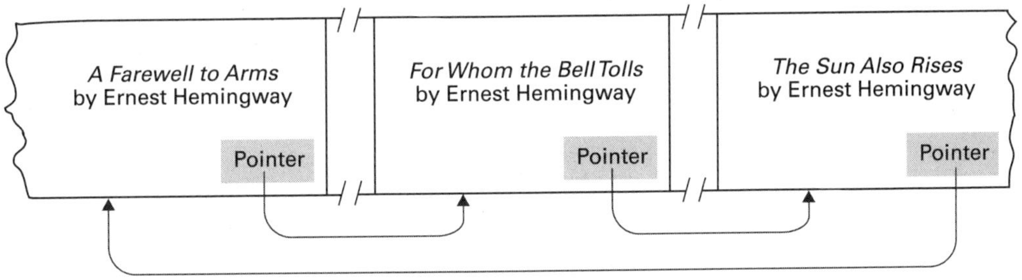

update the pointer to reflect the new address of the data. Later, when we need to access the item of data, we can find it by means of the pointer. Indeed, the pointer will always "point" to the data.

We have already encountered the concept of a pointer in our study of CPUs in Chapter 2. There we found that a register called a program counter is used to hold the address of the next instruction to be executed. Thus, the program counter plays the role of a pointer. In fact, another name for a program counter is **instruction pointer.**

As an example of the application of pointers, suppose we have a list of novels stored in a computer's memory alphabetically by title. Although convenient in many applications, this arrangement makes it difficult to find all the novels by a particular author—they are scattered throughout the list. To solve this problem, we can reserve an additional memory cell within each block of cells representing a novel and use this cell as a pointer to another block representing a book by the same author. In this manner the novels with common authorship can be linked in a loop (Figure 8.4). Once we find one novel by a given author, we can find all the others by following the pointers from one book to another.

Many modern programming languages include pointers as a primitive data type. That is, they allow the declaration, allocation, and manipulation of pointers in ways reminiscent of integers and character strings. Using such a language, a programmer can design elaborate networks of data within a machine's memory where pointers are used to link related items to each other.

Questions & Exercises

1. In what sense are data structures such as arrays, lists, stacks, queues, and trees abstractions?
2. Describe an application that you would expect to involve a static data structure. Then describe an application that you would expect to involve a dynamic data structure.
3. Describe contexts outside of computer science in which the pointer concept occurs.

8.3 Implementing Data Structures

Let us now consider ways in which the data structures discussed in the previous section can be stored in a computer's main memory. As we saw in Chapter 6, these structures are often provided as primitive structures in high-level programming languages. Our goal here is to understand how programs that deal with such structures are translated into machine-language programs that manipulate data stored in main memory.

Storing Arrays

We begin with techniques for storing arrays.

Suppose we want to store a sequence of 24 hourly temperature readings, each of which requires one memory cell of storage space. Moreover, suppose we want to identify these readings by their positions in the sequence. That is, we want to be able to access the first reading or the fifth reading. In short, we want to manipulate the sequence as though it were a one-dimensional array.

We can obtain this goal merely by storing the readings in a sequence of 24 memory cells with consecutive addresses. Then, if the address of the first cell in the sequence is x, the location of any particular temperature reading can be computed by subtracting one from the index of the desired reading and then adding the result to x. In particular, the fourth reading would be located at address $x + (4 - 1)$, as shown in Figure 8.5.

This technique is used by most translators of high-level programming languages to implement one-dimensional arrays. When the translator encounters a declaration statement such as

```
int Readings[24];
```

declaring that the term `Readings` is to refer to a one-dimensional array of 24 integer values, the translator arranges for 24 consecutive memory cells to be set aside. Later in the program, if it encounters the assignment statement

```
Readings[4] = 67;
```

requesting that the value 67 be placed in the fourth entry of the array `Readings`, the translator builds the sequence of machine instructions required to place the

Figure 8.5 The array of temperature readings stored in memory starting at address x

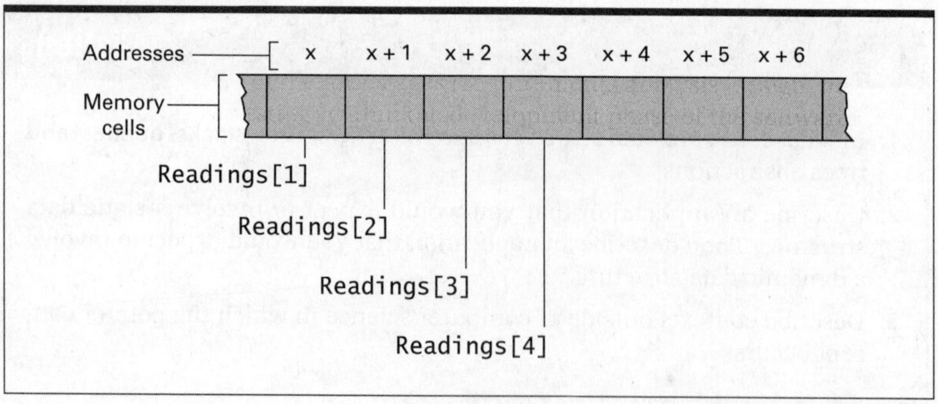

value 67 in the memory cell at address $x + (4 - 1)$, where x is the address of the first cell in the block associated with the array `Readings`. In this manner, the programmer is allowed to write the program as though the temperature readings were actually stored in a one-dimensional array. (Caution: In the languages Python, C, C++, C#, and Java, array indices start at 0 rather than 1, so the fourth reading would be referenced by `Readings[3]`. See question 3 at the end of this section.)

Now suppose we want to record the sales made by a company's sales force during a one-week period. In this case, we might envision the data arranged in a two-dimensional array, where the values across each row indicate the sales made by a particular employee, and the values down a column represent all the sales made during a particular day.

To accommodate this need, we first recognize that the array is static in the sense that its size does not vary as updates are made. We can therefore calculate the amount of storage area needed for the entire array and reserve a block of contiguous memory cells of that size. Next, we store the data in the array row by row. Starting at the first cell of the reserved block, we store the values from the first row of the array into consecutive memory locations; following this, we store the next row, then the next, and so on (Figure 8.6). Such a storage system is said to use **row major order** in contrast to **column major order** in which the array is stored column by column.

With the data stored in this manner, let us consider how we could find the value in the third row and fourth column of the array. Envision that we are at the first location in the reserved block of the machine's memory. Starting at this location, we find the data in the first row of the array followed by the second, then the third, and so on. To get to the third row, we must move beyond both the first and second rows. Since each row contains five entries (one for each day of the week from Monday through Friday), we must move beyond a total of 10 entries to reach the first entry of the third row. From there, we must move beyond another three entries to reach the entry in the fourth column of the row. Altogether, to reach the entry in the third row and fourth column, we must move beyond 13 entries from the beginning of the block.

Figure 8.6 A two-dimensional array with four rows and five columns stored in row major order

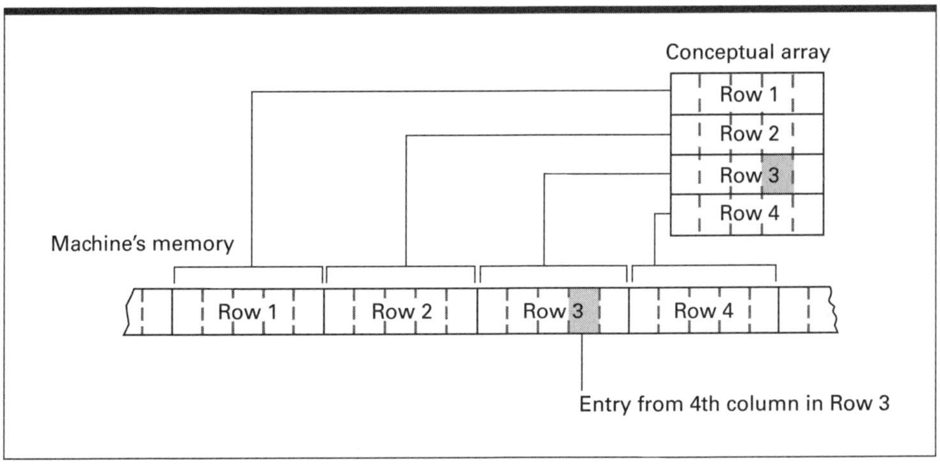

Implementing Contiguous Lists

The primitives for constructing and manipulating arrays that are provided in most high-level programming languages are convenient tools for constructing and manipulating contiguous lists. If the entries of the list are all the same primitive data type, then the list is nothing more than a one-dimensional array. A slightly more involved example is a list of ten names, each of which is no longer than eight characters, as discussed in the text. In this case, a programmer could construct the contiguous list as a two-dimensional array of characters with ten rows and eight columns, which would produce the structure represented in Figure 8.6 (assuming that the array is stored in row major order).

Many high-level languages incorporate features that encourage such implementations of lists. For example, suppose the two-dimensional array of characters proposed above was called `MemberList`. Then in addition to the traditional notation in which the expression `MemberList[3,5]` refers to the single character in the third row and fifth column, some languages adopt the expression `MemberList[3]` to refer to the entire third row, which would be the third entry in the list.

The preceding calculation can be generalized to obtain a formula for converting references in terms of row and column positions into actual memory addresses. In particular, if we let c represent the number of columns in an array (which is the number of entries in each row), then the address of the entry in the ith row and jth column will be

$$x + (c \times (i - 1)) + (j - 1)$$

where x is the address of the cell containing the entry in the first row and first column. That is, we must move beyond $i - 1$ rows, each of which contains c entries, to reach the ith row and then $j - 1$ more entries to reach the jth entry in this row. In our prior example $c = 5$, $i = 3$, and $j = 4$, so if the array were stored starting at address x, then the entry in the third row, fourth column would be at address $x + (5 \times (3 - 1)) + (4 - 1) = x + 13$. The expression $(c \times (i - 1)) + (j - 1)$ is sometimes called the **address polynomial.**

Once again, this is the technique used by most translators of high-level programming languages. When faced with the declaration statement

```
int Sales[8, 5];
```

declaring that the term `Sales` is to refer to a two-dimensional array of integer values with 8 rows and 5 columns, the translator arranges for 40 consecutive memory cells to be set aside. Later, if it encounters the assignment statement

```
Sales[3, 4] = 5;
```

requesting that the value 5 be placed in the entry at the third row and fourth column of the array `Sales`, it builds the sequence of machine instructions required to place the value 5 in the memory cell whose address is $x + 5 \times (3 - 1) + (4 - 1)$, where x is the address of the first cell in the block associated with the array `Sales`. In this manner, the programmer is allowed to write the program as though the sales were actually stored in a two-dimensional array.

Storing Aggregates

Now suppose we want to store an aggregate called **Employee** consisting of the three fields: **Name** of type character array, **Age** of type integer, and **SkillRating** of type float. If the number of memory cells required by each field is fixed, then we can store the aggregate in a block of contiguous cells. For example, suppose the field **Name** required at most 25 cells, **Age** required only one cell, and **SkillRating** required only one cell. Then, we could set aside a block of 27 contiguous cells, store the name in the first 25 cells, store the age in the 26th cell, and store the skill rating in the last cell (Figure 8.7a).

With this arrangement, it would be easy to access the different fields within the aggregate. A reference to a field can be translated to a memory cell by knowing the address where the aggregate begins, and the offset of the desired field within that aggregate. If the address of the first cell were x, then any reference to **Employee.Name** (meaning the **Name** field within the aggregate **Employee**) would translate to the 25 cells starting at address x and a reference to **Employee.Age** (the **Age** field within **Employee**) would translate to the cell at address $x + 25$. In particular, if a translator found a statement such as

```
Employee.Age = 22;
```

in a high-level program, then it would merely build the machine language instructions required to place the value 22 in the memory cell whose address is $x + 25$.

Figure 8.7 Storing the aggregate type **Employee**

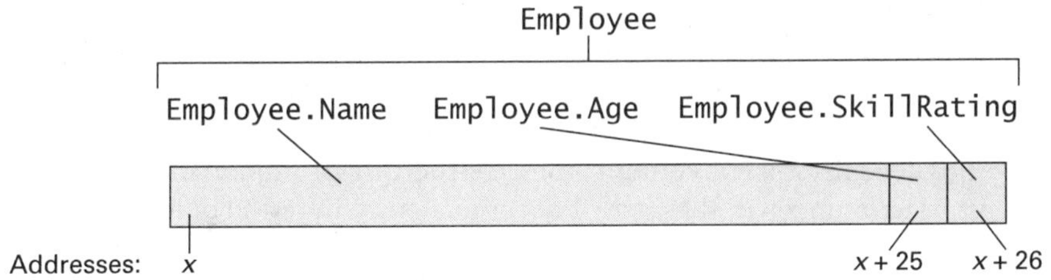

a. Aggregate stored in a contiguous block

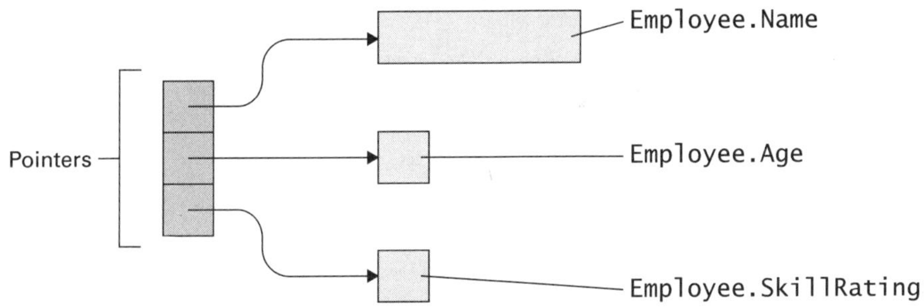

b. Aggregate fields stored in separate locations

An alternative to storing an aggregate in a block of contiguous memory cells is to store each field in a separate location and then link them together by means of pointers. More precisely, if the aggregate contains three fields, then we find a place in memory to store three pointers, each of which points to one of the fields (Figure 8.7b). If these pointers are stored in a block starting at address x, then the first field can be found by following the pointer stored at location x, the second field can be found by following the pointer at location $x + 1$, and so forth.

This arrangement is especially useful in those cases in which the size of the aggregate's fields is dynamic. For instance, by using the pointer system the size of the first field can be increased merely by finding an area in memory to hold the larger field and then adjusting the appropriate pointer to point to the new location. But if the aggregate were stored in a contiguous block, the entire structure would have to be altered.

Storing Lists

Let us now consider techniques for storing a list of names in a computer's main memory. One strategy is to store the entire list in a single block of memory cells with consecutive addresses. Assuming that each name is no longer than eight letters, we can divide the large block of cells into a collection of subblocks, each containing eight cells. Into each subblock we can store a name by recording its ASCII code using one cell per letter. If the name alone does not fill all the cells in the subblock allocated to it, we can merely fill the remaining cells with the ASCII code for a space. Using this system requires a block of 80 consecutive memory cells to store a list of 10 names.

The storage system just described is summarized in Figure 8.8. The significant point is that the entire list is stored in one large block of memory, with successive entries following each other in contiguous memory cells. Such an organization is referred to as a **contiguous list.**

A contiguous list is a convenient storage structure for implementing static lists, but it has disadvantages in the case of dynamic lists where the deletion and insertion of names can lead to a time-consuming shuffling of entries. In a worst-case scenario, the addition of entries could create the need to move the entire list to a new location to obtain an available block of cells large enough for the expanded list.

These problems can be simplified if we allow the individual entries in a list to be stored in different areas of memory rather than together in one large, contiguous block. To explain, let us reconsider our example of storing a list of names

Figure 8.8 Names stored in memory as a contiguous list

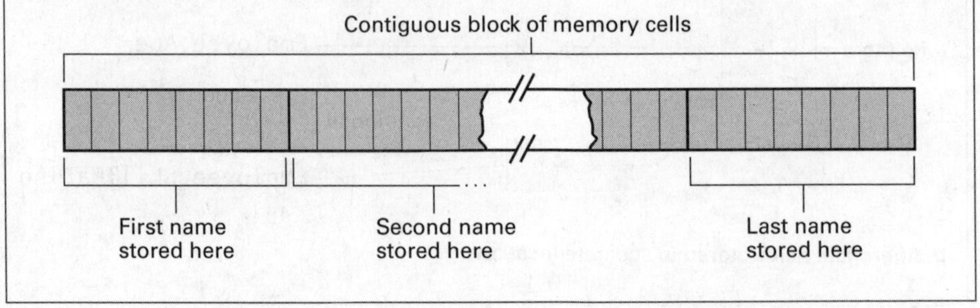

(where each name is no more than eight characters long). This time we store each name in a block of nine contiguous memory cells. The first eight of these cells are used to hold the name itself, and the last cell is used as a pointer to the next name in the list. Following this lead, the list can be scattered among several small nine-cell blocks linked together by pointers. Because of this linkage system, such an organization is called a **linked list.**

To keep track of the beginning of a linked list, we set aside another pointer in which we save the address of the first entry. Since this pointer points to the beginning, or head, of the list, it is called the **head pointer.**

To mark the end of a linked list, we use a **null pointer** (also known as a **NIL pointer** in some languages, or the `None` object in Python), which is merely a special bit pattern placed in the pointer cell of the last entry to indicate that no further entries are in the list. For example, if we agree never to store a list entry at address 0, the value zero will never appear as a legitimate pointer value and can therefore be used as the null pointer.

The final linked list structure is represented by the diagram in Figure 8.9, in which we depict the scattered blocks of memory used for the list by individual rectangles. Each rectangle is labeled to indicate its composition. Each pointer is represented by an arrow that leads from the pointer itself to the pointer's addressee. Traversing the list involves following the head pointer to find the first entry. From there, we follow the pointers stored with the entries to hop from one entry to the next until the null pointer is reached.

To appreciate the advantages of a linked list over a contiguous one, consider the task of deleting an entry. In a contiguous list this would create a hole, meaning that those entries following the deleted one would have to be moved forward to keep the list contiguous. However, in the case of a linked list, an entry can be deleted by changing a single pointer. This is done by changing the pointer that formerly pointed to the deleted entry so that it points to the entry following the deleted entry (Figure 8.10). From then on, when the list is traversed, the deleted entry is passed by because it no longer is part of the chain.

Inserting a new entry in a linked list is only a little more involved. We first find an unused block of memory cells large enough to hold the new entry and a pointer. Here we store the new entry and fill in the pointer with the address of the entry in the list that should follow the new entry. Finally, we change the pointer associated with the entry that should precede the new entry so that it points to

Figure 8.9 The structure of a linked list

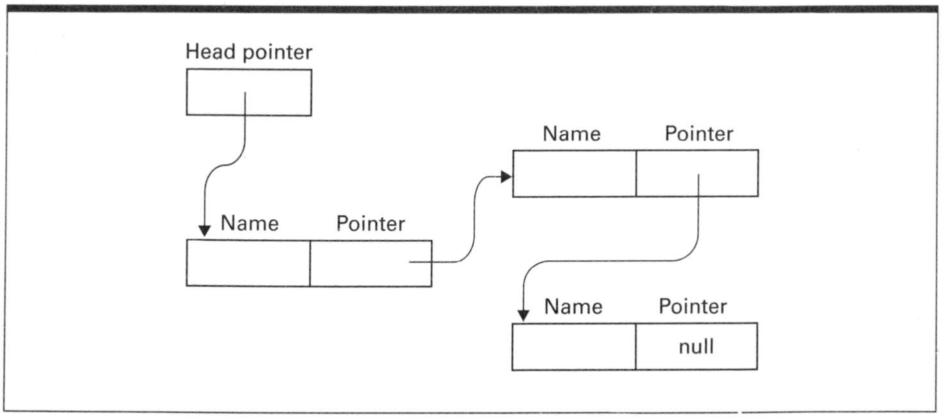

A Problem with Pointers

Just as the use of flowcharts led to tangled algorithm designs (Chapter 5), and the haphazard use of `goto` statements led to poorly designed programs (Chapter 6), undisciplined use of pointers has been found to produce needlessly complex and error-prone data structures. To bring order to this chaos, many programming languages restrict the flexibility of pointers. For example, Java does not allow pointers in their general form. Instead, it allows only a restricted form of pointers called references. One distinction is that a reference cannot be modified by an arithmetic operation. For example, if a Java programmer wanted to advance the reference `Next` to the next entry in a contiguous list, he or she would use a statement equivalent to

```
redirect Next to the next list entry
```

whereas a C programmer would use a statement equivalent to

```
assign Next the value Next + 1
```

Note that the Java statement better reflects the underlying goal. Moreover, to execute the Java statement, there must be another list entry, but if `Next` already pointed to the last entry in the list, the C statement would result in `Next` pointing to something outside the list—a common error for beginning, and even seasoned, C programmers.

the new entry (Figure 8.11). After we make this change, the new entry will be found in the proper place each time the list is traversed.

Storing Stacks and Queues

For storing stacks and queues, an organization similar to a contiguous list is often used. In the case of a stack, a block of memory, large enough to accommodate the stack at its maximum size, is reserved. (Determining the size of this block can often be a critical design decision. If too little room is reserved, the stack will ultimately exceed the allotted storage space; however, if too much room is reserved, memory space will be wasted.) One end of this block is designated as

Figure 8.10 Deleting an entry from a linked list

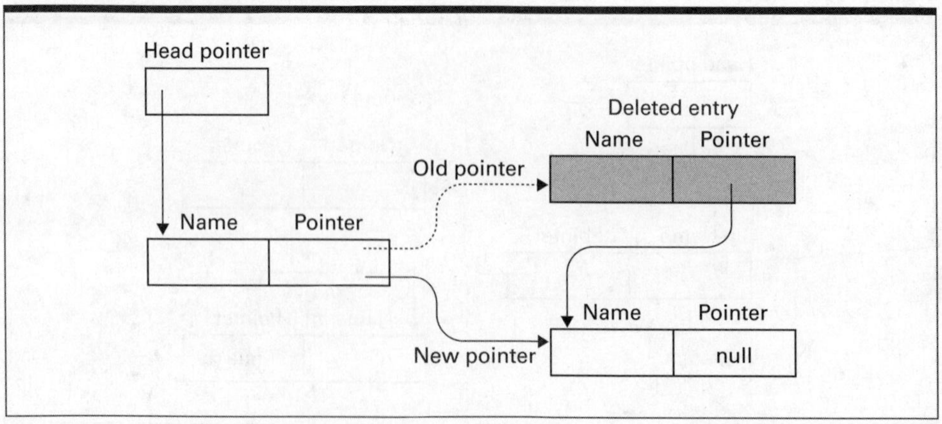

Figure 8.11 Inserting an entry into a linked list

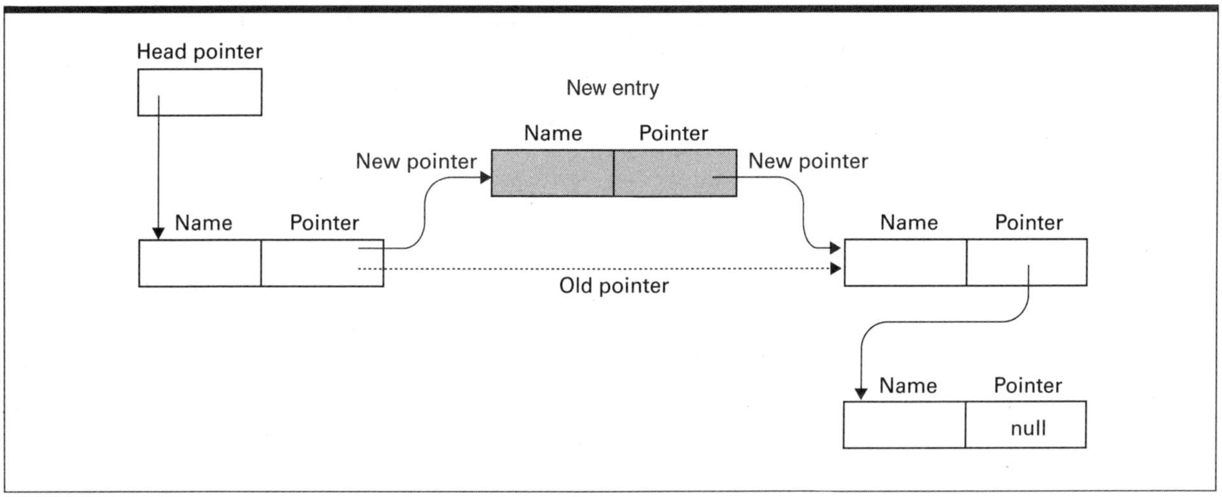

the stack's base. It is here that the first entry to be pushed onto the stack is stored. Then each additional entry is placed next to its predecessor as the stack grows toward the other end of the reserved block.

Observe that as entries are pushed and popped, the location of the top of the stack will move back and forth within the reserved block of memory cells. To keep track of this location, its address is stored in an additional memory cell known as the **stack pointer.** That is, the stack pointer is a pointer to the top of the stack.

The complete system, as illustrated in Figure 8.12, works as follows: To push a new entry on the stack, we first adjust the stack pointer to point to the vacancy just beyond the top of the stack and then place the new entry at this location. To pop an entry from the stack, we read the data pointed to by the stack pointer and then adjust the stack pointer to point to the next entry down on the stack.

The traditional implementation of a queue is similar to that of a stack. Again we reserve a block of contiguous cells in main memory large enough to hold the queue at its projected maximum size. However, in the case of a queue we need to perform operations at both ends of the structure, so we set aside two memory cells to use as pointers instead of only one as we did for a stack. One of these

Figure 8.12 A stack in memory

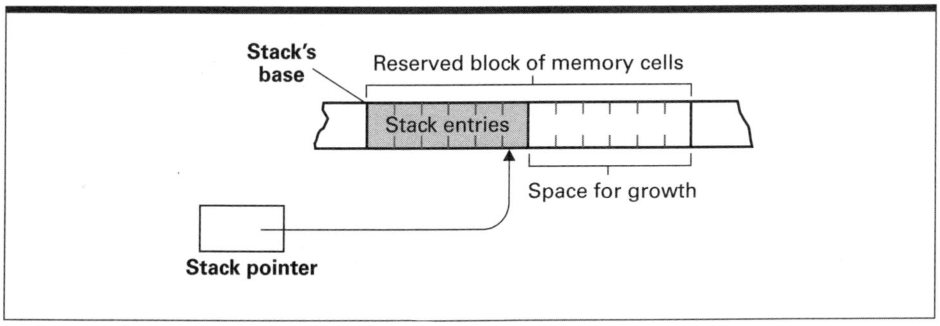

pointers, called the **head pointer,** keeps track of the head of the queue; the other, called the **tail pointer,** keeps track of the tail. When the queue is empty, both of these pointers point to the same location (Figure 8.13). Each time an entry is inserted into the queue, it is placed in the location pointed to by the tail pointer, and then the tail pointer is adjusted to point to the next unused location. In this manner, the tail pointer is always pointing to the first vacancy at the tail of the queue. Removing an entry from the queue involves extracting the entry pointed to by the head pointer and then adjusting the head pointer to point to the next entry in the queue.

A problem with the storage system as described thus far is that, as entries are inserted and removed, the queue crawls through memory like a glacier (see again Figure 8.13). Thus we need a mechanism for confining the queue to its reserved block of memory. The solution is simple. We let the queue migrate through the block. Then, when the tail of the queue reaches the end of the block, we start inserting additional entries back at the original end of the block, which by this time is vacant. Likewise, when the last entry in the block finally becomes the head of the queue and this entry is removed, the head pointer is adjusted back to the beginning of the block where other entries are, by this time, waiting. In this manner, the queue chases itself around within the block as though the ends of the

Figure 8.13 A queue implementation with head and tail pointers. Note how the queue crawls through memory as entries are inserted and removed

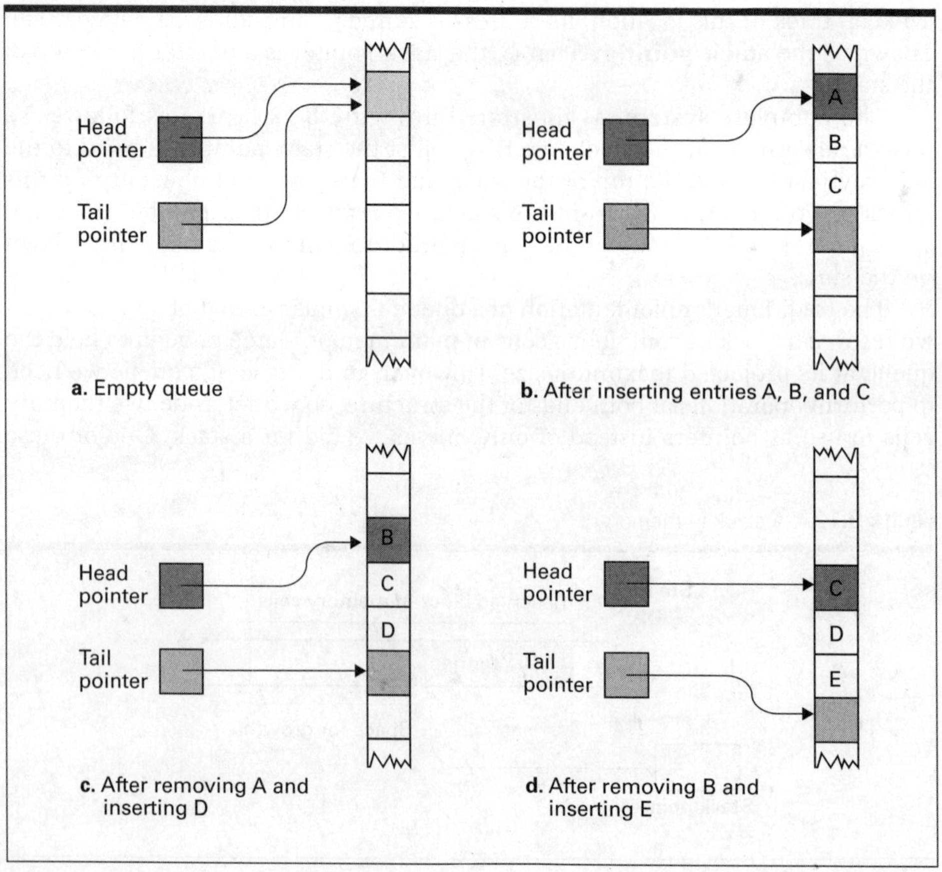

Figure 8.14 A circular queue containing the letters P through V

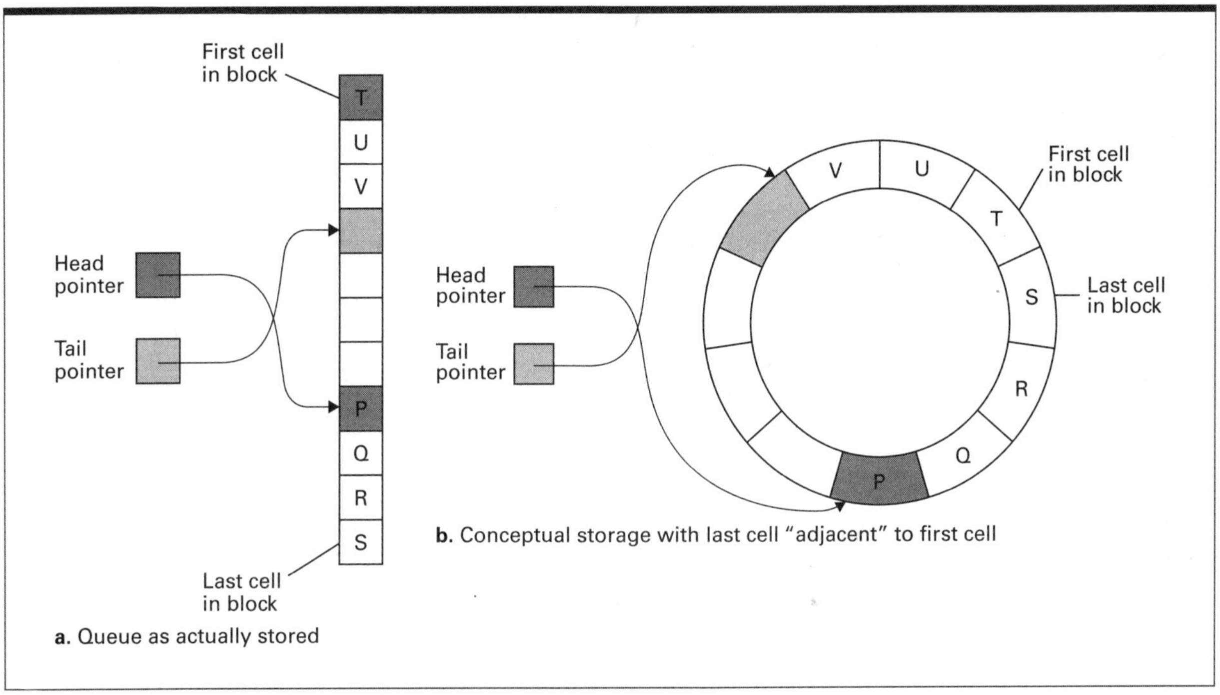

block were connected to form a loop (Figure 8.14). The result is an implementation called a **circular queue.**

Storing Binary Trees

For the purpose of discussing tree storage techniques, we restrict our attention to binary trees, which we recall are trees in which each node has at most two children. Such trees normally are stored in memory using a linked structure similar to that of linked lists. However, rather than each entry consisting of two components (the data followed by a next-entry pointer), each entry (or node) of the binary tree contains three components: (1) the data, (2) a pointer to the node's first child, and (3) a pointer to the node's second child. Although there is no left or right inside a machine, it is helpful to refer to the first pointer as the **left child pointer** and the other pointer as the **right child pointer** in reference to the way we would draw the tree on paper. Thus each node of the tree is represented by a short, contiguous block of memory cells with the format shown in Figure 8.15.

Figure 8.15 The structure of a node in a binary tree

Storing the tree in memory involves finding available blocks of memory cells to hold the nodes and linking these nodes according to the desired tree structure. Each pointer must be set to point to the left or right child of the pertinent node or assigned the null value if there are no more nodes in that direction of the tree. (This means that a terminal node is characterized by having both of its pointers assigned null.) Finally, we set aside a special memory location, called a **root pointer,** where we store the address of the root node. It is this root pointer that provides initial access to the tree.

An example of this linked storage system is presented in Figure 8.16, where a conceptual binary tree structure is exhibited along with a representation of how that tree might actually appear in a computer's memory. Note that the actual arrangement of the nodes within main memory might be quite different from the conceptual arrangement. However, by following the root pointer, one can find the root node and then trace any path down the tree by following the appropriate pointers from node to node.

An alternative to storing a binary tree as a linked structure is to use a single, contiguous block of memory cells for the entire tree. Using this approach, we store the tree's root node in the first cell of the block. (For simplicity, we assume that each node of the tree requires only one memory cell.) Then we store the left child of the root in the second cell, store the right child of the root in the third cell, and in general, continue to store the left and right children of the node found in cell n in the cells $2n$ and $2n + 1$, respectively. Cells within the block that represent locations not used by the tree are marked with a unique bit pattern that indicates the absence of data. Using this technique, the same tree shown in Figure 8.16 would be stored as shown in Figure 8.17. Note that the system is essentially that of storing the nodes across successively lower

Figure 8.16 The conceptual and actual organization of a binary tree using a linked storage system

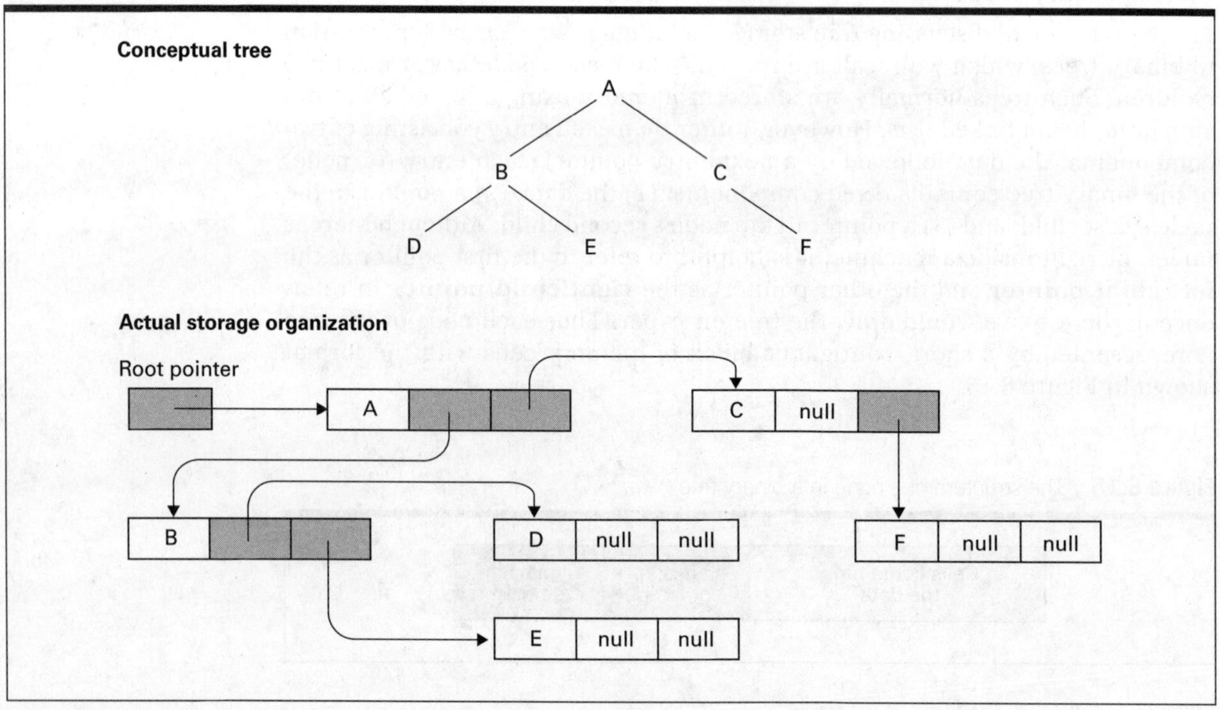

Figure 8.17 A tree stored without pointers

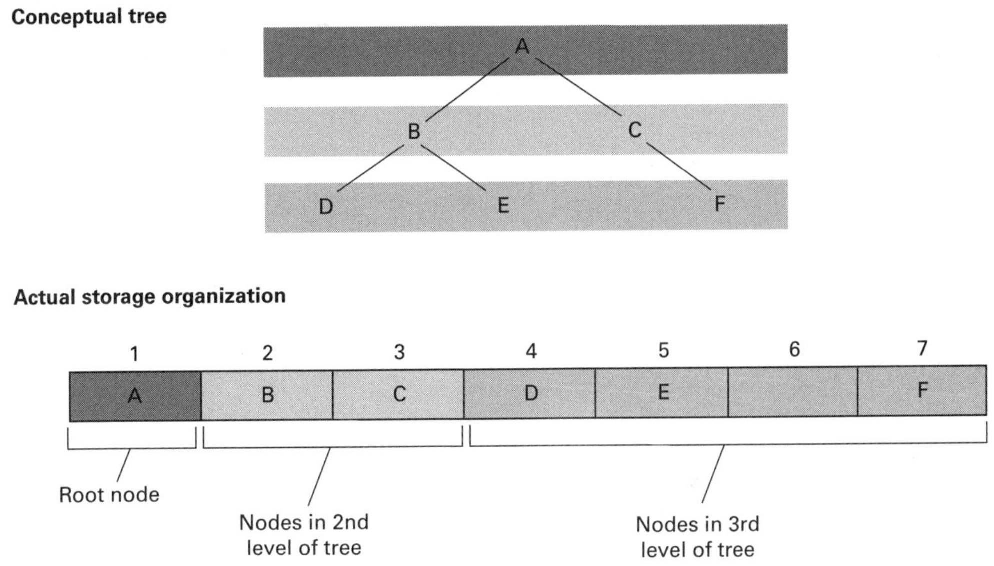

levels of the tree as segments, one after the other. That is, the first entry in the block is the root node, followed by the root's children, followed by the root's grandchildren, and so on.

In contrast to the linked structure described earlier, this alternative storage system provides an efficient method for finding the parent or sibling of any node. The location of a node's parent can be found by dividing the node's position in the block by 2 while discarding any remainder (the parent of the node in position 7 would be the node in position 3). The location of a node's sibling can be found by adding 1 to the location of a node in an even-numbered position or subtracting 1 from the location of a node in an odd-numbered position. For example, the sibling of the node in position 4 is the node in position 5, while the sibling of the node in position 3 is the node in position 2. Moreover, this storage system makes efficient use of space when the binary tree is approximately balanced (in the sense that both subtrees below the root node have the same depth) and full (in the sense that it does not have long, thin branches). For trees without these characteristics, though, the system can become quite inefficient, as shown in Figure 8.18.

Manipulating Data Structures

We have seen that the way data structures are actually stored in a computer's memory is not the same as the conceptual structure envisioned by the user. A two-dimensional array is not actually stored as a two-dimensional rectangular block, and a list or a tree might actually consist of small pieces scattered over a large area of memory.

Hence, to allow the user to access the structure as an abstract tool, we must shield the user from the complexities of the actual storage system. This means that instructions given by the user (and stated in terms of the abstract tool) must be converted into steps that are appropriate for the actual storage system. In the

Figure 8.18 A sparse, unbalanced tree shown in its conceptual form and as it would be stored without pointers

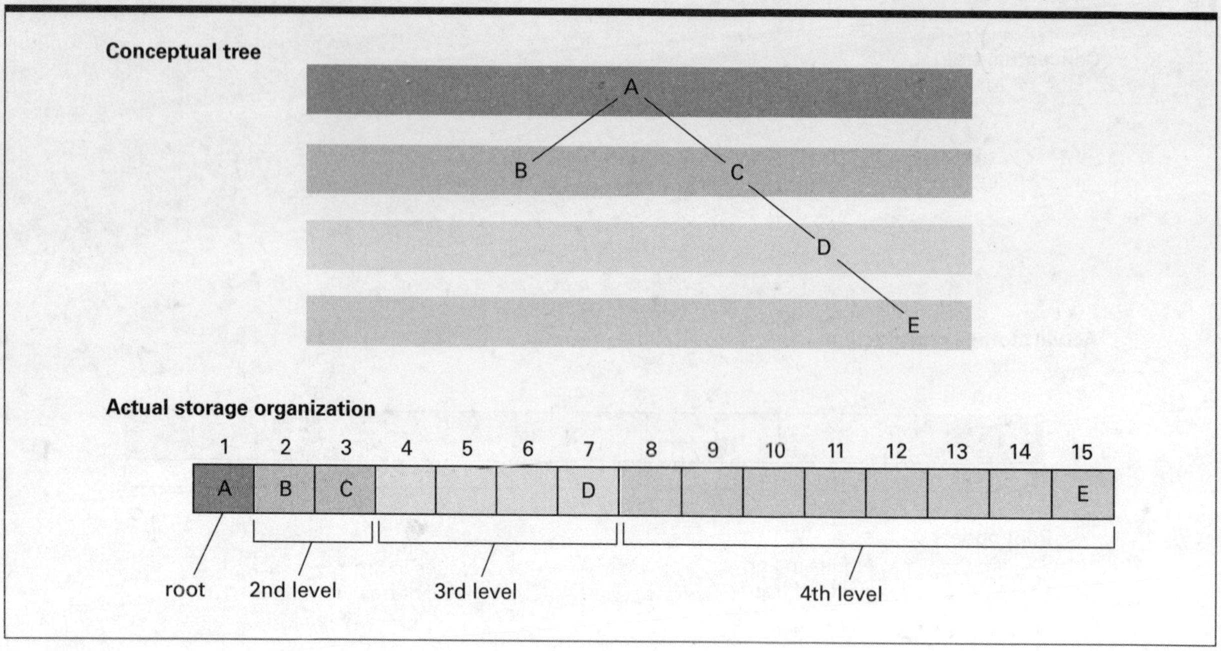

case of arrays, we have seen how this can be done by using an address polynomial to convert row and column indices into memory cell addresses. In particular, we have seen how the statement

```
Sales[3, 4] = 5;
```

written by a programmer who is thinking in terms of an abstract array can be converted into steps that perform the correct modifications to main memory. Likewise, we have seen how statements such as

```
Employee.Age = 22;
```

referring to an abstract aggregate type can be translated into appropriate actions depending on how the aggregate is actually stored.

In the case of lists, stacks, queues, and trees, instructions stated in terms of the abstract structure are usually converted into the appropriate actions by means of functions that perform the required task while shielding the user from the details of the underlying storage system. For example, if the function `insert` were provided for inserting new entries into a linked list, then J. W. Brown could be inserted in the list of students enrolled in Physics 208 merely by executing a function call such as

```
insert("Brown, J.W.", Physics208)
```

Note that the function call is stated entirely in terms of the abstract structure—the manner in which the list is actually implemented is hidden.

As a more detailed example, Figure 8.19 presents a function named `printList` for printing a linked list of values. This function assumes that the first entry of the list is pointed to by a field called `Head` within the aggregate called `List`, and that each entry in the list consists of two pieces: a value ("`Value`") and a pointer

Figure 8.19 A function for printing a linked list

```
def PrintList(List):
  CurrentPointer = List.Head
  while (CurrentPointer != None):
    print(CurrentPointer.Value)
    CurrentPointer = CurrentPointer.Next
```

to the next entry ("Next"). In the figure, the special Python value None is used as the null pointer. Once this function has been developed, it can be used to print a linked list as an abstract tool without being concerned for the steps actually required to print the list. For example, to obtain a printed class list for Economics 301, a user need only perform the function call

```
printList(Economics301ClassList)
```

to obtain the desired results. Moreover, if we should later decide to change the manner in which the list is actually stored, then only the internal actions of the function `printList` must be changed—the user would continue to request the printing of the list with the same function call as before.

Questions & Exercises

1. Show how the array below would be arranged in main memory when stored in row major order.

5	3	7
4	2	8
1	9	6

2. Give a formula for finding the entry in the *i*th row and *j*th column of a two-dimensional array if it is stored in column major order rather than row major order.
3. In the Python, C, C++, Java, and C# programming languages, indices of arrays start at 0 rather than at 1. Thus the entry in the first row, fourth column of an array named `Array` is referenced by `Array[0][3]`. In this case, what address polynomial is used by the translator to convert references of the form `Array[i][j]` into memory addresses?
4. What condition indicates that a linked list is empty?
5. Modify the function in Figure 8.19 so that it stops printing once a particular name has been printed.
6. Based on the technique of this section for implementing a stack in a contiguous block of cells, what condition indicates that the stack is empty?

7. Describe how a stack can be implemented in a high-level language in terms of a one-dimensional array.
8. When a queue is implemented in a circular fashion as described in this section, what is the relationship between the head and tail pointers when the queue is empty? What about when the queue is full? How can one detect whether a queue is full or empty?
9. Draw a diagram representing how the tree below appears in memory when stored using the left and right child pointers, as described in this section. Then, draw another diagram showing how the tree would appear in contiguous storage using the alternative storage system described in this section.

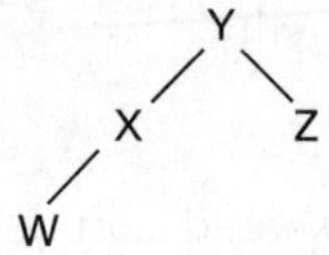

8.4 A Short Case Study

Let us consider the task of storing a list of names in alphabetical order. We assume that the operations to be performed on this list are the following:

search for the presence of an entry,
print the list in alphabetical order, and
insert a new entry

Our goal is to develop a storage system along with a collection of functions to perform these operations—thus producing a complete abstract tool.

We begin by considering options for storing the list. If the list were stored according to the linked list model, we would need to search the list in a sequential fashion, a process that, as we discussed in Chapter 5, could be very inefficient if the list becomes long. We will therefore seek an implementation that allows us to use the binary search algorithm (Section 5.5) for our search procedure. To apply this algorithm, our storage system must allow us to find the middle entry of successively smaller portions of the list. Our solution is to store the list as a binary tree. We make the middle list entry the root node. Then we make the middle of the remaining first half of the list the root's left child, and we make the middle of the remaining second half the root's right child. The middle entries of each remaining fourth of the list become the children of the root's children and so forth. For example, the tree in Figure 8.20 represents the list of letters A, B, C, D, E, F, G, H, I, J, K, L, and M. (We consider the larger of the middle two entries as the middle when the part of the list in question contains an even number of entries.)

Figure 8.20 The letters A through M arranged in an ordered tree

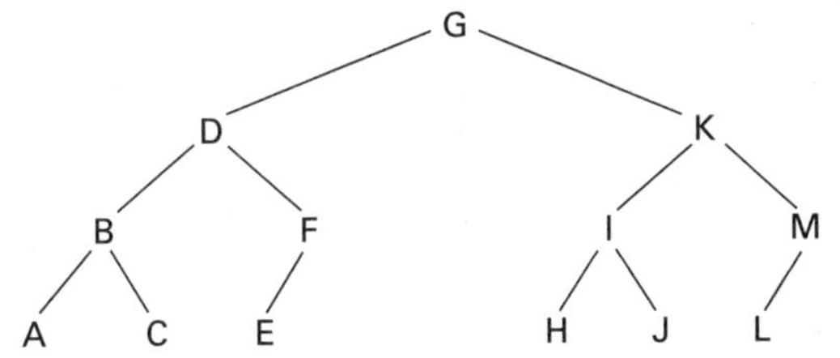

To search the list stored in this manner, we compare the target value to the root node. If the two are equal, our search has succeeded. If they are not equal, we move to the left or right child of the root, depending on whether the target is less than or greater than the root, respectively. There we find the middle of the portion of the list that is necessary to continue the search. This process of comparing and moving to a child continues until we find the target value (meaning that our search was successful) or we reach a null pointer (`None`) without finding the target value (meaning that our search was a failure).

Figure 8.21 shows how this search process can be expressed in the case of a linked tree structure. The Python `elif` keyword is a shortcut for "`else: if ...`". Note that this function is merely a refinement of the function in Figure 5.14, which is our original statement of the binary search. The distinction is largely cosmetic. Instead of stating the algorithm in terms of searching successively smaller segments of the list, we now state the algorithm in terms of searching successively smaller subtrees (Figure 8.22).

Having stored our "list" as a binary tree, you might think that the process of printing the list in alphabetical order would now be difficult. However, to print the list in alphabetical order, we merely need to print the left subtree in alphabetical order, print the root node, and then print the right subtree in alphabetical

Figure 8.21 The binary search as it would appear if the list were implemented as a linked binary tree

```
def Search(Tree, TargetValue):
  if (Tree is None):
    return None              # Search failed
  elif (TargetValue == Tree.Value):
    return Tree              # Search succeeded
  elif (TargetValue < Tree.Value):
    # Continue search in left subtree.
    return Search(Tree.Left, TargetValue)
  elif (TargetValue > Tree.Value):
    # Continue search in right subtree.
    return Search(Tree.Right, TargetValue)
```

Garbage Collection

As dynamic data structures grow and shrink, storage space is used and released. The process of reclaiming unused storage space for future use is known as **garbage collection.** Garbage collection is required in numerous settings. The memory manager within an operating system must perform garbage collection as it allocates and retrieves memory space. The file manager performs garbage collection as files are stored in and deleted from the machine's mass storage. Moreover, any process running under the control of the dispatcher might need to perform garbage collection within its own allotted memory space.

Garbage collection involves some subtle problems. In the case of linked structures, each time a pointer to a data item is changed, the garbage collector must decide whether to reclaim the storage space to which the pointer originally pointed. The problem becomes especially complex in intertwined data structures involving multiple paths of pointers. Inaccurate garbage collection routines can lead to loss of data or to inefficient use of storage space. For example, if garbage collection fails to reclaim storage space, the available space will slowly dwindle away, a phenomenon known as a **memory leak.**

order (Figure 8.23). After all, the left subtree contains all the elements that are less than the root node, while the right subtree contains all the elements that are greater than the root. A sketch of our logic so far looks like this:

```
if (tree not empty):
  print the left subtree in alphabetical order
  print the root node
  print the right subtree in alphabetical order
```

Figure 8.22 The successively smaller trees considered by the function in Figure 8.21 when searching for the letter J

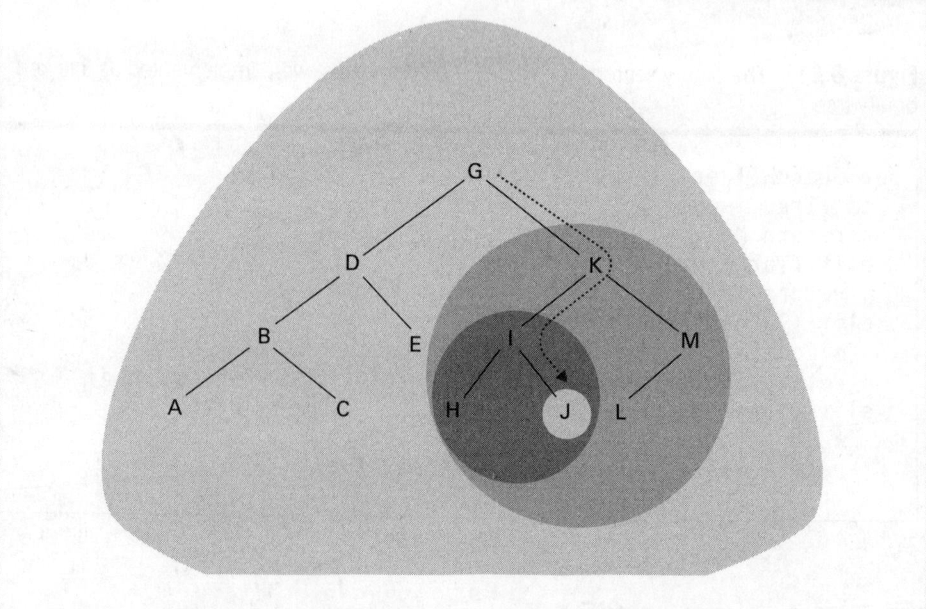

Figure 8.23 Printing a search tree in alphabetical order

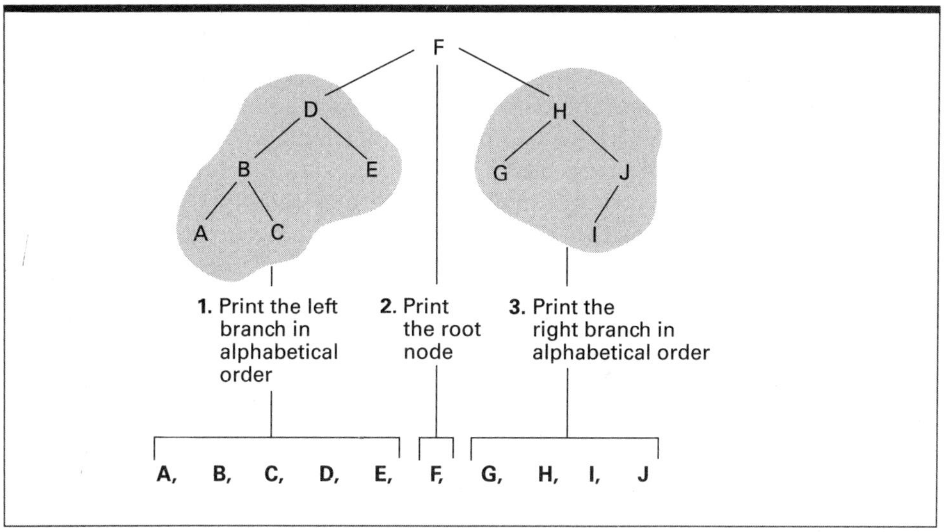

This outline involves the tasks of printing the left subtree and the right subtree in alphabetical order, both of which are essentially smaller versions of our original task. That is, solving the problem of printing a tree involves the smaller task of printing subtrees, which suggests a recursive approach to our tree printing problem.

Following this lead, we can expand our initial idea into a complete Python function for printing our tree as shown in Figure 8.24. We have assigned the function the name `PrintTree` and then requested the services of `PrintTree` for printing the left and right subtrees. Note that the termination condition of the recursive process (reaching a null subtree, "`None`") is guaranteed to be reached, because each successive activation of the function operates on a smaller tree than the one causing the activation.

The task of inserting a new entry in the tree is also easier than it might appear at first. Your intuition might lead you to believe that insertions might require cutting the tree open to allow room for new entries, but actually the node being added can always be attached as a new leaf, regardless of the value involved. To find the proper place for a new entry, we move down the tree along the path that we would follow if we were searching for that entry. Since the entry is not in

Figure 8.24 A function for printing the data in a binary tree

```
def PrintTree(Tree):
  if (Tree != None):
    PrintTree(Tree.Left)
    print(Tree.Value)
    PrintTree(Tree.Right)
```

the tree, our search will lead to a null pointer. At this point we will have found the proper location for the new node (Figure 8.25). Indeed, this is the location to which a search for the new entry would lead.

A function expressing this process in the case of a linked tree structure is shown in Figure 8.26. It searches the tree for the value being inserted (called `NewValue`) and then places a new leaf node containing `NewValue` at the proper location. Note that if the entry being inserted is actually found in the tree during the search, no insertion is made. The Python code in Figure 8.26 uses the function call `TreeNode()` to create a new aggregate to serve as a fresh leaf in the linked tree structure. This requires additional code outside of the figure to identify `TreeNode` as user-defined type, as we will see in the next section.

We conclude that a software package consisting of a linked binary tree structure together with our functions for searching, printing, and inserting provides a complete package that could be used as an abstract tool by our hypothetical application. Indeed, when properly implemented, this package could be used without concern for the actual underlying storage structure. By using the procedures in the package, the user could envision a list of names stored in alphabetical order, whereas the reality would be that the "list" entries are actually scattered among blocks of memory cells that are linked as a binary tree.

Figure 8.25 Inserting the entry M into the list B, E, G, H, J, K, N, P stored as a tree

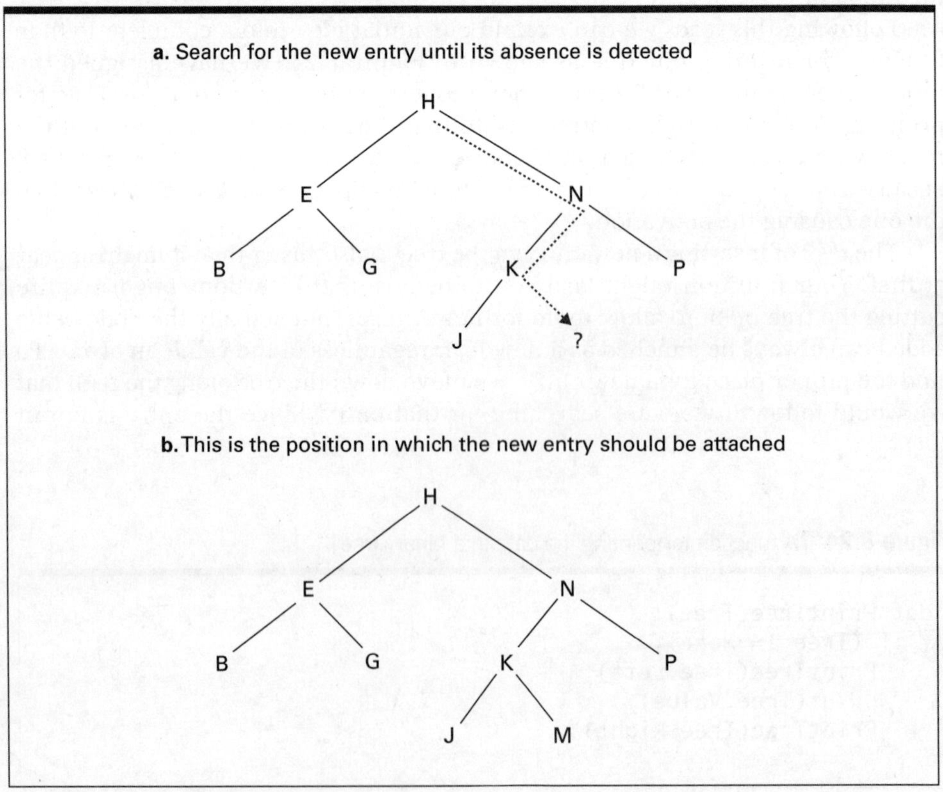

Figure 8.26 A function for inserting a new entry in a list stored as a binary tree

```
def Insert(Tree, NewValue):
  if (Tree is None):
    # Create a new leaf with NewValue
    Tree = TreeNode()
    Tree.Value = NewValue
  elif (NewValue < Tree.Value):
    # Insert NewValue into the left subtree
    Tree.Left = Insert(Tree.Left, NewValue)
  elif (NewValue > Tree.Value):
    # Insert NewValue into the right subtree
    Tree.Right = Insert(Tree.Right, NewValue)
  else:
    # Make no change.
  return Tree
```

Questions & Exercises

1. Draw a binary tree that you could use to store the list R, S, T, U, V, W, X, Y, and Z for future searching.
2. Indicate the path traversed by the binary search algorithm in Figure 8.21 when applied to the tree in Figure 8.20 in searching for the entry J. What about the entry P?
3. Draw a diagram representing the status of activations of the recursive tree-printing algorithm in Figure 8.24 at the time node K is printed within the ordered tree in Figure 8.20.
4. Describe how a tree structure in which each node has as many as 26 children could be used to encode the correct spelling of words in the English language.

8.5 Customized Data Types

In Chapter 6 we introduced the concept of a data type and discussed such elementary types as integer, float, character, and Boolean. These data types are provided in most programming languages as primitive data types. In this section we consider ways in which a programmer can define his or her own data types to fit more closely the needs of a particular application.

User-Defined Data Types

Expressing an algorithm is often easier if data types other than those provided as primitives in the programming language are available. For this reason, many modern programming languages allow programmers to define additional data types, using the primitive types as building blocks. The most elementary examples of such "home-made" data types are known as **user-defined data types,** which are essentially conglomerates of primitive types collected under a single name.

To explain, suppose we wanted to develop a program involving numerous variables, each with the same aggregate structure consisting of a name, age, and skill rating. One approach would be to define each variable separately as an aggregate type (Section 6.2). A better approach, however, would be to define the aggregate to be a new (user-defined) data type and then to use that new type as though it were a primitive.

Recalling the example from Section 6.2, in C the statement

```
struct
{
  char  Name[25];
  int   Age;
  float SkillRating;
} Employee;
```

defines a new aggregate, called `Employee`, containing fields called `Name` (of type character), `Age` (of type integer), and `SkillRating` (of type float).

In contrast, the C statement

```
struct EmployeeType
{
  char  Name[25];
  int   Age;
  float SkillRating;
};
```

does not define a new aggregate variable, but defines a new aggregate type, `EmployeeType`. This new data type could then be used to declare variables in the same way as a primitive data type. That is, in the same way that C allows the variable *x* to be declared as an integer using the statement

```
int x;
```

the variable `Employee1` could be declared to be of the type `Employee` with the statement

```
struct EmployeeType Employee1;
```

Then, later in the program, the variable `Employee1` would refer to an entire block of memory cells containing the name, age, and skill rating of an employee. Individual items within the block could be referenced by expressions such as `Employee1.Name` and `Employee1.Age`. Thus, a statement such as

```
Employee1.Age = 26;
```

might be used to assign the value 26 to the `Age` field within the block known as `Employee1`. Moreover, the statement

```
struct EmployeeType DistManager, SalesRep1, SalesRep2;
```

could be used to declare the three variables `DistManager`, `SalesRep1`, and `SalesRep2` to be of type `EmployeeType` just as a statement of the form

```
float Sleeve, Waist, Neck;
```

is normally used to declare the variables `Sleeve`, `Waist`, and `Neck` to be of the primitive type `float`.

It is important to distinguish between a user-defined data type and an actual item of that type. The latter is referred to as an **instance** of the type. A user-defined data type is essentially a template that is used in constructing instances of the type. It describes the properties that all instances of that type have but does not itself constitute an occurrence of that type (just as a cookie-cutter is a template from which cookies are made but is not itself a cookie). In the preceding example, the user-defined data type `EmployeeType` was used to construct three instances of that type, known as `DistManager`, `SalesRep1`, and `SalesRep2`.

Abstract Data Types

User-defined data types such as C's structs and Pascal's records play an important role in many programming languages, helping the software designer to tailor the representation of data to the needs for a particular program. Traditional user-defined data types, however, merely allow programmers to define new storage systems. They do not also provide operations to be performed on data with these structures.

An **abstract data type (ADT)** is a user-defined data type that can include both data (representation) and functions (behavior). Programming languages that support creation of ADTs generally provide two features: (1) syntax for defining the ADT as single unit, and (2) a mechanism for hiding the internal structure of the ADT from other parts of the program that will make use of it. The first feature is an important organizational tool for keeping the data and functions of an ADT together, which simplifies maintenance and debugging. The second feature provides reliability, by preventing other code outside of the ADT from accessing its data without going through the functions that have been provided for that purpose.

To clarify, suppose we wanted to create and use several stacks of integer values within a program. Our approach might be to implement each stack as an array of 20 integer values. The bottom entry in the stack would be placed (pushed) into the first array position, and additional stack entries would be placed (pushed) into successively higher entries in the array (see question 7 in Section 8.3). An additional integer variable would be used as the stack pointer. It would hold the index of the array entry into which the next stack entry should be pushed. Thus each stack would consist of an array containing the stack itself and an integer playing the role of the stack pointer.

To implement this plan, we could first establish a user-defined type called StackType with a C statement of the form

```
struct StackType
{
  int StackEntries[20];
  int StackPointer = 0;
};
```

(Recall that in languages such as C, C++, C#, and Java, indices for the array `StackEntries` range from 0 to 19, so we have initialized `StackPointer` to the value 0.) Having made this declaration, we could then declare stacks called StackOne, StackTwo, and StackThree via the statement

```
struct StackType StackOne, StackTwo, StackThree;
```

At this point, each of the variables StackOne, StackTwo, and StackThree would reference a unique block of memory cells used to implement an individual stack. But what if we now want to push the value 25 onto StackOne? We would like to avoid the details of the array structure underlying the stack's implementation and merely use the stack as an abstract tool—perhaps by using a function call similar to

```
push(25, StackOne);
```

But such a statement would not be available unless we also defined an appropriate function named push. Other operations we would like to perform on variables of type StackType would include popping entries off the stack, checking to see if the stack is empty, and checking to see if the stack is full—all of which would require definitions of additional functions. In short, our definition of the data type StackType has not included all the properties we would like to have associated with the type. Moreover, any function in the program can potentially access the StackPointer and StackEntries fields of our StackType variables, bypassing the careful checks we would design into our push and pop functions. A sloppy assignment statement in another part of the program could overwrite a data element stored in the middle of the stack data structure, or even destroy the LIFO behavior that is characteristic of all stacks.

What is needed is a mechanism for defining the operations that are allowed on our StackType, as well as for protecting the internal variables from outside interference. One such mechanism is the Java language's interface syntax. For example, in Java, we could write

```
interface StackType
{
  public int pop(); /* Return the item at top of stack */
  public void push(int item); /* Add a new item to stack */
  public boolean isEmpty(); /* Check if stack is emtpy */
  public boolean isFull(); /* Check if stack is full */
}
```

Alone, this abstract data type does not specify how the stack will be stored, or what algorithms will be used to execute the push, pop, isEmpty, and isFull functions. Those details (which have been *abstracted* away in this interface) will be specified in other Java code elsewhere. However, like our user-defined data type before, programmers are able to declare variables or function parameters to be of type StackType.

We could declare StackOne, StackTwo, and StackThree to be stacks with the statement

```
StackType StackOne, StackTwo, StackThree;
```

Later in the program (these three variables start out as null references and must be instantiated with concrete Java classes before use—but we are not concerned with those details here), we could push entries onto these stacks with statements such as

```
StackOne.push(25);
```

which means to execute the push function associated with StackOne using the value 25 as the actual parameter.

As opposed to the more elementary user-defined data types, abstract data types are complete data types, and their appearance in such languages as Ada in the 1980s represented a significant step forward in programming language design. Today, object-oriented languages provide for extended versions of abstract data types called classes, as we will see in the next section.

Questions & Exercises

1. What is the difference between a data type and an instance of that type?
2. What is the difference between a user-defined data type and an abstract data type?
3. Describe an abstract data type for implementing a list.
4. Describe an abstract data type for implementing checking accounts.

8.6 Classes and Objects

As we learned in Chapter 6, the object-oriented paradigm leads to systems composed of units called objects that interact with each other to accomplish tasks. Each object is an entity that responds to messages received from other objects. Objects are described by templates known as classes.

In many respects, these classes are actually descriptions of abstract data types (whose instances are called objects). For example, Figure 8.27 shows how a class known as StackOfIntegers can be defined in the languages Java and C#. (The equivalent class definition in C++ has the same structure but slightly different syntax.) Note that this class provides a body for each of the functions declared in the abstract data type StackType. In addition, this class contains an array of integers called StackEntries, and an integer used to identify the top of the stack within the array called StackPointer.

Using this class as a template, an object named StackOne can be created in a Java or C# program by the statement

```
StackType StackOne = new StackOfIntegers();
```

or in a C++ program by the statement

```
StackOfIntegers StackOne();
```

Later in the programs, the value 106 can be pushed onto StackOne using the statement

```
StackOne.push(106);
```

or the top entry from StackOne can be retrieved and placed in the variable OldValue using the statement

```
OldValue = StackOne.pop();
```

Figure 8.27 A stack of integers implemented in Java and C#

```
class StackOfIntegers implements StackType
{
  private int[] StackEntries = new int[20];
  private int StackPointer = 0;

  public void push(int NewEntry)
  {  if (StackPointer < 20)
        StackEntries[StackPointer++] = NewEntry;
  }

  public int pop()
  {  if (StackPointer > 0) return StackEntries[--StackPointer];
        else return 0;
  }

  public boolean isEmpty()
  {       return (StackPointer == 0);   }

  public boolean isFull()
  {       return (StackPointer >= MAX);    }
}
```

These features are essentially the same as those associated with abstract data types. There are, however, distinctions between classes and abstract data types. The former is an extension of the latter. For instance, as we learned in Section 6.5, object-oriented languages allow classes to inherit properties from other classes and to contain special methods called constructors that customize individual objects when they are created. Moreover, classes can be associated with varying degrees of encapsulation (Section 6.5), allowing the internal properties of their instances to be protected from misguided shortcuts, while exposing other fields to be available externally.

We conclude that the concepts of classes and objects represent another step in the evolution of techniques for representing data abstractions in programs. It is, in fact, the ability to define and use abstractions in a convenient manner that has led to the popularity of the object-oriented programming paradigm.

The Standard Template Library

The data structures discussed in this chapter have become standard programming structures—so standard, in fact, that many programming environments treat them very much like primitives. One example is found in the C++ programming environment, which is enhanced by the Standard Template Library (STL). The STL contains a collection of predefined classes that describe popular data structures. Consequently, by incorporating the STL into a C++ program, the programmer is relieved from the task of describing these structures in detail. Instead, he or she needs merely to declare identifiers to be of these types in the same manner that we declared `StackOne` to be of type `StackOfIntegers` in Section 8.6.

Questions & Exercises

1. In what ways are abstract data types and classes similar? In what ways are they different?
2. What is the difference between a class and an object?
3. Describe a class that would be used as a template for constructing objects of type queue-of-integers.

8.7 Pointers in Machine Language

In this chapter we have introduced pointers and have shown how they are used in constructing data structures. In this section we consider how pointers are handled in machine language.

Suppose that we want to write a program in the machine language described in Appendix C to pop an entry off the stack as described in Figure 8.12 and place that entry in a general-purpose register. In other words, we want to load a register with the contents of the memory cell that contains the entry on top of the stack. Our machine language provides two instructions for loading registers: one with op-code 2, the other with op-code 1. Recall that in the case of op-code 2, the operand field contains the data to be loaded, and in the case of op-code 1, the operand field contains the address of the data to be loaded.

We do not know what the contents will be, so we cannot use op-code 2 to obtain our goal. Moreover, we cannot use op-code 1, because we do not know what the address will be. After all, the address of the top of the stack will vary as the program is executed. However, we do know the address of the stack pointer. That is, we know the location of the address of the data we want to load. What we need, then, is a third op-code for loading a register, in which the operand contains the address of a pointer to the data to be loaded.

To accomplish this goal we could extend the language in Appendix C to include an op-code D. An instruction with this op-code could have the form DRXY, which would mean to load register R with the contents of the memory cell whose address is found at address XY (Figure 8.28). Thus if the stack pointer is in the memory cell at address AA, then the instruction D5AA would cause the data at the top of the stack to be loaded into register 5.

This instruction, however, does not complete the pop operation. We must also subtract one from the stack pointer so that it points to the new top of the stack. This means that, following the load instruction, our machine language program would have to load the stack pointer into a register, subtract one from it, and store the result back in memory.

By using one of the registers as the stack pointer instead of a memory cell, we could reduce this movement of the stack pointer back and forth between registers and memory. But this would mean that we must redesign the load instruction so that it expects the pointer to be in a register rather than in main memory. Thus, instead of the earlier approach, we might define an instruction with op-code D to have the form DR0S, which would mean to load register R

Figure 8.28 Our first attempt at expanding the machine language in Appendix C to take advantage of pointers

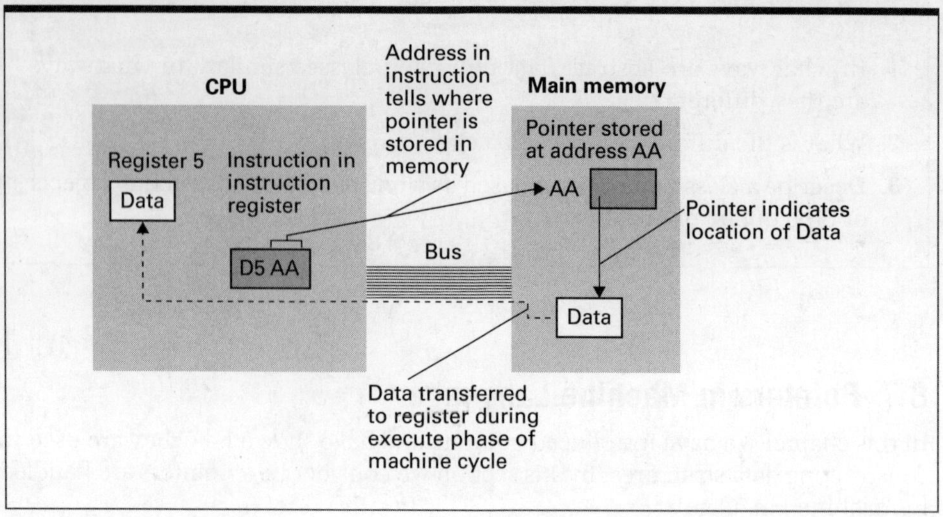

with the contents of the memory cell pointed to by register S (Figure 8.29). Then, a complete pop operation could be performed by following this instruction with an instruction (or instructions) to subtract one from the value stored in register S.

Note that a similar instruction is needed to implement a push operation. We might therefore extend the language described in Appendix C further by introducing the op-code E so that an instruction of the form ER0S would mean to store the contents of register R in the memory cell pointed to by register S. Again, to complete the push operation, this instruction would be followed by an instruction (or instructions) to add one to the value in register S.

Figure 8.29 Loading a register from a memory cell that is located by means of a pointer stored in a register

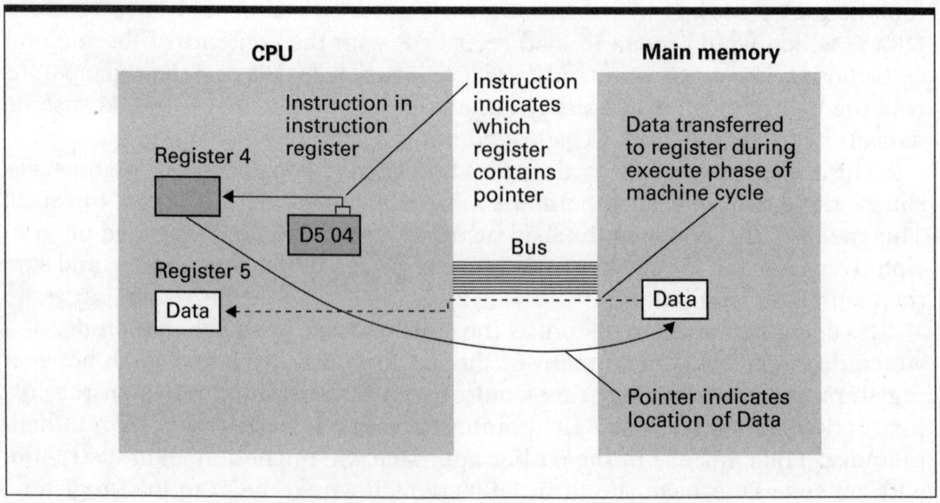

These new op-codes D and E that we have proposed not only demonstrate how machine languages are designed to manipulate pointers, they also demonstrate an addressing technique that was not present in the original machine language. As presented in Appendix C, the machine language uses two means of identifying the data involved in an instruction. The first of these is demonstrated by an instruction whose op-code is 2. Here, the operand field contains the data involved explicitly. This is called **immediate addressing.** The second means of identifying data is demonstrated by instructions with op-codes 1 and 3. Here the operand fields contain the address of the data involved. This is called **direct addressing.** However, our proposed new op-codes D and E demonstrate yet another form of identifying data. The operand fields of these instructions contain the address of the address of the data. This is called **indirect addressing.** All three are common in today's machine languages.

Questions & Exercises

1. Suppose the machine language described in Appendix C has been extended as suggested at the end of this section. Moreover, suppose register 8 contains the pattern DB, the memory cell at address DB contains the pattern CA, and the cell at address CA contains the pattern A5. What bit pattern will be in register 5 immediately after executing each of the following instructions?

   a. 25A5

   b. 15CA

   c. D508

2. Using the extensions described at the end of this section, write a complete machine language routine to perform a pop operation. Assume that the stack is implemented as shown in Figure 8.12, the stack pointer is in register F, and the top of the stack is to be popped into register 5.
3. Using the extensions described at the end of this section, write a program to copy the contents of five contiguous memory cells starting at address A0 to the five cells starting at address B0. Assume your program starts at address 00.
4. In the chapter, we introduced a machine instruction of the form DR0S. Suppose we extended this form to DRXS, meaning "Load register R with the data pointed to by the value in register S plus the value X." Thus the pointer to the data is obtained by retrieving the value in register S and then incrementing that value by X. The value in register S is not altered. (If register F contained 04, then the instruction DE2F would load register E with the contents of the memory cell at address 06. The value of register F would remain 04.) What advantages would this instruction have? What about an instruction of the form DRTS—meaning "Load register R with the data pointed to by the value in register S incremented by the value in register T"?

Chapter Review Problems

(Asterisked problems are associated with optional sections.)

1. Draw pictures showing how the array below appears in a machine's memory when stored in row major order and in column major order:

A	B	C	D
E	F	G	H
I	J	K	L

2. Suppose an array with six rows and eight columns is stored in row major order starting at address – 50 (base 10). If each entry in the array requires two memory cells, what is the address of the entry in the fifth row and seventh column? What if each entry requires three memory cells?

3. Rework question 2 assuming column major order rather than row major order.

4. Write a function such that if an element in an M × N matrix is 0, its entire row and column are set to 0.

5. Why is a contiguous list considered to be a convenient storage structure for implementing static lists, but not for implementing dynamic lists? Explain your answer.

6. Suppose you want to insert the number 3 in the list of numbers 1, 2, 4, 5, 6, 7, 8. What activities are required to insert the number 3 in the list, assuming that the order of the list is to be maintained?

7. The following table represents the contents of some cells in a computer's main memory along with the address of each cell represented. Note that some of the cells contain letters of the alphabet, and each such cell is followed by an empty cell. Place addresses in these empty cells so that each cell containing a letter together with the following cell form an entry in a linked list in which the letters appear in alphabetical order. (Use zero for the null pointer.) What address should the head pointer contain?

Address	Contents
11	C
12	
13	G
14	
15	E
16	
17	B
18	
19	U
20	
21	F
22	

8. The following table represents a portion of a linked list in a computer's main memory. Each entry in the list consists of two cells: The first contains a letter of the alphabet; the second contains a pointer to the next list entry. Alter the pointers so that the letter N is no longer in the list. Then replace the letter N with the letter G and alter the pointers so that the new letter appears in the list in its proper place in alphabetical order.

Address	Contents
30	J
31	38
32	B
33	30
34	X
35	46
36	N
37	40
38	K
39	36
40	P
41	34

9. The following table represents a linked list using the same format as in the preceding problems. If the head pointer contains the value 44, what name is represented by

the list? Change the pointers so that the list contains the name Jean.

Address	Contents
40	N
41	46
42	I
43	40
44	J
45	50
46	E
47	00
48	M
49	42
50	A
51	40

10. Which of the following routines correctly inserts `NewEntry` immediately after the entry called `PreviousEntry` in a linked list? What is wrong with the other routine?

Routine 1:

```
1. Copy the value in the pointer
   field of PreviousEntry into the
   pointer field of NewEntry.
2. Change the value in the pointer
   field of PreviousEntry to the
   address of NewEntry.
```

Routine 2:

```
1. Change the value in the pointer
   field of PreviousEntry to the
   address of NewEntry.
2. Copy the value in the pointer
   field of PreviousEntry into the
   pointer field of NewEntry.
```

11. Design a function to find the `Kth` element in a single linked list with `n` elements.

12. Design a function to check whether the elements of a single linked list with `n` elements, form a palindrome.

13. Design a function for counting the nodes of a linked list.

14. a. Suppose you were given a linked list with `n` elements. Design an algorithm to remove duplicates from an unsorted linked list.

b. If the use of a temporary buffer is not permitted to solve part (a), how would you solve the problem?

15. Sometimes a single linked list is given two different orders by attaching two pointers to each entry rather than one. Fill in the table below so that by following the first pointer after each letter one finds the name Carol, but by following the second pointer after each letter one finds the letters in alphabetical order. What values belong in the head pointer of each of the two lists represented?

Address	Contents
60	O
61	
62	
63	C
64	
65	
66	A
67	
68	
69	L
70	
71	
72	R
73	
74	

16. The table below represents a stack stored in a contiguous block of memory cells, as discussed in the text. If the base of the stack is at address 10 and the stack pointer contains the value 12, what value is retrieved by a pop instruction? What value is in the stack pointer after the pop operation?

Address	Contents
10	F
11	C
12	A
13	B
14	E

17. Draw a table showing the final contents of the memory cells if the instruction in question 16 had been to push the letter D on the stack rather than to pop a letter. What would the value in the stack pointer be after the push instruction?

18. How would you design a stack which, in addition to the traditional push and pop operations, also supports an operation called `min` which returns the element having the minimum value in the stack? `push`, `pop`, and `min` should all operate in O(1) time.

19. Describe how a single array can be used to implement three stacks.

20. Suppose you were given a stack and you were allowed to use one additional stack, without copying the elements into any other data structure. Write a program to sort the stack in ascending order (biggest items on the top). The stack supports `push`, `pop`, `peek`, and `isEmpty` operations.

21. Suppose you were given three stacks and you were only allowed to move entries one at a time from one stack to another. Design an algorithm for reversing two adjacent entries on one of the stacks.

22. Suppose we want to create a stack of names that vary in length. Why is it advantageous to store the names in separate areas of memory and then build the stack out of pointers to these names rather than allowing the stack to contain the names themselves?

23. Design a function called `TwoStacks` which implements a queue by using two stacks.

24. Suppose a stack consists of boxes of specific width, height, and depth. Boxes can be stacked on the top if the underlying box is larger in all dimensions, but cannot be rotated. Try to implement the tallest stack, where the height of a stack is the sum of the heights of each box.

25. Suppose the entries in a queue require one memory cell each, the head pointer contains the value 11, and the tail pointer contains the value 17. What are the values of these pointers after one entry is inserted and two are removed?

26. The Towers of Hanoi is a classic puzzle consisting of 3 towers, and N disks of different sizes which can slide onto any tower. The puzzle starts with the disks sorted in an ascending order from top to bottom. It has the following constraints:

    a. Only one disk can be moved at a time.
    b. A disk is moved from the top of one tower onto the next tower.
    c. A disk can only be placed on top of a larger disk.

    Write a program to move the disks from the first tower to the last using stacks.

27. Design a method that counts all the possible ways in which a person can run up the stairs, if he can jump one, two or three steps at a time.

28. Suppose you were given two queues and you were only allowed to move one entry at a time from the head of a queue to the tail of either. Design an algorithm for reversing two adjacent entries in one of the queues.

29. The table below represents a tree stored in a machine's memory. Each node of the tree consists of three cells. The first cell contains the data (a letter), the second contains a pointer to the node's left child, and the third contains a pointer to the node's right child. A value of 0 represents a null pointer. If the value of the root pointer is 55, draw a picture of the tree.

Address	Contents
40	G
41	0
42	0
43	X
44	0
45	0
46	J
47	49
48	0
49	M
50	0
51	0
52	F
53	43
54	40
55	W
56	46
57	52

30. The table below represents the contents of a block of cells in a computer's main memory. Note that some of the cells contain letters of the alphabet, and each of those cells is followed by two blank cells. Fill in the blank cells so that the memory block represents the tree that follows. Use the first cell following a letter as the pointer to that node's left child and the next cell as the pointer to the right child. Use 0 for null pointers. What value should be in the root pointer?

Address	Contents
30	C
31	
32	
33	H
34	
35	
36	K
37	
38	
39	E
40	
41	
42	G
43	
44	
45	P
46	
47	

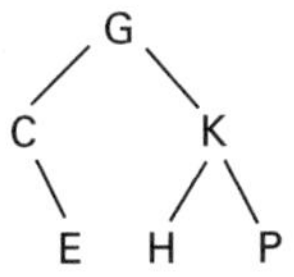

31. Write an algorithm to create a binary search tree with minimal height, for a given sorted array of integers.

32. Design a nonrecursive algorithm to replace the recursive one represented in Figure 8.24. Use a stack to control any backtracking that might be necessary.

33. Apply the recursive tree-printing algorithm of Figure 8.24. Draw a diagram representing the nested activations of the algorithm (and the current position in each) at the time node X is printed.

34. Implement a function to check if a binary tree is balanced. A balanced tree is defined to be a tree in which the heights of two subtrees of any node never differ by more than one.

35. Draw a diagram showing how the binary tree below appears in memory when stored without pointers using a block of contiguous memory cells as described in Section 8.3.

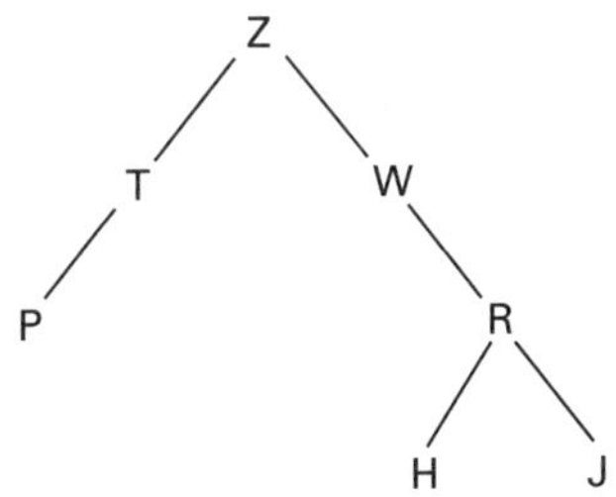

36. Suppose each node in a binary tree contains a value. Design a method that prints all the paths which sum to a specified value. The path can start at an arbitrary node.

37. Give an example in which you might want to implement a list (the conceptual structure) as a tree (the actual underlying structure). Give an example in which you might want to implement a tree (the conceptual structure) as a list (the actual underlying structure).

38. Suppose a binary tree Tl has millions of nodes, and another tree T2, has hundreds of nodes. Create an algorithm to decide whether T2 is a subtree of Tl. T2 would be a subtree of Tl if there is a node "n" in Tl whose subtree is identical to T2.

39. Design an algorithm to check whether a route between two nodes exists in a directed graph.

40. Identify the trees below whose nodes would be printed in alphabetical order by the algorithm in Figure 8.24.

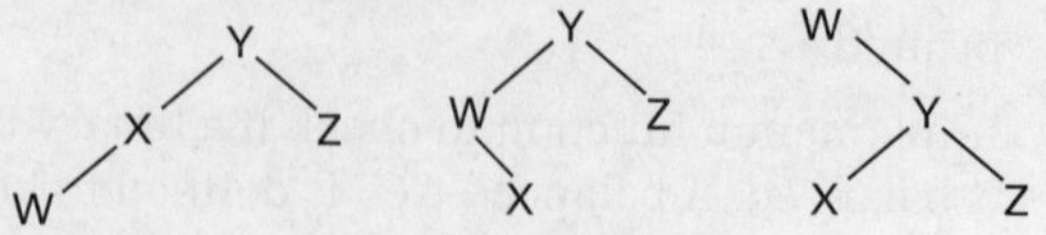

41. Modify the function in Figure 8.24 to print the "list" in reverse order.

42. Suppose a call center has three levels of employees—respondent, manager, and director. An incoming telephone call must first be allocated to a respondent who is free. If the respondent cannot handle the call, the call must be escalated to a manager. If the manager is occupied, then the call should be escalated to a director. Design the classes and data structures for this problem. Implement a method `dispatchCall()` which assigns a call to the first available employee.

43. Design a procedure for finding and deleting a given value from a tree stored in the fashion of Figure 8.20.

44. In the traditional implementation of a tree, each node is constructed with a separate pointer for each possible child. The number of such pointers is a design decision and represents the maximum number of children any node can have. If a node has fewer children than pointers, some of its pointers are simply set to null. But such a node can never have more children than pointers. Describe how a tree could be implemented without limiting the number of children a node could have.

45. Using pseudocode modeled on the C struct statement introduced in Section 8.5, define a user-defined data type representing data regarding an employee of a company (such as name, address, job assignment, pay scale, and so on).

46. Using pseudocode similar to the Java class syntax of Figure 8.27, sketch a definition of an abstract data type representing a list of names. In particular, what structure would contain the list and what functions would be provided to manipulate the list? (You do not need to include detailed descriptions of the functions.)

47. Using pseudocode similar to the Java class syntax of Figure 8.27, sketch a definition of an abstract data type representing a queue. Then give pseudocode statements showing how instances of that type could be created and how entries could be inserted in and deleted from those instances.

48. a. What is the difference between a user-defined data type and a primitive data type?
b. What is the difference between an abstract data type and a user-defined data type?

49. Identify the data structures and procedures that might appear in an abstract data type representing an address book.

50. Identify the data structures and procedures that might appear in an abstract data type representing a simple spacecraft in a video game.

51. Modify Figure 8.27 and the StackType interface from Section 8.5 so that the class defines a queue rather than a stack.

52. In what way is a class more general than a traditional abstract data type?

***53.** Using instructions of the form DR0S and ER0S as described at the end of Section 8.7, write a complete machine language routine to push an entry onto a stack implemented as shown in Figure 8.12. Assume that the stack pointer is in register F and that the entry to be pushed is in register 5.

***54.** Suppose a Boolean expression consisting of the symbols 0, 1, &, |, and A, and a desired Boolean result value is given. Implement a function to count the number of ways to parenthesize the expression, such that it evaluates to the result. For example, if the expression is 1 A 01011 and the desired result is false (0), the output will be 1A((010) 11) and 1 A (91 (011)).

***55.** What advantages does an instruction of the form DR0S as described in Section 8.7 have over an instruction of the form DRXY? What advantage does the form DRXS as described in question 4 of Section 8.7 have over the form DR0S?

Social Issues

The following questions are intended as a guide to the ethical/social/legal issues associated with the field of computing. The goal is not merely to answer these questions. You should also consider why you answered as you did and whether your justifications are consistent from one question to the next.

1. Suppose a software analyst designs a data organization that allows for efficient manipulation of data in a particular application. How can the rights to that data structure be protected? Is a data structure the expression of an idea (like a poem) and therefore protected by copyright or do data structures fall through the same legal loopholes as algorithms? What about patent law?
2. To what extent is incorrect data worse than no data?
3. In many application programs, the size to which a stack can grow is determined by the amount of memory available. If the available space is consumed, then the software is designed to produce a message such as "stack overflow" and terminate. In most cases this error never occurs, and the user is never aware of it. Who is liable if such an error occurs and sensitive information is lost? How could the software developer minimize his or her liability?
4. In a data structure based on a pointer system, the deletion of an item usually consists of changing a pointer rather than erasing memory cells. Thus when an entry in a linked list is deleted, the deleted entry actually remains in memory until its memory space is required by other data. What ethical and security issues result from this persistence of deleted data?
5. It is easy to transfer data and programs from one computer to another. Thus it is easy to transfer the knowledge held by one machine to many machines. In contrast, it sometimes takes a long time for a human to transfer knowledge to another human. For example, it takes time for a human to teach another human a new language. What implications could this contrast in knowledge transfer rate have if the capabilities of machines begin to challenge the capabilities of humans?
6. The use of pointers allows related data to be linked in a computer's memory in a manner reminiscent of the way many believe information is associated in the human mind. How are such links in a computer's memory similar to links in a brain? How are they different? Is it ethical to attempt to build computers that more closely mimic the human mind?
7. Has the popularization of computer technology produced new ethical issues or simply provided a new context in which previous ethical theories are applicable?
8. Suppose the author of an introductory computer science textbook wants to include program examples to demonstrate concepts in the text. However, to obtain clarity, many of the examples must be simplified versions of what would actually be used in professional-quality software. The author knows that the examples could be used by unsuspecting readers and ultimately could find their way into significant software applications in which more robust techniques would be more appropriate. Should the author use the simplified examples, insist that all examples be robust even if doing so decreases their demonstrative value, or refuse to use such examples unless clarity and robustness can both be obtained?

Additional Reading

Carrano, F. M., and T. Henry. *Data Abstraction and Problem Solving with C++: Walls and Mirrors,* 6th ed. Boston, MA: Addison-Wesley, 2012.

Gray, S. *Data Structures in Java: From Abstract Data Types to the Java Collections Framework.* Boston, MA: Addison-Wesley, 2007.

Main, M. *Data Structures and Other Objects Using Java,* 4th ed. Boston, MA: Addison-Wesley, 2011.

Main, M., and W. Savitch. *Data Structures and Other Objects Using C++,* 4th ed. Boston, MA: Addison-Wesley, 2010.

Prichard, J., and F.M. Carrano. *Data Abstraction and Problem Solving with Java: Walls and Mirrors,* 3rd ed. Boston, MA: Addison-Wesley, 2010.

Shaffer, C. A. *Practical Introduction to Data Structures and Algorithm Analysis,* 2nd ed. Upper Saddle River, NJ: Prentice Hall, 2001.

Weiss, M. A. *Data Structures and Problem Solving Using Java,* 4th ed. Boston, MA: Addison-Wesley, 2011.

Weiss, M. A. *Data Structures and Algorithm Analysis in C++,* 4th ed. Boston, MA: Addison-Wesley, 2013.

Weiss, M. A. *Data Structures and Algorithm Analysis in Java,* 3rd ed. Boston, MA: Addison-Wesley, 2011.

CHAPTER

9

Database Systems

A database is a system that converts a large collection of data into an abstract tool, allowing users to search for and extract pertinent items of information in a manner that is convenient to the user. In this chapter we explore this subject as well as take side excursions into the related fields of data mining, which seeks techniques for uncovering hidden patterns in large data collections, and traditional file structures, which provide many of the tools underlying today's database and data mining systems.

**Asterisks indicate suggestions for optional sections.*

Today's technology is capable of storing extremely large amounts of data, but such data collections are useless unless we are able to extract those particular items of information that are pertinent to the task at hand. In this chapter we will study database systems and learn how these systems apply abstraction to convert large data conglomerates into useful information sources. As a related topic, we will investigate the rapidly expanding field of data mining, whose goal is to develop techniques for identifying and exploring patterns within data collections. We will also examine the principles of traditional file structures, which provide the underpinnings for today's database and data mining systems.

9.1 Database Fundamentals

The term **database** refers to a collection of data that is multidimensional in the sense that internal links between its entries make the information accessible from a variety of perspectives. This is in contrast to a traditional file system (Section 9.5), sometimes called a **flat file,** which is a one-dimensional storage system, meaning that it presents its information from a single point of view. Whereas a flat file containing information about composers and their compositions might provide a list of compositions arranged by composer, a database might present all the works by a single composer, all the composers who wrote a particular type of music, and perhaps the composers who wrote variations of another composer's work.

The Significance of Database Systems

Historically, as computing machinery found broader uses in information management, each application tended to be implemented as a separate system with its own collection of data. Payroll was processed using the payroll file, the personnel department maintained its own employee records, and inventory was managed via an inventory file. This meant that much of the information required by an organization was duplicated throughout the company, while many different but related items were stored in separate systems. In this setting, database systems emerged as a means of integrating the information stored and maintained by a particular organization (Figure 9.1). With such a system, the same sales data could be used to produce restocking orders; create reports on market trends, direct advertisements, and product announcements to customers who are most likely to respond favorably to such information; and generate bonus checks for members of the sales force.

Such integrated pools of information provided a valuable resource with which management decisions could be made, assuming the information could be accessed in a meaningful way. In turn, database research focused on developing techniques by which the information in a database could be brought to the decision-making process. Much progress has been made in this regard. Today, database technology, combined with data mining techniques, is an important management tool, allowing the management of an organization to extract pertinent information from enormous amounts of data covering all aspects of the organization and its environment.

Moreover, database systems have become the underlying technology that supports many of the more popular sites on the World Wide Web. The underlying theme of sites such as Google, eBay, and Amazon is to provide an interface

Figure 9.1 A file versus a database organization

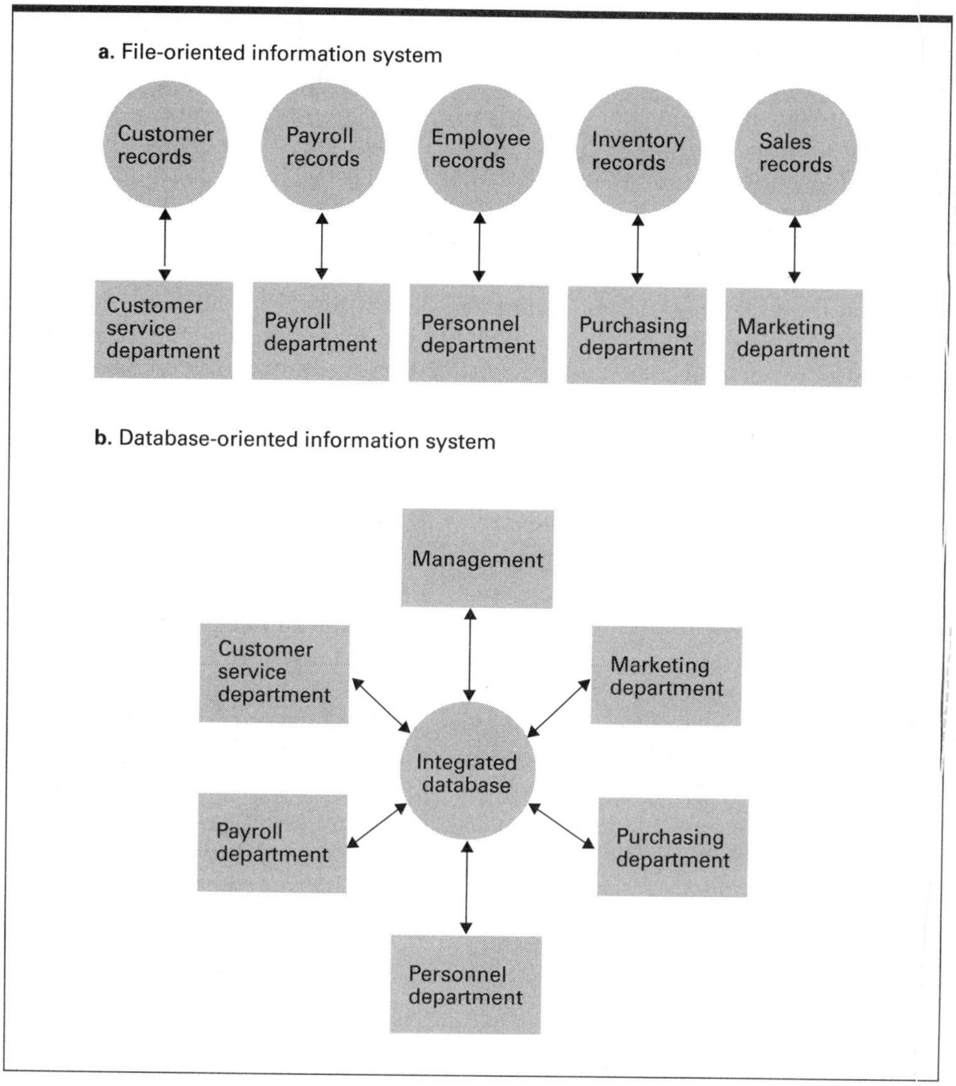

between clients and databases. To respond to a client's request, the server interrogates a database, organizes the results in the form of a Web page, and sends that page to the client. Such Web interfaces have popularized a new role for database technology in which a database is no longer a means of storing a company's records but, instead, is the company's product. Indeed, by combining database technology with Web interfaces, the Internet has become a major world-wide information source.

The Role of Schemas

Among the disadvantages of the proliferation of database technology is the potential of sensitive data being accessed by unauthorized personnel. Someone placing an order at a company's website should not have access to the company's financial data; similarly, an employee in a company's benefits department may need access to the company's employee records but should not have access to the corporation's inventory or sales records. Thus the ability to control access to the information in the database is as important as the ability to share it.

To provide different users access to different information within a database, database systems often rely on schemas and subschemas. A **schema** is a description of the entire database structure that is used by the database software to maintain the database. A **subschema** is a description of only that portion of the database pertinent to a particular user's needs. For example, a schema for a university database would indicate that each student record contains such items as the current address and phone number of that student in addition to the student's academic record. Moreover, it would indicate that each student record is linked to the record of the student's faculty adviser. In turn, the record for each faculty member would contain the person's address, employment history, and so on. Based on this schema, a linkage system would be maintained that ultimately connected the information about a student to the employment history of a faculty member.

To keep the university's registrar from using this linkage to obtain privileged information about the faculty, the registrar's access to the database must be restricted to a subschema whose description of the faculty records does not include employment history. Under this subschema, the registrar could find out which faculty member is a particular student's adviser but could not obtain access to additional information about that faculty member. In contrast, the subschema for the payroll department would provide the employment history of each faculty member but would not include the linkage between students and advisers. Thus the payroll department could modify a faculty member's salary but could not obtain the names of the students advised by that person.

Database Management Systems

A typical database application involves multiple software layers, which we will group into two major layers—an application layer and a database management layer (Figure 9.2). The application software handles the communication with the user of the database and may be quite complex, as exemplified by applications

Figure 9.2 The conceptual layers of a database implementation

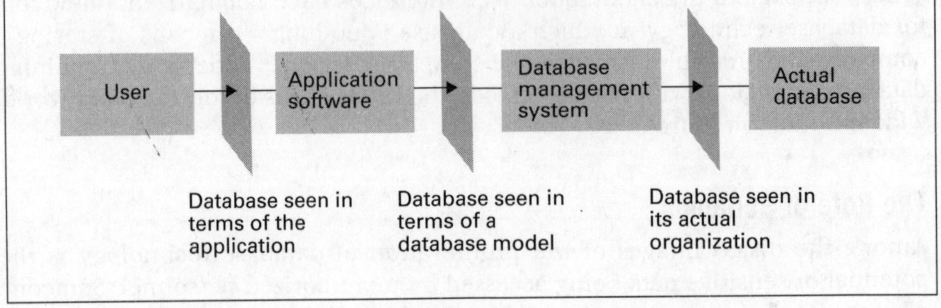

Distributed Databases

With the advancement of networking capabilities, database systems have grown to encompass databases, known as distributed databases, that consist of data residing on different machines. For instance, an international corporation might store and maintain local employee records at local sites yet link those records via a network to create a single distributed database.

A distributed database might contain fragmented and/or replicated data. The first case is exemplified by the previous employee-records example in which different fragments of the database are stored in different locations. In the second case, duplicates of the same database component are stored at different locations. Such replication might occur as a means of reducing information retrieval time. Both cases pose problems not present in more traditional centralized databases—how to disguise the distributed nature of the database so that it functions as a coherent system or how to ensure that replicated portions of a database remain duplicates of each other as updates occur. In turn, the study of distributed databases is a current area of research.

in which users access a database by means of a website. In that case the entire application layer consists of clients throughout the Internet and a server that uses the database to fill the requests from the clients.

Note that the application software does not directly manipulate the database. The actual manipulation of the database is accomplished by the **database management system (DBMS).** Once the application software has determined what action the user is requesting, it uses the DBMS as an abstract tool to obtain the results. If the request is to add or delete data, it is the DBMS that actually alters the database. If the request is to retrieve information, it is the DBMS that performs the required searches.

This dichotomy between the application software and the DBMS has several benefits. One is that it allows for the construction and use of abstract tools, which we have repeatedly found to be a major simplifying concept in software design. If the details of how the database is actually stored are isolated within the DBMS, the design of the application software can be greatly simplified. For instance, with a well-designed DBMS, the application software does not have to be concerned with whether the database is stored on a single machine or scattered among many machines within a network as a **distributed database.** Instead, the DBMS would deal with these issues, allowing the application software to access the database without concern for where the data is actually stored.

A second advantage of separating the application software from the DBMS is that such an organization provides a means for controlling access to the database. By dictating that the DBMS performs all access to the database, the DBMS can enforce the restrictions imposed by the various subschemas. In particular, the DBMS can use the entire database schema for its internal needs but can require that the application software employed by each user remain within the bounds described by that user's subschema.

Still another reason for separating the user interface and actual data manipulation into two different software layers is to achieve **data independence**—the ability to change the organization of the database itself without changing the application software. For example, the personnel department might need to add an additional field to each employee's record to indicate whether the corresponding employee chose to participate in the company's new health insurance program. If the application software dealt directly with the database, such a change in the data's format could require modifications to all application programs dealing with the database. As a result, the change instigated by the personnel department might cause changes to the payroll program as well as to the program for printing mailing labels for the company's newsletter.

The separation between application software and a DBMS removes the need for such reprogramming. To implement a change in the database required by a single user, one needs to change only the overall schema and the subschemas of those users involved in the change. The subschemas of all the other users remain the same, so their application software, which is based on the unaltered subschemas, does not need to be modified.

Database Models

We have repeatedly seen how abstraction can be used to hide internal complexities. Database management systems provide yet another example. They hide the complexities of a database's internal structure, allowing the user of the database to imagine that the information stored in the database is arranged in a more useful format. In particular, a DBMS contains routines that translate commands stated in terms of a conceptual view of the database into the actions required by the actual data storage system. This conceptual view of the database is called a **database model.**

In the following sections we will consider both the relational database model and the object-oriented database model. In the case of the relational database model, the conceptual view of the database is that of a collection of tables consisting of rows and columns. For example, information about a company's employees might be viewed as a table containing a row for each employee and columns labeled name, address, employee identification number, and so on. In turn, the DBMS would contain routines that would allow the application software to select certain entries from a particular row of the table or perhaps to report the range of values found in the salary column—even though the information is not actually stored in rows and columns.

These routines form the abstract tools used by the application software to access the database. More precisely, application software is often written in one of the general-purpose programming languages, such as those discussed in Chapter 6. These languages provide the basic ingredients for algorithmic expressions but lack instructions for manipulating a database. However, a program written in one of these languages can use the routines provided by the DBMS as prewritten subroutines—in effect extending the capabilities of the language in a manner that supports the conceptual image of the database model.

The search for better database models is an ongoing process. The goal is to find models that allow complex data systems to be conceptualized easily, lead to concise ways of expressing requests for information, and produce efficient database management systems.

Questions & Exercises

1. Identify two departments in a manufacturing plant that would have different uses for the same or similar inventory information. Then, describe how the subschema for the two departments might differ.
2. What is the purpose of a database model?
3. Summarize the roles of the application software and a DBMS.

9.2 The Relational Model

In this section we look more closely at the relational database model. It portrays data as being stored in rectangular tables, called **relations,** which are similar to the format in which information is displayed by spreadsheet programs. For example, the relational model allows information regarding the employees of a firm to be represented by a relation such as that shown in Figure 9.3.

A row in a relation is called a **tuple** (some say "TOO-pul," others say "TUH-pul"). In the relation of Figure 9.3, tuples consist of the information about a particular employee. Columns in a relation are referred to as **attributes** because each entry in a column describes some characteristic, or attribute, of the entity represented by the corresponding tuple.

Issues of Relational Design

A pivotal step in designing a relational database is to design the relations making up the database. Although this might appear to be a simple task, many subtleties are waiting to trap the unwary designer.

Suppose that in addition to the information contained in the relation of Figure 9.3, we want to include information about the jobs held by the employees. We might want to include a job history associated with each employee that consists of such attributes as job title (secretary, office manager, floor supervisor), a job identification code (unique to each job), the skill code associated with each job, the department in which the job exists, and the period during which the employee held the job in terms of a starting date and termination date. (We use an asterisk as the termination date if the job represents the employee's current position.)

Figure 9.3 A relation containing employee information

Empl Id	Name	Address	SSN
25X15	Joe E. Baker	33 Nowhere St.	111223333
34Y70	Cheryl H. Clark	563 Downtown Ave.	999009999
23Y34	G. Jerry Smith	1555 Circle Dr.	111005555
⋮	⋮	⋮	⋮

One approach to this problem is to extend the relation in Figure 9.3 to include these attributes as additional columns in the table, as shown in Figure 9.4. However, close examination of the result reveals several problems. One is a lack of efficiency due to redundancy. The relation no longer contains one tuple for each employee but rather one tuple for each assignment of an employee to a job. If an employee has advanced in the company through a sequence of several jobs, several tuples in the new relation must contain the same information about the employee (name, address, identification number, and Social Security number). For example, the personal information about Baker and Smith is repeated because they have held more than one job. Moreover, when a particular position has been held by numerous employees, the department associated with that job along with the appropriate skill code must be repeated in each tuple representing an assignment of the job. For example, the description of the floor manager job is duplicated because more than one employee has held this position.

Another, perhaps more serious, problem with our extended relation surfaces when we consider deleting information from the database. Suppose for example that Joe E. Baker is the only employee to hold the job identified as D7. If he were to leave the company and be deleted from the database represented in Figure 9.4, we would lose the information about job D7. After all, the only tuple containing the fact that job D7 requires a skill level of K2 is the tuple relating to Joe Baker.

You might argue that the ability to erase only a portion of a tuple could solve the problem, but this would in turn introduce other complications. For instance, should the information relating to job F5 also be retained in a partial tuple, or does this information reside elsewhere in the relation? Moreover, the temptation to use partial tuples is a strong indication that the design of the database can be improved.

The cause of all these problems is that we have combined more than one concept in a single relation. As proposed, the extended relation in Figure 9.4 contains information dealing directly with employees (name, identification number, address, Social Security number), information about the jobs available in the company (job identification, job title, department, skill code), and information

Figure 9.4 A relation containing redundancy

Empl Id	Name	Address	SSN	Job Id	JobTitle	Skill Code	Dept	Start Date	Term Date
25X15	Joe E. Baker	33 Nowhere St.	111223333	F5	Floor manager	FM3	Sales	9-1-2009	9-30-2010
25X15	Joe E. Baker	33 Nowhere St.	111223333	D7	Dept. head	K2	Sales	10-1-2010	*
34Y70	Cheryl H. Clark	563 Downtown Ave.	999009999	F5	Floor manager	FM3	Sales	10-1-2009	*
23Y34	G. Jerry Smith	1555 Circle Dr.	111005555	S25X	Secretary	T5	Personnel	3-1-1999	4-30-2010
23Y34	G. Jerry Smith	1555 Circle Dr.	111005555	S26Z	Secretary	T6	Accounting	5-1-2010	*
⋮	⋮	⋮	⋮	⋮	⋮	⋮	⋮	⋮	⋮

Database Systems for PCs

Personal computers are used in a variety of applications, ranging from elementary to sophisticated. In elementary "database" applications, such as storing Christmas card lists or maintaining bowling league records, spreadsheet systems are often used in lieu of database software since the application calls for little more than the ability to store, print, and sort data. There are, however, true database systems available for the PC market, one of which is Microsoft's Access. This is a complete relational database system as described in Section 9.2, as well as chart- and report-generation software. Access provides an excellent example of how the principles presented in this text form the backbone of popular products on the market today.

regarding the relationship between employees and jobs (start date, termination date). On the basis of this observation, we can solve our problems by redesigning the system using three relations—one for each of the preceding categories. We can keep the original relation in Figure 9.3 (which we now call the `EMPLOYEE` relation) and insert the additional information in the form of the two new relations called `JOB` and `ASSIGNMENT`, which produces the database in Figure 9.5.

Figure 9.5 An employee database consisting of three relations

EMPLOYEE relation

Empl Id	Name	Address	SSN
25X15	Joe E. Baker	33 Nowhere St.	111223333
34Y70	Cheryl H. Clark	563 Downtown Ave.	999009999
23Y34	G. Jerry Smith	1555 Circle Dr.	111005555

JOB relation

Job Id	JobTitle	Skill Code	Dept
S25X	Secretary	T5	Personnel
S26Z	Secretary	T6	Accounting
F5	Floor manager	FM3	Sales
•	•	•	•
•	•	•	•
•	•	•	•

ASSIGNMENT relation

Empl Id	Job Id	Start Date	Term Date
23Y34	S25X	3-1-1999	4-30-2010
34Y70	F5	10-1-2009	*
23Y34	S26Z	5-1-2010	*
•	•	•	•
•	•	•	•
•	•	•	•

A database consisting of these three relations contains the pertinent information about employees in the EMPLOYEE relation, about available jobs in the JOB relation, and about job history in the ASSIGNMENT relation. Additional information is implicitly available by combining the information from different relations. For instance, if we know an employee's identification number, we can find the departments in which that employee has worked by first finding all the jobs that employee has held using the ASSIGNMENT relation and then finding the departments associated with those jobs by means of the JOB relation (Figure 9.6). Through processes such as these, any information that could be obtained from the single large relation can be obtained from the three smaller relations without the problems previously cited.

Unfortunately, dividing information into various relations is not always as trouble-free as in the preceding example. For instance, compare the original relation in Figure 9.7, with attributes **EmplId**, **JobTitle**, and **Dept**, to the proposed decomposition into two relations. At first glance, the two-relation system might appear to contain the same information as the single-relation system, but, in fact, it does not. Consider for example the problem of finding the department in which a given employee works. This is easily done in the single-relation system by interrogating the tuple containing the employee identification number of the target employee and extracting the corresponding department. However, in the

Figure 9.6 Finding the departments in which employee 23Y34 has worked

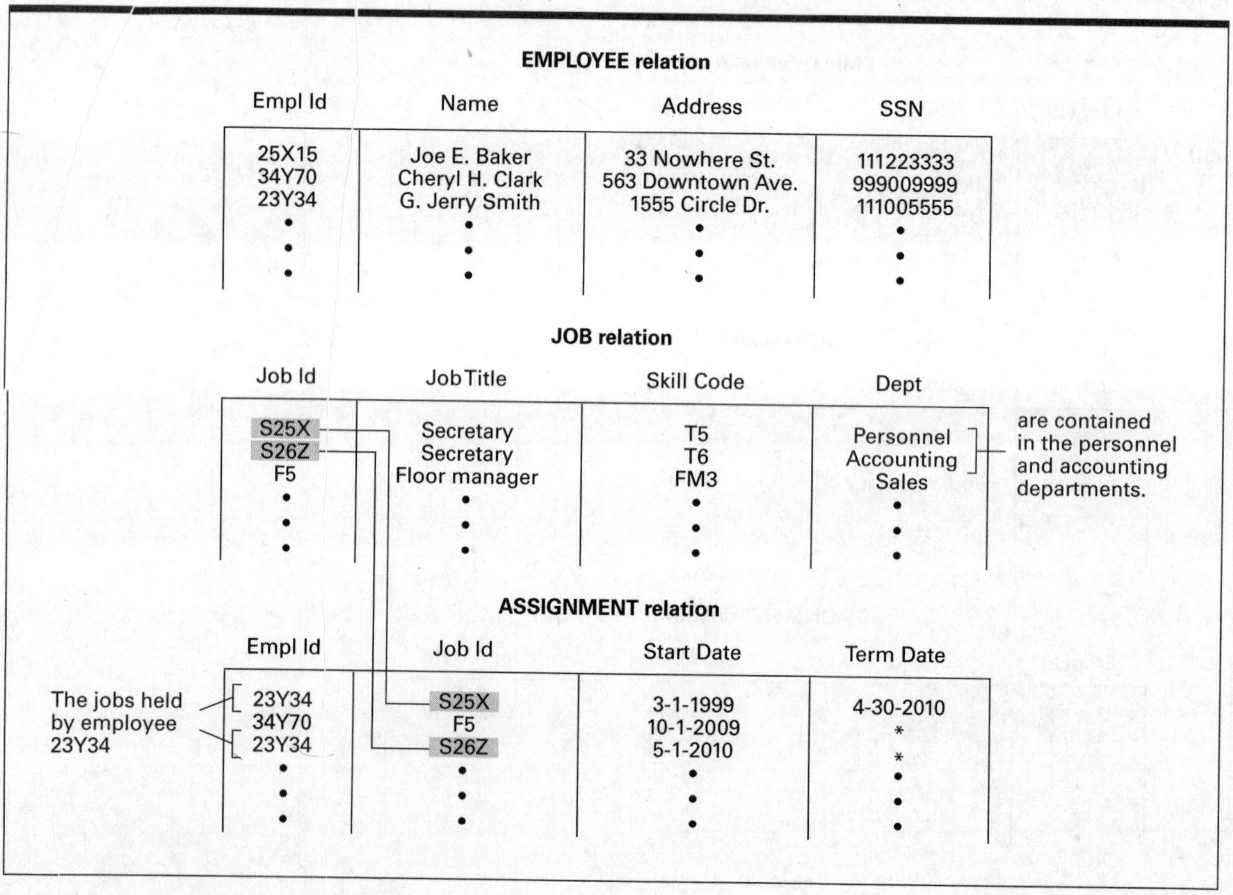

Figure 9.7 A relation and a proposed decomposition

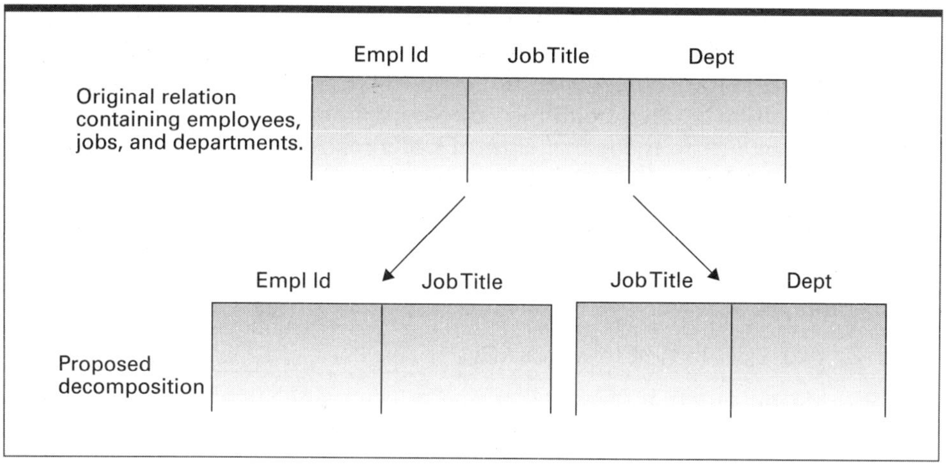

two-relation system, the desired information is not necessarily available. We can find the job title of the target employee and a department having such a job but this does not necessarily mean that the target employee works in that particular department, because several departments might have jobs with the same title.

We see, then, that sometimes dividing a relation into smaller relations causes the loss of information, and sometimes it does not. (The latter is called a **lossless decomposition**—or sometimes a **nonloss decomposition.**) Such relational characteristics are important design considerations. The goal is to identify the relational characteristics that can lead to problems in database design and find ways to reorganize those relations to remove these problematic characteristics.

Relational Operations

Now that you have a basic understanding of how data can be organized in terms of the relational model, it is time to see how information can be extracted from a database consisting of relations. We begin with a look at some operations that we might want to perform on relations.

At times we need to select certain tuples from a relation. To retrieve the information about an employee, we must select the tuple with the appropriate identification attribute value from the `EMPLOYEE` relation, or to obtain a list of the job titles in a certain department, we must select the tuples from the `JOB` relation having that department as their department attribute. The result of such a process is another relation consisting of the tuples selected from the parent relation. The outcome of selecting information about a particular employee results in a relation containing only one tuple from the `EMPLOYEE` relation. The outcome of selecting the tuples associated with a certain department results in a relation that probably contains several tuples from the `JOB` relation.

In short, one operation we might want to perform on a relation is to select tuples possessing certain characteristics and to place these selected tuples in a new relation. To express this operation, we adopt the syntax

```
NEW ← SELECT from EMPLOYEE where EmplId = '34Y70'
```

The semantics of this statement is to create a new relation called NEW containing those tuples (there should be only one in this case) from the relation EMPLOYEE whose EmplId attribute equals 34Y70 (Figure 9.8).

In contrast to the SELECT operation, which extracts rows from a relation, the PROJECT operation extracts columns. Suppose, for example, that in searching for the job titles in a certain department, we had already SELECTed the tuples from the JOB relation that pertained to the target department and placed these tuples in a new relation called NEW1. The list we are seeking is the JobTitle column within this new relation. The PROJECT operation allows us to extract this column (or columns if required) and place the result in a new relation. We express such an operation as

```
NEW2 ← PROJECT JobTitle from NEW1
```

The result is the creation of another new relation (called NEW2) that contains the single column of values from the JobTitle column of relation NEW1.

As another example of the PROJECT operation, the statement

```
MAIL ← PROJECT Name, Address from EMPLOYEE
```

can be used to obtain a listing of the names and addresses of all employees. This list is in the newly created (two-column) relation called MAIL (Figure 9.9).

Another operation used in conjunction with relational databases is the JOIN operation. It is used to combine different relations into one relation. The JOIN of two relations produces a new relation whose attributes consist of the attributes from the original relations (Figure 9.10). The names of these attributes are the same as those in the original relations except that each is prefixed by the relation of its origin. (If relation A containing attributes V and W is JOINed with relation B containing attributes X, Y, and Z, then the result has five attributes named A.V, A.W, B.X, B.Y, and B.Z.) This naming convention ensures that the attributes in the new relation have unique names, even though the original relations might have attribute names in common.

Figure 9.8 The SELECT operation

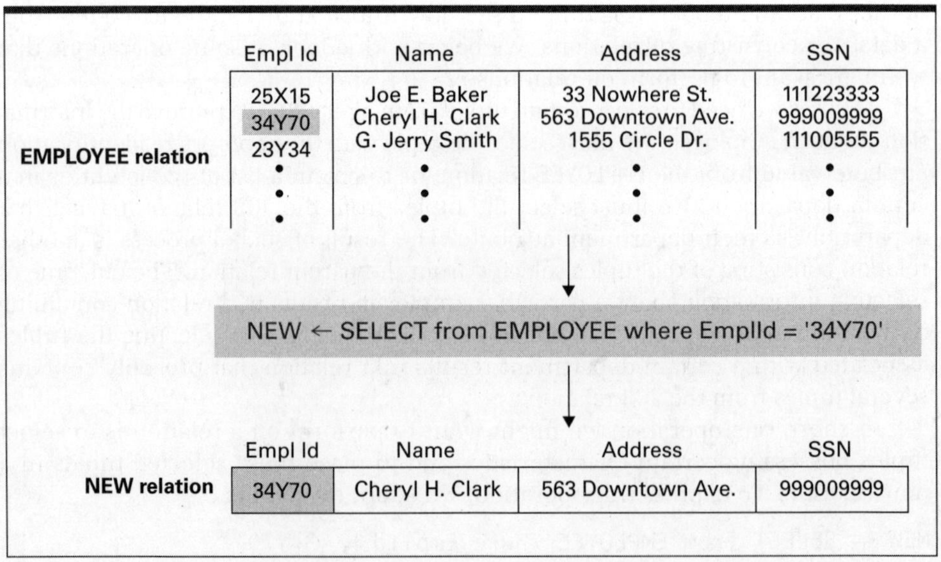

Figure 9.9 The PROJECT operation

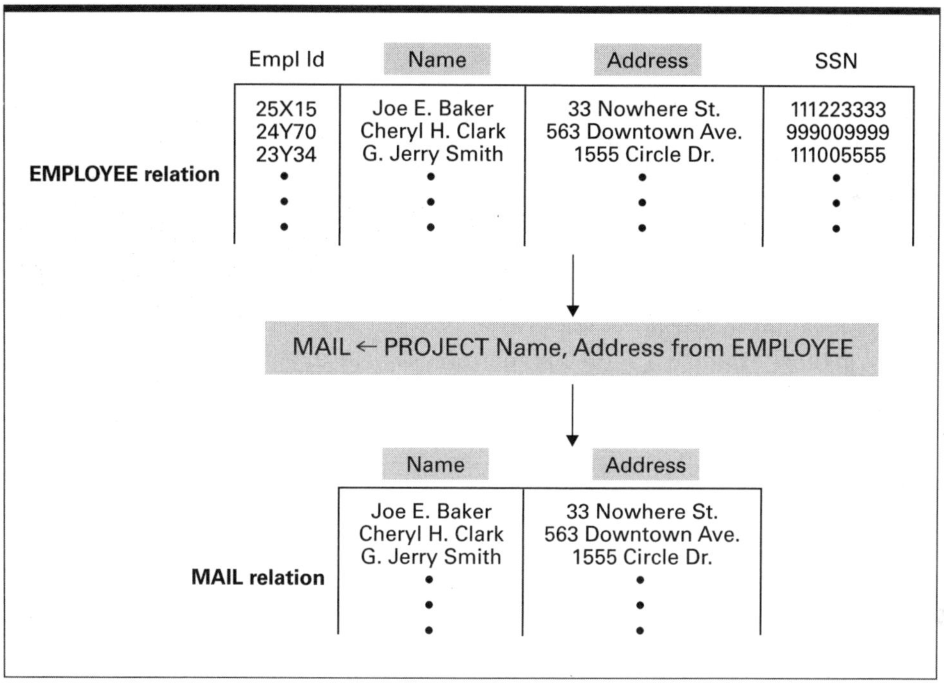

The tuples (rows) of the new relation are produced by concatenating tuples from the two original relations (see again Figure 9.10). Which tuples are actually joined to form tuples in the new relation is determined by the condition under which the JOIN is constructed. One such condition is that designated attributes

Figure 9.10 The JOIN operation

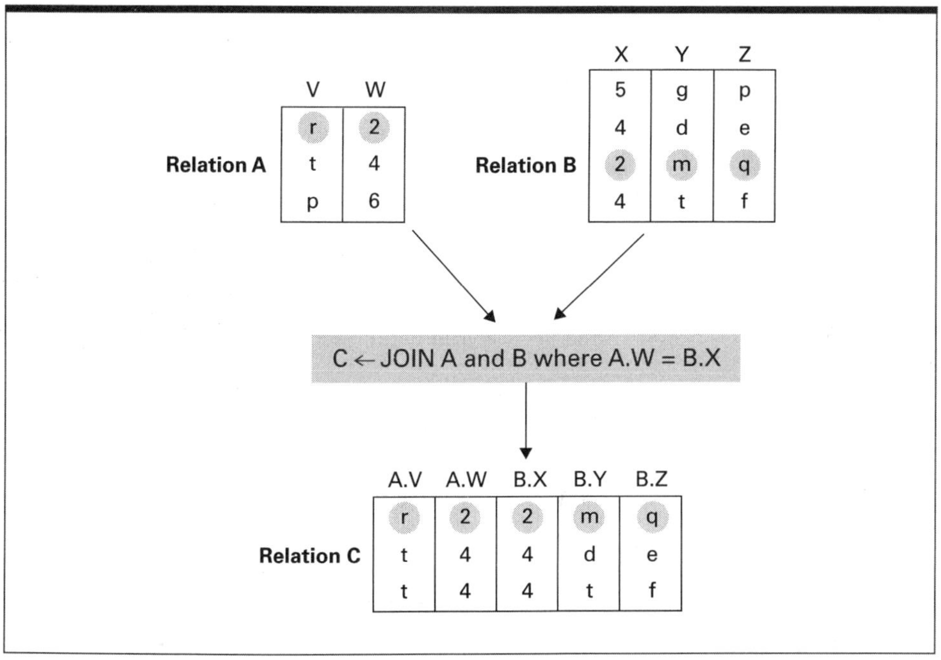

have the same value. This, in fact, is the case represented in Figure 9.10, where we demonstrate the result of executing the statement

```
C ← JOIN A and B where A.W = B.X
```

In this example, a tuple from relation A should be concatenated with a tuple from relation B in exactly those cases where the attributes W and X in the two tuples are equal. Thus the concatenation of the tuple (r, 2) from relation A with the tuple (2, m, q) from relation B appears in the result because the value of attribute W in the first equals the value of attribute X in the second. On the other hand, the result of concatenating the tuple (r, 2) from relation A with the tuple (5, g, p) from relation B does not appear in the final relation because these tuples do not share common values in attributes W and X.

As another example, Figure 9.11 represents the result of executing the statement

```
C ← JOIN A and B where A.W < B.X
```

Note that the tuples in the result are exactly those in which attribute W in relation A is less than attribute X in relation B.

Let us now see how the JOIN operation can be used with the database of Figure 9.5 to obtain a listing of all employee identification numbers along with the department in which each employee works. Our first observation is that the information required is distributed over more than one relation, and thus the process of retrieving the information must entail more than SELECTions and PROJECTions. In fact, the tool we need is the statement

```
NEW1 ← JOIN ASSIGNMENT and JOB
  where ASSIGNMENT.JobId = JOB.JobId
```

Figure 9.11 Another example of the JOIN operation

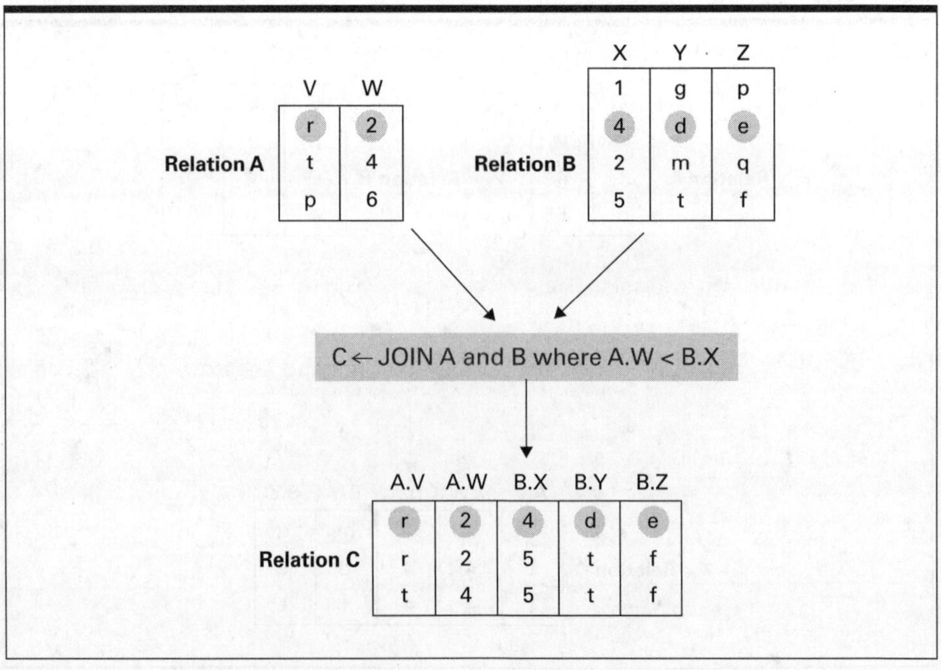

that produces the relation `NEW1`, as shown in Figure 9.12. From this relation, our problem can be solved by first `SELECT`ing those tuples in which `ASSIGNMENT.TermDate` equals `'*'` (which indicates "still employed") and then `PROJECT`ing the attributes `ASSIGNMENT.EmplId` and `JOB.Dept`. In short, the information we need can be obtained from the database in Figure 9.5 by executing the sequence

```
NEW1 ← JOIN ASSIGNMENT and JOB
  where ASSIGNMENT.JobId = JOB.JobId
NEW2 ← SELECT from NEW1 where ASSIGNMENT.TermDate = '*'
LIST ← PROJECT ASSIGNMENT.EmplId, JOB.Dept from NEW2
```

SQL

Now that we have introduced the basic relational operations, let us reconsider the overall structure of a database system. Remember that a database is actually stored in a mass storage system. To relieve the application programmer from the details of such systems, a database management system is provided that allows the application software to be written in terms of a database model, such as the relational model. The DBMS accepts commands in terms of the model and converts them into actions relative to the actual storage structure. This conversion is handled by a collection of routines within the DBMS that are used by the application software as abstract tools. Thus a DBMS based on the relational model would include routines to perform the `SELECT`, `PROJECT`, and `JOIN` operations, which

Figure 9.12 An application of the JOIN operation

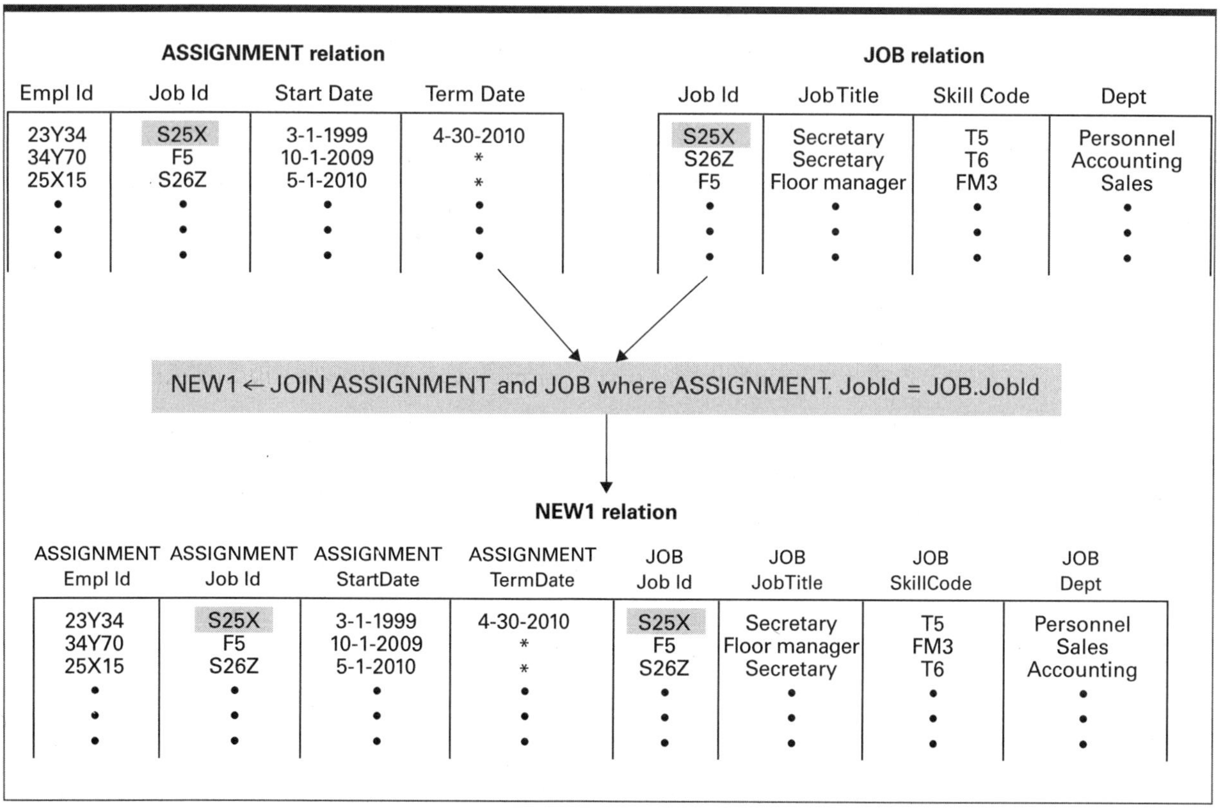

could then be called from the application software. In this manner the application software can be written as though the database were actually stored in the simple tabular form of the relational model.

Today's relational database management systems do not necessarily provide routines to perform the SELECT, PROJECT, and JOIN operations in their raw form. Instead, they provide routines that might be combinations of these basic steps. An example is the language SQL (Structured Query Language), which forms the backbone of most relational database query systems. For example, SQL is the underlying language in the relational database system MySQL (pronounced "My–S–Q–L") used by many database servers in the Internet.

One reason for SQL's popularity is that the American National Standards Institute has standardized it. Another reason is that it was originally developed and marketed by IBM and has thus benefited from a high level of exposure. In this section we explain how relational database queries are expressed in SQL.

Although we are about to find that a query stated in SQL is expressed in an imperative-sounding form, the reality is that it is essentially a declarative statement. You should read an SQL statement as a description of the information desired rather than a sequence of activities to be performed. The significance of this is that SQL relieves application programmers from the burden of developing algorithms for manipulating relations—they need merely to describe the information desired.

For our first example of an SQL statement, let us reconsider our last query in which we developed a three-step process for obtaining all employee identification numbers along with their corresponding departments. In SQL this entire query could be represented by the single statement

```
SELECT EmplId, Dept
FROM Assignment, Job
WHERE Assignment.JobId = Job.JobId
  AND Assignment.TermDate = '*';
```

As indicated by this example, each SQL query statement can contain three clauses: a select clause, a from clause, and a where clause. Roughly speaking, such a statement is a request for the result of forming the JOIN of all the relations listed in the from clause, SELECTing those tuples that satisfy the conditions in the where clause, and then PROJECTing those attributes listed in the select clause. (Note that the terminology is somewhat reversed since the select clause in an SQL statement identifies the attributes used in the PROJECT operation.) Let us consider some simple examples.

The statement

```
SELECT Name, Address
FROM Employee;
```

produces a listing of all employee names and addresses contained in the relation Employee. Note that this is merely a PROJECT operation.

The statement

```
SELECT EmplId, Name, Address, SSNum
FROM Employee
WHERE Name = 'Cheryl H. Clark';
```

produces all the information from the tuple associated with Cheryl H. Clark in the Employee relation. This is essentially a SELECT operation.

The statement

```
SELECT Name, Address
FROM Employee
WHERE Name = 'Cheryl H. Clark';
```

produces the name and address of Cheryl H. Clark as contained in the Employee relation. This is a combination of SELECT and PROJECT operations.

The statement

```
SELECT Employee.Name, Assignment.StartDate
FROM Employee, Assignment
WHERE Employee.EmplId = Assignment.EmplId;
```

produces a listing of all employee names and their dates of initial employment. Note that this is the result of JOINing the relations Employee and Assignment and then SELECTing and PROJECTing the appropriate tuples and attributes as identified in the where and select clauses.

We close by noting that SQL encompasses statements for defining the structure of relations, creating relations, and modifying the contents of relations as well as performing queries. For example, the following are examples of the INSERT INTO, DELETE FROM, and UPDATE statements.

The statement

```
INSERT INTO Employee
VALUES ('42Z12', 'Sue A. Burt', '33 Fair St.', '444661111');
```

adds a tuple to the Employee relation containing the values given;

```
DELETE FROM Employee
WHERE Name = 'G. Jerry Smith';
```

removes the tuple relating to G. Jerry Smith from the Employee relation; and

```
UPDATE Employee
SET Address = '1812 Napoleon Ave.'
WHERE Name = 'Joe E. Baker';
```

changes the address in the tuple associated with Joe E. Baker in the Employee relation.

Questions & Exercises

1. Answer the following questions based on the partial information given in the EMPLOYEE, JOB, and ASSIGNMENT relations in Figure 9.5:
   a. Who is the secretary in the accounting department with experience in the personnel department?
   b. Who is the floor manager in the sales department?
   c. What job does G. Jerry Smith currently hold?
2. Based on the EMPLOYEE, JOB, and ASSIGNMENT relations presented in Figure 9.5, write a sequence of relational operations to obtain a list of all job titles within the personnel department.

3. Based on the EMPLOYEE, JOB, and ASSIGNMENT relations presented in Figure 9.5, write a sequence of relational operations to obtain a list of employee names along with the employees' departments.
4. Convert your answers to questions 2 and 3 into SQL.
5. How does the relational model provide for data independence?
6. How are the different relations in a relational database tied together?

9.3 Object-Oriented Databases

Another database model is based on the object-oriented paradigm. This approach leads to an object-oriented database consisting of objects that are linked to each other to reflect their relationships. For example, an object-oriented implementation of the employee database from the previous section could consist of three classes (types of objects): `Employee`, `Job`, and `Assignment`. An object from the `Employee` class could contain such entries as `EmplId`, `Name`, `Address`, and `SSNum`; an object from the class `Job` could contain such entries as `JobId`, `JobTitle`, `SkillCode`, and `Dept`; and each object from the class `Assignment` could contain entries such as `StartDate` and `TermDate`.

A conceptual representation of such a database is shown in Figure 9.13 where the links between the various objects are represented by lines connecting the related objects. If we focus on an object of type `Employee`, we find it linked to a collection of objects of type `Assignment` representing the various assignments that that particular employee has held. In turn, each of these objects of type `Assignment` is linked to an object of type `Job` representing the job associated

Figure 9.13 The associations between objects in an object-oriented database

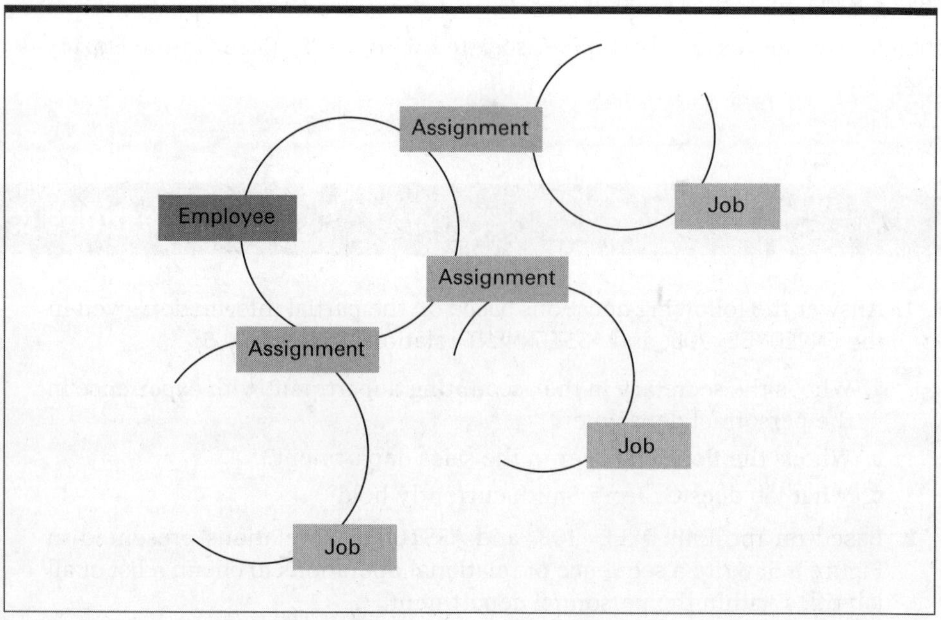

with that assignment. Thus all the assignments of an employee can be found by following the links from the object representing that employee. Similarly, all the employees who have held a particular job can be found by following the links from the object representing that job.

The links between objects in an object-oriented database are normally maintained by the DBMS, so the details of how these links are implemented are not a concern of the programmer writing application software. Instead, when a new object is added to the database, the application software merely specifies the other objects to which it should be linked. The DBMS then creates any linkage system that might be required to record these associations. In particular, a DBMS might link the objects representing the assignments of a given employee in a manner similar to a linked list.

Another task of an object-oriented DBMS is to provide permanent storage for the objects entrusted to it—a requirement that might seem obvious but is inherently distinct from the manner in which objects are normally treated. Normally, when an object-oriented program is executed, the objects created during the program's execution are discarded when the program terminates. In this sense the objects are considered transient. But objects that are created and added to a database must be saved after the program that created them terminates. Such objects are said to be **persistent.** Thus creating persistent objects is a significant departure from the norm.

Proponents of object-oriented databases offer numerous arguments to show why the object-oriented approach to database design is better than the relational approach. One is that the object-oriented approach allows the entire software system (application software, DBMS, and the database itself) to be designed in the same paradigm. This is in contrast to the historically common practice of using an imperative programming language to develop application software for interrogating a relational database. Inherent in such a task is the clash between imperative and relational paradigms. This distinction is subtle at our level of study but the difference has been the source of many software errors over the years. Even at our level, we can appreciate that an object-oriented database combined with an objected-oriented application program produces a homogeneous image of objects communicating with each other throughout the system. On the other hand, a relational database combined with an imperative application program conjures an image of two inherently different organizations trying to find a common interface.

To appreciate another advantage that object-oriented databases have over their relational counterparts, consider the problem of storing employee names in a relational database. If an entire name is stored as a single attribute in a relation, then inquiries regarding only surnames are awkward. However, if the name is stored as individual attributes, such as first name, middle name, and surname, then the number of attributes becomes problematic because not all names conform to a specific structure—even when the population is restricted to a single culture. In an object-oriented database, these issues can be hidden within the object that holds the employee's name. An employee's name can be stored as an intelligent object that is capable of reporting the related employee's name in a variety of formats. Thus, from outside these objects, it would be just as easy to deal with only surnames as with entire names, maiden names, or nicknames. The details involved with each perspective would be encapsulated within the objects.

This ability to encapsulate the technicalities of different data formats is advantageous in other cases as well. In a relational database, the attributes in a relation are part of the overall design of the database, and thus the types associated with these attributes permeate the entire DBMS. (Variables for temporary storage must be declared to be the appropriate type, and functions for manipulating data of the various types must be designed.) Thus, extending a relational database to include attributes of new types (audio and video) can be problematic. In particular, a variety of functions throughout the database design might need to be expanded to incorporate these new data types. In an object-oriented design, however, the same functions used to retrieve an object representing an employee's name can be used to retrieve an object representing a motion picture because the distinctions in type can be hidden within the objects involved. Thus the object-oriented approach appears to be more compatible with the construction of multimedia databases—a feature that is already proving to be a great advantage.

Still another advantage the object-oriented paradigm offers to database design is the potential for storing intelligent objects rather than merely data. That is, an object can contain methods describing how it should respond to messages regarding its contents and relationships. For example, each object of the class `Employee` in Figure 9.13 could contain methods for reporting and updating the information in the object as well as a method for reporting that employee's job history and perhaps a method for changing that employee's job assignment. Likewise, each object from the `Job` class could have a method for reporting the specifics of the job and perhaps a method for reporting those employees who have held that particular job. Thus to retrieve an employee's job history, we would not need to construct an elaborate function. Instead, we could merely ask the appropriate employee object to report its job history. This ability to construct databases whose components respond intelligently to inquiries offers an exciting array of possibilities beyond those of more traditional relational databases.

Questions & Exercises

1. What methods would be contained in an instance of an object from the `Assignment` class in the employee database discussed in this section?
2. What is a persistent object?
3. Identify some classes, as well as some of their internal characteristics, that can be used in an object-oriented database dealing with a warehouse inventory.
4. Identify an advantage that an object-oriented database can have over a relational database.

9.4 Maintaining Database Integrity

Inexpensive database management systems for personal use are relatively simple systems. They tend to have a single objective—to shield the user from the technical details of the database implementation. The databases maintained by these systems are relatively small and generally contain information whose loss or corruption would be inconvenient rather than disastrous. When a problem does arise, the user can usually correct the erroneous items directly or reload the database from a backup copy and manually make the modifications required to bring that copy up to date. This process might be inconvenient, but the cost of avoiding the inconvenience tends to be greater than the inconvenience itself. In any case, the inconvenience is restricted to only a few people, and any financial loss is generally limited.

In the case of large, multiuser, commercial database systems, however, the stakes are much higher. The cost of incorrect or lost data can be enormous and can have devastating consequences. In these environments, a major role of the DBMS is to maintain the database's integrity by guarding against problems such as operations that for some reason are only partially completed or different operations that might interact inadvertently to cause inaccurate information in the database. It is this role of a DBMS that we address in this section.

The Commit/Rollback Protocol

A single transaction, such as the transfer of funds from one bank account to another, the cancellation of an airline reservation, or the registration of a student in a university course, might involve multiple steps at the database level. For example, a transfer of funds between bank accounts requires that the balance in one account be decremented and the balance in the other be incremented. Between such steps the information in the database might be inconsistent. Indeed, funds are missing during the brief period after the first account has been decremented but before the other has been incremented. Likewise, when reassigning a passenger's seat on a flight, there might be an instant when the passenger has no seat or an instant when the passenger list appears to be one passenger greater than it actually is.

In the case of large databases that are subject to heavy transaction loads, it is highly likely that a random snapshot will find the database in the middle of some transaction. A request for the execution of a transaction or an equipment malfunction will therefore likely occur at a time when the database is in an inconsistent state.

Let us first consider the problem of a malfunction. The goal of the DBMS is to ensure that such a problem will not freeze the database in an inconsistent state. This is often accomplished by maintaining a log containing a record of each transaction's activities in a nonvolatile storage system, such as a magnetic disk. Before a transaction is allowed to alter the database, the alteration to be performed is first recorded in the log. Thus the log contains a permanent record of each transaction's actions.

The point at which all the steps in a transaction have been recorded in the log is called the **commit point.** It is at this point that the DBMS has the information it needs to reconstruct the transaction on its own if that should become necessary. At this point the DBMS becomes committed to the transaction in the sense that it accepts the responsibility of guaranteeing that the transaction's activities will be reflected in the database. In the case of an equipment malfunction, the DBMS can use the information in its log to reconstruct the transactions that have been completed (committed) since the last backup was made.

If problems should arise before a transaction has reached its commit point, the DBMS might find itself with a partially executed transaction that cannot be completed. In this case the log can be used to **roll back** (undo) the activities actually performed by the transaction. In the case of a malfunction, for instance, the DBMS could recover by rolling back those transactions that were incomplete (noncommitted) at the time of the malfunction.

Rollbacks of transactions are not restricted, however, to the process of recovering from equipment malfunctions. They are often a part of a DBMS's normal operation. For example, a transaction might be terminated before it has completed all its steps because of an attempt to access privileged information, or it might be involved in a deadlock in which competing transactions find themselves waiting for data being used by each other. In these cases, the DBMS can use the log to roll back a transaction and thus avoid an erroneous database due to incomplete transactions.

To emphasize the delicate nature of DBMS design, we should note that there are subtle problems lurking within the rollback process. The rolling back of one transaction might affect database entries that have been used by other transactions. For example, the transaction being rolled back might have updated an account balance, and another transaction might have already based its activities on this updated value. This might mean that these additional transactions must also be rolled back, which might adversely affect still other transactions. The result is the problem known as **cascading rollback.**

Locking

We now consider the problem of a transaction being executed while the database is in a state of flux from another transaction, a situation that can lead to inadvertent interaction between the transactions and produce erroneous results. For instance, the problem known as the **incorrect summary problem** can arise if one transaction is in the middle of transferring funds from one account to another when another transaction tries to compute the total deposits in the bank. This could result in a total that is either too large or too small depending on the order in which the transfer steps are performed. Another possibility is known as the **lost update problem,** which is exemplified by two transactions, each of which makes a deduction from the same account. If one transaction reads the account's current balance at the point when the other has just read the balance but has not yet calculated the new balance, then both transactions will base their deductions on the same initial balance. In turn, the effect of one of the deductions will not be reflected in the database.

To solve such problems, a DBMS could force transactions to execute in their entirety on a one-at-a-time basis by holding each new transaction in a queue until those preceding it have completed. But a transaction often spends a lot of time waiting for mass storage operations to be performed. By interweaving the execution of transactions, the time during which one transaction is waiting can be used by another transaction to process data it has already retrieved. Most large database management systems therefore contain a scheduler to coordinate time-sharing among transactions in much the same way that a multiprogramming operating system coordinates interweaving of processes (Section 3.3).

To guard against such anomalies as the incorrect summary problem and the lost update problem, these schedulers incorporate a **locking protocol** in which the items within a database that are currently being used by some transaction are marked as such. These marks are called locks; marked items are said to be locked. Two types of locks are common—**shared locks** and **exclusive locks.** They correspond to the two types of access to data that a transaction might require—shared access and exclusive access. If a transaction is not going to alter a data item, then it requires shared access, meaning that other transactions are also allowed to view the data. However, if the transaction is going to alter the item, it must have exclusive access, meaning that it must be the only transaction with access to that data.

In a locking protocol, each time a transaction requests access to a data item, it must also tell the DBMS the type of access it requires. If a transaction requests shared access to an item that is either unlocked or locked with a shared lock, that access is granted and the item is marked with a shared lock. If, however, the requested item is already marked with an exclusive lock, the additional access is denied. If a transaction requests exclusive access to an item, that request is granted only if the item has no lock associated with it. In this manner, a transaction that is going to alter data protects that data from other transactions by obtaining exclusive access, whereas several transactions can share access to an item if none of them are going to change it. Of course, once a transaction is finished with an item, it notifies the DBMS, and the associated lock is removed.

Various algorithms are used to handle the case in which a transaction's access request is rejected. One algorithm is that the transaction is merely forced to wait until the requested item becomes available. This approach, however, can lead to deadlock, since two transactions that require exclusive access to the same two data items could block each other's progress if each obtains exclusive access to one of the items and then insists on waiting for the other. To avoid such deadlocks, some database management systems give priority to older transactions. That is, if an older transaction requires access to an item that is locked by a younger transaction, the younger transaction is forced to release all of its data items, and its activities are rolled back (based on the log). Then, the older transaction is given access to the item it required, and the younger transaction is forced to start again. If a younger transaction is repeatedly preempted, it will grow older in the process and ultimately become one of the older transactions with high priority. This protocol, known as the **wound-wait protocol** (old transactions wound young transactions, young transactions wait for old ones), ensures that every transaction will ultimately be allowed to complete its task.

Questions & Exercises

1. What is the difference between a transaction that has reached its commit point and one that has not?
2. How could a DBMS guard against extensive cascading rollback?
3. Show how the uncontrolled interweaving of two transactions, one deducting \$100 from an account and the other deducting \$200 from the same account, could produce final balances of \$100, \$200, and \$300, assuming that the initial balance is \$400.

4. a. Summarize the possible results of a transaction requesting shared access to an item in a database.
   b. Summarize the possible results of a transaction requesting exclusive access to an item in a database.
5. Describe a sequence of events that would lead to deadlock among transactions performing operations on a database system.
6. Describe how the deadlock in your answer to question 5 could be broken. Would your solution require use of the database management system's log? Explain your answer.

9.5 Traditional File Structures

In this section we digress from our study of mutidimensional database systems to consider traditional file structures. These structures represent the historical beginning of data storage and retrieval systems from which current database technology has evolved. Many of the techniques developed for these structures (such as indexing and hashing) are important tools in the construction of today's massive, complex databases.

Sequential Files

A **sequential file** is a file that is accessed in a serial manner from its beginning to its end as though the information in the file were arranged in one long row. Examples include audio files, video files, files containing programs, and files containing textual documents. In fact, most of the files created by a typical personal computer user are sequential files. For instance, when a spreadsheet is saved, its information is encoded and stored as a sequential file from which the spreadsheet application software can reconstruct the spreadsheet.

Text files, which are sequential files in which each logical record is a single symbol encoded using ASCII or Unicode, often serve as a basic tool for constructing more elaborate sequential files such as an employee records file. One only needs to establish a uniform format for representing the information about each employee as a string of text, encode the information according to that format, and then record the resulting employee records one after another as one single string of text. For example, one could construct a simple employee file by agreeing to enter each employee record as a string of 31 characters, consisting of a field of 25 characters containing the employee's name (filled with enough blanks to complete the 25-character field), followed by a field of 6 characters representing the employee's identification number. The final file would be a long string of encoded characters in which each 31-character block represents the information about a single employee (Figure 9.14). Information would be retrieved from the file in terms of logical records consisting of 31-character blocks. Within each of these blocks, individual fields would be identified according to the uniform format with which the blocks were constructed.

Figure 9.14 The structure of a simple employee file implemented as a text file

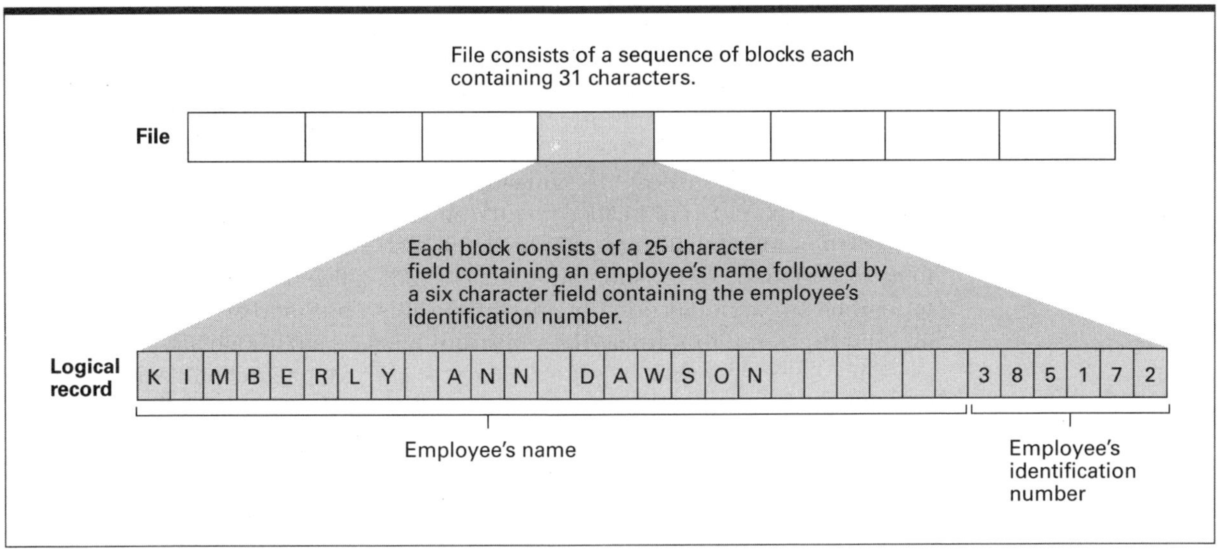

The data in a sequential file must be recorded in mass storage in such a way that the sequential nature of the file is preserved. If the mass storage system is itself sequential (as in the case of a magnetic tape or CD), this is a straightforward undertaking. We need merely record the file on the storage medium according to the sequential properties of the medium. Then processing the file is the task of merely reading and processing the file's contents in the order in which they are found. This is exactly the process followed in playing audio CDs, where the music is stored as a sequential file sector by sector along one continuous spiraling track.

In the case of magnetic disk storage, however, the file would be scattered over different sectors that could be retrieved in a variety of orders. To preserve the proper order, most operating systems (more precisely, the file manager) maintain a list of the sectors on which the file is stored. This list is recorded as part of the disk's directory system on the same disk as the file. By means of this list, the operating system can retrieve the sectors in the proper sequence as though the file were stored sequentially, even though the file is actually distributed over various portions of the disk.

Inherent in processing a sequential file is the need to detect when the end of the file is reached. Generically, we refer to the end of a sequential file as the **end-of-file (EOF).** There are a variety of ways of identifying the EOF. One is to place a special record, called a **sentinel,** at the end of the file. Another is to use the information in the operating system's directory system to identify a file's EOF. That is, since the operating system knows which sectors contain the file, it also knows where the file terminates. A classic example involving sequential files is payroll processing in a small company. Here we imagine a sequential file consisting of a series of logical records, each of which contains the information about an employee's pay (name, employee identification number, pay scale, and so on) from which checks must be printed on a routine basis. As each employee record is retrieved, that employee's pay is calculated, and the appropriate check produced. The activity of processing such a sequential file is exemplified by the statement

```
while (the EOF has not been reached):
  retrieve the next record from the file and process it
```

When the logical records within a sequential file are identified by key field values, the file is usually arranged so that the records appear in the order determined by the keys (perhaps alphabetical or numerical). Such an arrangement simplifies the task of processing the information in the file. For example, suppose that processing payroll requires that each employee record be updated to reflect the information on that employee's time sheet. If both the file containing the time sheet records and the file containing the employee records are in the same order according to the same keys, then this updating process can be handled by accessing both files sequentially—using the time sheet retrieved from one file to update the corresponding record from the other file. This is a significant improvement over the repeated searching process that would be required if the files were not in corresponding order. Thus updating classic sequential files is typically handled in multiple steps. First, the new information (such as the collection of time sheets) is recorded in a sequential file known as a transaction file, and this transaction file is sorted to match the order of the file to be updated, which is called the master file. Then, the records in the master file are updated by retrieving the records from both files sequentially.

A slight variation of this updating process is the process of merging two sequential files to form a new file containing the records from the two originals. The records in the input files are assumed to be arranged in ascending order according to a common key field, and it is also assumed that the files are to be merged in a manner that produces an output file whose keys are also in ascending order. The classic merge algorithm is summarized in Figure 9.15. The underlying theme is to build the output file as the two input files are scanned sequentially (Figure 9.16).

Figure 9.15 A function for merging two sequential files

```
def MergeFiles (InputFileA, InputFileB, OutputFile):
  if (both input files at EOF):
    Stop, with OutputFile empty.
  if (InputFileA not at EOF):
    Declare its first record to be its current record.
  if (InputFileB not at EOF):
    Declare its first record to be its current record.
  while (neither input file at EOF):
    Put the current record with the "smaller" key field
      value in OutputFile.
    if (that current record is the
      last record in its corresponding input file):
      Declare that input file to be at EOF.
    else:
      Declare the next record in that input file
        to be the file's current record.
  Starting with the current record in the input file that is not at
  EOF, copy the remaining records to OutputFile.
```

Figure 9.16 Applying the merge algorithm. (Letters are used to represent entire records. The particular letter indicates the value of the record's key field)

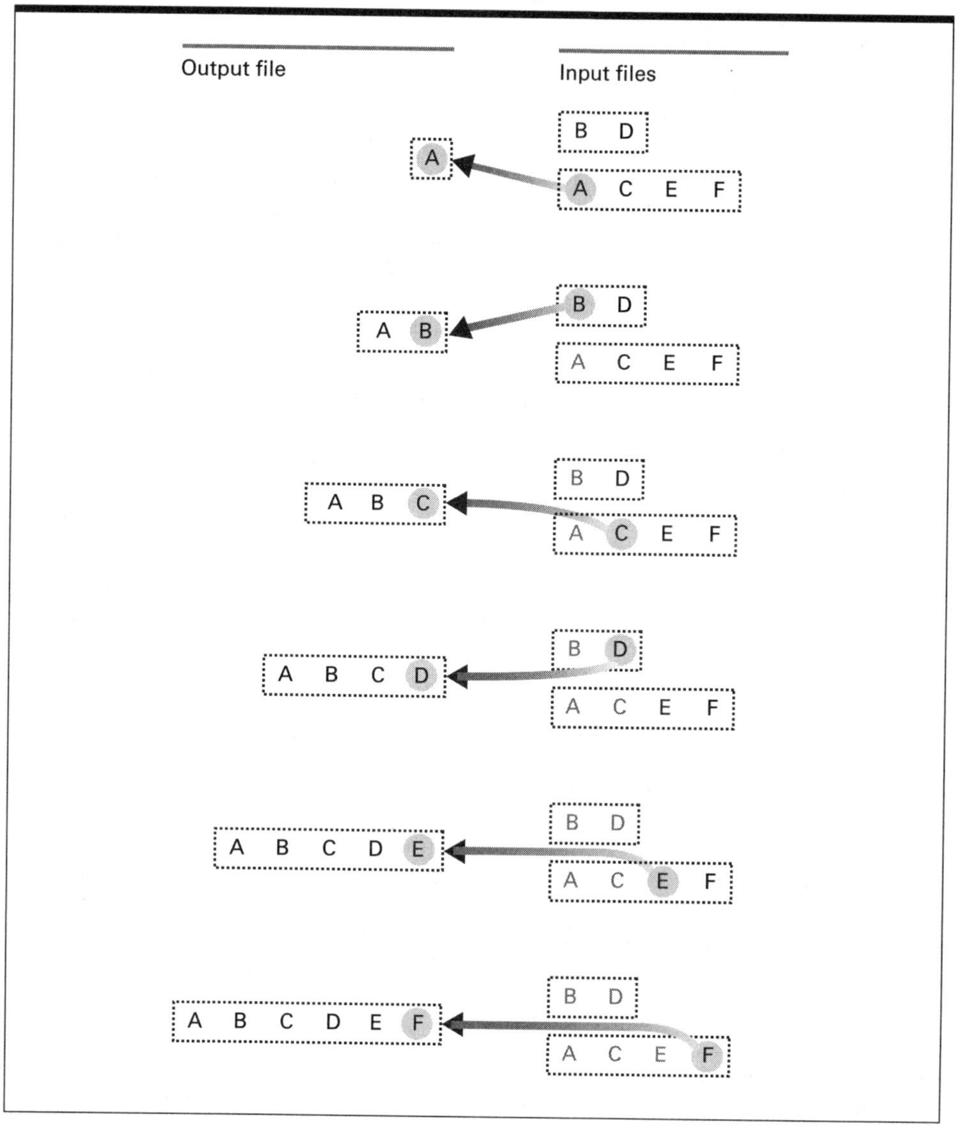

Indexed Files

Sequential files are ideal for storing data that will be processed in the order in which the file's entries are stored. However, such files are inefficient when records within the file must be retrieved in an unpredictable order. In such situations what is needed is a way to identify the location of the desired logical record quickly. A popular solution is to use an index for the file in much the same way that an index in a book is used to locate topics within the book. Such a file system is called an **indexed file.**

An index for a file contains a list of the keys stored in the file along with entries indicating where the record containing each key is stored. Thus to find a particular record, one finds the identifying key in the index and then retrieves the block of information stored at the location associated with that key.

A file's index is normally stored as a separate file on the same mass storage device as the indexed file. The index is usually transferred to main memory before file processing begins so that it is easily accessible when access to records in the file is required (Figure 9.17).

A classic example of an indexed file occurs in the context of maintaining employee records. Here an index can be used to avoid lengthy searches when you are retrieving an individual record. In particular, if the file of employee records is indexed by employee identification numbers, then an employee's record can be retrieved quickly when the employee's identification number is known. Another example is found on audio CDs where an index is used to allow relatively quick access to individual recordings.

Over the years numerous variations of the basic index concept have been used. One variation constructs an index in a hierarchical manner so that the index takes on a layered or tree structure. A prominent example is the hierarchical directory system used by most operating systems for organizing file storage. In such a case, the directories, or folders, play the role of indexes, each containing links to its subindexes. From this perspective, the entire file system is merely one large indexed file.

Hash Files

Although indexing provides relatively quick access to entries within a data storage structure, it does so at the expense of index maintenance. **Hashing** is a technique that provides similar access without such overhead. As in the case of an indexed system, hashing allows a record to be located by means of a key value. But, rather than looking up the key in an index, hashing identifies the location of the record directly from the key.

A hash system can be summarized as follows: The data storage space is divided into several sections, called **buckets,** each of which is capable of holding several records. The records are dispersed among the buckets according to an algorithm that converts key values into bucket numbers. (This conversion from key values to bucket numbers is called a **hash function.**) Each record is stored in the bucket identified by this process. Therefore, a record that has been placed in the storage structure can be retrieved by first applying the hash function to the

Figure 9.17 Opening an indexed file

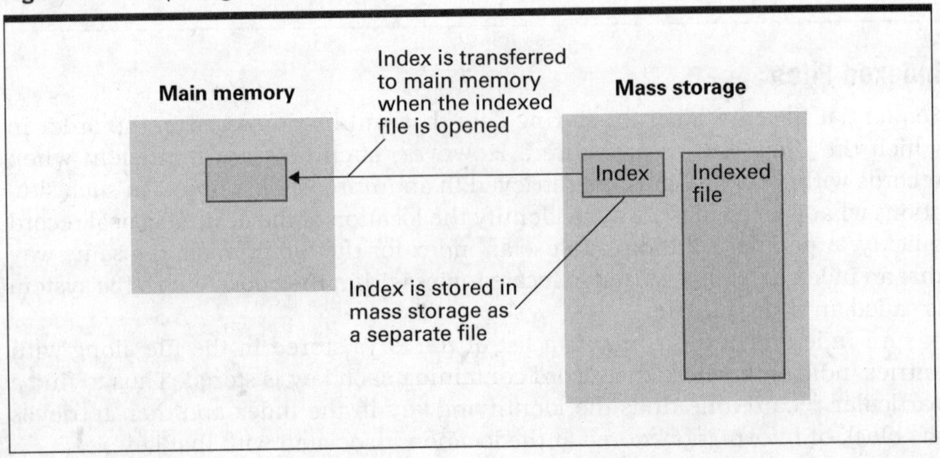

Authentication via Hashing

Hashing is much more than a means of constructing efficient data storage systems. For example, hashing can be used as a means of authenticating messages transferred over the Internet. The underlying theme is to hash the message in a secret way. This value is then transferred with the message. To authenticate the message, the receiver hashes the message received (in the same secret way) and confirms that the value produced agrees with the original value. (The odds of an altered message hashing to the same value are assumed to be very small.) If the value obtained does not agree with the original value, the message is exposed as being corrupted. Those who are interested might wish to search the Internet for information about MD5, which is a hash function used extensively in authentication applications.

It is enlightening to consider error detection techniques as an application of hashing for authentication. For example, the use of parity bits is essentially a hashing system in which a bit pattern is hashed to produce either a 0 or a 1. This value is then transferred along with the original pattern. If the pattern ultimately received does not hash to that same value, the pattern is considered corrupted.

record's identifying key to determine the appropriate bucket, then retrieving the contents of that bucket, and finally searching through the data retrieved for the desired record.

Hashing is not only used as a means of retrieving data from mass storage but also as a means of retrieving items from large blocks of data stored in main memory. When hashing is applied to a storage structure in mass storage, the result is called a **hash file.** When applied to a storage structure within main memory, the result is usually called a **hash table.**

Let us apply the hashing technique to the classic employee file in which each record contains information about a single employee in a company. First, we establish several available areas of mass storage that will play the role of buckets. The number of buckets and the size of each bucket are design decisions that we will consider later. For now, let us assume that we have created 41 buckets, which we refer to as bucket number 0, bucket number 1, through bucket number 40. (The reason we selected 41 buckets rather than an even 40 will be explained shortly.)

Let us assume that an employee's identification number will be used as the key for identifying the employee's record. Our next task, then, is to develop a hash function for converting these keys into bucket numbers. Although the employee identification "numbers" might have the form 25X3Z or J2X35 and are therefore not numeric, they are stored as bit patterns, and we can interpret the bit patterns as numbers. Using this numeric interpretation, we can divide any key by the number of buckets available and record the remainder, which in our case will be an integer in the range from 0 to 40. Thus we can use the remainder of this division process to identify one of the 41 buckets (Figure 9.18).

Using this as our hash function, we proceed to construct the file by considering each record individually, applying our divide-by-41 hash function to its key to obtain a bucket number, and then storing the record in that bucket (Figure 9.19). Later, if we need to retrieve a record, we need merely apply our hash function to the record's key to identify the appropriate bucket and then search that bucket for the record in question.

Figure 9.18 Hashing the key field value 25X3Z to one of 41 buckets

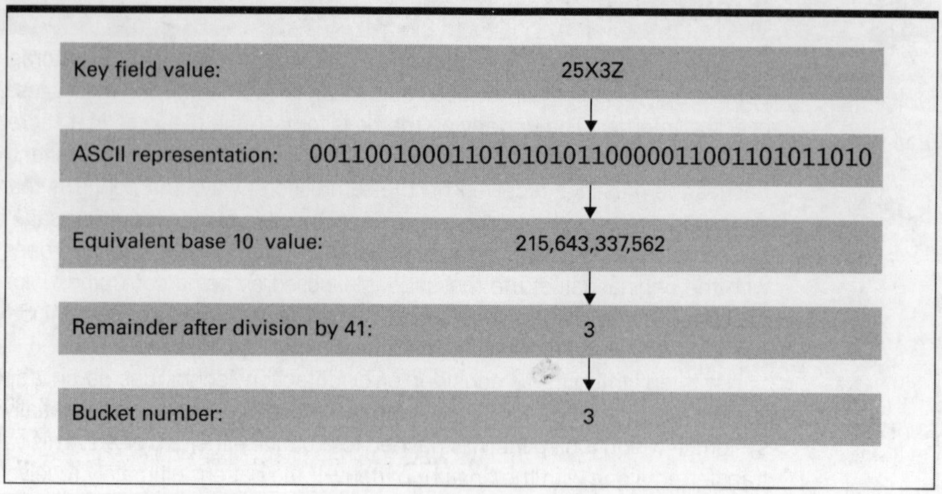

At this point let us reconsider our decision to divide the storage area into 41 buckets. First, note that to obtain an efficient hash system, the records being stored should be distributed evenly among the buckets. If a disproportionate number of keys happen to hash to the same bucket (a phenomenon called **clustering**), then a disproportionate number of records will be stored in a single bucket. In turn, retrieving a record from that bucket could require a time-consuming search, causing the loss of any benefits gained by hashing.

Now observe that if we had chosen to divide the storage area into 40 buckets rather than 41, our hash function would have involved dividing the keys by the value 40 rather than 41. But, if a dividend and a divisor both have a common

Figure 9.19 The rudiments of a hashing system

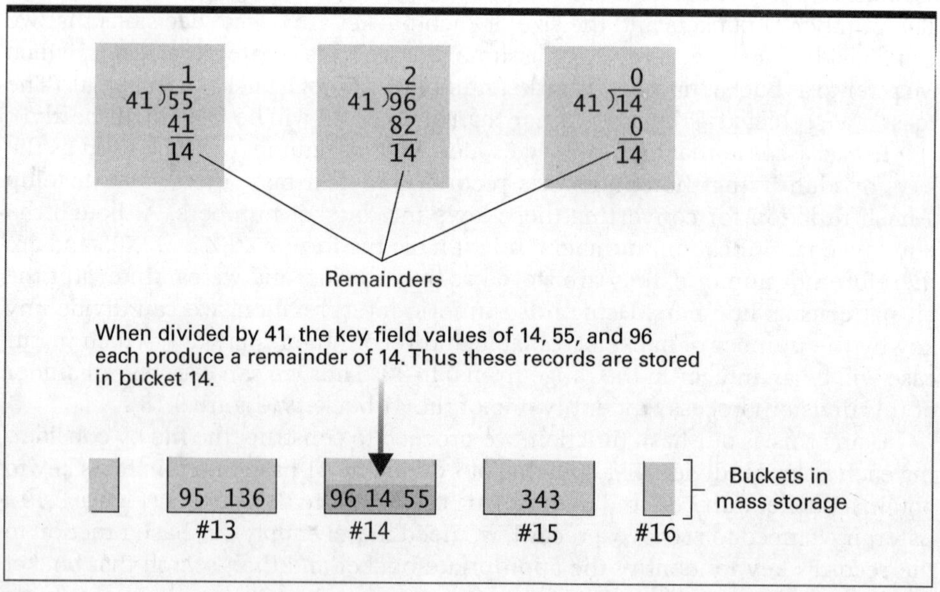

factor, that factor will be present in the remainder as well. In particular, if the keys to the entries stored in our hash file happened to be multiples of 5 (which is also a divisor of 40), then the factor of 5 would appear in the remainders when divided by 40, and the entries would cluster in those buckets associated with the remainders 0, 5, 10, 15, 20, 25, 30, and 35. Similar situations would occur in the case of keys that are multiples of 2, 4, 8, 10, and 20, because they are all also factors of 40. Consequently, we choose to divide the storage area into 41 buckets because the choice of 41, being a prime number, eliminated the possibility of common factors and therefore reduced the chance of clustering.

Unfortunately, the possibility of clustering can never be completely eliminated. Even with a well-designed hash function, it is highly likely that two keys will hash to the same value, a phenomenon called a collision, early in the file construction process. To understand why, consider the following scenario.

Suppose that we have found a hash function that arbitrarily distributes records among 41 buckets, that our storage system is empty, and that we are going to insert new records one at a time. When we insert the first record, it will be placed in an empty bucket. However, when we insert the next record, only 40 of the 41 buckets are still empty, so the probability that the second record will be placed in an empty bucket is only 40/41. Assuming that the second record is placed in an empty bucket, the third record finds only 39 empty buckets, and thus the probability of it being placed in one of them is 39/41. Continuing this process, we find that if the first seven records are placed in empty buckets, the eighth record has only a 34/41 probability of being placed in one of the remaining empty buckets.

This analysis allows us to compute the probability that all the first eight records will be placed in empty buckets—it is the product of the probabilities of each record being placed in an empty bucket, assuming that the preceding entries were so placed. This probability is

```
(41/41)(40/41)(39/41)(38/41) . . . (34/41) = .482
```

The point is that the result is less than one-half. That is, it is more likely than not that in distributing records among 41 buckets a collision will have occurred by the time the eighth record is stored.

The high probability of collisions indicates that, regardless of how well-chosen a hash function might be, any hash system must be designed with clustering in mind. In particular, it is possible that a bucket might fill up and overflow. One approach to this problem would be to allow the buckets to expand in size. Another approach is to allow buckets to spill into an overflow area that has been reserved for that purpose. In any case the occurrence of clustering and overflowing buckets can significantly degrade the performance of a hash file.

Research has shown that, as a general rule, hash files perform well as long as the ratio of the number of records to the total record capacity of the file (a ratio known as the **load factor**) remains below 50 percent. However, if the load factor begins to creep above 75 percent, the system's performance generally degrades (clustering raises its ugly head, causing some buckets to fill and possibly overflow). For this reason, a hash storage system is usually reconstructed with a larger capacity if its load factor approaches the 75 percent value. We conclude that the efficiency of record retrieval obtained by implementing a hash system is not gained without cost.

Questions & Exercises

1. Follow the merge algorithm presented in Figure 9.15, assuming that one input file contains records with key field values equal to B and E while the other contains A, C, D, and F.
2. The merge algorithm is the heart of a popular sort algorithm called the merge sort. Can you discover this algorithm? (Hint: Any nonempty file can be considered to be a collection of one-entry files.)
3. Is being sequential a physical or conceptual property of a file?
4. What are the steps required when retrieving a record from an indexed file?
5. Explain how a poorly chosen hash function can result in a hash storage system becoming little more than a sequential file.
6. Suppose a hash storage system is constructed using the division hash function as presented in the text but with six storage buckets. For each of the following key values, identify the bucket in which the record with that key is placed. What goes wrong and why?

a. 24	b. 30	c. 3	d. 18	e. 15
f. 21	g. 9	h. 39	i. 27	j. 0

7. How many people must be gathered together before the odds are that two members of the group will have birthdays on the same day of the year? How does this problem relate to the material in this section?

9.6 Data Mining

A rapidly expanding subject that is closely associated with database technology is data mining, which consists of techniques for discovering patterns in collections of data. Data mining has become an important tool in numerous areas including marketing, inventory management, quality control, loan risk management, fraud detection, and investment analysis. Data mining techniques even have applications in what might seem unlikely settings as exemplified by their use in identifying the functions of particular genes encoded in DNA molecules and characterizing properties of organisms.

Data mining activities differ from traditional database interrogation in that data mining seeks to identify previously unknown patterns as opposed to traditional database inquiries that merely ask for the retrieval of stored facts. Moreover, data mining is practiced on static data collections, called **data warehouses,** rather than "online" operational databases that are subject to frequent updates. These warehouses are often "snapshots" of databases or collections of databases. They are used in lieu of the actual operational databases because finding patterns in a static system is easier than in a dynamic one.

We should also note that the subject of data mining is not restricted to the domain of computing but has tentacles that extend far into statistics. In fact, many would argue that since data mining had its origins in attempts to perform statistical analysis on large, diverse data collections, it is an application of statistics rather than a field of computer science.

Two common forms of data mining are **class description** and **class discrimination.** Class description deals with identifying properties that characterize a given group of data items, whereas class discrimination deals with identifying properties that divide two groups. For example, class description techniques would be used to identify characteristics of people who buy small economical vehicles, whereas class discrimination techniques would be used to find properties that distinguish customers who shop for used cars from those who shop for new ones.

Another form of data mining is **cluster analysis,** which seeks to discover classes. Note that this differs from class description, which seeks to discover properties of members within classes that are already identified. More precisely, cluster analysis tries to find properties of data items that lead to the discovery of groupings. For example, in analyzing information about people's ages who have viewed a particular motion picture, cluster analysis might find that the customer base breaks down into two age groups—a 4-to-0 age group and a 25-to-40 age group. (Perhaps the motion picture attracted children and their parents?)

Still another form of data mining is **association analysis,** which involves looking for links between data groups. It is association analysis that might reveal that customers who buy potato chips also buy beer and soda or that people who shop during the traditional weekday work hours also draw retirement benefits.

Outlier analysis is another form of data mining. It tries to identify data entries that do not comply with the norm. Outlier analysis can be used to identify errors in data collections, to identify credit card theft by detecting sudden deviations from a customer's normal purchase patterns, and perhaps to identify potential terrorists by recognizing unusual behavior.

Finally, the form of data mining called **sequential pattern analysis** tries to identify patterns of behavior over time. For example, sequential pattern analysis might reveal trends in economic systems such as equity markets or in environmental systems such as climate conditions.

As indicated by our last example, results from data mining can be used to predict future behavior. If an entity possesses the properties that characterize a class, then the entity will probably behave like members of that class. However, many data mining projects are aimed at merely gaining a better understanding

Bioinformatics

Advances in database technology and data mining techniques are expanding the repertoire of tools available to biologists in research areas involving the identification of patterns and the classification of organic compounds. The result is a new field within biology called bioinformatics. Having originated in endeavors to decode DNA, bioinformatics now encompasses such tasks as cataloguing proteins and understanding sequences of protein interactions (called biochemical pathways). Although normally considered to be a part of biology, bioinformatics is an example of how computer science is influencing and even becoming ingrained in other fields.

of the data, as witnessed by the use of data mining in unraveling the mysteries of DNA. In any case, the scope of data mining applications is potentially enormous, and thus data mining promises to be an active area of research for years to come.

Note that database technology and data mining are close cousins, and thus research in one will have repercussions in the other. Database techniques are used extensively to give data warehouses the capability of presenting data in the form of **data cubes** (data viewed from multiple perspectives—the term *cube* is used to conjecture the image of multiple dimensions) that make data mining possible. In turn, as researchers in data mining improve techniques for implementing data cubes, these results will pay dividends in the field of database design.

In closing, we should recognize that successful data mining encompasses much more than the identification of patterns within a collection of data. Intelligent judgment must be applied to determine whether those patterns are significant or merely coincidences. The fact that a particular convenience store has sold a high number of winning lottery tickets should probably not be considered significant to someone planning to buy a lottery ticket, but the discovery that customers who buy snack food also tend to buy frozen dinners might constitute meaningful information to a grocery store manager. Likewise, data mining encompasses a vast number of ethical issues involving the rights of individuals represented in the data warehouse, the accuracy and use of the conclusions drawn, and even the appropriateness of data mining in the first place.

Questions & Exercises

1. Why is data mining not conducted on "online" databases?
2. Give an additional example of a pattern that might be found by each of the types of data mining identified in the text.
3. Identify some different perspectives that a data cube might allow when mining sales data.
4. How does data mining differ from traditional database inquiries?

9.7 Social Impact of Database Technology

With the development of database technology, information that was once buried in arcane records has become accessible. In many cases, automated library systems place a patron's reading habits within easy reach, retailers maintain records of their customers' purchases, and Internet search engines keep records of their clients' requests. In turn this information is potentially available to marketing firms, law enforcement agencies, political parties, employers, and private individuals.

This is representative of the potential problems that permeate the entire spectrum of database applications. Technology has made it easy to collect enormous amounts of data and to merge or compare different data collections to obtain relationships that would otherwise remain buried in the heap. The ramifications, both positive and negative, are enormous. These ramifications are not merely subjects for academic debate—they are realities.

In some cases the data collection process is readily apparent; in others it is subtle. Examples of the first case occur when one is explicitly asked to provide information. This may be done in a voluntary manner, as in surveys or contest registration forms, or it may be done in an involuntary manner, such as when imposed by government regulations. Sometimes whether it is voluntary depends on one's point of view. Is providing personal information when applying for a loan voluntary or involuntary? The distinction depends on whether receiving the loan is a convenience or a necessity. To use a credit card at some retailers now requires that you allow your signature to be recorded in a digitized format. Again, providing the information is either voluntary or involuntary depending on your situation.

More subtle cases of data collection avoid direct communication with the subject. Examples include a credit company that records the purchasing practices of the holders of its credit cards, websites that record the identities of those who visit the site, and social activists who record the license plate numbers on the cars parked in a targeted institution's parking lot. In these cases the subject of the data collection might not be aware that information is being collected and less likely to be aware of the existence of the databases being constructed.

Sometimes the underlying data-collection activities are self-evident if one merely stops to think. For example, a grocery store might offer discounts to its regular customers who register in advance with the store. The registration process might involve the issuance of identification cards that must be presented at the time of purchase to obtain the discount. The result is that the store is able to compile a record of the customers' purchases—a record whose value far exceeds the value of the discounts awarded.

Of course, the force driving this boom in data collection is the value of the data, which is amplified by advances in database technology that allow data to be linked in ways that reveal information that would otherwise remain obscure. For example, the purchasing patterns of credit card holders can be classified and cross-listed to obtain customer profiles of immense marketing value. Subscription forms for body-building magazines can be mailed to those who have recently purchased exercise equipment, whereas subscription forms for dog obedience magazines can be targeted toward those who have recently purchased dog food. Alternative ways of combining information are sometimes very imaginative. Welfare records have been compared to criminal records to find and apprehend parole violators, and in 1984 the Selective Service in the United States used old birthday registration lists from a popular ice cream retailer to identify citizens who had failed to register for the military draft.

There are several approaches to protecting society from abusive use of databases. One is to apply legal remedies. Unfortunately, passing a law against an action does not stop the action from occurring but merely makes the action illegal. A prime example in the United States is the Privacy Act of 1974 whose purpose was to protect citizens from abusive use of government databases. One provision of this act required government agencies to publish notice of their databases in the Federal Register to allow citizens to access and correct their personal information. However, government agencies were slow to comply with this provision. This does not necessarily imply malicious intent. In many cases the problem was one of bureaucracy. But, the fact that a bureaucracy might be constructing personnel databases that it is unable to identify is not reassuring.

Another, and perhaps more powerful, approach to controlling database abuse is public opinion. Databases will not be abused if the penalties outweigh the benefits; and the penalty businesses fear the most is adverse public opinion—this goes right to the bottom line. In the early 1990s it was public opinion that ultimately stopped major credit bureaus from selling mailing lists for marketing purposes. More recently, Google discontinued its Google Buzz social networking tool in 2011 after its automatic sharing of contact information from the popular Gmail tool was greeted with harsh public criticism. Even government agencies have bowed to public opinion. In 1997 the Social Security Administration in the United States modified its plan to make Social Security records available via the Internet when public opinion questioned the security of the information. In some of these cases results were obtained in days—a stark contrast to the extended time periods associated with legal processes.

Of course, in many cases database applications are beneficial to both the holder and the subject of the data, but in all cases there is a loss of privacy that should not be taken lightly. Such privacy issues are serious when the information is accurate, but they become gigantic when the information is erroneous. Imagine the feeling of hopelessness if you realized that your credit rating was adversely affected by erroneous information. Imagine how your problems would be amplified in an environment in which this misinformation was readily shared with other institutions. Privacy problems are, and will be, a major side effect of advancing technology in general and database techniques in particular. The solutions to these problems will require an educated, alert, and active citizenry.

Questions & Exercises

1. Should law enforcement agencies be given access to databases for the purpose of identifying individuals with criminal tendencies, even though the individuals might not have committed a crime?
2. Should insurance companies be given access to databases for the purpose of identifying individuals with potential medical problems, even though the individuals have not shown any symptoms?
3. Suppose you were financially comfortable. What benefits could you derive if this information were shared among a variety of institutions? What penalties could you suffer from the distribution of this same information? What if you were financially uncomfortable?
4. What role does a free press have in controlling database abuse? (For example, to what extent does the press affect public opinion or expose abuse?)

Chapter Review Problems

(Asterisked problems are associated with optional sections.)

1. What is the significance of database management systems?
2. What is a database model?
3. What is a lossless decomposition or a nonloss decomposition?
4. What is the difference between a tuple and an attribute?
5. Identify two benefits of separating application software from the DBMS.
6. Describe the similarities between an abstract data type (Chapter 8) and a database model.
7. Identify the level within a database system (user, programmer of application software, designer of the DBMS software) at which each of the following concerns or activities occur:
   a. How should data be stored on a disk to maximize efficiency?
   b. Is there a vacancy on flight 243?
   c. How should a relation be organized in mass storage?
   d. How many times should a user be allowed to mistype a password before the conversation is terminated?
   e. How can the PROJECT operation be implemented?
8. Which of the following tasks are handled by a DBMS?
   a. Ensure that a user's access to the database is restricted to the appropriate subschema.
   b. Translate commands stated in terms of the database model into actions compatible with the actual data storage system.
   c. Disguise the fact that the data in the database is actually scattered among many computers in a network.
9. Describe how the following information about railways, trains (for a particular day), and passengers would be represented in a relational database:

   Trains: Rolar, Omni, and Holiday

   Trains for Rolar: R221, R567, and R234

   Holiday special Trains: H897 and H008

   Trains for Omni: O999 and O815

   John has reservations on R221 (seat 34U), R567 (seat 23U), and R234 (seat 43L).

   Henry has reservations on O999 (seat 15L) and H008 (seat 18L).

   Duke has reservations on H897 (seat 7U) and O815 (seat 2L).
10. To what extent is the order in which SELECT and PROJECT operations are applied to a relation significant? That is, under what conditions will SELECTing and then PROJECTing produce the same results as first PROJECTing and then SELECTing?
11. Give an argument showing that the "where" clause in the JOIN operation as described in Section 9.2 is not necessary. (That is, show that any query that uses a "where" clause could be restated using a JOIN operation that concatenated every tuple in one relation with every tuple in the other.)
12. In terms of the relations shown below, what is the appearance of the relation FINAL after executing each of these instructions:

A relation

L	M	N
X	P	1
Y	Q	7
Z	R	6

B relation

X	Y
9	7
4	3

   a. FINAL ← SELECT from B where X = 9
   b. FINAL ← PROJECT L from A
   c. FINAL ← SELECT from A where L = Z
   d. FINAL ← JOIN A and B where A.N = B.Y

13. Using the commands SELECT, PROJECT, and JOIN, write a sequence of instructions to answer each of the following questions about branches and their courses in terms of the following database:

Course relation

CName	ID
Networks	IT655
DataBase	CS543
VLSI	EC653

Branch relation

BName	ID	Credits
Computer Science	CS543	4
Computer Science	EC653	5
Electronics & Communication	IT655	4
Electronics & Communication	EC653	5
Information Technology	CS543	4
Information Technology	IT655	4

a. Which branches offer IT665?
b. List all the branches present in Branch relation.
c. Which branches offer 4-credit courses?

14. Answer question 13 using SQL.

15. Using the commands SELECT, PROJECT, and JOIN, write sequences to answer the following questions about the information in the EMPLOYEE, JOB, and ASSIGNMENT relations in Figure 9.5:
a. Obtain the name of an employee whose Job ID is S25X.
b. Obtain a list of the department, skill code and job title of the employee named G. Jerry Smith.
c. Obtain a list of the name and address of the employee whose start date is 5-1-2010.

16. Answer question 14 using SQL.

17. Design a relational database containing information about authors, their titles, and their publishers. (Avoid redundancies similar to those in Figure 9.4.)

18. Design a relational database containing information about students, their courses, and their current semester along with their disciplines. (Avoid redundancies similar to those in Figure 9.4.)

19. Design a relational database containing information about employees of different companies and their salaries. (Avoid redundancies similar to those in Figure 9.4.)

20. Design a relational database containing information about fruits, colors, and the season of their availability. (Avoid redundancies similar to those in Figure 9.4.)

21. Design a relational database containing information about parts, suppliers, and customers. Each part might be supplied by several suppliers and ordered by many customers. Each supplier might supply many parts and have many customers. Each customer might order many parts from many suppliers; in fact, the same part might be ordered from more than one supplier. (Avoid redundancies similar to those in Figure 9.4.)

22. Write a sequence of instructions (using the operations `SELECT`, `PROJECT` and `JOIN`) to retrieve the `JobId`, `StartDate`, and `TermDate` for each job in the accounting department from the relational database described in Figure 9.5.

23. Answer the previous problem using SQL.

24. Write a sequence of instructions (using the operations `SELECT`, `PROJECT` and `JOIN`) to retrieve the `Name`, `Address`, `JobTitle`, and `Dept` of every current employee from the relational database described in Figure 9.5.

25. Answer the previous problem using SQL.

26. Write a sequence of instructions (using the operations `SELECT`, `PROJECT` and `JOIN`) to retrieve the `Name` and `JobTitle` of each current employee from the relational database described in Figure 9.5.

27. Answer the previous problem using SQL.

28. What is the difference in the information supplied by the single relation

Name	Department	TelephoneNumber
Jones	Sales	555-2222
Smith	Sales	555-3333
Baker	Personnel	555-4444

and the two relations

Name	Department
Jones	Sales
Smith	Sales
Baker	Personnel

Department	TelephoneNumber
Sales	555-2222
Sales	555-3333
Personnel	555-4444

29. Design a relational database containing information about novels, its authors and the number of pages in the novels. Be sure to allow for the fact that a novel may contain less number of pages in one version and at the same it may contain more number of pages in a new version.

30. Pick a popular website such as www.google.com, www.amazon.com, or www.ebay.com and design a relational database that you would propose to serve as the site's supporting database.

31. On the basis of the database represented in Figure 9.5, state the question that is answered by the following program segment:

```
TEMP ← SELECT from JOB
  where JobTitle = 'Secretary'
RESULT ← PROJECT SkillCode, Department
  from TEMP
```

32. Answer question 31 using SQL.

33. On the basis of the database represented in Figure 9.5, state the question that is answered by the following program segment:

```
INTER1 ← JOIN JOB and ASSIGNMENT
  where JOB.JobId =
    ASSIGNMENT.JobId
INTER2 ← SELECT from INTER1 where
  EmplId = '23Y34'
FINAL ← PROJECT TermDate, StartDate
  from INTER2
```

34. Answer question 33 using SQL.

35. On the basis of the database represented in Figure 9.5, state the question that is answered by the following program segment:

```
TEMP1 ← JOIN EMPLOYEE and JOB
  where EMPLOYEE.EmplId = JOB.EmplId
```

36. Translate the query in the previous problem into SQL.

37. Translate the SQL statement

```
SELECT Job.JobTitle
FROM Assignment, Job
WHERE Assignment.JoblId = Job.JobId
  AND Assignment.EmplId = '34Y70';
```

into a sequence of SELECT, PROJECT, and JOIN operations.

38. Translate the SQL statement

```
SELECT Assignment.StartDate
FROM Assignment, Employee
WHERE Assignment.EmplId =
  Employee.EmplId
  AND Employee.Name = 'Joe E.
    Baker';
```

into a sequence of SELECT, PROJECT, and JOIN operations.

39. Describe the effect that the following SQL statement would have on the database in Problem 13.

```
INSERT INTO Course
VALUES ('Computer Concepts', 'CS342');
```

40. Describe the effect that the following SQL statement would have on the database in question 13.

```
UPDATE Branch
  SET ID = 'CS555'
  WHERE BName = 'Computer Science'
    AND Credits = 5;
```

***41.** Identify some of the objects that you would expect to find in an object-oriented database used to maintain a grocery store's inventory. What methods would you expect to find within each of these objects?

***42.** Identify some of the objects that you would expect to find in an object-oriented database used to maintain records of a library's holdings. What methods would you expect to find within each of these objects?

***43.** What incorrect information is generated by the following schedule of transactions T1 and T2?

T1 is designed to compute the sum of accounts A and B; T2 is designed to transfer $100 from account A to account B. T1 begins by retrieving the balance of account A; then, T2 performs its transfer; and finally, T1 retrieves the balance of account B and reports the sum of the values it has retrieved.

***44.** What is the difference between incorrect summary problem and lost update problem? Explain your answer with examples.

***45.** What effect would the wound-wait protocol have on the sequence of events in question 43 if T1 was the younger transaction? If T2 was the younger transaction?

***46.** Suppose one transaction tries to add $100 to an account whose balance is $200 while another tries to withdraw $100 from the same account. Describe an interweaving of these transactions that would lead to a final balance of $100. Describe an interweaving of these transactions that would lead to a final balance of $300.

***47.** What is the difference between a transaction having exclusive access or shared access to an item in a database and why is the distinction important?

***48.** The problems discussed in Section 9.4 involving concurrent transactions are not limited to database environments. What similar problems would arise when accessing a document with word processors? (If you have a PC with a word processor, try to access the same document with two activations of the word processor and see what happens.)

***49.** Suppose a sequential file contains 50,000 records and 5 milliseconds is required to interrogate an entry. How long should we expect to wait when retrieving a record from the middle of the file?

***50.** List the steps that are executed in the merge algorithm in Figure 9.15 if one of the input files is empty at the start.

***51.** Modify the algorithm in Figure 9.15 to handle the case in which both input files contain a record with the same key field value. Assume that these records are identical and that only one should appear in the output file.

***52.** Design a system by which a file stored on a disk can be processed as a sequential file with either of two different orderings.

***53.** Describe how a sequential file containing information about a magazine's subscribers could be constructed using a text file as the underlying structure.

***54.** Design a technique by which a sequential file whose logical records are not a consistent size could be implemented as a text file. For example, suppose you wanted to construct a sequential file in which each logical record contained information about a novelist as well as a list of that author's works.

***55.** Explain the terms cluster analysis, association analysis, outlier analysis, and sequential pattern analysis in brief.

***56.** The chapter drew parallels between a traditional file index and the file directory system maintained by an operating system. In what ways does an operating system's file directory differ from a traditional index?

***57.** If a hash file is partitioned into 10 buckets, what is the probability of at least two of three arbitrary records hashing to the same bucket? (Assume the hash function gives no bucket priority over the others.) How many records must be stored in the file until it is more likely for collisions to occur than not?

***58.** Solve the previous problem, assuming that the file is partitioned into 100 buckets instead of 10.

***59.** If we are using the division technique discussed in this chapter as a hash function and the file storage area is divided into 23 buckets, which section should we search to find the record whose key, when interpreted as a binary value, is the integer 124?

***60.** Compare the implementation of a hash file to that of a homogeneous two-dimensional array. How are the roles of the hash function and the address polynomial similar?

***61.** Give one advantage that

a. a sequential file has over an indexed file.
b. a sequential file has over a hash file.
c. an indexed file has over a sequential file.
d. an indexed file has over a hash file.
e. a hash file has over a sequential file.
f. a hash file has over an indexed file.

***62.** Explain the technique of hashing. How is it related to a hash function and a hash table?

Social Issues

The following questions are intended as a guide to the ethical/social/legal issues associated with the field of computing. The goal is not merely to answer these questions. You should also consider why you answered as you did and whether your justifications are consistent from one question to the next.

1. In the United States, DNA records of all federal prisoners are now stored in a database for use in criminal investigations. Would it be ethical to release this information for other purposes—for example, for medical research? If so, for what purposes? If not, why not? What are the pros and cons in each case?
2. To what extent should a university be allowed to release information about its students? What about their names and addresses? What about grade distributions without identifying the students? Is your answer consistent with your answer to question 1?
3. What restrictions are appropriate regarding the construction of databases about individuals? What information does a government have a right to hold regarding its citizens? What information does an insurance company have a right to hold regarding its clients? What information does a company have a right to hold regarding its employees? Should controls in these settings be implemented and, if so, how?
4. Is it proper for a credit card company to sell the purchasing patterns of its clients to marketing firms? Is it acceptable for a sports car mail order business to sell its mailing list to a sports car magazine? Is it acceptable for the Internal Revenue Service in the United States to sell the names and addresses of those taxpayers with significant capital gains to stockbrokers? If you cannot answer with an unqualified yes or no, what would you propose as an acceptable policy?
5. To what extent is the designer of a database responsible for how the information in that database is used?
6. Suppose a database mistakenly allows unapproved access to information in the database. If that information is obtained and used adversely, to what degree do the database designers share responsibility for the misuse of the information? Does your answer depend on the amount of effort required by the perpetrator to discover the flaw in the database design and obtain the unauthorized information?
7. The prevalence of data mining raises numerous issues of ethics and privacy. Is your privacy infringed if data mining reveals certain characteristics about the overall population of your community? Does the use of data mining promote good business practice or bigotry? To what extent is it proper to force citizens to participate in a census, knowing that more information will be extracted from the data than is explicitly requested by the individual questionnaires? Does data mining give marketing firms an unfair advantage over unsuspecting audiences? To what extent is profiling good or bad?
8. To what extent should a person or corporation be allowed to collect and hold information about individuals? What if the information collected is already publicly available although scattered among several sources? To what extent should a person or company be expected to protect such information?

9. Many libraries offer a reference service so that patrons can enlist the assistance of a librarian when searching for information. Will the existence of the Internet and database technology render this service obsolete? If so, would that be a step forward or backward? If not, why not? How will the existence of the Internet and database technology affect the existence of libraries themselves?

10. To what extent are you exposed to the possibility of identity theft? What steps can you take to minimize that exposure? How could you be damaged if you were the victim of identity theft? Should you be liable when identity theft occurs?

Additional Reading

Berstein, A., M. Kifer, and P. M. Lewis. *Database Systems,* 2nd ed. Boston, MA: Addison-Wesley, 2006.

Connolly, T., and C.E. Beg. *Database Systems: A Practical Approach to Design, Implementation and Management,* 5th ed. Boston, MA: Addison-Wesley, 2009.

Date, C. J. *An Introduction to Database Systems,* 8th ed. Boston, MA: Addison-Wesley, 2004.

Date, C. J. *Databases, Types and the Relational Model,* 3rd ed. Boston, MA: Addison-Wesley, 2007.

Elmasri, R., and S. Navathe. *Fundamentals of Database Systems,* 6th ed. Boston, MA: Addison-Wesley, 2011.

Patrick, J. J. *SQL Fundamentals,* 3rd ed. Upper Saddle River, NJ: Prentice-Hall, 2009.

Silberschatz, A., H. Korth, and S. Sudarshan. *Database Systems Concepts,* 6th ed. New York: McGraw-Hill, 2009.

Ullman, J. D., and J. D. Widom. *A First Course in Database Systems,* 3rd ed. Upper Saddle River, NJ: Prentice-Hall, 2008.

Computer Graphics

CHAPTER **10**

In this chapter we explore the field of computer graphics—a field that is having a major impact in the production of motion pictures and interactive video games. Indeed, advances in computer graphics are freeing the visual media from restrictions of reality, and many argue that computer-generated animation may soon replace the need for traditional actors, sets, and photography throughout the motion picture and television industries.

**Asterisks indicate suggestions for optional sections.*

Computer graphics is the branch of computer science that applies computer technology to the production and manipulation of visual representations. It is associated with a wide assortment of topics including the presentation of text, the construction of graphs and charts, the development of graphical user interfaces, the manipulation of photographs, the production of video games, and the creation of animated motion pictures. However, the term *computer graphics* is increasingly being used in reference to the specific field called 3D graphics, and most of this chapter concentrates on this topic. We begin by defining 3D graphics and clarifying its role within the broader interpretation of computer graphics.

10.1 The Scope of Computer Graphics

With the emergence of digital cameras, the popularity of software for manipulating digitally encoded images has rapidly expanded. This software allows one to touch up photographs by removing blemishes and the dreaded "red eye," as well as cutting and pasting portions from different photographs to create images that do not necessarily reflect reality.

Similar techniques are often applied to create special effects in the motion picture and television industries. In fact, such applications were major motivating factors for these industries shifting from analog systems such as film to digitally encoded images. Applications include removing the appearance of support wires, overlaying multiple images, or producing short sequences of new images that are used to alter the action that was originally captured by a camera.

In addition to software for manipulating digital photographs and motion picture frames, there is now a wide variety of utility/application software packages that assist in producing two-dimensional images ranging from simple line drawings to sophisticated art. (A well-known elementary example is Microsoft's application called Paint.) At a minimum, these programs allow the user to draw dots and lines, insert simple geometric shapes such as ovals and rectangles, fill regions with color, and cut and paste designated portions of a drawing.

Note that all the preceding applications deal with the manipulation of flat two-dimensional shapes and images. They are, therefore, examples of two related fields of research: One is **2D graphics,** the other is **image processing.** The distinction is that 2D graphics focuses on the task of converting two-dimensional shapes (circles, rectangles, letters, etc.) into patterns of pixels to produce an image, whereas image processing, which we will meet later in our study of artificial intelligence, focuses on analyzing the pixels in an image in order to identify patterns that can be used to enhance or perhaps "understand" the image. In short, 2D graphics deals with producing images while image processing deals with analyzing images.

In contrast to converting two-dimensional shapes into images as in 2D graphics, the field of **3D graphics** deals with converting three-dimensional shapes into images. The process is to construct digitally encoded versions of three-dimensional scenes and then to simulate the photographic process to produce images of those scenes. The theme is analogous to that of traditional photography, except that the scene that is "photographed" using 3D graphics techniques does not exist as a physical reality but instead "exists" merely as a collection of data and algorithms. Thus, 3D graphics involves "photographing" virtual worlds, whereas traditional photography involves photographing the real world.

It is important to note that the creation of an image using 3D graphics encompasses two distinct steps. One is the creation, encoding, storage, and manipulation of the scene to be photographed. The other is the process of producing the image. The former is a creative, artistic process; the latter is a computationally intense process. These are topics that we will explore in the next four sections.

The fact that 3D graphics produces "photographs" of virtual scenes makes it ideal for use in interactive video games and animated motion picture productions where the shackles of reality would otherwise limit the action. An interactive video game consists of an encoded three-dimensional virtual environment with which the game player interacts. The images that the player sees are produced by means of 3D graphics technology. Animated motion pictures are created in a similar manner, except that it is the human animator who interacts with the virtual environment rather than the ultimate viewer. The product ultimately distributed to the public is a sequence of two-dimensional images as determined by the production's director/producer.

We will investigate the use of 3D graphics in animation more thoroughly in Section 10.6. For now, let us close this section by imagining where these applications may lead as 3D graphics technology advances. Today, motion pictures are distributed as sequences of two-dimensional images. Although the projectors that display this information have progressed from analog devices with reels of film to digital technology using DVD players and flat panel displays, they still deal only with two-dimensional representations.

Imagine, however, how this may change as our ability to create and manipulate realistic three-dimensional virtual worlds improves. Rather than "photographing" these virtual worlds and distributing a motion picture in the form of two-dimensional images, we could distribute the virtual worlds. A potential viewer would receive access to the motion picture set rather than just the motion picture. This three-dimensional set would then be viewed by means of a "3D graphics projector" in much the same way that video games are viewed by special-purpose "game boxes." One might first watch a "suggested plot" that would result in viewing the motion picture as the director/producer envisioned. But, the viewer could also interact with the virtual set in a manner reminiscent of a video game to produce other scenarios. The possibilities are extensive, especially when we also consider the potentials of the three-dimensional human-machine interfaces that are being developed.

Questions & Exercises

1. Summarize the distinction between image processing, 2D graphics, and 3D graphics.
2. How does 3D graphics differ from traditional photography?
3. What are the two major steps in producing a "photograph" using 3D graphics?

10.2 Overview of 3D Graphics

Let us begin our study of 3D graphics by considering the entire process of creating and displaying images—a process that consists of three steps: modeling, rendering, and displaying. The modeling step (which we will explore in detail in Section 10.3) is analogous to designing and constructing a set in the traditional motion picture industry, except that the 3D graphics scene is "constructed" from digitally encoded data and algorithms. Thus, the scene produced in the context of computer graphics may never exist in reality.

The next step is to produce a two-dimensional image of the scene by computing how the objects in the scene would appear in a photograph made by a camera at a specified position. This step is called **rendering**—the subject of Sections 10.4 and 10.5. Rendering involves applying the mathematics of analytic geometry to compute the projection of the objects in the scene onto a flat surface known as the **projection plane** in a manner analogous to a camera projecting a scene onto film (Figure 10.1). The type of projection applied is a **perspective projection,** which means that all objects are projected along straight lines, called **projectors,** that extend from a common point called the **center of projection,** or the **view point.** (This is in contrast to a **parallel projection** in which the projectors are parallel. A perspective projection produces a projection similar to that seen by the human eye, whereas a parallel projection produces a "true" profile of an object, which is often useful in the context of engineering drawings.)

The restricted portion of the projection plane that defines the boundaries of the final image is known as the **image window.** It corresponds to the rectangle that is displayed in the viewfinder of most cameras to indicate the boundaries of the potential picture. Indeed, the viewfinder of most cameras allows you to view more of the camera's projection plane than merely its image window. (You may see the top of Aunt Martha's head in the viewfinder, but unless the top of her head is within the image window, it will not appear in the final picture.)

Once the portion of the scene that projects into the image window is identified, the appearance of each pixel in the final image is computed. This

Figure 10.1 The 3D graphics paradigm

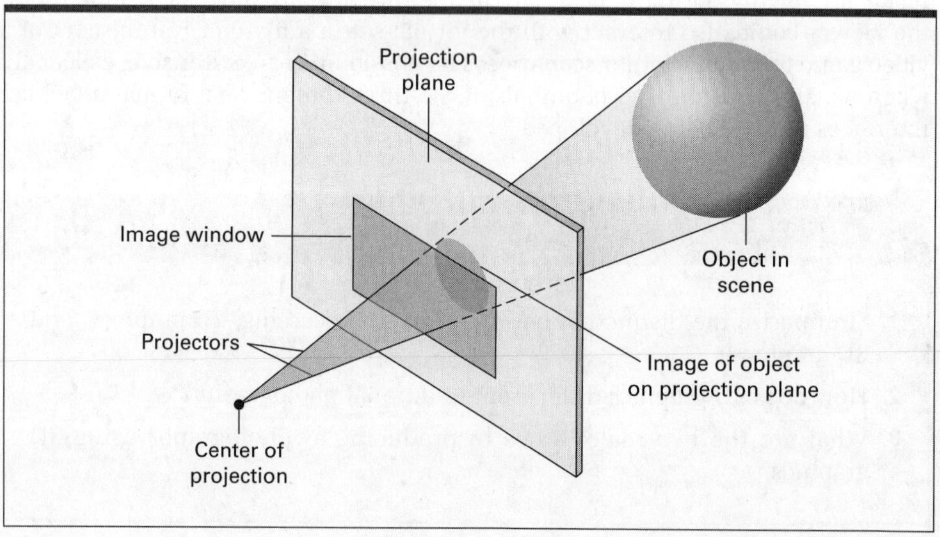

pixel-by-pixel process can be computationally complex because it requires determining how the objects in the scene interact with light—a hard, shiny surface in bright light should be rendered differently than a soft, transparent surface in indirect light. In turn, the rendering process borrows heavily from numerous fields including material science and physics. Moreover, determining the appearance of one object often requires knowledge about other objects in the scene. The object may be in the shadow of another object, or the object may be a mirror whose appearance is essentially that of another object.

As the appearance of each pixel is determined, the results are stored collectively as a bit map representation of the image in a storage area called the **frame buffer.** This buffer may be an area of main memory or, in the case of hardware designed specifically for graphics applications, it may be a block of special purpose memory circuitry.

Finally, the image stored in the frame buffer is either displayed for viewing or transferred to more permanent storage for later display. If the image is being produced for use in a motion picture, it may be stored and perhaps even modified before final presentation. However, in an interactive video game or flight simulator, images must be displayed as they are produced on a real-time basis, a requirement that often limits the quality of the images created. This is why the graphics quality of full-feature animated productions distributed by the motion picture industry exceeds that of today's interactive video games.

We close our introduction to 3D graphics by analyzing a typical video game system. The game itself is essentially an encoded virtual world together with software that allows that world to be manipulated by the game player. As the player manipulates that world, the game system repeatedly renders the scene and stores the image in the image buffer. To overcome real-world time constraints, much of this rendering process is handled by special-purpose hardware. Indeed, the presence of this hardware is a distinguishing feature between a game system and a generic personal computer. Finally, the display device in the game system displays the contents of the frame buffer, giving the player the illusion of a changing scene.

Questions & Exercises

1. Summarize the three steps involved in producing an image using 3D graphics.
2. What is the difference between the projection plane and the image window?
3. What is a frame buffer?

10.3 Modeling

A 3D computer graphics project begins in much the same way as a theatrical stage production—a set must be designed and the required props must be collected or constructed. In computer graphics terminology, the set is called a **scene** and the props are called **objects.** Keep in mind that a 3D graphics scene is virtual because it consists of objects that are "constructed" as digitally encoded models rather than tangible, physical structures.

In this section we will explore topics related to "constructing" objects and scenes. We begin with issues of modeling individual objects and conclude by considering the task of collecting those objects to form a scene.

Modeling Individual Objects

In a stage production, the extent to which a prop conforms to reality depends on how it will be used in the scene. We may not need an entire automobile, the telephone does not have to be functional, and the background scenery may be painted on a flat backdrop. Likewise, in the case of computer graphics, the degree to which the software model of an object accurately reflects the true properties of the object depends on the requirements of the situation. More detail is necessary to model objects in the foreground than objects in the background. Moreover, more detail can be produced in those cases that are not under stringent, real-time constraints.

Thus, some object models may be relatively simple whereas others may be extremely complex. As a general rule, more precise models lead to higher-quality images but longer rendering times. In turn, much of the ongoing research in computer graphics seeks the development of techniques for constructing highly detailed, yet efficient, object models. Some of this research deals with developing models that can provide different levels of detail depending on the object's ultimate role in the scene, the result being a single object model that can be used in a changing environment.

The information required to describe an object includes the object's shape as well as additional properties, such as surface characteristics that determine how the object interacts with light. For now, let us consider the task of modeling shape.

Shape The shape of an object in 3D graphics is usually described as a collection of small flat surfaces called **planar patches,** each of which is the shape of a polygon. Collectively, these polygons form a **polygonal mesh** that approximates the shape of the object being described (Figure 10.2). By using small planar patches, the approximation can be made as precise as needed.

The planar patches in a polygonal mesh are often chosen to be triangles because each triangle can be represented by its three vertices, which is the minimum number of points required to identify a flat surface in three-dimensional space. In any case a polygonal mesh is represented as the collection of the vertices of its planar patches.

A polygonal mesh representation of an object can be obtained in a variety of ways. One is to begin with a precise geometric description of the desired shape, and then use that description to construct a polygonal mesh. For example, analytic geometry tells us that a sphere (centered at the origin) with radius r is described by the equation

$$r^2 = x^2 + y^2 + z^2$$

Based on this formula, we can establish equations for lines of latitude and longitude on the sphere, identify the points where these lines intersect, and then use these points as the vertices of a polygonal mesh. Similar techniques can be applied to other traditional geometric shapes, and this is why characters in

Figure 10.2 A polygonal mesh for a sphere

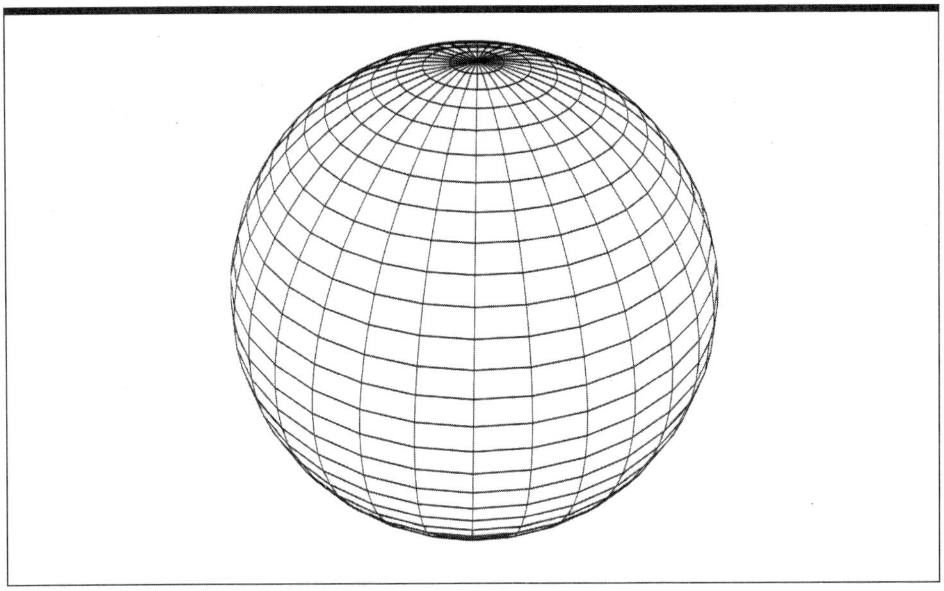

less-expensive computer-generated animations often appear to be pieced together from such structures as spheres, cylinders, and cones.

More general shapes can be described by more sophisticated analytical means. One is based on the use of **Bezier curves** (named after Pierre Bezier who developed the concept in the early 1970s as an engineer for the Renault car company), which allow a curved line segment in three-dimensional space to be defined by only a few points called control points—two of which represent the ends of the curve segment while the others indicate how the curve is distorted. As an example, Figure 10.3 displays a curve defined by four control points. Note how the curve appears to be pulled toward the two control points that do not identify the segment ends. By moving these points, the curve can be twisted into

Figure 10.3 A Bezier curve

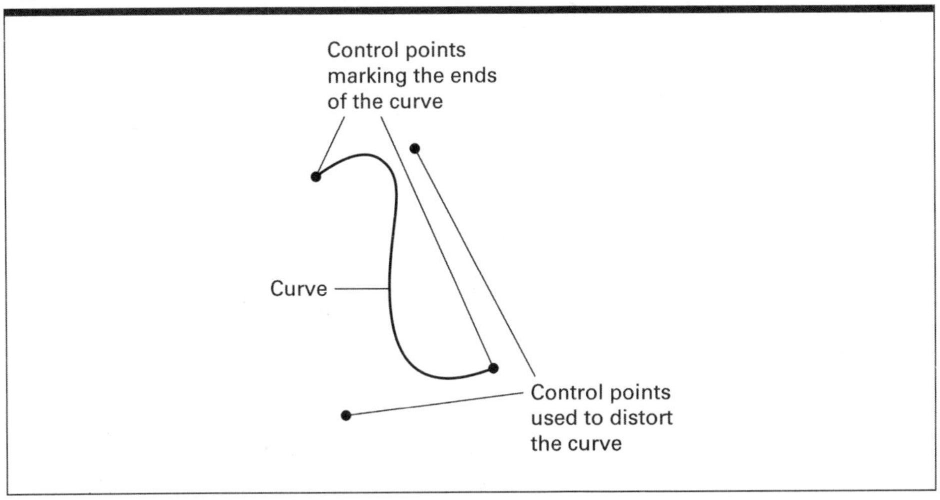

different shapes. (You may have experienced such techniques when constructing curved lines using drawing software packages such as Microsoft's Paint.) Although we will not pursue the topic here, Bezier's techniques for describing curves can be extended to describe three-dimensional surfaces, known as **Bezier surfaces.** In turn, Bezier surfaces have proven to be an efficient first step in the process of obtaining polygonal meshes for complex surfaces.

You may ask why it is necessary to convert a precise description of a shape, such as the concise formula of a sphere or the formulas describing a Bezier surface, into an approximation of the shape using a polygonal mesh. The answer is that representing the shape of all objects by polygonal meshes establishes a uniform approach to the rendering process—a trait that allows entire scenes to be rendered more efficiently. Thus, although geometric formulas provide precise descriptions of shapes, they serve merely as tools for constructing polygonal meshes.

Another way of obtaining a polygonal mesh is to construct the mesh in a brute force manner. This approach is popular in cases where a shape defies representation by elegant mathematical techniques. The procedure is to build a physical model of the object and then to record the location of points on the surface of the model by touching the surface with a pen device that records its position in three-dimensional space—a process known as **digitizing.** The collection of points obtained can then be used as vertices to obtain a polygonal mesh describing the shape.

Unfortunately, some shapes are so complex that obtaining realistic models by geometric modeling or manual digitizing is unfeasible. Examples include intricate plant structures such as trees, complex terrain such as mountain ranges, and gaseous substances such as clouds, smoke, or the flames of a fire. In these cases, polygonal meshes can be obtained by writing programs that construct the desired shape automatically. Such programs are collectively known as **procedural models.** In other words, a procedural model is a program unit that applies an algorithm to generate a desired structure.

As an example, procedural models have been used to generate mountain ranges by executing the following steps: Starting with a single triangle, identify the midpoints of the triangle's edges (Figure 10.4a). Then, connect these midpoints to form a total of four smaller triangles (Figure 10.4b). Now, while holding the original triangle's vertices fixed, move the midpoints in three-dimensional space (allowing the triangle's edge lines to stretch or contract), thus distorting the triangular shapes (Figure 10.4c). Repeat this process with each of the smaller triangles (Figure 10.4d), and continue repeating the process until the desired detail is obtained.

Procedural models provide an efficient means of producing multiple complex objects that are similar yet unique. For instance, a procedural model can be used to construct a variety of realistic tree objects—each with its own, yet similar, branching structure. One approach to such tree models is to apply branching rules to "grow" tree objects in much the same way that a parser (Section 6.4) constructs a parse tree from grammar rules. In fact, the collection of branching rules used in these cases is often called a grammar. One grammar may be designed for "growing" pine trees whereas another may be designed for "growing" oaks.

Another method of constructing procedural models is to simulate the underlying structure of an object as a large collection of particles. Such models are called **particle systems.** Usually particle systems apply certain predefined rules to move the particles in the system, perhaps in a manner reminiscent of molecular

Figure 10.4 Growing a polygonal mesh for a mountain range

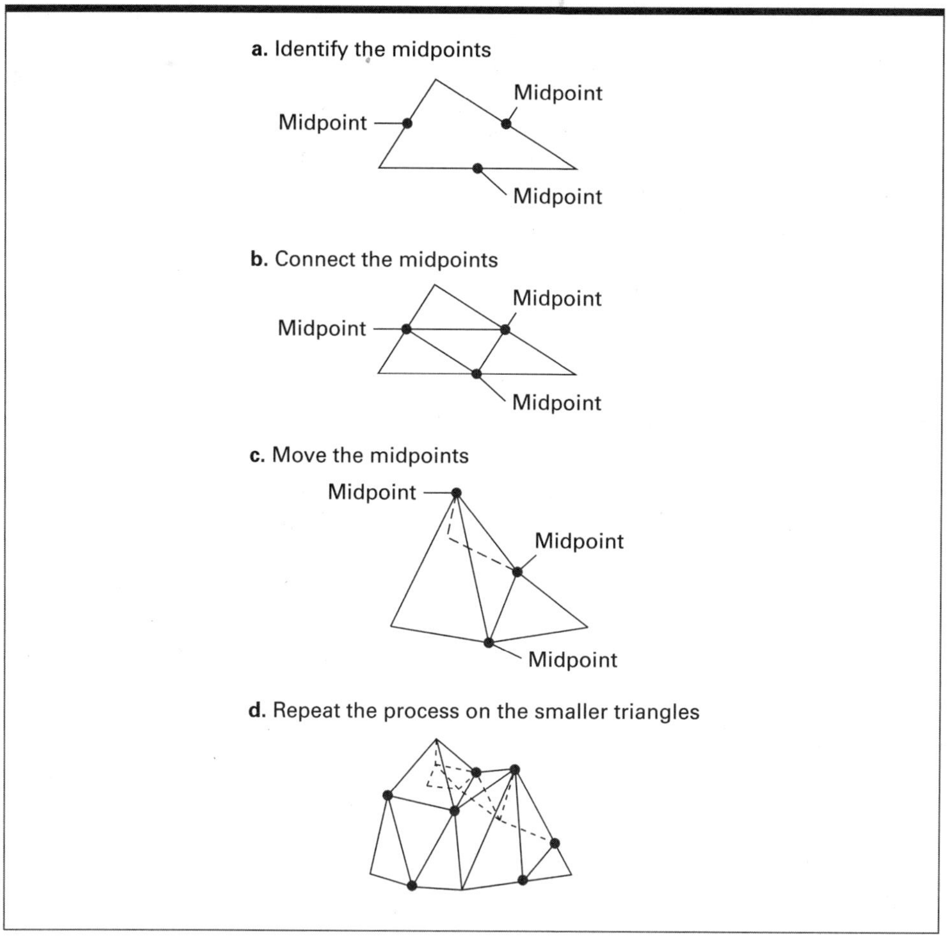

interactions, to produce the desired shape. As an example, particle systems have been used to produce an animation of sloshing water as we will see later in our discussion of animation. (Imagine a bucket of water modeled as a bucket of marbles. As the bucket rocks, the marbles tumble around, simulating the movement of water.) Other examples of particle system applications include flickering fire flames, clouds, and crowd scenes.

The output of a procedural model is usually a polygonal mesh that approximates the shape of the desired object. In some cases, such as generating a mountain range from triangles, the mesh is a natural consequence of the generating process. In other cases, such as growing a tree from branching rules, the mesh may be constructed as an additional, final step. For example, in the case of particle systems, the particles on the outer edge of the system are natural candidates for the vertices of the final polygonal mesh.

How precise the mesh generated by a procedural model may be depends on the situation. A procedural model for a tree in a scene's background may produce a course mesh that reflects only the basic shape of the tree, whereas a procedural model for a tree in the foreground may produce a mesh that distinguishes individual branches and leaves.

Fractals

The construction of a mountain range by means of a procedural model as described in the text (see Figure 10.4) is an example of the role that fractals play in 3D graphics. Technically speaking, a **fractal** is a geometric object whose "Hausdorff dimension is greater than its topological dimension." What this means intuitively is that the object is formed by "packing together" copies of an object of a lower dimension. (Think of the illusion of width created by "packing together" multiple parallel line segments.) A fractal is usually formed by means of a recursive process, where each activation in the recursion "packs together" additional (yet smaller) copies of the pattern being used to build the fractal. The fractal that results is self-similar in that each portion, when magnified, appears as a copy of itself.

A traditional example of a fractal is the von Koch snowflake that is formed by repeatedly replacing the straight-line segments in the structure

with smaller versions of the same structure. This leads to a sequence of refinements that proceeds as follows:

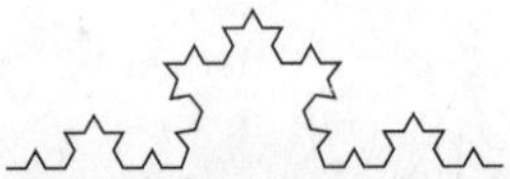

Fractals are often the backbone of procedural models in the field of 3D graphics. Indeed, they have been used to produce realistic images of mountain ranges, vegetation, clouds, and smoke.

Surface Characteristics A model consisting merely of a polygonal mesh captures only the shape of an object. Most rendering systems are capable of enriching such models during the rendering process to simulate various surface characteristics as requested by the user. For example, by applying different shading techniques (which we will introduce in Section 10.4) a user may specify that a polygonal mesh for a ball be rendered as a red smooth ball or a green rough ball. In some cases, such flexibility is desirable. But in situations requiring faithful rendering of an original object, more specific information about the object must be included in the model so that the rendering system will know what it should do.

There are a variety of techniques for encoding information about an object in addition to its shape. For instance, along with each vertex in a polygonal mesh, one might encode the color of the original object at that point on the object. This information could then be used during rendering to recreate the appearance of the original object.

In other instances, color patterns can be associated with an object's surface by means of a process known as **texture mapping.** Texture mapping is similar to the process of applying wallpaper in that it associates a predefined image with the surface of an object. This image might be a digital photograph, an artist's rendering, or perhaps a computer-generated image. Traditional texture images include brick walls, wood grained surfaces, and marble facades.

Suppose, for example, that we wanted to model a stone wall. We could represent the shape of the wall with a simple polygonal mesh depicting a long rectangular solid. Then, with this mesh we could supply a two-dimensional image of stone masonry. Later, during the rendering process, this image could be applied to the rectangular solid to produce the appearance of a stone wall. More precisely, each time the rendering process needed to determine the appearance of a point on the wall it would simply use the appearance of the corresponding point in the masonry image.

Texture mapping works best when applied to relatively flat surfaces. The result can look artificial if the texture image must be distorted significantly to cover a curved surface (imagine the problems of trying to wallpaper a beach ball) or if the texture image wraps completely around an object causing a seam where the texture pattern may not blend with itself. Nonetheless, texture mapping has proven to be an efficient means of simulating texture and is widely used in situations that are real-time sensitive—a prime example being interactive video games.

The Search for Realism Building object models that lead to realistic images is a topic of ongoing research. Of special interest are materials associated with living characters such as skin, hair, fur, and feathers. Much of this research is specific to a particular substance and encompasses both modeling and rendering techniques. For instance, to obtain realistic models of human skin, some researchers have incorporated the degree to which light penetrates the epidermal and dermal skin layers and how the contents of those layers affect the skin's appearance.

Another example involves the modeling of human hair. If hair is to be seen from a distance, then more traditional modeling techniques may suffice. But, for close-up views, realistic-appearing hair can be challenging. Problems include translucent properties, textural depth, draping characteristics, and the manner in which hair responds to external forces such as wind. To overcome these hurtles, some applications have resorted to modeling individual strands of hair—a daunting task because the number of hairs on a human head can be on the order of 100,000. More astounding, however, is that some researchers have constructed hair models that address the scaled texture, color variation, and mechanical dynamics of each individual strand.

Still another example in which considerable detail has been pursued is in modeling cloth. In this case the intricacies of weaving patterns have been used to produce proper textural distinctions between fabric types such as twill versus satin, and detailed properties of yarn have been combined with knitting pattern data to create models of knit fabric that lead to extremely realistic close-up images. In addition, knowledge of physics and mechanical engineering has been applied to individual threads to compute images of draped material that account for such aspects as stretching of threads and shearing of the weave.

The production of realistic images is an active area of research that, as we have said, incorporates techniques in both the modeling and rendering processes. Typically, as progress is made, the new techniques are first incorporated in applications that are not subject to real-time constraints, such as the graphics software of motion picture production studios where there is a significant delay between the modeling/rendering process and the ultimate presentation of images. As these new techniques are refined and streamlined, they find their way into real-time applications, and the quality of the graphics in these environments improves as well. Truly realistic real-time interaction with virtual worlds may not be too far in the future.

Modeling Entire Scenes

Once the objects in a scene have been adequately described and digitally encoded, they are each assigned a location, size, and an orientation within the scene. This collection of information is then linked to form a data structure called a **scene graph.** In addition, the scene graph contains links to special objects representing light sources as well as a particular object representing the camera. It is here that the location, orientation, and focal properties of the camera are recorded.

Thus, a scene graph is analogous to a studio set-up in traditional photography. It contains the camera, lights, props, and background scenery—everything that will contribute to the appearance of the photograph when the shutter is snapped—all in their proper places. The difference is that a traditional photography setup contains physical objects whereas a scene graph contains digitally encoded representations of objects. In short, the scene graph describes a virtual world.

The positioning of the camera within a scene has many repercussions. As we mentioned earlier, the detail with which objects are modeled depends on the object's location in the scene. Foreground objects require more detail than background objects, and the distinction between foreground and background depends on the camera position. If the scene is to be used in a context analogous to a theatrical stage setting, then the roles of foreground and background are well established and the object models can be constructed accordingly. If, however, the context requires that the camera's position be altered for different images, the detail provided by the object models might need to be adjusted between "photographs." This is an area of current research. One envisions a scene consisting of "intelligent" models that refine their polygonal meshes and other features as the camera moves within the scene.

An interesting example of a moving camera scenario occurs in virtual reality systems with which a human user is allowed to experience the sensation of

3D Television

Several technologies exist to produce 3D imagery in the context of television, but all rely on the same stereoscopic visual effect—two slightly different images arriving at the left and right eyes are interpreted by the brain as depth. The most inexpensive mechanisms for this require special glasses with filter lenses. Older colored lenses (used in cinema in the 1950s) or the more modern polarized lenses filter out different aspects of a single image from the screen, resulting in different images reaching different eyes. More costly technology involves "active" glasses that alternately shutter left and right lenses in synchronization with a 3D television that switches quickly between the left and right images. Finally, 3D televisions are being developed that do not require special glasses or head gear. They use elaborate arrays of filters or magnifying lens on the surface of the screen to project the left and right images toward a viewer's head at slightly different angles, meaning that the left and right eyes of the viewer see different images.

moving around within an imaginary three-dimensional world. The imaginary world is represented by a scene graph, and the human views this environment by means of a camera that moves within the scene as dictated by the movements of the human. Actually, to provide the depth perception of three dimensions, two cameras are used: one representing the human's right eye, the other representing the human's left eye. By displaying the image obtained by each camera in front of the appropriate eye, the human gets the illusion of residing inside the three-dimensional scene, and when audio and tactile sensations are added to the experience, the illusion can become quite realistic.

In closing, we should note that the construction of a scene graph resides at a pivotal position in the 3D graphics process. Because it contains all the information required to produce the final image, its completion marks the end of the artistic modeling process and the beginning of the computationally intensive process of rendering the image. Indeed, once the scene graph is constructed, the graphics task becomes that of computing projections, determining surface details at specific points, and simulating the effects of light—a collection of tasks that is largely independent of the particular application.

Questions & Exercises

1. The following are four points (encoded using the traditional rectangular coordinate system) that represent the vertices of a planar patch. Describe the shape of the patch. (For those without a background in analytic geometry, each triple tells you how to reach the point in question beginning at the corner of a room. The first number tells you how far to walk along the seam between the floor and the wall on your right. The second number tells you how far to walk out into the room in a direction parallel to the wall on your left. The third number tells you how far to climb up from the floor. If a number is negative, you will have to pretend that you are a ghost and can walk backward through walls and floors.)

   (0, 0, 0) (0, 1, 1) (0, 2, 1) (0, 1, 0)
2. What is a procedural model?
3. List some of the objects that might be present in a scene graph used to produce an image in a park.
4. Why are shapes represented by polygonal meshes even though they could be represented more precisely by geometric equations?
5. What is texture mapping?

10.4 Rendering

It is time now to consider the process of rendering, which involves determining how the objects in a scene graph would appear when projected onto the projection plane. There are several ways to accomplish the rendering task. This section focuses on the traditional approach that is used by most of the more popular graphics systems (video games, home computers, etc.) on the "consumer market" today. The following section investigates two alternatives to this approach.

We begin with some background information on the interaction between light and objects. After all, the appearance of an object is determined by the light emitted from that object, and thus determining an object's appearance ultimately becomes the task of simulating the behavior of light.

Light-Surface Interaction

Depending on the material properties of an object, light striking its surface may be absorbed, bounce off the surface as reflected light, or pass through the surface (and be bent) as refracted light.

Reflection Let us consider a ray of light that is reflected off a flat opaque surface. The ray arrives traveling in a straight line and strikes the surface at an angle called the **incidence angle.** The angle at which the ray is reflected is identical to the incidence angle. As shown in Figure 10.5, these angles are measured relative to a line perpendicular (or **normal**) to the surface. (A line normal to a surface is often referred to as simply "the normal" as in "The incidence angle is measured relative to the normal.") The incoming ray, the reflected ray, and the normal all lie in the same plane.

If a surface is smooth, parallel light rays (such as those arriving from the same light source) that strike the surface in the same area will be reflected in essentially the same direction and travel away from the object as parallel rays. Such reflected light is called **specular light.** Note that specular light can be observed only when the orientation of the surface and the light source causes the light to be reflected in the viewer's direction. Thus, it normally appears as bright highlights on a surface. Moreover, because specular light has minimal contact with the surface, it tends to portray the color of the original light source.

Surfaces, however, are rarely perfectly smooth, and therefore many light rays may strike the surface at points whose orientations differ from that of the prevailing surface. Moreover, light rays often penetrate the immediate boundary of a surface and ricochet among the surface particles before finally departing as reflected light. The result is that many rays will be scattered in different directions. This scattered light is called **diffuse light.** Unlike specular light,

Figure 10.5 Reflected light

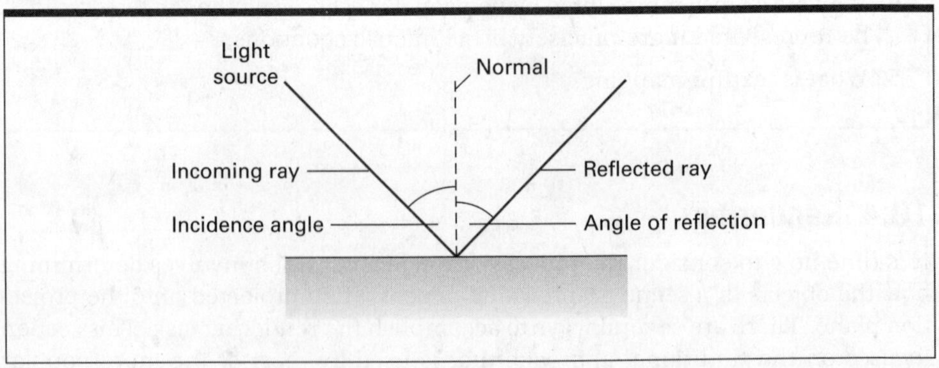

diffuse light is visible within a wide range of directions. And, because it tends to have prolonged contact with the surface, diffuse light is more susceptible to the absorption properties of the material and therefore tends to portray the color of the object.

Figure 10.6 presents a ball that is illuminated by a single light source. The bright highlight on the ball is produced by specular light. The rest of the hemisphere facing the light source is seen by means of diffuse light. Note that the hemisphere facing away from the primary light source is not visible by means of light being reflected directly from that source. The ability to see this portion of the ball is due to **ambient light,** which is "stray" or scattered light that is not associated with any particular source or direction. Portions of surfaces illuminated by ambient light often appear as a uniform dark color.

Most surfaces reflect both specular and diffuse light. The characteristics of the surface determine the proportion of each. Smooth surfaces appear shiny because they reflect more specular light than diffuse light. Rough surfaces appear dull because they reflect more diffuse light than specular light. Moreover, due to minute properties of some surfaces, the ratio of specular to diffuse light varies depending on the direction of the incoming light. Light striking such a surface from one direction may be reflected primarily as specular light, whereas light striking the surface from another direction may be reflected primarily as diffuse light. Thus, the appearance of the surface will shift from shiny to dull as it is rotated. Such surfaces are called **anisotropic surfaces,** as opposed to **isotropic surfaces** whose reflection patterns are symmetric. Examples of anisotropic surfaces are found in fabric such as satin, where the nap of the cloth alters the material's appearance depending on its orientation. Another example is the grassy surface of an athletic field, where the lie of the grass (usually determined by the manner in which the grass is cut) produces anisotropic visual effects such as light and dark striped patterns.

Figure 10.6 Specular versus diffuse light

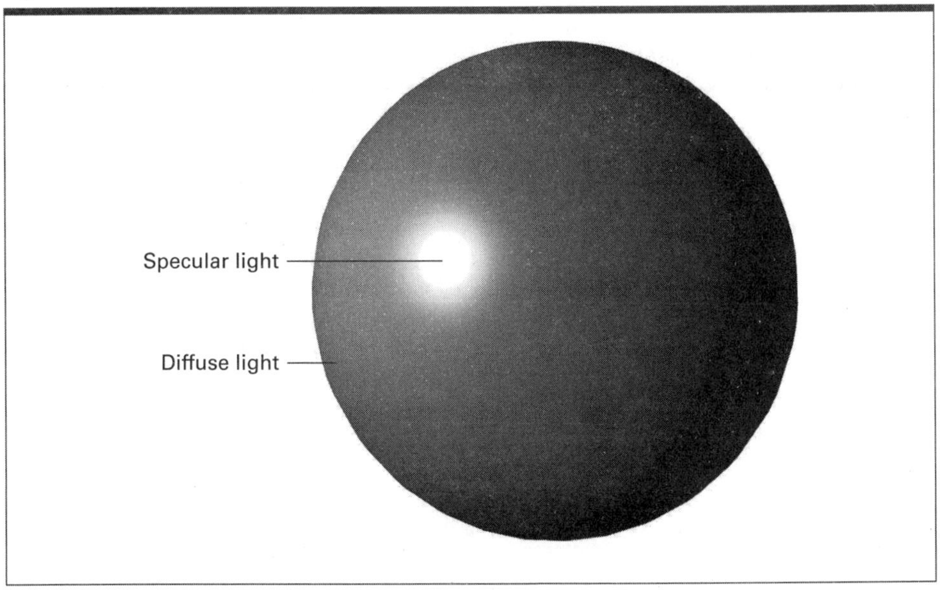

Refraction Now consider light striking an object that is transparent rather than opaque. In this case light rays pass through the object rather than bounce off its surface. As the rays penetrate the surface, their direction is altered—a phenomenon called **refraction** (Figure 10.7). The degree of refraction is determined by the refractive index of the materials involved. The refractive index is related to the density of the material. Dense materials tend to have a higher refractive index than less dense materials. As a light ray passes into a material with a higher reflective index (such as passing from air into water), it bends toward the normal at the point of entry. If it passes into a material with a lower refractive index, it bends away from the normal.

To render transparent objects properly, rendering software must know the refractive indexes of the materials involved. But this is not the whole story. The rendering software must also know which side of an object's surface represents the inside of an object as opposed to the outside. Is the light entering the object or exiting the object? Techniques for obtaining this information are sometimes quite subtle. For example, if we agree to always list the vertices of each polygon in a polygonal mesh in a counter-clockwise order as seen from outside the object, then the list cleverly encodes which side of the patch represents the outside of the object.

Clipping, Scan Conversion, and Hidden-Surface Removal

Let us now focus on the process of producing an image from a scene graph. Our approach for now is to follow the techniques used in most interactive video game systems. Collectively, these techniques form a well-established paradigm known as the **rendering pipeline.** We will consider some of the pros and cons of this approach at the end of this section and explore two alternatives in the following section. For now it is helpful to note that the rendering pipeline deals with opaque objects and thus refraction is not an issue. Moreover, it ignores interactions between objects so that, for now, we will not be concerned with mirrors and shadows.

Figure 10.7 Refracted light

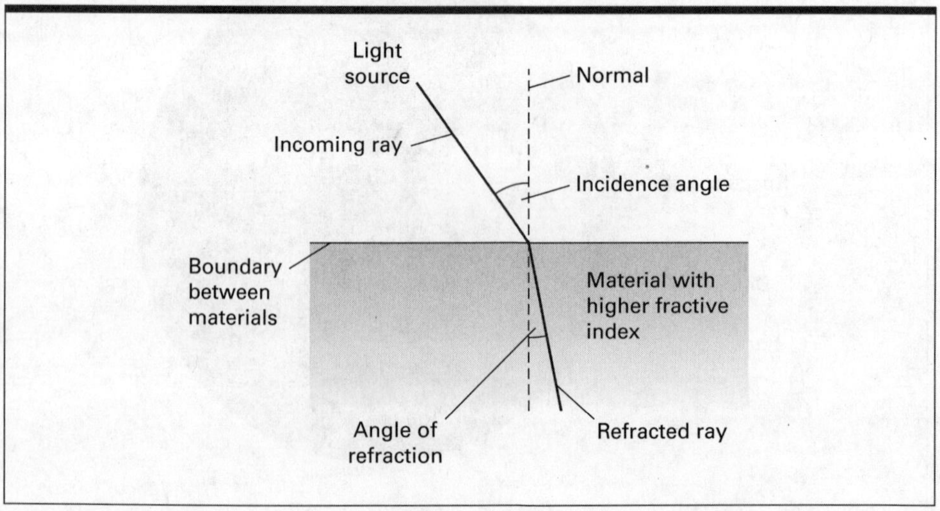

The rendering pipeline begins by identifying the region in a three-dimensional scene that contains the objects (or parts of objects) that can be "seen" by the camera. This region, called the **view volume,** is the space within the pyramid defined by straight lines extending from the center of projection through the corners of the image window (Figure 10.8).

Once the view volume is identified, the task is to discard from consideration those objects or parts of objects that do not intersect the view volume. After all, the projection of that portion of the scene will fall outside the image window and therefore not appear in the final image. The first step is to discard all those objects that are totally outside the view volume. To streamline this process, a scene graph may be organized in a tree structure in which objects in different regions of the scene are stored in different branches. In turn, large sections of the scene graph can be discarded merely by ignoring entire branches in the tree.

After identifying and discarding the objects that do not intersect the view volume, the remaining objects are trimmed by a process known as **clipping,** which essentially slices off the portion of each object that lies outside the view volume. More precisely, clipping is the process of comparing each individual planar patch to the boundaries of the view volume and trimming off those portions of the patch that fall outside. The results are polygonal meshes (of possibly trimmed planar patches) that lie entirely within the view volume.

The next step in the rendering pipeline is to identify the points on the remaining planar patches that are to be associated with pixel positions in the final image. It is important to realize that only these points will contribute to the final

Figure 10.8 Identifying the region of the scene that lies inside the view volume

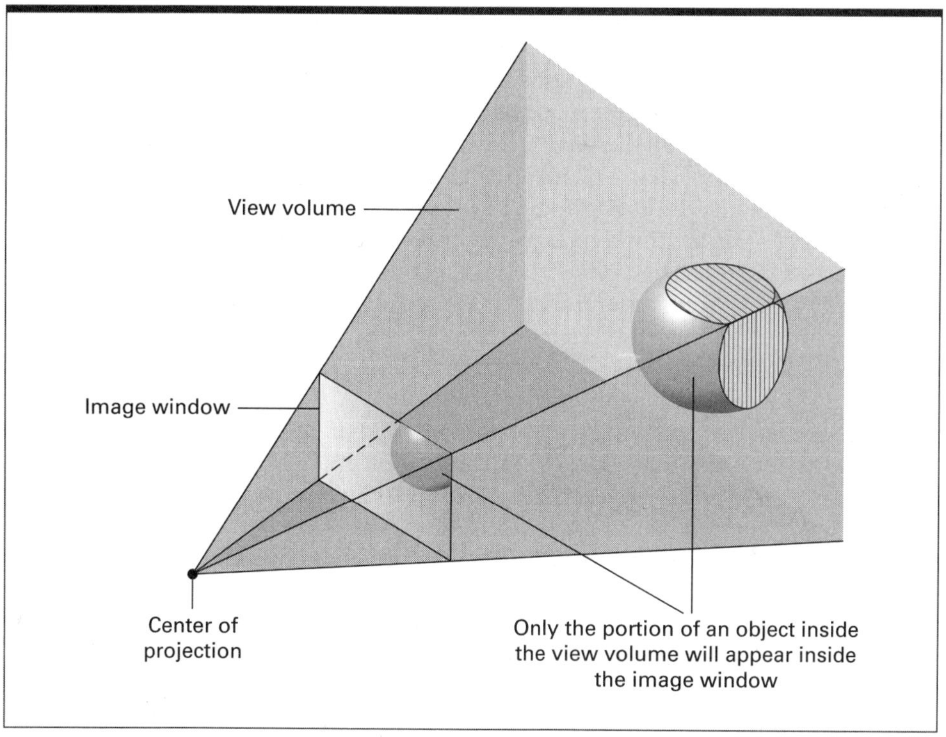

Aliasing

Have you ever noticed the weird "glittery" appearance that striped shirts and ties have on television screens? This is the result of the phenomenon called **aliasing,** which occurs when a pattern in the desired image meshes inappropriately with the density of the pixels comprising the image. As an example, suppose a portion of the desired image consists of alternating black and white stripes but the center of all the pixels happens to fall only on the black stripes. The object would then be rendered as being completely black. But, if the object moves slightly, the center of all the pixels may fall on the white stripes, meaning that the object would suddenly change to white. There are a variety of ways to compensate for this annoying effect. One is to render each pixel as the average of a small area in the image rather than as the appearance of a precise single point.

picture. If a detail on an object falls between the pixel positions, it will not be represented by a pixel and therefore not be visible in the final image. This is why pixel counts are heavily advertised in the digital camera market. The more pixels there are, the more likely that small details will be captured in a photograph.

The process of associating pixel positions with points in the scene is called **scan conversion** (because it involves converting the patches into horizontal rows of pixels called scan lines) or **rasterization** (because an array of pixels is known as a raster). Scan conversion is accomplished by extending straight lines (projectors) from the center of projection through each pixel position in the image window and then identifying the points at which these projectors intersect the planar patches. These, then, are the points on the patches at which we must determine an object's appearance. Indeed, these are the points that will be represented by the pixels in the final image.

Figure 10.9 depicts the scan conversion of a single triangular patch. Part a of the figure shows how a projector is used to associate a pixel position with a point on the patch. Part b shows the pixel image of the patch as determined by the scan conversion. The entire array of pixels (the raster) is represented by a grid, and the pixels associated with the triangle have been shaded. Note that the figure also demonstrates the distortion that can occur when scan converting a shape whose features are small relative to the size of the pixels. Such jagged edges are familiar to users of most personal computer display screens.

Unfortunately, scan conversion of an entire scene (or even a single object) is not as straightforward as scan converting a single patch. This is because when multiple patches are involved, one patch may block the view of another. Thus, even though a projector intersects a planar patch, that point on the patch may not be visible in the final image. Identifying and discarding points in a scene that are blocked from view is the process called **hidden-surface removal.**

A specific version of hidden-surface removal is **back face elimination,** which involves discarding from consideration those patches in a polygonal mesh that represent the "back side" of an object. Note that back face elimination is relatively straightforward because the patches on the back side of an object can be identified as those whose orientation faces away from the camera.

Solving the complete hidden-surface removal problem, however, requires much more than back face elimination. Imagine, for example, a scene of an

Figure 10.9 The scan conversion of a triangular patch

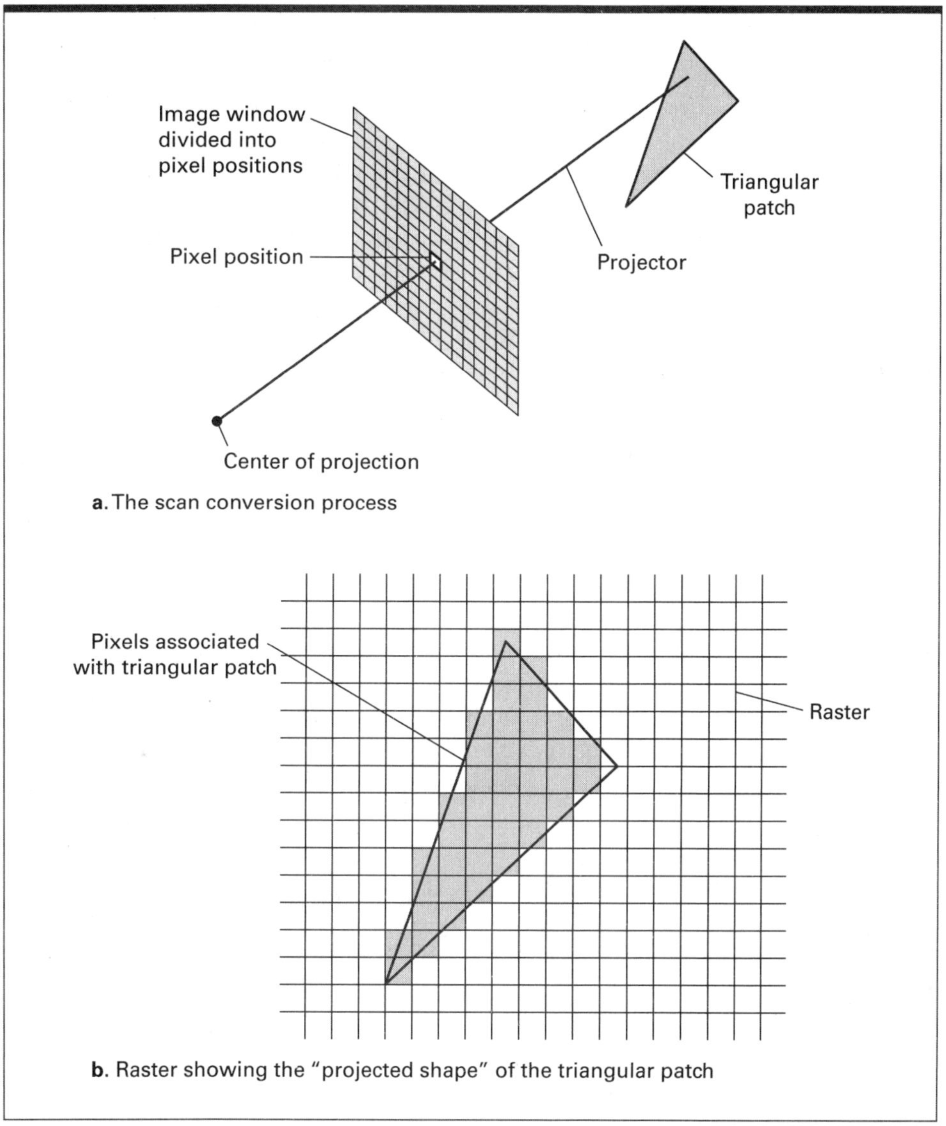

automobile in front of a building. Planar patches from both the automobile and the building will project into the same area of the image window. Where overlaps occur, the pixel data ultimately stored in the frame buffer should indicate the appearance of the object in the foreground (the automobile) rather than the object in the background (the building). In short, if a projector intersects more than one planar patch, it is the point on the patch nearest the image window that should be rendered.

A simplistic approach to solving this "foreground/background" problem, known as the **painter's algorithm,** is to arrange the objects in the scene according to their distances from the camera and then to scan convert the more distant objects first, allowing the results of scan converting closer objects to override any previous results. Unfortunately, the painter's algorithm fails to handle cases in which objects are intertwined. Part of a tree may be behind another object while another part of the tree may be in front of that object.

More encompassing solutions to the "foreground/background" problem are obtained by focusing on individual pixels rather than entire objects. A popular technique uses an extra storage area, called a **z-buffer** (also a depth buffer), which contains an entry for each pixel in the image (or, equivalently, each pixel entry in the frame buffer). Each position in the z-buffer is used to store the distance along the appropriate projector from the camera to the object currently represented by the corresponding entry in the frame buffer. Thus, with the aid of a z-buffer, the "foreground/background" problem can be resolved by computing and storing the appearance of a pixel only if data for that pixel has not yet been placed in the frame buffer or if the point on the object currently being considered is closer than that of the previously rendered object as determined by the distance information recorded in the z-buffer.

More precisely, when using a z-buffer, the rendering process can proceed as follows: Set all entries in the z-buffer to a value representing the maximum distance from the camera that an object will be considered for rendering. Then, each time a new point on a planar patch is considered for rendering, first compare its distance from the camera to the value in the z-buffer associated with the current pixel position. If that distance is less than the value found in the z-buffer, compute the appearance of the point, record the results in the frame buffer, and replace the old entry in the z-buffer with the distance to the point just rendered. (Note that if the distance to the point is greater than the value found in the z-buffer, no action needs to be taken because the point on the patch is too far away to be considered or it is blocked from view by a closer point that has already been rendered.)

Shading

Once scan conversion has identified a point on a planar patch that is to appear in the final image, the rendering task becomes that of determining the appearance of the patch at that point. This process is called **shading.** Note that shading involves computing the characteristics of the light projected toward the camera from the point in question, which, in turn, depends on the orientation of the surface at that point. After all, it is the orientation of the surface at the point that determines the degree of specular, diffuse, and ambient light witnessed by the camera.

A straightforward solution to the shading problem, called **flat shading,** is to use the orientation of a planar patch as the orientation of each point on the patch—that is, to assume the surface over each patch is flat. The result, however, is that the final image will appear faceted as depicted in Figure 10.10 rather than rounded as shown in Figure 10.6. In a sense, flat shading produces an image of the polygonal mesh itself rather than the object being modeled by the mesh.

To produce a more realistic image, the rendering process must blend the appearance of individual planar patches into a smoothly curved appearing surface. This is accomplished by estimating the true orientation of the original surface at each individual point being rendered.

Such estimation schemes normally begin with data indicating the surface orientation at the vertices of the polygonal mesh. There are several ways to obtain this data. One is to encode the orientation of the original surface at each vertex and attach this data to the polygonal mesh as part of the modeling process. This produces a polygonal mesh with arrows, called **normal vectors,** attached to each

Figure 10.10 A sphere as it might appear when rendered by flat shading

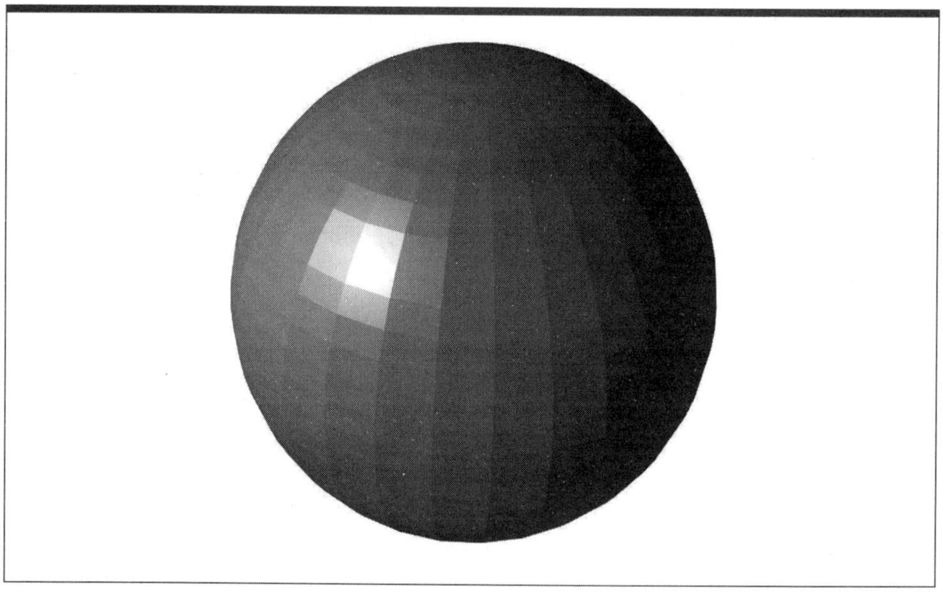

vertex. Each normal vector points outward in the direction perpendicular to the original surface. The result is a polygonal mesh that can be envisioned as shown in Figure 10.11. (Another approach is to compute the orientation of each patch adjacent to a vertex and then use an "average" of those orientations as an estimate of the surface's orientation at the vertex.)

Regardless of how the orientation of the original surface at a polygonal mesh's vertices is obtained, several strategies are available for shading a planar patch based on this data. These include **Gouraud shading** and **Phong shading,** the distinction between which is subtle. Both begin by using the information about the surface orientation at a patch's vertices to approximate the surface orientation along the boundaries of the patch. Gouraud shading then applies that information to determine the appearance of the surface along the patch boundaries and, finally, interpolates that boundary appearance to estimate the appearance of the surface at points in the interior of the patch. In contrast, Phong shading interpolates the orientation of the surface along the patch's boundaries to estimate the surface orientation at points within the patch's interior and only then considers questions of appearance. (In short, Gouraud shading converts orientation information into color information and then interpolates the color information. Phong

Figure 10.11 A conceptual view of a polygonal mesh with normal vectors at its vertices

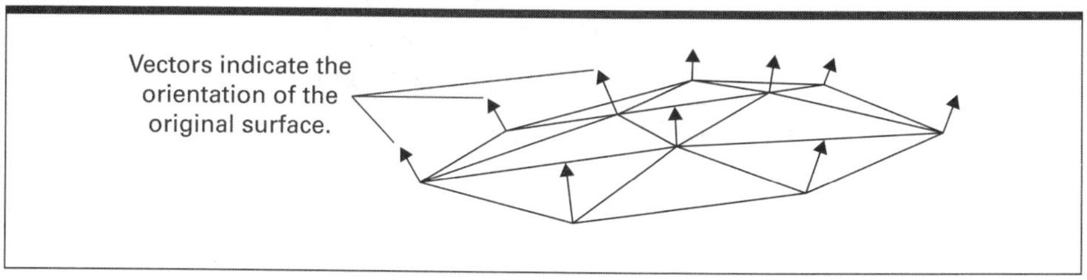

shading interpolates orientation information until the orientation of the point in question is estimated, and then converts that orientation information into color information.) The result is that Phong shading is more likely to detect specular light within a patch's interior because it is more responsive to changes in surface orientation. (See question 3 at the end of this section.)

Finally, we should note that basic shading techniques can be augmented to add the appearance of texture to a surface. An example, called **bump mapping,** is essentially a way of generating small variations in the apparent orientation of a surface so that the surface appears to be rough. More precisely, bump mapping adds a degree of randomness to the interpolation process applied by traditional shading algorithms so that the overall surface appears to have texture, as demonstrated in Figure 10.12.

Rendering-Pipeline Hardware

As we have already said, the processes of clipping, scan conversion, hidden- surface removal, and shading are viewed collectively as a sequence known as the rendering pipeline. Moreover, efficient algorithms for performing these tasks are well-known and have been implemented directly in electronic circuitry, which has been miniaturized by VLSI technology to produce chips that perform the entire rendering pipeline automatically. Today, even inexpensive examples are capable of rendering millions of planar patches per second.

Most computer systems that are designed for graphics applications, including video game machines, incorporate these devices in their design. In the case of more general-purpose computer systems, this technology can be added in the form of a **graphics card,** or **graphics adapter,** which is attached to the computer's bus as a specialized controller (see Chapter 2). Such hardware substantially reduces the time required to perform the rendering process.

Figure 10.12 A sphere as it might appear when rendered using bump mapping

Rendering-pipeline hardware also reduces the complexity of graphics application software. Essentially, all the software needs to do is provide the graphics hardware with the scene graph. The hardware then performs the pipeline steps and places the results in the frame buffer. Thus, from the software's perspective, the entire rendering pipeline is reduced to a single step using the hardware as an abstract tool.

As an example, let us again consider an interactive video game. To initialize the game, the game software transfers the scene graph to the graphics hardware. The hardware then renders the scene and places the image in the frame buffer from where it is automatically displayed on the monitor screen. As the game progresses, the game software merely updates the scene graph in the graphics hardware to reflect the changing game situation, and the hardware repeatedly renders the scene, each time placing the updated image in the frame buffer.

We should note, however, that the capabilities and communication properties of different graphics hardware vary substantially. Thus, if an application such as a video game were developed for a specific graphics platform, it would have to be modified if transferred to another environment. To reduce this dependence on the specifics of graphics systems, standard software interfaces have been developed to play an intermediary role between graphics hardware and application software. These interfaces consist of software routines that convert standardized commands into the specific instructions required by a particular graphics hardware system. Examples include **OpenGL** (short for **Open Graphics Library**), which is a nonproprietary system developed by Silicon Graphics and widely used in the video game industry, and **Direct3D,** which was developed by Microsoft for use in Microsoft Windows environments.

In closing we should note that, with all the advantages associated with the rendering pipeline, there are disadvantages as well—the most significant of which is the fact that the pipeline implements only a **local lighting model,** meaning that the pipeline renders each object independently of other objects. That is, under a local lighting model, each object is rendered in relation to the light sources as though it were the only object in the scene. The result is that light interactions between objects, such as shadows and reflections, are not captured. This is in contrast to a **global lighting model** in which interactions among objects are considered. We will discuss two techniques for implementing a global lighting model in the next section. For now we merely note that these techniques lie outside the real-time capabilities of current technology.

This does not mean, however, that systems using rendering-pipeline hardware are not able to produce some global lighting effects. Indeed, clever techniques have been developed to overcome some of the restrictions imposed by a local lighting model. In particular, the appearance of **drop shadows,** which are shadows cast on the ground, can be simulated within the context of a local lighting model by making a copy of the polygonal mesh of the object casting the shadow, squashing the duplicate mesh flat, placing it on the ground, and coloring it dark. In other words, the shadow is modeled as though it were another object, which can then be rendered by traditional rendering-pipeline hardware to produce the illusion of a shadow. Such techniques are popular in both "consumer level" applications such as interactive video games and "professional level" applications such as flight simulators.

Questions & Exercises

1. Summarize the distinction between specular light, diffuse light, and ambient light.
2. Define the terms *clipping* and *scan conversion*.
3. Gouraud shading and Phong shading can be summarized as follows: Gouraud shading uses the orientation of an object's surface along the boundaries of a patch to determine the appearance of the surface along the boundaries and then interpolates these appearances over the interior of the patch to determine the appearance of the particular points in question. Phong shading interpolates the boundary orientations to compute the orientations of points interior to the patch and then uses those orientations to determine the appearance of the particular points in question. How would the appearance of an object possibly differ?
4. What is the significance of the rendering pipeline?
5. Describe how reflections in a mirror might be simulated using a local lighting model.

10.5 Dealing with Global Lighting

Researchers are currently investigating two alternatives to the rendering pipeline, both of which implement a global lighting model and thus provide the potential of overcoming the local lighting model restrictions inherent in the traditional pipeline. One of these alternatives is ray tracing, the other is radiosity. Both are meticulous, time-consuming processes, as we are about to see.

Ray Tracing

Ray tracing is essentially the process of following a ray of light backward to find its source. The process starts by selecting a pixel to be rendered, identifying the straight line passing through that pixel and the center of projection, and then tracing the light ray that strikes the image window along that line. This tracing process involves following the line into the scene until it contacts an object. If that object is a light source, the ray tracing process terminates and the pixel is rendered as a point on the light source. Otherwise, the properties of the object's surface are evaluated to determine the direction of the incoming ray of light that was reflected to produce the ray the process is backtracking. The process then follows that incoming ray backward to find its source, at which point yet another ray may be identified and traced.

An example of ray tracing is depicted in Figure 10.13 where we see a ray traced backward through the image window to the surface of a mirror. From there the ray is traced to a shiny ball, from there back to the mirror, and from the mirror to the light source. Based on the information gained from this tracing process, the pixel in the image should appear as a point on the ball illuminated by the light source reflected in the mirror.

Figure 10.13 Ray tracing

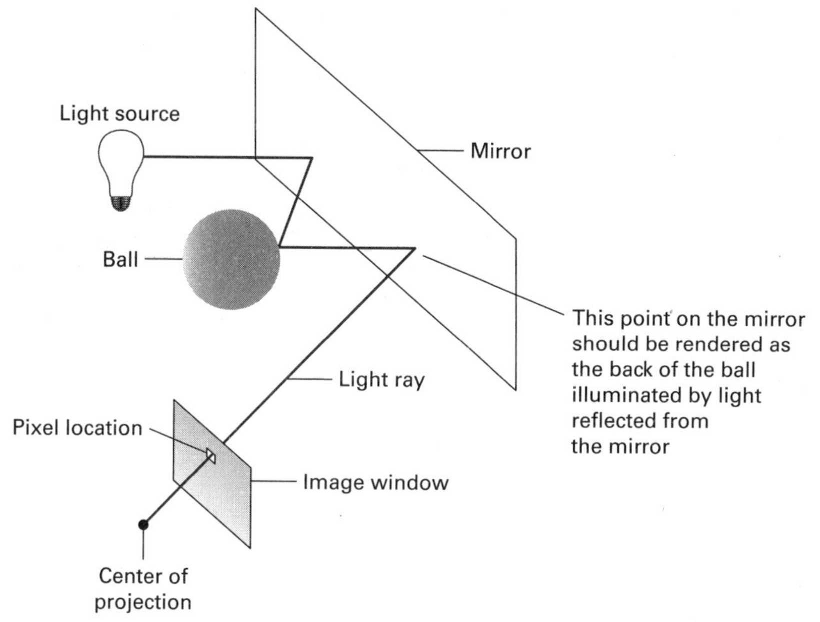

One drawback to ray tracing is that it traces only specular reflections. Thus, all the objects rendered by this method tend to have a shiny appearance. To counter this effect, a variation of ray tracing, called **distributed ray tracing,** can be applied. The difference is that rather than tracing a single ray backward from a point of reflection, distributed ray tracing traces multiple rays from that point, each extending in a slightly different direction.

Another variation to basic ray tracing is applicable when transparent objects are involved. In this case, two effects must be considered each time a ray is traced back to a surface. One is reflection, the other is refraction. In this case, the task of tracing the original ray splits into two tasks: tracing the reflection backwards and tracing the refraction backwards.

Ray tracing is normally implemented recursively, with each activation being asked to trace a ray to its source. The first activation may trace its ray to a shiny opaque surface. At that point it would recognize that its ray is the reflection of an incoming ray, compute the direction of that incoming ray, and call another activation to trace that incoming ray. This second activation would perform a similar task to find the source of its ray—a process that may result in calling still other activations.

A variety of conditions can be used to terminate recursive ray tracing. The ray being traced may reach a light source, the ray being traced may exit the scene without striking an object, or the number of activations may reach a predetermined limit. Still another termination condition can be based on the absorption properties of the surfaces encountered. If a surface is highly absorptive, such as a dark matte surface, then any incoming ray will have little effect on the surface's appearance and ray tracing can cease. Accumulative absorption can have a similar effect. That is, ray tracing can terminate after visiting several moderately absorptive surfaces.

Being based on a global lighting model, ray tracing avoids many of the restrictions inherent in the traditional rendering pipeline. For example, the problems of hidden-surface removal and detecting shadows are naturally solved in the ray tracing process. Unfortunately, ray tracing has the major drawback of being time consuming. As each reflection is traced back to its source, the number of computations required grows immensely—a problem that is compounded when allowing for refractions or applying distributed ray tracing. Hence, ray tracing is not implemented in consumer-level real-time systems such as interactive video games but instead may be found in professional-level applications that are not real-time sensitive such as the graphics software used by motion picture studios.

Radiosity

Another alternative to the traditional rendering pipeline is **radiosity.** Whereas ray tracing takes a point-by-point approach by tracing individual rays of light, radiosity takes a more regional approach by considering the total light energy radiated between pairs of planar patches. This radiated light energy is essentially diffuse light. The light energy that is radiated from an object is either generated by the object (as in the case of a light source) or reflected off the object. The appearance of each object is then determined by considering the light energy it receives from other objects.

The degree to which light radiated from one object affects the appearance of another is determined by parameters called **form factors.** A unique form factor is associated with each pair of patches in the scene to be rendered. These form factors take into account the geometric relationships between the patches involved such as separation distance and relative orientations. To determine the appearance of a patch in the scene, the amount of light energy received from all the other patches in the scene is computed using the appropriate form factor for each computation. The results are combined to produce a single color and intensity for each patch. These values are then interpolated among adjacent patches using techniques similar to Gouraud shading to obtain a smoothly contoured appearing surface rather than a faceted one.

Because there are numerous patches to be considered, radiosity is very computationally intense. In turn, like ray tracing, its application falls outside the capabilities of real-time graphics systems currently available in the consumer market. Another problem with radiosity is that because it deals with units consisting of entire patches rather than individual points, it fails to capture the details of specular light, meaning that all the surfaces rendered by radiosity tend to have a dull appearance.

Radiosity does, however, have its merits. One is that determining the appearance of objects using radiosity is independent of the camera. Thus, once the radiosity computations for a scene have been performed, the rendering of the scene can be completed quickly for various camera positions. Another is that radiosity captures many of the subtle characteristics of light such as **color bleeding** where the color of one object affects the hue of other objects around it. In turn, radiosity has its niches. One is in graphics software used in architectural design settings. Indeed, the light within a proposed building consists mainly of diffuse and ambient light so that specular effects are not significant, and the fact that new camera positions can be handled efficiently means that an architect can quickly view different rooms from different perspectives.

Questions & Exercises

1. Why does ray tracing follow rays backward from the image window to the light source rather than forward from the light source to the image window?
2. What is the difference between straightforward ray tracing and distributed ray tracing?
3. What are two disadvantages of radiosity?
4. In what ways are ray tracing and radiosity similar? In what ways are they different?

10.6 Animation

We turn now to the subject of computer animation, which is the use of computer technology to produce and display images that exhibit motion.

Animation Basics

We begin by introducing some basic animation concepts.

Frames Animation is achieved by displaying a sequence of images, called **frames,** in rapid succession. These frames capture the appearance of a changing scene at regular time intervals, and thus their sequential presentation creates the illusion of observing the scene continuously over time. The standard rate of display in the motion picture industry is twenty-four frames per second. The standard in broadcast video is sixty frames per second (although because every other video frame is designed to be interwoven with the preceding frame to produce a complete detailed image, video can also be classified as a thirty-frames-per- second system).

Kineographs

A kineograph is a book of animation frames that simulate motion when the pages are flipped rapidly. You can make your own kineograph out of this text (assuming that you have not already filled the margins with doodles). Simply place a dot in the margin of the first page and then, based on the position of the impression made on the third page, place another dot on the third page in a slightly different position than the dot on the first. Repeat this process on each consecutive odd page until you reach the end of the book. Now flip through the pages and watch the dot dance around. Presto! You have made your own kineograph and perhaps taken the first step toward a career in animation! As an experiment in kinematics, try drawing a stick figure instead of a simple dot and make the stick figure appear to walk. Now, experiment with dynamics by producing the image of a drop of water hitting the ground.

Frames can be produced by traditional photography or generated artificially by means of computer graphics. Moreover, the two techniques can be combined. For example, 2D graphics software is often used to modify images obtained via photography to remove the appearance of support wires, to superimpose images, and to create the illusion of **morphing,** which is the process of one object appearing to change into another.

A closer look at morphing provides interesting insights into the animation process. Constructing a morphing effect begins by identifying a pair of key frames that bracket the morphing sequence. One is the last image before the morph is to occur; the other is the first image after the morph has occurred. (In traditional motion picture production, this requires "filming" two sequences of action: one leading up to the occurrence of the morph, the other proceeding after the morph.) Features such as points and lines, called **control points,** in the frame preceding the morph are then associated with similar features in the postmorph frame, and the morph is constructed by applying mathematical techniques that incrementally distort one image into the other while using the control points as guides. By recording the images produced during this distortion process, a short sequence of artificially generated images is obtained that fills the gap between the original key frames and creates the morphing illusion.

The Storyboard A typical animation project begins with the creation of a **storyboard,** which is a sequence of two-dimensional images that tell the complete story in the form of sketches of scenes at key points in the presentation. The ultimate role of the storyboard depends on whether the animation project is implemented using 2D or 3D techniques. In a project using 2D graphics, the storyboard typically evolves into the final set of frames in much the same way that it did back in the Disney studios of the 1920s. In those days, artists, called master animators, would refine the storyboard into detailed frames, called **key frames,** that established the appearance of the characters and scenery at regular intervals of the animation. Assistant animators would then draw additional frames that would fill the gaps between the key frames so that the animation would appear continuous and smooth. This fill-in-the-gap process was called **in-betweening.**

The major distinction between this process and that used today is that animators now use image processing and 2D graphics software to draw key frames

Blurring

In the field of traditional photography, much effort has been expended toward the goal of producing sharp images of fast-moving objects. In the field of animation, the opposite problem arises. If each frame in a sequence depicting a moving object portrays the object as a sharp image, then the motion may appear jerky. However, sharp images are a natural byproduct of creating frames as individual images of stationary objects in a scene graph. Thus, animators often artificially distort the image of a moving object in a computer-generated frame. One technique, called **supersampling,** is to produce multiple images in which the moving object is only slightly displaced and then to overlay these images to produce a single frame. Another technique is to alter the shape of the moving object so that it appears elongated along the direction of motion.

and much of the in-betweening process has been automated so that the role of assistant animators has essentially disappeared.

3D Animation Most video game animation and full-feature animated productions are now created using 3D graphics. In these cases the project still begins with the creation of a storyboard consisting of two-dimensional images. However, rather than evolving into the final product as with 2D graphics projects, the storyboard is used as a guide in the construction of a three-dimensional virtual world. This virtual world is then repeatedly "photographed" as the objects within it are moved according to the script or the progression of the video game.

Perhaps we should pause here and clarify what it means for an object to move within a computer-generated scene. Keep in mind that the "object" is actually a collection of data stored in the scene graph. Among the data in this collection are values that indicate the location and orientation of the object. Thus, "moving" an object is accomplished merely by changing these values. Once these changes have been made, the new values will be used in the rendering process. Consequently, the object will appear to have moved in the final two-dimensional image.

Dynamics and Kinematics

The degree to which motion within a 3D graphics scene is automated or controlled by a human animator varies among applications. The goal, of course, is to automate the entire process. To this end, much research has been directed toward finding ways to identify and simulate the motion of naturally occurring phenomena. Two areas of mechanics have proven particularly useful in this regard.

One is **dynamics,** which deals with describing the motion of an object by applying the laws of physics to determine the effects of the forces acting on the object. For example, in addition to a location, an object in a scene might be assigned a direction of motion, speed, and mass. These items could then be used to determine the effects that gravity or collisions with other objects would have on the object, which would allow software to calculate the proper location of the object for the next frame.

As an example, consider the task of constructing an animated sequence depicting water sloshing in a container. We could use a particle system in the scene graph to represent the water, where each particle represents a small unit of water. (Think of the water consisting of large "molecules" the size of marbles.) Then, we could apply the laws of physics to compute the effects of gravity on the particles as well as the interaction among the particles themselves as the container rocks side to side. This would allow us to compute the location of each particle at regular time intervals, and by using the location of the outer particles as vertices of a polygonal mesh, we could obtain a mesh depicting the surface of the water. Our animation could then be obtained by repeatedly "photographing" this mesh as the simulation progresses.

The other branch of mechanics used to simulate motion is **kinematics,** which deals with describing an object's motion in terms of how parts of an object move with respect to each other. Applications of kinematics are prominent when animating articulated figures, where it is necessary to move appendages such as arms and legs. These motions are more easily modeled by simulating joint movement patterns than by computing the effects of the individual forces exerted by muscles and gravity. Thus, whereas dynamics might be the technique of choice when determining the path of a bouncing ball, the motion of an animated character's arm would be determined by applying kinematics to compute the proper shoulder, elbow, and wrist rotations. In turn, much research in animating living characters focuses on issues of anatomy and how joint and appendage structure influence motion.

A typical method of applying kinematics is to begin by representing a character by a stick figure that simulates the skeletal structure of the character being portrayed. Each section of the figure is then covered with a polygonal mesh representing the character's surface surrounding that section, and rules are established to determine how adjacent meshes should connect with each other. The figure can then be manipulated (either by software or a human animator) by repositioning the joints in the skeletal structure in the same manner that one manipulates a string puppet. The points at which the "strings" attach to the model are called **avars,** short for "articulation variables" (or more recently "animation variables").

Much research in the application of kinematics has been directed toward developing algorithms for automatically computing sequences of appendage positions that mimic natural occurring motion. Along these lines, algorithms are now available that generate realistic walking sequences.

However, much of the animation based on kinematics is still produced by directing a character through a preset sequence of joint-appendage positions. These positions may be established by the creativity of an animator or obtained by **motion capture,** which involves recording the positions of a living model as the model performs the desired action. More precisely, after applying reflective tape to strategic points on a human's body, the human can be photographed from multiple angles while throwing a baseball. Then, by observing the locations of the tape in the various photographs, the precise orientations of the human's arms and legs can be identified as the throwing action progresses, and these orientations can then be transferred to a character in an animation.

The Animation Process

The ultimate goal of research in animation is to automate the entire animation process. One imagines software that, given the proper parameters, would automatically produce the desired animated sequence. Progress in this direction is demonstrated by the fact that the motion picture industry now produces images of crowds, battle scenes, and stampeding animals by means of individual virtual "robots" that automatically move within a scene graph, each performing its allotted task.

An interesting case in point occurred when filming the fantasy armies of Orcs and humans for the *Lord of the Rings* trilogy. Each onscreen warrior was modeled as a distinct "intelligent" object with its own physical characteristics and a randomly assigned personality that gave it tendencies to attack or flee. In test simulations for the battle of Helms Deep in the second film, the Orcs had their tendency to flee set too high, and they simply ran away when confronted with the human warriors. (This was perhaps the first case of virtual extras considering a job too dangerous.)

Of course, much animation today is still created by human animators. However, rather than drawing two-dimensional frames by hand as in the 1920s, these animators use software to manipulate three-dimensional virtual objects in a scene graph in a manner reminiscent of controlling string puppets, as explained in our earlier discussion of kinematics. In this way, an animator is able to create a series of virtual scenes that are "photographed" to produce the animation. In some cases this technique is used to produce only the scenes for key frames, and then software is used to produce the in-between frames by automatically rendering the scene as the software applies dynamics and kinematics to move the objects in the scene graph from one key-frame scene position to the next.

As research in computer graphics progresses and technology continues to improve, more of the animation process will certainly become automated. Whether the role of human animators as well as human actors and physical sets will someday become obsolete remains to be seen, but many believe that day is not too far in the future. Indeed, 3D graphics has the potential of affecting the motion picture industry far more than the transition from silent movies to "talkies."

Questions & Exercises

1. Images seen by a human tend to linger in the human's perception for approximately 200 milliseconds. Based on this approximation, how many images per second must be presented to the human to create animation? How does this approximation compare to the number of frames per second used in the motion picture industry?
2. What is a storyboard?
3. What is in-betweening?
4. Define the terms *kinematics* and *dynamics.*

Chapter Review Problems

1. Which of the following are applications of 2D graphics and which are applications of 3D graphics?
   a. Designing the layout of magazine pages
   b. Drawing an image using Microsoft Paint
   c. Producing images from a virtual world for a video game
2. In the context of 3D graphics, what corresponds to each of the following items from traditional photography? Explain your answers.
   a. Film
   b. Rectangle in viewfinder
   c. Scene being photographed
3. When using a perspective projection, under what conditions will a sphere in the scene not produce a circle on the projection plane?
4. When using a perspective projection, can the image of a straight line segment ever be a curved line segment on the projection plane? Justify your answer.
5. Suppose one end of an eight-foot straight pole is four feet from the center of projection. Moreover, suppose that a straight line from the center of projection to one end of the pole intersects the projection plane at a point that is one foot from the center of projection. If the pole is parallel to the projection plane, how long is the image of the pole in the projection plane?
6. Explain the concepts of kinematics and dynamics as used in 3D animation.
7. How is blurring in animation different from image blurring?

8. What is a significant difference between applying 3D graphics to produce a motion picture and applying 3D graphics to produce the animation for an interactive video game? Explain your answer.

9. Identify some properties of an object that might be incorporated in a model of that object for use in a 3D graphics scene. Identify some properties that would probably not be represented in the model. Explain your answer.

10. Identify some physical properties of an object that are not captured by a model containing only a polygonal mesh. (Thus, a polygonal mesh alone does not constitute a complete model of the object.) Explain how one of those properties could be added to the object's model.

11. A triangle is displayed with approximate shading in Figure 10.9(b). Suggest a way to improve the accuracy of the shape.

12. Each collection that follows represents the vertices (using the traditional rectangular coordinate system) of a patch in a polygonal mesh. Describe the shape of the mesh.

```
Patch 1: (0, 0, 0) (0, 2, 0)
         (2, 2, 0) (2, 0, 0)
Patch 2: (0, 0, 0) (1, 1, 1)
         (2, 0, 0)
Patch 3: (2, 0, 0) (1, 1, 1)
         (2, 2, 0)
Patch 4: (2, 2, 0) (1, 1, 1)
         (0, 2, 0)
Patch 5: (0, 2, 0) (1, 1, 1)
         (0, 0, 0)
```

13. Each collection that follows represents the vertices (using the traditional rectangular coordinate system) of a patch in a polygonal mesh. Describe the shape of the mesh.

```
Patch 1: (0, 0, 0) (0, 4, 0)
         (2, 4, 0) (2, 0, 0)
Patch 2: (0, 0, 0) (0, 4, 0)
         (1, 4, 1) (1, 0, 1)
Patch 3: (2, 0, 0) (1, 0, 1)
         (1, 4, 1) (2, 4, 0)
Patch 4: (0, 0, 0) (1, 0, 1)
         (2, 0, 0)
Patch 5: (2, 4, 0) (1, 4, 1)
         (0, 4, 0)
```

14. Design a polygonal mesh representing a rectangular solid. Use the traditional rectangular coordinate system to encode the vertices and draw a sketch representing your solution.

15. Using no more than eight triangular patches, design a polygonal mesh to approximate the shape of a sphere with radius one. (With only eight patches, your mesh will be a very rough approximation of a sphere, but the goal is for you to display an understanding of what a polygonal mesh is rather than to produce a precise representation of a sphere.) Represent the vertices of your patches using the traditional rectangular coordinate system and draw a sketch of your mesh.

16. Why would the following four points not be the vertices of a planar patch?

```
(0, 0, 0) (1, 0, 0)
(0, 1, 0) (0, 0, 1)
```

17. Suppose the points (1, 0, 0), (1, 1, 1), and (1, 0, 2) are the vertices of a planar patch. Which of the following line segments is/are normal to the surface of the patch?
    a. The line segment from (1, 0, 0) to (1, 1, 0)
    b. The line segment from (1, 1, 1) to (2, 1, 1)
    c. The line segment from (1, 0, 2) to (0, 0, 2)
    d. The line segment from (1, 0, 0) to (1, 1, 1)

18. What is meant by flat shading?

19. What procedures can be adopted to obtain polygonal meshes for the following cases?
    a. A mob at a rock concert
    b. A building
    c. A sphere
    d. A painted canvas

20. Explain the following terms with the help of a labelled diagram:
    a. Projection plane
    b. Center of projection
    c. View volume
    d. Image window

21. Explain the terms hidden-surface removal, back face elimination, and z-buffer in brief.

22. What is meant by aliasing? Suggest one of the possible ways to overcome the problem of aliasing.

23. Suppose the surface of the planar patch with vertices (0, 0, 0), (0, 2, 0), (2, 2, 0), and (2, 0, 0) is smooth and shiny. If a light ray originates at the point (0, 0, 1) and strikes the surface at (1, 1, 0), through which of the following points will the reflected ray pass?
a. (0, 0, 1)
b. (1, 1, 1)
c. (2, 2, 1)
d. (3, 3, 1)

24. Suppose a buoy supports a light ten feet above the surface of still water. At what point on the water's surface will an observer see the reflection of the light if the observer is fifteen feet from the buoy and five feet above the water's surface?

25. If a fish is swimming below the surface of still water and an observer is viewing the fish from above the water, where will the fish appear to be from the observer's position?
a. Above and toward the background of its true position
b. At the true position
c. Below and toward the foreground of its true position

26. Suppose the points (1, 0, 0), (1, 1, 1), and (1, 0, 2) are the vertices of a planar patch and the vertices are listed in a counter-clockwise order as seen from outside the object. In each case that follows, indicate whether a ray of light originating at the given point would strike the surface of the patch from outside or inside the object.
a. (0, 0, 0)
b. (2, 0, 0)
c. (2, 1, 1)
d. (3, 2, 1)

27. In what way is the process of hidden-surface removal more complex than back face elimination? Explain your answer.

28. How is movement produced on screen in animation?

29. In our discussion of hidden-surface removal, we described the procedure for solving the "foreground/background" problem with the aid of a z-buffer. Express that procedure using the pseudocode introduced in Chapter 5.

30. Suppose the surface of an object is covered by alternating orange and blue vertical stripes, each of which is one centimeter wide. If the object is positioned in a scene so that the pixel positions are associated with points on the object spaced at two-centimeter intervals, what would be the possible appearances of the object in the final image? Explain your answer.

31. Although texture mapping and bump mapping are means of associating "texture" with a surface, they are considerably different techniques. Write a short paragraph comparing the two.

32. Give an example scenario where the painter's algorithm fails to solve the foreground/background problem.

33. You have two images of resolution 1024 × 1024 and 640 × 480. Which image would be more detailed?

34. In what way does the hardware in a computer designed for interactive video games differ from that of a general-purpose PC?

35. What are the various advantages and disadvantages of radiosity?

36. What is the distinction between anisotropic surfaces and isotropic surfaces?

37. What advantage does ray tracing have over the traditional rendering pipeline? What disadvantage does it have?

38. What advantage does distributed ray tracing have over traditional ray tracing? What disadvantage does it have?

39. What is the significance of graphics software interfaces in graphics processing? Explain your answer.

40. Write a pseudocode to draw a triangle with vertices at (0, 0), (2, 2) and (2, 0). Use the brute force approach to choose every pixel to be printed on screen.

41. How many frames would be required to produce a ninety-minute animated production to be shown in a motion picture theater?

42. What is the distinction between Bezier curves and Bezier surfaces? Explain your answer.

43. Explain how the use of a z-buffer could assist when creating an animation sequence depicting a single object moving within a scene.

44. Dynamics and kinematics have proven to be useful in simulating motion. Give a brief distinction between the two.

Social Issues

The following questions are intended as a guide to the ethical/social/legal issues associated with the field of computing. The goal is not merely to answer these questions. You should also consider why you answered as you did and whether your justifications are consistent from one question to the next.

1. Suppose computer animation reaches the point that real actors are no longer needed in the motion picture and television industries. What would the consequences be? What would be the ripple effect of no longer having "movie stars"?
2. With the development of digital cameras and related software, the ability to alter or fabricate photographs has been placed within the capabilities of the general public. What changes will this bring to society? What ethical and legal issues could arise?
3. To what extent should photographs be owned? Suppose a person places his or her photograph on a website and someone else downloads that photograph, alters it so that the subject is in a compromising situation, and circulates the altered version. What recourse should the subject of the photograph have?
4. To what extent is a programmer who helps develop a violent video game responsible for any consequences of that game? Should children's access to video games be restricted? If so, how and by whom? What about other groups in society, such as convicted criminals?

Additional Reading

Angel, E. and D. Shreiner. *Interactive Computer Graphics, A Top-Down Approach with Shader-Based OpenGL,* 6th ed. Boston, MA: Addison-Wesley, 2011.

Bowman, D. A., E. Kruijff, J. J. LaViola, Jr., and I. Poupyrev. *3D User Interfaces Theory and Practice.* Boston, MA: Addison-Wesley, 2005.

Hill, Jr., F. L., and S. Kelley. *Computer Graphics Using OpenGL.* 3rd ed. Upper Saddle River, NJ: Prentice-Hall, 2007.

McConnell, J. J. *Computer Graphics, Theory into Practice.* Sudbury, MA: Jones and Bartlett, 2006.

Parent, R. *Computer Animation, Algorithms and Techniques,* 3rd ed. San Francisco, CA: Morgan Kaufmann, 2012.

CHAPTER 11

Artificial Intelligence

In this chapter we explore the branch of computer science known as artificial intelligence. Although this field is relatively young, it has produced some astonishing results such as electronic game show contestants, computers that appear to learn and reason, and machines that coordinate their activities to achieve a common goal such as winning a soccer game. In artificial intelligence, today's science fiction might well be tomorrow's reality.

Artificial intelligence is the field of computer science that seeks to build autonomous machines—machines that can carry out complex tasks without human intervention. This goal requires that machines be able to perceive and reason. Such capabilities fall within the category of common sense activities that, although natural for the human mind, have historically proven difficult for machines. The result is that work in the field continues to be challenging. In this chapter we explore some of the topics in this vast area of research.

11.1 Intelligence and Machines

The field of artificial intelligence is quite large and merges with other subjects such as psychology, neurology, mathematics, linguistics, and electrical and mechanical engineering. To focus our thoughts, then, we begin by considering the concept of an agent and the types of intelligent behavior that an agent might exhibit. Indeed, much of the research in artificial intelligence can be categorized in terms of an agent's behavior.

Intelligent Agents

An **agent** is a "device" that responds to stimuli from its environment. It is natural to envision an agent as an individual machine such as a robot, although an agent may take other forms such as an autonomous airplane, a character in an interactive video game, or a process communicating with other processes over the Internet (perhaps as a client, a server, or a peer). Most agents have sensors by which they receive data from their environments and actuators by which they can affect their environments. Examples of sensors include microphones, cameras, range sensors, and air or soil sampling devices. Examples of actuators include wheels, legs, wings, grippers, and speech synthesizers.

Much of the research in artificial intelligence can be characterized in the context of building agents that behave intelligently, meaning that the actions of the agent's actuators must be rational responses to the data received though its sensors. In turn, we can classify this research by considering different levels of these responses.

The simplest response is a reflex action, which is merely a predetermined response to the input data. Higher levels of response are required to obtain more "intelligent" behavior. For example, we might empower an agent with knowledge of its environment and require that the agent adjust its actions accordingly. The process of throwing a baseball is largely a reflex action but determining how and where to throw the ball requires knowledge of the current environment. (There is one out with runners on first and third.) How such real-world knowledge can be stored, updated, accessed, and ultimately applied in the decision-making process continues to be a challenging problem in artificial intelligence.

Another level of response is required if we want the agent to seek a goal such as winning a game of chess or maneuvering through a crowded passageway. Such goal-directed behavior requires that the agent's response, or sequence of responses, be the result of deliberately forming a plan of action or selecting the best action among the current options.

In some cases an agent's responses improve over time as the agent learns. This could take the form of developing **procedural knowledge** (learning "how") or storing **declarative knowledge** (learning "what"). Learning procedural knowledge usually involves a trial-and-error process by which an agent learns appropriate actions by being punished for poor actions and rewarded for good ones. Following this approach, agents have been developed that, over time, improve their abilities in competitive games such as checkers and chess. Learning declarative knowledge usually takes the form of expanding or altering the "facts" in an agent's store of knowledge. For example, a baseball player must repeatedly adjust his or her database of knowledge (there is still just one out, but now runners are on first and second) from which rational responses to future events are determined.

To produce rational responses to stimuli, an agent must "understand" the stimuli received by its sensors. That is, an agent must be able to extract information from the data produced by its sensors, or in other words, an agent must be able to perceive. In some cases this is a straightforward process. Signals obtained from a gyroscope are easily encoded in forms compatible with calculations for determining responses. But in other cases extracting information from input data is difficult. Examples include understanding speech and images. Likewise, agents must be able to formulate their responses in terms compatible with their actuators. This might be a straightforward process or it might require an agent to formulate responses as complete spoken sentences—meaning that the agent must generate speech. In turn, such topics as image processing and analysis, natural language understanding, and speech generation are important areas of research.

The agent attributes that we have identified here represent past as well as current areas of research. Of course, they are not totally independent of each other. We would like to develop agents that possess all of them, producing agents that understand the data received from their environments and develop new response patterns through a learning process whose goal is to maximize the agent's abilities. However, by isolating various types of rational behavior and pursuing them independently, researchers gain a toehold that can later be combined with progress in other areas to produce more intelligent agents.

We close this subsection by introducing an agent that will provide a context for our discussion in Sections 11.2 and 11.3. The agent is designed to solve the eight-puzzle, which consists of eight square tiles labeled 1 through 8 mounted in a frame capable of holding a total of nine such tiles in three rows and three columns (Figure 11.1). Among the tiles in the frame is a vacancy into which any of the adjacent tiles can be pushed, allowing the tiles in the frame to be scrambled. The problem posed is to move the tiles in a scrambled puzzle back to their initial positions (Figure 11.1).

Our agent takes the form of a box equipped with a gripper, a video camera, and a finger with a rubber end so that it does not slip when pushing something

Figure 11.1 The eight-puzzle in its solved configuration

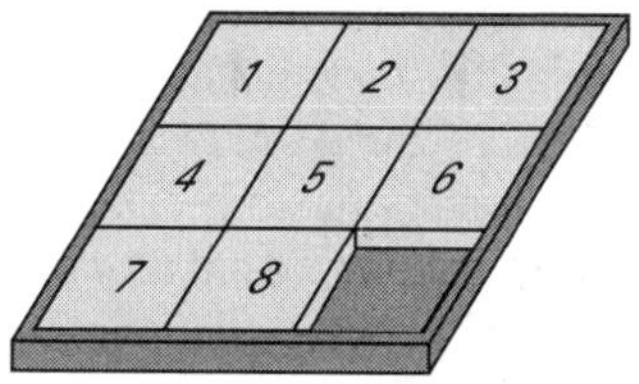

(Figure 11.2). When the agent is first turned on, its gripper begins to open and close as if asking for the puzzle. When we place a scrambled eight-puzzle in the gripper, the gripper closes on the puzzle. After a short time the machine's finger lowers and begins pushing the tiles around in the frame until they are back in their original positions. At this point the machine releases the puzzle and turns itself off.

This puzzle-solving machine exhibits two of the agent attributes that we have identified. First, it must be able to perceive in the sense that it must extract the current puzzle state from the image it receives from its camera. We will address issues of understanding images in Section 11.2. Second, it must develop and implement a plan for obtaining a goal. We will address these issues in Section 11.3.

Research Methodologies

To appreciate the field of artificial intelligence, it is helpful to understand that it is being pursued along two paths. One is the engineering track in which researchers are trying to develop systems that exhibit intelligent behavior. The other is a theoretical track in which researchers are trying to develop a computational understanding of animal—especially human—intelligence. This dichotomy is clarified by considering the manner in which the two tracks are pursued. The engineering approach leads to a performance-oriented methodology because the underlying goal is to produce a product that meets certain performance goals. The theoretical approach leads to a simulation-oriented methodology because the underlying goal is to expand our understanding of intelligence and thus the emphasis is on the underlying process rather than the exterior performance.

As an example, consider the fields of natural language processing and linguistics. These fields are closely related and benefit from research in each other, yet the underlying goals are different. Linguists are interested in learning how humans process language and thus tend toward more theoretical

Figure 11.2 Our puzzle-solving machine

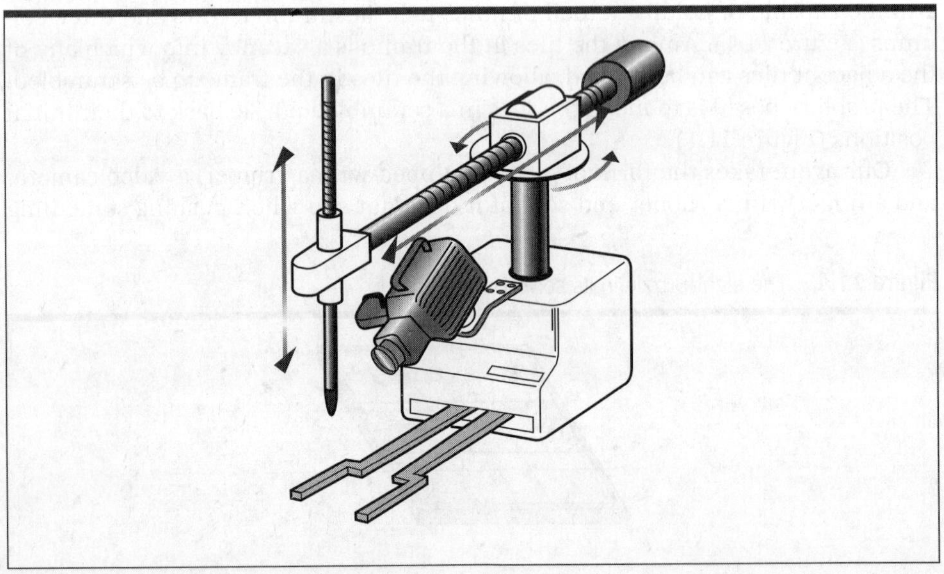

pursuits. Researchers in the field of natural language processing are interested in developing machines that can manipulate natural language and therefore lean in the engineering direction. Thus, linguists operate in simulation-oriented mode-building systems whose goals are to test theories. In contrast, researchers in natural language processing operate in performance-oriented mode-building systems to perform tasks. Systems produced in this latter mode (such as document translators and systems by which machines respond to verbal commands) rely heavily on knowledge gained by linguists but often apply "shortcuts" that happen to work in the restricted environment of the particular system.

As an elementary example, consider the task of developing a shell for an operating system that receives instructions from the outside world through verbal English commands. In this case, the shell (an agent) does not need to worry about the entire English language. More precisely, the shell does not need to distinguish between the various meanings of the word *copy*. (Is it a noun or a verb? Should it carry the connotation of plagiarism?) Instead, the shell needs merely to distinguish the word *copy* from other commands such as *rename* and *delete*. Thus the shell could perform its task just by matching its inputs to predetermined audio patterns. The performance of such a system may be satisfactory to an engineer, but the way it is obtained would not be aesthetically pleasing to a theoretician.

The Turing Test

In the past the **Turing test** (proposed by Alan Turing in 1950) has served as a benchmark in measuring progress in the field of artificial intelligence. Today the significance of the Turing test has faded although it remains an important part of the artificial intelligence folklore. Turing's proposal was to allow a human, whom we call the interrogator, to communicate with a test subject by means of a typewriter system without being told whether the test subject was a human or a machine. In this environment, a machine would be declared to behave intelligently if the interrogator was not able to distinguish it from a human. Turing predicted that by the year 2000 machines would have a 30 percent chance of passing a five-minute Turing test—a conjecture that turned out to be surprisingly accurate.

The Origins of Artificial Intelligence

The quest to build machines that mimic human behavior has a long history, but many would agree that the modern field of artificial intelligence had its origins in 1950. This was the year that Alan Turing published the article "Computing Machinery and Intelligence" in which he proposed that machines could be programmed to exhibit intelligent behavior. The name of the field—*artificial intelligence*—was coined a few years later in the now legendary proposal written by John McCarthy who suggested that a "study of artificial intelligence be carried out during the summer of 1956 at Dartmouth College" to explore "the conjecture that every aspect of learning or any other feature of intelligence can in principle be so precisely described that a machine can be made to simulate it."

One reason that the Turing test is no longer considered to be a meaningful measure of intelligence is that an eerie appearance of intelligence can be produced with relative ease. A well-known example arose as a result of the program DOCTOR (a version of the more general system called ELIZA) developed by Joseph Weizenbaum in the mid-1960s. This interactive program was designed to project the image of a Rogerian analyst conducting a psychological interview; the computer played the role of the analyst while the user played the patient. Internally, all that DOCTOR did was restructure the statements made by the patient according to some well-defined rules and direct them back to the patient. For example, in response to the statement "I am tired today," DOCTOR might have replied with "Why do you think you're tired today?" If DOCTOR was unable to recognize the sentence structure, it merely responded with something like "Go on" or "That's very interesting."

Weizenbaum's purpose in developing DOCTOR dealt with the study of natural language communication. The subject of psychotherapy merely provided an environment in which the program could "communicate." To Weizenbaum's dismay, however, several psychologists proposed using the program for actual psychotherapy. (The Rogerian thesis is that the patient, not the analyst, should lead the discussion during the therapeutic session, and thus, they argued, a computer could possibly conduct a discussion as well as a therapist could.) Moreover, DOCTOR projected the image of comprehension so strongly that many who "communicated" with it became subservient to the machine's question-and- answer dialogue. In a sense, DOCTOR passed the Turing test. The result was that ethical, as well as technical, issues were raised, and Weizenbaum became an advocate for maintaining human dignity in a world of advancing technology.

More recent examples of Turing test "successes" include Internet viruses that carry on "intelligent" dialogs with a human victim in order to trick the human into dropping his or her malware guard. Moreover, phenomena similar to Turing tests occur in the context of computer games such as chess-playing programs. Although these programs select moves merely by applying brute-force techniques (similar to those we will discuss in Section 11.3), humans competing against the computer often experience the sensation that the machine possesses creativity and even a personality. Similar sensations occur in robotics where machines have been built with physical attributes that project intelligent characteristics. Examples include toy robot dogs that project adorable personalities merely by tilting their heads or lifting their ears in response to a sound.

Questions & Exercises

1. Identify several types of "intelligent" actions that might be made by an agent.
2. A plant placed in a dark room with a single light source grows toward the light. Is this an intelligent response? Does the plant possess intelligence? What, then, is your definition of intelligence?
3. Suppose a vending machine is designed to dispense various products depending on which button is pressed. Would you say that such a machine is "aware" of which button is pressed? What, then, is your definition of awareness?

4. If a machine passes the Turing test, would you agree that it is intelligent? If not, would you agree that it appears to be intelligent?
5. Suppose you used a chat room to chat with someone over the Internet (or used Instant Messenger) and carried on a meaningful coherent conversation for ten minutes. If later you found out that you had conversed with a machine, would you conclude that the machine was intelligent? Why or why not?

11.2 Perception

To respond intelligently to the input from its sensors, an agent must be able to understand that input. That is, the agent must be able to perceive. In this section we explore two areas of research in perception that have proven to be especially challenging—understanding images and language.

Understanding Images

Let us consider the problems posed by the puzzle-solving machine introduced in the previous section. The opening and closing of the gripper on the machine presents no serious obstacle, and the ability to detect the presence of the puzzle in the gripper during this process is straightforward because our application requires very little precision. Even the problem of focusing the camera on the puzzle can be handled simply by designing the gripper to position the puzzle at a particular predetermined position for viewing. Consequently, the first intelligent behavior required by the machine is the extraction of information through a visual medium.

It is important to realize that the problem faced by our machine when looking at the puzzle is not that of merely producing and storing an image. Technology has been able to do this for years as in the case of traditional photography and television systems. Instead, the problem is to understand the image in order to extract the current status of the puzzle (and perhaps later to monitor the movement of the tiles).

In the case of our puzzle-solving machine, the possible interpretations of the puzzle image are relatively limited. We can assume that what appears is always an image containing the digits 1 through 8 in a well-organized pattern. The problem is merely to extract the arrangement of these digits. For this, we imagine that the picture of the puzzle has been encoded in terms of bits in the computer's memory, with each bit representing the brightness level of a particular pixel. Assuming a uniform size of the image (the machine holds the puzzle at a predetermined location in front of the camera), our machine can detect which tile is in which position by comparing the different sections of the picture to prerecorded templates consisting of the bit patterns produced by the individual digits used in the puzzle. As matches are found, the condition of the puzzle is revealed.

This technique of recognizing images is one method used in optical character readers. It has the drawback, however, of requiring a certain degree of uniformity for the style, size, and orientation of the symbols being read. In particular, the bit pattern produced by a physically large character does not match the template for a smaller version of the same symbol, even though the shapes are the same. Moreover, you can imagine how the problems increase in difficulty when trying to process handwritten material.

Another approach to the problem of character recognition is based on matching the geometric characteristics rather than the exact appearance of the symbols. In such cases the digit 1 might be characterized as a single vertical line, 2 might be an opened curved line joined with a horizontal straight line across the bottom, and so on. This method of recognizing symbols involves two steps: The first is to extract the features from the image being processed, and the second is to compare the features to those of known symbols. As with the template-matching approach, this technique for recognizing characters is not foolproof. For instance, minor errors in the image can produce a set of entirely different geometric features, as in the case of distinguishing between an O and a C or, in the case of the eight-puzzle, a 3 and an 8.

We are fortunate in our puzzle application because we do not need to understand images of general three-dimensional scenes. Consider, for example, the advantage we have by being assured that the shapes to be recognized (the digits 1 through 8) are isolated in different parts of the picture rather than appearing as overlapping images, as is common in more general settings. In a general photograph, for instance, one is faced not only with the problem of recognizing an object from different angles but also with the fact that some portions of the object might be hidden from view.

The task of understanding general images is usually approached as a two-step process: (1) **image processing,** which refers to identifying characteristics of the image, and (2) **image analysis,** which refers to the process of understanding what these characteristics mean. We have already observed this dichotomy in the context of recognizing symbols by means of their geometric features. In that situation, we found image processing represented by the process of identifying the geometric features found in the image and image analysis represented by the process of identifying the meaning of those features.

Image processing entails numerous topics. One is edge enhancement, which is the process of applying mathematical techniques to clarify the boundaries between regions in an image. In a sense, edge enhancement is an attempt to convert a photograph into a line drawing. Another activity in image analysis is known as

Strong AI versus Weak AI

The conjecture that machines can be programmed to exhibit intelligent behavior is known as **weak AI** and is accepted, to varying degrees, by a wide audience today. However, the conjecture that machines can be programmed to possess intelligence and, in fact, consciousness, which is known as **strong AI,** is widely debated. Opponents of strong AI argue that a machine is inherently different from a human and thus can never feel love, tell right from wrong, and think about itself in the same way that a human does. However, proponents of strong AI argue that the human mind is constructed from small components that individually are not human and are not conscious but, when combined, are. Why, they argue, would the same phenomenon not be possible with machines?

The problem in resolving the strong AI debate is that such attributes as intelligence and consciousness are internal characteristics that cannot be identified directly. As Alan Turing pointed out, we credit other humans with intelligence because they behave intelligently—even though we cannot observe their internal mental states. Are we, then, prepared to grant the same latitude to a machine if it exhibits the external characteristics of consciousness? Why or why not?

region finding. This is the process of identifying those areas in an image that have common properties such as brightness, color, or texture. Such a region probably represents a section of the image that belongs to a single object. (It is the ability to recognize regions that allows computers to add color to old-fashioned black-and-white motion pictures.) Still another activity within the scope of image processing is smoothing, which is the process of removing flaws in the image. Smoothing keeps errors in the image from confusing the other image-processing steps, but too much smoothing can cause the loss of important information as well.

Smoothing, edge enhancement, and region finding are all steps toward identifying the various components in an image. Image analysis is the process of determining what these components represent and ultimately what the image means. Here one faces such problems as recognizing partially obstructed objects from different perspectives. One approach to image analysis is to start with an assumption about what the image might be and then try to associate the components in the image with the objects whose presence is conjectured. This appears to be an approach applied by humans. For instance, we sometimes find it hard to recognize an unexpected object in a setting in which our vision is blurred, but once we have a clue to what the object might be, we can easily identify it.

The problems associated with general image analysis are enormous, and much research in the area remains to be done. Indeed, image analysis is one of the fields that demonstrates how tasks that are performed quickly and apparently easily by the human mind continue to challenge the capabilities of machines.

Language Processing

Another perception problem that has proven challenging is that of understanding language. The success obtained in translating formal high-level programming languages into machine language (Section 6.4) led early researchers to believe that the ability to program computers to understand natural language was only a few years away. Indeed, the ability to translate programs gives the illusion that the machine actually understands the language being translated. (Recall from Section 6.1 the story told by Grace Hopper about managers who thought she was teaching computers to understand German.)

What these researchers failed to understand was the depth to which formal programming languages differ from natural languages such as English, German, and Latin. Programming languages are constructed from well-designed primitives so that each statement has only one grammatical structure and only one meaning. In contrast, a statement in a natural language can have multiple meanings depending on its context or even the manner in which it is communicated. Thus, to understand natural language, humans rely heavily on additional knowledge.

For example, the sentences

Norman Rockwell painted people.

and

Cinderella had a ball.

have multiple meanings that cannot be distinguished by parsing or translating each word independently. Instead, to understand these sentences requires the ability to comprehend the context in which the statement is made. In other instances the true meaning of a sentence is not the same as its literal translation. For example,

Do you know what time it is?

often means "Please tell me what time it is," or if the speaker has been waiting for a long time, it might mean "You are very late."

To unravel the meaning of a statement in a natural language therefore requires several levels of analysis. The first of these is **syntactic analysis,** whose major component is parsing. It is here that the subject of the sentence

Mary gave John a birthday card.

is recognized as *Mary*, while the subject of

John got a birthday card from Mary.

is found to be *John*.

Another level of analysis is called **semantic analysis.** In contrast to the parsing process, which merely identifies the grammatical role of each word, semantic analysis is charged with the task of identifying the semantic role of each word in the statement. Semantic analysis seeks to identify such things as the action described, the agent of that action (which might or might not be the subject of the sentence), and the object of the action. It is through semantic analysis that the sentences "Mary gave John a birthday card" and "John got a birthday card from Mary" would be recognized as saying the same thing.

A third level of analysis is **contextual analysis.** It is at this level that the context of the sentence is brought into the understanding process. For example, it is easy to identify the grammatical role of each word in the sentence

The bat fell to the ground.

We can even perform semantic analysis by identifying the action involved as *falling,* the agent as *bat,* and so on. But it is not until we consider the context of the statement that the meaning of the statement becomes clear. In particular, it has a different meaning in the context of a baseball game than it does in the context of cave exploration. Moreover, it is at the contextual level that the true meaning of the question "Do you know what time it is?" would finally be revealed.

We should note that the various levels of analysis—syntactic, semantic, and contextual—are not necessarily independent. The subject of the sentence

Stampeding cattle can be dangerous.

is the noun *cattle* (modified by the adjective *stampeding*) if we envision the cattle stampeding on their own. But the subject is the gerund *stampeding* (with object *cattle*) in the context of a troublemaker whose entertainment consists of starting stampedes. Thus the sentence has more than one grammatical structure—which one is correct depends on the context.

Another area of research in natural language processing concerns an entire document rather than individual sentences. Here the problems of concern fall into two categories: **information retrieval** and **information extraction.** Information retrieval refers to the task of identifying documents that relate to the topic at hand. An example is the problem faced by users of the World Wide Web as they try to find the sites that relate to a particular topic. The current state of the art is to search sites for key words, but this often produces an avalanche of false leads and can overlook an important site because it deals with "automobiles" instead of "cars." What is needed is a search mechanism that understands the contents of the sites being considered. The difficulty of obtaining such understanding is the reason many are turning to techniques such as XML to produce a semantic Web, as introduced in Section 4.3.

Information extraction refers to the task of extracting information from documents so that it takes a form that is useful in other applications. This might mean identifying the answer to a specific question or recording the information in a form from which questions can be answered at a later date. One such form is known as a **frame,** which is essentially a template in which specifics are recorded. For example, consider a system for reading a newspaper. The system might make use of a variety of frames, one for each type of article that might appear in a newspaper. If the system identifies an article as reporting on a burglary, it would proceed by trying to fill in the slots in the burglary frame. This frame would probably request such items as the address of the burglary, the time and date of the burglary, the items taken, and so on. In contrast, if the system identifies an article as reporting on a natural disaster, it would fill in the natural disaster frame, which would lead the system toward identifying the type of disaster, amount of damage, and so on.

Another form in which information extractors record information is known as a **semantic net.** This is essentially a large linked data structure in which pointers are used to indicate associations among the data items. Figure 11.3 shows part of a semantic net in which the information obtained from the sentence

Mary hit John.

has been highlighted.

Figure 11.3 A semantic net

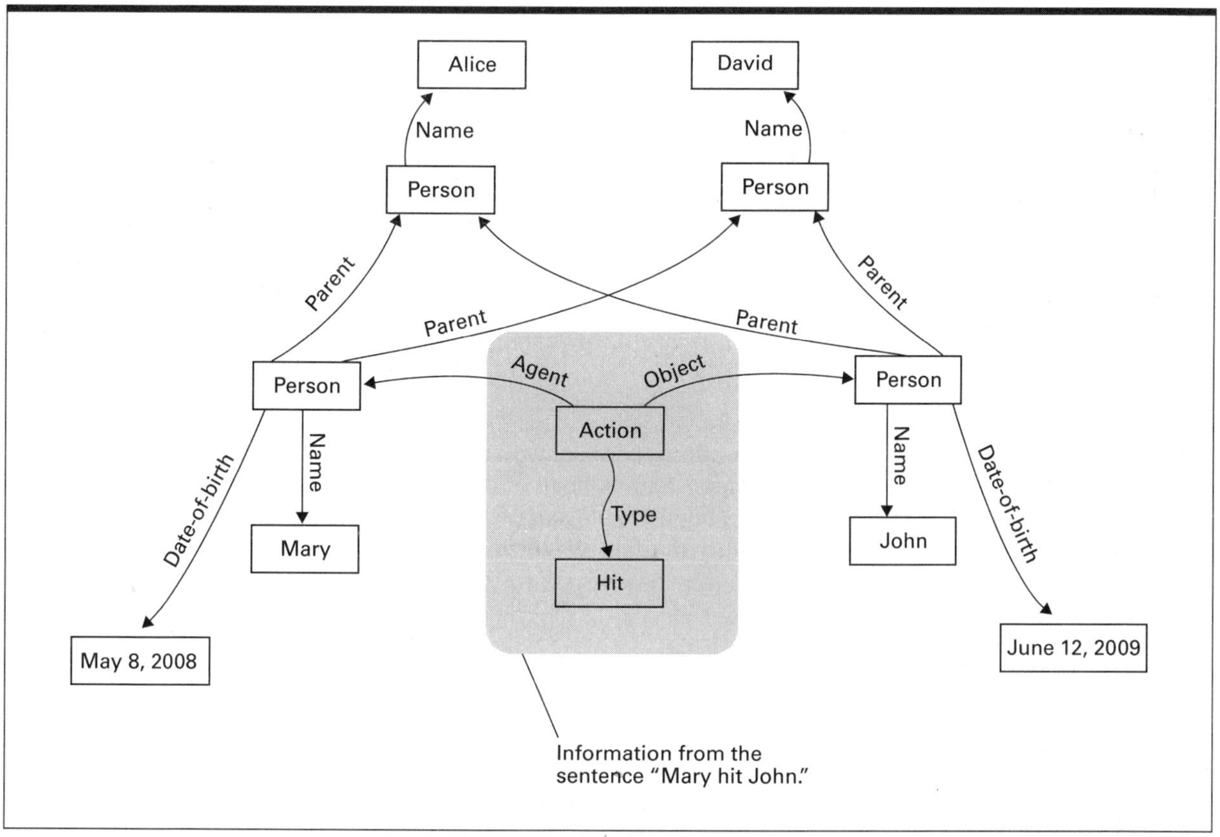

Artificial Intelligence in the Palm of Your Hand

Artificial intelligence techniques are increasingly showing up in smartphone applications. For example, Google has developed Google Goggles, a smartphone application providing a visual search engine. Just take a picture of a book, landmark, or sign using a smartphone's camera and Goggles will perform image processing, image analysis, and text recognition, and then initiate a Web search to identify the object. If you are an English speaker visiting in France, you can take a picture of a sign, menu, or other text and have it translated to English. Beyond Goggles, Google is actively working on voice-to-voice language translation. Soon you will be able to speak English into your phone and have your words spoken in Spanish, Chinese, or another language. Smartphones will undoubtedly get smarter as AI continues to be utilized in innovative ways.

Questions & Exercises

1. How do the requirements of a video system on a robot differ if the robot itself uses them to control its activities rather than relaying them to a human who controls the robot remotely?
2. What tells you that the following drawing is nonsense? How can this insight be programmed into a machine?

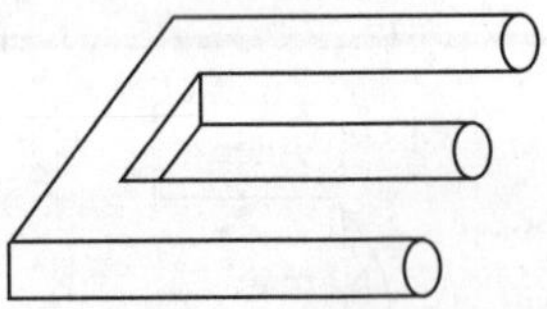

3. How many blocks are in the stack represented next? How could a machine be programmed to answer such questions accurately?

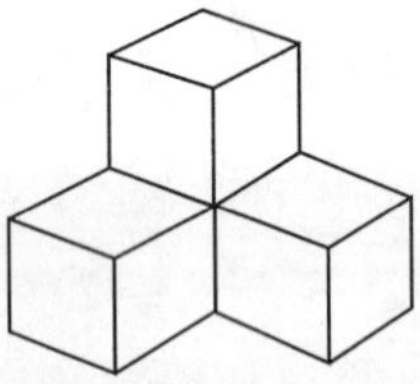

4. How do you know that the two statements "Nothing is better than complete happiness" and "A bowl of cold soup is better than nothing" do not imply that "A bowl of cold soup is better than complete happiness"? How can your ability to make this differentiation be transferred to a machine?
5. Identify the ambiguities involved in translating the sentence "They are racing horses."
6. Compare the results of parsing the following two sentences. Then, explain how the sentences differ semantically.

   The farmer built the fence in the field.

   The farmer built the fence in the winter.
7. Based on the semantic net in Figure 11.3, what is the family relationship between Mary and John?

11.3 Reasoning

Let us now use the puzzle-solving machine introduced in Section 11.1 to explore techniques for developing agents with elementary reasoning abilities.

Production Systems

Once our puzzle-solving machine has deciphered the positions of the tiles from the visual image, its task becomes that of figuring out what moves are required to solve the puzzle. An approach to this problem that might come to mind is to preprogram the machine with solutions to all possible arrangements of the tiles. Then the machine's task would merely be to select and execute the proper program. However, the eight-puzzle has over 100,000 configurations, so the idea of providing an explicit solution for each is not inviting. Thus, our goal is to program the machine so that it can construct solutions to the eight-puzzle on its own. That is, the machine must be programmed to perform elementary reasoning activities.

The development of reasoning abilities within a machine has been a topic of research for many years. One of the results of this research is the recognition that there is a large class of reasoning problems with common characteristics. These common characteristics are isolated in an abstract entity known as a **production system,** which consists of three main components:

1. A *collection of states.* Each **state** is a situation that might occur in the application environment. The beginning state is called the **start** (or initial) **state;** the desired state (or states) is called the **goal state.** (In our case, a state is a configuration of the eight-puzzle; the start state is the configuration of the puzzle when it is handed to the machine; the goal state is the configuration of the solved puzzle as shown in Figure 11.1.)
2. A *collection of productions (rules or moves).* A **production** is an operation that can be performed in the application environment to move from one state to another. Each production might be associated with preconditions; that is, conditions might exist that must be present in the environment before a production can be applied. (Productions in our case are the movements of tiles. Each movement of a tile has the precondition that the vacancy must be next to the tile in question.)
3. A *control system.* The **control system** consists of the logic that solves the problem of moving from the start state to the goal state. At each step in the process the control system must decide which of those productions whose preconditions are satisfied should be applied next. (Given a particular state in our eight-puzzle example, there would be several tiles next to the vacancy and therefore several applicable productions. The control system must decide which tile to move.)

Note that the task assigned to our puzzle-solving machine can be formulated in the context of a production system. In this setting the control system takes the form of a program. This program inspects the current state of the eight-puzzle, identifies a sequence of productions that leads to the goal state, and executes this sequence. It is therefore our task to design a control system for solving the eight-puzzle.

An important concept in the development of a control system is that of a **problem space,** which is the collection of all the states, productions, and preconditions in a production system. A problem space is often conceptualized in the form of a **state graph.** Here the term *graph* refers to a structure that mathematicians would call a **directed graph,** meaning a collection of locations called **nodes** connected by arrows. A state graph consists of a collection of nodes representing the states in the system connected by arrows representing the productions that shift the system from one state to another. Two nodes are connected by an arrow in the state graph if and only if there is a production that transforms the system from the state at the origin of the arrow to the state at the destination of the arrow.

We should emphasize that just as the number of possible states prevented us from explicitly providing preprogrammed solutions to the eight-puzzle, the problem of magnitude prevents us from explicitly representing the entire state graph. A state graph is therefore a way of conceptualizing the problem at hand but not something that we would consider drawing in its entirety. Nonetheless, you might find it helpful to consider (and possibly extend) the portion of the state graph for the eight-puzzle displayed in Figure 11.4.

When viewed in terms of the state graph, the problem faced by the control system becomes that of finding a sequence of arrows that leads from the start state to the goal state. After all, this sequence of arrows represents a sequence of productions that solves the original problem. Thus, regardless of the application, the task of the control system can be viewed as that of finding a path through a state graph. This universal view of control systems is the prize that we obtain by analyzing problems requiring reasoning in terms of production systems. If a problem can be characterized in terms of a production system, then its solution can be formulated in terms of searching for a path.

To emphasize this point, let us consider how other tasks can be framed in terms of production systems and thus performed in the context of control systems

Figure 11.4 A small portion of the eight-puzzle's state graph

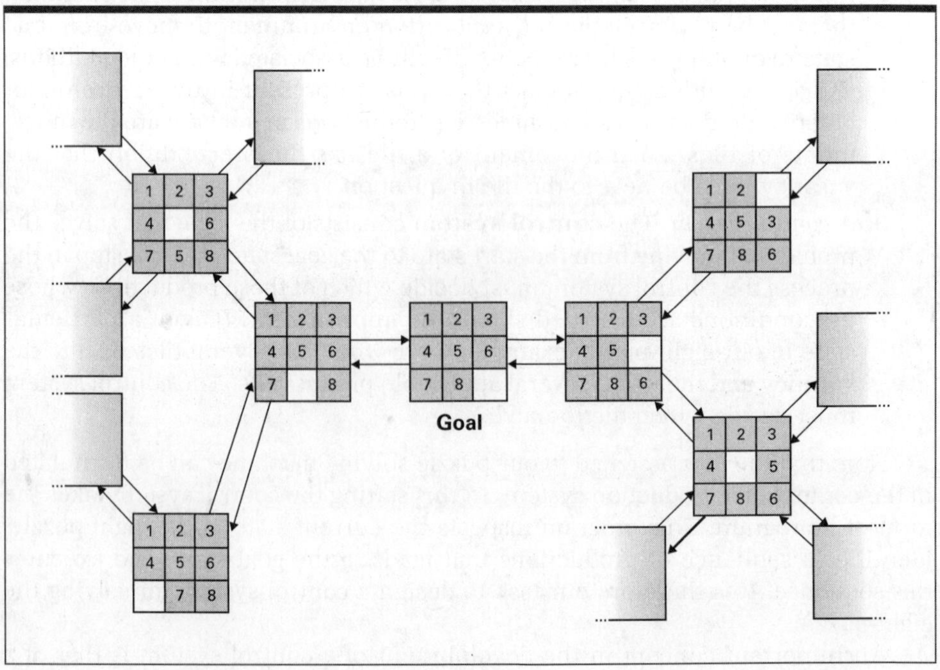

finding paths through state graphs. One of the classic problems in artificial intelligence is playing games such as chess. These games involve moderate complexity in a well-defined context and hence provide an ideal environment for testing theories. In chess the states of the underlying production system are the possible board configurations, the productions are the moves of the pieces, and the control system is embodied in the players (human or otherwise). The start node of the state graph represents the board with the pieces in their initial positions. Branching from this node are arrows leading to those board configurations that can be reached after the first move in a game; branching from each of those configurations are arrows to those configurations that are reachable by the next move; and so on. With this formulation, we can imagine a game of chess as consisting of two players, each trying to find a path through a large state graph to a goal node of his or her own choosing.

Perhaps a less obvious example of a production system is the problem of drawing logical conclusions from given facts. The productions in this context are the rules of logic, called **inference rules,** that allow new statements to be formed from old ones. For example, the statements "All super heroes are noble" and "Superman is a super hero" can be combined to produce "Superman is noble." States in such a system consist of collections of statements known to be true at particular points in the deduction process: The start state is the collection of basic statements (often called axioms) from which conclusions are to be drawn, and a goal state is any collection of statements that contain the proposed conclusion.

As an example, Figure 11.5 shows the portion of a state graph that might be traversed when the conclusion "Socrates is mortal" is drawn from the collection

Figure 11.5 Deductive reasoning in the context of a production system

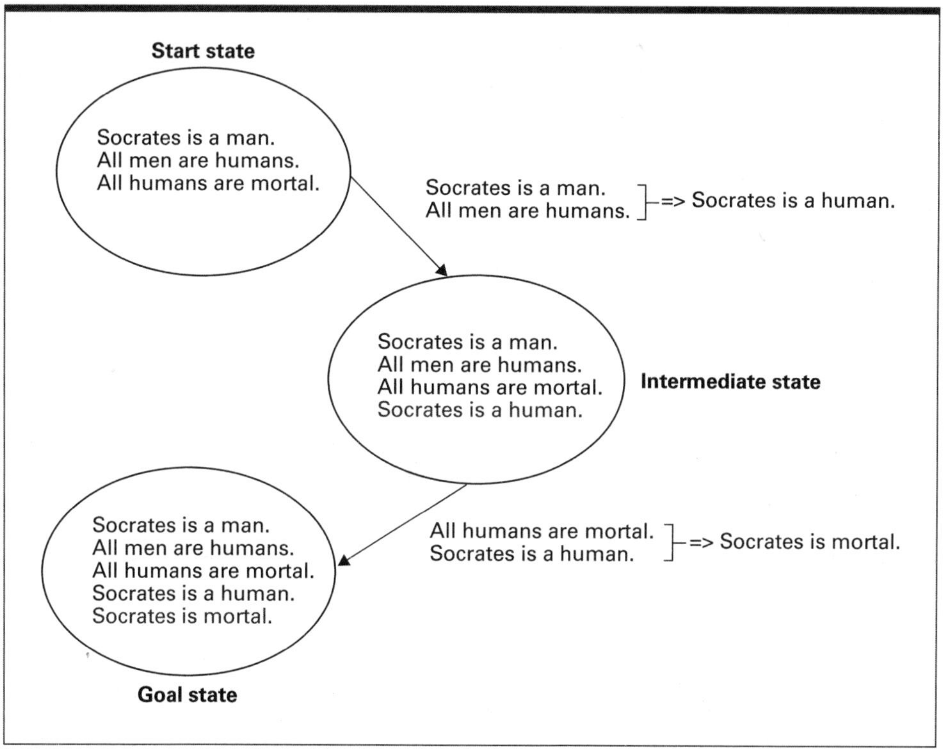

of statements "Socrates is a man," "All men are humans," and "All humans are mortal."

There we see the body of knowledge shifting from one state to another as the reasoning process applies appropriate productions to generate additional statements. Today, such reasoning systems, often implemented in logic programming languages (Section 6.7), are the backbone of most **expert systems,** which are software packages designed to simulate the cause-and-effect reasoning that human experts would follow if confronted with the same situations. Medical expert systems, for example, are used to assist in diagnosing ailments or developing treatments.

Search Trees

We have seen that, in the context of a production system, a control system's job involves searching the state graph to find a path from the start node to a goal. A simple method of performing this search is to traverse each of the arrows leading from the start state and in each case record the destination state, then traverse the arrows leaving these new states and again record the results, and so on. The search for a goal spreads out from the start state like a drop of dye in water. This process continues until one of the new states is a goal, at which point a solution has been found, and the control system needs merely to apply the productions along the discovered path from the start state to the goal.

The effect of this strategy is to build a tree, called a **search tree,** that consists of the part of the state graph that has been investigated by the control system. The root node of the search tree is the start state, and the children of each node are those states reachable from the parent by applying one production. Each arc between nodes in a search tree represents the application of a single production, and each path from the root to a leaf represents a path between the corresponding states in the state graph.

The search tree that would be produced in solving the eight-puzzle from the configuration shown in Figure 11.6 is illustrated in Figure 11.7. The leftmost branch of this tree represents an attempt to solve the problem by first moving the 6 tile up, the center branch represents the approach of moving the 2 tile to the right, and the rightmost branch represents moving the 5 tile down. Furthermore, the search tree shows that if we do begin by moving the 6 tile up, then the only production allowable next is to move the 8 tile to the right. (Actually, at that point we could also move the 6 tile down but that would merely reverse the previous production and thus be an extraneous move.)

The goal state occurs in the last level of the search tree of Figure 11.7. Since this indicates that a solution has been found, the control system can terminate its search procedure and begin constructing the instruction sequence that will be used to solve the puzzle in the external environment. This turns out to be the simple process of walking up the search tree from the location of the goal node

Figure 11.6 An unsolved eight-puzzle

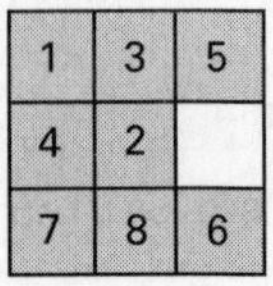

Figure 11.7 A sample search tree

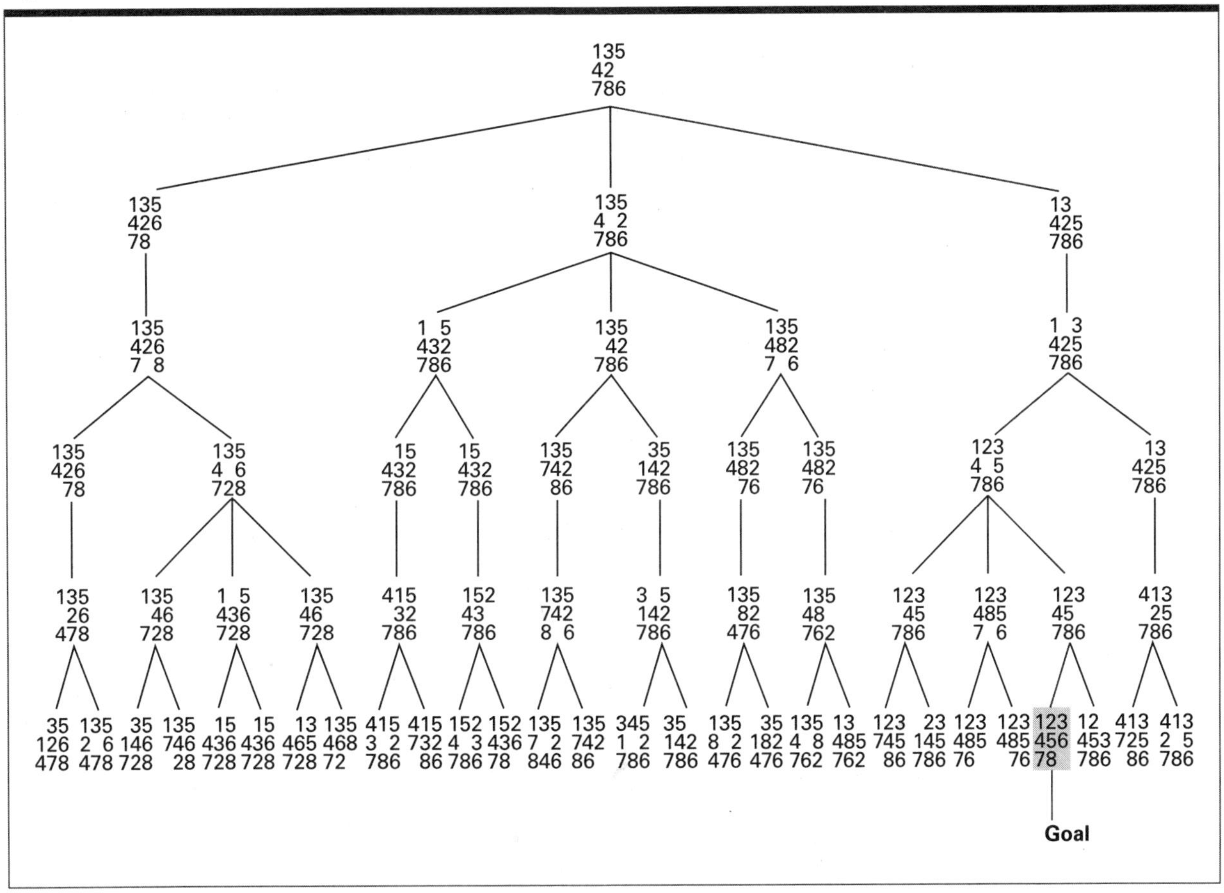

while pushing the productions represented by the tree arcs on a stack as they are encountered. Applying this technique to the search tree in Figure 11.7 produces the stack of productions in Figure 11.8. The control system can now solve the puzzle in the outside world by executing the instructions as they are popped from this stack.

There is one more observation that we should make. Recall that the trees we discussed in Chapter 8 use a pointer system that points *down* the tree, thereby allowing us to move from a parent node to its children. In the case of a search

Figure 11.8 Productions stacked for later execution

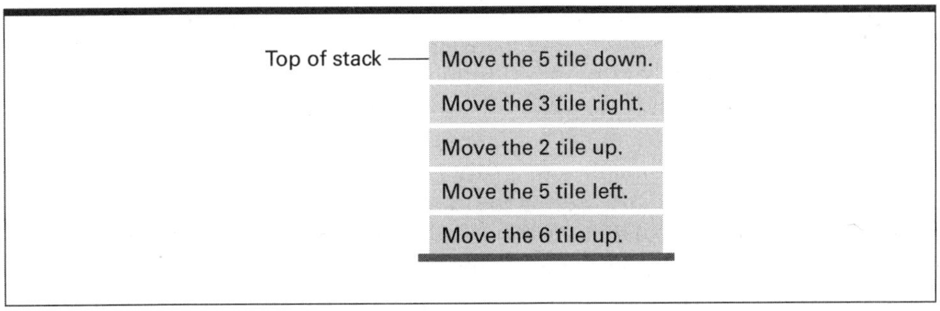

tree, however, the control system must be able to move from a child to its parent as it moves *up* the tree from the goal state to the start state. Such trees are constructed with their pointer systems pointing up rather than down. That is, each child node contains a pointer to its parent rather than the parent nodes containing pointers to their children. (In some applications, both sets of pointers are used to allow movement within the tree in both directions).

Heuristics

For our example in Figure 11.7, we chose a starting configuration that produces a manageable search tree. In contrast, the search tree generated in an attempt to solve a more complex problem could grow much larger. In a game of chess, there are twenty possible first moves so the root node of the search tree in such a case would have twenty children rather than the three in the case of our example. Moreover, a game of chess can easily consist of thirty to thirty-five pairs of moves. Even in the case of the eight-puzzle, the search tree can become quite large if the goal is not quickly reached. As a result, developing a full search tree can become as impractical as representing the entire state graph.

One strategy for countering this problem is to change the order in which the search tree is constructed. Rather than building it in a **breadth-first** manner (meaning that the tree is constructed layer by layer), we can pursue the more promising paths to greater depths and consider the other options only if these original choices turn out to be false leads. This results in a **depth-first** construction of the search tree, meaning that the tree is constructed by building vertical paths rather than horizontal layers. More precisely, this approach is often called a **best-first** construction in recognition of the fact that the vertical path chosen for pursuit is the one that appears to offer the best potential.

The best-first approach is similar to the strategy that we as humans would apply when faced with the eight-puzzle. We would rarely pursue several options at the same time, as modeled by the breadth-first approach. Instead, we probably would select the option that appeared most promising and follow it first. Note that we said *appeared* most promising. We rarely know for sure which option is best at a particular point. We merely follow our intuition, which may, of course, lead us astray. Nonetheless, the use of such intuitive information seems to give humans an advantage over the brute-force methods in which each option was given equal attention, and it would therefore seem prudent to apply intuitive methods in automated control systems.

To this end, we need a way of identifying which of several states appears to be the most promising. Our approach is to use a **heuristic,** which in our case is a quantitative value associated with each state that attempts to measure the "distance" from that state to the nearest goal. In a sense, our heuristic is a measure of projected cost. Given a choice between two states, the one with the smaller heuristic value is the one from which a goal can apparently be reached with the least cost. This state, therefore, would represent the direction we should pursue.

A heuristic should have two characteristics. First, it should constitute a reasonable estimate of the amount of work remaining in the solution if the associated state were reached. This means that it can provide meaningful information when selecting among options—the better the estimate provided by the heuristic, the better will be the decisions that are based on the information. Second, the heuristic should be easy to compute. This means that its use has a chance of benefiting the search process rather than of becoming a burden. If computing the heuristic

Behavior-Based Intelligence

Early work in artificial intelligence approached the subject in the context of explicitly writing programs to simulate intelligence. However, many argue today that human intelligence is not based on the execution of complex programs but instead by simple stimulus-response functions that have evolved over generations. This theory of "intelligence" is known as *behavior-based intelligence* because "intelligent" stimulus response functions appear to be the result of behaviors that caused certain individuals to survive and reproduce while others did not.

Behavior-based intelligence seems to answer several questions in the artificial intelligence community such as why machines based on the von Neumann architecture easily outperform humans in computational skills but struggle to exhibit common sense. Thus behavior-based intelligence promises to be a major influence in artificial intelligence research. As described in the text, behavior-based techniques have been applied in the field of artificial neural networks to teach neurons to behave in desired ways, in the field of genetic algorithms to provide an alternative to the more traditional programming process, and in robotics to improve the performance of machines through reactive strategies.

is extremely complicated, then we might as well spend our time conducting a breadth-first search.

A simple heuristic in the case of the eight-puzzle would be to estimate the "distance" to the goal by counting the number of tiles that are out of place—the conjecture being that a state in which four tiles are out of place is farther from the goal (and therefore less appealing) than a state in which only two tiles are out of place. However, this heuristic does not take into account how far out of position the tiles are. If the two tiles are far from their proper positions, many productions could be required to move them across the puzzle.

A slightly better heuristic, then, is to measure the distance each tile is from its destination and add these values to obtain a single quantity. A tile immediately adjacent to its final destination would be associated with a distance of one, whereas a tile whose corner touches the square of its final destination would be associated with a distance of two (because it must move at least one position vertically and another position horizontally). This heuristic is easy to compute and produces a rough estimate of the number of moves required to transform the puzzle from its current state to the goal. For instance, the heuristic value associated with the configuration in Figure 11.9 is seven (because tiles 2, 5, and 8 are

Figure 11.9 An unsolved eight-puzzle

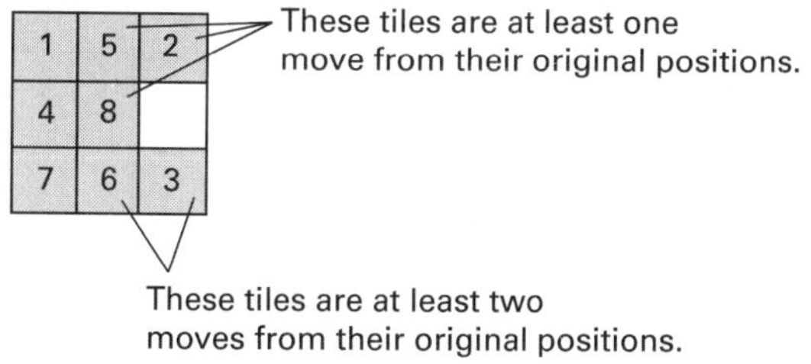

Figure 11.10 An algorithm for a control system using heuristics

```
Establish the start node of the state graph as the root of the
  search tree and record its heuristic value.
while (the goal node has not been reached):
  Select the leftmost leaf node with the smallest heuristic
    value of all leaf nodes.
  To this selected node attach as children those nodes that
    can be reached by a single production.
  Record the heuristic of each of these new nodes next to the
    node in the search tree
Traverse the search tree from the goal node up to the root, pushing
  the production associated with each arc traversed onto a stack.
Solve the original problem by executing the productions as they
  are popped off the stack.
```

each a distance of one from their final destinations while tiles 3 and 6 are each a distance of two from home). In fact, it actually takes seven moves to return this puzzle configuration to the solved configuration.

Now that we have a heuristic for the eight-puzzle, the next step is to incorporate it into our decision-making process. Recall that a human faced with a decision tends to select the option that appears closest to the goal. Thus our search procedure should consider the heuristic of each leaf node in the search tree and pursue the search from a leaf node associated with the smallest value. This is the strategy adopted in Figure 11.10, which presents an algorithm for developing a search tree and executing the solution obtained.

Let us apply this algorithm to the eight-puzzle, starting from the initial configuration in Figure 11.6. First, we establish this initial state as the root node and record its heuristic value, which is five. Then, the first pass through the body of the while statement instructs us to add the three nodes that can be reached from the initial state, as shown in Figure 11.11. Note that we have recorded the heuristic value of each leaf node in parentheses beneath the node.

The goal node has not been reached, so we again pass through the body of the while statement, this time extending our search from the leftmost node ("the

Figure 11.11 The beginnings of our heuristic search

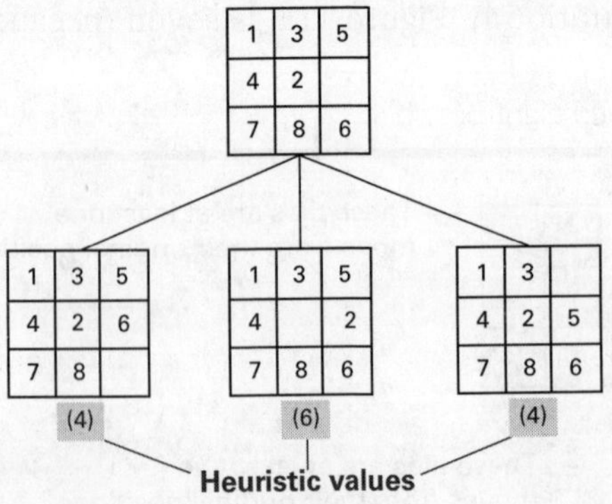

Figure 11.12 The search tree after two passes

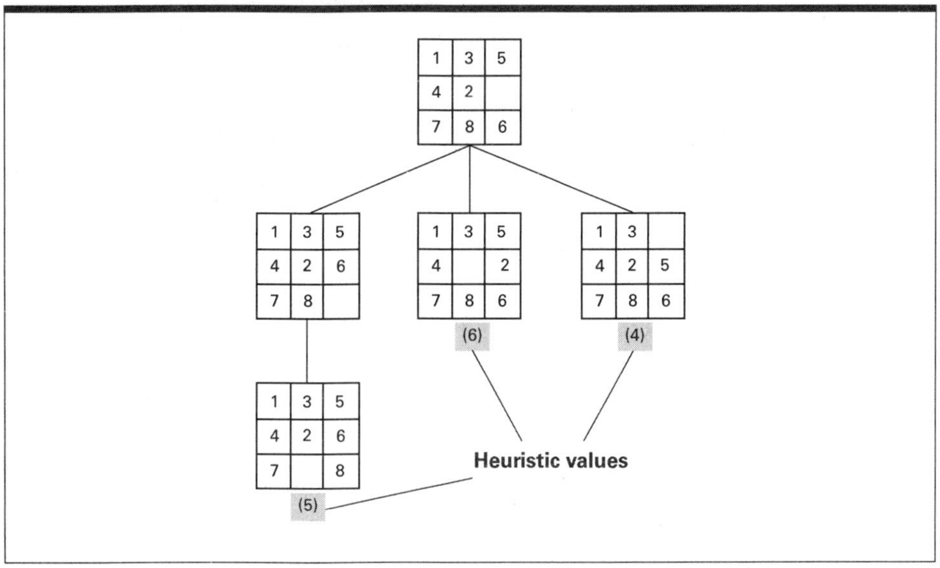

leftmost leaf node with the smallest heuristic value"). After this, the search tree has the form displayed in Figure 11.12.

The heuristic value of the leftmost leaf node is now five, indicating that this branch is perhaps not a good choice to pursue after all. The algorithm picks up on this and in the next pass through the while statement instructs us to expand the tree from the rightmost node (which now is the "leftmost leaf node with the smallest heuristic value"). Having been expanded in this fashion, the search tree appears as in Figure 11.13.

At this point the algorithm seems to be on the right track. Because the heuristic value of this last node is only three, the while statement instructs us to continue

Figure 11.13 The search tree after three passes

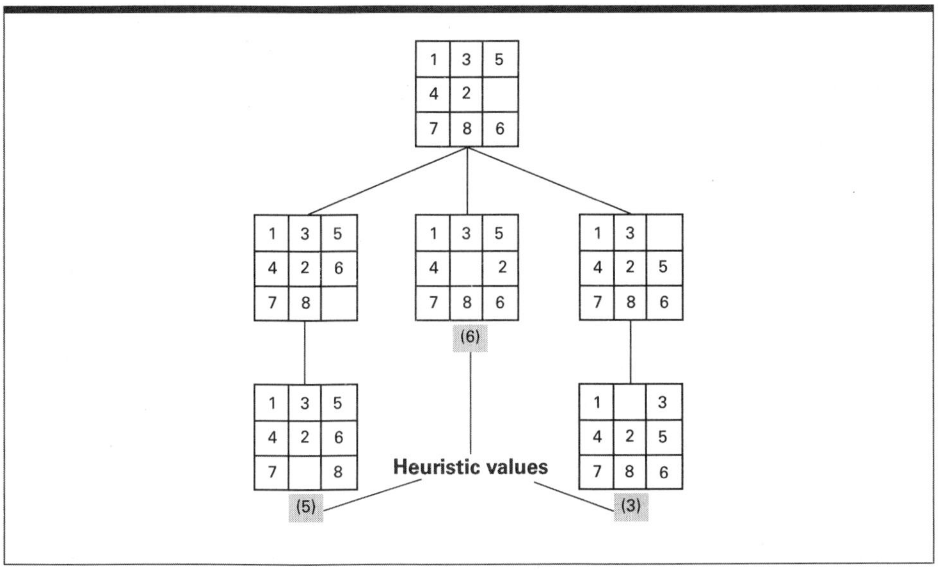

pursuing this path, and the search focuses toward the goal, producing the search tree appearing in Figure 11.14. Comparing this with the tree in Figure 11.7 shows that, even with the temporary wrong turn taken early on by the new algorithm, the use of heuristic information has greatly decreased the size of the search tree and produced a much more efficient process.

After reaching the goal state, the while statement terminates, and we move on to traverse the tree from the goal node up to the root, pushing the productions encountered onto a stack as we go. The resultant stack appears as depicted earlier in Figure 11.8.

Finally, we are instructed to execute these productions as they are popped from the stack. At this point, we would observe the puzzle-solving machine lower its finger and begin to move the tiles.

One final comment regarding heuristic searching is in order. The algorithm we have proposed in this section, which is often called the best-fit algorithm, is not guaranteed to find be the best solution in all applications. For example, when searching for a path to a city using a Global Positioning System (GPS) in an automobile, one would like to find the shortest path rather than just any path. The **A* algorithm** (pronounced "A star algorithm") is a modified version of our

Figure 11.14 The complete search tree formed by our heuristic system

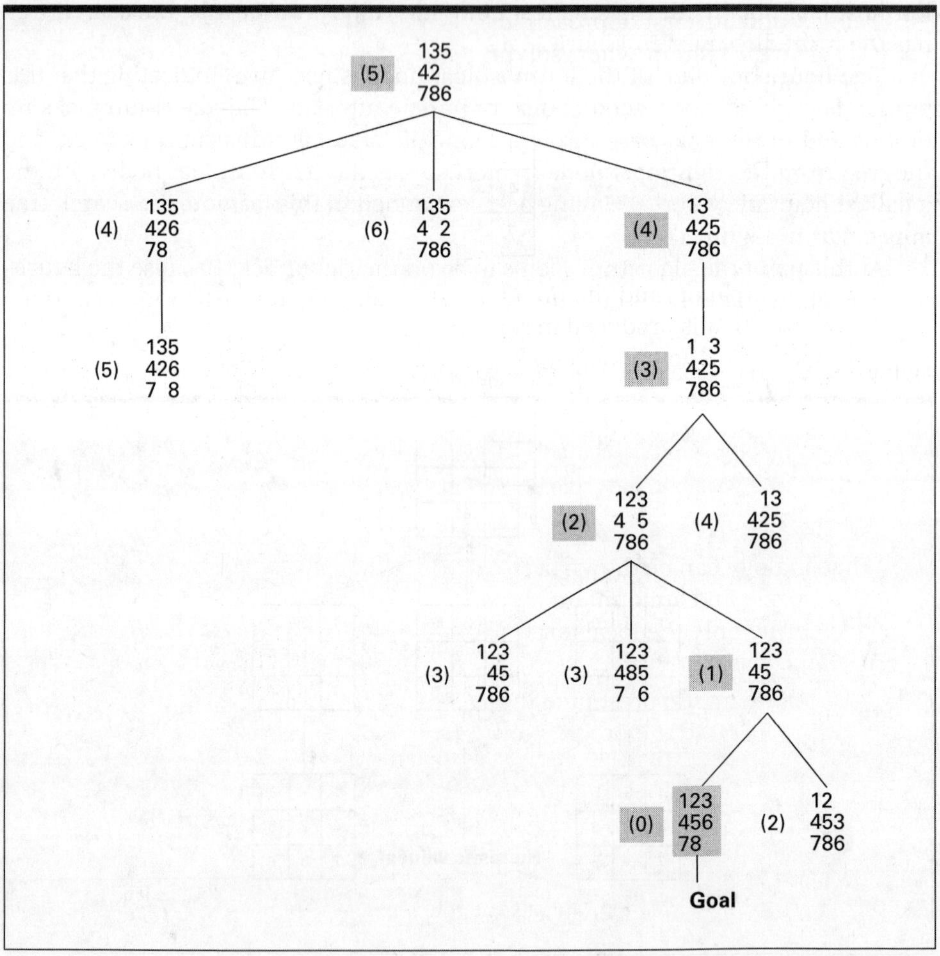

best-fit algorithm that finds an optimal solution. The major difference between the two algorithms is that, in addition to a heuristic value, the A* algorithm takes into account the "accumulated cost" incurred to reach each leaf node when selecting the next node to expand. (In the case of an automobile's GPS, this cost is the distance traveled that the GPS obtains from its internal database.) Thus, the A* algorithm bases its decisions on estimates of the cost of complete potential paths rather than merely on projections of remaining costs.

Questions & Exercises

1. What is the significance of production systems in artificial intelligence?
2. Draw a portion of the state graph for the eight-puzzle surrounding the node representing the following state:

4	1	3
	2	6
7	5	8

3. Using a breadth-first approach, draw the search tree that is constructed by a control system when solving the eight-puzzle from the following start state:

1	2	3
4	8	5
7	6	

4. Use pencil, paper, and the breadth-first approach to try to construct the search tree that is produced in solving the eight-puzzle from the following start state. (You do not have to finish.) What problems do you encounter?

4	3	
2	1	8
7	6	5

5. What analogy can be drawn between our heuristic system for solving the eight-puzzle and a mountain climber who attempts to reach the peak by considering only the local terrain and always proceeding in the direction of steepest ascent?
6. Using the heuristic presented in this section, apply the best-fit algorithm of Figure 11.10 to the problem of solving the following eight-puzzle:

1	2	3
4		8
7	6	5

7. Refine our method of computing the heuristic value for a state of the eight-puzzle so that the search algorithm of Figure 11.10 does not make the wrong choice, as it did in the example in this section. Can you find an example in which your heuristic still causes the search to go astray?
8. Draw to the search tree produced by the best-fit algorithm (Figure 11.10) in finding the route from Leesburg to Bedford. Each node in the search tree will be a city on the map. Begin with a node for Leesburg. When expanding a node, add only the cities that are directly connected to the city being expanded. Record in each node the straight-line distance to Bedford and use this as the heuristic value. What is the solution found by the best-fit algorithm? Is the found solution the shortest route?

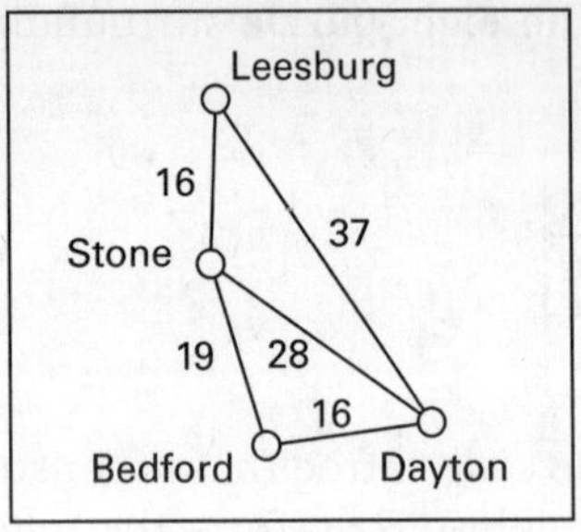

Straight-line distance to Bedford from

Dayton	16
Leesburg	34
Stone	19

9. The A* algorithm modifies the best-fit algorithm in two significant ways. First, it records the actual cost to reach a state. In the case of a route on a map, the actual cost is the distance traveled. Second, when selecting a node to expand, it chooses the node whose sum of the actual cost plus heuristic value is the smallest. Draw the search tree of question 8 that would result from these two modifications. Record in each node the distance traveled to the city, the heuristic value to reach the goal, and their sum. What is the found solution? Is the found solution the shortest route?

11.4 Additional Areas of Research

In this section we explore issues of handling knowledge, learning, and dealing with very complex problems, which continue to challenge researchers in the field of artificial intelligence. These activities involve capabilities that appear to be easy for human minds but apparently tax the capabilities of machines. For now, much of the progress in developing "intelligent" agents has been achieved essentially by avoiding direct confrontation with these issues—perhaps by applying clever shortcuts or limiting the scope in which a problem arises.

Representing and Manipulating Knowledge

In our discussion of perception we saw that understanding images requires a significant amount of knowledge about the items in the image and that the meaning of a sentence might depend on its context. These are examples of the role played by the warehouse of knowledge, often called **real-world knowledge,** maintained by human minds. Somehow, humans store massive amounts of information and draw from that information with remarkable efficiency. Giving machines this capability is a major challenge in artificial intelligence.

The underlying goal is to find ways to represent and store knowledge. This is complicated by the fact that, as we have already seen, knowledge occurs in both declarative and procedural forms. Thus, representing knowledge is not merely the representation of facts, but instead encompasses a much broader spectrum. Whether a single scheme for representing all forms of knowledge will ultimately be found is therefore questionable.

The problem, however, is not just to represent and store knowledge. The knowledge must also be readily accessible, and achieving this accessibility is a challenge. Semantic nets, as introduced in Section 11.2, are often used as a means of knowledge representation and storage, but extracting information from them can be problematic. For example, the significance of the statement "Mary hit John" depends on the relative ages of Mary and John. (Are the ages 2 and 30 or vice versa?) This information would be stored in the complete semantic net suggested by Figure 11.3, but extracting such information during contextual analysis could require a significant amount of searching through the net.

Yet another problem dealing with accessing knowledge is identifying knowledge that is implicitly, instead of explicitly, related to the task at hand. Rather than answering the question "Did Arthur win the race?" with a blunt "No," we want a system that might answer with "No, he came down with the flu and was not able to compete." In the next section we will explore the concept of associative memory, which is one area of research that is attempting to solve this related information problem. However, the task is not merely to retrieve related information. We need systems that can distinguish between related information and relevant information. For example, an answer such as "No, he was born in January and his sister's name is Lisa" would not be considered a worthy response to the previous question, even though the information reported is in some way related.

Another approach to developing better knowledge extraction systems has been to insert various forms of reasoning into the extraction process, resulting in what is called **meta-reasoning**—meaning reasoning about reasoning. An example, originally used in the context of database searches, is to apply the **closed-world assumption,** which is the assumption that a statement is false unless it can be explicitly derived from the information available. For example, it is the closed-world assumption that allows a database to conclude that Nicole Smith does not subscribe to a particular magazine even though the database does not contain any information at all about Nicole. The process is to observe that Nicole Smith is not on the subscription list and then apply the closed-world assumption to conclude that Nicole Smith does not subscribe.

On the surface the closed-world assumption appears trivial, but it has consequences that demonstrate how apparently innocent meta-reasoning techniques can have subtle, undesirable effects. Suppose, for example, that the only knowledge we have is the single statement

Mickey is a mouse OR Donald is a duck.

From this statement alone we cannot conclude that Mickey is in fact a mouse. Thus the closed-world assumption forces us to conclude that the statement

Mickey is a mouse.

is false. In a similar manner, the closed-world assumption forces us to conclude that the statement

Donald is a duck.

is false. Thus, the closed-world assumption has led us to the contradictory conclusion that although at least one of the statements must be true, both are false. Understanding the consequences of such innocent-looking meta-reasoning techniques is a goal of research in the fields of both artificial intelligence and database, and it also underlines the complexities involved in the development of intelligent systems.

Finally, there is the problem, known as the **frame problem,** of keeping stored knowledge up to date in a changing environment. If an intelligent agent is going to use its knowledge to determine its behavior, then that knowledge must be current. But the amount of knowledge required to support intelligent behavior can be enormous, and maintaining that knowledge in a changing environment can be a massive undertaking. A complicating factor is that changes in an environment often alter other items of information indirectly and accounting for such indirect consequences is difficult. For example, if a flower vase is knocked over and broken, your knowledge of the situation no longer contains the fact that water is in the vase, even though spilling the water was only indirectly involved with breaking the vase. Thus, to solve the frame problem not only requires the ability to store and retrieve massive amounts of information in an efficient manner, but it also demands that the storage system properly react to indirect consequences.

Learning

In addition to representing and manipulating knowledge, we would like to give intelligent agents the ability to acquire new knowledge. We can always "teach" a computer-based agent by writing and installing a new program or explicitly adding to its stored data, but we would like intelligent agents to be able to learn on their own. We want agents to adapt to changing environments and to perform tasks for which we cannot easily write programs in advance. A robot designed for household chores will be faced with new furniture, new appliances, new pets, and even new owners. An autonomous, self-driving car must adapt to variations in the boundary lines on roads. Game-playing agents should be able to develop and apply new strategies.

One way of classifying approaches to computer learning is by the level of human intervention required. At the first level is learning by **imitation,** in which a person directly demonstrates the steps in a task (perhaps by carrying out a sequence of computer operations or by physically moving a robot through a sequence of motions) and the computer simply records the steps. This form of learning has been used for years in application programs such as spreadsheets and word processors, where frequently occurring sequences of commands are recorded and later replayed by a single request. Note that learning by imitation places little responsibility on the agent.

At the next level is learning by **supervised training.** In supervised training a person identifies the correct response for a series of examples and then the agent generalizes from those examples to develop an algorithm that applies to new cases. The series of examples is called the **training set.** Typical applications of supervised training include learning to recognize a person's handwriting or voice, learning to distinguish between junk and welcome email, and learning how to identify a disease from a set of symptoms.

A third level is learning by **reinforcement.** In learning by reinforcement, the agent is given a general rule to judge for itself when it has succeeded or failed at a task during trial and error. Learning by reinforcement is good for learning how to play a game like chess or checkers, because success or failure is easy to define. In contrast to supervised training, learning by reinforcement allows the agent to act autonomously as it learns to improve its behavior over time.

Learning remains a challenging field of research since no general, universal principle has been found that covers all possible learning activities. However, there are numerous examples of progress. One is ALVINN (Autonomous Land Vehicle in a Neural Net), a system developed at Carnegie Mellon University to learn to steer a van with an on-board computer using a video camera for input. The approach used was supervised training. ALVINN collected data from a human driver and used that data to adjust its own steering decisions. As it learned, it would predict where to steer, check its prediction against the human driver's data, and then modify its parameters to come closer to the human's steering choice. ALVINN succeeded well enough that it could steer the van at 70 miles an hour, leading to additional research that has produced control systems that have successfully driven at highway speeds in traffic.

Finally, we should recognize a phenomenon that is closely related to learning: discovery. The distinction is that learning is "target based" whereas discovery is not. The term *discovery* has a connotation of the unexpected that is not present in learning. We might set out to learn a foreign language or how to drive a car, but we might discover that those tasks are more difficult than we expected. An explorer might discover a large lake, whereas the goal was merely to learn what was there. Developing agents with the ability to discover efficiently requires that the agent be able to identify potentially fruitful "trains of thought." Here, discovery relies heavily on the ability to reason and the use of heuristics. Moreover, many potential applications of discovery require that an agent be able to distinguish meaningful results from insignificant ones. A data mining agent, for example, should not report every trivial relationship it finds.

Knowledge in Logic Programming

An important concern in representing and storing knowledge is that it be done in a way that is compatible with the system that must access the knowledge. It is in this context that logic programming (see Section 6.7) often proves beneficial. In such systems knowledge is represented by "logic" statements such as

Dumbo is an elephant.

and

X is an elephant implies X is gray.

Such statements can be represented using notational systems that are readily accessible to the application of inference rules. In turn, sequences of deductive reasoning, such as we saw in Figure 11.5, can be implemented in a straightforward manner. Thus, in logic programming the representation and storage of knowledge are well integrated with the knowledge extraction and application process. One might say that logic programming systems provide a "seamless" boundary between stored knowledge and its application.

Examples of success in computer discovery systems include Bacon, named after the philosopher Sir Francis Bacon, that has discovered (or maybe we should say "rediscovered") Ohm's law of electricity, Kepler's third law of planetary motion, and the conservation of momentum. Perhaps more persuasive is the system AUTOCLASS that, using infrared spectral data, has discovered new classes of stars that were previously unknown in astronomy—a true scientific discovery by a computer.

Genetic Algorithms

The A* algorithm (introduced in the previous section) will find the optimal solution to many search problems; however, there are some problems that are too complex to be solved (execution exceeds available memory or cannot be completed within a reasonable amount of time) by such search techniques. For these problems, a solution can sometimes be discovered through an evolutionary process involving many generations of trial solutions. This strategy is the foundation for what is called **genetic algorithms.** In essence, genetic algorithms will discover a solution by random behavior combined with a simulation of reproductive theory and the evolutionary process of natural selection.

A genetic algorithm begins by generating a random pool of trial solutions. Each solution is just a guess. (In the case of the eight-puzzle, a trial solution can be a random sequence of tile movements.) Each trial solution is called a **chromosome** and each component of the chromosome is a called a **gene** (a single tile movement in the case of the eight-puzzle).

Since each initial chromosome is a random guess, it is very unlikely that it will represent a solution to the problem at hand. Thus, the genetic algorithm proceeds to generate a new pool of chromosomes whereby each chromosome is an offspring (child) of two chromosomes (parents) of the previous pool. The parents are randomly selected from the pool giving a probabilistic preference to those chromosomes that appear to provide the best chance of leading to a solution, thereby emulating the evolutionary principle of survival of the fittest. (Determining which chromosomes are the best candidates for parenthood is perhaps the most problematic step in the generic algorithm process.) Each offspring is a random combination of genes from the parents. In addition, a resulting offspring may occasionally be mutated in some random way (switch two moves). Hopefully, by repeating this process over and over, better and better trial solutions will evolve until a very good one, if not the best, is discovered. Unfortunately, there is no assurance that the genetic algorithm will ultimately find a solution, yet research has demonstrated that genetic algorithms can be effective in solving a surprisingly wide range of complex problems.

When applied to the task of program development, the genetic algorithm approach is known as **evolutionary programming.** Here the goal is to develop programs by allowing them to evolve rather than by explicitly writing them. Researchers have applied evolutionary programming techniques to the program development process using functional programming languages. The approach has been to start with a collection of programs that contain a rich variety of functions. The functions in this starting collection form the "gene pool" from which future generations of programs will be constructed. One then allows the evolutionary process to run for many generations, hoping that by producing each generation from the best performers in the previous generation, a solution to the target problem will evolve.

Questions & Exercises

1. What is meant by the term *real-world knowledge,* and what is its significance in artificial intelligence?
2. A database about magazine subscribers typically contains a list of subscribers to each magazine but does not contain a list of those who do not subscribe. How, then, does such a database determine that a person does not subscribe to a particular magazine?
3. Summarize the frame problem.
4. Identify three ways of training a computer. Which one does not involve direct human intervention?
5. How do evolutionary techniques differ from more traditional problem-solving techniques?

11.5 Artificial Neural Networks

With all the progress that has been made in artificial intelligence, many problems in the field continue to tax the abilities of computers using traditional algorithmic approaches. Sequences of instructions do not seem capable of perceiving and reasoning at levels comparable to those of the human mind. For this reason, many researchers are turning to approaches that leverage phenomena observed in nature. One such approach is genetic algorithms presented in the previous section. Another approach is the artificial neural network.

Basic Properties

Artificial neural networks provide a computer processing model that mimics networks of neurons in living biological systems. A biological neuron is a single cell with input tentacles called dendrites and an output tentacle called the axon (Figure 11.15). The signals transmitted via a cell's axon reflect whether the cell is in an inhibited or excited state. This state is determined by the combination of signals received by the cell's dendrites. These dendrites pick up signals from the

Figure 11.15 A neuron in a living biological system

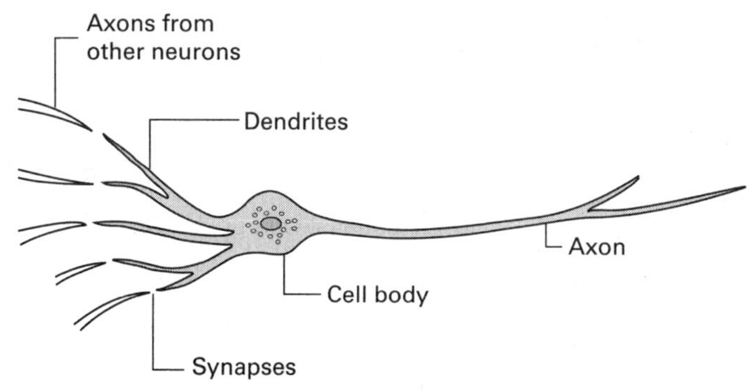

axons of other cells across small gaps known as synapses. Research suggests that the conductivity across a single synapse is controlled by the chemical composition of the synapse. That is, whether the particular input signal will have an exciting or inhibiting effect on the neuron is determined by the chemical composition of the synapse. Thus it is believed that a biological neural network learns by adjusting these chemical connections between neurons.

A neuron in an artificial neural network is a software unit that mimics this basic understanding of a biological neuron. It produces an output of 1 or 0, depending on whether its effective input exceeds a given value, which is called the neuron's **threshold** value. This effective input is a weighted sum of the actual inputs, as represented in Figure 11.16. In this figure, a neuron is represented with an oval and connections between neurons are represented with arrows. The values obtained from the axons of other neurons (denoted by v_1, v_2, and v_3) are used as inputs to the depicted neuron. In addition to these values, each connection is associated with a **weight** (denoted by w_1, w_2, and w_3). The neuron receiving these input values multiplies each by the associated weight for the connection and then adds these products to form the effective input ($v_1w_1 + v_2w_2 + v_3w_3$). If this sum exceeds the neuron's threshold value, the neuron produces an output of 1 (simulating an excited state); otherwise, the neuron produces a 0 as its output (simulating an inhibited state).

Following the lead of Figure 11.16, we adopt the convention of representing neurons as circles. Where each input connects to a neuron, we record the weight associated with that input. Finally, we write the neuron's threshold value in the middle of the circle. As an example, Figure 11.17 represents a neuron with a threshold value of 1.5 and weights of −2, 3, and −1 associated with each of its input connections. Therefore, if the neuron receives the inputs 1, 1, and 0, its effective input is $(1)(-2) + (1)(3) + (0)(-1) = 1$, and thus its output is 0. But, if the neuron receives 0, 1, and 1, its effective input is $(0)(-2) + (1)(3) + (1)(-1) = 2$, which exceeds the threshold value. The neuron's output will thus be 1.

The fact that a weight can be positive or negative means that the corresponding input can have either an inhibiting or exciting effect on the receiving neuron. (If the weight is negative, then a 1 at that input position reduces the weighted sum and thus tends to hold the effective input below the threshold value. In contrast, a positive weight causes the associated input to have an increasing effect on the weighted sum and thus increase the chances of that sum exceeding the threshold value.) Moreover, the actual size of the weight controls the degree to which the corresponding input is allowed to inhibit or excite the receiving neuron. Consequently, by adjusting the values of the weights throughout an artificial

Figure 11.16 The activities within a neuron

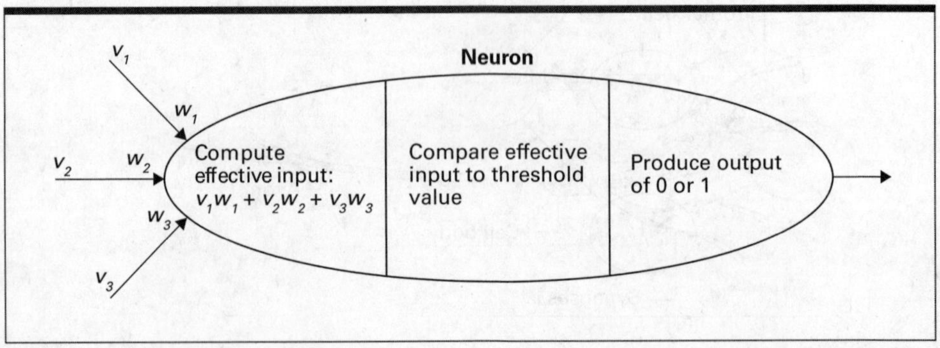

Figure 11.17 Representation of a neuron

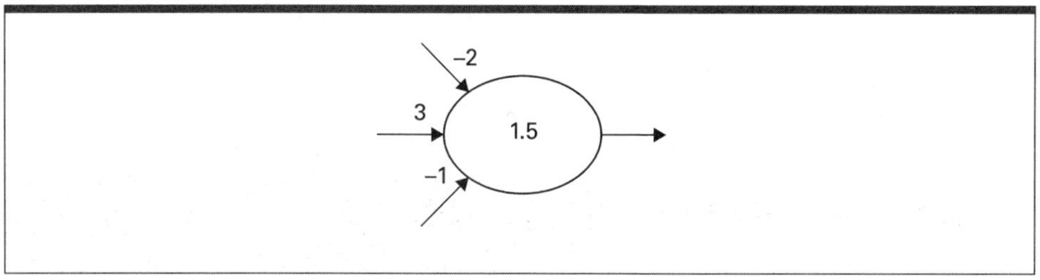

neural network, we can program the network to respond to different inputs in a predetermined manner.

Artificial neural networks are typically arranged in a topology of several layers. The input neurons are in the first layer and the output neurons are in the last. Additional layers of neurons (called hidden layers) may be included between the input and output layers. Each neuron of one layer is interconnected with every neuron in the subsequent layer. As an example, the simple network presented in Figure 11.18a is programmed to produce an output of 1 if its two inputs differ and an output of 0 otherwise. If, however, we change the weights to those shown in Figure 11.18b, we obtain a network that responds with a 1 if both of its inputs are 1s and with a 0 otherwise.

We should note that the network configuration in Figure 11.18 is far more simplistic than an actual biological network. A human brain contains approximately 1011 neurons with about 104 synapses per neuron. Indeed, the dendrites of a biological neuron are so numerous that they appear more like a fibrous mesh than the individual tentacles represented in Figure 11.15.

Training Artificial Neural Networks

An important feature of artificial neural networks is that they are not programmed in the traditional sense but instead are trained. That is, a programmer does not determine the values of the weights needed to solve a particular problem and

Figure 11.18 A neural network with two different programs

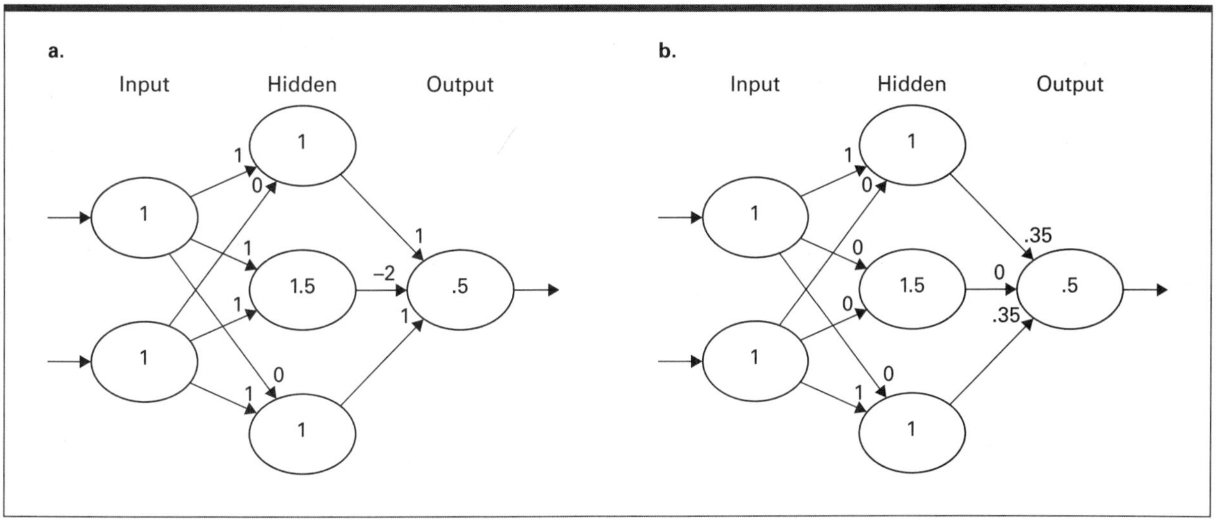

then "plug" those values into the network. Instead, an artificial neural network learns the proper weight values via supervised training (Section 11.4) involving a repetitive process in which inputs from the training set are applied to the network and then the weights are adjusted by small increments so that the network's performance approaches the desired behavior.

It is interesting to note how genetic algorithm techniques have been applied to the task of training artificial neural networks. In particular, to train a neural network, a number of sets of weights for the network can be randomly generated—each set of which will serve as a chromosome for the genetic algorithm. Then, in a step-by-step process, the network can be assigned the weights represented by each chromosome and tested over a variety of inputs. The chromosomes producing fewest errors during this testing process can then be given a greater probability of being selected as parents for the next generation. In numerous experiments this approach has ultimately led to a successful set of weights.

Let us consider an example in which training an artificial neural network to solve a problem has been successful and perhaps more productive than trying to provide a solution by means of traditional programming techniques. The problem is one that might be faced by a robot when trying to understand its environment via the information it receives from its video camera. Suppose, for example, that the robot must distinguish between the walls of a room, which are white, and the floor, which is black. At first glance, this would appear to be an easy task: Simply classify the white pixels as part of a wall and the black pixels at part of the floor. However, as the robot looks in different directions or moves around in the room, various lighting conditions can cause the wall to appear gray in some cases whereas in other cases the floor may appear gray. Thus, the robot needs to learn to distinguish between walls and floor under a wide variety of lighting conditions.

To accomplish this, we could build an artificial neural network whose inputs consist of values indicating the color characteristics of an individual pixel in the image as well as a value indicating the overall brightness of the entire image. We could then train the network by providing it with numerous examples of pixels representing parts of walls and floors under various lighting conditions.

Beyond simple learning problems (such as the classification of pixels), artificial neural networks have been used to learn sophisticated intelligent behavior, as testified by the ALVINN project cited in the previous section. Indeed, ALVINN was an artificial neural network whose composition was surprisingly simple (Figure 11.19). Its input was obtained from a 30 by 32 array of sensors, each of which observed a unique portion of the video image of the road ahead and reported its findings to each of four neurons on a hidden layer. (Thus, each of these four neurons had 960 inputs.) The output of each of these four neurons was connected to each of thirty output neurons, whose outputs indicated the direction to steer. Excited neurons at one end of the thirty-neuron row indicated a sharp turn to the left, while excited neurons at the other end indicated a sharp turn to the right.

ALVINN was trained by "watching" a human drive while it made its own steering decisions, comparing its decisions to those of the human, and making slight modifications to its weights to bring its decisions closer to those of the human. There was, however, an interesting side issue. Although ALVINN learned to steer following this simple technique, ALVINN did not learn how to recover from mistakes. Thus, the data collected from the human was artificially enriched to include recovery situations as well. (One approach to this recovery training

Figure 11.19 The structure of ALVINN (Autonomous Land Vehicle in a Neural Net)

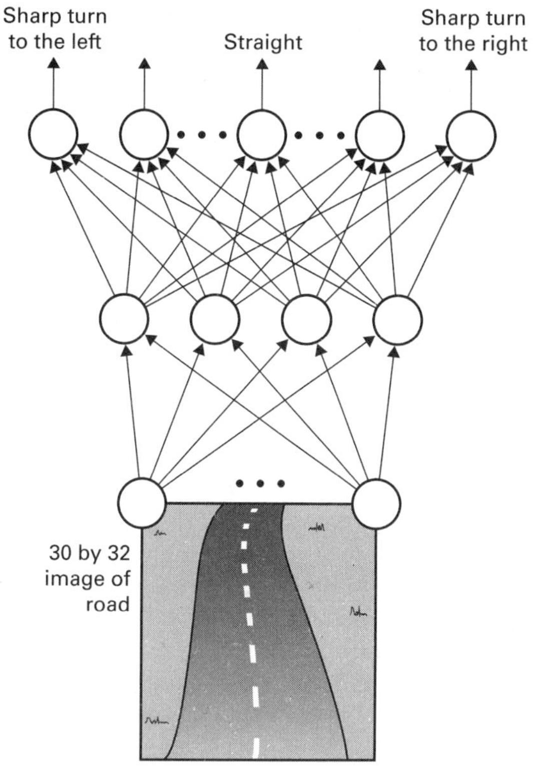

that was initially considered was to have the human swerve the vehicle so that ALVINN could watch the human recover and thus learn how to recover on its own. But unless ALVINN was disabled while the human performed the initial swerve procedure, ALVINN learned to swerve as well as to recover—an obviously undesirable trait.)

Associative Memory

The human mind has the amazing ability to retrieve information that is associated with a current topic of consideration. When we experience certain smells, we might readily recall memories of our childhood. The sound of a friend's voice might conjure an image of the person or perhaps memories of good times. Certain music might generate thoughts of particular holiday seasons. These are examples of **associative memory**—the retrieval of information that is associated with, or related to, the information at hand.

To construct machines with associative memory has been a goal of research for many years. One approach is to apply techniques of artificial neural networks. For instance, consider a network consisting of many neurons that are interconnected to form a web with no inputs or outputs. (In some designs, called Hopfield networks, the output of each neuron is connected as inputs to each of the other neurons; in other cases, the output of a neuron may be connected only to its immediate neighbors.) In such a system, the excited neurons will tend to excite other neurons, whereas the inhibited neurons will tend to inhibit others. In turn, the entire system may be in a constant state of change, or it may be that the system will find its way to a stable configuration where the excited neurons remain excited and the inhibited neurons remain inhibited. If we start the network in a nonstable configuration that is close to a stable one, we would expect it to wander to that stable configuration. In a sense, when given a part of a stable configuration, the network might be able to complete the configuration.

Now suppose that we represent an excited state by 1 and an inhibited state by 0 so that the condition of the entire network at any time can be envisioned as a configuration of 0s and 1s. Then, if we set the network to a bit pattern that is close to a stable pattern, we could expect the network to shift to the stable pattern. In other words, the network might find the stable bit pattern that is close to the pattern it was given. Thus if some of the bits are used to encode smells and others are used to encode childhood memories, then initializing the smell bits according to a certain stable configuration could cause the remaining bits to find their way to the associated childhood memory.

Now consider the artificial neural network shown in Figure 11.20. Following the conventions used to depict artificial neural networks, each circle in the figure represents a neuron whose threshold value is recorded inside the circle. Instead of arrows, the lines connecting the circles represent two-way connections between the corresponding neurons. That is, a line connecting two neurons indicates that the output of each neuron is connected as an input to the other. Thus the output of the center neuron is connected as an input to each of the neurons around the perimeter, and the output of each of the neurons around the perimeter is connected as an input to the center neuron as well as an input to each of its immediate neighbors on the perimeter. Two connected neurons associate the same weight with each other's output. This common weight is recorded next to the line connecting the neurons. Thus the neuron at the top of the diagram associates a weight of −1 with the input it receives from the center neuron and a weight of 1 with the inputs it receives from its two neighbors on the perimeter.

Figure 11.20 An artificial neural network implementing an associative memory

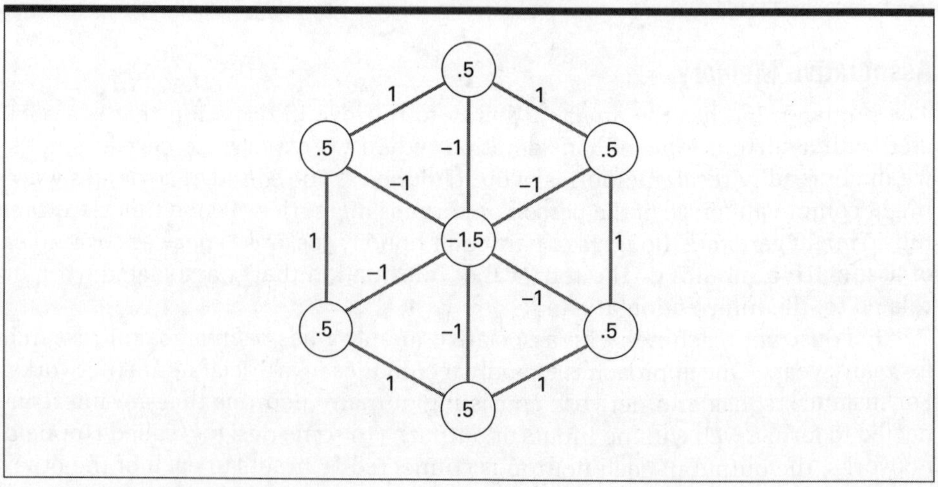

Likewise, the center neuron associates a weight of −1 with each of the values it receives from the neurons around the perimeter.

The network operates in discrete steps in which all neurons respond to their inputs in a synchronized manner. To determine the next configuration of the network from its current configuration, we determine the effective inputs of each neuron throughout the network and then allow all the neurons to respond to their inputs at the same time. The effect is that the entire network follows a coordinated sequence of compute effective inputs, respond to inputs, compute effective inputs, respond to inputs, etc. Consider the sequence of events that would occur if we initialized the network with its two rightmost neurons inhibited and the other neurons excited (Figure 11.21a). The two leftmost neurons would have effective inputs of 1, so they would remain excited. But, their neighbors on the perimeter would have effective inputs of 0, so they would become inhibited. Likewise, the center neuron would have an effective input of −4, so it would become inhibited. Thus the entire network would shift to the configuration shown in Figure 11.21b in which only the two leftmost neurons are excited. Since the center neuron would now be inhibited, the excited conditions of the leftmost neurons would cause the top and bottom neurons to become excited again. Meanwhile, the center neuron would remain inhibited since it would have an effective input of −2. Thus the network would shift to the configuration in Figure 11.21c, which would then lead to the configuration in Figure 11.21d. (You might wish to confirm that a blinking phenomenon would

Figure 11.21 The steps leading to a stable configuration

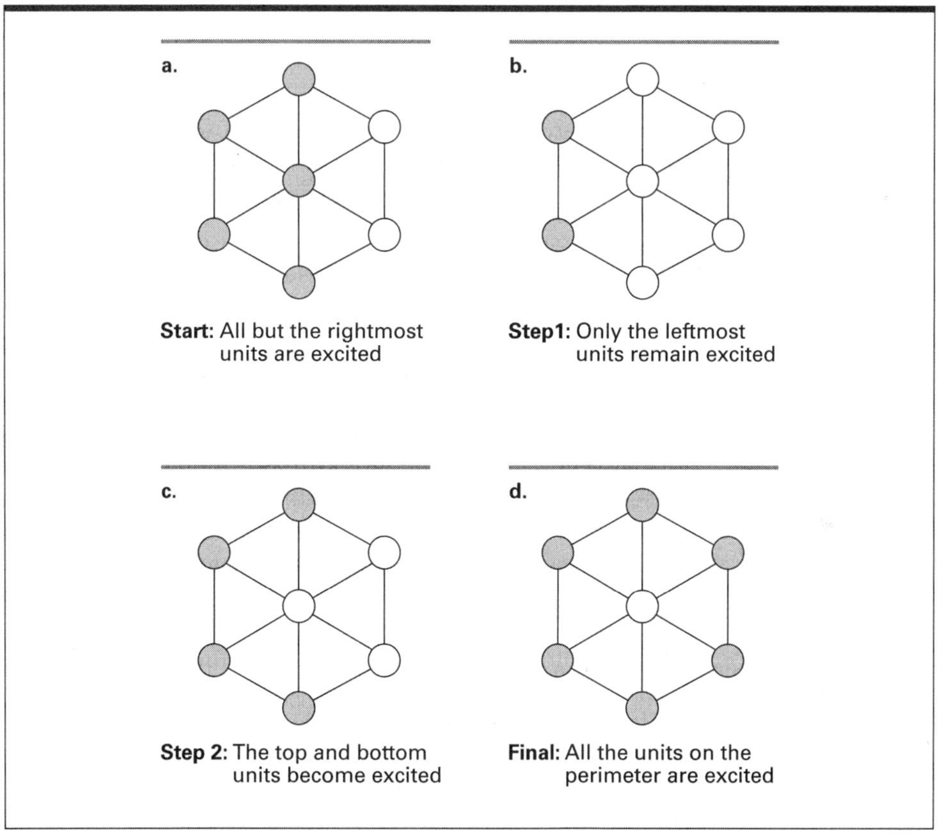

occur if the network were initialized with only the upper four neurons excited. The top neuron would remain excited while its two neighbors on the perimeter and the center neuron would alternate between being excited and inhibited.)

Finally, observe that the network has two stable configurations: one in which the center neuron is excited and the others are inhibited, and another configuration in which the center neuron is inhibited and the others are excited. If we initialize the network with the center neuron excited and no more than two of the other neurons excited, the network will wander to the former stable configuration. If we initialize the network with at least four adjacent neurons on the perimeter in their excited states, the network will wander to the latter configuration. Thus we could say that the network associates the former stable configuration with initial patterns in which its center neuron and fewer than three of its perimeter neurons are excited and associates the latter stable configuration with initial patterns in which four or more of its perimeter neurons are excited. In short, the network represents an elementary associative memory.

Questions & Exercises

1. What is the output of the following neuron when both its inputs are 1s? What about the input patterns 0, 0; 0, 1; and 1, 0?

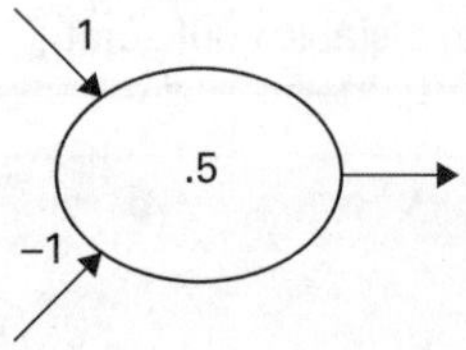

2. Adjust the weights and threshold value of the following neuron so that its output is 1 if and only if at least two of its inputs are 1s.

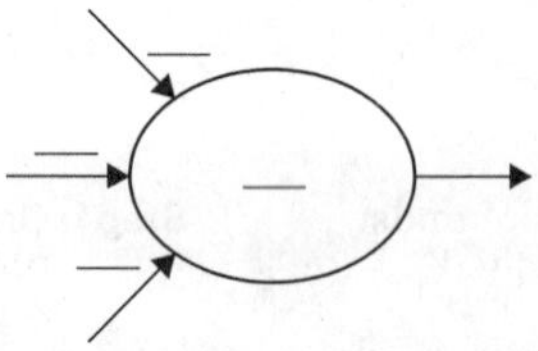

3. Identify a problem that might occur in training an artificial neural network.
4. To which stable configuration will the network in Figure 11.21 wander if it is initialized with all its neurons inhibited?

11.6 Robotics

Robotics is the study of physical, autonomous agents that behave intelligently. As with all agents, robots must be able to perceive, reason, and act in their environment. Research in robotics thereby encompasses all areas of artificial intelligence as well as drawing heavily from mechanical and electrical engineering.

To interact with the world, robots need mechanisms to manipulate objects and to move about. In the early days of robotics, the field was closely allied with the development of manipulators, most often mechanical arms with elbows, wrists, and hands or tools. Research dealt not only with how such devices could be maneuvered but also with how knowledge of their location and orientation could be maintained and applied. (You are able to close your eyes and still touch your nose with your finger because your brain maintains a record of where your nose and finger are.) Over time robots' arms have become more dexterous to where, with a sense of touch based on force feedback, they can handle eggs and paper cups successfully.

Recently, the development of faster, lighter weight computers has led to greater research in mobile robots that can move about. Achieving this mobility has led to an abundance of creative designs. Researchers in robot locomotion have developed robots that swim like fish, fly like dragonflies, hop like grasshoppers, and crawl like snakes.

Wheeled robots are very popular since they are relatively easy to design and build, but they are limited in the type of terrain they can traverse. Overcoming this restriction, using combinations of wheels or tracks to climb stairs or roll over rocks, is the goal of current research. As an example, the NASA Mars rovers used specially designed wheels to move on rocky soil.

Legged robots offer greater mobility but are significantly more complex. For instance, two-legged robots, designed to walk as humans, must constantly

Robots Making History

a. Two teams of robots play against each other in soccer at the 2013 RoboCup German Open tournament on April 26, 2013 in Magdeburg, Germany. (Jens Schlueter/Stringer/GettyImages). **b.** Tartan Racing's "Boss"—winner of the Urban Challenge, a contest sponsored by DARPA to have vehicles drive themselves through an urban environment (© DARPA). **c.** One of NASA's Rovers—a robot geologist exploring the surface of Mars (Courtesy NASA/JPL-Caltech).

monitor and adjust their stance or they will fall. However, such difficulties can be overcome, as exemplified by the two-legged humanoid robot named Asimo, developed by Honda, that can walk up stairs and even run.

Despite great advances in manipulators and locomotion, most robots are still not very autonomous. Industrial robot arms are typically rigidly programmed for each task and work without sensors, assuming parts will be given to them in exact positions. Other mobile robots such as the NASA Mars rovers and military unmanned aerial vehicles (UAVs) rely on human operators for their intelligence.

Overcoming this dependency on humans is a major goal of current research. One question deals with what an autonomous robot needs to know about its environment and to what degree it needs to plan its actions in advance. One approach is to build robots that maintain detailed records of their environments, containing an inventory of objects and their locations with which they develop precise plans of action. Research in this direction depends heavily on progress in knowledge representation and storage as well as improved reasoning and plan-development techniques.

An alternative approach is to develop reactive robots that, rather than maintaining complex records and expending great efforts in constructing detailed plans of action, merely apply simple rules for interacting with the world to guide their behavior moment by moment. Proponents of reactive robotics argue that when planning a long trip by car, humans do not make all-encompassing, detailed plans in advance. Instead, they merely select the major roads, leaving such details as where to eat, what exits to take, and how to handle detours for later consideration. Likewise, a reactive robot that needs to navigate a crowded hallway or to go from one building to another does not develop a highly detailed plan in advance, but instead applies simple rules to avoid each obstacle as it is encountered. This is the approach taken by the best-selling robot in history, the iRobot Roomba vacuum cleaner, which moves about a floor in a reactive mode without bothering to remember the details of furniture and other obstacles. After all, the family pet will probably not be in the same place next time.

Of course, no single approach will likely prove the best for all situations. Truly autonomous robots will most likely use multiple levels of reasoning and planning, applying high-level techniques to set and achieve major goals and lower-level reactive systems to achieve minor sub-goals. An example of such multilevel reasoning is found in the Robocup competition—an international competition of robot soccer teams—that serves as a forum for research toward developing a team of robots that can beat world-class human soccer teams by the year 2050. Here the emphasis is not just to build mobile robots that can "kick" a ball but to design a team of robots that cooperate with each other to obtain a common goal. These robots not only have to move and to reason about their actions, but they have to reason about the actions of their teammates and their opponents.

Another example of research in robotics is the field known as evolutionary robotics in which theories of evolution are applied to develop schemes for both low-level reactive rules and high-level reasoning. Here we find the survival-of-the-fittest theory being used to develop devices that over multiple generations acquire their own means of balance or mobility. Much of the research in this area distinguishes between a robot's internal control system (largely software) and the physical structure of its body. For example, the control system for a swimming tadpole robot was transferred to a similar robot with legs. Then evolutionary techniques were applied within the control system to obtain a robot that crawled. In other instances, evolutionary techniques have been applied to a robot's physical body to discover positions for sensors that are optimal for performing a particular task. More challenging research seeks ways to evolve software control systems simultaneously with physical body structures.

To list all the impressive results from research in robotics would be an overwhelming task. Our current robots are far from the powerful robots in fictional movies and novels, but they have achieved impressive successes on specific tasks. We have robots that can drive in traffic, behave like pet dogs, and guide weapons to their targets. However, while relishing in these successes, we should note that the affection we feel for an artificial pet dog and the awesome power of smart weapons raise social and ethical questions that challenge society. Our future is what we make it.

Questions & Exercises

1. In what way does the reactive approach to robot behavior differ from the more traditional "plan-based" behavior?
2. What are some current topics of research in the field of robotics?
3. What are two levels at which evolutionary theories are being applied to robot development?

11.7 Considering the Consequences

Without a doubt, advances being made in artificial intelligence have the potential of benefiting humankind, and it is easy to become caught up in the enthusiasm generated by the potential benefits. However, there are also potential perils lurking in the future whose ramifications could be as devastating as their counterparts are beneficial. The distinction is often merely one's point of view or perhaps one's position in society—one person's gain might be another's loss. It is fitting then that we take a moment to look at advancing technology from alternative perspectives.

Some view the advancement of technology as a gift to humanity—a means of freeing humans from boring, mundane tasks and opening the door to more enjoyable lifestyles. But others see this same phenomenon as a curse that robs citizens of employment and channels wealth toward those with power. This, in fact, was a message of the devoted humanitarian Mahatma Gandhi of India. He repeatedly argued that India would be better served by replacing large textile mills with spinning wheels placed in the homes of the peasants. In this way, he claimed, centralized mass production that employed only a few would be replaced by a distributed mass production system that would benefit multitudes.

History is full of revolutions with roots in the disproportionate distribution of wealth and privilege. If today's advancing technology is allowed to entrench such discrepancies, catastrophic consequences could result.

But the consequences of building increasingly intelligent machines is more subtle—more fundamental—than those dealing with power struggles between different segments of society. The issues strike at the very heart of humanity's self-image. In the nineteenth century, society was appalled by Charles Darwin's theory of evolution and the thought that humans might have evolved from lesser life forms. How then will society react if faced with the onslaught of machines whose mental capabilities challenge those of humans?

In the past, technology has developed slowly, allowing time for our self-image to be preserved by readjusting our concept of intelligence. Our ancient ancestors would have interpreted the mechanical devices of the nineteenth century as having supernatural intelligence, but today we do not credit these machines with any intelligence at all. But how will humanity react if machines truly challenge the intelligence of humans, or, more likely, if the capabilities of machines begin to advance faster than our ability to adapt?

We might get a clue to humanity's potential reaction to machines that challenge our intellect by considering society's response to IQ tests in the middle of the twentieth century. These tests were considered to identify a child's level of intelligence. Children in the United States were often classified by their performances on these tests and channeled into educational programs accordingly. In turn, educational opportunities were opened to those children who performed well on these tests, whereas children who performed poorly were directed toward remedial programs of study. In short, when given a scale on which to measure an individual's intelligence, society tended to disregard the capabilities of those who found themselves on the lower end of the scale. How then would society handle the situation if the "intellectual" capabilities of machines became comparable, or even appeared to be comparable, with those of humans? Would society discard those whose abilities were seen as "inferior" to those of machines? If so, what would be the consequences for those members of society? Should a person's dignity be subject to how he or she compares to a machine?

We have already begun to see the intellectual powers of humans challenged by machines in specific fields. Machines are now capable of beating experts in chess; computerized expert systems are capable of giving medical advice; and simple programs managing investment portfolios often outperform investment professionals. How do such systems affect the self-image of the individuals involved? How will an individual's self-esteem be affected as that individual is outperformed by machines in more and more areas?

Many argue that the intelligence possessed by machines will always be inherently different from that of humans since humans are biological and machines are not. Thus, they argue, machines will never reproduce a human's decision-making process. Machines might reach the same decisions as humans but those decisions would not be made on the same basis as those made by humans. To what extent, then, are there different kinds of intelligence, and would it be ethical for society to follow paths proposed by nonhuman intelligence?

In his book, *Computer Power and Human Reason,* Joseph Weizenbaum argues against the unchecked application of artificial intelligence as follows:

> Computers can make judicial decisions, computers can make psychiatric judgments. They can flip coins in much more sophisticated ways than can the most patient human being. The point is that they *ought* not be given such tasks. They might even be able to arrive at "correct" decisions in some cases—but always and necessarily on bases no human being should be willing to accept.
>
> There have been many debates on "Computers and Mind." What I conclude here is that the relevant issues are neither technological nor even mathematical; they are

> ethical. They cannot be settled by asking questions beginning with "can." The limits of the applicability of computers are ultimately statable only in terms of oughts. What emerges as the most elementary insight is that, since we do not now have any ways of making computers wise, we ought not now to give computers tasks that demand wisdom.

You might argue that much of this section borders on science fiction rather than computer science. It was not too long ago, however, that many dismissed the question "What will happen if computers take over society?" with the same it-will-never-happen attitude. But in many respects, that day has now arrived. If a computerized database erroneously reports that you have a bad credit rating, a criminal record, or an overdrawn checking account, is it the computer's statement or your claim of innocence that will prevail? If a malfunctioning navigational system indicates that a fog-covered runway is in the wrong place, where will the aircraft land? If a machine is used to predict the public's reaction to various political decisions, which decision does a politician make? How many times has a clerk been unable to help you because "the computer is down"? Who (or what), then, is in charge? Have we not already surrendered society to machines?

Questions & Exercises

1. How much of today's population would survive if the machines developed over the last 100 years were removed? What about the last fifty years? What about twenty years? Where would the survivors be located?
2. To what extent is your life controlled by machines? Who controls the machines that affect your life?
3. Where do you get the information on which you base your daily decisions? What about your major decisions? What confidence do you have in the accuracy of that information? Why?

Chapter Review Problems

(Asterisked problems are associated with optional sections.)

1. As demonstrated in Section 11.2, humans might use a question for a purpose other than asking. Another example is "Do you know that your tire is flat?" which is used to inform rather than to ask. Give examples of questions used to reassure, to warn, and to criticize.
2. Analyze a soda dispensing machine as an agent. What are its sensors? What are its actuators? What level of response (reflex, knowledge-based, goal-based) does it exhibit?
3. Identify each of the following responses as being reflex, knowledge based, or goal based. Justify your answers.
   a. A computer program translating text from German to English
   b. A thermostat turning on the furnace when the temperature in a house drops below the current setting
   c. A pilot landing a plane safely on a runway

4. If a researcher uses computer models for studying the memorization capabilities of the human mind, do the programs developed for the machine necessarily memorize to the best of the machine's abilities? Explain.

5. Give some examples of declarative knowledge. Give some examples of procedural knowledge.

*6. In the context of object-oriented programming, what parts of an object are used to store declarative knowledge? What parts are used to store procedural knowledge?

7. Which of the following activities do you expect to be performance oriented and which are simulation oriented?
   a. The design of an automated shuttle system (often used at airports between terminals)
   b. The design of a model predicting the path of a hurricane
   c. The design of a Web search database used to derive and maintain indices for documents stored on the World Wide Web
   d. The design of a model of a nation's economy for testing theories
   e. The design of a program for monitoring a patient's vital signs

8. Today, some telephone calls to businesses are handled by automated answering systems that use speech and voice recognition to converse with the caller. Do these systems pass the Turing test? Explain your answer.

9. Identify a small set of geometric properties that can be used to distinguish between the symbols F, E, L, and T.

*10. Describe the similarities between the technique of identifying characteristics by comparing them to templates and the error-correcting codes discussed in Chapter 1.

11. Describe two interpretations of the following line drawing based on whether the "corner" marked A is convex or concave:

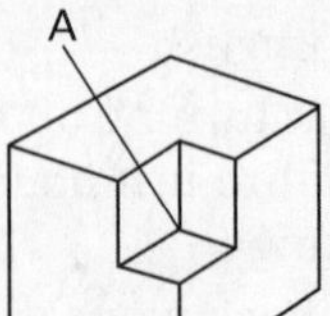

12. Compare the roles of the prepositional phrases in the following two sentences (which differ by only one word). How could a machine be programmed to make such distinctions?

    The pigpen was built by the barn.
    The pigpen was built by the farmer.

13. How do the results of parsing the following two sentences differ? How do the results of semantic analysis differ?

    An awesome sunset was seen by Andrea.
    Andrea saw an awesome sunset.

14. How do the results of parsing the following two sentences differ? How do the results of semantic analysis differ?

    If $X < 10$ then subtract 1 from X else add 1 from X.

    If $X > 10$ then add 1 to X else subtract 1 from X.

15. In the text we briefly discussed the problems of understanding natural languages as opposed to formal programming languages. As an example of the complexities involved in the case of natural languages, identify situations in which the question "Do you know what time it is?" has different meanings.

16. Changes in the context of a sentence can change the significance of the sentence as well as its meaning. In the context of Figure 11.3, how would the significance of the sentence "Mary hit John" change if the birth dates were in the late 2000s? What if one were in the 1980s and the other in the late 2000s?

17. Draw a semantic net representing the information in the following paragraph.

    Donna threw the ball to Jack, who hit it into center field. The center fielder tried to catch it, but it bounced off the wall instead.

18. Sometimes the ability to answer a question depends as much on knowing the limits of knowledge as it does on the facts themselves. For example, suppose databases A and B both contain a complete list of employees who belong to the company's health insurance program, but only database A is aware that the

list is complete. What could database A conclude about a member who was not on its list that database B could not?

19. Give an example in which the closed-world assumption leads to a contradiction.

20. Give two examples where the closed-world assumption is commonly used.

21. In the context of a production system, what is the difference between a state graph and a search tree?

22. Analyze the task of solving the Rubik's cube in terms of a production system. (What are the states, the productions, and so on?)

23. a. Suppose a search tree is a binary tree and reaching the goal requires eight productions. What is the largest number of nodes that could be in the tree when the goal state is reached if the tree is constructed with a breadth-first manner?

    b. Explain how the total number of nodes considered during the search could be reduced by conducting two searches at the same time—one beginning at the initial state while the other searches backward from the goal—until the two meet. (Assume that the search tree recording the states found in the backward search is also a binary tree and that both searches progress at the same rate.)

24. In the text we mentioned that a production system is often used as a technique for drawing conclusions from known facts. The states of the system are the facts known to be true at each stage of the reasoning process, and the productions are the rules of logic for manipulating the known facts. Identify some rules of logic that allow the conclusion "John is tall" to be obtained from the facts that "John is a basketball player," "Basketball players are not short," and "John is either short or tall."

25. The following tree represents possible moves in a competitive game, showing that player X currently has a choice between move A and move B. Following the move of player X, player Y is allowed to select a move, and then player X is allowed to select the last move of the game. The leaf nodes of the tree are labeled W, L, or T, depending on whether that ending represents a win, loss, or tie for player X. Should player X select move A or move B? Why? How does selecting a "production" in a competitive atmosphere differ from a one-person game such as the eight-puzzle?

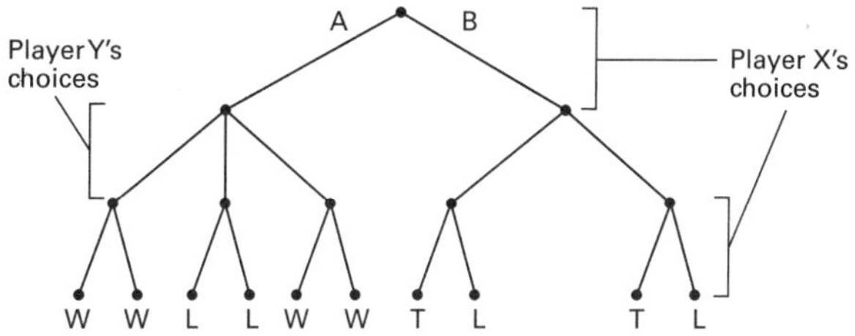

26. Analyze the game of checkers as a production system and describe a heuristic that could be used to determine which of two states is closer to the goal. How would the control system in this setting differ from that of a one-person game such as the eight-puzzle?

27. By considering the manipulation rules of algebra as productions, problems involving the simplification of algebraic expressions can be solved in the context of a production system. Identify a set of algebraic productions that allow the equation $3/(2x - 1) = 6/(3x + 1)$ to be reduced to the form $x = 3$. What are some general rules (that is, heuristic rules) used when performing such algebraic simplifications?

28. Draw the search tree that is generated by a breadth-first search in an attempt to solve the eight-puzzle from the following start state without using the assistance of any heuristic information.

	1	3
4	2	5
7	8	6

29. Draw the search tree that is generated by the best-fit algorithm of Figure 11.10 in an attempt to solve the eight-puzzle from the start state in problem 28 if the number of tiles out of place is used as a heuristic.

30. Draw the search tree that is generated by the best-fit algorithm of Figure 11.10 in an attempt to solve the eight-puzzle from the following start state, assuming the heuristic used is the same as that developed in Section 11.3.

1	2	3
5	7	6
4		8

31. When solving the eight-puzzle, why would the number of tiles out of place not be as good a heuristic as the one used in Section 11.3?

32. What is the distinction between the technique of deciding which half of the list to consider when performing a binary search (Section 5.5) and deciding which branch to pursue when performing a heuristic search?

33. Note that if a state in the state graph of a production system has an extremely low heuristic value in comparison to the other states and if there is a production from that state to itself, the algorithm in Figure 11.10 can get caught in the loop of considering that state over and over again. Show that if the cost of executing any production in the system is at least one, then by computing the projected cost to be the sum of the heuristic value plus the cost of reaching the state along the path being traversed, this endless looping process will be avoided.

34. What heuristic do you use when searching for a route between two cities on a large road map?

35. Draw to four levels the search tree produced by the best-fit algorithm of Figure 11.10 in finding the route from Trent to Wildwood. Each node in the search tree will be a city on the map. Begin with a node for Trent. When expanding a node, add only the cities that are directly connected to the city being expanded. Record in each node the straight-line distance to Wildwood and use this as the heuristic value. Does the best-fit algorithm have a defect in its processing? If so, what correction is needed?

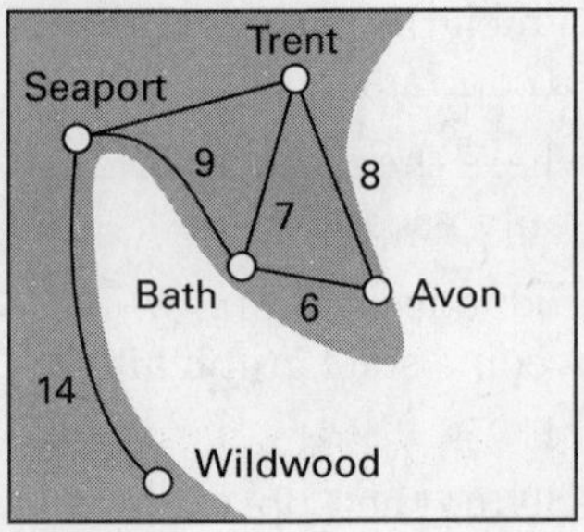

Straight line distance to Wildwood from

Avon	10
Bath	8
Trent	15
Seaport	13

36. The A* algorithm modifies the best-fit algorithm in two significant ways. First, it records the actual cost to reach a state. In the case of a route on a map, the actual cost is the distance traveled. Second, when selecting a node to expand, it chooses the node whose sum of the actual cost plus heuristic value is the smallest. Draw the search tree of problem 35 that would result from these two modifications. Record in each node the distance traveled to the city, the heuristic value to reach the goal, and their sum. What is the found path from Dearborn to Wildwood?

37. List two properties that a heuristic should have if it is to be useful in a production system.

38. Suppose you have two buckets. One has a capacity of exactly three liters; the other has a capacity of five liters. You can pour water from one bucket to another, empty a bucket, or fill a bucket at any time. Your problem is to place exactly four liters of water in the five-liter bucket. Describe how this problem could be framed as a production system.

39. Suppose your job is to supervise the loading of two trucks, each of which can carry at most fourteen tons. The cargo is a variety of crates whose total weight is twenty-eight tons but whose individual weights vary from crate to crate. The weight of each crate is marked on its side. What heuristic would you use for dividing the crates between the two trucks?

40. Which of the following are examples of meta-reasoning?
    a. He has been gone long so he must have gone far.
    b. Since I usually make the wrong decision and the last two decisions I made were correct, I will reverse my next decision.
    c. I am getting tired so I am probably not thinking clearly.
    d. I am getting tired so I think I will take a nap.

41. Describe how a human's ability to solve the frame problem helps the human find lost articles.

42. a. In what sense is learning by imitation similar to learning by supervised training?
    b. In what sense is learning by imitation different from learning by supervised training?

43. The following diagram represents an artificial neural network for an associative memory as discussed in Section 11.5. What pattern does it associate with any pattern in which only two neurons that are separated by a single neuron are excited? What will happen if the network is initialized with all its neurons inhibited?

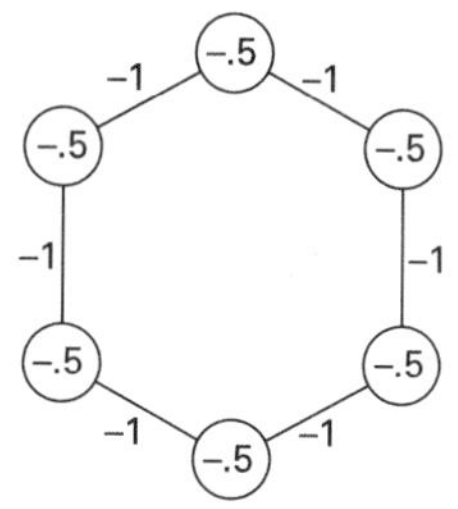

44. The following diagram represents an artificial neural network for an associative memory as discussed in Section 11.5. What stable configuration does it associate with any initial pattern in which at least three of the neurons on the perimeter are excited and the center neuron is inhibited? What would happen if it were given an initial pattern in which only two neurons that are opposite each other on the perimeter were excited?

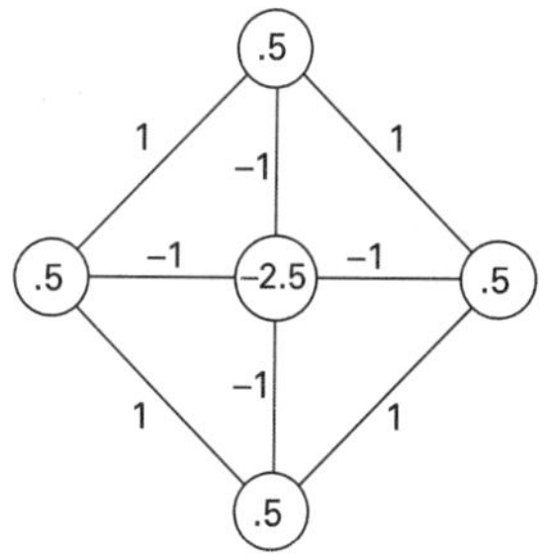

45. Design an artificial neural network for an associative memory (as discussed in Section 11.5) consisting of a rectangular array of neurons that tries to move toward stable patterns in which a single vertical column of neurons is excited.

46. Adjust the weights and threshold values in the artificial neural network in Figure 11.18 so that its output is 1 when both inputs are the same (both 0 or both 1) and 0 when the inputs are different (one being 0 while the other is 1).

47. Draw a diagram similar to Figure 11.5 representing the process of simplifying the algebraic expression $7x + 3 = 3x - 5$ to the expression $x = -2$.

48. Expand your answer to the previous problem to show other paths that a control system might pursue when attempting to solve the problem.

49. Draw a diagram similar to Figure 11.5 representing the reasoning process involved when concluding that "Polly can fly" from the initial facts "Polly is a parrot," "A parrot is a bird," and "All birds can fly."

50. In contrast to the statement in the preceding problem, some birds, such as an ostrich or a robin with a broken wing, cannot fly. However, it would not seem reasonable to construct a deductive reasoning system in which all the exceptions to the statement "All birds can fly" are explicitly listed. How then do we as humans decide whether a particular bird can or cannot fly?

51. Explain how the meaning of the sentence "I read the new tax law" depends on the context.

52. Describe how the problem of traveling from one city to another could be framed as a production system. What are the states? What are the productions?

53. Suppose you must perform three tasks, A, B, and C, that can be performed in any order (but not simultaneously). Describe how this problem can be framed as a production system and draw its state graph.

54. How does the state graph in the previous problem change if task C must be performed before task B?

55. a. If the notation (*i*, *j*), where *i* and *j* are positive integers, is used to mean "if the entry in the *i*th position in the list is greater than the entry in the *j*th position, interchange the two entries," which of the following two sequences does a better job of sorting a list of length three?

    (1, 3) (3, 2)
    (1, 2) (2, 3) (1, 2)

    b. Note that by representing sequences of interchanges in this manner, sequences can be broken into sub-sequences that can then be reconnected to form new sequences. Use this approach to describe a genetic algorithm for developing a program that sorts lists of length ten.

56. Suppose each member in a group of robots is to be equipped with a pair of sensors. Each sensor can detect an object directly in front of it within a range of two meters. Each robot is shaped like a round trash can and can move in any direction. Design a sequence of experiments to determine where the sensors should be placed to produce a robot that successfully pushes a basketball in a straight line. How does your sequence of experiments compare to an evolutionary system?

57. Do you tend to make decisions in a reactive or plan-based mode? Does your answer depend on whether you are deciding on what to have for lunch or making a career decision?

Social Issues

The following questions are intended as a guide to the ethical/social/legal issues associated with the field of computing. The goal is not merely to answer these questions. You should also consider why you answered as you did and whether your justifications are consistent from one question to the next.

1. To what extent should researchers in nuclear power, genetic engineering, and artificial intelligence be held responsible for the way the results of their work are used? Is a scientist responsible for the knowledge revealed by his or her research? What if the resulting knowledge was an unexpected consequence?
2. How would you distinguish between intelligence and simulated intelligence? Do you believe there is a difference?
3. Suppose a computerized medical expert system gains a reputation within the medical community for giving sound advice. To what extent should a physician allow that system to alter his or her decisions regarding the treatment of patients? If the physician applies a treatment contrary to that proposed by the expert system and the system turns out to be right, is the physician guilty of malpractice? In general, if an expert system becomes well-known within a field, to what degree could it hamper, rather than enhance, the ability of human experts when making their own judgments?

4. Many would argue that a computer's actions are merely consequences of how it was programmed, and thus a computer cannot possess free will. In turn, a computer should not be held responsible for its actions. Is a human's mind a computer? Are humans preprogrammed at birth? Are humans programmed by their environments? Are humans responsible for their actions?

5. Are there avenues that science should not pursue even though it might be capable of doing so? For instance, if it becomes possible to construct a machine with perception and reasoning skills comparable to those of humans, would the construction of such a machine be appropriate? What issues could the existence of such a machine raise? What are some of the issues being raised today by advancements in other scientific fields?

6. History abounds with instances in which the work of scientists and artists was affected by the political, religious, or other social influences of their times. In what ways are such issues affecting current scientific efforts? What about computer science in particular?

7. Many cultures today take at least some responsibility toward helping to retrain those whose jobs have been made redundant by advancing technology. What should/can society do as technology makes more and more of our capabilities redundant?

8. Suppose you receive a computer-generated bill for \$0.00. What should you do? Suppose you do nothing and 30 days later you receive a second notice of \$0.00 due in your account. What should you do? Suppose you do nothing and 30 days later you receive another notice of \$0.00 due in your account along with a note stating that, unless the bill is paid promptly, legal action will be taken. Who is in charge?

9. Are there times when you associate personalities with your personal computer? Are there times when it seems vindictive or stubborn? Do you ever get mad at your computer? What is the difference between being mad *at* your computer and being mad *as a result of* your computer? Does your computer ever get mad at you? Do you have similar relationships with other objects such as cars, televisions, and ballpoint pens?

10. On the basis of your answers to question 9, to what extent are humans willing to associate an entity's behavior with the presence of intelligence and awareness? To what extent should humans make such associations? Is it possible for an intelligent entity to reveal its intelligence in some way other than its behavior?

11. Many feel that the ability to pass the Turing test does not imply that a machine is intelligent. One argument is that intelligent behavior does not, in itself, imply intelligence. Yet the theory of evolution is based on the survival of the fittest, which is a behavior-based test. Does the theory of evolution imply that intelligent behavior is a predecessor to intelligence? Would the ability to pass the Turing test imply that machines were on their way to becoming intelligent?

12. Medical treatment has advanced to the point that numerous parts of the human body can now be replaced with artificial parts or parts from human donors. It is conceivable that this might someday include parts of the brain. What ethical problems would such capabilities raise? If a patient's neurons were replaced one at a time with artificial neurons, would the patient remain

the same person? Would the patient ever notice a difference? Would the patient remain human?

13. A GPS in an automobile provides a friendly voice notifying the driver of upcoming turns and other actions. In the event the driver makes a mistake, it will automatically make adjustments and provide directions to get back on route without undue emotion. Do you feel that a GPS reduces a driver's stress when driving to a new destination? In what ways does a GPS contribute to stress?
14. Suppose your smartphone provided voice-to-voice language translation, would you feel comfortable using this feature? Would you trust it to convey the correct meaning? Would you have any concerns?

Additional Reading

Banzhaf, W., P. Nordin, R. E. Deller, and F. D. Francone. *Genetic Programming: An Introduction.* San Francisco, CA: Morgan Kaufmann, 1998.

Lu, J., and J. Wu. *Multi-Agent Robotic Systems.* Boca Raton, FL: CRC Press, 2001.

Luger, G. F. *Artificial Intelligence: Structures and Strategies for Complex Problem Solving,* 6th ed. Boston, MA: Addison-Wesley, 2008.

Mitchell, M. *An Introduction to Genetic Algorithms.* Cambridge, MA: MIT Press, 1998.

Negnevitsky, M. *Artificial Intelligence: A Guide to Intelligent Systems,* 2nd ed. Boston, MA: Addison-Wesley, 2005.

Nilsson, N. *Artificial Intelligence: A New Synthesis.* San Francisco, CA: Morgan Kaufmann, 1998.

Nolfi, S., and D. Floreano. *Evolutionary Robotics.* Cambridge, MA: MIT Press, 2000.

Rumelhart, D. E., and J. L. McClelland. *Parallel Distributed Processing.* Cambridge, MA: MIT Press, 1986.

Russell, S., and P. Norvig. *Artificial Intelligence: A Modern Approach,* 3rd ed. Upper Saddle River, NJ: Prentice-Hall, 2009.

Shapiro, L. G., and G. C. Stockman. *Computer Vision.* Englewood Cliffs, NJ: Prentice-Hall, 2001.

Shieber, S. *The Turing Test.* Cambridge, MA: MIT Press, 2004.

Weizenbaum, J. *Computer Power and Human Reason.* New York: W. H. Freeman, 1979.

CHAPTER 12

Theory of Computation

In this chapter we will consider the theoretical foundations of computer science. In a sense, it is the material in this chapter that gives computer science the status of a true science. Although somewhat abstract in nature, this body of knowledge has many very practical applications. In particular, we will explore its implications regarding the power of programming languages and see how it leads to a public-key encryption system that is widely used in communication over the Internet.

**Asterisks indicate suggestions for optional sections.*

In this chapter we consider questions regarding what computers can and cannot do. We will see how simple machines, known as Turing machines, are used to identify the boundary between problems that are solvable by machines and problems that are not. We will identify a particular problem, known as the halting problem, whose solution falls beyond the powers of algorithmic systems and therefore beyond the capabilities of today's as well as tomorrow's computers. Moreover, we will find that even among the machine-solvable problems, there are problems whose solutions are so complex that they are unsolvable from any practical point of view. We close by considering how knowledge in the field of complexity can be used to construct a public-key encryption system.

12.1 Functions and Their Computation

Our goal in this chapter is to investigate the capabilities of computers. We want to understand what machines can and cannot do and what features are required for machines to reach their full potential. We have seen many examples of Python functions in previous chapters, but here we begin with the more general concept of computing mathematical functions.

A **function** in its mathematical sense is a correspondence between a collection of possible input values and a collection of output values so that each possible input is assigned a single output. An example is the function that converts measurements in yards into meters. With each measurement in yards, it assigns the value that would result if the same distance were measured in meters. Another example, which we could call the sort function, assigns each input list of numeric values to an output list whose entries are the same as those in the input list but are arranged in the order of increasing value. Still another example is the addition function whose inputs are pairs of values and whose outputs are values representing the sum of each input pair.

The process of determining the particular output value that a function assigns to a given input is called *computing the function.* The ability to compute functions is important because it is by means of computing functions that we are able to solve problems. To solve an addition problem we must compute the addition function; to sort a list we must compute the sort function. In turn, a fundamental task of computer science is to find techniques for computing the functions that lie beneath the problems we want to solve.

Consider, for example, a system in which a function's inputs and outputs can be predetermined and recorded in a table. Each time the output of the function

Recursive Function Theory

Nothing tantalizes human nature more than to be told something cannot be done. Once researchers began to identify problems that are unsolvable in the sense that they have no algorithmic solutions, others began to study these problems to try to understand their complexity. Today, this field of research is a major part of the subject known as recursive function theory, and much has been learned about these super-difficult problems. Indeed, just as mathematicians have developed number systems that reveal "quantitative" levels beyond infinity, recursive function theorists have uncovered multiple levels of complexity within problems that exist well beyond the capabilities of algorithms.

is required, we merely look for the given input in the table where we find the required output. Thus the computation of the function is reduced to the process of searching the table. Such systems are convenient but limited in power because many functions cannot be represented completely in tabular form. An example is shown in Figure 12.1, which is an attempt to display the function that converts measurements in yards into equivalent measurements in meters. Because there is no limit to the list of possible input/output pairs, the table is destined to be incomplete.

A more powerful approach to computing functions is to follow directions provided by an algebraic formula rather than trying to display all possible input/output combinations in a table. We could, for example, use the algebraic formula

$$V = P(1 + r)^n$$

to describe how to compute the value of an investment of P after earning an annually compounded interest rate of r for n years.

But the expressive power of algebraic formulas has its limitations as well. There are functions whose input/output relationships are too complex to be described by algebraic manipulations. Examples include the trigonometric functions such as sine and cosine. If pressed to calculate the sine of 38 degrees, you might draw the appropriate triangle, measure its sides, and calculate the desired ratio—a process that cannot be expressed in terms of algebraic manipulations of the value 38. Your pocket calculator also struggles with the task of computing the sine of 38 degrees. In reality, it is forced to apply rather sophisticated mathematical techniques to obtain a very good approximation to the sine of 38 degrees, which it reports to you as the answer.

We see, then, that as we consider functions with increasing complexity, we are forced to apply more powerful techniques for computing them. Our question is whether we can always find a system for computing functions, regardless of their complexity. The answer is no. A striking result from mathematics is that there are functions that are so complex that there is no well-defined, step-by-step process for determining their outputs based on their input values. In turn, the computation of these functions lies beyond the abilities of any algorithmic system. These functions are said to be noncomputable, whereas the functions whose output values can be determined algorithmically from their input values are said to be **computable.**

The distinction between computable and noncomputable functions is important in computer science. Because machines can only perform tasks described

Figure 12.1 An attempt to display the function that converts measurements in yards into meters

Yards (input)	Meters (output)
1	0.9144
2	1.8288
3	2.7432
4	3.6576
5	4.5720
.	.
.	.
.	.

by algorithms, the study of computable functions is the study of the ultimate capabilities of machines. If we can identify capabilities that allow a machine to compute the entire set of computable functions and then build machines with these capabilities, we will be assured that the machines we build are as powerful as we can make them. Likewise, if we discover that the solution to a problem requires the computation of a noncomputable function, we can conclude that the solution to that problem lies beyond the capabilities of machines.

Questions & Exercises

1. Identify some functions that can be represented completely in tabular form.
2. Identify some functions whose outputs can be described as an algebraic expression involving their inputs.
3. Identify a function that cannot be described in terms of an algebraic formula. Is your function nonetheless computable?
4. Ancient Greek mathematicians used a straight-edge and compass to draw shapes. They developed techniques for finding the midpoint on a straight line, constructing a right angle, and drawing an equilateral triangle. However, what were some "computations" that their "computational system" could not perform?

12.2 Turing Machines

In an effort to understand capabilities and limitations of machines, many researchers have proposed and studied various computational devices. One of these is the Turing machine, which was proposed by Alan M. Turing in 1936 and is still used today as a tool for studying the power of algorithmic processes.

Turing Machine Fundamentals

A **Turing machine** consists of a control unit that can read and write symbols on a tape by means of a read/write head (Figure 12.2). The tape extends indefinitely at both ends and is divided into cells, each of which can contain any one of a finite set of symbols. This set is called the machine's alphabet.

Figure 12.2 The components of a Turing machine

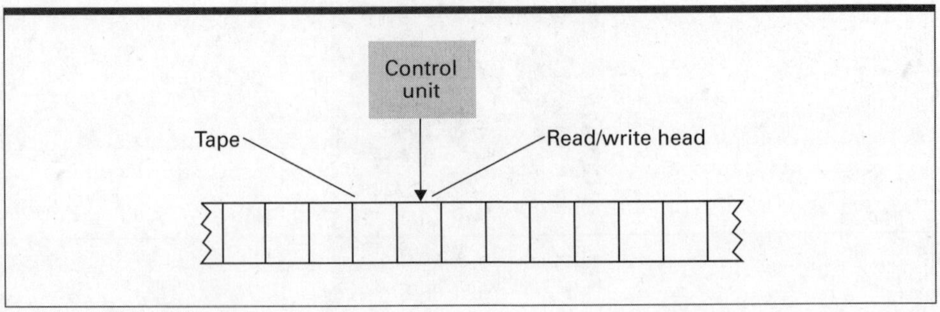

The Origins of Turing Machines

Alan Turing developed the concept of a Turing machine in the 1930s, well before technology was capable of providing the machines we know today. In fact, Turing's vision was that of a human performing computations with pencil and paper. Turing's goal was to provide a model by which the limits of "computational processes" could be studied. This was shortly after the publication in 1931 of Gödel's famous paper exposing the limitations of computational systems, and a major research effort was being directed toward understanding these limitations. In the same year that Turing presented his model (1936), Emil Post presented another model (now known as Post production systems) that has been shown to have the same capabilities as Turing's. As a testimony to the insights of these early researchers, their models of computational systems (such as Turing machines and Post production systems) still serve as valuable tools in computer science research.

At any time during a Turing machine's computation, the machine must be in one of a finite number of conditions, called states. A Turing machine's computation begins in a special state called the start state and ceases when the machine reaches another special state known as the halt state.

A Turing machine's computation consists of a sequence of steps that are executed by the machine's control unit. Each step consists of observing the symbol in the current tape cell (the one viewed by the read-write head), writing a symbol in that cell, possibly moving the read-write head one cell to the left or right, and then changing states. The exact action to be performed is determined by a program that tells the control unit what to do based on the machine's state and the contents of the current tape cell.

Let us consider an example of a specific Turing machine. For this purpose, we represent the machine's tape as a horizontal strip divided into cells in which we can record symbols from the machine's alphabet. We indicate the current position of the machine's read/write head by placing a label under the current tape cell. The alphabet for our example consists of the symbols 0, 1, and *. The tape of our machine might appear as follows:

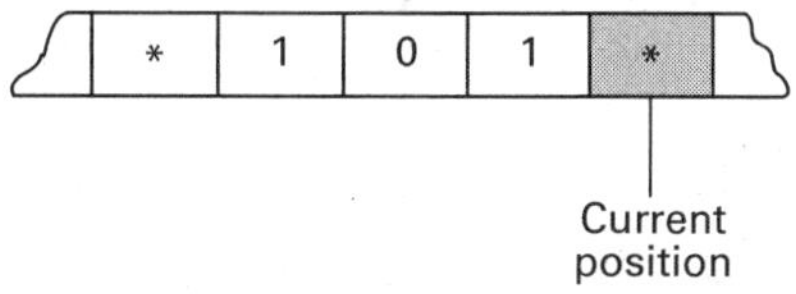

By interpreting a string of symbols on the tape as representing binary numbers separated by asterisks, we recognize that this particular tape contains the value 5. Our Turing machine is designed to increment such a value on the tape by 1. More precisely, it assumes that the starting position is at an asterisk marking the right end of a string of 0s and 1s, and it proceeds to alter the bit pattern to the left so that it represents the next larger integer.

The states for our machine are START, ADD, CARRY, OVERFLOW, RETURN, and HALT. The actions corresponding to each of these states and the content of the current cell are described in the table in Figure 12.3. We assume that the machine always begins in the START state.

Let us apply this machine to the tape pictured earlier, which contains the value 5. Observe that when in the START state with the current cell containing * (as is our case), we are instructed by the table to rewrite the *, move the read/write head one cell to the left, and enter the ADD state. Having done this, the machine can be described as follows:

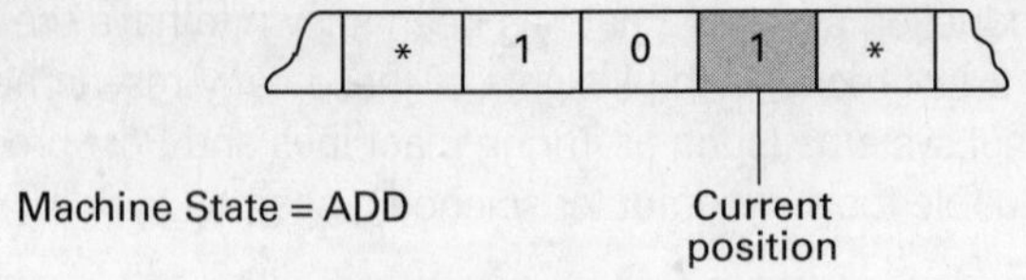

To proceed, we look at the table to see what to do when in the ADD state with the current cell containing 1. The table tells us to replace the 1 in the current cell with 0, move the read/write head one cell to the left, and enter the CARRY state. Thus the configuration of the machine becomes:

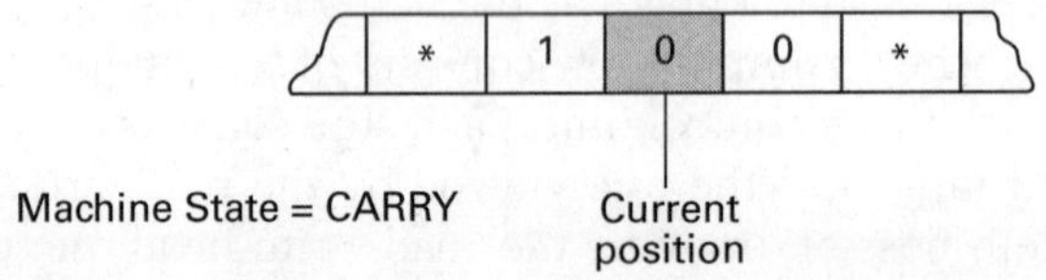

We again refer to the table to see what to do next and find that when in the CARRY state with the current cell containing 0, we should replace the 0 with 1,

Figure 12.3 A Turing machine for incrementing a value

Current state	Current cell content	Value to write	Direction to move	New state to enter
START	*	*	Left	ADD
ADD	0	1	Right	RETURN
ADD	1	0	Left	CARRY
ADD	*	*	Right	HALT
CARRY	0	1	Right	RETURN
CARRY	1	0	Left	CARRY
CARRY	*	1	Left	OVERFLOW
OVERFLOW	(Ignored)	*	Right	RETURN
RETURN	0	0	Right	RETURN
RETURN	1	1	Right	RETURN
RETURN	*	*	No move	HALT

move the read/write head one cell to the right, and enter the RETURN state. After we do this, the machine's configuration is as follows:

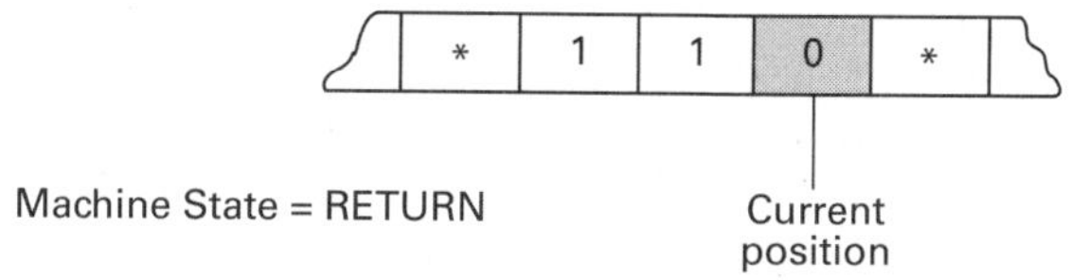

From this situation, the table instructs us to proceed by replacing the 0 in the current cell with another 0, move the read/write head one cell to the right, and remain in the RETURN state. Consequently, we find our machine in the following condition:

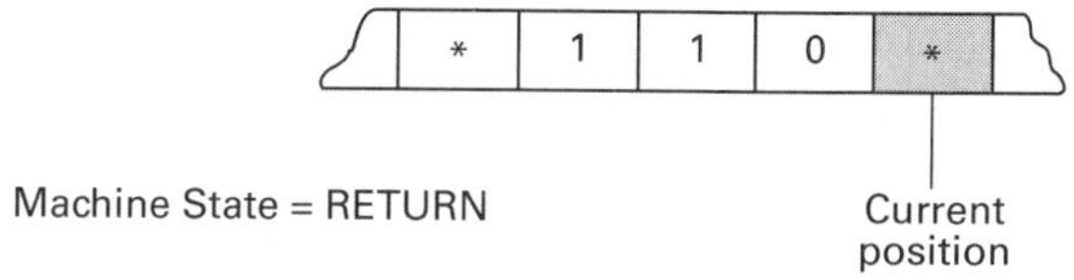

At this point, we see that the table instructs us to rewrite the asterisk in the current cell and HALT. The machine thus stops in the following configuration (the symbols on the tape now represent the value 6 as desired):

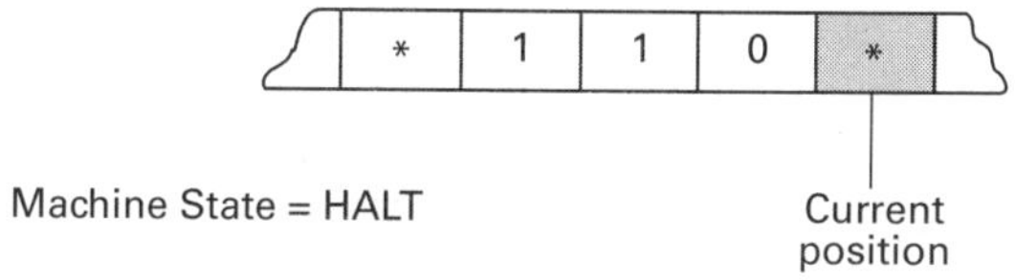

The Church-Turing Thesis

The Turing machine in the preceding example can be used to compute the function known as the successor function, which assigns each nonnegative integer input value n to the output value $n + 1$. We need merely place the input value in its binary form on the machine's tape, run the machine until it halts, and then read the output value from the tape. A function that can be computed in this manner by a Turing machine is said to be **Turing computable.**

Turing's conjecture was that the Turing-computable functions were the same as the computable functions. In other words, he conjectured that the computational power of Turing machines encompasses that of any algorithmic system or, equivalently, that (in contrast to such approaches as tables and algebraic formulas) the Turing machine concept provides a context in which solutions to all the computable functions can be expressed. Today, this conjecture is often referred to as the **Church–Turing thesis,** in reference to the contributions made by both Alan Turing and Alonzo Church. Since Turing's initial work, much evidence has been collected to support this thesis, and today the Church–Turing thesis is widely accepted. That is, the computable functions and the Turing-computable functions are considered the same.

The significance of this conjecture is that it gives insight to the capabilities and limitations of computing machinery. More precisely, it establishes the capabilities of Turing machines as a standard to which the powers of other computational systems can be compared. If a computational system is capable of computing all the Turing-computable functions, it is considered to be as powerful as any computational system can be.

Questions & Exercises

1. Apply the Turing machine described in this section (Figure 12.3), starting with the following initial status:

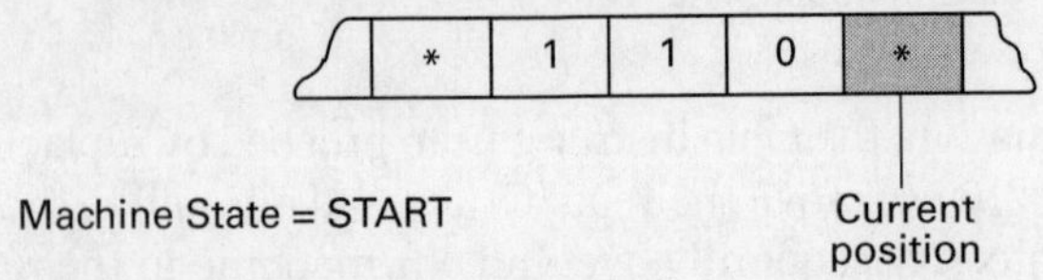

2. Describe a Turing machine that replaces a string of 0s and 1s with a single 0.
3. Describe a Turing machine that decrements the value on the tape if it is greater than zero or leaves the value unaltered if it is zero.
4. Identify an everyday situation in which calculating takes place. How is that situation analogous to a Turing machine?
5. Describe a Turing machine that ultimately halts for some inputs but never halts for others.

12.3 Universal Programming Languages

In Chapter 6 we studied a variety of features found in high-level programming languages. In this section we apply our knowledge of computability to determine which of these features are actually necessary. We will find that most features in today's high-level languages merely enhance convenience rather than contribute to the fundamental power of the language.

Our approach is to describe a simple imperative programming language that is rich enough to allow us to express programs for computing all the Turing-computable functions (and thus all the computable functions). Hence, if a future programmer finds that a problem cannot be solved using this language, the reason will not be a fault of the language. Instead, it will be that there is no algorithm for solving the problem. A programming language with this property is called a **universal programming language.**

You might find it surprising that a universal language need not be complex. Indeed, the language we are about to present is quite simple. We will call it Bare Bones because it isolates the minimal set of requirements of a universal programming language.

The Bare Bones Language

Let us begin our presentation of Bare Bones by considering the variables found in other programming languages. Variables allow programmers the luxury of thinking in terms of data structures and data types (such as lists of numbers and strings of alphabetic characters) even though the machine itself merely manipulates bit patterns without any knowledge of what the patterns represent. Before being presented to a machine for execution, a high-level instruction dealing with elaborate data types and structures must be translated into machine-level instructions that manipulate bit patterns to simulate the actions requested.

For convenience, we can interpret these patterns as numeric values represented in binary notation. Thus, all computations performed by a computer could be expressed as numeric computations involving nonnegative integers—it is all in the eye of the beholder. Moreover, programming languages could be simplified by requiring programmers to express algorithms in these terms (although this would place a larger burden on the programmer).

Because our goal in developing Bare Bones is to develop the simplest language possible, we will follow this lead. All variables in Bare Bones will be considered to represent bit patterns that, for convenience, we interpret as nonnegative integers in binary notation. Thus a variable currently assigned the pattern 10 will be said to contain the value two, whereas a variable assigned the pattern 101 will be said to contain five.

Using this convention, all variables in a Bare Bones program are of the same type so the language does not need operations for converting between value types or declarative statements by which variable names and their associated properties are described. When using Bare Bones, as in Python, a programmer can simply begin using a new variable name when it is needed, with the understanding that it refers to a bit pattern interpreted as a nonnegative integer.

Of course, a translator for our Bare Bones language must be able to distinguish variable names from the other terms. This is done by designing the syntax of Bare Bones so that the role of any term can be identified by syntax alone. For this purpose, we specify that variable names must begin with a letter from the English alphabet, which can be followed by any combination of letters and digits (0 through 9). Thus the strings `XYZ`, `B747`, `abcdefghi`, and `X5Y` can be used as variable names, whereas `2G5`, `%o`, and `x.y` cannot.

Let us now consider the procedural statements in Bare Bones. There are three assignment statements and one control structure representing a loop. Following Python-inspired syntax, we adopt the policy of writing only one statement per line, and use indentation to mark the body of a loop structure.

Each of the three assignment statements requests that the contents of the variable identified in the statement be modified. The first allows us to associate the value zero with a variable. Its syntax is

```
clear name
```

where *name* can be any variable name.

The other assignment statements are essentially opposites of each other:

```
incr name
```

and

```
decr name
```

Again, `name` represents any variable name. The first of these statements causes the value associated with the identified variable to be incremented by one. Thus, if the variable `Y` were assigned the value five before the statement

```
incr Y
```

is executed, then the value assigned to `Y` afterward would be six.

In contrast, the decr statement is used to decrement the value associated with the identified variable by one. An exception is when the variable is already associated with zero, in which case this statement leaves the value unaltered. Therefore, if the value associated with Y is five before the statement

```
decr Y
```

is executed, the value four would be associated with Y afterward. However, if the value of Y had been zero before executing the statement, the value would remain zero after execution.

Bare Bones provides only one control structure represented by while. The statement sequence

```
while name not 0:
  .
  .
  .
```

(where name represents any variable name) causes any statement or statement sequence indented below the while statement to be repeated as long as the value of the variable name is not zero. To be more precise, when a while structure is encountered during program execution, the value of the identified variable is first compared to zero. If it is zero, the structure is skipped, and execution continues with the statement following the indented body. If, however, the variable's value is not zero, the indented statement sequence within the while structure is executed and control is returned to the while statement, whereupon the comparison is conducted again. Note that the burden of loop control is partially placed on the programmer, who must explicitly request that the variable's value be altered within the loop body to avoid an infinite loop. For instance, the sequence

```
incr X
while X not 0:
  incr Z
```

results in an infinite process because once the while statement is reached, the value associated with X can never be zero, whereas the sequence

```
clear Z
while X not 0:
  incr Z
  decr X
```

ultimately terminates with the effect of transferring the value initially associated with X to the variable Z.

Observe that while statements might appear within the instructions being repeated by another while statement. In such a case the multiple levels of indention will indicate which instructions belong to the body of inner nested while statements.

As a closing example, the instruction sequence in Figure 12.4 results in the product of the values associated with X and Y being assigned to Z, although it has the side effect of destroying any nonzero value that might have been associated with X. (The while structure controlled by the variable W has the effect of restoring the original value of Y.)

Figure 12.4 A Bare Bones program for computing X × Y

```
clear Z
while X not 0:
  clear W
  while Y not 0:
    incr Z
    incr W
    decr Y
  while W not 0:
    incr Y
    decr W
  decr X
```

Programming in Bare Bones

Keep in mind that our goal in presenting the language Bare Bones is to investigate what is possible, not what is practical. Bare Bones would prove to be awkward if used in an applied setting. On the other hand, we will soon see that this simple language fulfills our goal of providing a no-frills universal programming language. For now, we will merely demonstrate how Bare Bones can be used to express some elementary operations.

We first note that with a combination of the assignment statements, any value (any nonnegative integer) can be associated with a given variable. For example, the following sequence assigns the value three to the variable X by first assigning it the value zero and then incrementing its value three times:

```
clear X
incr X
incr X
incr X
```

Another common activity in programs is to copy data from one location to another. In terms of Bare Bones, this means that we need to be able to assign the value of one variable to another variable. This can be accomplished by first clearing the destination and then incrementing it an appropriate number of times. In fact, we have already observed that the sequence

```
clear Z
while X not 0:
  incr Z
  decr X
```

transfers the value associated with X to Z. However, this sequence has the side effect of destroying the original value of X. To correct for this, we can introduce an auxiliary variable to which we first transfer the subject value from its initial location. We then use this auxiliary variable as the data source from which we restore the original variable while placing the subject value in the desired destination. In this manner, the movement of `Today` to `Yesterday` can be accomplished by the sequence shown in Figure 12.5.

We adopt the syntax

```
copy name1 to name2
```

Figure 12.5 A Bare Bones implementation of the instruction "copy Today to Tomorrow"

```
clear Aux
clear Tomorrow
while Today not 0:
  incr Aux
  decr Today
while Aux not 0:
  incr Today
  incr Tomorrow
  decr Aux
```

(where `name1` and `name2` represent variable names) as a shorthand notation for a statement structure of the form in Figure 12.5. Thus, although Bare Bones itself does not have an explicit copy instruction, we often write programs as though it did, with the understanding that to convert such informal programs into real Bare Bones programs, we must replace the copy statements with their equivalent `while` structures using an auxiliary variable whose name does not clash with a name already used elsewhere in the program.

The Universality of Bare Bones

Let us now apply the Church-Turing thesis to confirm our claim that Bare Bones is a universal programming language. First, we observe that any program written in Bare Bones can be thought of as directing the computation of a function. The function's input consists of values assigned to variables prior to executing the program, and the function's output consists of the values of variables when the program terminates. To compute the function, we merely execute the program, starting with proper variable assignments, and then observe the variables' values when the program terminates.

Under these conditions the program

```
incr X
```

directs the computation of the same function (the successor function) that is computed by the Turing machine example of Section 12.2. Indeed, it increases the value associated with X by one. Likewise, if we interpret the variables X and Y as inputs and the variable Z as the output, the program

```
copy Y to Z
while X not 0:
  incr Z
  decr X
```

directs the computation of the addition function.

Researchers have shown that the Bare Bones programming language can be used to express algorithms for computing all the Turing-computable functions. Combining this with the Church-Turing thesis implies that any computable function can be computed by a program written in Bare Bones. Thus Bare Bones is a universal programming language in the sense that, if an algorithm exists for solving a problem, then that problem can be solved by some Bare Bones program. In turn, Bare Bones could theoretically serve as a general-purpose programming language.

We say *theoretically* because such a language is certainly not as convenient as Python or the high-level languages introduced in Chapter 6. However, each of those languages essentially contains the features of Bare Bones as its core. It is, in fact, this core that ensures the universality of each of those languages; all the other features in the various languages are included for convenience.

Although not practical in an application programming environment, languages such as Bare Bones find use within theoretical computer science. For example, in Appendix E we use Bare Bones as a tool to settle the question regarding the equivalence of iterative and recursive structures raised in Chapter 5. There we find that our suspicion of equivalence was, in fact, justified.

Questions & Exercises

1. Show that the statement `invert X` (whose action is to convert the value of X to zero if its initial value is nonzero and to 1 if its initial value is zero) can be simulated by a Bare Bones program segment.
2. Show that even our simple Bare Bones language contains more statements than necessary by showing that the `clear` statement can be replaced with combinations of other statements in the language.
3. Show that the if-else structure can be simulated using Bare Bones. That is, write a program sequence in Bare Bones that simulates the action of the statement

   ```
   if X not 0:
     S1
   else:
     S2
   ```

   where S1 and S2 represent arbitrary statement sequences.
4. Show that each of the Bare Bones statements can be expressed in terms of the machine language of Appendix C. (Thus Bare Bones can be used as a programming language for such a machine.)
5. How can negative numbers be dealt with in Bare Bones?
6. Describe the function computed by the following Bare Bones program, assuming the function's input is represented by X and its output by Z:

   ```
   clear Z
   while X not 0:
     incr Z
     incr Z
     decr X
   ```

12.4 A Noncomputable Function

We now identify a function that is not Turing computable and so, by the Church-Turing thesis, is widely believed to be noncomputable in the general sense. Thus it is a function whose computation lies beyond the capabilities of computers.

The Halting Problem

The noncomputable function we are about to reveal is associated with a problem known as the **halting problem,** which (in an informal sense) is the problem of trying to predict in advance whether a program will terminate (or halt) if started under certain conditions. For example, consider the simple Bare Bones program

```
while X not 0:
  incr X
```

If we execute this program with the initial value of X being zero, the loop will not be executed and the program's execution will quickly terminate. However, if we execute the program with any other initial value of X, the loop will be executed forever, leading to a nonterminating process.

In this case, then, it is easy to conclude that the program's execution will halt only when it is started with X assigned the value zero. However, as we move to more complex examples, the task of predicting a program's behavior becomes more complicated. In fact, in some cases the task is impossible, as we shall see. But first we need to formalize our terminology and focus our thoughts more precisely.

Our example has shown that whether a program ultimately halts can depend on the initial values of its variables. Thus if we hope to predict whether a program's execution will halt, we must be precise in regard to these initial values. The choice we are about to make for these values might seem strange to you at first, but do not despair. Our goal is to take advantage of a technique called **self-reference**—the idea of an object referring to itself. This ploy has repeatedly led to amazing results in mathematics from such informal curiosities as the sentence "This statement is false" to the more serious paradox represented by the question "Does the set of all sets contain itself?" What we are about to do, then, is set the stage for a line of reasoning similar to "If it does, then it doesn't; but, if it doesn't, then it does."

In our case self-reference will be achieved by assigning the variables in a program an initial value that represents the program itself. To this end, observe that each Bare Bones program can be encoded as a single long bit pattern in a one-character-per-byte format using ASCII, which can then be interpreted as the binary representation for a (rather large) nonnegative integer. It is this integer value that we assign as the initial value for the variables in the program.

Let us consider what would happen if we did this in the case of the simple program

```
while X not 0:
  incr X
```

We want to know what would happen if we started this program with X assigned the integer value representing the program itself (Figure 12.6). In this case the answer is readily apparent. Because X would have a nonzero value, the program

Figure 12.6 Testing a program for self-termination

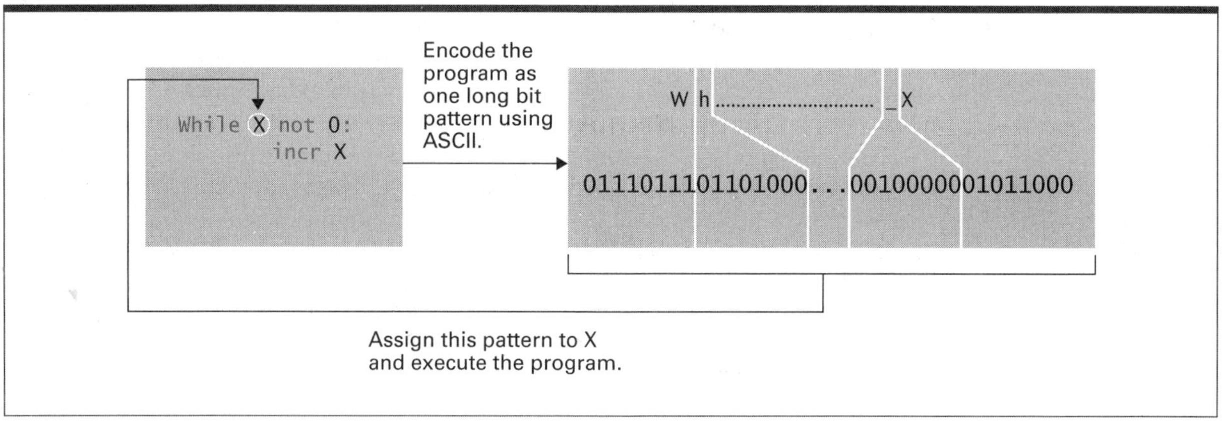

would become caught in the loop and never terminate. On the other hand, if we performed a similar experiment with the program

```
clear X
while X not 0:
  incr X
```

the program would terminate because the variable X would have the value zero by the time the while structure is reached regardless of its initial value.

Let us, then, make the following definition: A Bare Bones program is **self-terminating** if executing the program with all its variables initialized to the program's own encoded representation leads to a terminating process. Informally, a program is self-terminating if its execution terminates when started with itself as its input. Here, then, is the self-reference that we promised.

Note that whether a program is self-terminating probably has nothing to do with the purpose for which the program was written. It is merely a property that each Bare Bones program either possesses or does not possess. That is, each Bare Bones program is either self-terminating or not.

We can now describe the halting problem in a precise manner. It is the problem of determining whether Bare Bones programs are or are not self-terminating. We are about to see that there is no algorithm for answering this question in general. That is, there is no single algorithm that, when given any Bare Bones program, is capable of determining whether that program is or is not self-terminating. Thus the solution to the halting problem lies beyond the capabilities of computers.

The fact that we have apparently solved the halting problem in our previous examples and now claim that the halting problem is unsolvable might sound contradictory, so let us pause for clarification. The observations we used in our examples were unique to those particular cases and would not be applicable in all situations. What the halting problem requests is a single, generic algorithm that can be applied to any Bare Bones program to determine whether it is self-terminating. Our ability to apply certain isolated insights to determine whether a particular program is self-terminating in no way implies the existence of a single, generic approach that can be applied in all cases. In short, we might be able to build a machine that can solve a particular halting problem, but we cannot build a single machine that we could use to solve any halting problem that arises.

The Unsolvability of the Halting Problem

We now want to show that solving the halting problem lies beyond the capabilities of machines. Our approach is to show that to solve the problem would require an algorithm for computing a noncomputable function. The inputs of the function in question are encoded versions of Bare Bones programs; its outputs are limited to the values 0 and 1. More precisely, we define the function so that an input representing a self-terminating program produces the output value 1 while an input representing a program that is not self-terminating produces the output value 0. For the sake of conciseness, we will refer to this function as the *halting function.*

Our task is to show that the halting function is not computable. Our approach is the technique known as "proof by contradiction." In short, we prove that a statement is false by showing that it cannot be true. Let us, then, show that the statement "the halting function is computable" cannot be true. Our entire argument is summarized in Figure 12.7.

If the halting function is computable, then (because Bare Bones is a universal programming language) there must be a Bare Bones program that computes it. In other words, there is a Bare Bones program that terminates with its output equal to 1 if its input is the encoded version of a self-terminating program and terminates with its output equal to 0 otherwise.

To apply this program we do not need to identify which variable is the input variable but instead merely to initialize all the program's variables to the encoded representation of the program to be tested. This is because a variable that is not an input variable is inherently a variable whose initial value does not affect the ultimate output value. We conclude that if the halting function is computable, then there is a Bare Bones program that terminates with its output equal to 1 if all its variables are initialized to the encoded version of a self-terminating program and terminates with its output equal to 0 otherwise.

Assuming that the program's output variable is named X (if it is not we could simply rename the variables), we could modify the program by attaching the statement

```
while X not 0:
```

at its end, producing a new program. This new program must be either self-terminating or not. However, we are about to see that it can be neither.

In particular, if this new program were self-terminating and we ran it with its variables initialized to the program's own encoded representation, then when its execution reached the `while` statement that we added, the variable X would contain a 1. (To this point the new program is identical to the original program that produced a 1 if its input was the representation of a self-terminating program.) At this point, the program's execution would be caught forever in the `while` structure because we made no provisions for X to be decremented within the loop. But this contradicts our assumption that the new program is self-terminating. Therefore we must conclude that the new program is not self-terminating.

If, however, the new program were not self-terminating and we executed it with its variables initialized to the program's own encoded representation, it would reach the added `while` statement with X being assigned the value 0. (This occurs because the statements preceding the `while` statement constitute the original program that produces an output of 0 when its input represents a program

Figure 12.7 Proving the unsolvability of the halting program

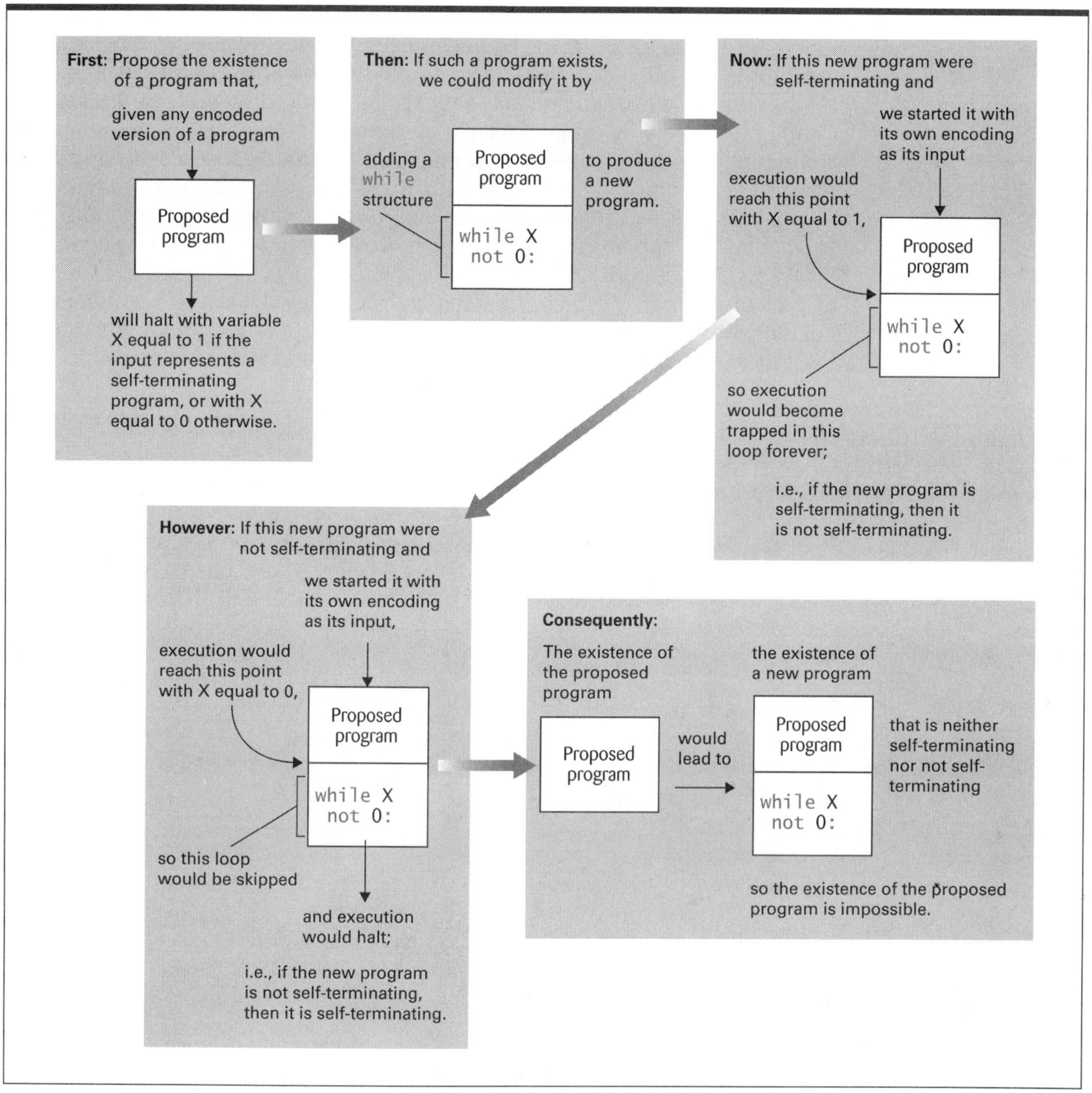

that is not self-terminating.) In this case, the loop in the `while` structure would be avoided and the program would halt. But this is the property of a self-terminating program, so we are forced to conclude that the new program is self-terminating, just as we were forced to conclude earlier that it is not self-terminating.

In summary, we see that we have the impossible situation of a program that on the one hand must be either self-terminating or not and on the other hand can be neither. Consequently, the assumption that led to this dilemma must be false.

We conclude that the halting function is not computable, and because the solution to the halting problem relies on the computation of that function we must conclude that solving the halting problem lies beyond the capabilities of any algorithmic system. Such problems are called **unsolvable problems.**

In closing, we should relate what we have just discussed to the ideas in Chapter 11. There, a major underlying question was whether the powers of computing machines include those required for intelligence itself. Recall that machines can solve only problems with algorithmic solutions, and we have now found that there are problems without algorithmic solutions. The question, then, is whether the human mind embodies more than the execution of algorithmic processes. If it does not, then the limits we have identified here are also limits of human thought. Needless to say, this is a highly debatable and sometimes emotional issue. If, for example, human minds are no more than programmed machines, then one would conclude that humans do not possess free will.

Questions & Exercises

1. Is the following Bare Bones program self-terminating? Explain your answer.

```
incr X
decr Y
```

2. Is the following Bare Bones program self-terminating? Explain your answer.

```
copy X to Y
incr Y
incr Y
while X not 0:
  decr X
  decr X
  decr Y
  decr Y
decr Y
while Y not 0:
```

3. What is wrong with the following scenario?

   In a certain community, everyone owns his or her own house. The house painter of the community claims to paint all those and only those houses that are not painted by their owners.

   (*Hint:* Who paints the house painter's house?)

12.5 Complexity of Problems

In Section 12.4 we investigated the solvability of problems. In this section we are interested in the question of whether a solvable problem has a practical solution. We will find that some problems that are theoretically solvable are so complex that they are unsolvable from a practical point of view.

Measuring a Problem's Complexity

We begin by returning to our study of algorithm efficiency that we started in Section 5.6. There we used big-theta notation to classify algorithms according to the time required to execute them. We found that the insertion sort algorithm is in the class $\Theta(n^2)$, The sequential search algorithm is in $\Theta(n)$, and the binary search algorithm is in $\Theta(\log_2 n)$. We now use this classification system to help us identify the complexity of problems. Our goal is to develop a classification system that tells us which problems are more complex than others and ultimately which problems are so complex that their solutions lie beyond practicality.

The reason that our present study is based on our knowledge of algorithm efficiency is that we wish to measure the complexity of a problem in terms of the complexity of its solutions. We consider a simple problem to be one that has a simple solution; a complex problem is one that does not have a simple solution. Note that the fact that a problem has a difficult solution does not necessarily mean that the problem itself is complex. After all, a problem has many solutions, one of which is bound to be complex. Thus to conclude that a problem itself is complex requires that we show that none of its solutions are simple.

In computer science, the problems of interest are those that are solvable by machines. The solutions to these problems are formulated as algorithms. Thus the complexity of a problem is determined by the properties of the algorithms that solve that problem. More precisely, the complexity of the simplest algorithm for solving a problem is considered to be the complexity of the problem itself.

But how do we measure the complexity of an algorithm? Unfortunately, the term *complexity* has different interpretations. One deals with the amount of decision making and branching involved in the algorithm. In this light, a complex algorithm would be one that involves a twisted, entwined set of directions. This interpretation might be compatible with the point of view of a software engineer who is interested in issues relating to algorithm discovery and representation, but it does not capture the concept of complexity from a machine's point of view. A machine does not really make decisions when selecting the next instruction for execution but merely follows its machine cycle over and over, each time executing the instruction that is indicated by the program counter. Consequently, a machine can execute a set of tangled instructions as easily as it can execute a list of instructions in a simple sequential order. This interpretation of complexity, therefore, tends to measure the difficulty encountered in an algorithm's representation rather than the complexity of the algorithm itself.

An interpretation that more accurately reflects the complexity of an algorithm from a machine's point of view is to measure the number of steps that must be performed when executing the algorithm. Note that this is not the same as the number of instructions appearing in the written program. A loop whose body consists of a single statement but whose control requests the body's execution 100 times is equivalent to 100 statements when executed. Such a routine is therefore considered more complex than a list of 50 individually written statements, even though the latter appears longer in written form. The point is that this meaning of *complexity* is ultimately concerned with the time it takes a machine to execute a solution and not with the size of the program representing the solution.

We therefore consider a problem to be complex if all its solutions require a lot of time. This definition of complexity is referred to as **time complexity.** We have already met the concept of time complexity indirectly through our study of algorithm efficiency in Section 5.6. After all, the study of an algorithm's efficiency is the study of the algorithm's time complexity—the two are merely inverses of each other. That is, "more efficient" equals "less complex." Thus, in terms of time complexity, the sequential search algorithm (which we found to be in $\Theta(n)$) is a more complex solution to the problem of searching a list than is the binary search algorithm (which we found to be in $\Theta(\log_2 n)$).

Let us now apply our knowledge of the complexity of algorithms to obtain a means of identifying the complexity of problems. We define the (time) complexity of a problem to be $\Theta(f(n))$, where f(n) is some mathematical expression in n, if there is an algorithm for solving the problem whose time complexity is in $\Theta(f(n))$ and no other algorithm for solving the problem has a lower time complexity. That is, the (time) complexity of a problem is defined to be the (time) complexity of its best solution. Unfortunately, finding the best solution to a problem and knowing that it is the best is often a difficult problem in itself. In such situations, a variation of big-theta notation called **big O notation** (pronounced "big oh notation") is used to represent what is known about a problem's complexity. More precisely, if f(n) is a mathematical expression in n and if a problem can be solved by an algorithm in $\Theta(f(n))$ then we say that the problem is in $O(f(n))$ (pronounced "big oh of f(n)"). Thus, to say that a problem belongs to $O(f(n))$ means that it has a solution whose complexity is in $\Theta(f(n))$ but it could possibly have a better solution.

Our investigation of searching and sorting algorithms tells us that the problem of searching within a list of length n (when all we know is that the list has previously been sorted) is in $O(\log_2 n)$ because the binary search algorithm solves the problem. Moreover, researchers have shown that the searching problem is actually in $\Theta(\log_2 n)$ so the binary search represents an optimal solution for that problem. In contrast, we know that the problem of sorting a list of length n (when we know nothing about the original distribution of the values in it) is in O(n2) because the insertion sort algorithm solves the problem. The problem of sorting, however, is known to be in $\Theta(n \log_2 n)$, which tells us that the insertion sort algorithm is not an optimal solution (in the context of time complexity).

An example of a better solution to the sorting problem is the merge sort algorithm. Its approach is to merge small, sorted portions of the list to obtain larger sorted portions that can then be merged to obtain still larger sorted portions. Each merging process applies the merge algorithm that we encountered when discussing sequential files (Figure 9.15). For convenience, we present it again in Figure 12.8, this time in the context of merging two lists. The complete (recursive) merge sort algorithm is presented as the function called `MergeSort` in Figure 12.9. When asked to sort a list, this function first checks to see if the list is shorter than two entries. If so, the function's task is complete. If not, the function divides the list into two pieces, asks other copies of the function `MergeSort` to sort these pieces, and then merges these sorted pieces together to obtain the final sorted version of the list.

To analyze the complexity of this algorithm, we first consider the number of comparisons between list entries that must be made in merging a list of length r with a list of length s. The merge process proceeds by repeatedly comparing an entry from one list with an entry from the other and placing the "smaller" of the two entries in the output list. Thus each time a comparison is made, the number of entries still to be considered is reduced by one. Because there are only $r + s$ entries to begin with, we conclude that the process of merging the two lists will involve no more than $r + s$ comparisons.

We now consider the entire merge sort algorithm. It attacks the task of sorting a list of length n in such a way that the initial sorting problem is reduced to two

Figure 12.8 A `MergeLists` function for merging two lists

```
def MergeLists(InputListA, InputListB, OutputList):

  if (both input lists are empty):
    Stop, with OutputList empty.
  if (InputListA is empty):
    Declare it to be exhausted.
  else:
    Declare its first entry to be its current entry.
  if (InputListB is empty):
    Declare it to be exhausted.
  else:
    Declare its first entry to be its current entry.
  while (neither input list is exhausted):
    Put the "smaller" current entry in OutputList.
    if (that current entry is the last entry in its corresponding input list):
      Declare that input list to be exhausted.
    else:
      Declare the next entry in that input list to be the list's current entry.
  Starting with the current entry in the input list that is not exhausted,
      copy the remaining entries to OutputList.
```

smaller problems, each of which is asked to sort a list of length approximately n/2. These two problems are in turn reduced to a total of four problems of sorting lists of length approximately n/4. This division process can be summarized by the tree structure in Figure 12.10, where each node of the tree represents a single problem in the recursive process and the branches below a node represent the smaller problems derived from the parent. Hence, we can find the total number of comparisons that occur in the entire sorting process by adding together the number of comparisons that occur at the nodes in the tree.

Let us first determine the number of comparisons made across each level of the tree. Observe that each node appearing across any level of the tree has the task of sorting a unique segment of the original list. This is accomplished by the merge process and therefore requires no more comparisons than there are entries in the list segment, as we have already argued. Hence, each level of the tree requires no more comparisons than the total number of entries in the list segments, and because the segments across a given level of the tree represent disjoint portions of the original list, this total is no greater than the length of the

Figure 12.9 The merge sort algorithm implemented as a function `MergeSort`

```
def MergeSort(List):
  if (List has more than one entry):
    MergeSort(the first half of List)
    MergeSort(the second half of List)
    MergeLists(the first and second halves of List) to produce
        a sorted version of List.
```

Figure 12.10 The hierarchy of problems generated by the merge sort algorithm

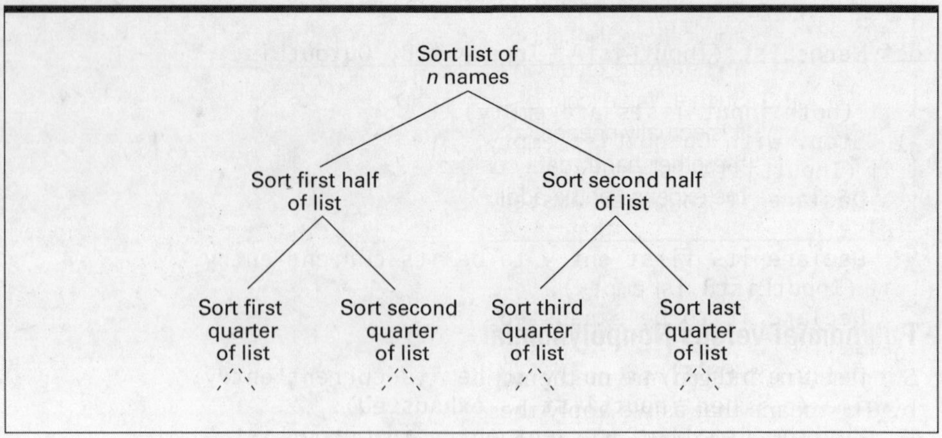

original list. Consequently, each level of the tree involves no more than n comparisons. (Of course the lowest level involves sorting lists of length less than two, which involves no comparisons at all.)

Now we determine the number of levels in the tree. For this, observe that the process of dividing problems into smaller problems continues until lists of length less than two are obtained. Thus the number of levels in the tree is determined by the number of times that, starting with the value n, we can repeatedly divide by two until the result is no larger than one, which is $\log_2 n$. More precisely, there are no more than $\lceil \log_2 n \rceil$ levels of the tree that involve comparisons, where the notation $\lceil \log_2 n \rceil$ represents the value of $\log_2 n$ rounded up to the next integer.

Finally, the total number of comparisons made by the merge sort algorithm when sorting a list of length n is obtained by multiplying the number of comparisons made at each level of the tree by the number of levels in which comparisons are made. We conclude that this is no larger than $n \lceil \log_2 n \rceil$. Because the graph of $n \lceil \log_2 n \rceil$ has the same general shape as the graph of $n \log_2 n$, we conclude that the merge sort algorithm belongs to $O(n \log_2 n)$. Combining this with the fact that researchers tell us that the sorting problem has complexity $\Theta(n \log_2 n)$ implies that the merge sort algorithm represents an optimal solution to the sorting problem.

Space Complexity

An alternative to measuring complexity in terms of time is to measure storage space requirements instead—resulting in a measure known as **space complexity.** That is, the space complexity of a problem is determined by the amount of storage space required to solve the problem. In the text we have seen that the time complexity of sorting a list with n entries is $O(n \lg n)$. The space complexity of the same problem is no more than $O(n + 1) = O(n)$. After all, sorting a list with n entries using the insertion sort requires space for the list itself plus space to store a single entry on a temporary basis. Thus, if we were asked to sort longer and longer lists, we would find that the time required for each task would increase more rapidly than the space required. This is in fact a common phenomenon. Because it takes time to use space, a problem's space complexity never grows more rapidly than its time complexity.

There are often tradeoffs made between time and space complexity. In some applications it might be advantageous to perform certain computations in advance and store the results in a table from which they can be retrieved quickly when needed. Such a "table lookup" technique decreases the time required to obtain a result once it is actually needed, at the expense of the additional space required by the table. On the other hand, data compression is often used to reduce storage requirements at the expense of the additional time required to compress and decompress the data.

Polynomial versus Nonpolynomial Problems

Suppose f(n) and g(n) are mathematical expressions. To say that g(n) is bounded by f(n) means that as we apply these expressions to larger and larger values of n, the value of f(n) will ultimately become greater than that of g(n) and remain greater than g(n) for all larger values of n. In other words, that g(n) is bounded by f(n) means that the graph of f(n) will be above the graph of g(n) for "large" values of n. For instance, the expression $\log_2 n$ is bounded by the expression n (Figure 12.11a), and $n \log_2 n$ is bounded by n^2 (Figure 12.11b).

We say that a problem is a **polynomial problem** if the problem is in O(f(n)), where the expression f(n) is either a polynomial itself or bounded by a polynomial. The collection of all polynomial problems is represented by **P.** Note that our previous investigations tell us that the problems of searching a list and of sorting a list belong to P.

To say that a problem is a polynomial problem is a statement about the time required to solve the problem. We often say that a problem in P can be solved in polynomial time or that the problem has a polynomial time solution. Identifying the problems that belong to P is of major importance in computer science because it is closely related to questions regarding whether problems have practical solutions. Indeed, problems that are outside the class P are characterized as having extremely long execution times, even for inputs of moderate size. Consider, for example, a problem whose solution requires 2^n steps. The exponential expression 2^n is not bounded by any polynomial—if f(n) is a polynomial, then as we increase

Figure 12.11 Graphs of the mathematical expressions n, $\log_2$ n, n $\log_2$ n, and n^2

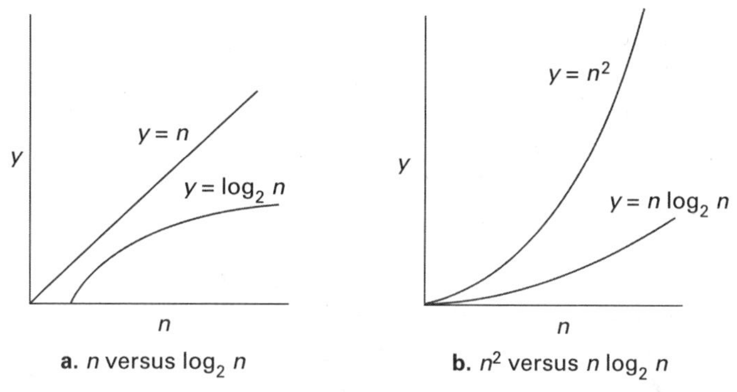

the value of n, we will find that the values of 2^n will ultimately be larger than those of f(n). This means that an algorithm with complexity $\Theta(2n)$ will generally be less efficient, and thus require more time, than an algorithm with complexity $\Theta(f(n))$. An algorithm whose complexity is identified by an exponential expression is said to require exponential time.

As a particular example, consider the problem of listing all possible subcommittees that can be formed from a group of n people. Because there are $2^n - 1$ such subcommittees (we allow a subcommittee to consist of the entire group but do not consider the empty set to be a subcommittee), any algorithm that solves this problem must have at least $2^n - 1$ steps and thus a complexity at least that large. But, the expression $2^n - 1$, being an exponential expression, is not bounded by any polynomial. Hence any solution to this problem becomes enormously time-consuming as the size of the group from which the committees are selected increases.

In contrast to our subcommittee problem, whose complexity is large merely because of the size of its output, problems exist whose complexities are large even though their ultimate output is merely a simple yes or no answer. An example involves the ability to answer questions about the truth of statements involving the addition of real numbers. For instance, we can easily recognize that the answer to the question "Is it true that there is a real number that when added to itself produces the value 6?" is yes, whereas the answer to "Is it true that there is a nonzero real number which when added to itself is 0?" is no. However, as such questions become more involved, our ability to answer them begins to fade. If we found ourselves faced with many such questions, we might be tempted to turn to a computer program for assistance. Unfortunately, the ability to answer these questions has been shown to require exponential time, so even a computer ultimately fails to produce answers in a timely manner as the questions become more involved.

The fact that the problems that are theoretically solvable but are not in P have such enormous time complexities leads us to conclude that these problems are essentially unsolvable from a practical point of view. Computer scientists call these problems intractable. In turn, the class P has come to represent an important boundary that distinguishes intractable problems from those that might have practical solutions. Thus an understanding of the class P has become an important pursuit within computer science.

NP Problems

Let us now consider the traveling salesperson problem, which involves a traveling salesperson who must visit each of her clients in different cities without exceeding her travel budget. His problem, then, is to find a path (starting from her home, connecting the cities involved, and returning to her home) whose total length does not exceed her allowed mileage.

The traditional solution to this problem is to consider the potential paths in a systematic manner, comparing the length of each path to the mileage limit until either an acceptable path is found or all possibilities have been considered. This approach, however, does not produce a polynomial time solution. As the number of cities increases, the number of paths to be tested grows more rapidly than any polynomial. Thus, solving the traveling salesperson problem in this manner is impractical for cases involving large numbers of cities.

We conclude that to solve the traveling salesperson problem in a reasonable amount of time, we must find a faster algorithm. Our appetite is whetted by the observation that if a satisfactory path exists and we happen to select it first, our present algorithm terminates quickly. In particular, the following list of instructions can be executed quickly and has the potential of solving the problem:

```
Pick one of the possible paths, and compute its total distance.
if (this distance is not greater than the allowable mileage):
  Declare a success.
else:
  Declare nothing.
```

However, this set of instructions is not an algorithm in the technical sense. Its first instruction is ambiguous in that it does not specify which path is to be selected nor does it specify how the decision is to be made. Instead it relies on the creativity of the mechanism executing the program to make the decision on its own. We say that such instructions are nondeterministic, and we call an "algorithm" containing such statements a **nondeterministic algorithm.**

Note that as the number of cities increases, the time required to execute the preceding nondeterministic algorithm grows relatively slowly. The process of selecting a path is merely that of producing a list of the cities, which can be done in a time proportional to the number of cities involved. Moreover, the time required to compute the total distance along the chosen path is also proportional to the number of cities to be visited, and the time required to compare this total to the mileage limit is independent of the number of cities. In turn, the time required to execute the nondeterministic algorithm is bounded by a polynomial. Thus it is possible to solve the traveling salesperson problem by a nondeterministic algorithm in polynomial time.

Of course, our nondeterministic solution is not totally satisfactory. It relies on a lucky guess. But its existence is enough to suggest that perhaps there is a deterministic solution to the traveling salesperson problem that runs in polynomial time. Whether this is true remains an open question. In fact, the traveling salesperson problem is one of many problems that are known to have nondeterministic solutions that execute in polynomial time but for which no deterministic polynomial time solution has yet been found. The tantalizing efficiency of the nondeterministic solutions to these problems causes some to hope that efficient deterministic solutions will be found someday, yet most believe that these problems are just complex enough to escape the capabilities of efficient deterministic algorithms.

A problem that can be solved in polynomial time by a nondeterministic algorithm is called a **nondeterministic polynomial problem,** or an **NP problem** for short. It is customary to denote the class of NP problems by **NP.** Note that all the problems in P are also in NP, because any (deterministic) algorithm can have a nondeterministic instruction added to it without affecting its performance.

Whether all of the NP problems are also in P, however, is an open question, as demonstrated by the traveling salesperson problem. This is perhaps the most widely known unsolved problem in computer science today. Its solution could have significant consequences. For example, in the next section we will learn that encryption systems have been designed whose integrity relies on the enormous time required to solve problems similar to the traveling salesperson problem. If it turns out that efficient solutions to such problems exist, these encryption systems will be compromised.

Efforts to resolve the question of whether the class NP is, in fact, the same as the class P have led to the discovery of a class of problems within the class NP known as the **NP-complete problems.** These problems have the property that a polynomial time solution for any one of them would provide a polynomial time solution for all the other problems in NP as well. That is, if a (deterministic) algorithm can be found that solves one of the NP-complete problems in polynomial time, then that algorithm can be extended to solve any other problem in NP in polynomial time. In turn, the class NP would be the same as the class P. The traveling salesperson problem is an example of an NP-complete problem.

In summary, we have found that problems can be classified as either solvable (having an algorithmic solution) or unsolvable (not having an algorithmic solution), as depicted in Figure 12.12. Moreover, within the class of solvable problems are two subclasses. One is the collection of polynomial problems that contains those problems with practical solutions. The second is the collection of nonpolynomial problems whose solutions are practical for only relatively small or carefully selected inputs. Finally, there are the mysterious NP problems that thus far have evaded precise classification.

Deterministic versus Nondeterministic

In many cases, there is a fine line between a deterministic and a nondeterministic "algorithm." However, the distinction is quite clear and significant. A deterministic algorithm does not rely on the creative capabilities of the mechanism executing the algorithm, whereas a nondeterministic "algorithm" might. For instance, compare the instruction

```
Go to the next intersection and turn either right or left.
```

and the instruction

```
Go to the next intersection and turn right or left depending on
what the person standing on the corner tells you to do.
```

In either case the action taken by the person following the directions is not determined prior to actually executing the instruction. However, the first instruction requires the person following the directions to make a decision based on his or her own judgment and is therefore nondeterministic. The second instruction makes no such requirements of the person following the directions—the person is told what to do at each stage. If several different people follow the first instruction, some might turn right, while others might turn left. If several people follow the second instruction and receive the same information, they will all turn in the same direction. Herein lies an important distinction between deterministic and nondeterministic "algorithms." If a deterministic algorithm is executed repeatedly with the same input data, the same actions will be performed each time. However, a nondeterministic "algorithm" might produce different actions when repeated under identical conditions.

Figure 12.12 A graphic summation of the problem classification

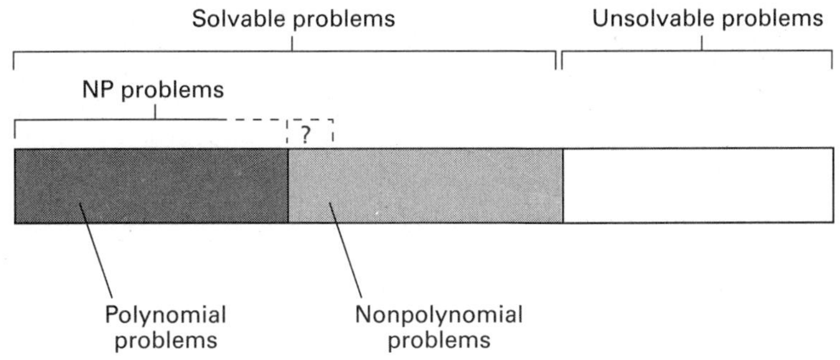

Questions & Exercises

1. Suppose a problem can be solved by an algorithm in $\Theta(2^n)$. What can we conclude about the complexity of the problem?
2. Suppose a problem can be solved by an algorithm in $\Theta(n^2)$ as well as another algorithm in $\Theta(2^n)$. Will one algorithm always outperform the other?
3. List all of the subcommittees that can be formed from a committee consisting of the two members Alice and Bill. List all the subcommittees that can be formed from the committee consisting of Alice, Bill, and Carol. What about the subcommittees from Alice, Bill, Carol, and David?
4. Give an example of a polynomial problem. Give an example of a nonpolynomial problem. Give an example of an NP problem that as yet has not been shown to be a polynomial problem.
5. If the complexity of algorithm X is greater than that of algorithm Y, is algorithm X necessarily harder to understand than algorithm Y? Explain your answer.

12.6 Public-Key Cryptography

In some cases the fact that a problem is difficult to solve has been turned into an asset rather than a liability. Of particular interest is the problem of finding the factors of a given integer—a problem for which an efficient solution has yet to be found, if one even exists. For example, armed with only paper and pencil, you might find the task of finding the factors of relatively small values such as 2,173 to be time consuming, and if the number involved was so large that its representation required several hundred digits, the task would be intractable even if modern technology were applied using the best factoring techniques currently known.

The failure to find an efficient way of determining the factors of large integers has long been a thorn in the side of many mathematicians, but in the field of cryptography it has been applied to produce a popular method of encrypting and decrypting messages. This method is known as the **RSA algorithm**—a name chosen to honor its inventors Ron Rivest, Adi Shamir, and Len Adleman. It is a means of encrypting messages using one set of values known as the **encrypting keys** and decrypting those messages using another set of values known as the **decrypting keys.** People who know the encrypting keys can encrypt messages, but they cannot decrypt messages. The only person who can decrypt messages is the one holding the decrypting keys. Thus the encrypting keys can be widely distributed without violating the security of the system.

Such cryptography systems are called **public-key encryption** systems, a term that reflects the fact that the keys used to encrypt messages can be public knowledge without degrading the system's security. Indeed, the encrypting keys are often called the **public keys,** whereas the decrypting keys are called the **private keys** (Figure 12.13).

Modular Notation

To describe the RSA public-key encryption system, it is convenient to use the notation $x \% m$, which is read "x modulo m" or usually just "x mod m," to represent the remainder obtained when the value x is divided by m. Thus, 9 % 7 is 2 because 9 ÷ 7 produces a remainder of 2. Similarly, 24 % 7 is 3 because 24 ÷ 7 produces a remainder of 3, and 14 % 7 is 0 because 14 ÷ 7 produces a remainder of 0. Note that x % m is x itself if x is an integer in the range 0 to m − 1. For example, 4 % 9 is 4.

Mathematics tells us that if p and q are prime numbers and m is an integer between 0 and pq (the product of p and q) then

$$1 = m^{k(p-1)(q-1)} \% pq$$

for any positive integer k. Although we will not justify this claim here, it is advantageous to consider an example to clarify the statement. Suppose, then, that p and

Figure 12.13 Public key cryptography

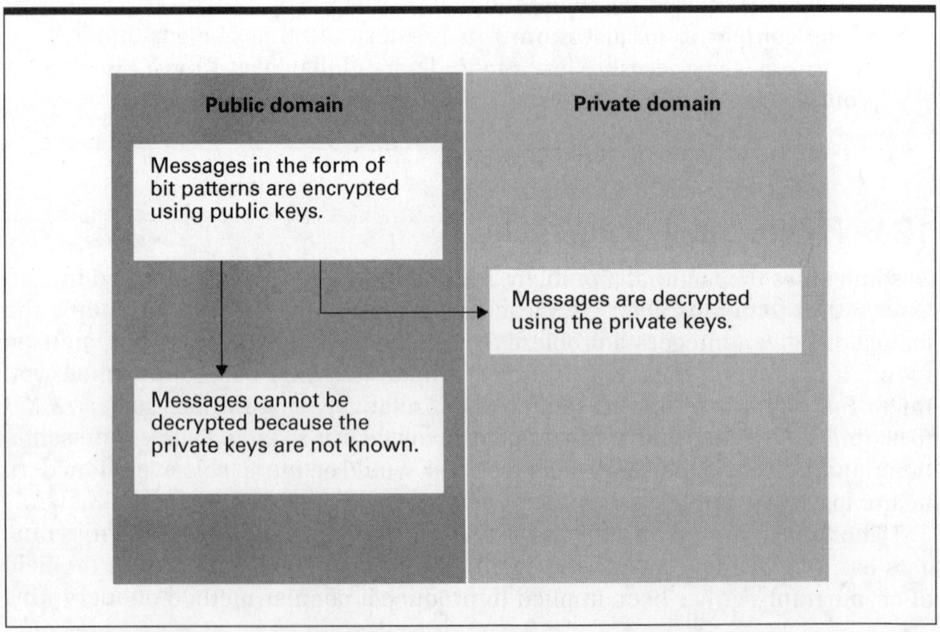

q are the prime numbers 3 and 5, respectively, and m is the integer 4. Then the statement claims that for any positive integer k, the value $m^{k(p-1)(q-1)}$ divided by 15 (the product of 3 and 5) will produce the remainder 1. In particular, if $k = 1$, then

$$m^{k(p-1)(q-1)} = 4^{1(3-1)(5-1)} = 4^8 = 65{,}536$$

which when divided by 15 produces the remainder 1 as claimed. Moreover, if $k = 2$, then

$$m^{k(p-1)(q-1)} = 4^{2(3-1)(5-1)} = 4^{16} = 4{,}294{,}967{,}296$$

which when divided by 15 again produces the remainder 1. Indeed, we would obtain the remainder 1 regardless of the positive integer chosen for k.

RSA Public-Key Cryptography

We are now prepared to construct and analyze a public-key encryption system based on the RSA algorithm. First we pick two distinct prime numbers p and q, whose product we will represent by n. Then we pick two other positive integers e and d such that $e \times d = k(p - 1)(q - 1) + 1$, for some positive integer k. We are calling these values e and d because they will be part of the encryption and decryption process, respectively. (The fact that values e and d can be chosen to satisfy the preceding equation is another fact from mathematics that we will not pursue here.)

Thus we have selected five values: p, q, n, e, and d. The values e and n are the encrypting keys. The values d and n are decrypting keys. The values p and q are only used for constructing the encryption system.

Let us consider a specific example for clarification. Suppose we choose 7 and 13 as the values for p and q. Then $n = 7 \times 13 = 91$. Moreover, the values 5 and 29 could be used for e and d because $5 \times 29 = 145 = 144 + 1 = 2(7 - 1)(13 - 1) + 1 = 2(p - 1)(q - 1) + 1$ as required. Thus, the encrypting keys are $n = 91$ and $e = 5$, and the decrypting keys are $n = 91$ and $d = 29$. We distribute the encrypting keys to anyone who might want to send us messages, but we keep the decrypting keys (as well as the values of p and q) to ourselves.

We now consider how messages are encrypted. To this end, suppose a message is currently encoded as a bit pattern (perhaps using ASCII or Unicode) and the value of the pattern, when interpreted as a binary representation, is less than n. (If it is not less than n, we would chop the message into smaller segments and encrypt each segment individually.)

Let us assume that our message, when interpreted as a binary representation, represents the value m. Then, the encrypted version of the message is the binary representation of the value $c = m^e \% n$. That is, the encrypted message is the binary representation of the remainder obtained by dividing m^e by n.

In particular, if someone wanted to encrypt the message 10111 using the encrypting keys $n = 91$ and $e = 5$ as developed in the previous example, he or she would first recognize that 10111 is the binary representation for 23, then compute $23^e = 23^5 = 6{,}436{,}343$, and finally divide this value by $n = 91$ to obtain the remainder 4. The encrypted version of the message would therefore be 100, which is the binary representation of 4.

To decrypt a message that represents the value c in binary notation, we compute the value $c^d \% n$. That is, we compute the value c^d, divide the result by n, and retain the remainder. Indeed, this remainder will be the value m of the original message because

$$\begin{aligned} c^d \% n &= m^{e \times d} \% n \\ &= m^{k(p-1)(q-1)+1} \% n \\ &= m \times m^{k(p-1)(q-1)} \% n \\ &= m \% n \\ &= m \end{aligned}$$

Here we have used the facts that $m^{k(p-1)(q-1)} \% n = m^{k(p-1)(q-1)} \% pq = 1$ and that $m \% n = m$ (because $m < n$), as previously claimed.

Continuing with the preceding example, if we received the message 100, we would recognize this as the value 4, compute the value $4^d = 4^{29} = 288, 230, 376, 151, 711, 744$, and divide this value by $n = 91$ to obtain the remainder 23, which produces the original message 10111 when expressed in binary notation.

In summary, an RSA public-key encryption system is generated by selecting two prime integers, p and q, from which the values n, e, and d are generated. The values n and e are used to encrypt messages and are therefore the public keys. The values n and d are used to decrypt messages and are the private keys (Figure 12.14). The beauty of the system is that knowing how to encrypt messages does not allow one to decrypt messages. Thus the encrypting keys n and e can be widely distributed. If your adversaries were to obtain these keys, they would still not be able to decrypt the messages they intercept. Only a person who knows the decrypting keys can decrypt messages.

Figure 12.14 Establishing an RSA public key encryption system

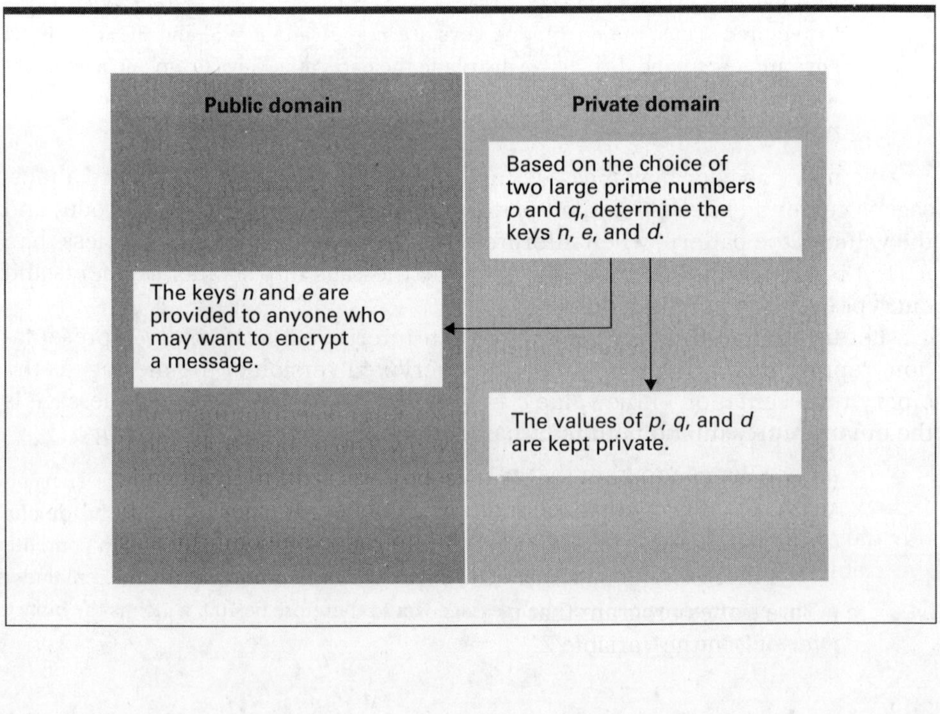

The security of this system is based on the assumption that knowing the encrypting keys n and e does not allow one to compute the decrypting keys n and d. However, there are algorithms for doing exactly that! One approach would be to factor the value n to discover the values p and q, and then to determine d by finding a value k such that $k(p - 1)(q - 1) + 1$ is evenly divided by e (the quotient would then be d). On the other hand, the first step in this process can be time-consuming—especially if the values of p and q were chosen to be large. In fact, if p and q are so large that their binary representations require hundreds of digits, then the best known factoring algorithms would require years before the identities of p and q could be revealed from n. In turn, the content of an encrypted message would remain secure long after its significance had deteriorated.

To this date, no one has found an efficient way of decrypting messages based on RSA cryptography without knowing the decrypting keys, and thus public-key encryption based on the RSA algorithm is widely used to obtain privacy when communicating over the Internet.

Questions & Exercises

1. Find the factors of 66,043. (Don't waste too much time on this one. The point is that it can be time-consuming.)
2. Using the public keys $n = 91$ and $e = 5$, encrypt the message 101.
3. Using the private keys $n = 91$ and $d = 29$, decrypt the message 10.
4. Find the appropriate value for the decrypting keys n and d in an RSA public-key cryptography system based on the primes $p = 7$ and $q = 19$ and the encryption key $e = 5$.

Chapter Review Problems

1. Show how a structure of the form

```
while X equals 0:
    .
    .
    .
```

can be simulated with Bare Bones.

2. Write a Bare Bones program that places a 1 in the variable Z if the variable X is less than or equal to the variable Y, and places a 0 in the variable Z otherwise.

3. Write a Bare Bones program that places the Xth power of 2 in the variable Z.

4. In each of the following cases write a program sequence in Bare Bones that performs the indicated activity:
   a. Assign 0 to Z if the value of X is even; otherwise assign 1 to Z.
   b. Calculate the sum of the integers from 0 to X.

5. Write a Bare Bones routine that divides the value of X by the value of Y. Disregard any remainder; that is, 1 divided by 2 produces 0, and 5 divided by 3 produces 1.

6. Describe the function computed by the following Bare Bones program, assuming the

function's inputs are represented by X and Y and its output by Z:

```
copy X to Z
copy Y to Aux
while Aux not 0:
  decr Z
  decr Aux
```

7. Describe the function computed by the following Bare Bones program, assuming the function's inputs are represented by X and Y and its output by Z:

```
clear Z
copy X to Aux1
copy Y to Aux2
while Aux1 not 0:
  while Aux2 not 0:
    decr Z
    decr Aux2
  decr Aux1
```

8. Write a Bare Bones program that computes the exclusive-OR of the variables X and Y, leaving the result in the variable Z. You might assume that X and Y start only with integer values of 0 and 1.

9. Show that if we allow instructions in a Bare Bones program to be labeled with integer values and replace the while loop structure with the conditional branch represented by the form

```
if name not 0:
  goto label
```

where name is any variable and label is an integer value used elsewhere to label an instruction, then the new language will still be a universal programming language.

10. In this chapter we saw how the statement

```
copy name1 to name2
```

could be simulated in Bare Bones. Show how that statement could still be simulated if the while loop structure in Bare Bones were replaced with a posttest loop expressed in the form

```
repeat:...
  until (name equals 0)
```

11. Show that the Bare Bones language would remain a universal language if the while statement were replaced with a posttest loop expressed in the form

```
repeat:
  ...
  until (name equals 0)
```

12. Give an example of a language that is not deterministic.

13. Design a Turing machine that recognizes the set of palindromes in {a, b}* such that the number of as is a multiple of three.

14. Suppose a pattern of 0s and 1s on the tape of a Turing machine is delimited by asterisks at either end. Design a Turing machine that rotates this pattern one cell to the left, assuming that the machine starts with the current cell being the asterisk at the right end of the pattern.

15. Design a Turing machine that places 0s and 1s in all the cells to the right of the current cell until it reaches a cell containing a plus symbol.

16. Summarize the Church–Turing thesis.

17. Is the following Bare Bones program self-terminating? Explain your answer.

```
copy X to Y
incr Y
incr Y
while X not 0:
  decr X
  decr X
  decr Y
  decr Y
decr Y
while Y not 0:
  incr X
  decr Y
while X not 0:
```

18. Is the following Bare Bones program self-terminating? Explain your answer.

```
while X not 0:
```

19. Is the following Bare Bones program self-terminating? Explain your answer.

```
while X not 0:
  decr X
```

20. Analyze the validity of the following pair of statements:

```
The next statement is true.
The previous statement is false.
```

21. Analyze the validity of the statement "The cook on a ship cooks for all those and only those who do not cook for themselves." (Who cooks for the cook?)

22. Suppose you were in a country where each person was either a truth teller or a liar. (A truth teller always tells the truth, a liar always lies.) What single question could you ask a person that would allow you to detect whether that person was a truth teller or a liar?

23. When is a function said to be Turing computable? Explain your answer.

24. What is meant by a halting problem? Explain how a halting problem is undecidable.

25. Suppose you needed to find out if anyone in a group of people had a birthday on a particular date. One approach would be to ask the members one at a time. If you took this approach, the occurrence of what event would tell you that there was such a person? What event would tell you that there was no such person? Now suppose that you wanted to find out if at least one of the positive integers has a particular property and you applied the same approach of systematically testing the integers one at a time. If, in fact, some integer has the property, how would you find out? If, however, no integer has the property, how would you find out? Is the task of testing to see if a conjecture is true necessarily symmetric with the task of testing to see if it is false?

26. Is the problem of searching through a binary tree for a particular value a polynomial problem? Justify your answer.

27. Design an algorithm for calculating the Fibonacci series of a given number. Is your solution efficient? Is your solution a polynomial or nonpolynomial one?

28. Give an example of a scenario in which there is a fine line of distinction between deterministic and nondeterministic algorithms.

29. Design a Turing machine for a palindrome detector. The program should check a string of symbols on the tape and return a `true(1)` if it is a palindrome, else `false(0)`.

30. Charlie Programmer is given the problem of dividing a group (of an even number of people) into two disjoint subgroups of equal size so that the difference between the total ages of each subgroup is as large as possible. He proposes the solution of forming all possible subgroup pairs, computing the difference between the age totals of each pair, and selecting the pair with the largest difference. Mary Programmer, on the other hand, proposes that the original group first be sorted by age and then divided into two subgroups by forming one subgroup from the younger half of the sorted group and the other from the older half. What is the complexity of each of these solutions? Is the problem itself of polynomial, NP, or nonpolynomial complexity?

31. Prove that if L is recognized by a Turing machine with a two-way infinite tape, it can be recognized by a Turing machine with a one-way infinite tape.

32. Suppose a lottery is based on correctly picking four integer values, each in the range from 1 to 50. Moreover, suppose that the jackpot grows so large that it becomes profitable to buy a separate lottery ticket for each possible combination. If it takes one second to buy a single ticket, how long would it take to buy one ticket for each combination? How would the time requirement change if the lottery required picking five numbers instead of four? What does this problem have to do with the material from this chapter?

33. Is the following algorithm deterministic? Explain your answer.

```
def mystery(Number):
  if (Number > 5):
    answer "yes"
  else:
    pick a value less than 5 and give
      this number as the answer
```

34. Is the following algorithm deterministic? Explain your answer.

```
Drive straight ahead.
At the third intersection, ask the
   person standing on the corner if you
   should turn right or left.
Turn according to that person's
   directions.
Drive two more blocks and stop
   there.
```

35. Identify the points of nondeterminism in the following algorithm:

```
Select three numbers between 1 and 100.
if (the sum of the selected
   numbers is greater than 150):
   answer "yes"
else:
   select one of the chosen numbers
     and give that number as the
     answer
```

36. Does the following algorithm have a polynomial or nonpolynomial time complexity? Explain your answer.

```
def mystery(ListOfNumbers):
   Pick a collection of numbers from
     ListOfNumbers.
   if (the numbers in that collection
     add to 125):
     answer "yes"
   else:
     do not give an answer
```

37. Which of the following problems are in the class P?

a. For a given set S of n integers, sort S.
b. The traveling salesperson problem.
c. The Hamilton Path problem.
d. The Node Cover problem.

38. Summarize the distinction between stating that a problem is a polynomial problem and stating that it is a nondeterministic polynomial problem.

39. Explain how a Turing machine can be used to determine whether a given number is prime.

40. Suppose you are given two algorithms for solving the same problem. One algorithm has time complexity n^4 and the other has time complexity 4n. For what size inputs is the former more efficient than the latter?

41. Suppose we were faced with solving the traveling salesperson problem in a context involving 15 cities in which any two cities were connected by a unique road. How many different paths through the cities would there be? How long would it take to compute the length of all of these paths assuming that the length of a path can be computed in one microsecond?

42. How many comparisons between names are made if the merge sort algorithm (Figures 12.9 and 12.8) is applied to the list Alice, Bob, Carol, and David? How many are required if the list is Alice, Bob, Carol, David, and Elaine?

43. How does a universal Turing machine function? Explain with an example.

44. Design an algorithm for finding integer solutions for equations of the form $x^2 + y^2 = n$, where n is some given positive integer. Determine the time complexity of your algorithm.

45. Another problem that falls in the NP-complete category is the **knapsack problem,** which is the problem of finding which numbers from a list are the ones whose sum is a particular value. For example, the numbers 257, 388, and 782 are the entries in the list

```
642 257 771 388 391 782 304
```

whose sum is 1427. Find the entries whose sum is 1723. What algorithm did you apply? What is the complexity of that algorithm?

46. Identify similarities between the traveling salesperson problem and the knapsack problem (see question 45).

47. The following algorithm for sorting a list is called the bubble sort. How many comparisons between list entries does the bubble sort require when applied to a list of n entries?

```
def BubbleSort(List):
  Counter = 1
  while (Counter < number of entries
    in List):
    N = the number of entries in List
    while (N > 1):
```

```
if (the Nth List entry is less
  than the entry preceding it):
  interchange the Nth entry with
    the preceding entry
N = N - 1
```

48. Use RSA public-key encryption to encrypt the message 1111 using the public keys $n = 119$ and $e = 5$.

49. Use RSA public-key encryption to decrypt the message 1101 using the private keys $n = 911$ and $d = 5$.

50. Suppose you know that the public keys to a public-key encryption system based on the RSA algorithm are $n = 3233$ and $e = 17$. What are the private keys? Can you solve this problem in a reasonable amount of time?

51. Find the factors of 211,397. How does this problem relate to this chapter?

52. What can be concluded if the positive integer n has no integer factors in the range from 2 to the square root of n? What does this tell you about the task of finding the factors of a positive integer?

Social Issues

The following questions are intended as a guide to the ethical/social/legal issues associated with the field of computing. The goal is not merely to answer these questions. You should also consider why you answered as you did and whether your justifications are consistent from one question to the next.

1. Suppose the best algorithm for solving a problem would require 100 years to execute. Would you consider the problem to be tractable? Why?
2. Should citizens have the right to encrypt messages in such a manner that precludes monitoring from government agencies? Does your answer provide for "proper" law enforcement? Who should decide what "proper" law enforcement is?
3. If the human mind is an algorithmic device, what consequences does Turing's thesis have in regard to humanity? To what extent do you believe that Turing machines encompass the computational abilities of the human mind?
4. We have seen that there are different computational models (finite tables, algebraic formulae, Turing machines, and so on) having different computational abilities. Are there differences in the computational capabilities of different organisms? Are there differences in the computational capabilities of different humans? If so, should humans with higher abilities be able to use those abilities to obtain higher lifestyles?
5. Today there are websites that provide road maps of most cities. These sites assist in finding particular addresses and provide zooming capabilities for viewing the layout of small neighborhoods. Starting with this reality, consider the following fictitious sequence. Suppose these map sites were enhanced with satellite photographs with similar zooming capabilities. Suppose these zooming capabilities were increased to give a more detailed image of individual buildings and the surrounding landscape. Suppose these images were enhanced to include real-time video. Suppose these video images were enhanced with infrared technology. At this point others could watch you inside your own home 24 hours a day. At what point in this progression were

your privacy rights first violated? At what point in this progression do you think we moved beyond the capabilities of current spy-satellite technology? To what degree is this scenario fictitious?

6. Suppose a company develops and patents an encryption system. Should the national government of the company have the right to use the system as it sees fit in the name of national security? Should the national government of the company have the right to restrict the company's commercial use of the system in the name of national security? What if the company is a multinational organization?
7. Suppose you buy a product whose internal structure is encrypted. Do you have the right to decrypt the underlying structure? If so, do you have the right to use that information in a commercial manner? What about a noncommercial manner? What if the encryption was done using a secret encryption system, and you discover the secret. Do you have the right to share that secret?
8. Some years ago the philosopher John Dewey (1859–1952) introduced the term "responsible technology." Give some examples of what you would consider to be "responsible technology." Based on your examples, formulate your own definition of "responsible technology." Has society practiced "responsible technology" over the last 100 years? Should actions be taken to ensure that it does? If so, what actions? If not, why?

Additional Reading

Garey, M. R., and D. S. Johnson. *Computers and Intractability.* New York: W. H. Freeman, 1979.

Hamburger, H., and D. Richards. *Logic and Language Models for Computer Science.* Englewood Cliffs, NJ: Prentice-Hall, 2002.

Hofstadter, D. R. *Gödel, Escher, Bach: An Eternal Golden Braid.* St. Paul, MN: Vintage, 1980.

Hopcroft, J. E., R. Motwani, and J. D. Ullman. *Introduction to Automata Theory, Languages, and Computation,* 3rd ed. Boston, MA: Addison-Wesley, 2007.

Lewis, H. R., and C. H. Papadimitriou. *Elements of the Theory of Computation,* 2nd ed. Englewood Cliffs, NJ: Prentice-Hall, 1998.

Rich, E. *Automata. Computability, and Complexity: Theory and Application.* Upper Saddle River, NJ: Prentice-Hall, 2008.

Sipser, M. *Introduction to the Theory of Computation,* 3rd ed. Boston, MA: Cengage Learning, 2012.

Smith, C., and E. Kinber. *Theory of Computing: A Gentle Introduction.* Englewood Cliffs, NJ: Prentice-Hall, 2001.

Sudkamp, T. A. *Languages and Machines: An Introduction to the Theory of Computer Science,* 3rd ed. Boston, MA: Addison-Wesley, 2006.

Appendixes

- A ASCII
- B Circuits to Manipulate Two's Complement Representations
- C A Simple Machine Language
- D High-Level Programming Languages
- E The Equivalence of Iterative and Recursive Structures
- F Answers to Questions & Exercises

appendix

A

ASCII

The following is a partial listing of ASCII code, in which each bit pattern has been extended with a 0 on its left to produce the 8-bit pattern commonly used today. The hexadecimal value of each 8-bit pattern is given in the third column.

Symbol	ASCII	Hex	Symbol	ASCII	Hex	Symbol	ASCII	Hex
line feed	00001010	0A	>	00111110	3E	^	01011110	5E
carriage return	00001011	0B	?	00111111	3F	_	01011111	5F
space	00100000	20	@	01000000	40	`	01100000	60
!	00100001	21	A	01000001	41	a	01100001	61
"	00100010	22	B	01000010	42	b	01100010	62
#	00100011	23	C	01000011	43	c	01100011	63
$	00100100	24	D	01000100	44	d	01100100	64
%	00100101	25	E	01000101	45	e	01100101	65
&	00100110	26	F	01000110	46	f	01100110	66
'	00100111	27	G	01000111	47	g	01100111	67
(	00101000	28	H	01001000	48	h	01101000	68
)	00101001	29	I	01001001	49	i	01101001	69
*	00101010	2A	J	01001010	4A	j	01101010	6A
+	00101011	2B	K	01001011	4B	k	01101011	6B
'	00101100	2C	L	01001100	4C	l	01101100	6C
.	00101101	2D	M	01001101	4D	m	01101101	6D
/	00101110	2E	N	01001110	4E	n	01101110	6E
0	00101111	2F	O	01001111	4F	o	01101111	6F
1	00110000	30	P	01010000	50	p	01110000	70
2	00110001	31	Q	01010001	51	q	01110001	71
3	00110010	32	R	01010010	52	r	01110010	72
4	00110011	33	S	01010011	53	s	01110011	73
5	00110100	34	T	01010100	54	t	01110100	74
6	00110101	35	U	01010101	55	u	01110101	75
7	00110110	36	V	01010110	56	v	01110110	76
8	00110111	37	W	01010111	57	w	01110111	77
9	00111000	38	X	01011000	58	x	01111000	78
:	00111001	39	Y	01011001	59	y	01111001	79
;	00111010	3A	Z	01011010	5A	z	01111010	7A
<	00111011	3B	[	01011011	5B	{	01111011	7B
=	00111100	3C	\	01011100	5C	|	01111100	7C
	00111101	3D	]	01011101	5D	}	01111101	7D

appendix

B

Circuits to Manipulate Two's Complement Representations

This appendix presents circuits for negating and adding values represented in two's complement notation. We begin with the circuit in Figure B.1 that converts a four-bit two's complement representation to the representation for the negative of that value. For example, given the two's complement representation of 3, the circuit produces the representation for −3. It does this by following the same algorithm as presented in the text. That is, it copies the pattern from right to left until a 1 has been copied and then complements each remaining bit as it is moved from the input to the output. Because one input of the rightmost XOR gate is fixed at 0, this gate will merely pass its other input to the output. However, this output is also passed to the left as one of the inputs to the next XOR gate. If this output is 1, the next XOR gate will complement its input bit as it passes to the output. Moreover, this 1 will also be passed to the left through the OR gate to affect the next gate as well. In this manner, the first 1 that is copied to the output will also be passed to the left, where it will cause all the remaining bits to be complemented as they are moved to the output.

Figure B.1 A circuit that negates a two's complement pattern

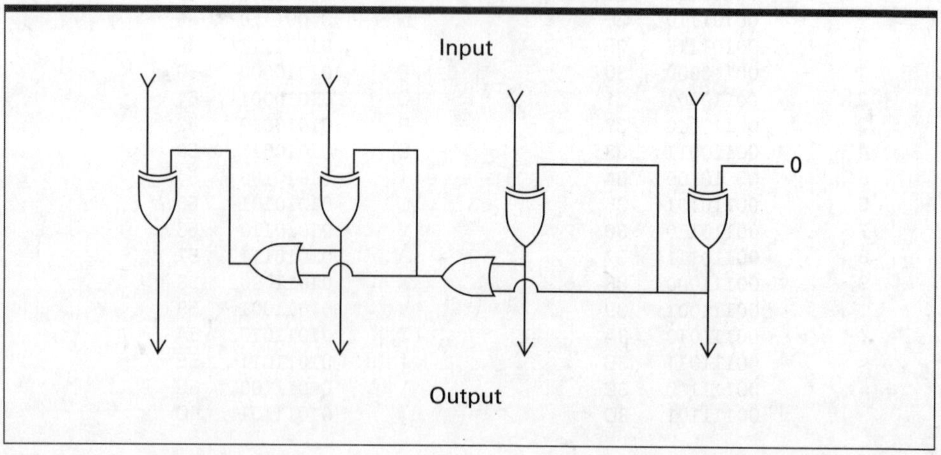

Next, let us consider the process of adding two values represented in two's complement notation. In particular, when solving the problem

+ 0110
+ 1011

we proceed from right to left in a column-by-column manner, executing the same algorithm for each column. Thus once we obtain a circuit for adding one column of such a problem, we can construct a circuit for adding many columns merely by repeating the single-column circuit.

The algorithm for adding a single column in a multiple-column addition problem is to add the two values in the current column, add that sum to any carry from the previous column, write the least significant bit of this sum in the answer, and transfer any carry to the next column. The circuit in Figure B.2 follows this same algorithm. The upper XOR gate determines the sum of the two input bits. The lower XOR gate adds this sum to the value carried from the previous column. The two AND gates together with the OR gate pass any carry to the left. In particular, a carry of 1 will be produced if the original two input bits in this column were 1 or if the sum of these bits and the carry were both 1.

Figure B.2 A circuit to add a single column in a multiple-column addition problem

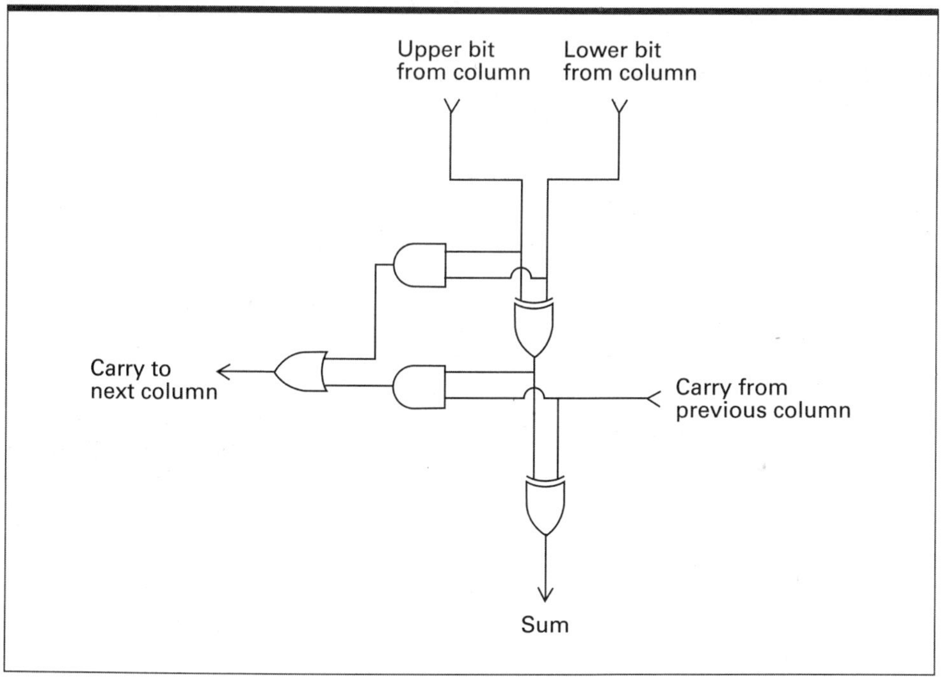

Figure B.3 shows how copies of this single-column circuit can be used to produce a circuit that computes the sum of two values represented in a four-bit two's complement system. Each rectangle represents a copy of the single-column addition circuit. Note that the carry value given to the rightmost rectangle is always 0 because there is no carry from a previous column. In a similar manner, the carry produced from the leftmost rectangle is ignored.

The circuit in Figure B.3 is known as a *ripple adder* because the carry information must propagate, or ripple, from the rightmost to the leftmost column. Although simple in composition, such circuits are slower to perform their functions than more clever versions, such as the lookahead carry adder, which minimize this column-to-column propagation. Thus the circuit in Figure B.3, although sufficient for our purposes, is not the circuit that is used in today's machines.

Figure B.3 A circuit for adding two values in a two's complement notation using four copies of the circuit in Figure B.2

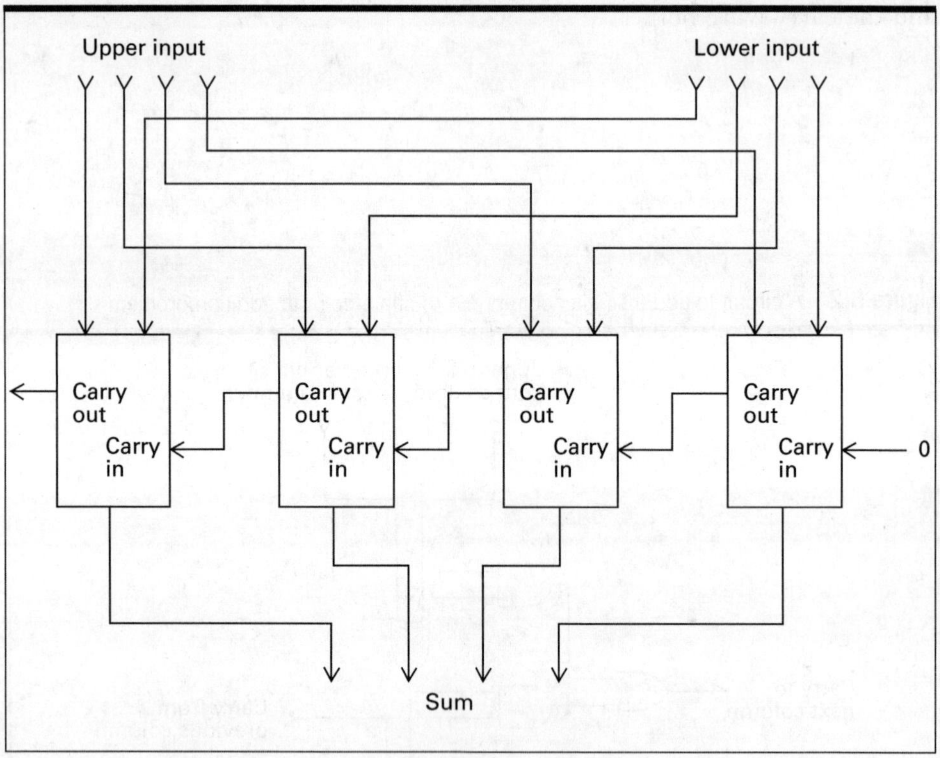

appendix

C

A Simple Machine Language

In this appendix we present a simple but representative machine language. We begin by explaining the architecture of the machine itself.

The Machine's Architecture

The machine has 16 general-purpose registers numbered 0 through F (in hexadecimal). Each register is one byte (eight bits) long. For identifying registers within instructions, each register is assigned the unique four-bit pattern that represents its register number. Thus register 0 is identified by 0000 (hexadecimal 0), and register 4 is identified by 0100 (hexadecimal 4).

There are 256 cells in the machine's main memory. Each cell is assigned a unique address consisting of an integer in the range of 0 to 255. An address can therefore be represented by a pattern of eight bits ranging from 00000000 to 11111111 (or a hexadecimal value in the range of 00 to FF).

Floating-point values are assumed to be stored in an eight-bit format discussed in Section 1.7 and summarized in Figure 1.24.

The Machine's Language

Each machine instruction is two bytes long. The first 4 bits provide the op-code; the last 12 bits make up the operand field. The table that follows lists the instructions in hexadecimal notation together with a short description of each. The letters R, S, and T are used in place of hexadecimal digits in those fields representing a register identifier that varies depending on the particular application of the instruction. The letters X and Y are used in lieu of hexadecimal digits in variable fields not representing a register.

Op-code	Operand	Description
1	RXY	LOAD the register R with the bit pattern found in the memory cell whose address is XY. *Example:* 14A3 would cause the contents of the memory cell located at address A3 to be placed in register 4.
2	RXY	LOAD the register R with the bit pattern XY. *Example:* 20A3 would cause the value A3 to be placed in register 0.

Op-code	Operand	Description
3	RXY	STORE the bit pattern found in register R in the memory cell whose address is XY. *Example:* 35B1 would cause the contents of register 5 to be placed in the memory cell whose address is B1.
4	0RS	MOVE the bit pattern found in register R to register S. *Example:* 40A4 would cause the contents of register A to be copied into register 4.
5	RST	ADD the bit patterns in registers S and T as though they were two's complement representations and leave the result in register R. *Example:* 5726 would cause the binary values in registers 2 and 6 to be added and the sum placed in register 7.
6	RST	ADD the bit patterns in registers S and T as though they represented values in floating-point notation and leave the floating-point result in register R. *Example:* 634E would cause the values in registers 4 and E to be added as floating-point values and the result to be placed in register 3.
7	RST	OR the bit patterns in registers S and T and place the result in register R. *Example:* 7CB4 would cause the result of ORing the contents of registers B and 4 to be placed in register C.
8	RST	AND the bit patterns in registers S and T and place the result in register R. *Example:* 8045 would cause the result of ANDing the contents of registers 4 and 5 to be placed in register 0.
9	RST	EXCLUSIVE OR the bit patterns in registers S and T and place the result in register R. *Example:* 95F3 would cause the result of EXCLUSIVE ORing the contents of registers F and 3 to be placed in register 5.
A	R0X	ROTATE the bit pattern in register R one bit to the right X times. Each time place the bit that started at the low-order end at the high-order end. *Example:* A403 would cause the contents of register 4 to be rotated 3 bits to the right in a circular fashion.
B	RXY	JUMP to the instruction located in the memory cell at address XY if the bit pattern in register R is equal to the bit pattern in register number 0. Otherwise, continue with the normal sequence of execution. (The jump is implemented by copying XY into the program counter during the execute phase.) *Example:* B43C would first compare the contents of register 4 with the contents of register 0. If the two were equal, the pattern 3C would be placed in the program counter so that the next instruction executed would be the one located at that memory address. Otherwise, nothing would be done and program execution would continue in its normal sequence.
C	000	HALT execution. *Example:* C000 would cause program execution to stop.

appendix

D

High-Level Programming Languages

This appendix contains a brief background of each of the languages used as examples in Chapter 6.

Ada

The language Ada, named after Augusta Ada Byron (1815–1851), who was an advocate of Charles Babbage and the daughter of poet Lord Byron, was developed at the initiative of the U.S. Department of Defense in an attempt to obtain a single, general-purpose language for all its software development needs. A major emphasis during Ada's design was to incorporate features for programming real-time computer systems used as a part of larger machines such as missile guidance systems, environmental control systems within buildings, and control systems in automobiles and small home appliances. Ada thus contains features for expressing activities in parallel processing environments as well as convenient techniques for handling special cases (called exceptions) that might arise in the application environment. Although originally designed as an imperative language, newer versions of Ada have embraced the object-oriented paradigm.

The design of the Ada language has consistently emphasized features that lead to the efficient development of reliable software, a characteristic exemplified by the fact that all of the internal control software in the Boeing 777 aircraft was written in Ada. This is also a major reason that Ada was used as a starting point in the development of the language SPARK, as indicated in Chapter 5.

C

The language C was developed by Dennis Ritchie at Bell Laboratories in the early 1970s. Although originally designed as a language for developing system software, C has achieved popularity throughout the programming community and has been standardized by the American National Standards Institute.

C was originally envisioned as merely a step up from machine language. Consequently, its syntax is terse compared with other high-level languages that use complete English words to express some primitives that are represented by special symbols in C. This terseness allows for efficient representations of complex algorithms, which is a major reason for C's popularity. (Often a concise representation is more readable than a lengthy one.)

C++

The language C++ was developed by Bjarne Stroustrup at Bell Laboratories as an enhanced version of the language C. The goal was to produce a language compatible with the object-oriented paradigm. Today, C++ is not only a prominent object-oriented language in its own right but it has served as a starting point for the development of two other leading object-oriented languages: Java and C#.

C#

The language C# was developed by Microsoft to be a tool in the .NET Framework, which is a comprehensive system for developing application software for machines running Microsoft system software. The C# language is very similar to C++ and Java. Indeed, the reason Microsoft introduced C# as a different language was not that it is truly new in the language sense, but that, as a different language, Microsoft could customize specific features of the language without concern for standards that were already associated with other languages or for proprietary rights of other corporations. Thus the novelty of C# is in its role as a prominent language for developing software utilizing the .NET Framework. With Microsoft's backing, C# and the .NET Framework promise to be prominent players in the world of software development for years to come.

FORTRAN

FORTRAN is an acronym for FORmula TRANslator. This language was one of the first high-level languages developed (it was announced in 1957) and one of the first to gain wide acceptance within the computing community. Over the years its official description has undergone numerous extensions, meaning that today's FORTRAN language is much different from the original. Indeed, by studying the evolution of FORTRAN, one would witness the effects of research in programming language design. Although originally designed as an imperative language, newer versions of FORTRAN now encompass many object-oriented features. FORTRAN continues to be a popular language within the scientific community. In particular, many numerical analysis and statistical packages are, and will probably continue to be, written in FORTRAN.

Java

Java is an object-oriented language developed by Sun Microsystems in the early 1990s. Its designers borrowed heavily from C and C++. The excitement over Java is due, not to the language itself, but to the language's universal implementation and the vast number of predesigned templates that are available in the Java programming environment. The universal implementation means that a program written in Java can be executed efficiently over a wide range of machines; and the availability of templates means that complex software can be developed with relative ease. For example, templates such as applet and servlet streamline the development of software for the World Wide Web.

appendix

E

The Equivalence of Iterative and Recursive Structures

In this appendix, we use our Bare Bones language of Chapter 12 as a tool to answer the question posed in Chapter 5 regarding the relative power of iterative and recursive structures. Recall that Bare Bones contains only three assignment statements (`clear`, `incr`, and `decr`) and one control structure (constructed from a `while` statement). This simple language has the same computing power as a Turing machine; thus, if we accept the Church-Turing thesis, we might conclude that any problem with an algorithmic solution has a solution expressible in Bare Bones.

The first step in the comparison of iterative and recursive structures is to replace the iterative structure of Bare Bones with a recursive structure. We do this by removing the `while` statement from the language and in its place providing the ability to divide a Bare Bones program into units along with the ability to call one of these units from another location in the program. More precisely, we propose that each program in the modified language consist of a number of syntactically disjoint program units. We suppose that each program must contain exactly one unit called `MAIN` having the syntactic structure of

```
def MAIN():
  .
  .
  .
```

(where the dots represent other indented Bare Bones statements) and perhaps other units (semantically subordinate to `MAIN`) that have the structure

```
def unit():
  .
  .
  .
```

(where `unit` represents the unit's name that has the same syntax as variable names). The semantics of this partitioned structure is that the program always begins execution at the beginning of the unit `MAIN` and halts when that unit's indented body is completed. Program units other than `MAIN` can be called as functions by means of the conditional statement

```
if name not 0:
  unit()
```

(where `name` represents any variable name and `unit` represents any of the program unit names other than `MAIN`). Moreover, we allow the units other than `MAIN` to call themselves recursively.

With these added features, we can simulate the `while` structure found in the original Bare Bones. For example, a Bare Bones program of the form

```
while X not 0:
  S
```

(where `S` represents any sequence of Bare Bones statements) can be replaced by the unit structure

```
def MAIN():
  if X not 0:
    unitA()
def unitA():
  S
  if X not 0:
    unitA()
```

Consequently, we conclude that the modified language has all the capabilities of the original Bare Bones.

It can also be shown that any problem that can be solved using the modified language can be solved using Bare Bones. One method of doing this is to show how any algorithm expressed in the modified language could be written in the original Bare Bones. However, this involves an explicit description of how recursive structures can be simulated with the `while` structure of Bare Bones.

For our purpose, it is simpler to rely on the Church-Turing thesis as presented in Chapter 12. In particular, the Church-Turing thesis, combined with the fact that Bare Bones has the same power as Turing machines, dictates that no language can be more powerful than our original Bare Bones. Therefore, any problem solvable in our modified language can also be solved using Bare Bones.

We conclude that the power of the modified language is the same as that of the original Bare Bones. The only distinction between the two languages is that one provides an iterative control structure and the other provides recursion. Thus the two control structures are in fact equivalent in terms of computing power.

appendix

F

Answers to Questions & Exercises

Chapter 1

Section 1.1

1. One and only one of the upper two inputs must be 1, and the lowest input must be 1.
2. The 1 on the lower input is negated to 0 by the NOT gate, causing the output of the AND gate to become 0. Thus both inputs to the OR gate are 0 (remember that the upper input to the flip-flop is held at 0) so the output of the OR gate becomes 0. This means that the output of the AND gate will remain 0 after the lower input to the flip-flop returns to 0.
3. The output of the upper OR gate will become 1, causing the upper NOT gate to produce an output of 0. This will cause the lower OR gate to produce a 0, causing the lower NOT gate to produce a 1. This 1 is seen as the output of the flip-flop as well as being fed back to the upper OR gate, where it holds the output of that gate at 1, even after the flip-flop's input has returned to 0.
4. a. The entire circuit is equivalent to a single OR gate.
   b. This entire circuit is also equivalent to a single XOR gate.
5. a. 6AF2 b. E85517 c. 48
6. a. 0101111110110010111
   b. 0110000100001010
   c. 101010 1111001101
   d. 0000000100000000

Section 1.2

1. In the first case, memory cell number 6 ends up containing the value 5. In the second case, it ends up with the value 8.
2. Step 1 erases the original value in cell number 3 when the new value is written there. Consequently, Step 2 does not place the original value from cell number 3 in cell number 2. The result is that both cells end up with

the value that was originally in cell number 2. A correct procedure is the following:

Step 1. Move the contents of cell number 2 to cell number 1.

Step 2. Move the contents of cell number 3 to cell number 2.

Step 3. Move the contents of cell number 1 to cell number 3.

3. 32768 bits

Section 1.3

1. Faster retrieval of data and higher transfer rates
2. The point to remember here is that the slowness of mechanical motion compared with the speed of the internal functioning of the computer dictates that we minimize the number of times we must move the read/write heads. If we fill a complete surface before starting the next, we must move the read/write head each time we finish with a track. The number of moves therefore is approximately the same as the total number of tracks on the two surfaces. If, however, we alternate between surfaces by electronically switching between the read/write heads, we must move the read/write heads only after each cylinder has been filled.
3. In this application, information must be retrieved from mass storage in a random manner, which would be time consuming in the context of the spiral system used on CDs and DVDs. (Moreover, current technology does not allow individual portions of data to be updated on a CD or DVD.)
4. CD, DVD, and Blu-ray disks are all the same physical size and use the same spiral track layout for placing data on the platter. A player equipped with multiple lasers is able to read all three types of optical disk.
5. Flash drives do not require physical motion so they have shorter response times and do not suffer from physical wear.
6. Magnetic hard disks are faster and have higher capacities than other forms of magnetic media, such as floppy disks and magnetic tape. Speed, capacity, and rewriting ability compare favorably to optical media. Price per units of storage on magnetic disks continues to be lower than solid-state disks, although this advantage has steadily eroded in recent years.

Section 1.4

1. Computer Science
2. The two patterns are the same, except that the sixth bit from the low-order end is always 0 for uppercase and 1 for lowercase.
3. a.

00100010	01010011	01110100	01101111
01110000	00100001	00100010	00100000
01000011	01101000	01100101	01110010
01111001	01101100	00100000	01110011
01101000	01101111	01110101	01110100
01100101	01110100	00101110	

b. 01000100 01101111 01100101 01110011
00100000 00110010 00100000 00101011
00100000 00110011 00100000 00111101
00100000 00110101 00111111

4. 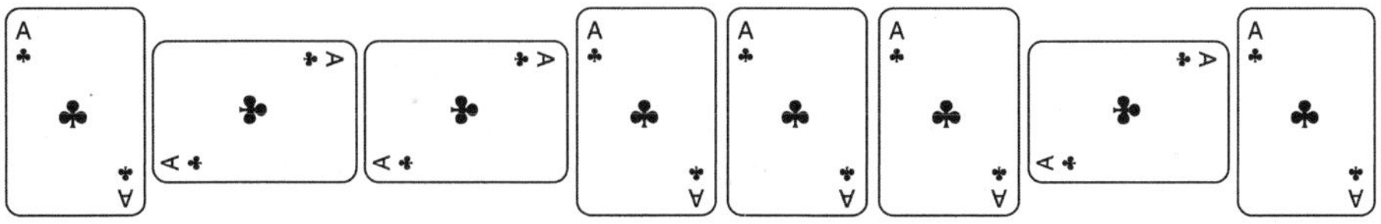

5. a. 5 b. 9 c. 11 d. 6 e. 16 f. 18

6. a. 110 b. 1101 c. 1011 d. 10010 e. 11011 f. 100

7. In 24 bits, we can store three symbols using ASCII. Thus we can store values as large as 999. However, if we use the bits as binary digits, we can store values up to 16,777,215.

8. a. 15.15 b. 51.0.128 c. 10.160

9. Geometric representations are more conducive to changes in scale than images encoded as bit maps. However, geometric representations do not typically provide the same photographic quality that bit maps produce. Indeed, as discussed in Section 1.9, JPEG representations of bit maps are very popular in photography.

10. With a sample rate of 44,100 samples per second, one hour of stereo music would require 635,040,000 bytes of storage. Thus, it would just about fill a CD whose capacity is slightly more than 600MB.

Section 1.5

1. a. 42 b. 33 c. 23 d. 6 e. 31

2. a. 100000 b. 1000000 c. 1100000 d. 1111 e. 11011

3. a. $3\frac{1}{4}$ b. $5\frac{7}{8}$ c. $2\frac{1}{2}$ d. $6\frac{3}{8}$ e. $\frac{5}{8}$

4. a. 100.1 b. 10.11 c. 1.001 d. 0.0101 e. 101.101

5. a. 100111 b. 1011.110 c. 100000 d. 1000.00

Section 1.6

1. a. 3 b. 15 c. −4 d. −6 e. 0 f. −16

2. a. 00000110 b. 11111010 c. 11101111
d. 00001101 e. 11111111 f. 00000000

3. a. 11111111 b. 10101011 c. 00000100
d. 00000010 e. 00000000 f. 10000001

4. a. With 4 bits the largest value is 7 and the smallest is −8.
b. With 6 bits the largest value is 31 and the smallest is −32.
c. With 8 bits the largest value is 127 and the smallest is −128.

5. a. 0111 $(5 + 2 = 7)$ b. 0100 $(3 + 1 = 4)$ c. 1111 $(5 + (-6) = -1)$
d. 0001 $(-2 + 3 = 1)$ e. 1000 $(-6 + (-2) = -8)$

6. a. 0111 b. 1011 (overflow) c. 0100 (overflow)
   d. 0001 e. 1000 (overflow)

7.

a.	b.	c.	d.	e.
0110	0011	0100	0010	0001
+ 0001	+ 1110	+ 1010	+ 0100	+1011
0111	0001	1110	0110	1100

8. No. Overflow occurs when an attempt is made to store a number that is too large for the system being used. When adding a positive value to a negative value, the result must be between the values being added. Therefore the result will be small enough to be stored without error.

9. a. 6 because $1110 \rightarrow 14 - 8$
   b. -1 because $0111 \rightarrow 7 - 8$
   c. 0 because $1000 \rightarrow 8 - 8$
   d. -6 because $0010 \rightarrow 2 - 8$
   e. -8 because $0000 \rightarrow 0 - 8$
   f. 1 because $1001 \rightarrow 9 - 8$

10. a. 1101 because $5 + 8 = 13 \rightarrow 1101$
    b. 0011 because $-5 + 8 = 3 \rightarrow 0011$
    c. 1011 because $3 + 8 = 11 \rightarrow 1011$
    d. 1000 because $0 + 8 = 8 \rightarrow 1000$
    e. 1111 because $7 + 8 = 15 \rightarrow 1111$
    f. 0000 because $-8 + 8 = 0 \rightarrow 0000$

11. No. The largest value that can be stored in excess eight notation is 7, represented by 1111. To represent a larger value, at least excess 16 (which uses patterns of 5 bits) must be used. Similarly, 6 cannot be represented in excess four notation. (The largest value that can be represented in excess four notation is 3.)

Section 1.7

1. a. $^5/_8$ b. $3^1/_4$ c. $^9/_{32}$ d. $-1^1/_2$ e. $-(^{11}/_{64})$

2. a. 01101011 b. 01111010 (truncation error)
   c. 01001100 d. 11101110 e. 11111000 (truncation error)

3. 01001001 ($^9/_{16}$) is larger than 00111101 ($^{13}/_{32}$). The following is a simple way of determining which of two patterns represents the larger value:

   Case 1. If the sign bits are different, the larger is the one with 0 sign bit.

   Case 2. If the sign bits are both 0, scan the remaining portions of the patterns from left to right until a bit position is found where the two patterns differ. The pattern containing the 1 in this position represents the larger value.

   Case 3. If the sign bits are both 1, scan the remaining portions of the patterns from left to right until a bit position is found where the two patterns differ. The pattern containing the 0 in this position represents the larger value. The simplicity of this comparison process is one of the reasons for representing the exponent in floating-point systems with an excess notation rather than with two's complement.

4. The largest value would be $7\frac{1}{2}$, which is represented by the pattern 01111111. As for the smallest positive value, you could argue that there are two "correct" answers. First, if you stick to the coding process described in the text, which requires the most significant bit of the mantissa to be 1 (called normalized form), the answer is $1/32$, which is represented by the pattern 00001000. However, most machines do not impose this restriction for values close to 0. For such a machine, the correct answer is $1/256$ represented by 00000001.

Section 1.8

1. Python is considered an *interpreted language* because users can type program fragments interactively at a prompt, rather than having to save the script, invoke a compiler, and then execute the program.
2. a. `print('Computer Science Rocks' + '!')`
   b. `print(42)`
   c. `print(3.1416)`
3. a. `rockstar = 'programmer'`
   b. `seconds_per_hour = 60 * 60`
   or
   `seconds_per_hour = 3600`
   c. `bodyTemp = 98.6`
4. `metricBodyTemp = (bodyTemp - 32)/1.8`

Section 1.9

1. Run-length encoding, frequency-dependent encoding, relative encoding, and dictionary encoding
2. 121321112343535
3. Color cartoons consist of blocks of solid color with sharp edges. Moreover, the number of colors involved is limited.
4. No. Both GIF and JPEG are lossy compression systems, meaning that details in the image will be lost.
5. JPEG's baseline standard takes advantage of the fact that the human eye is not as sensitive to changes in color as it is to changes in brightness. Thus it reduces the number of bits used to represent color information without noticeable loss in image quality.
6. Temporal masking and frequency masking
7. When encoding information, approximations are made. In the case of numeric data, these approximations are compounded when computations are performed, which can lead to erroneous results. Approximations are not as critical in the cases of images and sound because the encoded data are normally only stored, transferred, and reproduced. If, however, images or sound were repeatedly reproduced, rerecorded, and then reencoded, these approximations could compound and ultimately lead to worthless data.

Section 1.10

1. b, c, and e
2. Yes. If an even number of errors occurs in one byte, the parity technique does not detect them.
3. In this case, errors occur in bytes a and d of Question 1. The answer to Question 2 remains the same.
4. a.

100100010	101010011	101110100
101101111	001110000	100100001
100100010	000100000	001000011
001101000	101100101	101110010
001111001	101101100	000100000
001110011	001101000	101101111
001110101	101110100	101100101
001100100	100101110	

b.

101000100	101101111	101100101
001110011	100100000	000110010
000100000	100101011	000100000
100110011	000100000	000111101
000100000	100110101	100111111

5. a. BED   b. CAB   c. HEAD
6. One solution is the following:
   A 00000
   B 11100
   C 01111
   D 10011

Chapter 2

Section 2.1

1. On some machines this is a two-step process consisting of first reading the contents from the first cell into a register and then writing it from the register into the destination cell. On most machines, this is accomplished as one activity without using an intermediate register.
2. The value to be written, the address of the cell in which to write, and the command to write
3. General-purpose registers are used to hold the data immediately applicable to the operation at hand; main memory is used to hold data that will be needed in the near future; and mass storage is used to hold data that will likely not be needed in the near future.

Section 2.2

1. The term *move* often carries the connotation of removing from one location and placing in another, thus leaving a hole behind. In most cases within a machine, this removal does not take place. Rather, the object being moved is most often copied (or cloned) into the new location.

2. A common technique, called relative addressing, is to state how far rather than where to jump. For example, an instruction might be to jump forward three instructions or jump backward two instructions. You should note, however, that such statements must be altered if additional instructions are later inserted between the origin and the destination of the jump.
3. This could be argued either way. The instruction is stated in the form of a conditional jump. However, because the condition that 0 be equal to 0 is always satisfied, the jump will always be made as if there were no condition stated at all. You will often find machines with such instructions in their repertoires because they provide an efficient design. For example, if a machine is designed to execute an instruction with a structure such as "If . . . jump to. . . " this instruction form can be used to express both conditional and unconditional jumps.
4. 156C = 0001010101101100
   166D = 0001011001101101
   5056 = 0101000001010110
   306E = 0011000001101110
   C000 = 1100000000000000
5. a. STORE the contents of register 6 in memory cell number 8A.
   b. JUMP to location DE if the contents of register A equals that of register 0.
   c. AND the contents of registers 3 and C, leaving the result in register 0.
   d. MOVE the contents of register F to register 4.
6. The instruction 15AB requires that the CPU query the memory circuitry for the contents of the memory cell at address AB. This value, when obtained from memory, is then placed in register 5. The instruction 25AB does not require such a request of memory. Rather, the value AB is placed in register 5.
7. a. 2356 b. A503 c. 80A5

Section 2.3

1. Hexadecimal 34
2. a. 0F b. C3
3. a. 00 b. 01 c. four times
4. It halts. This is an example of what is often called self-modifying code. That is, the program modifies itself. Note that the first two instructions place hexadecimal C0 at memory location F8, and the next two instructions place 00 at location F9. Thus, by the time the machine reaches the instruction at F8, the halt instruction (C000) has been placed there.

Section 2.4

1. a. 00001011 b. 10000000 c. 00101101
   d. 11101011 e. 11101111 f. 11111111
   g. 11100000 h. 01101111 i. 11010010
2. 00111100 with the AND operation
3. 00111100 with the XOR operation

4. a. The final result is 0 if the string contained an even number of 1s. Otherwise it is 1.
   b. The result is the value of the parity bit for even parity.
5. The logical XOR operation mirrors addition except for the case where both operands are 1, in which case the XOR produces a 0, whereas the sum is 10. (Thus the XOR operation can be considered an addition operation with no carry.)
6. Use AND with the mask 11011111 to change lowercase to uppercase. Use OR with 00100000 to change uppercase to lowercase.
7. a. 01001101 b. 11100001 c. 11101111
8. a. 57 b. B8 c. 6F d. 6A
9. 5
10. 00110110 in two's complement; 01011110 in floating-point. The point here is that the procedure used to add the values is different depending on the interpretation given the bit patterns.
11. One solution is as follows:

    12A7 (LOAD register 2 with the contents of memory cell A7.)
    2380 (LOAD register 3 with the value 80.)
    7023 (OR registers 2 and 3 leaving the result in register 0.)
    30A7 (STORE contents of register 0 in memory cell A7.)
    C000 (HALT.)
12. One solution is as follows:

    15E0 (LOAD register 5 with the contents of memory cell E0.)
    A502 (ROTATE the contents of register 5 to the left by 2 bits.)
    260F (LOAD register 6 with the value 0F.)
    8056 (AND registers 5 and 6, leaving the result in register 0.)
    30E1 (STORE the contents of register 0 in memory cell E1.)
    C000 (HALT.)

Section 2.5

1. a. 37B5
   b. One million times
   c. No. A typical page of text contains less than 4000 characters. Thus the ability to print five pages in a minute indicates a printing rate of no more than 20,000 characters per minute, which is much less than one million characters per second. (The point is that a computer can send characters to a printer much faster than the printer can print them; thus the printer needs a way of telling the computer to wait.)
2. The disk will make 50 revolutions in one second, meaning that 800 sectors will pass under the read/write head in a second. Because each sector contains 1024 bytes, bits will pass under the read/write head at approximately 6.5 Mbps. Thus communication between the controller and the disk drive will have to be at least this fast if the controller is going to keep up with the data being read from the disk.

3. A 300-page novel represented in Unicode consists of about 2MB or 16,000,000 bits. Thus approximately 0.3 seconds would be required to transfer the entire novel at 54 Mbps.

Section 2.6

1. The `int()` function calls used when inputting the side lengths will truncate any floating-point values entered to integer values. However, the `math.sqrt()` function returns a floating-point value, regardless of whether its parameters were integers or floats. To output an integer instead, the final line of the script can be replaced with

   ```
   print(int(hypotenuse))
   ```

   or the assignment statement for hypotenuse can be replaced with

   ```
   hypotenuse = int(math.sqrt(sideA**2 + sideB**2))
   ```

2. Replacing both `int()` calls in the original script with `float()` produces a script that works with floating-point values.
3. One example of Python code that would produce cleaner output is:

   ```
   print('Your speed is ' + str(mph) + ' mph')
   . . .
   print('Your total elapsed time is ' + str(elapsed_minutes) +
         ' minutes, ' + str(elapsed_seconds) + ' seconds')
   ```

4. One example would be:

   ```
   number = int(input('Enter a base-10 number: '))
   print('Binary representation is: ' + str(bin(number)))
   ```

5. One example would be:

   ```
   number = int(input('Enter a number to encrypt or decrypt: '))
   number = number ^ 0x55555555
   print('Result is: ' + str(number))
   ```

6. Unexpected inputs in simple scripts such as these will generally cause errors or unexpected behavior. More complex scripts would check the input for suitability before trying to convert it to an integer, or would include conditionals to check for negative side lengths, etc.

Section 2.7

1. The pipe would contain the instructions B1B0 (being executed), 5002, and perhaps even B0AA. If the value in register 1 is equal to the value in register 0, the jump to location B0 is executed, and the effort already expended on the instructions in the pipe is wasted. On the other hand, no time is wasted because the effort expended on these instructions did not require extra time.
2. If no precautions are taken, the information at memory locations F8 and F9 is fetched as an instruction before the previous part of the program has had a chance to modify these cells.

3. a. The CPU that is trying to add 1 to the cell can first read the value in the cell. Following this the other CPU reads the cell's value. (Note that at this point both CPUs have retrieved the same value.) If the first CPU now finishes its addition and writes its result back in the cell before the second finishes its subtraction and writes its result, the final value in the cell reflects only the activity of the second CPU.
   b. The CPUs might read the data from the cell as before, but this time the second CPU might write its result before the first. Thus only the activity of the first CPU is reflected in the cell's final value.

Chapter 3

Section 3.1

1. A traditional example is the line of people waiting to buy tickets to an event. In this case there might be someone who tries to "break in line," which would violate the FIFO structure.
2. Options (b), (c), and (e)
3. Embedded systems often focus on dedicated tasks, whereas PCs are general-purpose computers. Embedded systems frequently have more limited resources than PCs of comparable age, but may face strict deadlines with minimal human intervention.
4. Time-sharing refers to more than one user accessing a machine at the same time. Multitasking refers to a user performing more than one task at the same time.

Section 3.2

1. *Shell:* Communicates with the machine's environment.

   File manager: Coordinates the use of the machine's mass storage.

   Device drivers: Handle communication with the machine's peripheral devices.

   Memory manager: Coordinates the use of the machine's main memory.

   Scheduler: Coordinates the processes in the system.

   Dispatcher: Controls the assignment of processes to CPU time.
2. The line is vague, and the distinction is often in the eye of the beholder. Roughly speaking, utility software performs basic, universal tasks, whereas application software performs tasks unique to the machine's application.
3. Virtual memory is the imaginary memory space whose apparent presence is created by the process of swapping data and programs back and forth between main memory and mass storage.
4. When the machine is turned on, the CPU begins executing the bootstrap, which resides in ROM. This bootstrap directs the CPU through the process of transferring the operating system from mass storage into the volatile area of main memory. When this transfer is complete, the bootstrap directs the CPU to jump to the operating system.

Section 3.3

1. A program is a set of directions. A process is the action of following those directions.
2. The CPU completes its current machine cycle, saves the state of the current process, and sets its program counter to a predetermined value (which is the location of the interrupt handler). Thus the next instruction executed will be the first instruction within the interrupt handler.
3. They could be given higher priorities so that they would be given preference by the dispatcher. Another option would be to give the higher-priority processes longer time slices.
4. If each process consumed its entire time slice, the machine could provide a complete slice to almost 20 processes in one second. If processes did not consume their entire time slices, this value could be much higher, but then the time required to perform a context switch might become more significant (see Question 5).
5. A total of $^{5000}/_{5001}$ of the machine's time would be spent actually performing processes. However, when a process requests an I/O activity, its time slice is terminated while the controller performs the request. Thus if each process made such a request after only one microsecond of its time slice, the efficiency of the machine would drop to 1/2. That is, the machine would spend as much time performing context switches as it would executing processes.

Section 3.4

1. This system guarantees that the resource is not used by more than one process at a time; however, it dictates that the resource be allocated in a strictly alternating fashion. Once a process has used and relinquished the resource, it must wait for the other process to use the resource before the original process can access it again. This is true even if the first process needs the resource right away and the other process will not need it for some time.
2. If two cars enter opposite ends of the tunnel at the same time, they will not be aware of the other's presence. The process of entering and turning on the lights is another example of a critical region, or in this case we might call it a critical process. In this terminology, we could summarize the flaw by saying that cars at opposite ends of the tunnel could execute the critical process at the same time.
3. a. This guarantees that the nonsharable resource is not required and allocated on a partial basis; that is, a car is given the whole bridge or nothing at all.
   b. This means that the nonsharable resource can be forcibly retrieved.
   c. This makes the nonsharable resource shareable, which removes the competition.
4. A sequence of arrows that forms a closed loop in the directed graph. It is on this observation that techniques have been developed that allow some operating systems to recognize the existence of deadlock and consequently to take appropriate corrective action.

Section 3.5

1. Names and dates are considered poor candidates because they are common choices and therefore represent easy targets for password guessers. The use of complete words is also considered poor because password guessers can easily write a program to try the words found in a dictionary. Moreover, passwords containing only characters are discouraged because they are formed from a limited character set.
2. Four is the number of different bit patterns that can be formed using 2 bits. If more privilege levels were required, the designers would need at least 3 bits to represent the different levels and would therefore probably choose to use a total of 8 levels. In the same manner, the natural choice for fewer than 4 privilege levels would be 2, which is the number of patterns that can be represented with 1 bit.
3. The process could alter the operating system program so that the dispatcher gave every time slice to that process.

Chapter 4

Section 4.1

1. An open network is one whose specifications and protocols are public, allowing different vendors to produce compatible products.
2. Both connect two buses to form a larger bus network. However, a bridge forwards only those messages destined for the other side of the bridge, whereas a switch has multiple connections that each may act as a bridge.
3. A router is a device that directs messages between networks in an internet.
4. How about a mail-order business and its clients, a bank teller and the bank's customers, or a pharmacist and his or her customers?
5. There are numerous protocols involved in traffic flow, verbal telephone communication, and etiquette.
6. Cluster computing typically involves multiple, dedicated computers to provide high-availability or load-balanced distributed computing. Grid computing is more loosely coupled than cluster computing, and could involve machines that join the distributed computation when they are otherwise idle.

Section 4.2

1. Tier-1 and tier-2 ISPs provide the Internet's communication "core," whereas access ISPs provide access to that core to their customers.
2. The DNS (Domain Name System) is the Internet-wide collection of name servers that allow translation from mnemonic addresses to IP addresses (and in the other direction as well).
3. The expression 3.6.9 represents the three-byte pattern 000000110000011000001001. The bit pattern 0001010100011100 would be represented as 21.28 in dotted decimal notation.

4. There could be several answers to this. One is that both progress from the specific to the general. Internet addresses in mnemonic form begin with the name of a particular machine and progress to the name of the TLD. Postal addresses begin with the name of an individual and progress to increasingly larger regions such as city, state, and country. This order is reversed in IP addresses, which start with the bit pattern identifying the domain.
5. Name servers help translate mnemonic addresses into IP addresses. Mail servers send, receive, and store email messages. FTP servers provide file transfer service.
6. Protocols can describe the format of messages that are exchanged, the proper ordering of messages in an exchange, and the meaning of messages.
7. They relieve the initial server from the burden of sending individual messages to each client. The P2P approach shifts this burden to the clients (peers) themselves, whereas multicast shifts this burden to the Internet routers.
8. Criteria to consider may include cost, portability, the practicality of using your computer as your phone, the need to preserve any existing analog phones, emergency 911 service, and the reliability and service areas of the various providers involved.

Section 4.3

1. A URL is essentially the address of a document in the World Wide Web. A browser is a program that assists a user in accessing hypertext.
2. A markup language is a system for inserting explanatory information in a document.
3. HTML is a particular markup language. XML is a standard for producing markup languages.
4. a. <html> marks the beginning of an HTML document.
   b. <head> marks the beginning of a document's head.
   c. </p> marks the end of a paragraph.
   d. </a> marks the end of an item that is linked to another document.
5. Client side and server side are terms used to identify whether an activity is performed at the client's computer or the server's computer.

Section 4.4

1. The link layer receives the message and hands it to the network layer. The network layer determines the direction in which the message should be forwarded and gives the message back to the link layer to be forwarded. The higher layers are not required for routing, although advanced routers may use the transport or application layers to provide additional services such as selective filtering or tiered quality of service.
2. Unlike TCP, UDP is a connectionless protocol that does not confirm that the message was received at the destination.

3. The transport layer uses transport protocol port numbers to determine which unit within the application layer should receive an incoming message.
4. Nothing really. A programmer at any host could modify the software at that host to keep such records. This is why sensitive data should be encrypted.

Section 4.5

1. Phishing is a technique for obtaining sensitive information by asking users for their passwords, credit card numbers, etc., through email while masquerading as a legitimate entity such as the user's bank or the campus IT department. Computers are not secured against phishing; users must rely on sound judgment when revealing sensitive data to others without proper verification.
2. A region's gateway is a router that merely forwards packets (parts of messages) as they pass through. Thus a firewall at the gateway cannot filter traffic by its content but merely by its address information.
3. The use of passwords protects data (and therefore information as well). The use of encryption protects information.
4. In the case of a public-key encryption system, knowing how messages are encrypted does not allow messages to be decrypted.
5. The problems are international in nature and therefore not subject to the laws of a single government. Moreover, legal remedies merely provide recourse to injured parties rather than preventing the injuries.

Chapter 5

Section 5.1

1. A process is the activity of executing an algorithm. A program is a representation of an algorithm.
2. In the introductory chapter we cited algorithms for playing music, operating washing machines, constructing models, and performing magic tricks, as well as the Euclidean algorithm. Many of the "algorithms" you meet in everyday life fail to be algorithms according to our formal definition. The example of the long-division algorithm was cited in the text. Another is the algorithm executed by a clock that continues to advance its hands and ring its chimes day after day.
3. The informal definition fails to require that the steps be ordered and unambiguous. It merely hints at the requirements that the steps be executable and lead to an end.
4. There are two points here. The first is that the instructions define a nonterminating process. In reality, however, the process will ultimately reach the state in which there are no coins in your pocket. In fact, this might be the starting state. At this point the problem is that of ambiguity. The algorithm, as represented, does not tell us what to do in this situation.

Section 5.2

1. One example is found in the composition of matter. At one level, the primitives are considered molecules, yet these particles are actually composites made up of atoms, which in turn are composed of electrons, protons, and neutrons. Today, we know that even these "primitives" are composites.
2. Once a function is correctly constructed, it can be used as a building block for larger program structures without reconsidering the function's internal composition.
3.
```
X = the larger input
Y = the smaller input
while (Y not zero):
  Remainder = remainder after dividing X by Y
  X = Y
  Y = Remainder
GCD = X
```
4. All other colors of light can be produced by combining red, blue, and green. Thus a television picture tube is designed to produce these three basic colors.

Section 5.3

1. a.
```
if (n == 1 or n == 2):
  the answer is the list containing the single value n
else:
  Divide n by 3, obtaining a quotient q and a remainder r
  if (r == 0):
    the answer is the list containing q 3s
  if (r == 1):
    the answer is the list containing (q - 1) 3s and two 2s
  if (r == 2):
    the answer is the list containing q 3s and one 2
```
   b. The result would be the list containing 667 threes.
   c. You probably experimented with small input values until you began to see a pattern.
2. a. Yes. Hint: Place the first tile in the center so that it avoids the quadrant containing the hole while covering one square from each of the other quadrants. Each quadrant then represents a smaller version of the original problem.
   b. The board with a single hole contains $2^{2n} - 1$ squares, and each tile covers exactly three squares.
   c. Parts (a) and (b) of this question provide an excellent example of how knowing a solution to one problem helps solve another. See Polya's fourth phase.
3. It says, "This is the correct answer."
4. Simply trying to assemble the pieces would be a bottom-up approach. However, by looking at the puzzle box to see what the picture is supposed to look like adds a top-down component to your approach.

Section 5.4

1. Change the test in the `while` statement to read "target value != current entry and there remain entries to be considered."

2.
```
Z = 0
X = 1
repeat:
   Z = Z + X
   X = X + 1
   until (X == 6)
```

3. This has proven to be a problem with the C language. When the do and `while` key words are separated by several lines, readers of a program often stumble over the proper interpretation of a `while` clause. In particular, the `while` at the end of a do statement is often interpreted as the beginning of a `while` statement. Thus experience would say that it is better to use different key words to represent pretest and posttest loop structures.

4.

Cheryl	Alice	Alice
Gene	Cheryl	Brenda
Alice	Gene	Cheryl
Brenda	Brenda	Gene

5. It is a waste of time to insist on placing the pivot above an identical entry in the list. For instance, make the proposed change and then try the new program on a list in which all entries are the same.

6.
```
def sort (List):
   N = 1
   while (N is less than the length of List):
     J = N + 1
     while (J is not greater than length of List):
       if (the entry in position J is less than the entry in
           position N):
           interchange the two entries
       J = J + 1
     N = N + 1
```

7. The following is an inefficient solution. Can you make it more efficient?

```
def sort (List):
   N = the length of List
   while (N > 1):
     J = the length of List
     while (J > 1):
       if (the entry in position J < the entry in
           position J - 1):
           interchange the two entries
       J = J - 1
     N = N - 1
```

Section 5.5

1. The first name considered would be Henry, the next would be Larry, and the last would be Joe.
2. 8, 17
3. 1, 2, 3, 3, 2, 1
4. The termination condition is "N is bigger than or equal to 3" (or "N is not less than 3"). This is the condition under which no additional activations are created.

Section 5.6

1. If the machine can sort 100 names in one second, it can perform $\frac{1}{4}(10{,}000 - 100)$ comparisons in one second. This means that each comparison takes approximately 0.0004 second. Consequently, sorting 1000 names [which requires an average of $\frac{1}{4}(1{,}000{,}000 - 1000)$ comparisons] requires roughly 100 seconds or $1\frac{2}{3}$ minutes.
2. The binary search belongs to $\Theta(\log_2 n)$, the sequential search belongs to $\Theta(n)$, and the insertion sort belongs to $\Theta(n^2)$.
3. The class $\Theta(\log_2 n)$ is most efficient, followed by $\Theta(n)$, $\Theta(n^2)$, and $\Theta(n^3)$.
4. No. The answer is not correct, although it might sound right. The truth is that two of the three cards are the same on both sides. Thus the probability of picking such a card is two-thirds.
5. No. If the dividend is less than the divisor, such as in $\frac{3}{7}$, the answer given is 1, although it should be 0.
6. No. If the value of X is zero and the value of Y is nonzero, the answer given will not be correct.
7. Each time the test for termination is conducted, the statement "Sum $= 1 + 2 + \ldots + K$ and K less than or equal to N" is true. Combining this with the termination condition "K greater than or equal to N" produces the desired conclusion "Sum $= 1 + 2 + \ldots + N$." Because K is initialized at zero and incremented by one each time through the loop, its value must ultimately reach that of N.
8. Unfortunately, no. Problems beyond the control of hardware and software design, such as mechanical malfunctions and electrical problems, can affect computations.

Chapter 6

Section 6.1

1. A program in a third-generation language is machine independent in the sense that its steps are not stated in terms of the machine's attributes such as registers and memory cell addresses. On the other hand, it is machine dependent in the sense that arithmetic overflow and truncation errors will still occur.

2. The major distinction is that an assembler translates each instruction in the source program into a single machine instruction, whereas a compiler often produces many machine-language instructions to obtain the equivalent of a single source program instruction.
3. The declarative paradigm is based on developing a description of the problem to be solved. The functional paradigm forces the programmer to describe the problem's solution in terms of solutions to smaller problems. The object-oriented paradigm places emphasis on describing the components in the problem's environment.
4. The third-generation languages allow the program to be expressed more in terms of the problem's environment and less in terms of computer gibberish than do the earlier-generation languages.

Section 6.2

1. Using a descriptive constant can improve the accessibility of the program.
2. A declarative statement describes terminology; an imperative statement describes steps in an algorithm.
3. Integer, float, character, and Boolean
4. The `if-else` and `while` loop structures are very common.
5. All components of an array have the same type.

Section 6.3

1. The scope of a variable is the range of the program in which that variable is accessible.
2. A fruitful function is a function that returns a value associated with the function's name.
3. Because that is what they are. I/O operations are actually calls to routines within the machine's operating system.
4. A formal parameter is an identifier within a function. It serves as a place holder for the value, the actual parameter, that is passed to the function when the function is called.
5. A function that passes parameters call-by-reference can potentially make changes to the parameters that will be visible to the caller; call-by-value parameters are copies, and changes made to them within the function will not be visible from outside.

Section 6.4

1. Lexical analysis: the process of identifying tokens.
   Parsing: the process of recognizing the grammatical structure of the program.
   Code generation: the process of producing the instructions in the object program.
2. A symbol table is the record of information the parser has obtained from the program's declarative statements.

3. In the syntax diagrams, terms that appear in ovals are terminals. Terms that require further description are in rectangles, and are called "nonterminals."

4.

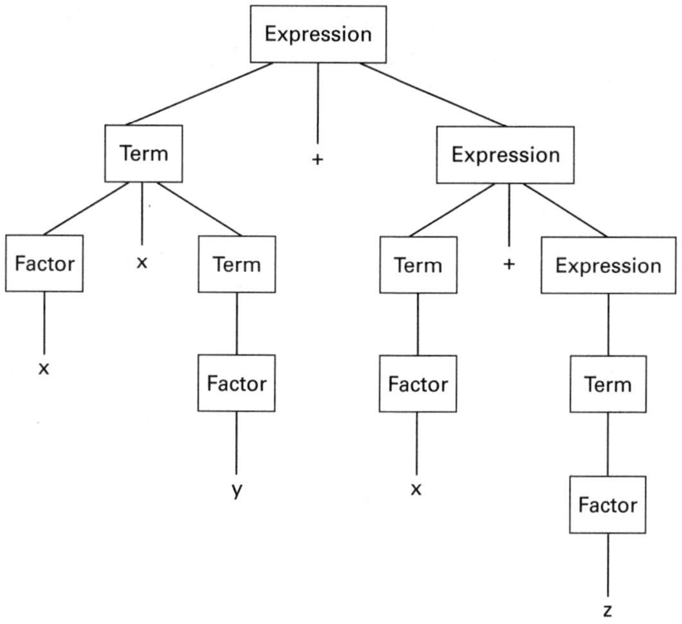

5. The strings that conform to the structure Chacha consist of one or more of the following substrings:
forward backward cha cha cha
backward forward cha cha cha
swing right cha cha cha
swing left cha cha cha

6. Python keywords appear in this color. Module names, functions and classes appear in this color, as do first time variable assignments. String constants and comments appear in this color. All other Python code appears in this color.

Section 6.5

1. A class is the description of an object.
2. One would probably be `MeteorClass` from which the various meteors would be constructed. Within the class `LaserClass` one might find an instance variable named `AimDirection` indicating the direction in which the laser is aimed. This variable would probably be used by the `fire`, `turnRight`, and `turnLeft` methods.
3. The `Employee` class might contain features relating to an employee's name, address, years in service, etc. The `FullTimeEmployee` class might contain features relating to retirement benefits. The `PartTimeEmployee` class might contain features relating to hours worked per week, hourly wage, etc.

4. A constructor is a special method in a class that is executed when an instance of the class is created.
5. Some items in a class are designated as private to keep other program units from gaining direct access to those items. If an item is private, then the repercussions of modifying that item should be restricted to the interior of the class.

Section 6.6

1. The list would include techniques for initiating the execution of concurrent processes and techniques for implementing interprocess communication.
2. One is to place the burden on the processes, another is to place the burden on the data. The latter has the advantage of concentrating the task at a single point in the program.
3. These include weather forecasting, air traffic control, simulation of complex systems (from nuclear reactions to pedestrian traffic), computer networking, and database maintenance.

Section 6.7

1. R, T, and V. For instance, we can show that R is a consequence by adding its negation to the collection and showing that resolution can lead to the empty statement, as shown here:

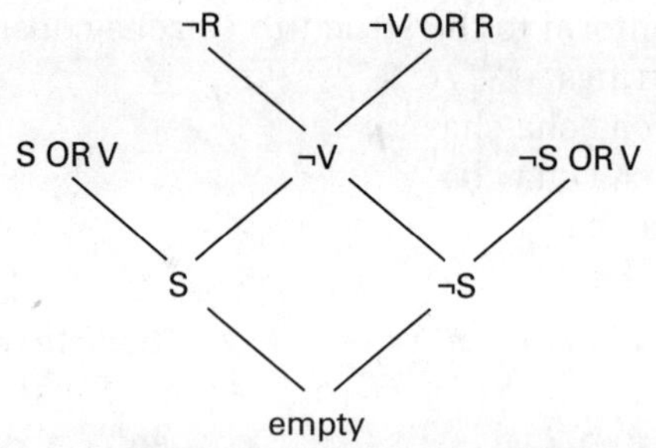

2. No. The collection is inconsistent, because resolution can lead to the empty statement, as shown here:

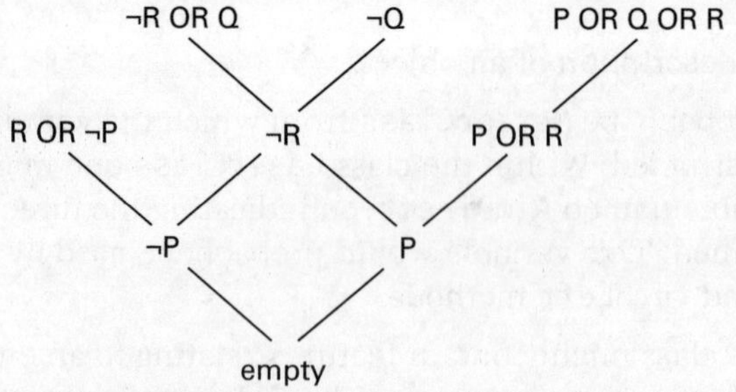

3.
```
mother(X, Y) :- parent(X, Y), female(X).
father(X, Y) :- parent(X, Y), male(X).
```

4. Prolog will conclude that `carol` is her own sibling. To solve this problem, the rule needs to include the fact that X cannot be equal to Y, which in Prolog is written X \ = Y. Thus an improved version of the rule would be

```
sibling (X, Y) :-X \= Y, parent(Z, X), parent(Z, Y).
```

which says that X is Y's sibling if X and Y are not equal and have a common parent. The following version would insist that X and Y are siblings only if they have both parents in common:

```
sibling (X, Y) :- X \= Y, Z \= W
parent (Z, X), parent (Z, Y),
parent (W, X), parent (W, Y).
```

Chapter 7

Section 7.1

1. A long sequence of assignment statements is not as complex in the context of program design as a few nested `if` statements.
2. How about the number of errors found after a fixed period of use? One problem here is that this value cannot be measured in advance.
3. The point here is to think about how software properties can be measured. One approach for estimating the number of errors in a piece of software is to intentionally place some errors in the software when it is designed. Then, after the software has supposedly been debugged, check to see how many of the original errors are still present. For example, if you intentionally place seven errors in the software and find that five have been removed after debugging, then you might conjecture that only $5/7$ of the total errors in the software have been removed.
4. Possible answers include the discovery of metrics, the development of prefabricated components, the development of CASE tools, the move toward standards. Another, which is covered later in Section 7.5, is the development of modeling and notational systems such as UML.

Section 7.2

1. Small efforts made during development can pay enormous dividends during maintenance.
2. The requirements analysis phase concentrates on what the proposed system must accomplish. The design phase concentrates on how the system accomplishes its goals. The implementation phase concentrates on the actual construction of the system. The testing phase concentrates on making sure that the system does what it is intended to do.
3. A software requirements specification is a written agreement between a client and a software engineering firm stating the requirements and specifications of the software to be developed.

Section 7.3

1. The traditional waterfall approach dictates that the requirements analysis, design, implementation, and testing phases be performed in a linear manner. The newer models allow for a more relaxed trial-and-error approach.
2. How about the incremental model, the iterative model, and XP?
3. Traditional evolutionary prototyping is performed within the organization developing the software, whereas open-source development is not restricted to an organization. In the case of open-source development the person overseeing the development does not necessarily determine what enhancements will be reported, whereas in the case of traditional evolutionary prototyping the person managing the software development assigns personnel to specific enhancement tasks.
4. This is one for you to think about. If you were an administrator in a software development company, would you be able to adopt the open-source methodology for the development of software to be sold by your company?

Section 7.4

1. The chapters of a novel build on one another, whereas the sections in an encyclopedia are largely independent. Hence, a novel has more coupling between its chapters than an encyclopedia has between its sections. However, the sections within an encyclopedia probably have a higher level of cohesion than the chapters in a novel.
2. The accumulated score would be an example of data coupling. Other "couplings" that might exist would include fatigue, momentum, knowledge gained about an opponent's strategy, and perhaps self-confidence. In many sports the cohesion of the units is increased by terminating the action and restarting the next unit from a fresh beginning. For example, in baseball each inning starts without any base runners, even though the team might have finished the previous inning with the bases loaded. In other cases the units are scored separately as in tennis where each set is won or lost without regard for the other sets.
3. This is a tough one. From one point of view, we could start by placing everything in a single module. This would result in little cohesion and no coupling at all. If we then begin to divide this single module into smaller ones, the result would be an increase in coupling. We might therefore conclude that increasing cohesion tends to increase coupling. On the other hand, suppose the problem at hand naturally divides into three very cohesive modules, which we will call A, B, and C. If our original design did not observe this natural division (for example, half of task A might be placed with half of task B, and so on), we would expect the cohesion to be low and the coupling high. In this case, redesigning the system by isolating tasks A, B, and C into separate modules would most likely decrease intermodule coupling as intramodule cohesion increases.
4. Coupling is linking between modules. Cohesion is the connectedness within a module. Information hiding is the restriction of information sharing.

5. You should probably add an arrow indicating that `ControlGame` must tell `UpdateScore` who won the volley and another arrow in the other direction indicating that `UpdateScore` will report the current status (such as "set over" or "match over") when it returns control to `ControlGame`.
6. Delete all the horizontal arrows in Figure 7.5 except for the first and last. That is, the judge should evaluate `Player A's` serve and directly send the `updateScore` message to `Score`. (This, of course, ignores the chance for a second serve. How could you modify the program design to allow for double faults?)
7. A traditional programmer writes programs in terms of statements such as those introduced in Chapter 6. A component assembler builds programs by linking prefabricated blocks called components.
8. There are many answers to this question. One combination is to have the calendar automatically set an alarm in a clock to notifying the user of an upcoming appointment. Furthermore, the calendar application could use the components of a map application to provide the directions to the address of the appointment.

Section 7.5

1. Make sure that your diagram deals with the flow of data (not the movement of books). The following diagram indicates that book identifications (from patrons) and patron records (from the library files) are combined to form loan records that are stored in the library files.

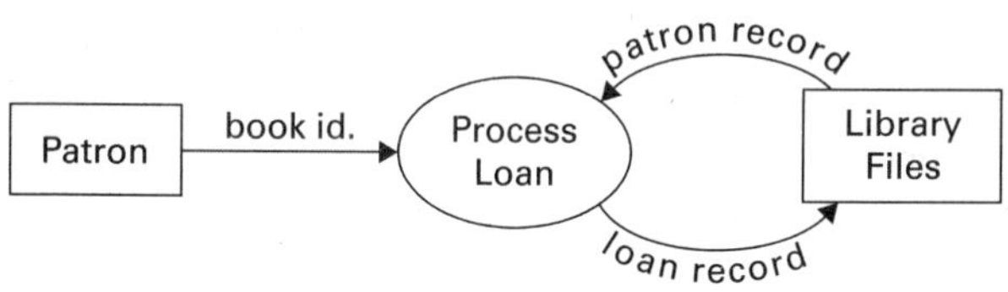

2.

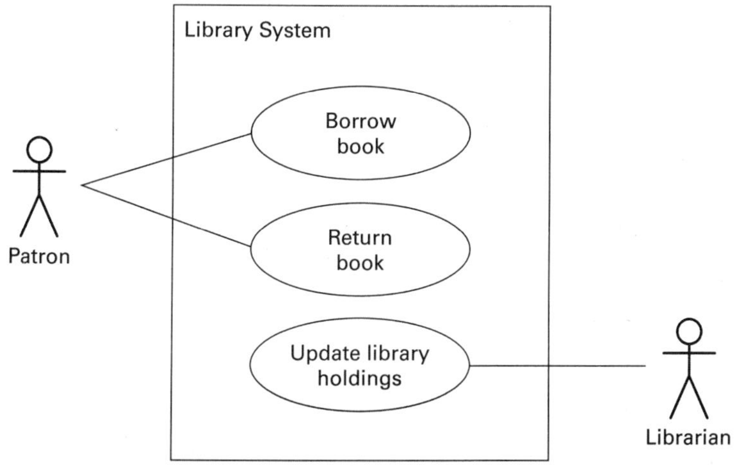

3. 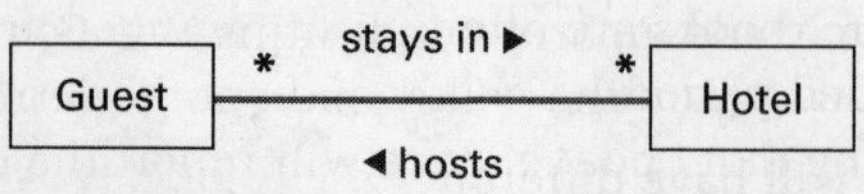

4. 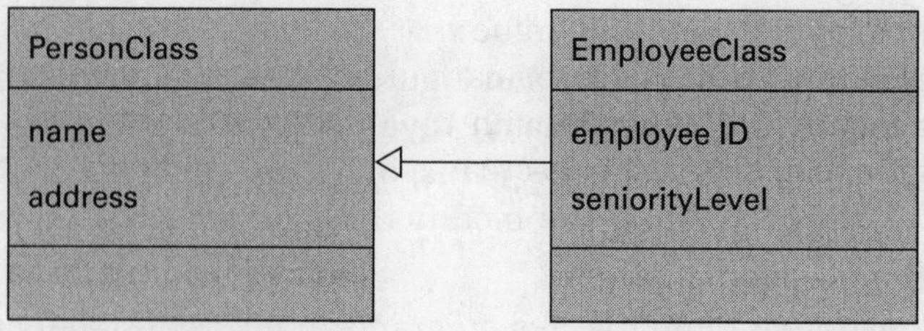

5. Simply draw a rectangle around the figure and add a "sd" label in the upper left-hand corner as in Figure 7.13.
6. Design patterns provide standardized, well-developed approaches for implementing recurring software themes.

Section 7.6

1. The SQA (software quality assurance) group oversees and enforces the quality control systems adopted by the organization.
2. Humans have a tendency not to record the steps (decisions, actions, etc.) that they take during a project. (There are also issues of personality conflicts, jealousies, and ego clashes.)
3. Record keeping and reviewing.
4. The purpose of testing software is to find errors. In a sense, then, a test that does not reveal an error is a failure.
5. One would be to consider the amount of branching in the modules. For instance, a procedural module containing numerous loops and `if-else` statements would probably be more prone to errors than a module with a simple logical structure.
6. Boundary value analysis would suggest that you test the software on a list with 100 entries as well as a list with no entries. You might also perform a test with a list that is already in the correct order.

Section 7.7

1. Documentation takes the form of user documentation, system documentation, and technical documentation. It might appear in accompanying manuals, within the source program in the form of comments and well-written code, through interactive messages that the program itself writes at a terminal, through data dictionaries, and in the form of design documents such as structure charts, class diagrams, dataflow diagrams, and entity-relationship diagrams.
2. In both the development and modification phases. The point is that modifications must be documented as thoroughly as the original program. (It is also true that software is documented while in its use phase. For example, a user of the system might discover problems, which, rather than being fixed, are merely reported in future editions of the system user's manual.

Moreover, "how to" books are often produced after the software has been in use for an extended period.)

3. Different people will have different opinions on this one. Some will argue that the program is the point of the whole project and thus is naturally the more important. Others will argue that a program is worth nothing if it is not documented, because if you cannot understand a program, you cannot use it or modify it. Moreover, with good documentation, the task of creating the program can be "easily" re-created.

Section 7.8

1. a. How about the ability to adjust the tilt of a display or the shape of a mouse? On smartphones, how about the use of touch screens instead of a mouse, or tilting the phone to provide input?
   b. How about the layout of a window on the display including the design of toolbars, scroll elevators, and pull-down menus? On a smartphone, isn't titling the camera to point at the items of interest in line with the way humans think?
2. a. It would be impractical and inconvenient to use a mouse (or even a stylus) on a smartphone. Furthermore, the reduced size of the display screen requires that nonessential elements of the display be constrained to limited space. For this reason, scrollbars are often omitted. If present, scrollbars are shown as thin lines.
   b. A sliding touch on the display screen is a natural gesture to the way we think. We may move papers or other items by sliding them around on a desk. An augment can be made that this is more natural than the use of scrollbars on a desktop computer. While indeed the scrollbar moves as expected, the area being scrolled moves in the opposite direction. For a user who has never used a computer, this behavior may seem counterintuitive.
3. You could answer "the role of human characteristics." Another good answer would be that interface design focuses on the external, rather than the internal, characteristics of a software system.
4. The three that are discussed in the text are the formation of habits, the narrowness of attention, and limited multiprocessing capabilities. Can you imagine others? How about the tendency to make assumptions?

Section 7.9

1. The copyright notice asserts ownership of the work and identifies personnel authorized to use the work. All works including requirements specifications, design documents, source code, and the final product usually involve a considerable investment to produce. An individual or corporation should take the steps to insure that their ownership rights are reserved and that all intellectual property is not used by undesired parties.
2. Copyright and patent laws benefit society because they encourage creators of new products to make them available to the public. Without such protection, companies would hesitate to make major investments in new products.
3. A disclaimer does not protect a company against negligence.

Chapter 8

Section 8.1

1. List: A listing of the members of a sports team.
   Stack: The stack of trays in a cafeteria.
   Queue: The line at a cafeteria.
   Tree: The organization chart of many governments.
2. Stacks and queues can be thought of as special types of lists. In the case of a general list, entries can be inserted and removed at any location. In the case of a stack, entries can be inserted and removed only at the head. In the case of a queue, entries can be inserted only at the tail, and entries can be removed only at the head.
3. The letters on the stack from top to bottom would be E, D, B, and A. If a letter were popped off the stack, it would be the letter E.
4. The letters in the queue from head to tail would be B, C, D, and E. If a letter were removed from the queue, it would be the letter B.
5. The leaf (or terminal) nodes are D and C. B must be the root node because all the other nodes have parents.

Section 8.2

1. Data within a computer's main memory is actually stored in individually addressable memory cells. Structures such as arrays, lists, and trees are simulated to make the data more accessible to the data's users.
2. If you were to write a program for playing a game of checkers, the data structure representing the checkerboard would probably be a static structure because the size of the board does not change during the game. However, if you were to write a program for playing a game of dominoes, the data structure representing the pattern of dominoes constructed on the table would probably be a dynamic structure because this pattern varies in size and cannot be predetermined.
3. A telephone directory is essentially a collection of pointers (telephone numbers) to people. The clues left at the scene of a crime are (perhaps encrypted) pointers to the perpetrator.

Section 8.3

1. 5 3 7 4 2 8 1 9 6
2. If R is the number of rows in the matrix, the formula is R(J − 1) + (I − 1).
3. (c − i) + j
4. The head pointer contains the NIL value.
5.
```
def PrintList (List):
    Last = the last name to be printed
    Finished = False
    CurrentPointer = List.Head
```

```
while ((CurrentPointer != None) and (Finished != False)):
  print(CurrentPointer.Value)
  if (name just printed == Last):
    Finished = True
  CurrentPointer = CurrentPointer.Next
```

6. The stack pointer points to the cell immediately below the base of the stack.
7. Represent the stack as a one-dimensional array and the stack pointer as a variable of integer type. Then use this stack pointer to maintain a record of the position of the stack's top within the array rather than of the exact memory address.
8. Both empty and full conditions are indicated by the equal head and tail pointers. Thus additional information is required to distinguish between the two conditions.
9.

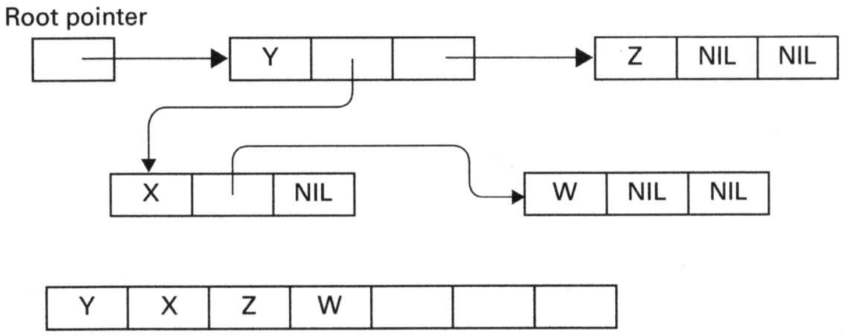

Section 8.4

1.

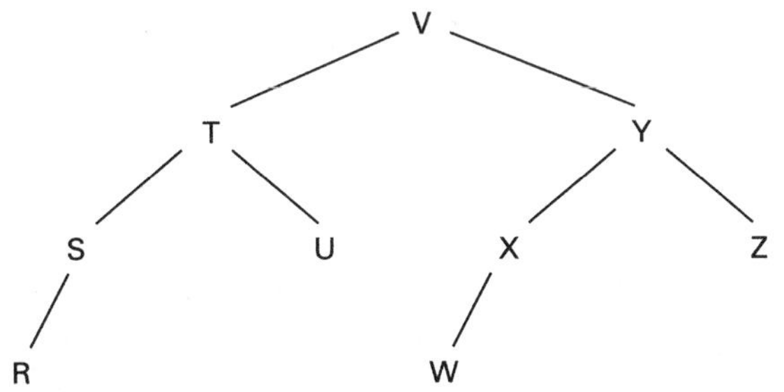

2. When searching for J:

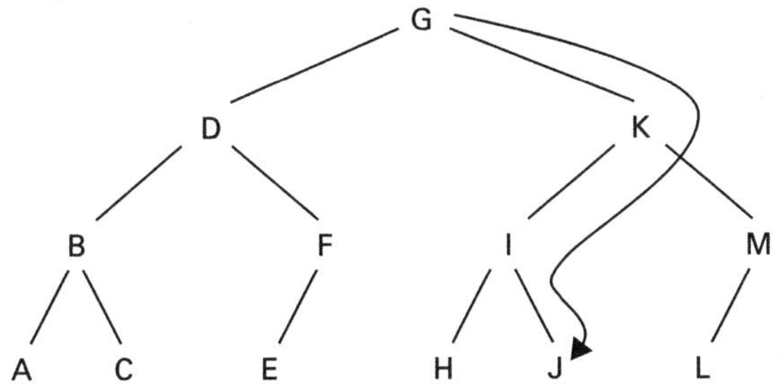

When searching for P:

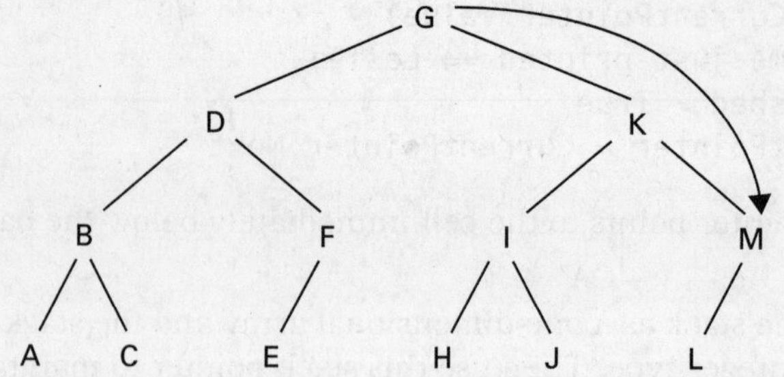

3.

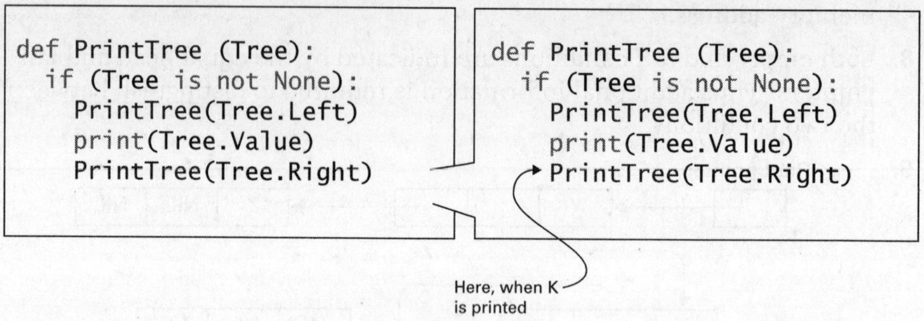

4. At each node, each child pointer could be used to represent a unique letter in the alphabet. A word could be represented by a path down the tree along the sequence of pointers representing the spelling of the word. A node could be marked in a special way if it represented the end of a correctly spelled word.

Section 8.5

1. A type is a template; an instance of that type is an actual entity built from that template. As an analogy, dog is a type of animal, whereas Lassie and Rex are instances of that type.
2. A user-defined data type is a description of data organization, whereas an abstract data type includes operations for manipulating the data.
3. A point to be made here is that you have a choice between implementing the list as a contiguous list or a linked list. The choice you make will affect the structure of the functions for inserting new entries, deleting old ones, and finding entries of interest. However, this choice should not be visible to a user of an instance of the abstract data type.
4. The abstract data type would at least contain a description of a data structure for storing the account balance and functions for making a deposit and making a withdrawal via a check.

Section 8.6

1. Both abstract data types and classes are templates for constructing instances of a type. Classes, however, are more general in that they are associated with inheritance and might describe a collection of only functions.

2. A class is a template from which objects are constructed.
3. The class might contain a circular queue along with functions for adding entries, removing entries, testing to see if the queue is full, and testing to see if the queue is empty.

Section 8.7

1. a. A5 b. A5 c. CA
2. D50F, 2EFF, 5FFE
3. 2EA0, 2FB0, 2101, 20B5, D50E, E50F, 5EE1, 5FF1, BF14, B008, C000
4. When traversing a linked list in which each entry consists of two memory cells (a data cell followed by a pointer to the next entry), an instruction of the form DR0S could be used to retrieve the data and DR1S could be used to retrieve the pointer to the next entry. If the form DRTS were used, then the exact memory cell being referenced could be adjusted by modifying the value in register T.

Chapter 9

Section 9.1

1. The purchasing department would be interested in inventory records to place orders for more raw goods, whereas the accounting department would need the information to balance the books.
2. A database model provides an organizational perspective of a database that is more compatible with applications than the actual organization. Thus defining a database model is the first step toward allowing the database to be used as an abstract tool.
3. The application software translates the user's requests from the terminology of the application into terminology compatible with the database model that is supported by the database management system. The database management system in turn converts these requests into actions on the actual database.

Section 9.2

1. a. Jerry Smith b. Cheryl H. Clark c. S26Z
2. One solution is

```
TEMP ← SELECT from JOB
  where Dept = "PERSONNEL"
LIST ← PROJECT JobTitle from TEMP
```

   In some systems this results in a list with a job title repeated, depending on how many times it occurred in the personnel department. That is, our list might contain numerous occurrences of the title secretary. It is more common, however, to design the PROJECT operation so that it removes duplicate tuples from the resulting relation.

3. One solution is

```
TEMP1 ← JOIN JOB and ASSIGNMENT
                where JOB.JobId = ASSIGNMENT.JobId
TEMP2 ← SELECT from TEMP1
                where TermDate = '*'
TEMP3 ← JOIN EMPLOYEE and TEMP2
                where EMPLOYEE.EmplId = TEMP2.EmplId
RESULT ← PROJECT Name, Dept from TEMP3
```

4.
```
SELECT JobTitle
  FROM Job
  WHERE Dept = 'PERSONNEL';

SELECT Employee.Name, Job.Dept
  FROM Job, Assignment, and Employee
  WHERE (Job.Job = Assignment.JobId) and
     (Assignment.EmplId = Employee.EmplID)
      and (Assignment.TermDate = '*');
```

5. The model itself does not provide data independence. This is a property of the data management system. Data independence is achieved by providing the data management system the ability to present a consistent relational organization to the application software even though the actual organization might change.

6. Through common attributes. For instance, the `EMPLOYEE` relation in this section is tied to the `ASSIGNMENT` relation via the attribute `EmplId`, and the `ASSIGNMENT` relation is tied to the `JOB` relation by the attribute `JobId`. Attributes used to connect relations like this are sometimes called connection attributes.

Section 9.3

1. There might be methods for assigning and retrieving the `StartDate` as well as the `TermDate`. Another method might be provided for reporting the total time in service.
2. A persistent object is an object that is stored indefinitely.
3. One approach is to establish an object for each type of product in inventory. Each of these objects could maintain the total inventory of its product, the cost of the product, and links to the outstanding orders for the product.
4. As indicated at the beginning of this section, object-oriented databases appear to handle composite data types more easily than relational databases. Moreover, the fact that objects can contain methods that take an active role in answering questions promises to give object-oriented databases an advantage over relational databases whose relations merely hold the data.

Section 9.4

1. Once a transaction has reached its commit point, the database management system accepts the responsibility of seeing that the complete transaction is performed on the database. A transaction that has not reached its commit

point does not have such assurance. If problems arise, it might have to be resubmitted.

2. One approach would be to stop interweaving transactions for an instant so that all current transactions can be completed in full. This would establish a point at which a future cascading rollback would terminate.

3. A balance of $100 would result if the transactions were executed one at a time. A balance of $200 would result if the first transaction were executed after the second transaction retrieved the original balance and before that second transaction stored its new balance. A balance of $300 would result if the second transaction were executed after the first retrieved the original balance and before the first transaction stored its new balance.

4. a. If no other transaction has exclusive access, the shared access will be granted.
   b. If another transaction already has some form of access, the database management system will normally make the new transaction wait, or it could roll back the other transactions and give access to the new transaction.

5. Deadlock would occur if each of two transactions acquired exclusive access to different items and then required access to the other.

6. The preceding deadlock could be removed by rolling back one of the transactions (using the log) and giving the other transaction access to the data item previously held by the first.

Section 9.5

1. You should be led through these initial stages:

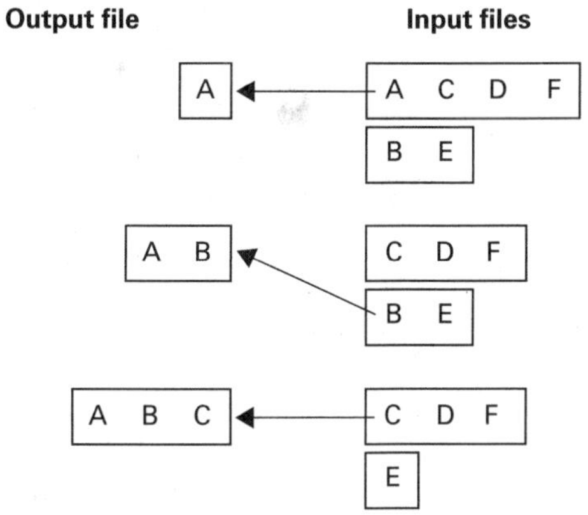

2. The idea is to first divide the file to be stored into many separate files containing one record each. Next, group the one-record files into pairs, and apply the merge algorithm to each pair. This results in half as many files, each with two records. Furthermore, each of these two-record files is sorted. We can group them into pairs and again apply the merge algorithm to the pairs. Again we find ourselves with fewer but larger files, each of which is sorted. Continuing in this fashion, we are ultimately left with only one file that consists of all the original records but in sorted order. (If an odd

number of files occurs at any stage of this process, we need merely to set the odd one aside and pair it with one of the larger files in the next stage.)

3. If the file is stored on tape or CD, its physical organization is most likely sequential. However, if the file is stored on magnetic disk, then it is most likely scattered over various sectors on the disk and the sequential nature of the file is a conceptual property that is supported by a pointer system or some form of a list in which the sectors on which the file is stored are recorded.
4. First find the target key in the file's index. From there, obtain the location of the target record. Then retrieve the record at that location.
5. A poorly chosen hash algorithm results in more clustering than normal and thus in more overflow. Because the overflow from each section of mass storage is organized as a linked list, searching through the overflow records is essentially searching a sequential file.
6. The section assignments are as follows:

a. 0	b. 0	c. 3	d. 0	e. 3
f. 3	g. 3	h. 3	i. 3	j. 0

   Thus all the records hash into buckets 0 and 3, leaving buckets 1, 2, 4, and 5 empty. The problem here is that the number of buckets being used (6) and the key values have the common factor of 3. (You might try rehashing these key values using 7 buckets and see what improvement you find.)
7. The point here is that we are essentially applying a hash algorithm to place the people in the group into one of 365 categories. The hash algorithm, of course, is the calculation of one's birthday. The amazing thing is that only twenty-three people are required before the probability is in favor of at least two of the birthdays being the same. In terms of a hashed file, this indicates that when hashing records into 365 available buckets of mass storage, clustering is likely to be present after only twenty-three records have been entered.

Section 9.6

1. Searching for patterns in dynamic data is problematic.
2. Class description—Identify characteristics of subscribers to a certain magazine.
   Class discrimination—Identify features that distinguish between subscribers of two magazines.
   Cluster analysis—Identify magazines that tend to attract similar subscribers.
   Association analysis—Identify links between subscribers to various magazines and different purchasing habits.
   Outlier analysis—Identify subscribers to a magazine who do not conform to the profile of normal subscribers.
   Sequential pattern analysis—Identify trends in magazine subscription.
3. The data cube might allow sales data to be viewed as sales by month, sales by geographic region, sales by product class, etc.
4. Traditional database inquiries retrieve facts stored in the database. Data mining looks for patterns among the facts.

Section 9.7

1. The point here is to compare your answer to this question with that of the next. The two raise essentially the same question but in different contexts.
2. See previous problem.
3. You might receive announcements or advertisements for opportunities that you would not have otherwise received, but you might also become the subject of solicitation or the target of crime.
4. The point here is that a free press can alert the public to abuses or potential abuses and thus bring public opinion into play. In most of the cases cited in the text, it was a free press that initiated corrective action by alerting the public.

Chapter 10

Section 10.1

1. Image processing deals with analyzing two-dimensional images, 2D graphics deals with converting two-dimensional shapes into images, and 3D graphics deals with converting three-dimensional scenes into images.
2. Traditional photography produces images of actual scenes, whereas 3D graphics produces images of virtual scenes.
3. The first is "building" the virtual scene. The second is capturing the image.

Section 10.2

1. The steps are modeling (building the scene), rendering (producing a picture), and displaying (displaying the picture).
2. The image window is the portion of the projection plane that constitutes the image.
3. A frame buffer is a memory area that contains an encoded version of an image.

Section 10.3

1. It is a rhombus (a squashed square).
2. A procedural model is a program segment that directs the construction of an object.
3. The list could include the grass-covered ground, a stone walkway, a gazebo, trees, shrubbery, clouds, sun, and actors. The point here is to emphasize the scope of a scene graph—it can contain a lot of detail.
4. Representing all objects by polygonal meshes provides a uniform approach to the rendering process. (In most cases, rendering is approached as the task of rendering planar patches rather than rendering objects.)
5. Texture mapping is a means of associating a two-dimensional image with the surface of an object.

Section 10.4

1. Specular light is light that is "directly" reflected off a surface. Diffuse light is light that is "scattered" off a surface. Ambient light is light that does not have a precise source.
2. Clipping is the process of discarding those objects (and parts of objects) that do not lie within the view volume.
3. Suppose a highlight should appear in the middle of a patch. That highlight is caused by a specific surface orientation at that point of the patch. Because Gouraud shading considers only the surface orientations along the boundaries of the patch, it will miss the highlight. But, because Phong shading attempts to determine the surface orientations within the patch interior, it may detect the highlight.
4. The rendering pipeline provides a standardized approach to rendering, which ultimately leads to more efficient rendering systems. In particular, the rendering pipeline can be implemented in firmware, meaning that the rendering process can be performed more quickly than if the task were implemented via traditional software.
5. The purpose of this question is to get you to think about the distinctions between local and global lighting models rather than to produce a specific predetermined answer. Potential solutions that you might propose include placing appropriately modified copies of the objects to be reflected behind the mirror while considering the mirror transparent or trying to handle images in the mirror as a form of drop shadows.

Section 10.5

1. We are interested only in the rays that ultimately reach the image window. If we started at the light source, we would not know which rays to follow.
2. Distributed ray tracing tries to avoid the inherent shiny appearance produced by traditional ray tracing by tracing multiple rays.
3. Radiosity is time consuming and fails to capture specular affects.
4. Both ray tracing and radiosity implement a global lighting model, and both are computationally intense. However, ray tracing tends to produce shiny-appearing surfaces, whereas radiosity leads to dull-appearing surfaces.

Section 10.6

1. There is not an exact answer. If an image lingers for 200 milliseconds and we projected five frames per second, each frame would have just faded away by the time the next frame was projected. This would probably result in a pulsating image that would be uncomfortable to watch for an extended time but still produce an animated effect. (In fact, slower rates can produce rough animation.) Note that the rate of five frames per second is well below the motion picture standard of twenty-four frames per second.
2. A storyboard is a "pictorial outline" of the desired animation sequence.
3. In-betweening is the process of creating frames that fill in the gaps between key frames.

4. Dynamics is the branch of mechanics that analyzes motion as the consequence of forces. Kinematics is the branch of mechanics that analyzes motion without regard for the forces that cause the motion.

Chapter 11

Section 11.1

1. Those introduced in the chapter include reflex actions, actions based on real-world knowledge, goal seeking actions, learning, and perception.
2. Our purpose here is not to give a decisive answer to this issue but to use it to show how delicate the argument over the existence of intelligence really is.
3. Although most of us would probably say no, we would probably claim that if a human dispensed the same products in a similar atmosphere, awareness would be present even though we might not be able to explain the distinction.
4. There is not a right or wrong answer. Most would agree that the machine at least appears to be intelligent.
5. There is not a right or wrong answer. It should be noted that chat bots, programs designed to emulate a person chatting, have difficulty carrying on a meaningful conversation for even a short period of time. Chat bots are easily identified as machines.

Section 11.2

1. In the remote control case, the system needs only to relay the picture, whereas to use the picture for maneuvering, the robot must be able to "understand" the meaning of the picture.
2. The possible interpretations for one section of the drawing do not match any of those of another section. To embed this insight into a program, you might isolate the interpretations allowable for various line junctions and then write a program that tries to find a set of compatible interpretations (one for each junction). In fact, if you stop and think about it, this is probably what your own senses did in trying to evaluate the drawing. Did you detect your eyes scanning back and forth between the two ends of the drawing as your senses tried to piece possible interpretations together? (If this subject interests you, you will want to read about the work of people such as D. A. Huffman, M. B. Clowes, and D. Waltz.)
3. There are four blocks in the stack but only three are visible. The point is that understanding this apparently simple concept requires a significant amount of "intelligence."
4. Interesting, isn't it? Such subtle distinctions in meaning present significant problems in the field of natural language understanding.
5. Is the sentence describing what kind of horses they are, or is it telling what some people are doing?
6. The parsing process produces identical structures, but the semantic analysis recognizes that the prepositional phrase in the first sentence tells where the fence was built, whereas the phrase in the second sentence tells when the fence was built.
7. They are brother and sister.

Section 11.3

1. Production systems provide a uniform approach to a variety of problems. That is, although apparently different in their original form, all problems reformulated into terms of production systems become the problem of finding a path through a state graph.

2. 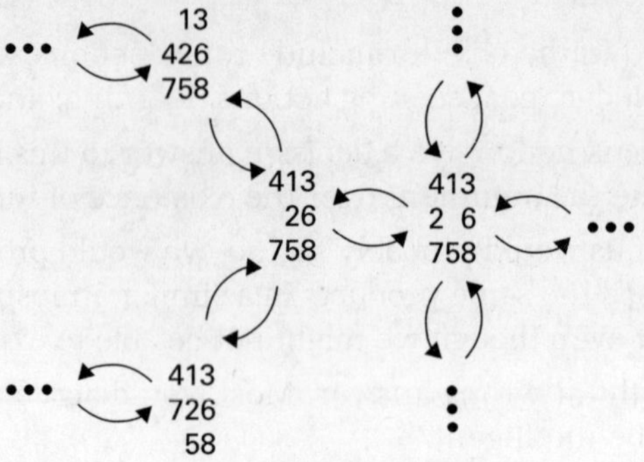

3. The tree is four moves deep. The upper portion appears as follows:

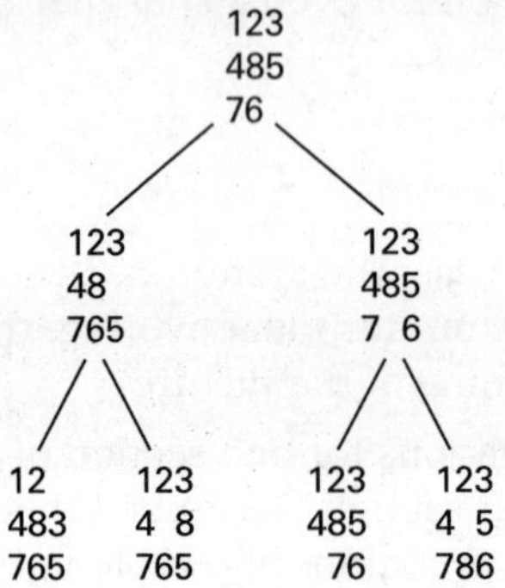

4. The task requires too much paper as well as too much time.

5. Our heuristic system for solving the eight-puzzle is based on an analysis of the immediate situation, just as that of the mountain climber. This shortsightedness is what allowed our algorithm to proceed initially along the wrong path in the example of this section just as a mountain climber can be led into trouble by always plotting a course based only on the local terrain. (This analogy often causes heuristic systems based on local or immediate information to be called hill-climbing systems.)

6. The system rotates the 5, 6, and 8 tiles either clockwise or counterclockwise until the goal state is reached.

7. The problem here is that our heuristic scheme ignores the value of keeping the hole adjacent to the tiles that are out of place. If the hole is surrounded by tiles in their correct position, some of these tiles must be moved before those tiles still seeking their correct place can be moved. Thus it is incorrect to consider all those tiles surrounding the hole as actually being correct. To fix this flaw, we might first observe that a tile in its correct position but blocking the hole from incorrectly positioned tiles must be moved away from its correct position and later moved back. Thus each correctly positioned tile on a path between the hole and the nearest incorrectly

positioned tile accounts for at least two moves in the remaining solution. We can therefore modify our projected cost calculation as follows:

First, calculate the projected cost as before. However, if the hole is totally isolated from the incorrectly positioned tiles, find a shortest path between the hole and an incorrectly positioned tile, multiply the number of tiles on this path by two, and add the resulting value to the previous projected cost.

With this system, the leaf nodes in Figure 11.10 have projected costs of 6, 6, and 4 (from left to right), and thus the correct branch is pursued initially.

Our new system is not foolproof. For example, consider the following configuration. The solution is to slide the 5 tile down, rotate the top two rows clockwise until those tiles are correct, move the 5 tile back up, and finally move the 8 tile to its correct position. However, our new heuristic system wants us to start by moving the 8 tile, because the state obtained by this initial move has a projected cost of only 6 compared with the other options that have costs of 8.

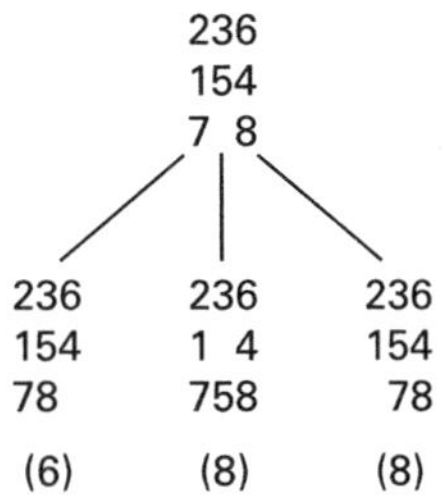

8. The solution found by the best fit algorithm is the path from Leesburg to Dayton and then to Bedford. This path is not the shortest route.

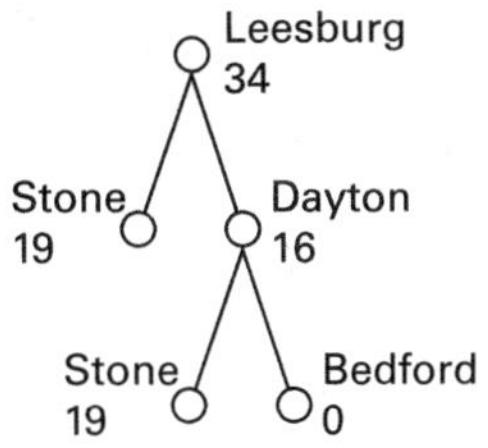

9. The solution found is the path from Leesburg to Stone, and then to Bedford. This path is the shortest route.

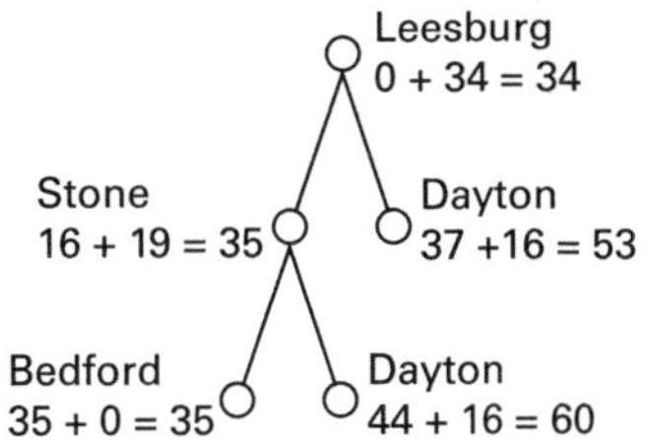

Section 11.4

1. Real-world knowledge is the information about the environment that a human uses to understand and reason. Developing methods for representing, storing, and recalling this information is a major goal of research in artificial intelligence.

2. It uses the closed-world assumption.
3. The frame problem is the problem of correctly updating a machine's store of knowledge as events occur. The task is complicated by the fact that many events have indirect consequences.
4. Imitation, supervised training, and reinforcement. Reinforcement does not involve direct human intervention.
5. Traditional techniques derive a single computer system. Evolutionary techniques involve multiple generations of trial systems from which a "good" system may be discovered.

Section 11.5

1. All patterns produce an output of 0 except for the pattern 1, 0, which produces an output of 1.
2. Assign a weight of 1 to each input, and assign the unit a threshold value of 1.5.
3. A major problem identified in the text is that the training process might oscillate, repeating the same adjustments over and over.
4. The network will wander to the configuration in which the center neuron is excited and all others are inhibited.

Section 11.6

1. Rather than developing a complete plan of action, the reactive approach is to wait and make decisions as options arise.
2. The point here is for you to think about how broad the field of robotics is. It encompasses the entire scope of artificial intelligence as well as numerous topics in other fields. The goal is to develop truly autonomous machines that can move about and react intelligently with their environments.
3. Internal control and physical structure.

Section 11.7

1. There is no right or wrong answer.
2. There is no right or wrong answer.
3. There is no right or wrong answer.

Chapter 12

Section 12.1

1. How about the boolean operations AND, OR, and XOR. In fact, we used tables in Chapter 1 when introducing these functions.
2. The computation of a loan payment, the area of a circle, or a car's mileage.
3. Mathematicians call such functions transcendental functions. Examples include the logarithmic and trigonometric functions. These particular

examples can still be computed but not by algebraic means. For example, the trigonometric functions can be calculated by actually drawing the triangle involved, measuring its sides, and only then turning to the algebraic operation of dividing.

4. One example is the problem of trisecting an angle. That is, they were unable to construct an angle that was one-third the size of a given angle. The point is that the Greeks' straight-edge and compass computational system is another example of a system with limitations.

Section 12.2

1. The result is the following diagram:

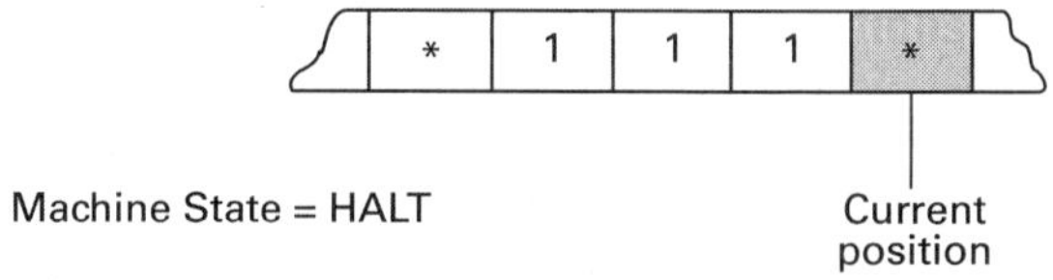

2.

Current state	Current cell content	Value to write	Direction to move	New state to enter
START	*	*	left	STATE 1
STATE 1	0	0	left	STATE 2
STATE 1	1	0	left	STATE 2
STATE 1	*	0	left	STATE 2
STATE 2	0	*	right	STATE 3
STATE 2	1	*	right	STATE 3
STATE 2	*	*	right	STATE 3
STATE 3	0	0	right	HALT
STATE 3	1	0	right	HALT

3.

Current state	Current cell content	Value to write	Direction to move	New state to enter
START	*	*	left	SUBTRACT
SUBTRACT	0	1	left	BORROW
SUBTRACT	1	0	left	NO BORROW
BORROW	0	1	left	BORROW
BORROW	1	0	left	NO BORROW
BORROW	*	*	right	ZERO
NO BORROW	0	0	left	NO BORROW
NO BORROW	1	1	left	NO BORROW
NO BORROW	*	*	right	RETURN
ZERO	0	0	right	ZERO
ZERO	1	0	right	ZERO
ZERO	*	*	no move	HALT
RETURN	0	0	right	RETURN
RETURN	1	1	right	RETURN
RETURN	*	*	no move	HALT

4. The point here is that the concept of a Turing machine is supposed to capture the meaning of "to compute." That is, any time a situation occurs in which computing is taking place, the components and activities of a Turing machine should be present. For example, a person figuring income tax is doing a certain degree of computing. The computing machine is the person and the tape is represented by the paper on which values are recorded.

5. The machine described by the following table halts if started with an even input but never halts if started with an odd input:

Current state	Cell content	Value to write	Direction to move	New state to enter
START	*	*	left	STATE 1
STATE 1	0	0	right	HALT
STATE 1	1	1	no move	STATE 1
STATE 1	*	*	no move	STATE 1

Section 12.3

1.
```
clear AUX
incr AUX
while X not 0:
  clear X
  clear AUX
while AUX not 0:
  incr X
  clear AUX
```

2.
```
while X not 0:
  decr X
```

3.
```
copy X to AUX
while AUX not 0:
  S1
  clear AUX
copy X to AUX
invert AUX (See Question #1)
while AUX not 0:
  S2
  clear AUX
while X not 0:
  clear AUX
  clear X
```

4. If we assume that X refers to the memory cell at address 40 and that each program segment starts at location 00, we have the following conversion table:

```
clear X
incr X
decr X
```

```
while X not 0:
   .
   .
   .
```

5. Just as in a real machine, negative numbers could be dealt with via a coding system. For example, the rightmost bit in each string can be used as a sign but with the remaining bits used to represent the magnitude of the value.
6. The function is multiplication by 2.

Section 12.4

1. Yes. In fact, this program halts regardless of the initial values of its variables, and therefore it must halt if its variables are initialized to the program's encoded representation.
2. The program halts only if the initial value of X ends in a 1. Because the ASCII representation of a semicolon is 00111011, the encoded version of the program must end in a 1. Therefore the program is self-terminating.
3. The point here is that the logic is the same as in our argument that the halting problem does not have an algorithmic solution. If the house painter paints his or her own house, then he or she does not and vice versa.

Section 12.5

1. We could conclude only that the problem has complexity $\Theta(2^n)$. If we could show that the "best algorithm" for solving the problem belongs to $\Theta(2^n)$, we could conclude that the problem belongs to $\Theta(2^n)$.
2. No. As a general rule, the algorithm in $\Theta(n^2)$ will outperform the one in $\Theta(2^n)$, but for small input values an exponential algorithm often outperforms a polynomial algorithm. In fact, it is true that exponential algorithms are sometimes preferred to polynomial ones when the application involves only small inputs.
3. The point is that the number of subcommittees is growing exponentially, and from this point on, the job of listing all the possibilities becomes a laborious task.
4. Within the class of polynomial problems is the sorting problem, which can be solved by polynomial algorithms such as the insertion sort. Within the class of nonpolynomial problems is the task of listing all the subcommittees that could be formed from a given parent committee. Any polynomial problem is an NP problem. The Traveling Salesman problem is an example of an NP problem that has not been shown to be a polynomial problem.
5. No. Our use of the term *complexity* refers to the time required to execute an algorithm—not to how hard the algorithm might be to understand.

Section 12.6

1. $211 - 313 = 66043$
2. The message 101 is the binary representation for 5. $5^e = 5^5 = 15625$. 15625 (mod 91) = 64, which is 1000000 in binary notation. Thus, 1000000 is the encrypted version of the message.
3. The message 10 is the binary representation for 2. $2^d = 2^{29} = 536870912$. 536870912 (mod 91) = 32, which is 100000 in binary notation. Thus, 100000 is the decrypted version of the message.
4. $n = p - q = 7 - 19 = 133$. To find d we need a positive integer value k such that $k(p - 1)(q - 1) + 1 = k(6 - 18) + 1 = 108k + 1$ is evenly divisible by $e = 5$. The values $k = 1$ and $k = 2$ are not satisfactory, but $k = 3$ produces $108k + 1 = 325$, which is divisible by 5. The quotient 65 is the value of d.

index